Dick Clement and Ian La Frenais have forged one of the most successful writing partnerships ever seen in the entertainment business. Now based in Hollywood, Clement and La Frenais are responsible for many successful TV shows, such as *The Likely Lads* and *Auf Wiedersehen, Pet*, and numerous film scripts, including *The Commitments* and *Still Crazy*.

Richard Webber is a journalist specialising in showbusiness. He has contributed to a host of newspapers and magazines, including the *Daily Mirror*, *Sunday Express*, *TV Times*, *OK!* and *Woman's Weekly*. He is the author of many previous books about classic television programmes.

Porridge: The Complete Scripts and Series Guide

Richard Webber, Dick Clement and Ian La Frenais

headline

First published in 2001 and 2002
by HEADLINE BOOK PUBLISHING

This edition first published in 2005
by HEADLINE BOOK PUBLISHING

1

ISBN 0 7553 1535 9

Typeset by Palimpsest Book Production Limited,
Polmont, Stirlingshire

Printed and bound in Great Britain by
Mackays of Chatham plc, Chatham, Kent

Headline's policy is to use papers that are natural, renewable and
recyclable products and made from wood grown in sustainable
forests. The logging and manufacturing processes are expected
to conform to the environmental regulations of the country of origin.

HEADLINE BOOK PUBLISHING
A division of Hodder Headline
338 Euston Road
London NW1 3BH

www.headline.co.uk
www.hodderheadline.com

CONTENTS

SERIES GUIDE

THE SCRIPTS

PILOT

1 SERIES ONE

2 SERIES TWO

3 SERIES THREE

CHRISTMAS SPECIALS

Porridge: The Series Guide

ACKNOWLEDGEMENTS

I would like to thank a great number of people, all of whom have helped in various ways during the writing of this book. First of all, I'd like to thank Dick Clement and Ian La Frenais for authorising this book, for giving up time to discuss the programme and contributing to the material you're just about to read. Equally helpful have been Sydney Lotterby and Jimmy Gilbert – thanks to you both.

During the course of my research, I've spoken to many of the actors and members of the production team associated with the sitcom. For sharing memories about life at Slade Prison or *Going Straight*, thanks go to you all, especially Brian Wilde, Tony Osoba, Ken Jones, Sam Kelly, Patricia Brake, Philip Madoc, John Dair, Philip Jackson, Christopher Biggins, Paul McDowell, Terence Soall, Tony Aitken, Maurice Denham, Paul Angelis, Colin Farrell, Johnny Wade, Ray Butt, Judy Loe, Mike Crisp, Christine Walmesley-Cotham, Max Harris and Ann Ailes-Stevenson. Special thanks go to Mary Husband and Ronnie Barker, whose support and help was crucial to the success of this project.

Thanks also to Christine Dunbobbin, Rosalie Dodson, Matthew Lacey, Barbara Barrington, Allan McKeown, Rannoch Daly (for agreeing to be interviewed about making the movie at his prison, and for then writing about it as well), John Rich (for sharing memories about his American production), George Forder, Garry Morton, Peter Hunt, Chris Muzzall, everyone at Headline and, of course, my agent, Jeffrey Simmons. As always, Hilary Johnson's advice has been invaluable.

Last, but not least, I would like to acknowledge the support of my wife, Paula.

Richard Webber, July 2003

FOREWORD

by Ronnie Barker

This book is terrific – a must for all *Porridge*
aficionados. It contains information that even I didn't
know: names, dates, comments from all the actors,
even viewing figures – it's all in there. Fancy the
Christmas show 'The Desperate Hours' getting twenty
million viewers! Fancy the director in his box cursing
Fulton Mackay! Fancy Clive James fancying my
daughter Ingrid!

A mine of information – it brings it all back. What
a show. What a book.

Ronnie Barker, March 2001

'Norman Stanley Fletcher, you have pleaded guilty to the charges brought by this court and it is now my duty to pass sentence. You're a habitual criminal who accepts arrest as an occupational hazard and, presumably, accepts imprisonment in the same casual manner. We therefore feel constrained to commit you to the maximum term allowed for these offences; you will go to prison for five years.'

INTRODUCTION

Nothing else in my experience was quite as painless as *Porridge* because literally nothing went wrong. It's true we'd already done a 'one-off', where Fletcher is escorted to prison, but by its end the doors had still not slammed on him.

Once we were commissioned to write the series we visited various prisons by way of research. We had a sherry with the Governor of Brixton at the time, in the RAC Club. He was a humane, civilised man and I remember asking him what he would change about the system if he had one wish. He gave it serious thought and said he'd like to be in charge only of people who deserved to be in prison, instead of alcoholics, drug addicts or the mentally unstable.

We became profoundly depressed because there is nothing funny about the reality of prison. Then, I suppose, Fletcher started to speak to us, just as he later did to Godber. 'Bide your time, keep your nose clean. Little victories, that's what keeps you going in here.'

Later, we were in Manchester, rehearsing our stage musical, *Billy*, and writing the first series of *Porridge* in between. And we felt that since prison is about being locked up it would be less than honest not to write one episode which was set entirely in a cell. So we wrote 'A Night In', not knowing at the time that Godber would be played by the superb Richard Beckinsale. That's what I mean by nothing going wrong. Every piece of casting, for which the credit goes to Syd Lotterby, enhanced what we'd written.

This is in danger of sounding bland, but I don't remember a serious difference of opinion or a cross word. We went each week to the read-through of each episode and our main concern was ensuring that the script was the right length. Ronnie usually came up with a few embellishments and more often than not they bought their way in. Then we went away until the day of the recording. That went seamlessly and we were in the bar by nine o'clock – you don't want to hear any more of this, you want to hear about the people who loathed each other, the fights, the feuds, the tempers, the tantrums. Sorry.

Well, there was one moment in the editing room before we'd chosen a title for the series. Titles can be tricky, they either come to you or they don't. Ronnie came in and announced that he'd got the perfect one. 'So have we!' we countered. A heated argument ensued for about ten seconds until we settled who was to go first. Ronnie won the coin toss. 'Porridge!' he announced triumphantly. 'That's our title!' we said. 'Swear to God!' End of debate, dispute over, off to the bar.

Dick Clement

THE PILOT

It's New Year's Eve and Fletcher is transferred from Brixton to Slade Prison, situated miles from anywhere in the wilderness of Cumberland. Sharing a train compartment with Mr Mackay and Mr Barrowclough, who'll become his greatest foes while serving his five-year prison sentence, he heads north for another spell behind bars.

To help while the time away, Barrowclough strikes up a conversation with Fletcher during which he explains that Slade is an experimental prison, regarded as a provider of 'sympathy and understanding' rather than of 'correction and punishment' – not that you would think so, with the bellowing Mackay around.

After disembarking at a rural station, Fletcher is in such desperate need of a toilet that he's told to relieve himself around the back of the van. Little do the warders know that it's all a cunning plan: Fletch, always the opportunist, urinates into the van's petrol tank!

En route to the prison, high on the moors, the minibus breaks down. With darkness closing in, Mackay sets off for help while Fletcher remains handcuffed to Barrowclough in the van. As the temperature drops, Fletcher puts the frighteners on Barrowclough by claiming they'll perish if they don't find somewhere warm. He persuades the weak-willed warder to shelter in a nearby deserted cottage, where they toast the New Year with a hot drink topped up with Scotch courtesy of Mackay's pocket!

While Fletcher keeps plying him with drink, a gloom-laden Barrowclough discusses life's sorrows and eventually agrees to release the handcuffs. But when the prison warder nods off, Fletcher grasps the opportunity to escape into the night. After hours on the run, he breaks into an empty cottage only to find he's back where he started!

'Prisoner and Escort' was one instalment from a set of pilots transmitted by the BBC in a search for a new comedy vehicle for Ronnie Barker. The project – titled *Seven of One* – was steered from its inception by executive producer Jimmy Gilbert and was part of a larger-scale project instigated when the BBC secured the services of Ronnie Barker and Ronnie Corbett from London Weekend Television. 'They were both promised a light-entertainment show, a Special each, plus a scripted comedy each, and *Seven of One* was the way of finding a situation comedy for Ronnie Barker,' explains Jimmy.

To ensure he received top-quality scripts, he turned to writers he knew. 'I commissioned more than the seven I needed. Two came from Roy Clarke, two from Clement and La Frenais, two from Hugh Leonard, one from a writer called Gerald Frow – which Yorkshire later made into a series with Clive Dunn – one written by Ronnie Barker himself, and one from N. F. Simpson.' Having selected those he wanted to pursue, Jimmy – with the help of his directors, Harold Snoad and Sydney Lotterby – put them into production.

One of the ideas submitted by Dick Clement and Ian La Frenais was based on life in prison, a theme largely untested in the genre of situation comedy and one that some people doubted had the staying power required for a long-running show. The show's chief player, Ronnie Barker, didn't share such doubts. He had always wanted to develop the idea of a prison-based show. 'When I was preparing a previous set of pilots I'd recorded, *Six Dates with Barker* – from which *The Phantom Raspberry-Blower* originated and was developed into a serial for *The Two Ronnies* – I'd write down various situations as ideas. One of these jottings simply said 'prison'; I always wanted to make a prison series and couldn't believe it when I spoke to Dick and Ian and discovered they'd come up with a similar idea.

'They were thinking, initially, about an open prison but I didn't think that had enough threat to it, whereas my idea was much more frivolous than *Porridge* – like *Bilko* in prison: smuggling women in, that sort of thing.'

Clement and La Frenais had built their success in sitcom around scripts containing more realism than Ronnie's idea afforded, so after a little deliberating they agreed on a closed prison – a setting in which the writers could exploit the daily dilemmas facing inmates. Ronnie was happy with Dick and Ian's desire to write something with a degree of reality. 'It was definitely the best way to go because my idea would have been geared much more towards laughs, whereas theirs possessed more bite.'

It was a judicious move to focus on the realism of the chosen situation. This allowed Clement and La Frenais the freedom – particularly during the actual series – to probe not only moments of grim reality for the prisoners of Slade Prison but compensatory elements too, such as the emergence of Fletcher as a father figure for young Godber.

When the writers sat down to pen the pilot, the script took off in an unexpected direction, as Dick Clement explains. 'We started writing the piece for Ronnie and found we couldn't stop; it went beyond just one episode and before we knew it we'd written an entire series.'

'It wasn't about a guy in prison, but about someone who'd just come out only to find his wife was having an affair with his best friend. Before long, we had written about fifty pages based on this situation, and envisaged Ronnie being the ex-prisoner. As we knew we had an entire series here, we put it aside,' adds Ian La Frenais.

Knowing they had exceeded Jimmy Gilbert's original requirements, Clement and La Frenais titled the scripts *Thick as Thieves* and sold the series to LWT. 'Meantime, Ronnie was still expecting something about prison, so we sat down and wrote "Prisoner and Escort". Later on, people asked why we were so obsessed with criminality, but it was just a coincidence: we set out to write a script for Ronnie but soon realised there was more than one episode in the idea.'

Clement and La Frenais didn't experience any difficulties writing the pilot script, and enjoyed the process. 'It was enormous fun,' says Ian. 'Once we'd established the main character in our minds, we were away. Of course, it helped knowing you were writing for Ronnie Barker – after all, he was so popular. We knew that if we didn't screw it up we had a real chance of success.'

As soon as Sydney Lotterby, who directed 'Prisoner and Escort', saw the pilot script, he knew they were on to a winner. 'It was wonderful and just pleading to be done – it was so clever. The script revealed the essence of Dick and Ian's writing: they don't write gags; they write situations and explore the personalities of the characters, which is why they score so well. Their scripts contain character and situation jokes, not just gags. With *Porridge*, their work was very accurate and seemed to reveal how a prisoner felt – it's almost as if they'd experienced prison life themselves!'

Casting for 'Prisoner and Escort', as well as for the other pilots, was Jimmy Gilbert's responsibility. In addition to Fletcher, the two main characters in the script were Mr Mackay and Mr Barrowclough. 'It was Ronnie's idea to recruit Brian Wilde to play Barrowclough,' explains Jimmy. 'He'd worked with him before, I believe, but I'd also known Brian from my RADA days. Ronnie thought he'd be marvellous in it and, of course, he was absolutely right.'

Jimmy Gilbert, meanwhile, knew Fulton Mackay. Since studying at drama school together, and then working at Glasgow's Citizens' Theatre as actors in the early 1950s, they'd become good friends. Jimmy recalls: 'It was whilst serving in India that he met a sergeant who pulled his neck in a funny way – something he later copied while playing Mr Mackay. I directed a series with Terry-Thomas, and Fulton played a similar character – a colonial sergeant in the police. He was great in that, so when the part of the prison warder – who by sheer coincidence was also called Mackay – came up, he was my first choice.'

Fletcher plies the joyless
Mr Barrowclough
with alcohol

But before offering the part to his old friend, Jimmy Gilbert contacted Clement and La Frenais. 'It's important you involve the writers because you don't want to suddenly find they've got a phobia about somebody. So I rang Dick and said: "How about Fulton Mackay for the part of Mackay?" Dick replied: "He'd be marvellous but do you think he'd do it?" I thought Fulton would be interested, so gave him a copy of the script and he jumped at the chance.'

The casting was spot-on. 'The three of them [Ronnie Barker, Fulton Mackay and Brian Wilde] worked well together, and they had great respect for each other,' says Jimmy. 'Brian – with his wonderful put-upon demeanour – and Fulton were the perfect balance for each other. There's a wonderful selection of characters in *Porridge* that are realistic and different. It was the same with Fulton: he brought something of his own personality to the role; he created this totally real authoritarian character. He was so funny.'

Because the pilot script centred on the transfer of Fletcher to the remote Cumberland prison, location shooting had to be organised. Jimmy Gilbert had already travelled to Wales to record 'I'll Fly You for A Quid' and knew immediately the location was ideal for 'Prisoner and Escort', despite the script being set mainly in Cumberland. 'I thought that the hills above the valleys of Caerphilly resembled the north of England; and, as the area was easy to reach, we ended up filming all the moorland scenes for "Prisoner and Escort" there.' Jimmy enjoyed making the pilot. 'I remember watching the filming and thinking how funny the scenes were, even though, at that point, they hadn't been pieced together.'

Ronnie Barker, meanwhile, recalls the inclement weather they endured while filming. 'It was terribly cold, which wasn't ideal because I did a lot of running across the moors; but then, I always remember cold weather whenever I think about BBC filming!' Overall, Ronnie was pleased with how the pilot panned out. 'The filming was successful, it was well shot and the reaction from the audience when we recorded the studio scenes was excellent.'

One of the scenes from the pilot is classed as among the 'finest memories' for writer Dick Clement. As he explains: 'It's when Fletcher escapes from the cottage, wanders around all night and breaks into a building; we had to conceal from the audience the fact that he was back in the same place – otherwise we wouldn't have got the laugh – which Sydney did superbly.'

Working alongside Sydney Lotterby as production manager was Ray Butt, who remained part of the team for the first series of *Porridge*. As production manager, his responsibilities involved finding locations. 'On a new programme, where nothing has been established, you're looking for one key location. Once found, you try to find any other locations nearby, so you're not travelling all the time.'

The series of pilots was successful in finding not one but two hit shows for Ronnie Barker: while 'Prisoner and Escort' was commissioned and re-titled *Porridge*, Roy Clarke's 'Open All Hours' kept its name and later became a successful series for the comedy actor. There was a third script Ronnie would like to have progressed. Written by Clement and La Frenais, 'I'll Fly You for a Quid' focussed on a Welsh gambling family who'd have a flutter on anything. 'It started off with them gambling on how long the sermon would last at church. It was an excellent script.'

The decision regarding which pilot would be made into a full-blown series was made at a restaurant. Around the table were Jimmy Gilbert, Duncan Wood (then Head of Comedy) and Ronnie Barker. They chewed over the merits of each show until two were left in the frame: 'Prisoner and Escort' and 'I'll Fly You for a Quid'. While Ronnie was keen on the latter, Jimmy Gilbert felt the idea lacked the stamina to survive. He says: 'It was a perfect short story but I couldn't see beyond the pilot.'

Jimmy and Duncan Wood favoured 'Prisoner and Escort', although they knew the writers were initially unsure how they could develop the situation into an on-going series. 'I thought "Prisoner and Escort" was tremendous in every way, and with Brian Wilde and Fulton Mackay it was really a three-hander,' says Jimmy. But he appreciated the task facing Clement and La Frenais. 'Not only did they have to place them all inside prison, but also what had been a tightly scripted and plotted pilot had to be expanded to include many more characters.'

When Clement and La Frenais were consulted about the decision to develop 'Prisoner and Escort' into a series, they felt the right choice had been made. 'I think it had the edge on "I'll Fly You for A Quid",' says Dick. 'Somebody once said that sitcom is all about a captive situation – and you can't get more captive than prison!'

THE PILOT — PRISONER AND ESCORT

Initial transmission: Sunday 1 April 1973 BBC2, 8.15 p.m.

CAST

Norman Fletcher . . . . **Ronnie Barker**
Mr Barrowclough . . . . **Brian Wilde**
Mr Mackay . . . . **Fulton Mackay**
Prison Warder . . . . **Hamish Roughead**

PRODUCTION TEAM

Written by . . . . **Dick Clement
and Ian La Frenais**
Music . . . . **Max Harris**
Film Cameraman . . . . **Alan Featherstone**
Film Editor . . . . **Ray Millichope**
Make-up . . . . **Penny Delamar**
Costume . . . . **Penny Lowe**
Lighting . . . . **Peter Smee**
Sound . . . . **Mike McCarthy**
Design . . . . **Tim Gleeson**
Executive Producer . . . . **James Gilbert**
Producer/Director . . . . **Sydney Lotterby**

WHAT A SCENE!

During the train journey to Slade Prison, Fletcher gives Mackay lip and is warned not to try it on.

FLETCHER
I wouldn't, Mr Mackay, I wouldn't, would I? Otherwise you'll wait till the train gets a bit of speed up outside Hemel Hempstead and chuck me out the window, wouldn't you? Put it down on the official report as attempted escape.

BARROWCLOUGH
He wouldn't do that.

FLETCHER
No, s'pose not . . . he couldn't spell Hemel Hempstead, he'd wait till we got to Rugby.

MACKAY
Now look! (Clenching his fist) I'm a reasonable man, but one more allegation of brutality and I'm going to let you have it.

Seven of One

The series was made up of seven pilots and transmitted on BBC2 between 25 March and 6 May 1973.

1. 'Open All Hours' (written by Roy Clarke)

2. 'Prisoner and Escort' (written by Dick Clement and Ian La Frenais)

3. 'My Old Man' (written by Gerald Frow)

4. 'Spanner's Eleven' (written by Roy Clarke)

5. 'Another Fine Mess' (written by Hugh Leonard)

6. 'One Man's Meat' (written by Jack Goetz, alias Ronnie Barker)

7. 'I'll Fly You for a Quid' (written by Dick Clement and Ian La Frenais)

MAKING *PORRIDGE*

Porridge was more than a sitcom: it was comedy drama of
the highest order, played out in a claustrophobic environment
that exuded a degree of tension Clement and La Frenais
could exploit. Inmates, locked away with their freedom held
in the hands of others and forced to bide their time with all
sorts of unsavoury individuals, were rich veins of conflict just
waiting to be tapped, as Messrs Clement and La Frenais
discovered. And the scriptwriters made the most of their
golden opportunity, delivering script after script of crisp,
inventive writing, epitomised beautifully in the episode 'A
Night In'. The entire episode centres on Fletcher and Godber
locked up in their cell, with the young, first-time offender
confiding in the more experienced lag, unveiling his fears and
anxieties concerning surviving life inside. The episode
contains many poignant moments, with Fletch, an emerging
father figure for young Godber, dishing out advice on how to
survive prison. In this momentary expression of humanity,
human frailties and kindness are exposed in a fine display of
just how subtle and rewarding Clement and La Frenais'
comedy can be.

Glowing radiantly like a beacon, *Porridge* outshone its
rivals in this congested genre of British television. The twenty
scripts brought to life on screen between September 1974 and
March 1977 were of a striking quality, so it is surprising to
learn that Clement and La Frenais initially questioned
whether they could extract enough humour from the grim
setting of Slade Prison. 'We visited Brixton Prison and met
with the governor, but after being shown around the place
felt really deflated, thinking we'd definitely picked the wrong
pilot from the *Seven of One* series to pursue,' admits Ian.

'We also visited Wormwood Scrubs and Wandsworth
Prison,' adds Dick. 'We became very daunted: writing
"Prisoner and Escort" was one thing, but we came out of the
prisons and said to each other: "How the hell do we make a
whole series based in prison funny?" At the end of the day,

prisons are grim and we knew our show also had to reflect that; it would have been dishonest and cheap to trivialise it, thereby not dealing with the fact that it really is a heavy place.' Clement and La Frenais purposely addressed such truths early on in series one – with 'A Night In'. 'The one thing you could do on TV, probably better than any other medium, was to have an entire episode set inside a cell. Prison is about being locked up, so we decided to do this episode early on as a way of facing the fact that prison isn't funny: Lennie being scared and depressed reflected the harshness of the situation.'

The next stage in their research was pivotal in ridding their minds of the lingering doubt about their ability to make a prison-based sitcom entertaining. Realism and humour go hand in hand in Clement and La Frenais' work, yet the dearth of humorous moments found during their research visits to real-life prisons concerned them. Key players in helping show them the light were Jonathan Marshall and Jimmy Gilbert. 'At first, Dick and Ian felt it would be difficult to open up the story,' recalls Jimmy, 'so I referred them to Jonathan, who'd been introduced to me by a neighbour. He'd just written a book – which was later published – titled *How to Survive in the Nick*, and agreed to meet with Dick and Ian.'

Clement and La Frenais remember sitting down for a drink in Richmond and discussing prison life with Marshall. 'Just talking about the routine of prison life was valuable,' says Dick. 'In terms of providing the kind of basic inform-ation you need before you can start writing a series, Jonathan was a great help.'

'He taught us a lot about the slang used in prison,' says Ian, 'and was helpful in providing plenty of hints. But the hardest thing was how to work a plot in such a small, enclosed captive world each week, where the parameters are so tight; this is why the show turned out more character-driven than most series.'

A phrase uttered by Marshall focussed the writers' minds and injected a grain of optimism, as Ian recalls. 'Jonathan started telling us stories about being inside and kept using the phrase "little victories", which struck a chord. Dick and I thought that maybe this was the key: we could make the show about a man with a fondness for earning "little victories" – beating the system on a daily basis, even in the most trivial ways.'

That everyday survival had become the driving force of the show that encouraged Clement and La Frenais enough to begin writing the first episode, 'New Faces, Old Hands'. This they

Designer Tim Gleeson built a remarkable set at Ealing Film Studios

undertook from a Manchester hotel room: their successful stage musical *Billy* was playing in the city, prior to its move to London's Drury Lane; between rehearsals, they returned to the Midland Hotel and worked on the *Porridge* scripts.

As soon as the scripts started arriving at Television Centre, producer Sydney Lotterby and Jimmy Gilbert were impressed with what they saw. 'Their writing had it all,' says Jimmy. 'Dick might have been more into plot, and Ian into dialogue, but they were the perfect partnership. Dick, being a director – and a very good one – thought visually; he knew what the medium was all about.'

Although he'd enjoyed the pilot, Sydney Lotterby had doubted whether the idea for a prison-based sitcom was sufficiently strong to carry an entire series – until he got his

hands on the scripts. 'A director's job, and an actor's, is easy when you receive quality scripts because all you're doing is interpreting something you know is right. Your job is much more difficult if the scripts aren't of a high standard: that's when everyone pulls out the stops to make it work. But making bad scripts work is difficult.'

Fletcher carried a lot of influence within the walls of Slade Prison

Appointing Sydney to direct the series was welcomed by all quarters. Jimmy Gilbert, the man who recruited Lotterby to the team, regarded him as a 'most excellent director, who directed for total reality'. Meanwhile Dick Clement and Ian La Frenais felt reassured that someone they respected and with whom they had worked before (Lotterby had helped Clement through his first piece of small-screen directing, *The Likely Lads*) was at the helm.

'I was delighted Sydney was directing the series,' explains Dick, 'and I think it was his finest work. Take, for example, 'A Night In', from the first series, where Sydney was challenged with making an entire half-hour television comedy inside a prison cell. He didn't let that put him off and found every possible way to shoot two people in a small cell. He shot it brilliantly and never missed a trick; he cast all the parts beautifully, too. We were thrilled to have him on the show.'

Ian La Frenais also has nothing but gratitude for Sydney steering the show along. 'I admired him enormously and knew that, providing we didn't screw up and become sloppy with the scripts, *Porridge* was in safe hands.'

Ronnie Barker, too, was pleased with the choice of director. 'Sydney is a very gentle, calm character, and we never had rows or shouted at each other. He's an experienced director, which showed in how he went about his work.'

Creating the Characters

When the BBC commissioned the first series, Dick Clement and Ian La Frenais knew they had three characters already in place.

Fletcher, Mackay and Barrowclough had all featured in 'Prisoner and Escort', but the writers were keen to create one more main character, as Ian explains. 'We wanted a newcomer to prison, a guy who could act as our audience in many ways, allowing Fletch to become a sort of mentor.' In doing so, all the slang, procedures and general information about prisons that the writers wanted to impart could be conveyed through Fletcher. 'You can only do that by telling someone who's scared and never been inside before. If both Fletch and Godber were old lags they wouldn't have had those conversations, but with Fletch explaining everything to a newcomer we were able to deliver all these facts in a digestible way.'

One influence behind the series' central character, Fletcher, came from a book – a Czech classic Dick had picked up. 'It sounds slightly pretentious – and I'm not even sure I read the whole book – but it was about a man not dissimilar to Fletcher, in that he was at the bottom of the totem pole but survived by his wits and was, in a way, indefatigably cheerful: somebody whose attitude was all about "getting by".'

The nearest the writers came to meeting a real-life Fletcher was in America, while they were conducting research for the American version, *On the Rocks*, which ran to twenty-three episodes on ABC and was shown between 1975 and 1976.

Dick recalls the moment. 'We started to do the American version before we'd finished the English show, so we were visiting American prisons and carrying out research while still writing series three for the UK. This prisoner, who turned out to be a murderer, had similar attitudes to Fletcher. One of the guards said: "He never gives us any bother because he isn't a repeat offender." And they'd made him the prison photographer – which explained why he followed us around taking very inept photographs. Finding a cushy number like that was exactly what Fletcher would have done. He had all the cheeriness of Fletcher, too.'

While they queued in this prison's canteen, Clement and La Frenais experienced a scene that could have been lifted directly from a *Porridge* script. 'We were in the food line, trying to choose what we wanted, when someone said that we were only allowed one piece of chicken. At that moment, the guy serving the food gave me an extra bit.' This was an entirely cussed action, yet another attempt to beat the system in any way possible, and something the writers viewed as an attitude familiar in *Porridge*.

When Clement and La Frenais created Fletcher, they already knew that Ronnie Barker would play their character; this partly influenced the way they developed the old lag. 'Ronnie is a brilliant comic actor and approached the part totally from an actor's point of view, rather than wanting us to write a star vehicle for him,' recalls Dick.

Representative of the establishment were the ineffectual Mr Barrowclough and the inimitable Mr Mackay, both created (along with Norman Fletcher) for the pilot episode. 'They were a great contrast: one was a total bastard who you had to watch out for at every moment, the other a pushover,' remarks Dick. 'You could play one against the other, and it seemed logical to have two characters like that.'

Clement and La Frenais admit they didn't appreciate the true potential of the characters until the first series was in the can and they had time to reflect. Ian says: 'We underused them throughout the first series, not realising just how good they were – particularly Mr Mackay.' But he understands why this happened. 'We were still trying to find Fletcher, as well as establishing Godber, so developing other characters took time.'

Dick concedes that another reason they didn't capitalise on the likes of Mackay was because they didn't spend much time beforehand thinking their characters through. 'Nowadays, people writing sitcoms spend ages analysing their characters before putting pen to paper; that way, they can establish who's important and make sure they're given a fair share of the lines. But we were writing by the seat of our pants! We should have known by looking at the pilot that Mr Mackay in particular was going to be an asset, because he was absolutely brilliant.' Dick adds, however, 'We may have underused him at the start, but gradually gave him more and more to do.'

As Mackay got stronger, the importance of Mr Barrowclough somewhat dimmed. This was disappointing for actor Brian Wilde, who played the warder, especially because the character had been so prominent in the pilot. 'In many ways, I don't think that character had anywhere to go,' says Dick, 'whereas Mr Mackay's did, because it was richer.'

When it came to finding names for the series' protagonists, Dick and Ian's past came into play. Just as for many of their other shows, particularly *The Likely Lads*, names weren't necessarily plucked from thin air. Lennie Godber stemmed from the writers' London-based hairdresser, Denny Godber, while Dick had a close friend, Norman Stanley Gordon, whose name was adapted and became Norman Stanley Fletcher. 'We also wanted a name you could abbreviate, and Fletch sounded good,' says Ian.

It was pure coincidence that the writers picked the surname Mackay for a character to be played by his name-sake Fulton Mackay, and Mr Barrowclough was a name that simply sounded right, as Dick explains. 'It sounds like a northern name, which is what we wanted, and there was a lovely rhythm to the phrase: "Pull yourself together, Mr Barrowclough!" You have to experiment with names and see how they sound in certain situations – and they all seemed fine to us.'

'I like the name Barrowclough,' adds Ian. 'It's a wonderfully old-fashioned kind of East Riding name. It was the name of a Newcastle footballer and of a street in the Newcastle area, but I don't know of anyone in particular that could have influenced our choice.'

Another decision Clement and La Frenais faced when the series was commissioned was what to call the sitcom. 'Prisoner and Escort' was apposite for the pilot, but hardly suited the programme once Fletcher arrived at Slade Prison. The importance of a suitable-sounding title cannot be under-estimated, but making a decision wasn't easy, as Ian explains. 'We toyed with one or two, then thought about words like "stir" and "inside", from which the word *Porridge* emerged; at first, it seemed a bit daft, but the more we thought about it, the more it grew on us.'

But they weren't the only ones to come up with that title. Dick recalls: 'We were with Ronnie Barker, who said: "By the way, I've got a title." I replied: "So have we." He told us *Porridge*, and we said: "My God – that's the same as ours!" Quite independently we'd come up with the same title. It's obviously a slang term but it's just one word, which is desirable, and immensely memorable.'

Many noteworthy characters were seen during the sitcom's run, including Grouty – expertly played by Peter Vaughan – and Judge Rawley, brought to life briefly by veteran character actor Maurice Denham. Clement and La Frenais were equally adept at creating supplementary characters. 'The idea behind Grouty was that he's the enemy within,' explains Dick. 'Your enemy is not just the screws but also other prisoners, as any prison series or movie will tell you. You're just as scared of the people within as you are of the authorities, so when we wrote 'The Harder They Fall' we felt it was about time we introduced Grouty. Peter Vaughan created a very sinister yet funny prisoner who became a huge addition to the team.'

The idea to introduce the judge responsible for sentencing Fletcher evolved from the scripts Clement and La Frenais had written for the American version. As Dick recalls: 'The American TV company wanted twenty-three scripts in a year, and when we'd run out of adapting *Porridge* scripts we had to write new episodes. When it came to writing series three for the UK, we used storylines that had been completed in the States. We were constantly translating material that had been used in the States for the UK, whereas earlier we had adapted the British scripts for the American market – it was an extraordinary situation.'

Casting

Although three of the main characters for *Porridge* had already been placed for the pilot, 'Prisoner and Escort', a host of prisoners and warders had to be recruited to occupy Slade Prison. So, with the scripts complete, Sydney Lotterby's mind turned to casting the remaining team, and it was with his assistant, Judy Loe, that he set about the task. Judy worked alongside Sydney Lotterby for more than thirty years, initially as his production secretary and later as a production assistant. She was involved in all sorts of duties connected with *Porridge*, including running the production office. 'I'd normally be the first person to work with the producer on the programme, before anyone else joined the team,' Judy explains. 'I was involved in everything from getting the scripts typed to arranging the casting.' Judy has nothing but happy memories of working on *Porridge*. 'It was enjoyable and everyone got on well together – it was a nice little unit.'

Of those roles left to fill, the most important was that of naïve first offender Lennie Godber. To do this, Ronnie Barker suggested Paul Henry, who made his name playing woolly-hatted Benny in *Crossroads*. 'I'd just worked with him, and thought he was well suited for the role, but Sydney wanted Richard Beckinsale. I remember him saying to me: "I think this chap Richard Beckinsale, who's done *The Lovers*, would be good – have a look at this tape of the show." Sydney thought Richard was right for the part because of his sensitivity as an actor.'

Ronnie kept an open mind and watched the tape: he was impressed with what he saw and had no objections to Beckinsale being offered the role. It wasn't long before he knew the director had made the right choice. 'It was the first time I'd worked with Richard and as soon as we'd finished the read-through I knew Sydney was correct to suggest him.'

It was imperative that the principal actors worked well together, especially as most of the action was played out in the confines of a tiny cell; where such a restrictive environment would magnify the interplay between the actors, any underlying weaknesses or incompatibilities would stick out like a sore thumb. But there were no such worries on the set of *Porridge* because Ronnie knew immediately that he'd form a fruitful working relationship with Richard. 'Very rarely have I worked with someone I hate; it makes the job a hundred times more difficult. In *The Two Ronnies* people would comment on the fact we were using the same people, but with such a short rehearsal-time you've got to know from day one that whoever you're working with will know his lines, is reliable and a nice guy.

'I sensed the comedian in Richard straight away; it was like working with David Jason – a riot from start to finish. Richard was very funny and his comic timing impeccable; I loved working with him.' Although Beckinsale grew restless with the 'innocent young male roles' he was increasingly offered, and despite the character of Godber being just as young and easily led as others he'd played, Ronnie never noticed any concerns regarding the role. Perhaps this was because *Porridge* was more solemn than other sitcoms he'd worked on. 'I never felt he wanted to do anything more serious, or pithy,' says Ronnie.

'He had such a facility for being sympathetic and playing the naïve characters, although in real life he wasn't, of course. You could sense all the mothers saying: "Aah, isn't he sweet." He just exuded charm, his timing was excellent and he had a great sense of fun.'

Sydney had seen Richard in several shows and knew he'd be perfect as Godber. 'He was just right, although initially he had trouble with the Birmingham accent. Just like the scar on Fletcher's chin in the early episodes, the Brummie accent got lost and we finally settled for a Nottingham accent, which is where Richard was born.'

Clement and La Frenais acknowledge the part Sydney Lotterby played in making *Porridge* one of the BBC's most successful sitcoms. 'He cast the original pilot beautifully, then later recruited Richard and all the other key players – it was a fantastic piece of work.' Dick remembers Sydney calling to tell them about bringing Richard Beckinsale into the fold. 'We admired Richard so much, and Sydney was casting higher than our original expectations, which was fine with us. We hadn't really seen the part of Lennie being that big, but, once Beckinsale had been cast, he was so damned good and bonded so well with Ronnie that we just wanted to use him more and more.'

Dick considers the qualities Beckinsale brought to the role injected into it an enormous humanity and believability. 'He was also very honest and appealing, which helped as well because one found oneself on his side. There was an unmistakable truth in his acting, even though he was a terrible reader at the read-throughs,' says Dick, with a smile. 'The rest of the cast, who knew what he was like, would almost groan if they knew he had a long speech because they had to sit through his stuttering; he was a lousy reader and we used to joke about how the hell he got his first job! But during the four days' rehearsal everything always came together, and his performance during the recording was almost effortless, as well as wonderfully true.'

Ian La Frenais, too, was surprised and taken aback when he first heard Richard read. 'He was hopeless. He'd sit there, look at the script and give the most terrible reading. But he was always very laid back, knew he was a bad reader and had confidence in his own abilities to make sure he was word-perfect for the first run-through on the floor – and was.

'Despite all of that, the chemistry between Richard and Ronnie was wonderful. Richard was a rising young performer, a unique talent, while Ronnie was the master. A lot of actors are uncomfortable with that strange hybrid of activity and television with an audience; it's a bit strange and unnerving for many actors, but Ronnie loved it.'

'Ronnie was a pure genius,' says Dick. 'He always brought little additions to the scripts. At the read-throughs he'd always throw in an extra ad-lib and ask: "Is that all right?" He wanted the laugh but not if it was a cheap laugh or out of character. He was wonderfully funny and had such a quick brain, which was ideal because Fletcher was a man who lived by his wits. We needed a man who was quick on his feet, with a lively mind, and Ronnie was right for the role. He was a joy to work with and not in any way a selfish actor.'

Dick and Ian were also happy with the casting of Fulton Mackay and Brian Wilde, who carried their characters forward from 'Prisoner and Escort'. 'I adored Fulton, he was one of my favourite human beings in the world – and I still miss him,' comments Dick. 'Syd used to say Fulton never wanted to stop rehearsing, he would go on forever. But what came with that was this wonderful enthusiasm: he loved what he was doing, so you didn't mind that foible one little bit. He was a perfectionist, working away all the time, and you knew he was after the best performance he could possibly achieve. I saw a lot of his work and thought he was fantastic; he was an enormously well rounded human being, an interesting man who could strike up a conversation about anything.

Christopher Biggins, David Jason, Ronnie Barker and Richard Beckinsale act out a perfect scene

'Brian, meanwhile, brought something wonderfully lugubrious to his character, which was slightly reminiscent of Robb Wilton: I remember him from my childhood and his misery was funny. Rather like Captain Mainwaring in *Dad's Army*, Mr Barrowclough had a terrible marriage, and the way Fletcher exploited him was funny.'

Plenty of other established actors were spotted in Slade Prison, including David Jason, who went on to work with Ronnie Barker in another hit show, *Open All Hours*. 'An older character, called Blanco, was created,' says Sydney Lotterby, 'and as soon as Ronnie saw the script he said: "That's a part for David Jason." I replied: "Who?" David wasn't a big name then, and was also a young man, so when he turned up I was worried we'd made the wrong choice.' But as soon as make-up was applied and Jason started performing, Sydney was able to relax. 'He did terribly well; he's such an accomplished performer, and had worked with Ronnie before, which helped.'

Another character, Judge Rawley, was played by veteran stage- and screen-actor Maurice Denham. Sydney recalls that he fitted in well and was very conscientious about his performance, and production manager Mike Crisp also enjoyed working with him. 'It was a happy experience; Maurice was a very sweet man and well liked by the entire cast,' he says. Mike remembers the day he met a real-life judge with the same name. 'One of the first things a production manager does as soon as he receives a script is to make sure – where possible – that there isn't a person with the same name.

'Normally this is a job that would be farmed out to the reference library, although it remains the production manager's responsibility. Similarly, if someone gives out a phone number in the script, it has to be a dead line. When I saw there was a character called Judge Rawley in the script, I got the library to check; I was told there wasn't a judge with that name, so didn't think any more about it.'

It was six weeks before the cast recorded the episode in the studio. 'After an incident-free recording, I noticed a

Veteran actor Maurice Denham
played Judge Rawley, a friend
of the Governor Mr Venables
(the late Michael Barrington)

very distinguished man standing at the bottom of the audience rostrum,' continues Mike. 'It turned out he was with his son, and he said to me: "Oh, Mr Crisp, I would just like to say how much my son and I have enjoyed tonight's performance." When he introduced himself, I nearly fell through the floor because the judge was his namesake! It was an understandable mistake, because his surname was spelt differently to the one we'd checked, and fortunately he didn't mind.'

Authenticity is always important, even in situation comedy, and Mike, who worked on a Christmas Special and the third series, was keen to ensure this was achieved. 'I did some research and discovered that most prisoners are aged between eighteen and thirty and representative of an ethnic mix, whereas the people used as extras in the series were all old lag look-alikes – mainly white and aged between fifty and sixty. When I took over, I changed all that and brought in a range of people to play non-speaking roles. Overall, I think it worked well.'

Set-building

It was hoped that most interior scenes would be shot inside a real jail, but plans fell through at the eleventh hour. This was when Tim Gleeson, an experienced designer who had worked at the BBC since 1957, was summoned. Tim is now retired from the Beeb, but during his time there worked on many hit shows, including *Keeping Up Appearances* and *Yes, Minister*. When he became involved with *Porridge*, he was familiar with the show, having been the designer on 'Prisoner and Escort' and other pilots in the *Seven of One* series, but the requirements in this instance were much greater than anything previously tackled. While prison cells and offices could be filmed in the BBC studios, the association area – where the prisoners gather to play games or watch television, and where Fletcher is seen walking along to his cell in the opening credits – was too large for any studio at Television Centre. Sydney Lotterby had to put his thinking cap on.

Tim recalls the moment he was asked to help. 'Time was slipping away and Syd said: "Tim, we're desperate, is there any way we can conjure up a multilevel prison at Ealing Studios?" The timescale involved was incredibly short – it was only weeks until he wanted to start filming – so everything became telescoped.

'Magically, I discovered there was an old tank at Ealing, which was used for underwater filming-sequences and any other scenes involving water. The tank enabled me to build a multilevel structure. When you built scenery there was an accepted rule that no individual item could be made that two men couldn't handle, which was reasonable because everything had to be carried on and off trucks, up and down stairs, in and out of the studio. But it's not always easy, especially when you're faced with building walkways that have to bear the weight of several people.

'The tank itself was about nine feet deep, but by good fortune I was able to cantilever the walkways out over the top of it. Two thirds of the entire structure were fixed to the studio floor, allowing the other third to project outwards.'

All location shots for each series were done together, usually during a week's filming at Ealing Studios, after which the structure was dismantled. However, certain episodes contained scenes that necessitated the reassembling of segments of the construction within the studio. 'Some shots required the association area and the gantry suspended above, although no one would walk on it,' explains Tim.

No one can underestimate the magnitude of the task he faced. 'It was a massive job,' he admits, 'probably one of the most difficult I've designed, considering the timescale involved and the lack of co-operation from the authorities, which meant I was prevented from modelling the set on a real prison.

'As well as constructing the set, we also had to make it look realistic. We probably made the prison look dirtier than it perhaps would have been in real life.' Tim and his team used a technique know as 'blowing down': after the scenery has been built, a coat of paint is applied to it; the painters then delicately apply a light layer of dark-grey liquid spray. This produces an instantly aged effect, making the scenery appear old and worn.

Sydney Lotterby was enamoured of Tim's achievements at Ealing. 'Fletch's cell and the association area were relatively straightforward, but sometimes I wanted a bigger vista than that, which is where the tank came into play. The ground floor of the prison was built on the floor of the tank, the ground floor of the film studio became the first floor of the prison, with cells positioned along the passageway, and then Tim built another floor on top of that, which could be walked on. It was a very clever design.'

One of the first sequences Sydney recalls filming on the new structure was the opening titles, which evocatively captured the sounds associated with prison life. 'After visiting various prisons as part of his research, Dick Clement told me that you constantly hear the jingling of keys and shutting of doors. This triggered me into thinking that perhaps we could use these sounds in the titles, thereby setting the scene for the programme. Prior to this, the opening-titles sequence for comedy programmes consisted mainly of music and graphics, but I didn't think that was the right style for *Porridge*, so took a different approach. To be honest, when I shot the titles at Ealing I was concerned people wouldn't like the end result. But everything turned out fine.'

People did like the style adopted for the opening credits. In *The Times* on 6 September 1974, Stanley Reynolds remarked how the title sequence 'seemed grim as an old Warner Brothers prison movie, with only the exaggerated military swagger of Fulton Mackay as the bantam-cock prison officer giving the comic game away'.

When a programme is recorded in front of an audience, the designer faces extra challenges. *Porridge* was no exception to this rule, as Tim explains. 'The audience takes up half the studio, leaving little space for artistic development. You have to try and turn the sets to face the audience, but, with all the cameras and equipment, some people haven't a clear view of what's going on and end up watching on the monitors fixed round the studio. But anything with Ronnie Barker in it will always be great, and I enjoyed the show immensely.'

Designing the Costumes by Mary Husband

In 1972 I designed the costumes for *The Two Ronnies* and my happy and artistically fulfilling period working with Ronnie Barker began – and it continued for the next fifteen years. We had previously met on *Before the Fringe*, directed by Robin Nash and introduced by Alan Melville. *The Two Ronnies* was something different: wittier than *Morecambe and Wise*, colourful and musical. And with scope for me: for period-costume design and the opportunity to design for dancers, such as Pan's People.

After my first series with the Ronnies, I set up costumes for *Open All Hours*, also directed by Sydney Lotterby – with whom I'd worked on *The Liver Birds* – so it was no surprise when I was asked to do the costumes for *Porridge*.

I didn't feel that being sent to jail was a lot of fun, so decided not to use the dark-navy prison uniforms. I thought that on the small screen they would be far too dark, en masse, and too similar to the prison officers' uniforms. I decided instead to dress the prisoners in grey battle-dress-style uniforms with the standard striped shirt. Having seen the film version recently on television, for which the designer used the navy uniforms, I think I made the right decision.

I went into fittings with Ronnie Barker, Brian Glover, Richard Beckinsale, Peter Vaughan, Tony Osoba, Sam Kelly, Ken Jones and an exciting cast of regular artistes. Fulton Mackay was an added joy: a sharp and brilliant performance as the chief prison officer. He wanted a flat, guards' cap with an officers' peak, which I altered specially, and the boots had to be perfect. Brian Wilde was the foil to Fulton: homely, laconic and a joy to work with.

Filming, though lots of fun, was very busy. Derek Sumner, an ex-actor (who in retirement returned to acting), was Ronnie's favourite dresser and my right-hand man. We filmed at both Ealing Studios, in Tim Gleeson's remarkable set, and at a psychiatric hospital that looked like an old Victorian prison, where we were met daily by fascinated inmates.

To help me bring reality and authenticity to my costumes I had the help of an advisor, Jonathan Marshall, a charmer who had done a spell of 'porridge' himself and written a book about his experiences. He told me all about boots, nightwear, arm bands for trusties and generally helped me pull the whole picture together. Working on *Porridge* was a joy.

Out in the Open Air

Although *Porridge* was largely shot in studios at Ealing and Television Centre, locations were occasionally sought for outdoor shots – such as that of the large, intimidating gates of Slade Prison shown during the opening titles. The responsibility for hunting down suitable locations for the programme was given to Ray Butt, the production assistant on series one. Ray, who retired from the BBC in 1987, after completing thirty-two years' service, had worked with

Sydney since the days of *The Liver Birds*, but their relationship dates back to 1956 when he joined the Beeb. 'Sydney
used to be a cameraman, and when I joined as a kid at the
bottom of the crew he was not only senior cameraman but
also my boss. So, over the years, we've got to know each
other well.'

As Sydney Lotterby points out, Ray's job wasn't an easy
one. 'The prison authorities weren't very helpful. They
wouldn't let us film anywhere, even *outside* a prison. And,
although Dick Clement and Ian La Frenais were allowed in
while they were conducting their research, neither the
designer nor myself were allowed to look around.'

Being refused permission to film outside a real prison
posed problems for Sydney and Ray, but the solution came
in the shape of numerous psychiatric hospitals dotted
around the London area. Ray retraces the steps he took in
finding suitable locations. 'It was disappointing the Home
Office refused us permission; if we'd been making a docu-
mentary or drama they might have considered our application, but not for a comedy. The institutions we found made
suitable alternatives. We started at a grim-looking place

Fletch became a father
figure to the naïve first-
time offender Lennie
Godber

near Watford. It reminded me of a Victorian workhouse – a dreadful building.' With all the windows and walkways barred, it resembled a prison. 'We only wanted to use the building for long shots, so it worked fine.' In fact, the selected location was so convincing that some viewers wrote to the production office asking which prison had been used.

Ray also found the gatehouse represented so effectively in the opening credits. Once marking the entrance to St Albans' Prison, the building became a military-detention barracks in 1915. A ten-year spell of non-occupancy followed before the local council acquired it and turned it into a depot for their highways department. Today, the building is used as a sales and marketing HQ for a leading mineral-water company.

No one would have guessed that behind those giant gates stood rows of dustcarts because, thanks to a few props – such as the prison nameplate and the barring of nearby windows – HMP Slade was born. 'Tim Gleeson made the exterior look as good as it did; but it was great finding the site with its authentic prison gates, even though they hadn't been used for some time,' says Ray.

The rest of the filming for the opening sequence then had to be organised, as Ray explains. 'We used some stock shots of doors closing, while the close-ups of hands turning keys were taken at cells in Shepherd's Bush police station. For timing purposes, we still needed a couple more shots, so I nipped down with a cameraman to the police station, where I'd established a few contacts since filming episodes of *Dixon of Dock Green* around there.' The opening-titles sequence was altered later in the series, showing Fletcher walking about the prison.

When he was assigned to the production team for *Porridge*, Ray was among those with initial reservations about the show's chances of longevity. However, his worries rapidly dispersed when the scripts arrived. 'I couldn't see how the idea could be developed for a whole series, but when I saw the scripts everything became clear. The laughs were cleverly written and had depth, while the characters were solid, three-dimensional figures.'

The production team was presented with a further headache at the start of the third series, when permission to film at the psychiatric hospital was withdrawn after complaints were received from those hospital visitors who were unhappy about the building representing a prison on TV. When scripts arrived, one of the jobs allocated to the production manager was to work through them and identify what scenes would be recorded using an outside location. Thus the incumbent Mike Crisp set about finding a new venue.

'When the hospital used in the first two series became unavailable, I looked around and found an institution in Ealing, which was ideal because it was near BBC's filming unit,' says Mike. The next step was to visit the establishment. 'The official showing me around suggested filming by a laundry block; he then took me to the hospital's Victorian square, which looked grim. I knew that it was going to be a fairly easy job for someone of Tim Gleeson's talent to make it resemble a prison, especially once he'd put a few fake bars up at the windows.'

While touring the establishment, Mike noticed that both the post box and telephone kiosk were painted blue. Curiosity soon got the better of him. 'I found it slightly odd, so asked if it was because we were on government property. The official giving me the guided tour replied: "Oh, no. One of our inmates has a particular problem whereby he puts litter in anything painted red. We had no choice but to paint them a different colour."'

Production secretary Judy Loe also remembers filming at the psychiatric institutes, but there is one particular moment that sticks in her mind. 'We were completing a scene where Lennie Godber was fighting while Fletcher and some other characters walked towards the scuffle; during the action, one of the hospital inmates threw urine at the actors! I couldn't believe it!'

Rehearsals and Recordings

Porridge – like many other BBC sitcoms – was recorded in front of a live audience. This would take place on Sundays at Television Centre, after a week of rehearsing. Any location filming required was completed prior to rehearsals. As soon as the scripts arrived, scenes necessitating outside shots or the use of the tank at Ealing Studios were identified. Usually a two-week period was set aside to shoot, edit and dub the filmed sequences prior to the relevant studio recording, during which they were shown to the audience.

The weekly timetable was tight, as Sydney explains. 'After Sunday's recording, Monday was a day off – before rehearsals started again on Tuesday. We'd rehearse right through until Saturday morning, after which we'd all go home for lunch. If the actors hadn't got it right by then, they never would.'

Series writers Clement and La Frenais were usually present during the read-throughs, a crucial stage in the production cycle. Ian elaborates: 'The read-through tells you a lot about how the script will work, although you usually come away with some rewrites. We'd normally return on the Thursday for the technical run, when a few more adjustments might be made.'

The quality of the scripts was such that extensive rewriting was unheard of. 'It seemed such an effortless process,' recalls Ian. 'During the third series, we were in America and missed quite a few of the read-throughs. Occasionally we'd carry out rewrites over the phone, but the scripts didn't change much.' While they were busy in the States, they relied heavily on Ronnie Barker's instincts. 'He was so good, and provided plenty of great one-liners, but it was awful being so far away and not part of the production. But we had little choice because by then we were starting to write the American version, *On the Rocks*. It was a busy time.'

Tony Osoba, who played McLaren, enjoyed everything about *Porridge*, even attending rehearsals. A milieu was created that was conducive to making a successful show. 'I looked forward to being with everyone, not just the cast but the whole production team, too,' says Tony. 'It was a positive experience, less troubled than some jobs I've been involved with. Often at rehearsals there's huge anxiety, and there can be tantrums, too. But there was none of that on *Porridge*; everything ran smoothly – we just got together, had a good time and the show seemed to have a natural momentum.'

During recording, Fulton Mackay's drive for perfection often led to retakes – something that frustrated Mike Crisp when he took over as production manager for the 1975 Christmas Special, 'The Desperate Hours', and series three. 'There's one shot I recall where Fulton comes into frame, adjusts his hat, pulls his trademark neck movement, then walks off. I lost count of the takes we did for that. It drove me up the wall because one of the production manager's responsibilities is the budget, and all these takes were costing us money.'

Sydney Lotterby remembers other such occasions involving Fulton. 'Fulton had to get his moves right. I remember one scene he walked into a cell and couldn't get his feet positioned right. He'd often walk into the cell on the wrong foot and say: "Sorry, I've done this wrong, can I start again?" Sometimes it became a bit wearing, especially after five or six takes, but the end result was always fine.'

But Mike, who left the BBC in 1996, admits he was never happy as a production manager, and saw it as a stepping-stone to becoming a director – a role he later held for many years. 'As production manager, you're pulling the whole project together, and if anything goes wrong, it's inevitably your fault!' he says, smiling. 'Somebody said to me once: "You're a lucky devil, aren't you? Whenever you do shows there's never any panic, nor rows – you must have a guardian angel." I felt like saying, "Don't you realise I work bloody hard?" To ensure everything ran smoothly, I always arrived an hour before anyone else just to think about what could possibly create chaos, thereby allowing me the chance to sort it out before anything blew up.'

Some actors find recording in front of a live audience unsettling – Ronnie Barker is not among them. 'The adrenaline flows when you have an audience in the studio,' he says. 'It always seemed like the scenes recorded in front of the audience got plenty of laughs, whereas the audience's reaction and laughter subsided when they watched the filmed sequences via the monitors in the studio. In my view, the audience is very important.'

Ronnie's vast experience in the profession has taught him that tension often exists in the television studio, and he has a method for smoothing the atmosphere, as Mike Crisp explains. 'A sitcom recording is about the most uncomfortable experience anybody could ever have. Not only are the seats excruciatingly uncomfortable, but also half a ton of hardware comes between you and what you want to see. Barker realised that tension in an audience would stop them laughing so used a regular ploy to relax everyone. Within the first few minutes, he'd deliberately dry, make a cock-up or blow a raspberry, which meant the scene had to be recorded again. He'd remark that it was his fault, then proceeded to play it as straight as he could, by which time the audience had relaxed.'

Among those watching the recordings were Dick Clement and Ian La Frenais. 'They were always great fun,' recalls Dick. 'Ronnie often did the warm-ups, which I don't think he enjoyed too much, and if there was a recording stop for any reason, he would always talk to the audience and keep them happy.

'Writing a series about prison is a hard sell, but with Ronnie Barker in the lead it immediately made it easy – because the moment he walked on the screen, there was an air of reassurance and you knew the show was going to be funny. He totally diffused any initial worries I had about the subject matter, and played a huge part in the show's success.'

Looking back, Sydney Lotterby has nothing but fond memories of making *Porridge*. These include the time Fulton Mackay was covered in soot while recording the episode 'The Hustler'. 'In the episode, Fletch and a few of the prisoners sneak into the boiler room to gamble on a game of snakes and ladders,' Sydney recalls. 'When Mackay finds out, he arranges for a delivery of coal to be poured through a hole into the boiler room. The next scene saw Ronnie and the others rushing out of the door.

'I started filming and noticed there wasn't any soot coming out of the door. So I asked the special effects man if he could make it more visible. He agreed. However, the worst thing you can say to an effects man is: "Can you do it a bit more?" This time the door opened and a great cloud of soot poured out. Brian Wilde and Fulton were standing against the wall opposite; when they moved, a soot outline was left behind. Fulton had soot in his ears for ages!'

Making-up

In terms of preparing actors for the recording of an episode, the genre of situation comedy invariably poses fewer problems for the make-up designer than other types of programme do. Make-up artist Ann Ailes-Stevenson spent twenty-seven years with the Beeb before going freelance, and during

It took over an hour to apply David Jason's make-up whenever he appeared as old man Blanco

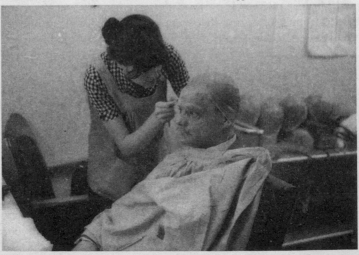

the 1960s and 1970s worked on plenty of comedies before concentrating mainly on period dramas. She was in charge of make-up for the second series of *Porridge*, and the biggest challenge she faced involved David Jason. She explains. 'David played Blanco, and we had to make him look old – something we achieved with the help of latex, which was stippled on. In those days it wasn't so sophisticated as it is now, because you didn't have so many latex pieces pre-made; you did everything on the day. And, to create the signs of ageing, you'd pinch the latex, forming creases.

'We then put a cap on his head, together with a fine wig, which allowed you to see bald patches. It took about an hour and a half every time we prepared him.'

Ronnie Barker's needs stretched to hair colouring. 'His natural colour is white, so we used a brown and reddish spray. It took about twenty minutes, because you had to be careful you didn't spray his scalp – getting the roots coloured entailed applying the spray with a toothbrush. Luckily, the spray didn't run under the heat of the lights, but it ran quite a lot when you applied it so you were always armed with a supply of cotton wool.'

Ann says that during her career she's enjoyed working on every show she's done. And it seems *Porridge* was no exception: 'There wasn't any difficulty with *Porridge*; everybody got on well together and it was like a big family.'

Making its Small-Screen Debut

The first series of *Porridge* kicked off with 'New Faces, Old Hands' on 5 September 1974. The episode centred on the arrival of three prisoners at Slade Prison: Fletcher, Godber and a simpleton called Heslop. The following day, Dick Clement was shooting a commercial and overheard the crew discussing the sitcom. 'No one realised I was involved in the series,' he says, 'so when they started talking about *Porridge*, my ears began flapping. It was very interesting because I got an immediate sense that the show had made a connection; the episode had been a hit and here was instant feedback –

it's hard to create that kind of buzz these days.'

Including the two Christmas Specials, a further nineteen episodes followed. Often, sitcoms can't sustain their momentum and tail off in terms of quality towards the end of their run, but this was not the case with *Porridge*. The quality remained high throughout, as acknowledged by Dick Clement – although he's the first to admit that some episodes were weaker than others. 'I felt happy with the standard of writing, and the second series was probably the best. During the first series we were feeling our way a bit, and there were a couple of episodes that didn't quite reach the level we wanted (an example of this is the episode 'A Day Out'). But by the second series, the plots were much tighter and we began writing for the strengths we'd identified within the show.'

One of the beauties of Clement and La Frenais' writing is their propensity for mixing a fair dosage of realism into comedic scripts, as exemplified masterfully by the first-series episode 'A Night In'. Behind the funny situations and humorous lines lies a resonance usually reserved for more serious studies of social and human behaviour. Fearful of his first night inside, Godber is shown the key to survival by the ripened criminal Fletcher, who quickly adopts parental-like feelings towards the young inmate sharing his cell. 'It was important we studied such issues,' says Dick. 'In a way, this episode gave us a focus for the series. The relationship between Fletcher and Godber became a kind of mentor-protégé situation; that scenario developed organically, we didn't sit down and plan it like that.'

Dick Clement admits that Galton and Simpson's writing influenced both Ian and him. 'We always wanted our scripts to have depth, just like Galton and Simpson's *Steptoe*. In that series, there's a real sense of sadness and frustration, which became something of a trend at the time. Without doubt, the best situation comedy has something more going for it; we wanted that as part of our work, too.'

By the time the third series had been commissioned, Dick and Ian were living in America, from where the scripts were written. Inevitably, their presence was missed on the set, but the writers believe the series still contained some good material. Their confidence – not only in their own writing but also in the capabilities of the team they'd left behind – was high. Dick and Ian were happy for alterations to be made to their scripts, although the necessity for such was remarkably rare. Jimmy Gilbert recalls the respect they held for Ronnie Barker. 'They knew he was a good writer and, as they were back and forth to America, they had total confidence in Ronnie's good faith and judgement, knowing he wouldn't change something for the sake of it. So, if I had problems getting hold of them, I knew they were happy if Ronnie, for example, wanted to make tiny changes to ensure a particular line was more comfortable for him.'

Jimmy Gilbert felt the sitcom scored top marks in all aspects, including the style of recording. 'Although it was shot in front of an audience, Syd Lotterby always did fourth-wall shots at the end, as pick-up shots. Normally you wouldn't be able to do that, because one wall of a room or set has to be kept open because the audience and cameras are all out front facing in. But Syd wanted the fourth-wall shot, to add that extra bit of reality.'

Sydney Lotterby explains: 'I got tired of always facing the same way in the cell, so I asked Tim Gleeson to paint a cloth that could be used to extend the cell. But as soon as someone opened a door on the stage the whole cloth moved, making it look as if the back of the cell was moving. We soon put a stop to that and found it gave the set some depth.'

Where Did You Get That Name?

Dick Clement and Ian La Frenais have a propensity for using old friends' names for their fictional characters, a trait first seen in *The Likely Lads* and used in most of their work since. *Porridge* was no exception, with Godber's namesake being a London-based hairdresser who cut Dick and Ian's hair from his salon. 'My name is Denny Godber, and my junior at that time was Lennie, so I think Dick and Ian swapped the names around and came up with Lennie Godber.'

Denny sold his salon fifteen years ago, but still cuts Dick and Ian's hair, as well as Jenny Clement's, Dick's ex-wife. 'Whenever the boys are over from America, they'll always visit my home, where I have a new salon in the basement.'

Born in Cornwall, Denny attended art school in Plymouth before leaving the Southwest for the bright lights of London. After retraining, he found work at Sweeney's, one of the first male hairdressing salons in the capital, whose clientele included rock stars and actors. Denny, who's now fifty-four, was initially employed as a junior but by 1975 had bought the salon. He later took a year off and toured with various pop stars – including Rod Stewart, Queen and Led Zeppelin – in his capacity as a hairdresser.

Origins of 'Porridge'

The derivation of the term 'porridge' is uncertain, but Bloomsbury's *Euphemisms* states that the word may have been inspired by 'stodgy prison food, which has to be stirred . . . an allusion to the slang *stir*, which means prison'. It's thought that the term dates back to the 1830s.

Meanwhile, Rannoch Daly, who was Assistant Governor at Chelmsford Prison when the *Porridge* movie was made, explains: 'By tradition, if a prisoner does not finish eating all his porridge for breakfast on his last day in prison he'll have to return to finish it later. Thus the phrase "doing porridge" applies to second and subsequent periods of imprisonment and is particularly appropriate to the old lag Norman Stanley Fletcher.'

Reviewing the Success

With more than sixteen million people tuning in to watch the opening instalment, *Porridge* became an instant hit. While evaluating a show's success isn't the easiest of tasks – why one show clicks and another flops defies logic at times – it

was fairly obvious why Clement and La Frenais' slice of
prison life was so readily accepted. 'Not only did they deliver
brilliant scripts – it was also arguably Ronnie Barker's best-
ever performance; he was wonderful,' enthuses Jimmy
Gilbert.

'If you think about the ingredients of a successful situation
comedy, it's clear the characters must be more than just life-
like: they also have to be interdependent, rather like *Steptoe
and Son*, where the two of them can't live with each other
but couldn't survive without the other. They were locked into
a situation, and it never worked so well when Galton and
Simpson sent them on holiday, or put them into a different
environment.

'With *Porridge*, the characters also found themselves
locked into their own little world. And there were threats all
around: from fellow prisoners, from the screws and the
system. All these elements added the tension that situation
comedy requires.'

The media's reviewers were almost unanimous in their
adulation for Clement and La Frenais' masterpiece. In his
aforementioned *Times* article of September 1974, Stanley
Reynolds wrote: 'How quickly *Porridge* . . . established the
main characters, the comic situation, and its style of play in
its first half-hour.' Clive James commented in the *Observer*,
'Those scripts by Clement and La Frenais were good in every
molecule.'

The *Guardian*, meanwhile, carried an article by Peter
Fiddick, who commented that it would require a 'great deal
of ingenuity' to make the series work. 'Setting a comedy
series in a prison imposes restrictions that seem to close
visibly like an Edgar Allan Poe cell the more you think of
them.' But he was nonetheless impressed by what he saw of
the new sitcom: 'Clement and La Frenais seem to have
absorbed something about prisons and their constraints, on
which to build. It could be a new source of comedy.'

When asked to nominate his favourite episodes, Ronnie
Barker cites 'A Night In' as one of which he's particularly
fond. 'Syd's idea of building a second set of the cell to obtain

an all-round feel meant we could cut between the two; it worked well and gave a claustrophobic feel to the episode. You never felt disappointed with any of the scripts, and another one that was good fun was "A Day Out". But I think more humour came from the concentrated situations inside the jail.'

'A Night In' is also one of Ian's favourite episodes, though he has a few regrets about the first series. 'Although there were a couple of great episodes, it was the weakest series. Dick and I felt we couldn't write the series without an episode showing what it's really like being locked away. "A Night In" really holds up, but there are one or two others that are too broad, such as "A Day Out". This was probably because we were still finding our way with the tone of the show, whereas by the second and third series the episodes were very solid.'

As for Dick, he's also keen on 'A Night In', as well as 'The Harder They Fall' and 'Just Desserts'. 'I'm very fond of that one because it's a whole episode about one tiny thing. In a way, that was the key to the series: picking something minute and constructing an episode around it.'

While Dick and Ian had initially worried about the plots, they eventually realised that the show was so character-driven they could rely on the simplest of storylines. (One episode, 'Just Desserts', for example, revolved around the disappearance of a can of pineapple.) 'As the series progressed, we built up the confidence to focus on much simpler themes, whereas previously some of the plots and storylines were too convoluted, resulting in the episodes being broader than they merited,' says Ian La Frenais.

As far as Sydney Lotterby is concerned, 'Just Desserts' and 'The Harder They Fall' are his favourite episodes from a sitcom he regards as among the best he's produced. 'It's a toss-up between *Porridge; Yes, Minister* and *Yes, Prime Minister*, but Clement and La Frenais' work was excellent.'

For least favoured episodes, Sydney points to 'No Peace For the Wicked', from series two, while Dick Clement didn't enjoy 'A Day Out'. 'It was the weakest in series one. We thought we needed a breath of fresh air, to get out of prison once in a while, but as soon as we had recorded it we realised it was best to stick with the limitations of the prison setting. In hindsight, I think we'd written "A Day Out" out of panic, thinking we couldn't possibly write six episodes based entirely in prison – but, of course, we could.'

With regular airings on terrestrial and satellite television, and the recent release of a boxed set of videos containing every episode, *Porridge* lives on – not that Jimmy Gilbert is surprised. 'There are few comedies that don't date; you even have to be careful with many of the classics now if you're selecting something for a repeat run, but crime and punishment are universal themes that won't date – which is great news for *Porridge* fans.'

Dick is occasionally asked by friends to show an episode of the sitcom. 'I'm very proud of the series and think it holds up well, even after all these years. It still makes me laugh and I never tire of watching it; in fact, I could sit down and watch most of the episodes any time.

'The show got off to a flying start. There was so much interest in it; I remember doing lots of interviews before the series came out, and felt it was going to attract a big audience. Fortunately, most people stuck with it. There had been an enormous amount of anticipation because of Ronnie Barker appearing in a prison series written by us. The main elements in the show appealed to people, including the idea of the guys bucking the system against all the odds, and, with the tremendous chemistry between everyone, it had plenty going for it. Unlike the success of some of our other shows, *Porridge*'s popularity didn't really take us by surprise.'

As for its continued success on British screens, Dick says: 'Its theme is pretty timeless; prison hasn't changed much, and the thought of people trying to survive and make the best of a bad situation is appreciated by all.'

Mike Crisp feels much of the credit for the show's success lies with Barker and Beckinsale. 'They got on so well professionally and never rowed. But, of course, there were other factors, including the quality of the scripts and the writers choosing an absolutely classic situation. Comedy comes from friction, which is in plentiful supply when people from all walks of life are trapped together – and you can't get anymore trapped than prison.'

Director Sydney Lotterby, meanwhile, believes one of the show's greatest strengths is its believability, even though it's outside the sphere of most people's experience. 'The characters are accepted as truthful, and the situation regarded as fairly representative of prison life. You have to suspend belief in any comedy, but most of the better sitcoms are realistic.'

In hindsight, there's little Sydney would change if he were making *Porridge* today. 'When Fletcher and Godber are in their cell there's hardly any noise in the background and now I'm disappointed with that aspect. At the time it was felt background noise would be a distraction; it's a shame I didn't do something because there's always noise in prison. But that's the only thing I would do differently.'

Dick Clement has little he'd alter second time around. 'I would have used Fulton more, particularly in the early days when I felt we were a bit profligate with Mackay.' He would also have ensured every episode unfolded within the confines of the prison walls. 'I wouldn't have gone outside like we did with "A Day Out"; it was better keeping the characters contained.'

Making Music

Given the job of writing the music for the theme tune, with lyrics sung by Ronnie Barker himself, was Max Harris, who'd worked with Jimmy Gilbert on numerous television productions. Max was commissioned to write the signature tunes for other pilots within the *Seven of One* series, including 'Open All Hours'.

Max, whose tune is mainly heard with the closing titles, wasn't briefed on what was expected; he was simply sent the script and it was left to his discretion what he came up with.

'In "Prisoner and Escort" the main character – Fletcher –

was a Cockney character, so, when it came to writing the
signature tune, I felt it needed a Cockney tune – most of
which are associated with music-hall themes. So that's the
kind of sound which eventually evolved,' says Max, who has
written more than fifty signature tunes for television
programmes, including *Mind Your Language, Doomwatch,
Sherlock Holmes* and *The Strange World of Gurney Slade.*

After kicking ideas around in his brain for some time, it
took Max only a couple of hours to actually write the
composition; then followed a three-hour session in the
studio. He still gets pleasure from hearing his theme tune
whenever *Porridge* is repeated. 'And I still collect some
royalties, which is nice – it keeps my bank manager a bit
happier, I suppose!'

Bringing Down the Curtain on Slade Prison

Ronnie Barker's wish to move on to pastures new was the
fundamental reason that the third series of life at Slade was
the last. Sydney Lotterby admits that everyone was sad when
the closing episode, 'Final Stretch', was complete, but also
knew there was no chance of a further series. 'You don't
persuade Ronnie; he's a very strong character. Once he'd
made up his mind that he didn't want to do any more, there
was no going back. It was disappointing, but there were new
projects to move on to.'

Dick Clement and Ian La Frenais would willingly have
written a further series of *Porridge*, as Ian explains. 'We
ended with a kind of compromise by doing *Going Straight.*
We just felt we couldn't abandon the character – people still
wanted to see him. I think *Porridge* would have taken
another series, but Ronnie is a prolific entertainer and had
lots on his plate; he was always working and wanted to
move on.' Ian didn't try changing Ronnie's mind. 'We all
agreed in the end, although Dick and I knew we could do
something else with it after a little pause. Then, of course,
Lew Grade had told us he wanted to make a feature film of
it, so we also had that to write.'

'I'm sure we could have written another series,' adds Dick, 'but on reflection we felt we'd just about done it all. I wasn't particularly disappointed – I didn't think of it in those terms. It was time to move on and I thought of the series with nothing but pleasure, because it really was totally painless.'

It's now more than thirty years since the pilot episode was first transmitted, and the series is still going strong. A year doesn't go by without *Porridge* repeats being shown by the BBC and the satellite station UK Gold. No one seems to tire of Fletcher and co., and the series always attracts glowing reviews whenever it's shown. Writing for the *Western Mail* back in July 1984, journalist Gethyn Stoodley Thomas remarked how 'far ahead of any new comedy series' it was, while Garry Bushell said in the *Sun* in 1990: 'Aren't those *Porridge* repeats the business? Ronnie Barker's wily old lag Fletcher is a classic comedy creation and the scripts are a joy.' And even in 1992 the show was still warmly received. So impressed was Richard Last by the series that he wrote in an article in the *Daily Telegraph*: 'Sometimes I wonder if the BBC is doing itself any favours by re-transmitting this eighteen-year-old series. It is so perfectly scripted, so beautifully acted, so full of humanity and so stomach-clutchingly funny, that it makes almost every contemporary TV comedy look wan.'

Without doubt, *Porridge* has become one of the elite in the sitcom genre, a ratings-winner that can be relied upon to hold its own against its more up-front, brash, younger siblings. Journalist Hilary Doling, writing in the *Sunday Express* back in 1984, summed up beautifully the calibre of the show when she said: 'It must be the only porridge that gets better with age.' How right she is.

THE WRITERS

Dick Clement

Even as a young boy, Dick Clement aspired to making people laugh. The youngest of five children, he admired his elder brother's ability to have the rest of the family in stitches. 'I saw how much Arthur got away with and knew I wanted to emulate him. I've always liked the feeling of making people laugh; when the family did laugh for the first time in response to one of my jokes, it was very satisfying,' recalls Dick, who tried his hand at writing from an early age.

His attempt to pen a radio show fell short of requirements, but the seed had been sown for what would become a glittering career. 'I was about eight when I tried writing an episode for the *Paul Temple* series, except it only lasted three minutes instead of thirty!'

When it dawned on Dick that he'd have to make a living, writing didn't seem a viable option. It was only later, while working for the BBC, that he rekindled his interest in writing. 'It's strange that it was only then that I remembered this foreshadowing that I had tried writing at a young age – I'd forgotten all about it.'

Born in Westcliff-on-Sea in Essex in 1937, Dick savoured a happy childhood on the coast. 'One of the things Ian and I have in common is that we both grew up in seaside towns: Ian in Whitley Bay, me in Westcliff. It was fun having the sea nearby. I remember the immediate post-war years, when mines were slowly being removed from the beaches and I explored bombed-out houses with other kids.'

Dick's father ran a successful milk business that employed his two brothers, but Dick was determined to pursue a different path. Although keen on writing, Dick's early ambition was to become an actor. 'The most important thing I did at school was act in school plays – I took it very seriously. I'm not sure if I would have made a very good actor, but the exposure was valuable later when I began directing and writing. There's an enormous overlap between the skills of acting and directing or producing; so the more experienced you are, the better you'll understand the business as a whole.'

Someone who encountered Dick's bent for acting is his old school-friend Terry Taylor. They met at Bishop's Stortford College, while in their early teens. 'Dick was in the dramatic society, and we were both in a puppet club as well,' says Terry. With the help of rudimentary tape recorders they visited local schools. 'We'd use string puppets, and Dick was always good with the voices on the recorder.

'Culturally, he was a big influence on me. He was always first into things, like Hemingway and other authors of the day. Once he asked whether I listened to *The Goon Show*. I didn't, but made sure I did the following week. We'd then imitate all the voices.' Terry also recalls putting their Saturday-morning study periods to good use. 'We'd creep off and listen to the repeat; it was a joy hearing it all over again. Dick was a boarder and I was a day-boy – I don't know how we chummed up. I think we used to laugh at each other's jokes and consequently became good friends.'

After leaving school, Terry worked in accountancy while Dick crossed the Atlantic on an exchange visit with an American school. He values those twelve months spent in the States. 'It's one of the most important things that has happened to me,' he says. 'During my sixth-form year, I became friends with an American who was on an exchange deal. I kept thinking how fantastic it must be to spend a year at school in a different country, learning about a completely new culture.'

After mulling over the opportunity, Dick applied for a place on the exchange scheme and was accepted. 'I'm proud I had the nous to go for it. Selection was based on an inter- view, and I'm reasonably good at talking, so felt confident about securing one of the eighteen spaces available to thirty-five applicants.'

Dick sailed to the States in 1955 on the *Queen Mary* and returned on the *Queen Elizabeth* a year later, having experienced in America a rehearsal for where life would eventually lead him. 'It was a real love affair, I had a wonderful time,' he enthuses. 'We were like ambassadors in many ways, so we had to behave, but I found the work very easy and felt it was a fantastic experience.' Dick believes the confidence he gained stood him in good stead for completing his national service upon returning. 'It helped me bullshit my way into a commission, separating me from the herd,' he says. 'It was a very important experience for an eighteen-year-old.'

Joining the RAF, Dick was stationed in Norfolk. Based at the same training camp at Bircham Newton was Michael Burridge, who played a key role in Dick's life after demob: not only did he play a part in introducing Dick to Ian La Frenais, but also helped with his search for employment. 'After we'd finished national service, I noticed in a newspaper advert that the BBC were looking for studio managers. I sent it to Dick, suggesting he apply – which, of course, he did.'

Michael's not surprised Dick has become one of the country's greatest comedy writers, having experienced his wit first hand. 'He was always very funny; the humour of life never escaped him. The way his career has turned out is no surprise to me.'

Back on civvy street, Dick knew it was time to establish a footing in the working world. After considering applying for RADA, he decided instead to respond to the BBC's advert for studio managers, and was successful in his application. 'I still wasn't entirely sure what I really wanted to do with my life, but joined the Corporation because I felt in the vaguest possible way that it was the right direction for me.'

Dick started his media career as a studio manager, or what he terms a 'glorified sound-man'. After training, he joined Bush House, where broadcasts were transmitted all over the world. 'It was very interesting at first and, although the work got boring after a while, the people were great. Most of the time you were putting out new broadcasts, perhaps in Albanian or Polish, and you couldn't understand a word.'

His subsequent transfer to the African Service afforded him the chance to complete his first piece of professional writing. 'I wrote a script in English, which was translated into Somali: that's the first time I put words on paper in a specialist capacity.'

While working for the BBC, Dick started writing for pleasure, contributing sketches and ideas to the Corporation's own drama group, the Ariel Players. His involvement with the Players grew as he began using the revues as a vehicle for developing his writing of comedy and satire. His association with the group was memorable in other ways: it was during the after-show party of the 1961 performance that Dick met his first wife. Jenny had played no part in the performance, but was invited along by Brenda Punshon (née Shepherd), who'd appeared in seven of the sketches and arranged the dance numbers for the Christmas show. 'I shared a flat with Jenny, while Dick shared a flat with Terry Taylor, who I went out with for a while,' she says.

The party was held at Dick's flat in Earls Court, and Brenda recalls introducing them to each other. 'That was the end of Jenny for me!' laughs Brenda. 'We'd planned to go to America together the following year, but she pulled out and ended up marrying Dick instead. I was still in the States at the time, much to my annoyance, but I managed to phone them at the wedding from San Francisco.' Jenny later returned the compliment by introducing Brenda to her husband, Richard.

Jenny remembers hitting it off with Dick immediately, partly because of their penchant for a little bear! 'We both adore Winnie-the-Pooh,' she explains, 'and were able to quote huge sections from stories as well as reciting the poems to each other. I found Dick quite imposing when we first met, because he's very tall. But intellectually we hit it off from the start, and began dating straight away. We continued talking about Winnie-the-Pooh from that first meeting and, as you can imagine, our children were brought up on the bear as well.'

Back at the BBC, Dick's duties started to encompass magazine programmes, voice work and producing. After five years, however, he was ready for a change. 'I was desperate to get into mainstream broadcasting, I felt in an incredible backwater,' he says. To achieve his aim he was accepted on a BBC directors' course; this led to the filming of a sketch titled 'Double Date', on the strength of which Dick and Ian were commissioned to write their first television sitcom: *The Likely Lads*. Dick was still employed by the Beeb when the series started life, but left to pursue a career as a freelance scriptwriter as its success picked up momentum.

Nowadays Dick is based in the States, where he lives with his second wife, Nancy. When it comes to recreation, his main interest is playing tennis in the Californian sun. 'I play as often as I can, usually two or three games a week. It's good fun and ideal for keeping fit. It's also a great way to unwind, especially after a hard day's work.'

Ian La Frenais

Like so many teenagers on the verge of leaving school, Ian La Frenais didn't know what he wanted from life. His father was a corporate accountant, but Ian, an only child, knew that wasn't the career for him. 'I was interested in art, but also had a leaning towards writing – or wanting to write – but didn't know how to progress the idea,' he says. 'In addition to writing essays at school, I wrote for pleasure, so for a while I considered being a journalist.'

Mike Thompson – who's known Ian since junior school and grew up in an adjoining street in Whitley Bay – says Ian's ambition to write existed from a young age. 'At school he was good at English and always keen to get into writing, but I think he probably saw himself as a novelist rather than writing for television. One of his great talents is instant recall of situations and conversations he'd had, or overheard, stretching back to his childhood, which has made him a good raconteur.'

Fellow schoolmate Horace Jeffcock remembers Ian as a 'fun guy'. 'He was always imagining funny situations, trying to create an amusing scene out of something we were looking at or talking about. That sense of humour was built in to him.'

Ian's uncertainty about a future career extended beyond his school days. After leaving the Dame Allan's School he had a year to kill before university. It was during this period that he decided against higher education and to complete his national service in the army. 'Even then I'd tell people I was going to be a writer, but it was a lie because I didn't have any clear ideas about what I wanted to do – it just sounded a glamorous thing to say.'

Although he spent his national service at Blenheim Barracks, Aldershot, Ian regularly returned home, as old friend Vin Welch recalls. 'He managed to get a job in the office issuing passes, so ended up with an inordinate amount of weekend passes!' Vin remembers a time when Ian went AWOL. 'After coming back for a weekend, a few friends went to the station to see him off before going on to a party. Ian was so annoyed about missing the do that he decided not to return.' He went to the party with his friends and the following day visited his doctor, feigning illness, thus preventing trouble when he reached his army base. .

Another of Ian's friends was David Hallwood, who attended Bygate Infant School at Monkseaton, and Park Primary in Whitley Bay with Ian. The pair joined up on the same day. 'We thought it best to get national service over and done with,' he says. 'Put on the London train by our folks in September 1955, neither of us had spent time away from home before; but we ended up laughing from dawn till dusk as Ian came to terms with the army. The "regular" NCOs couldn't get their brains round the name La Frenais so Ian was known as "Lee Francis" for the term of our square-bashing.

'Ian was constantly inventing characters in his imagin-ation. One was a mild little creature who dribbled and kept looking up into the eyes of his corporal and did everything he was told to the letter! If he saw a railway-hoarding advising people to go to Margate for their summer holidays, then Ian's make-believe character was off to Kent.

'Another of his ruses was to get the whole platoon, when marching from one place to another, to stamp on every seventh step, causing drill corporals near seizures as they struggled to work out what was happening. Ian was liked by all the rookie soldiers, even though we were a mixed bunch – with university graduates, public-school-leavers, ordinary working-class lads and one or two thugs. We all mixed in together and produced a winning "B" Company in the drill competition at the end of ten weeks.'

After returning to civvy street, Ian moved between jobs before parental pressure forced a decision. 'For a while it felt as if my life was in limbo, and it was quite nice,' he admits. But his father had begun to urge him to make something of his life, so he joined the tobacco company Gallahers as a sales trainee and spent the next two years working throughout the British Isles. 'I spent a lot of my youth smoking free cigarettes!'

Ian's life reached a crucial juncture during 1961, when some of his friends ditched their jobs and moved to London. Brian Flint, who started off as a teacher before going into advertising, and Maurice Hardaker, a physicist, wanted to break into the world of entertainment themselves. While living in the Northeast, they had secured a weekly slot on Tyne Tees – the regional independent television station – performing a satirical song, as Maurice explains. 'While Brian wrote the words, I composed the music. We appeared every week for a couple of years, back in the late fifties. We enjoyed it so much, we moved to London to see if we could make a career out of it. We'd already agreed that if we didn't make a lot of money we'd pack it in and return to something sensible.'

With another of his friends, Horace Jeffcock, already in London, Ian started getting itchy feet for the capital's bright lights. 'During that period, when economically everything was going well, "Going to London" had a certain significance,' Ian explains, 'and didn't beg the question: "What are you going to do when you get there?" It was simply a state of mind, I had no idea what I was going to do!'

So, having decided that his future lay south, Ian headed for London, escorted by Mike Thompson. 'A friend and I took him down as he went to start his career as the author of the century!' smiles Mike. 'He had ambitions of being interviewed by John Freeman on *Face to Face*, having written his first novel.' Initially he lived with Maurice and Brian in Earls Court before sharing a flat with Brian Flint in Pont Street, Knightsbridge.

To earn some cash, Ian worked for a cleaning company and had other jobs before joining Marketing Advisory Service, a market-research company. He was recruited by George Murray, who later set up his own company, Marketing Economics, and invited Ian to join him. They became good friends. 'Ian was always an amusing character,' says George, who was aware of his employee's writing ambitions. 'He was working for me when *The Likely Lads* first started. He has a very creative and distinctive talent, so I wasn't surprised when he eventually went part-time, then gradually filtered out altogether to spend more time writing.'

George enjoyed working with Ian. 'I wouldn't say he was a born market-researcher, but he had a good analytical mind, could do research and was able to write reports – I wouldn't have employed him if he hadn't been competent.'

One thing George remembers clearly about Ian was his eye for a fast car. 'When he was working for me, he demanded a company car. I thought he was going to choose a Ford

Cortina or something, but he wanted our red Sunbeam Alpine. Later, when he had a bit more money he bought himself an E-type Jag, then a Rolls-Royce – he even had his own chauffeur for a while.'

Writer Patrick Tilley, who'd already written several episodes of the Rediffusion series *Crane* when he first met Ian, also recalls this passion for cars. 'When Ian and Dick's stardom was beginning to go into ascendancy, Ian came round to my house in Highgate and asked me to look out the window. There was this dark-blue E-type Jag; it was a real "bird-puller". He was absolutely thrilled with it, and had bought it on the strength of the money he'd received for one of *The Likely Lads* series.' Patrick asked whether his family was happy about his success. 'He replied: "Yes, but my mother told me not to give up the day job!"'

Eventually Ian – who's now married to Doris and has one stepson, Michael – decided it was time to quit market research and concentrate on writing full-time. 'Throughout the period Dick and I wrote the first two series of *The Likely Lads*, as well as our first screenplay, *The Jokers*, I continued working in market research. But I began feeling I was missing out on all the fun of recording the episodes – and when the BBC ordered a third series of *The Likely Lads*, it seemed the ideal moment to put "professional writer" on the passport!'

The Writing Partnership

There aren't many writing partnerships that have lasted as long as the one forged nearly four decades ago by Dick Clement and Ian La Frenais. When they started penning skits for the amateur productions of the BBC's Ariel Players, they had no idea their talents would take them to Hollywood. Without question, theirs is one of the most respected and sought-after teams in the entertainment business – as proven by their ever-increasing lists of credits and awards.

Since the mid-1970s, Dick and Ian have lived in Beverly Hills. 'We sort of explored the idea of moving here in 1974,' explains Ian. 'But it wasn't until the end of '75 that we actually moved. Even though we were based in the States, we were constantly working for the British market throughout the remainder of the seventies and early eighties, which meant commuting for some time. Even in 1979, when we formed a production company and had offices in America and England, nearly all the work was London-generated. Gradually the writers accepted that the States had become their home, and began to settle. 'As the years passed and I married an American, established more and more American friends, I began realising my future lay here,' Ian continues.

Initially, Dick and Ian moved to the States to be near the centre of the movie industry. Following the success of their early sitcoms, they branched out into writing film scripts, starting with *The Jokers* in 1967, then *Otley*, a year later, which Dick also directed, and *Hannibal Brooks*, telling the story of a POW escaping over the Alps with an elephant. With Hollywood being the hub of the movie world, living within close proximity seemed crucial for Clement and La Frenais' future. But it was the writers' track record in sitcoms that agents seized upon when they touched down on American soil, and it wasn't long before they were involved in negotiations concerning an American version of *Porridge*. *On the Rocks* was screened in 1976 but never progressed beyond the first series.

Neither Dick nor Ian would consider returning to England: they enjoy their lives in Beverly Hills too much. 'It's a hard-working town, very work orientated,' says Dick. 'We have a routine: Ian comes around at about nine-thirty each morning, and we work till four-thirty. He's better at dialogue, while I'm better at structure; so together we work well.

'I'm very happy being based here, but we'd never stop writing for Britain: we still find that writing with a British voice is easier than writing with an American one. We like showing we're flexible and capable of more than one style, but it's enormously comfortable writing with a British voice.'

Although they've written for the American market, it's

something they find difficult and not particularly gratifying. 'We haven't been very successful at it, apart from writing for *The Tracey Ullman Show*, which is great fun,' says Dick. 'But that's for cable, where you have a lot more freedom; in fact, it's the nearest we've come to the freedom we were given on British television.'

Dick claims that writing for network television in the States is a 'young man's game'. 'You also need a lot of stamina because it's not really a writer's medium, it's a producer's. But that's not to say all American TV isn't funny: the best American comedy is fantastic – and in many ways they're better at writing comedy than the British.'

Much of the duo's success is down to their deep under-standing of each other, something that has developed over the years. 'It's been an enormously long and successful working marriage,' says Dick. 'But we've also worked on our own: Ian has written *Lovejoy* and *Spender*, while I've directed movies and a stage play. The break always proves productive and refreshing, but we've never wanted to break up the part-nership. It's more fun writing a script together: you can prop each other up as well as make each other laugh.'

Although they've enjoyed many successes during their careers, Clement and La Frenais are unable to pick a favourite. 'I have great respect for *The Likely Lads* because it was the series that got us started, but I wouldn't put it ahead of *Porridge* or *Auf Wiedersehen, Pet* – they're equally impor-tant,' says Dick.

'You write shows at different periods of your career, so it's difficult pinpointing one in particular,' Ian agrees. 'I enjoyed writing *Porridge*, and it was definitely the hardest to pull off. But you continue to learn; I feel we're better writers now than we were three or four years ago, which means it's not easy picking the best work we've done.'

One person who can testify to the quality of scripts in *Porridge* is Ronnie Barker, who feels that Clement and La Frenais' work oozed quality. 'The wonderful thing was you just picked up the script and did it. It was complete and well rounded, everything was there; you never needed to add a word. I never thought, 'This line isn't good enough', or 'This sequence doesn't work', because it always did.

'Occasionally I would add the odd word if I felt it would make something work better. I rarely did that sort of thing on the recording night because it's very dangerous – but if things were going well I couldn't resist it sometimes,' smiles Ronnie. 'I remember there was a prison visitors' scene and I was sitting with Patricia Brake – who was playing Fletcher's daughter – and Fulton started making this strange noise, so I turned to Patricia and said, "He does bird impressions now", which got a laugh. But Dick and Ian's work was always spot-on.'

One of Clement and La Frenais' trademarks is the strength of their characters. Pick up any one of their scripts and you won't find a barrowful of gags. Instead, you will see a depth of character an actor can really get his teeth into. 'We're not gag writers,' says Ian, 'we obtain humour from the characters themselves.' You need look no further than *Porridge* and *The Likely Lads* for proof that this works: the situation in both sitcoms is harsh, but the colour of the characters cleverly balances the grimness.

Patrick Tilley co-wrote a number of sketches for the Ariel Players and, later, novelised several scripts for a BBC book based on *Whatever Happened to the Likely Lads?* He has known Dick and Ian for years, and admires their work. 'They're on the same wavelength, and have a certain magic between them. It's a unique collaboration and fascinating to watch.' And Patrick's been fortunate enough to do just that. 'While Ian was walking around, Dick was sprawled out on a chaise longue, scribbling everything down. They work directly on to a computer these days, but when I saw them, Ian would spark off things, perhaps snatches of dialogue, and Dick would organise it and write it all down. It was great to observe.'

Though it is success that we readily associate with Clement and La Frenais, they have also endured the odd disappointment. Not everything they touch turns to gold – their 1993 comedy-drama for ITV, *Full Stretch*, being a prime case in point. 'I really felt that would work,' says Ian, 'but the programme wasn't given a chance to settle, because there were changes taking place in ITV at the time. It was a shame because the casting was wonderful and we felt we had created the new *Minder*.'

That said, many writers would give anything to taste a little of the success Dick and Ian have experienced in the field of sitcoms. They won The Society of Film and Television Arts award for both *Whatever Happened to the Likely Lads?* and *Porridge*, as well as picking up a Screen Writers' Guild award for their prison-based series. And yet, despite the critical acclaim they've enjoyed with their classic contribution to the genre, Dick and Ian are in no rush to return to it. 'Situation comedy is not my favourite genre,' Dick admits. 'I like everything we do to contain comedy, but I don't really want to go back to that. I find the tyranny of having to be funny all the time exhausting. I like it when you can be both. It's still tremendously satisfying hearing people laugh at something you've written, but it's gratifying to occasionally write a scene where the audience go quiet and are touched by what they see. In a way, the juxtaposition of the two is the ideal.'

But whatever they write in the future, humour will always be an integral component. 'I'd never want to write something without humour,' says Dick, 'because I think it's essential. Even in the darkest, most heavy movie it's important because life contains humour – often in the most inappropriate places – and I like that.'

It seems that writing situation comedy is an enervating exercise and not to be taken lightly. 'It's great when you finish it, but, boy, it's hard work,' Dick explains. 'When you set out to be funny and people don't laugh, you've failed one hundred per cent. And you know it because you can hear the silence; whereas if you write a thriller and people are fairly thrilled, it's not such a dramatic failure. It's only comedy where you have this absolute situation: do they laugh or not. And when they don't, it's very, very painful.'

FILM CREDITS include

The Jokers   The Likely Lads   Villain   Otley

Porridge   The Prisoner of Zenda   Still Crazy

Hannibal Brooks

THEATRE

Billy   CREDITS include

Porridge sketch for
The Two Ronnies stage show

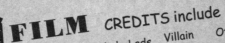

TV CREDITS include

Whatever Happened to   Mog   Porridge

The Likely Lads   the Likely Lads?   Going Straight

Mr Aitch   The New Adventures
of Lucky Jim   Freddie and Max

The Further Adventures
of Lucky Jim   Seven of One ('Prisoner and Escort'
and 'I'll Fly You for a Quid')

Auf Wiedersehen, Pet   The Highwayman

The Old Boy Network

Full Stretch   The Tracey Ullman Show (US)

Over the Rainbow

Rita Moreno Show (US)

Billy Liar (pilot for US)

Thick as Thieves

On The Rocks (US)

Dick also directed the second series of Not Only . . . But Also in 1966, as
well as writing material for the show.

NORMAN FLETCHER

PRISONER'S RECORD CARD

Name: **Norman Stanley Fletcher** **(known as Fletch)**	Prisoner No: **2215**
Home Address: 107 Alexandra Park Crescent, London N5	
Age: 42	

Family:
Married to Isobel (who used to work in the hardware department of
a shop) while doing porridge. They stayed together twenty-four
years. Has three children: Raymond, fourteen, Marion, nineteen, and
twenty-four-year-old Ingrid, who was named after his mother, who in
turn had been given the name of her mother's favourite film star,
Ingrid Bergman. It's claimed that Fletcher's eldest daughter was
conceived in Highgate Cemetery.

Length of Sentence:
Five years (transferred from Brixton), for robbery. After Post Office-
and housebreaking, he decided to try his luck at something different:
robbing a lorry. However, the brakes failed because it was overloaded, and he crashed through three gardens and a brick wall
before ending up in someone's tool shed.

Previous Form:
His entire life has been spent c/o Her Majesty's establishments, or so
it seems. As a youngster he had a spell in Borstal, where he gained a
diploma in plastering. Unfortunately, this earlier taste of prison life
did little to prevent him turning into a jailbird: he served time at
both Maidstone and Brixton prisons prior to Slade. Even his days as
a schoolboy were spent at a special school because he was constantly
playing truant.
His record is not surprising when you consider crime
is in the blood of the Fletcher family. His great-
granddad, William Wellington Fletcher, was the last
person to be hung in England for sheep stealing.

HM PRISON
SLADE

PRISONER'S RECORD CARD

Background:

Earlier in his life, he adopted the name Frankie Fletcher and used to sing in clubs around North London. During the 1950s he was King of the Teds in Muswell Hill, where he grew up. In terms of siblings, we hear only of a brother, George, who sends him a Christmas card – illustrated with a naked lady because he's 'only allowed it once a year'!

Fletcher left school without any qualifications and, as he couldn't follow the careers he wanted (namely as a stockbroker, or a tennis coach at a girls' school), he declined the chance to work in a cardboard-box factory and instead robbed a sub Post Office off London's North Circular.

He did his national service in Malaya, working in the stores in Kuala Lumpur. His parents are still alive and recently celebrated their diamond wedding anniversary.

Personality:

Very droll, possessing a dry, sarcastic sense of humour – you need to watch him! Is also one of life's cynics.

Hobbies and Interests:

Passionate about film star Rita Hayworth. Studied carpentry while at Slade but was not the most successful of students.

Unusual Habits:

Frequently sings a line from the hit song 'You Belong to Me'. Gets a little irritating after a while, as does the constant gum-chewing.

Review of Time in Slade:

Treated with deference by fellow inmates, many of whom often turned to him for advice or when they needed a shoulder to cry on. Held several jobs at Slade: initially he was swilling out the pigs at the prison farm, then he worked in the library until an incident involving throwing a vicar off the balcony saw him transferred to a less cushy number. Got back into the governor's good books, though, and was assigned a job in the admin block.

Post-Prison Update:

After serving three and a half years of his sentence, Fletch was released from Slade only to find that his wife had left him. Lives in Muswell Hill with his daughter Ingrid and son Raymond. He has taken a job as a night porter, working from eleven to seven.

HM PRISON
SLADE

Ronnie Barker

Ronnie Barker encountered no problems playing Fletcher, partly because he based some of the character's traits on himself. 'There was a lot of me in there – not that I break into post offices, of course!' Ronnie is eager to point out. 'There was plenty of my father in Fletch, too. Although the character was a Cockney and I was born in Oxford, he was working class and I could relate to him. He was easy to play and I didn't have to think much about it – unlike with Arkwright in *Open All Hours*, where I had to consider a different background entirely.

'Fletcher was obviously a wide-boy, out for everything he could get. Whatever he did was to his own benefit: you think he's helping someone out but he's working it to his own advantage; there are lots of examples of this in the scripts.' But Ronnie agrees that Fletch was likeable. 'You must always

have charm in a character. Even if you're playing an old tramp you need a bit of charm.'

Everyone involved in *Porridge* worked well together and found they could breeze through rehearsals. 'We'd often start at ten and finish by one because we all knew what we were doing,' says Ronnie, who knew he was carrying a lot of responsibility on his shoulders but never felt anything other than total support from those around him. 'You knew no one was going to let you down, ruin a gag or bit of timing.'

Upon reflection, Ronnie can spot certain milestones that acted as turning points in his long and exciting career. 'There are about five instances where I happened to be in the right place at the right time,' he says. 'I can't remember an occasion when I've been unlucky.' The first of these markers was his acceptance by a small repertory company in Aylesbury at the beginning of his career. Following this was his breakthrough to Oxford Rep, then his West End debut courtesy of Peter Hall. The other key moments involved his television career: appearing in *The Frost Report* alongside Ronnie Corbett was an important juncture, as Ronnie explains. 'As a result, David Frost signed us up for his production company; we had a five-year contract covering a sitcom and a series of *The Two Ronnies* each year. The show brought us into the limelight and helped establish our names with the Beeb.'

Ronnie was born in Bedford in 1929 and moved to Oxford at the age of four, when his father was relocated by Shell, for whom he was a clerk. Money was tight in the Barker household, but that didn't prevent Ronnie's father splashing out occasionally on a trip to the local theatre. His English master further encouraged his interest in the world of acting. 'It was during the Second World War, so the school was short-staffed because most of the teachers had joined the forces. A decision was taken not to continue with any theatre productions, but that didn't stop our English master doing a bit of reading in class. I remember playing the part of Shylock in *The Merchant of Venice* – it was great fun.'

Although he enjoyed the experience immensely, it wasn't until he'd left school and worked as clerk for a local bank that he acquired his taste for the stage. 'A pal I'd been at school with suggested I join a theatre group for something to do socially. He said: "There are a lot of girls there – and you don't need to be an actor; you can always help with the scenery."' But it wasn't long before Ronnie made his stage debut with The Theatre Players, his local amateur company. 'I was cast in a small part, then did a few more roles and suddenly realised it was what I wanted to do.'

After watching the Manchester Repertory Company perform at Aylesbury, Ronnie plucked up the courage to change direction and resign from the bank. 'I found the work very boring anyhow.' Ronnie's status as a junior clerk meant him being lumbered with many of the menial tasks. 'Everything had to be recorded by hand in thick ledgers, which terrified me – if you blotted them you were in terrible trouble.' He wrote a letter to the Aylesbury Rep asking for a job; and was soon employed as assistant stage manager, mainly working behind-the-scenes. Then: 'Within a couple of weeks I was offered a comedy part – and I can remember getting my first laugh even now.'

Ronnie found working in repertory theatre exhausting but exciting. 'While you were performing in one play, you'd also be rehearsing the next; and being involved in props meant I had to think about the one after that, too! But it was great training. Reps were wonderful because people came to see what actors and actresses were doing that week. They were more interested in the performers than the play, saying things like, "Oh, what's he playing?" or "Oh, look, he's got a moustache on this week."'

Ronnie feels that audiences in those pre-television days were much more naïve in their attitudes towards the trade than they are now. 'Audiences were less sophisticated. In the 1930s they'd say, "Let's go to that show in the West End where that man wears those funny suits." That was the height of the sophistication: they'd go and see a man in funny suits! The audiences were still a bit like that when I started, in 1948.'

It was evident from the start that Ronnie Barker had a natural talent for comedy; he enjoyed the genre and was skilled at it, even as a callow actor moving to Rhyl with the Aylesbury Rep.

When the company disbanded, Ronnie joined a rep at Bramhall, Cheshire, and there met Glenn Melvyn – who would later offer him his first taste of television, on *I'm Not Bothered*. But Ronnie at that time hankered after a return to his hometown, so wrote to the Oxford Playhouse and accepted a job in publicity as a way back. He went on to spend three years on the Playhouse stage before making his London and – shortly after – West End debuts.

The latter part of the 1950s saw Ronnie break into radio, with a regular role on *The Floggits* and parts on *Variety Playhouse* and *The Navy Lark*. He also made his film debut, as a head waiter in 1958's *Wonderful Things!* By the sixties, he was an established performer in all media, and the small screen had begun to take a higher priority in his career. While he made cameo appearances in dramas like *The Saint* and *The Avengers*, it was in *The Frost Report*, which began in 1966, and the equally irreverent *Not Only . . . But Also* that he established himself for television audiences. By now Ronnie had met the man who'd help him form one of television's strongest partnerships, *The Two Ronnies*, a relationship that would last twenty-two years.

In 1968, Ronnie was given his first series of pilot shows in *The Ronnie Barker Playhouse*. Three years later, *Six Dates with Barker* gave him the chance to experiment with a further batch. Although none of the pilot shows were picked up at that point, one was revisited nearly two decades later when Ronnie adapted Hugh Leonard's *The Removals Person* and created *Clarence*, the story of a short-sighted half-wit.

The sitcom turned out to be Ronnie's last, by which time he'd become one of comedy's true greats thanks to a body of work spanning the entire profession. 'I always thought the pilot would make a good series, so I rewrote the first episode to fit in with the rest that followed. I enjoyed making *Clarence*, partly because it was filmed around Oxfordshire.

The cottage featured in the series was built specially; it was beautiful and several people wanted to buy it.'

As well as for a dozen series of *The Two Ronnies* and numerous Christmas Specials, Ronnie is probably best remembered for playing Arkwright, the stingy shopkeeper in four series of *Open All Hours*, and Fletcher in *Porridge*. Unlike some actors, Ronnie Barker did not become typecast after appearing in a successful sitcom and has moved between roles with ease. He has, however, always worried about outstaying his welcome, and it was for this reason that he gave up his prison life as Fletch. 'I think Dick and Ian would have happily continued, but I didn't want to – although I agreed to do one more series [*Going Straight*] when Fletcher came out of prison.'

Ronnie feels he owes much to *Porridge*. 'It was probably the best and most important show I did, but *Open All Hours* topped it as far as fun was concerned. I loved doing both sitcoms but because of David Jason in *Open All Hours* it was slightly better, because of the laughs we had.

'I always worried about getting stuck with a character; I didn't want that. So after deciding to call it a day with *Porridge* I told Bill Cotton, Head of Comedy at that point, that I wanted to move on and do *Open All Hours*. He tried persuading me to stick with *Porridge* but it was no use.'

The first series of *Open All Hours* was recorded and transmitted in 1976 on BBC2, but it was five years before another series was seen. 'The first series only attracted about two and a half million viewers, which it would do on BBC2. I complained it was on the wrong channel, and when we finally made the second series it was shown on BBC1. It went on to become a massive hit.'

Ronnie has been the recipient of many awards in recognition of his services to the industry, including several BAFTAs. But none is more memorable than the award he collected at the Water Rats' Annual Dinner. 'It was an award for *Porridge*, so I thought it would be fun if I went in my uniform, handcuffed to Fulton. I asked him and he was delighted to do it. A limo was sent for us and just as we got to the venue we decided to put the handcuffs on – only to find we'd locked ourselves around a strap inside the car and couldn't get out. Eventually the chauffeur sorted that out.

'So in we went, and as we marched into the room there were great cheers and rounds of applause. But, although Fulton had the key, he couldn't open the cuffs. One of the people attending the dinner came up and said: 'Don't worry, I'm a member of the Magic Circle, I can get you out.' He spent twenty minutes trying but couldn't. We started to panic a bit but thankfully someone eventually prised us out of them.'

Ronnie Barker has now officially retired from the acting business. A number of factors were behind his decision. 'I'd run out of ideas and, to be honest, I'd done everything I wanted to do. And, I'm sorry to say, the material coming through wasn't such good quality.' As far as today's offerings on television are concerned, Ronnie isn't particularly impressed. 'I find it difficult to laugh at shows nowadays. I like programmes such as *As Time Goes By* and *Kiss Me Kate*, but I find some just too vulgar. Bad language in scripts can turn people away and much of it is unnecessary. 'One of the problems is that everyone wants to write their own scripts now; the performers write and feel they have to resort to lines concerning bodily functions. Producers are trying desperately to appeal to younger viewers, but they're not watching television – they're out with their chums. Producers should concentrate on older viewers if they want to increase audience figures.'

LENNIE GODBER

PRISONER'S RECORD CARD

Name:	Prisoner No:
Leonard Arthur Godber **(known as Lennie)**	**3470**

Home Address:
Not disclosed

Age:
23

Family:
Single, although had a fiancée, Denise, when incarcerated. This relationship fizzled out during his time behind bars. Lennie's mother was relieved at the split as she never liked Denise, partly because she wore green nail-varnish and went around braless!

Length of Sentence:
Two years, for breaking and entering.

Previous Form:
First offender, although he was lucky not to have been caught for a previous offence. He was planning to turn over a house in Sutton Coldfield where the chimney was his only source of access. He ended up getting stuck and his intended victims arrived home to find his legs sticking out of the fireplace. He managed to escape, but as a result of the incident he now suffers from claustrophobia.

HM PRISON
SLADE

PORRIDGE

PRISONER'S RECORD CARD

Background:
Grew up in a Birmingham back street, but Godber is proud of his upbringing because his mother kept her children spotless despite money being scarce. He is very close to his mother, but doesn't know where his father is.

Personality:
A likeable, hard-working prisoner, although easily led. A little naïve.

Hobbies and Interests:
Interested in making up for lost time and improving on the one O level (geography) he holds. Attended as many classes as possible while at Slade, including pottery and elementary plumbing. Also studied for a history O level.

A keen footballer and follower of Aston Villa, his favourite television programme is Kojak.

Unusual Habits:
Doesn't drink tea and dislikes brown toast!

Review of Time in Slade:
A quiet, conscientious prisoner who worked in the kitchen during his sentence.

Post-Prison Update:
Since his release, Godber has moved back to Birmingham. He secured employment as a long-distance lorry driver but spent more and more time in Muswell Hill, courting none other than Fletcher's daughter Ingrid. He would annoy Fletcher by parking an articulated lorry outside his home, blocking the sunlight from entering the windows. Ended up marrying Ingrid and honeymooning in Lanzarote.

HM PRISON SLADE

Richard Beckinsale

Richard Beckinsale's sudden death at the age of thirty-one was tragic. Not only did it rob his family of a loving husband and father, but it also deprived the world of showbusiness of one of its greatest talents, an actor whose career promised even greater things than he'd already achieved. Actor Christopher Biggins worked alongside Richard in several episodes of Porridge and admired his talent. 'He would have moved through each decade and have become, in my view, a huge name – he'd probably have become a movie star by now.'

With several hit shows under his belt, Richard was a sought-after actor, particularly in the world of television. Although he held a desire to expand his portfolio of characterisations beyond the naïve, callow, likeable men he was usually asked to play, his portrayal of such roles was always top class, his abilities affording him seamless performances.

When he was interviewed back in the seventies by Yorkshire Television, Richard expressed his desire to progress to more mature roles. With The Lovers and Rising Damp each showing him as an impressionable young man, he said, 'I'm getting a bit old for this type of role. I want to play older parts.' But he always made a success of the comedy roles he played, and never regretted accepting roles like Alan in Rising Damp, Geoffrey in The Lovers and, of course, Lennie Godber in Porridge. 'I've always been selective, especially where comedy series are concerned. I have been lucky in that I accepted three offers in television comedy within a relatively short space of time that became hits. But I have also turned down several offers which I feel pretty sure would not have been hits.'

Tony Osoba, who became friends with Richard during the days of Porridge, was aware he was keen to progress to more mature roles, but points out that the reason he was continuously offered such jobs was because he played them so well. 'We didn't know each other that well beforehand, even though we both played football for a showbusiness team and had a few mutual friends; but, as the show went along, we got to

71

know each other better and began socialising quite a bit.

'Part of that shy naïveté came from Richard, but there was a lot more to his acting than that. And one of the great things about him was that you could watch him and never see him act, which is an art. It appeared that he was doing it effortlessly and whatever character he played was real; that's a superb skill because it isn't easy.

'In Godber, he had a character who was much more than just a foil for Fletcher. He had to explore a range of emotions: there were moments where he had to be strong, others where he was struggling coming to terms with prison and had to be helped along; Richard conveyed that superbly.'

Born in Nottingham in 1947, Richard left school at sixteen determined to become an actor. Before his dream came true, he worked as an upholsterer, in an iron-pipe factory and as a clerk in the accounts department at the local gas board, while studying English and art at night school. But when he was offered a place at RADA in 1966, he headed for London and a new career.

After graduating from drama school, Richard – whose daughters Kate and Samantha are both actresses – worked in rep, initially at Crewe, before more extensive theatre roles came his way, such as that of Romeo in a production of *Romeo and Juliet* at the Leeds Playhouse in 1971. He was soon offered a number of small parts on television, including one in a 1969 episode of *Coronation Street* (playing PC Wilcox, he was responsible for arresting Ena Sharples).

But his big break came in 1970, when alongside Paula Wilcox he played Geoffrey in Granada's sitcom *The Lovers*. Two series were transmitted and his performance as the young Mancunian bank clerk won him an award as Best TV Newcomer for 1971. The show became a big hit with viewers and, by the time *Porridge* and *Rising Damp* – in which he played medical student Alan – were up and running in the mid-1970s, Richard Beckinsale had become a household name. Other television credits included *Couples, Second House, Tales of Piccadilly, Elephant Eggs in a Rhubarb Tree, Give and Take, Truscott's Luck* and *Consequences.*

Although the success he achieved in sitcom brought security, Richard was always on the hunt for fresh challenges on screen and stage. In 1975 he was offered a straight role in the TV film *Last Summer*, while the theatre saw him in productions of Shakespeare as well as in various musicals and satires. In 1979 he'd moved on to a new BBC sitcom, *Bloomers*, written by James Saunders, when he suffered a fatal heart attack. Rehearsals were due to begin on the sixth episode of the series when he died suddenly at his home; the five episodes already recorded were later transmitted with the blessing of his widow, actress Judy Loe.

Christopher Biggins recalls the moment he heard about Richard's death. 'I was making a film called *The Tempest* for Derek Jarman. We were filming in Northumberland and were staying in this rickety old hotel. It was freezing cold and I was having a lie down after filming on the beaches, when suddenly the manager came to me and said: "Mr Biggins, the *Sun* newspaper wants a comment from you." When I asked him on what subject, he replied: "Richard Beckinsale has just died." I was totally gobsmacked and could not believe it.'

News of Beckinsale's death was equally shocking for Ronnie Barker to accept. It was producer Sydney Lotterby who told him about the tragic event. 'He phoned and simply said, "Richard's dead!" I didn't understand what he was saying at first so he repeated himself. I couldn't believe what I was hearing. As far as I know he hadn't had anything wrong with his heart. We'd just finished the film and we'd both undergone insurance medicals, which we'd passed. It was such a shock.'

MR MACKAY

PRISON OFFICER'S EMPLOYMENT CARD

Name:	Job Title:
Mr Mackay	**Senior Prison Officer**

Age:
55

Length of Service:
Twenty-five years

Family:
Married for seventeen years. Seems a happy marriage, especially as his wife regularly presses his uniform!

Background:
Endured a tough childhood in the shadows of the Lanarkshire coal-fields. Money was scarce, so through necessity he left school at four-teen and became a boy soldier in order to help pay the bills in his impoverished household – although one of the prisoners, Fletcher, always claimed it was really a way of hiding behind a 'mantle of security'. His father was almost permanently unemployed, a depressing situation with eight children to support.

During the sixteen years he served with the 1st Battalion of the Argyll and Sutherland Highlanders, he climbed the promotion ladder to the rank of sergeant major. He also served as a drill sergeant, and travelled to far-flung corners of the world, including Malaya.

When he eventually returned to life as a civilian, he ran a boarding house, The Strathclyde, with his wife for two years (1951–53) in Peebles. The venture was far from successful, swallowing up most of Mackay's savings and demob pay, so he sold up. After a failed attempt to re-enlist, he plumped for the prison service instead.

HM PRISON
SLADE

PRISON OFFICER'S EMPLOYMENT CARD

Personality:
Parades around like a peacock, with a back so rigid it wouldn't be a surprise to find a board stuffed up his jacket!

Hobbies and Interests:
Few: it appears that the prison service is his life. However, he has a history in boxing, having fought for Midlothian Boys and for his army battalion.

Unusual Habits:
Has an infuriating habit of wrenching his neck at moments of confrontation or stress.

Suitability for Job:
Ran Slade Prison with a fist of iron, but it wouldn't do any harm if he were to adopt a more contemporary attitude towards how the establishment should be run. A little sense of humour wouldn't go amiss either.

Stop Press! In contrast to the meteoric climb up the promotion ladder he probably expected, Mackay left the service after a quarter of a century without reaching the ranks of management and with a bitter taste in his mouth.

HM PRISON
SLADE

Fulton Mackay

Such is the power of television, Fulton Mackay will always
be remembered for playing his televisual namesake in
Porridge. His top-notch portrayal of Slade Prison's stern
warder may have been an early excursion into small-screen
comedy, but the versatile Scottish actor had for years previously plied his trade in the theatre. When he pulled on his
warder's uniform for the first time it was clear his had been a
piece of first-class casting. Ronnie Barker enjoyed playing
alongside Fulton. 'He was immensely likeable, a charming
man, while in character he was the person you loved to hate.
Fulton had plenty of charisma and I thought he played the
part impeccably.' But Ronnie always wondered where Fulton
thought his character was supposed to be from. 'He told me
he based the character on a PT instructor he'd encountered in
the forces, a man who used to swagger about, but Fulton
always did a strange accent that wasn't quite Scottish – I
never dared ask him whether it was Cockney.'

A smile crosses Ronnie's face as he recalls how Fulton
bagged most of the rehearsal time. 'He was a great actor but
occasionally would say, "I can't play this scene, Ronnie."
About three-quarters of the rehearsal time was devoted to
him, which initially I didn't mind. But eventually I had to say
things like: "In this episode I've got twenty-five minutes,
you've got five, so can I do a bit of rehearsing as well?"'

Someone else who experienced Fulton's attention to detail
was Sam Kelly, who played Warren, one of the inmates at
Slade Prison. 'He put in a brilliant performance as Mr
Mackay. He'd come from years of serious, straight Scottish
theatre, yet took to comedy like a duck to water. But he was
very pernickety – I remember one day sitting in the
producer's box with Syd Lotterby, who shouted: "Oh, come
on, Fulton, for God's sake!" Fulton couldn't hear him, of
course, but he was absolutely furious with him over something – and I suspect that sort of thing went on more often
than we knew. Although Fulton was very particular, the end
result was extremely good.'

Jimmy Gilbert, Head of Comedy at the Beeb when
Porridge was commissioned, became a close friend of Fulton's
and believes any domination in terms of rehearsal time was
due to his quest for perfection. 'He was a total perfectionist
and very self-critical,' says Jimmy. 'Perfectionists can sometimes be a bit prickly – and Fulton *could* be difficult, but he
was a delightful man. As a friend he was such fun and very
loyal; I regarded him as family.'

Fulton was born in Paisley, Renfrewshire, in 1922. His
mother died when he was just a boy so, with his father
working in the NAAFI, an aunt in Clydebank raised him.
Upon leaving school, he was employed as a quantity
surveyor for a time before volunteering for the RAF in
1941. But a perforated eardrum prevented him from
joining up and he turned instead to the army, going on to
complete five years' service, three of which were spent in
India.

On his return to civvy street, he enrolled at RADA in
1945; after graduating he embarked on a theatrical career,
working many years in rep, including nine seasons at
Glasgow's Citizens' Theatre. He was also employed at
Edinburgh's Royal Lyceum Theatre before offers of work in
London came his way, beginning at the Arts Theatre Club,
where in 1960 he appeared in *Naked Island*, a production
about POWs in Singapore. Between 1962 and 1963 he
worked for the Old Vic Company, while a spell with the
Royal Shakespeare Company involved playing Squeers in the
original production of the Company's *The Life and
Adventures of Nicholas Nickleby*.

His talents extended to writing, and he contributed plays
for BBC radio and television, including *Girl with Flowers in
Her Hair* and *Semper Fidelis*. He also appeared in several
films, including *Local Hero*, with Burt Lancaster, *The Brave
Don't Cry, Gumshoe, Defence of the Realm, Nothing But
the Night, Laxdale Hall* and *Britannia Hospital*. He made
many small-screen appearances, too: among his credits are
roles in *Some Mothers Do 'Ave 'Em, Three Fables of
Orkney*, a series of *Special Branch, Ghosts, The*

Troubleshooters, Master of Ballantrae, Clay, Slip-Up, A Sense of Freedom, The Foundation, The Palace and Going Gently. But, despite his prolific career, Fulton Mackay will always be remembered by most for his portrayal of Slade Prison's strict disciplinarian.

Away from acting, one of Fulton's passions was art, as Tony Osoba, who struck up a friendship with Fulton during the filming of *Porridge*, explains. 'I think it might surprise some people to know that Fulton – who many people think of as this tough, rugged prison officer – enjoyed sitting in his garden painting pictures of flowers and trees. He was a very private man, so I felt privileged when he invited me to his home where he showed me his collection of paintings. Fulton was also a writer, and completed several romantic plays about Scotland.'

Fulton died in 1987, aged sixty-four. It was a shock to everyone, not least to close friend Jimmy Gilbert. 'I was heading off to the Montreux Film Festival and saw Fulton just before leaving. He said he was going into hospital to have an operation but made light of it. I remember saying to him, "For God sake, don't do something silly like keeling over." He laughed and said he'd see me when I returned. By the time I got back he'd had the operation, but it turned out to be stomach cancer and he died within a week. I miss him dearly.'

Fulton has left a legacy of fine portrayals on stage and screen; but, in terms of television comedy, it's difficult to find a better piece of work than his rich, colourful creation known as Mr Mackay.

MR BARROWCLOUGH

PRISON OFFICER'S EMPLOYMENT CARD

Name: **Henry Barrowclough**	Job Title: **Prison Officer**
Age: Not prepared to divulge such personal information.	
Length of Service: Twenty-three years' unblemished service.	

Family:

Unhappily married to Alice. Has openly admitted that the 'sun rarely shines in his household', which partly explains his brief affair with Dorothy Jamieson, the Governor's secretary.

His wife doesn't like his job; nor where they live, missing the amenities offered by a city. Barrowclough has painted a rather gruesome picture of her, claiming she's bitter, restless, bad-tempered and has spots. Their marriage has been on the rocks for some time, and she's enjoyed liaisons with other men – most recently with a marriage counsellor. To Barrowclough's dismay, invariably, she soon returns.

Background:

Refers to his background as 'a bit of a mixture', probably because previous generations of the Barrowclough family contain Scottish, English, Irish and Polish blood running through their veins. His granddad was an ironmonger in Accrington.

Completed national service with the RAF in Singapore, working in the equipment section, before joining the prison service – something he claimed he did because of always wanting a vocation that would 'satisfy his desire to do work of public usefulness'. (However, it's also been rumoured that the free house and uniform were key motivations behind his application.)

HM PRISON SLADE

PORRIDGE

PRISON OFFICER'S EMPLOYMENT CARD

Personality:
Described by prisoner 2215 (Fletcher) as looking like 'Arthur Askey on stilts'.

Hobbies and Interests:
Has a passion for astronomy and botany. Occasionally takes prisoners out on to the fell to explore the countryside.

Unusual Habits:
None known.

Suitability for Job:
Never going to set the prison-service career ladder on fire! Views himself as a modern-day humanitarian but his beliefs are occasionally far from considered. A bit wet, he's far too easily led and influenced to be considered for demanding managerial responsibilities.

He's an overly nervous individual who believes he's got an inferiority complex. He also feels he's holding down his job by the skin of his teeth, and has visited the prison psychiatric unit because of his lack of self-confidence.

HM PRISON
SLADE

80

Brian Wilde

Brian Wilde believes Mackay and Barrowclough probably
reflected the culture within the prison service at the time of
Porridge's first run. 'You had the old hard-bitten warders
who felt prisoners were inside to be punished, and a new
wave of officers coming through who were interested in
rehabilitating prisoners.'

Brian knew early on that *Porridge* possessed the necessary
ingredients for success. 'The writers were excellent; they
knew what they were doing and made it easier for the actors
to play their characters. The series was also well cast, even
down to the smaller parts; then we had Syd Lotterby, a very
good director and excellent at casting, who was helped by an
excellent assistant, Judy Loe. When you put it all together it's
not surprising the show worked so well.'

When asked to select a favourite episode, Brian quickly
points to 'Prisoner and Escort', the pilot which afforded him
the lion's share of the scenes with Ronnie Barker. 'I had lots
to do in it, whereas in other episodes I wasn't given so
much,' he says, admittedly disappointed that his character
wasn't allowed to develop to the extent he would have
wished. 'In the series, Barrowclough wasn't as important as
in the pilot, which was sad.'

Away from his duties patrolling the landings at Slade
Prison, Mr Barrowclough endured a miserable home life. So
unhappy was the warder, he'd even open his heart to Fletcher
about his tribulations, conjuring up the worst possible images
of his insufferable wife – who we never saw. 'It was left to
the audience to use their imagination about what she looked
like. To have shown her would have ruined the effect.'

Reflecting on his time playing Slade's ineffectual warder,
Brian feels that overall it was a happy period in his career.
'We had a good company. You can't spend a lot of time with
people without either falling out bitterly or getting on; fortunately we all got on well together.'

When *Porridge* came to an end in 1977, it was a sad time
for the cast who'd worked together during three series and

two Christmas Specials. But Brian acknowledges that the time was right to call it a day. 'There's nothing worse than letting a series drag on and I think it stopped at just the right time, when the episodes were still strong.' He wasn't so keen on the film, though. 'I don't think it worked and it had an air of tiredness about it.'

Two long-running, highly successful characters have dominated Brian's career: Barrowclough in *Porridge* and Foggy in *Last of the Summer Wine*. Brian again refers to the quality of the scripts as the reason behind the latter show's phenomenal success. 'Actors depend so much on the people who write the scripts and Roy Clarke was another good author. It makes life so much easier if the script tells you what to do, is clear and watertight. You then have confidence in the programme.'

He first appeared as Foggy in 1976 and stayed eight years before taking a break from the show. In 1990 he returned to the fold but eventually a minor indisposition forced him to give up the role.

As well as long-running parts in two of Britain's most popular sitcoms, Brian's TV career has included a debut in 1951's *Black Limelight*, Sir Thomas Landers in 1954's *The Scarlet Pimpernel*, a cemetery attendant in 1961's *Jango*, Happy Dwyer in a 1964 episode of *The Protectors*, several roles in *The Man in Room 17* a year later and appearances in *The Avengers, The Dustbinmen, Out of the Unknown, The Sweeney, The Love of Mike, Elizabeth R* and the lead in *Wyatt's Watchdogs*. Unfortunately the 1988 sitcom about a retired army major who formed a neighbourhood watch only lasted one series. 'We tried it but it didn't work for some reason – it was a good idea, though.'

Lancashire-born Brian grew up in Hertfordshire before training at RADA. But his life as a professional actor couldn't have got off to a worse start when he spent six months unemployed. He finally earned his first wage packet on stage at St Andrew's in Scotland before joining Liverpool Rep. The swift turnaround of plays in repertory theatre afforded Brian the chance to play different characters – a rich learning curve for any actor, though he wasn't conscious of it at the time. 'You just play the roles and hope it helps, but most of the time you didn't have time to think about how valuable it might all be.'

During the fifties and sixties he worked extensively in the theatre, with credits including *The Power and the Glory, The Ring of Truth, The Visit* and Peter Ustinov's *The Moment of Truth*, which was the first West End production in which Brian had a 'decent' part. He was the first member of his family to tread the boards. 'If anyone else in the family had done it I probably wouldn't have, because I'd have spotted all the pitfalls. I knew nothing about them, so I went in with every confidence – then realised what a hit-and-miss profession it is: you may click or may not. I thank God for the marvellous opportunities I had in *Porridge* and *Last of the Summer Wine*.'

After years of gaining what were mainly cameo roles in TV – in shows like *Doomwatch* and *Our Mutual Friend* – the two sitcoms meant Brian was thrust suddenly into the media spotlight and his career duly rewarded. 'I was doing quite well but it was nice to have something more than the odd episode here and there. It's lovely having regular work, because you feel more secure and can get on with acting instead of worrying.'

As well as working on the stage and television, Brian has appeared in a handful of films, such as *Simon and Laura, Street Corner, Will Any Gentleman . . .?, Tiger in the Smoke, Night of the Demon, Girls at Sea, On the Run, Rattle of a Simple Man, Darling, The Informers, Carry On Doctor, One Brief Summer* and *The Jokers*. While the latter part of his career has been dominated by comedy – particularly on TV – his early appearances were mainly in dramas. 'I used to play a lot of heavies at one time,' he admits.

He's quick to brush off the significance of his film roles, regarding them as 'inconsequential', and didn't particularly enjoy working in the medium. 'My appearances were just spits and coughs, nothing to speak of. Although I had a reasonable part in *The Jokers*, the rest were just one- or two-day jobs, so insignificant I can't remember them.'

Looking back over his long career, he finds it difficult choosing a favourite medium. 'I enjoy television but there's nothing like the excitement of the theatre, especially when the curtain goes up: you see the audience waiting for you, and you know you've got to get on with it and make it work.' Conversely, however, Brian's desires these days have changed: 'I don't work in the theatre because I couldn't stand the boredom of performing the same play every night, whereas in television you record a scene and it's over.' Today, Brian is semi-retired and taking life a little easier. 'I'm not actively seeking work – but if something interesting on TV came along, I'd consider it.'

THE WRITERS ON THE ACTORS

Clement on Barker

When I was set to direct my first movie, *Otley*, I tried to cast Ronnie as a professional assassin – the part eventually played by Leonard Rossiter. I was looking for a superb comic actor, my theory being that if you can play comedy you can play anything.

I still believe that. I wish we had seen Ronnie extend himself more as an actor because I never saw limits to his talent. He brought with him a rare intelligence. First to the script, where his quick mind offered up new or improved jokes, always with great respect. 'Is that all right?' he'd ask and as a rule, once we'd stopped laughing, we'd nod okay. When blocking a scene he was ahead of me as a director, usually sensing where the camera had to be for the master shot.

The day of the taping made him nervous. He didn't like to 'warm up' the studio audience, needing to concentrate on the job in hand. Yet once under way, if something went wrong, he was the one who stepped into the breach, explaining the problem and making them laugh.

Many actors are thrown off balance by the audience. They rehearse all week without them and then their response on the day of the taping throws their timing completely. It's a strange, hybrid medium – an awkward cross between theatre and film. But I can think of nobody who worked a studio audience better than Ronnie.

Take a moment in the pilot episode, 'Prisoner and Escort', when Fletcher, having been on the moors all night, discovers at dawn that he is back where he started from. We artfully concealed this fact from the studio audience and it got a huge laugh. But watch the tape and see what wonders Ronnie did with the moment.

Other actors would have got two laughs out of it – he got three. And without mugging or going out of character.

Porridge was the perfect marriage of an actor to a part. It was not the series Ronnie had envisaged – he'd seen it more as a prison version of *Bilko*. But once we'd gone round Wandsworth, Brixton and the Scrubs we knew we couldn't write that. For a while we didn't know how to write anything. Perhaps what kept us going was the thought that at a certain point Ronnie Barker was going to appear and the audience, at home as well as in the studio, would relax, knowing they were in safe hands – the hands of a comic genius.

He's also a warm and generous friend. After the *Porridge* movie, when he went to Australia for a year, he gave Ian and me his Jaguar! I think I drove it on odd days and Ian on even ones. In those days Ronnie usually had at least three years work planned in advance. He'd struggled in the early years and seemed to fear unemployment. Then suddenly, just after Peter Hall asked him to play Falstaff at the National, he decided to stop completely. I've never really understood why and I think it's a great loss. But thank you, Ronnie, for the great pleasure you have given all of us. And the Jaguar – though it needed a new silencer. Did I ever mention that?

La Frenais on Beckinsale

Richard didn't seem like any actor I'd ever met. By *Porridge* I'd been 'around' actors for a few years and as much as I loved and respected them, found them a breed of complex contradictions: self-absorbed and neurotic, obnoxious, vulnerable, ambitious and humble, egotistical and insecure; not surprising given the nature of their profession in which rejection is an inevitable constant.

Richard was different, and whatever drove him didn't appear to be fuelled by ambition and ego. He was the typical 'great bloke' that you remembered fondly from school. The one who stayed in the same home town, the same steady job and in the same marriage and whose view of the world was completely free of envy or malice.

The term 'laid back' didn't exist in the mid-seventies, but if it had there would have been a picture of Richard next to the dictionary definition. He was a terrible reader, which is the first part of an actor's investiture in a new role: the moment when he has nothing but a notion of the character and the unread, 'cold' script. Richard was hopeless, it's a wonder that he progressed from his earliest auditions!

He was even bad after he'd had the script for a few days and we all assembled for the cast read-through. Then something amazing happened, as it did every week when Richard's performances went from hesitancy and incoherence to the truth and brilliance with which he invested all his work. His acting, like himself, was without artifice or guile. He left the stage ridiculously early and I think his talent was irreplaceable.

Clement on Mackay

Fulton was a lovely man, brim full of life, love and enthusiasm. A well-rounded, spiritual man. Syd Lotterby told me that Fulton would rehearse forever if you let him, never too tired to have another try to see if he could make his performance even better. It was true, but it came from a deep desire for perfection, and at the same time a zestful energy for doing something he loved.

He did certain things in *Porridge* which were inimitable. I think of Mr Mackay's reaction when he knows Fletcher has put one over on him – first a cold fury that he's been had, followed by a mute warning of dire retribution to come. Ian and I can always make each other laugh by remembering his reading of a line from the movie, where he's showing the ropes to a new screw. 'The prison officers have a club. It is *known* . . . [a long, drawn out emphasis on this word, while his left hand paints the title on an imaginary door] . . . as The Prison Officers' Club.'

When an actor makes a part his own to that degree you can't imagine how you ever wrote it in the first place without seeing him in your mind's eye. I think it took us a few shows before we realised what a priceless asset he was, and what a brilliant adversary for Fletcher.

But I remember him, too, as a painter and philosopher, enormously kind and ever optimistic. I really miss him.

87

La Frenais on Wilde

The casting of *Porridge* was astonishing. Remember it wasn't the pilot episode of an intended series with all the pressure that entails, when the stakes are so much higher and every decision comes under so much scrutiny. 'Prisoner and Escort' was devised as a 'one off' play, in a series of seven whose only common link was that each would showcase Ronnie Barker's remarkable talent. If we'd known it was a series would the casting process have been more intense or selective? I can't imagine it could have been more perfect, and it was a brilliant achievement for producer Syd Lotterby.

Brian belonged to that stock of character actors whose work, understated and subtle, is consistently excellent and consistently unheralded. I think of Brian as the civil servant overlooked for his expected promotion; the man in the raincoat at the bus stop who's jostled aside and left standing in the rain. Or the clerk who lives with his invalid mother and who pines secretly, and hopelessly, for the girl in the accounts department.

Brian's characters don't stand out in the crowd. They blend in with the background, camouflaged against the spotlight. A little like the man himself whom we never got to know really well but grew to respect with growing affection for his dry humour and superb acting instincts.

Inevitably, the success of the series did thrust Brian more into the spotlight, as much as he tried to shield himself from its transitory glare. But at least a large and enthusiastic public got to recognise his craft and his talent.

He brought much more to the character of Barrowclough than I think, in truth, Dick and I put on the page. It was too easy just to be a patsy to Fletcher's cunning or the downtrodden husband. Brian ennobled Mister Barrowclough with compassion, and a sweet-natured perseverance that never allowed him to be pitiful or ridiculous. With his furrowed brow and lugubrious features he made us laugh unexpectedly, and frequently. And he did so by finding the truth of the character. And his humanity.

EPISODE GUIDE – *PORRIDGE*

SERIES ONE   NEW FACES, OLD HANDS

Original transmission: 📺 Thursday 5 September 1974,
BBC1, 8.30 p.m.

CAST

Norman Fletcher....	**Ronnie Barker**
Mr Barrowclough....	**Brian Wilde**
Mr Mackay....	**Fulton Mackay**
Lennie Godber....	**Richard Beckinsale**
Cyril Heslop....	**Brian Glover**
Medical Officer....	**John Bennett**
The Governor....	**Michael Barrington**
Other Prison Officers....	**Ronald Musgrove**
....	**Edward Cogdale**
....	**Keith Norrish**

Mackay introduces three new arrivals to life at Slade Prison:
while Cyril Heslop and Norman Fletcher are old hands,
Lennie Godber is a first offender, so Mackay asks Fletch to
describe a typical day, beginning at 7 a.m. with a 'persistent
and deafening bell'.

After their possessions are confiscated – a process Fletcher
describes as their 'dehumanisation' – he helps Godber come
to terms with his predicament and tries convincing him he
can survive the 'grim nightmare of his next two years'.

No longer a novice to prison life, Fletch expects special
attention, perhaps even his own cell, and one that's south-
facing! But there's a shock in store when he discovers Godber
is allocated his own cell and he's forced to share with Heslop
and the electric light-bulb-eating Evans. Just to rub salt into
the wound, Godber and Heslop are given cushy jobs while
Fletch is assigned pig-swilling duties.

WHAT A SCENE!

Three new arrivals (Fletcher, Godber and Heslop) are standing to attention, while Mr Mackay looks out through the barred windows.

MACKAY

What a beautiful day, for the time of year, quite astonishing. Beautiful day.

FLETCHER

(Sarcastically) Oh, lovely. Perhaps we can go out later on for a cycle ride!

Original transmission: 📺 **Thursday 12 September 1974**
BBC1, 8.30 p.m.

CAST

Norman Fletcher....	**Ronnie Barker**
Mr Barrowclough....	**Brian Wilde**
Mr Mackay....	**Fulton Mackay**
Lennie Godber....	**Richard Beckinsale**
Heslop....	**Brian Glover**
Ives....	**Ken Jones**
Lukewarm....	**Christopher Biggins**
Evans....	**Ray Dunbobbin**
Mr Appleton....	**Graham Ashley**
Prison Officer....	**John Quarmby**

Gambling is rife inside Slade Prison. Prisoners are so desperate for a flutter they'll bet on anything, including flies crawling up the wall and which hymns will be sung in the chapel. So it's good news when Fletch receives permission from Grouty to run a dice game.

On Saturday afternoon, while the warders challenge E Wing to a football match, a gathering of prisoners in the boiler room roll the dice. But Ives, who wasn't allowed to participate, has bet eight ounces of snout against them completing the game before the warders find out. Angry at being excluded from the game, he seeks revenge by informing Mackay of Fletch's illegal game of snakes and ladders; but instead of storming the secret location, the Chief Warder awaits a delivery of coal to help him out!

WHAT A SCENE!

Fletcher is organising some betting. He chats to Godber.

GODBER
What do you play for, big stakes?

FLETCHER
Yeah, if we can nick any out of the meat safe, yeah.

91

SERIES ONE — A NIGHT IN

Original transmission: Thursday 19 September 1974
BBC1, 8.30 p.m.

CAST

Norman Fletcher .... **Ronnie Barker**
Lennie Godber .... **Richard Beckinsale**
Prison Officer .... **Paul McDowell**

Fletch's peace is shattered when he's forced to share his cell with Lennie Godber, but they settle down after pointing out all the rules. It's not long before Godber is confiding in Fletch, telling him how he's struggling to adapt to terms with life inside – especially as he's got 698 days to go! He's also worried whether his fiancée, Denise, will wait for him.

During the long, cold night the two inmates discuss the woes of the world. Fletch reminds Godber about the importance of dreams, where there are 'no locked doors' to restrict the imagination, and helps his young cellmate survive the night, marking the beginning of a strong friendship.

WHAT A SCENE!

Godber, who has to share Fletch's cell, discusses his old cellmate, Banks, who caused a riot on his landing.

GODBER
He smuggled this kitten into his cell and from the way he handled it you could see the gentle side of his nature.

FLETCHER
You what? Before he lit his mattress I heard he threw a screw off the top landing.

GODBER
Well he wasn't hurt, he hit the safety net.

Original transmission: 📺   **Thursday 26 September 1974**
BBC1, 8.30 p.m.

CAST

Norman Fletcher . . . . **Ronnie Barker**
Mr Barrowclough . . . . **Brian Wilde**
Mr Mackay . . . . **Fulton Mackay**
Lennie Godber . . . . **Richard Beckinsale**
Ives . . . . **Ken Jones**
Navy Rum . . . . **Paul Angelis**
Dylan . . . . **Philip Jackson**
Scrounger . . . . **Johnny Wade**
Vicar . . . . **Robert Gillespie**
Verger . . . . **John Rutland**
Chief Prison Officer . . . . **Arnold Peters**
Landlord . . . . **Ralph Watson**
Nurse . . . . **Peggy Mason**

Fletcher and Godber enjoy the fresh air when they join a party digging drainage ditches for the council. Under Mackay's strict supervision the men keep on task, but when he pops down to the local village to buy spare parts for his lawnmower – a good excuse for a quick snifter – Barrowclough is put in charge.

True to form, the men take advantage of the situation. When Ives gets stung on the behind and writhes in agony, Fletch persuades Barrowclough to let him dash down to the village to fetch medication. Borrowing a quid from the gullible warder, he heads for the nearest pub, but as he sinks a drink Mackay appears on the scene and Fletch has to make a quick exit. But there's more drama in store before the day is out.

WHAT A SCENE!

Fletch and Godber discuss why they're pleased to be spending a day away from Slade Prison.

FLETCHER

Yeah, I must admit, I'm looking forward to going out today, yeah, yeah. Get the smell of disinfectant out of my nostrils – not to mention your festering feet!

GODBER

I change my socks every day.

FLETCHER

Oh yeah. Pity you can't change your feet, innit?

WAYS AND MEANS

Original transmission: 📺 **Thursday 3 October 1974**
BBC1, 8.30 p.m.

CAST

Norman Fletcher . . . . **Ronnie Barker**
Mr Barrowclough . . . . **Brian Wilde**
Mr Mackay . . . . **Fulton Mackay**
Ives . . . . **Ken Jones**
The Governor . . . . **Michael Barrington**
McLaren . . . . **Tony Osoba**

After upsetting Mr Mackay, Fletch is stripped of his cushy farm job and forced to make fishing nets. Needlework wreaks havoc with his hands, so he asks Barrowclough – who owes him a favour after accepting his advice on domestic affairs – to secure him a job in the library.

Fletch tries hard getting back into the Governor's good books, but also finds time to tender advice to McLaren about curbing his aggressive nature, which sees him red-carded for the third time in four football matches. McLaren's anger overspills and he climbs on to the prison roof and won't come down until his demands are met. Spotting an opportunity to ingratiate himself with the Governor, Fletch comes to the rescue – with a little help from McLaren himself – and ends up being rewarded with his job in the library.

WHAT A SCENE!

**McLaren and Fletch have a confrontation. Fletch
loses his temper and grabs him.**

FLETCHER

I don't want no trouble with you, McLaren. Listen to me,
you. I know you're a hard case, we all know that. We all
know you're full of nasty militant feelings, but if you
ever talk to me again like that I'm going to twist your
head round like a cork in a bottle of Beaujolais, all right?

MCLAREN

Yes.

FLETCHER

I'm going to pull it off and give it to that poof in B Wing
to keep his wigs on.

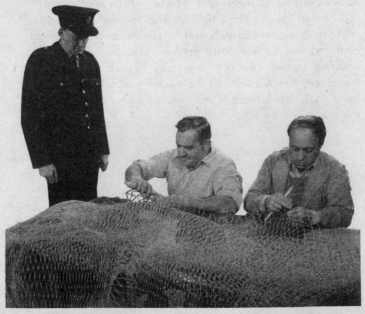

MEN WITHOUT WOMEN

Original transmission: **Thursday 10 October 1974**
BBC1, 8.30 p.m.

CAST

Norman Fletcher	**Ronnie Barker**
Mr Barrowclough	**Brian Wilde**
Mr Mackay	**Fulton Mackay**
Warren	**Sam Kelly**
Heslop	**Brian Glover**
The Governor	**Michael Barrington**
Lukewarm	**Christopher Biggins**
Sergeant Norris	**Royston Tickner**
Tolly	**Emlyn Price**
Isobel	**June Ellis**
Ingrid Fletcher	**Patricia Brake**
Norma	**Susan Littler**
Iris	**Andonia Katsaros**
Elaine	**Rosalind Elliot**
Trevor	**Donald Groves**

When the illiterate Warren, a fellow inmate, receives a letter
from his wife, he asks Fletcher to read it. It's clear from the
downbeat tone that his beloved's affections have strayed.
Fletch tells a group of lags that Warren's letter is indicative of
a woman's state of mind when her hubby has been inside
between eight and twelve months; he claims that, although
they make their vows, it's difficult to prevent them straying.

With visiting day approaching, Fletcher drafts a letter and
suggests his friends send it to their loved ones, feeling confident the subtlety of his writing will do the trick.

Warren believes Fletch's letter has done the trick when he
receives a reassuring reply, suggesting he has nothing to
worry about. All the wives turn up on visiting day – except
Fletcher's. His daughter Ingrid arrives instead to break the
news that his wife has run off with a heating engineer who
drives a mustard-coloured Ford Capri!

Fletcher is so stunned that the prison's welfare officer
recommends forty-eight hours' compassionate leave to help
sort matters out. Escorted home by Sergeant Norris of the

local constabulary, Fletch confronts his wife, Isobel, but what the authorities don't realise is that it's all a ruse enabling them to spend a weekend together.

WHAT A SCENE!

It's locking-up time at the prison and Barrowclough has a final word with Fletcher.

BARROWCLOUGH
You know, Fletcher, this is the part of the job I hate, you know, locking men up, caging them in.

FLETCHER
Yeah, 'tis a pity, too, just when the good telly is starting and all. It's a shame, ain't it? All we ever see is the news, ain't it? News and Nationwide. What's the good of Nationwide when you're stuck in here, eh?

BARROWCLOUGH
No, I've never got used to bolting these doors, you know. I think of all of you locked in these little cells and I . . . I think of me going out of here and . . . going home to my little house and my wife, who's waiting for me. (He looks forlorn)

FLETCHER
What's the matter, Mr Barrowclough?

BARROWCLOUGH
I sometimes wish I was in here with you lot!

Original transmission: 📺 **Friday 24 October 1975**
BBC1, 8.30 p.m.

CAST

Norman Fletcher	**Ronnie Barker**
Mr Barrowclough	**Brian Wilde**
Mr Mackay . .	**Fulton Mackay**
Lennie Godber	**Richard Beckinsale**
Ives	**Ken Jones**
Warren	**Sam Kelly**
McLaren	**Tony Osoba**
Lukewarm	**Christopher Biggins**
Banyard	**Eric Dodson**
Mr Appleton	**Graham Ashley**
Mr Birchwood . . .	**John Rudling**
Gay Gordon	**Felix Bowness**

There's a thief inside Slade Prison and Fletcher's disgusted. It may be acceptable outside but pilfering from fellow lags is inexcusable, especially as Fletch becomes the latest victim when his tin of pineapple chunks (acquired courtesy of Slade's kitchen) is swiped.

Fletcher holds an inquiry, but the meeting is broken up by the prowling Mackay who disbelieves Fletch's lame explanation that it's a gathering of the newly formed Slade Prison Cowboy Club.

After losing his chunks, Fletcher realises his trust has been misplaced and that prison is a 'jungle'; it's time he concentrated on looking after number one. Later, Mr Barrowclough informs Fletch he has found the tin of chunks while conducting a random security check; he knows it was stolen from the kitchen but won't report it so long as Fletch keeps his nose clean. When it's discovered that Mrs Barrowclough has eaten the chunks by mistake, they formulate a plan to replace the tin . . . but it runs anything but smoothly.

WHAT A SCENE!

Mackay is talking to Fletch about the increase in pilfering when Godber arrives dressed in his kitchen uniform.

MACKAY

This is a very unfortunate combination, isn't it?

FLETCHER

I dunno, sir.

MACKAY

Godber with his opportunities to steal from the kitchen and you with your distribution network.

GODBER

'Ere, I don't steal. I resent that.

MACKAY

Oh, you resent that, do you? I suppose butter wouldn't melt in your mouth?

FLETCHER

(Sarcastically) 'Ere that's a good idea, how much could you get in your mouth?

SERIES TWO — HEARTBREAK HOTEL

Original transmission:  **Friday 31 October 1975**
BBC1, 8.30 p.m.

CAST

Norman Fletcher. . . . **Ronnie Barker**
Mr Barrowclough. . . . **Brian Wilde**
Mr Mackay. . . . **Fulton Mackay**
Lennie Godber. . . . **Richard Beckinsale**
Ingrid . . . . **Patricia Brake**
Mrs Godber. . . . **Maggie Flint**

Fletch is shocked to hear that Godber is up in front of the
Governor after attacking Jackdaw with a soup ladle in the
kitchen. Such irrational behaviour from one of Slade's more
placid inmates takes everyone by surprise, but mitigating
circumstances save him from a spell in the cooler.

Godber's bad news arrived in a letter from Denise, his
fiancée, who announces in it that she's married someone else
– a third engineer in the merchant navy called Kenneth. But
Godber's bout of melancholia is short-lived when Fletcher's
daughter, the bubbly Ingrid, appears on the scene.

WHAT A SCENE!

Mackay questions Fletch because six soft toilet rolls have disappeared from the Governor's personal toilet.

FLETCHER
Oh dear, would you adam and eve it, whatever next?

MACKAY
Knowing you, Fletcher, probably the seat.

(Godber laughs)

FLETCHER
Don't look at me, sir.

(Mackay turns to Godber)

GODBER
Nor me, it's writing paper I'm short of.

MACKAY
Well it's not right. We've had to give the Governor standard prison-issue tissue.

GODBER
That's rough.

FLETCHER
Rough? I'd say it is. That'll wipe the smile off his face.

O— SERIES TWO DISTURBING THE PEACE

Original transmission: 📺 **Friday 7 November 1975**
BBC1, 8.30 p.m.

CAST

Norman Fletcher.... **Ronnie Barker**
Mr Barrowclough.... **Brian Wilde**
Mr Mackay.... **Fulton Mackay**
Lennie Godber.... **Richard Beckinsale**
Mr Wainwright.... **Peter Jeffrey**
Williams.... **Philip Madoc**
Warren.... **Sam Kelly**
McLaren.... **Tony Osoba**
The Governor.... **Michael Barrington**
Secretary (Mrs Heskith).... **Madge Hindle**

When the cat's away the mice will play, so with Mackay
attending a course, the prisoners plan working a few fiddles –
it's even suggested they could restart frog racing. But their
hopes are quickly dashed when Mackay's replacement turns
out to be the acid-tongued bully Wainwright, whom Fletcher
had the displeasure of meeting at Brixton. It's not long before
he's making his presence felt by curtailing the hours prisoners
can watch TV, banning talking in the exercise area and
removing the prisoners' ping-pong table; he even classes
Barrowclough as unfit to work anywhere except the prison
farm.

It's time action was taken against Wainwright's dictato-
rial behaviour and a riot is staged in the dining room. The
warders fail to regain control but when Fletcher tells the
Governor that Wainwright has inflamed the problem – and
that the only person who can quell the riot is
Barrowclough – the mild-mannered warder is brought in
from the cold.

WHAT A SCENE!

Barrowclough and Fletch discuss the ping-pong table, which has been moved to the warders' mess.

BARROWCLOUGH
Yes, well that's only till our billiard table is re-covered, you see.

FLETCHER
Oh yeah, well, yeah.

BARROWCLOUGH
Well, it was your fault it wanted re-covering.

FLETCHER
Our fault?

BARROWCLOUGH
Well some prisoner certainly tampered with it.

FLETCHER
Can you prove that?

BARROWCLOUGH
Well, we can surmise it. When Nosher Garrett went over the wall he was picked up in Blackpool wearing a green baize suit!

Original transmission: 📺 Friday 14 November 1975
BBC1, 8.30 p.m.

CAST

Norman Fletcher	**Ronnie Barker**
Mr Barrowclough	**Brian Wilde**
Mr Mackay	**Fulton Mackay**
Blanco	**David Jason**
Warren	**Sam Kelly**
McLaren	**Tony Osoba**
Banyard	**Eric Dodson**
The Governor	**Michael Barrington**
Mr Collinson	**Paul McDowell**
Vicar	**Tony Aitken**
Prison Visitors	**Ivor Roberts**
. . . .	**Barbara New**
. . . .	**Geoffrey Greenhill**

It's Saturday afternoon and, while everyone is out in the fresh air playing football, or down in the hobbies room, Fletch is relaxing on his bunk reading a dirty magazine. Several people ask him to play football, or join the prison's amateur dramatic society: no one believes that all Fletch wants is to be left alone. By the time Blanco arrives, Fletch has had enough and decides to stretch his legs by wandering down to Mr Collinson's office and stealing a couple of his Jaffa Cakes.

Later, as he's settling down again, Barrowclough pops in and they end up discussing prison life around the world, before Mackay and three Home Office officials arrive. However, the prison chaplain coming around is the final straw and Fletch throws him over the balcony. The Governor sentences him to three days in isolation, but Fletch is disappointed and pleads for more.

WHAT A SCENE!

Fletch and Barrowclough discuss the prison system abroad. Fletch wishes Slade would allow wives to stay.

FLETCHER
They have special apartments, you see, where the wife comes to stay the weekend, and then you spend the whole time manifesting your long-felt want.

BARROWCLOUGH
I don't know of any prison where . . .

FLETCHER
Maybe not here but certainly in Holland and also, I believe, in America, where they have a more enlightened penal system anyway.

BARROWCLOUGH
(Shocked) You mean the wives just visit and spend the whole weekend . . .

FLETCHER
Conjugating, yeah.

BARROWCLOUGH
That's more than I'm allowed at home!

Original transmission: Friday 21 November 1975
BBC1, 8.30 p.m.

CAST

Norman Fletcher	**Ronnie Barker**
Mr Barrowclough	**Brian Wilde**
Mr Mackay	**Fulton Mackay**
Lennie Godber	**Richard Beckinsale**
Blanco	**David Jason**
Norris	**Colin Farrell**
Mr Collinson	**Paul McDowell**
Medical Officer	**Terence Soall**

After the Carlisle General Hospital confirms that Fletcher has broken his ankle, he spends three weeks in the prison infirmary – a fact that angers Mackay. Fletch shares the ward with Blanco and the unlikeable Norris. When he learns that Norris has diddled the aged Blanco of his worldly goods during a card game, he devises a plan to reclaim his friend's possessions.

The crafty scheme seems to be working when Norris, on the eve of his release, overhears Blanco telling Fletch he's buried thousands of pounds in Leeds. Desperate to get his grubby little hands on the location map, he returns Blanco's possessions in exchange. But he's arrested before long for digging a hole in the middle of a football pitch!

WHAT A SCENE!

Blanco and Fletch are both in the prison infirmary, and the old man wakes up Fletch to tell him something, but all Fletcher wants to do is sleep.
BLANCO
There were three of us. We'd done a job on a wages van on its way to a fridge factory near Otley. Do you remember reading about it?

FLETCHER

No, I don't, no.

BLANCO

Well it was all in the Yorkshire Post.

FLETCHER

Yeah, well unless it made the Muswell Hill Standard or Titbits I'd have missed it.

BLANCO

Suppose so. Anyway it was an untidy job, a lot of things went wrong.

FLETCHER

Yeah, well you wouldn't be in here if it hadn't, would you?

BLANCO

No, no. Now the other two lads, they were brothers. There was Jack Barrett and Harry . . . (He can't remember the name)

FLETCHER

Barrett, was it?

BLANCO

That's right, did you know him?

FLETCHER

No, only through his brother, like.

BLANCO

'Cause you see, their escape was in the Yorkshire Post and all; they got away in a fishing boat from Bridlington.

FLETCHER

Yes, is this going to take long, Blanco, only my foot's gone to sleep and I'd like to catch it up, know what I mean?

Original transmission: 📺 Friday 28 November 1975
BBC1, 8.30 p.m.

CAST

Norman Fletcher . . . . **Ronnie Barker**
Mr Barrowclough . . . . **Brian Wilde**
Mr Mackay . . . . **Fulton Mackay**
Lonnie Godber . . . . **Richard Beckinsale**
Harry Grout . . . . **Peter Vaughan**
Jackdaw . . . . **Cyril Shaps**
PTI . . . . **Roy Sampson**

Godber's chuffed when he's chosen for the boxing team, but Grouty is more excited because sport means betting. Keen to earn some cash, he asks Fletcher to study the form. Fletch reports that Godber looks a firm favourite for his bout and Grouty tells him to fix the fight so that he falls in the second round, thus ensuring Grouty wins a packet from his opponent, Nesbitt. Fletcher realises he's got a problem when Godber announces he's already promised Billy Moffat he'll go down in the first. A change of plan finds Fletcher trying to nobble Nesbitt and making Godber win . . . so what happens when both fighters hit the canvas?

WHAT A SCENE!

Fletch tells Mackay and Godber about an old friend who used to be a boxer.

FLETCHER
Well, I don't reckon boxing is such a noble art, anyway.

MACKAY
No, of course you wouldn't.

FLETCHER
No. I haven't told you this: I had a friend once, he was a

---

good boy, he was, light-heavy, you know, good strong lad.
He won a few fights. Then, of course, he thought he was
the bee's knees, didn't he, hey? Fast cars, loose women.
Classic story: too much too soon; he just blew up, got
into debt. Do you know where he finished up? In a
boxing booth in a fairground. Four fights a night, seven
nights a week. Well, the body can't take that sort of
punishment, can it? The brain just went soft, reflexes
went, got punchy. He just became a vegetable, an incoherent, non-thinking zombie.

MACKAY

What became of him?

FLETCHER

He joined the prison service as a warder. He's doing very
well.

Original transmission: **Wednesday 24 December 1975
BBC1, 8.25 p.m.**

CAST

Norman Fletcher	**Ronnie Barker**
Mr Barrowclough	**Brian Wilde**
Mr Mackay	**Fulton Mackay**
Lennie Godber	**Richard Beckinsale**
Harry Grout	**Peter Vaughan**
Prison Doctor	**Graham Crowden**
Warren	**Sam Kelly**
Lukewarm	**Christopher Biggins**
Sandra	**Carol Hawkins**
Nurse	**Elisabeth Day**

Slade's Godfather, Harry Grout, is helping fellow inmate
Tommy Slocombe tunnel his way to freedom in time for
Christmas – and he expects everyone to pull their weight. But
Fletch thinks it's bad news, because if he succeeds everyone else
will suffer.

To wriggle his way out of helping, he feigns injury in an
attempt to get hospitalised for the duration of the festive
period. But relying on his old cartilage trouble doesn't
convince the prison doctor, proud of his infirmary's low
admission record, to give him a bed. Insisting that he be
taken seriously, Fletcher is referred to a civilian hospital for
examination.

News of Fletch's trip outside is music to Grouty's ears,
and he forces him into collecting an important package
containing a blank passport for Slocombe. The X-rays reveal
a healthy knee, but just before Fletch leaves hospital a nurse
hands him the secret package.

A relieved Fletcher hands over the passport upon his
return to Slade Prison. Just when he thinks his good deeds
are complete, however, he's given another job – one that
results in him being hospitalised after all.

WHAT A SCENE!

Fletch discusses with Godber the benefits of Slade Prison's Christmas tree.

GODBER
We've got such a lot to look forward to: concert coming up, and the carol service – and the tree.

FLETCHER
Yeah, very useful that tree.

GODBER
Useful?

FLETCHER
Yeah, for stashing Christmas contraband. All them dingly-danglies hide a multitude of sins, you know. Even the fairy on the top's got two ounces of tobacco stuffed up her tutu!

GODBER
(Smiling) No wonder she looks uncomfortable.

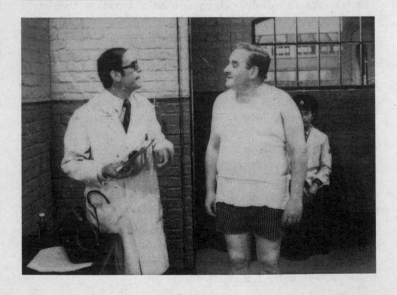

CHRISTMAS SPECIAL: THE DESPERATE HOURS

Original transmission: Friday 24 December 1976
BBC1, 8 p.m.

CAST

Norman Fletcher	Ronnie Barker
Mr Barrowclough	Brian Wilde
Mr Mackay	Fulton Mackay
Lennie Godber	Richard Beckinsale
Reg Urwin	Dudley Sutton
Warren	Sam Kelly
McLaren	Tony Osoba
The Governor	Michael Barrington
Keegan	Ken Wynne
Tulip	Michael Redfern
Mrs Jamieson	Jane Wenham

Unbeknown to everyone, Fletcher and Godber have been fermenting illicit liquor for months and it's reaching maturity just in time for the festive season. Meanwhile, the Governor hates Christmas time inside and prays that the period will pass peacefully. But no such luck – Mackay catches Fletcher and Godber, red-handed, indulging in their booze.

They're marched off to the Governor's office but while they're waiting, Reg Urwin – who's replaced Keegan as the Governor's tea boy – pops in. Finding Barrowclough alone in the office, he seizes his opportunity and takes the warder hostage, demanding ten grand and a helicopter or else he won't be responsible for his actions.

A plan is hatched to resolve the problem and Mackay, who's banished from the office, returns with cups of coffee, one laced with a tranquilliser. But Fletcher is mistakenly handed the cup and before long is fast asleep. Upon recovering, a newscaster on the radio states that three prisoners are involved in the incident. Annoyed that he's been implicated, Fletch decides it's time to persuade Urwin to give himself up.

WHAT A SCENE!

**Fletch asks some of his inmates about the real
meaning of Christmas.**

GODBER
Chestnuts roasting on an open fire.

FLETCHER
Yeah, yeah, yeah, very good, yeah.

MCLAREN
Hey, what about Mr Mackay roasting on an open fire?

FLETCHER
(Laughs) That's Guy Fawkes' Night.

SERIES THREE — A STORM IN A TEACUP

Original transmission: 📺 Friday 18 February 1977
BBC1, 8.30 p.m.

CAST

Norman Fletcher....	**Ronnie Barker**
Mr Barrowclough....	**Brian Wilde**
Mr Mackay....	**Fulton Mackay**
Lennie Godber....	**Richard Beckinsale**
Harry Grout....	**Peter Vaughan**
Harris....	**Ronald Lacey**
Warren....	**Sam Kelly**
McLaren....	**Tony Osoba**
Lukewarm....	**Christopher Biggins**
Spider....	**John Moore**
Crusher....	**John Dair**

While Fletcher enjoys a cuppa in the recreation area, Mackay searches Harris on the landing, suspecting him of pinching pills from the medical room. But before Mackay discovers them, the bottle drops into the unsuspecting Fletcher's mug of tea.

When Grouty discovers pills have been nabbed he demands Fletcher's help: if they're not returned to the medical room within the hour, Mackay will order a thorough stock-take, exposing Grouty's lucrative drug-peddling business in the process. With Fletcher working in the admin block, Grouty feels he could whip some pills from one of the women workers to replace the stolen pack.

A little arm-twisting saves the day for Fletch and he secures some replacement tablets in time, but before the evening is out he discovers the bottle that fell into his mug. With Mackay on the warpath, there's no alternative but to swallow the evidence.

WHAT A SCENE!

Warren disturbs Fletcher.

WARREN
What are you reading, Fletch?

FLETCHER
(Looks at his novel) A book.

WARREN
No, I mean what sort of book?

FLETCHER
Paperback sort of book, you know the sort of thing: lots of bits of paper all stuck down together, down the left-hand side.

WARREN
Is it a good book?

FLETCHER
Dunno until I finish it, do I? It might turn out rotten in the end. I shan't finish it, either, if I get these continuing interruptions, shall I?

WARREN
I'd read books if I could read. Is it a dirty book?

FLETCHER
Yeah, filthy, dropped it in a puddle coming back from lunch.

SERIES THREE POETIC JUSTICE

Original transmission: Friday 25 February 1977
BBC1, 8.30 p.m.

CAST

Norman Fletcher....	**Ronnie Barker**
Mr Barrowolough....	**Brian Wilde**
Mr Mackay....	**Fulton Mackay**
Lennie Godber....	**Richard Beckinsale**
Rawley....	**Maurice Denham**
Harris...	**Ronald Lacey**
Warren....	**Sam Kelly**
McLaren....	**Tony Osoba**
The Governor....	**Michael Barrington**
Mr Collinson....	**Paul McDowell**

Fletch goes bananas when he discovers he'll have to share his cell with a third inmate. But he feels even worse when the new arrival turns out to be Rawley, a close friend of the Governor's and, more shockingly, the judge who sentenced Fletcher. Fletch regards the judge as representing the establishment – and soon puts him in his place when he catches Godber making Rawley's bed.

As the cell door slams at the end of his first day inside, Rawley is suddenly aware of what prison life is like. Adjusting to his new surroundings isn't easy for a man who's enjoyed the finer things in life; before the episode closes, he faces being beaten up – until Fletcher intervenes.

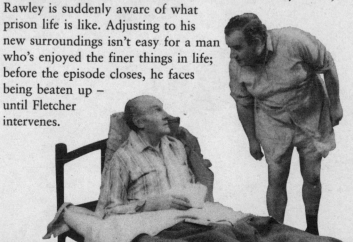

117

WHAT A SCENE!

Godber and Harris move a new bed into Fletcher's cell.

GODBER
Fletcher's not going to like this, Mr Barrowclough.

HARRIS
He naffing won't.
(Looking at Godber)
He didn't like you moving in, let alone a third.

BARROWCLOUGH
Fletcher will have no choice in the matter; we're running a prison not a hotel. Prisons are very overcrowded this time of year.

GODBER
Not surprising, it's bitter out.

Original transmission: 📺 **Friday 4 March 1977
BBC1, 8.30 p.m.**

CAST

Norman Fletcher	**Ronnie Barker**
Mr Barrowclough	**Brian Wilde**
Mr Mackay	**Fulton Mackay**
Lennie Godber	**Richard Beckinsale**
Rawley	**Maurice Denham**
Harris	**Ronald Lacey**
Warren	**Sam Kelly**
McLaren	**Tony Osoba**

While Rawley awaits his appeal, Fletcher presents him with a business proposition: he suggests dishing out legal advice to fellow prisoners in a partnership which would entail Fletch securing the trade and the judge imparting his knowledge. Rawley, however, isn't interested.

Fletch might have warmed a little towards his new cell-mate, but not everyone feels the same. Harris especially is unsympathetic, having been relegated to swilling pigs while Rawley ends up with a cushy clerical job. So when the judge's watch goes missing, Harris is chief suspect. To resolve the matter, Fletch calls a special court hearing with Rawley reluctantly presiding over the case.

It's not long until the case is dismissed due to lack of evidence, but it's surprising what a little arm-twisting, courtesy of McLaren, can do: before long, Harris has confessed and returned the watch.

There is more good news for Rawley: he wins his appeal and leaves Slade Prison, stating that he'll do whatever he can to improve the prison system.

WHAT A SCENE!

Warren asks Fletch to write him a letter.

FLETCHER
Don't you think you could have taken advantage of the educational facilities in 'ere and cured your illiteracy?

WARREN
I'm not illiterate, Fletch.

FLETCHER
Oh, I'm sorry. I thought that was the word we used for people who can't read or write.

WARREN
I'm not illiterate. I suffer from dyslexia. (Fletch looks puzzled) You don't know what it means, do ya?

FLETCHER
Well, obviously it's got to be some sort of acid stomach, hasn't it? But why that should stop you reading and writing I cannot imagine.

WARREN
No, no, you're wrong, dyslexia is word blindness, like. I can't make out words when they're written down, you see, they all get jumbled up in my head.

FLETCHER
Well, plenty of room, isn't there?

SERIES THREE PARDON ME

Original transmission: 📺 **Friday 11 March 1977**
BBC1, 8.30 p.m.

CAST

Norman Fletcher . . . . **Ronnie Barker**
Mr Barrowclough . . . . **Brian Wilde**
Mr Mackay . . . . **Fulton Mackay**
Lennie Godber . . . . **Richard Beckinsale**
Blanco . . . . **David Jason**

When old-timer Blanco's parole is granted, Lukewarm, Godber and Fletcher's congratulations are short-lived when Blanco protests his innocence and refuses parole – fearing he'd be admitting guilt for his crime.

To help their old inmate retain his pride as well as his freedom, Fletch, Lukewarm and Godber launch CROW (Campaign for the Release of Old Webb). Their campaign has two objectives: to demand a retrial, or to force the Governor to ask the Home Office for a pardon. To draw attention to their crusade Fletch informs Mr Venables that Blanco is considering a hunger strike; the last thing the Governor needs in Slade Prison is a martyr.

To save face and avoid any nasty publicity, Venables drops the Home Office a line and soon Blanco is awarded a pardon. But he's not as innocent as he looks.

WHAT A SCENE!

Fletch, Lukewarm, Blanco and Godber discuss what they were doing in 1959, the year Blanco was imprisoned.

GODBER

I was in junior school in 1959. Sat next to Ann Podmore; she was left-handed.

FLETCHER

(Turning to Lukewarm) Fascinating. I bet he got on the right side of her!

A TEST OF CHARACTER

SERIES THREE

Original transmission: Friday 18 March 1977
BBC1, 8.30 p.m.

CAST

Norman Fletcher . . . . **Ronnie Barker**
Mr Barrowclough . . . . **Brian Wilde**
Mr Mackay . . . . **Fulton Mackay**
Lennie Godber . . . . **Richard Beckinsale**
Spraggon . . . . **Alun Armstrong**
Warren . . . . **Sam Kelly**
McLaren . . . . **Tony Osoba**

Godber's swotting for his history O level, but he's finding it
tough thanks to constant interruptions from the likes of
Fletcher and Warren. When he storms out of the cell, Fletch
and Warren realise how much the exam means to him – and
that failure might send him back to crime upon his
impending release. To help their friend pass the O level, they
steal the exam paper.

But Godber doesn't want anything to do with it; he feels
he's cheated all his life and wants to pass through his own
merits – just as well, because the illiterate Warren has nicked
the biology papers by mistake!

WHAT A SCENE!

**Mackay tells Fletcher and Godber about his hard
childhood.**

MACKAY
I had to leave school at fourteen to help bring a living
wage into the house – hard times on those Lanarkshire
coal fields. My father was an unemployed miner, but
there were still eight children to provide for.

FLETCHER
Oh, eight kids, eh. He wasn't unemployed the whole of
the time, then?

Original transmission: 📺 **Friday 25 March 1977**
BBC1, 8.30 p.m.

CAST

Norman Fletcher. . . .	**Ronnie Barker**
Mr Barrowclough. . . .	**Brian Wilde**
Mr Mackay. . . .	**Fulton Mackay**
Lennie Godber. . . .	**Richard Beckinsale**
Jarvis. . . .	**David Daker**
Warren. . . .	**Sam Kelly**
Ingrid. . . .	**Patricia Brake**
Crusher. . . .	**John Dair**

Godber is up for parole soon and, as Fletch tells Ingrid, who's become his pen pal, his 'boyhood charm' will see him through. But he jeopardises his prospects when he's offended by remarks made by tough-nut Jarvis and starts a brawl. Even Fletcher's advice to steer clear of the Mancunian thug falls on deaf ears as Godber insists that 'a man's got to do what a man's got to do' – even if it means kissing goodbye to freedom.

Desperate to help his cellmate, Fletch discusses with Warren what they can do. After chewing over several ideas, including using drugs from the prison farm to tranquillise Jarvis, there seems only one option: Fletch will have to confront Jarvis himself, even if it means blotting his own copybook. Any aggro should result in Jarvis being locked away until after the parole hearing. Fletch, however, finds it hard getting the reaction he wants from Jarvis; but then Crusher unwittingly saves the day.

Godber's parole is granted and in an emotional final scene he thanks Fletcher for all his help. Then he breaks the news that he's got a new sweetheart: Ingrid!

WHAT A SCENE!

Ingrid visits Fletch and they discuss Marion, who he feels is lazy.

FLETCHER
Does she still work in Woolworths?

INGRID
No, not now, she don't need to, Dad. Her boyfriend, Ricky, is ever so well off. He's got three cars. He gave her one for Christmas.

FLETCHER
Yeah, I bet he did. Did she get a present as well?

INGRID
Dad! If she marries Ricky she'll want for nothing.

FLETCHER
If. What does he do?

INGRID
He runs these cheap charter aeroplane-trips.

FLETCHER
Oh yeah, what are they called: Gullible's Travels?

PRODUCTION TEAM

ALL EPISODES WRITTEN BY
Dick Clement and Ian La Frenais

MUSIC
Max Harris

FILM CAMERAMEN
Len Newson (S1/episodes 1–3 & 6); Keith Taylor (S1/episodes 4–5);
Ken Willicombe (S2/episodes 2–4 & 6); Kenneth MacMillan (S2/episode 5);
John Tiley ('No Way Out'); John McGlashan (S3)

FILM EDITORS
Geoffrey Botterill (S1/episodes 1–2); Ray Millichope (S1/episodes 3–6;
S2/episodes 2–6;
'No Way Out'); John Dunstan (S3)

FILM SOUND
Ron Blight (credited on 'No Way Out')

MAKE-UP
Sylvia James (S1); Ann Ailes-Stevenson (S2; 'No Way Out');
Suzanne Broad ('The Desperate Hours'; S3)

COSTUMES
Mary Husband (S1; S3); Betty Aldiss (S2); Susan Wheal ('No Way Out');
Robin Stubbs ('The Desperate Hours')

LIGHTING
Peter Smee (S1/episodes 1–4 & 6; S2/episodes 1–4; 'No Way Out'); Peter
Wesson (S1/episode 5; S3);
Brian Clemett (S2/episode 5); Sam Barclay ('The Desperate Hours')

SOUND
Anthony Philpot (S1; S2; 'The Desperate Hours'); Jeff Booth ('No Way
Out'); John Holmes (S3)

PRODUCTION ASSISTANT
Ray Butt (S1); Dave Perrottet (S2); Alan Bell ('No Way Out'); Mike Crisp
('The Desperate Hours'; S3)

TECHNICAL ADVISER
Jonathan Marshall (credited on S1/episodes 1–4)

DESIGNER
Tim Gleeson (S1/episodes 1–2 & 5–6; S2/episode 1; 'No Way Out'; 'The
Desperate Hours'; S3);
David Chandler (S1/episodes 3 & 6); Gerry Scott (S1/episodes 4–5); John
Pusey (S2/episodes 2–6)

PRODUCER/DIRECTOR
Sydney Lotterby

MEET THE OTHER INMATES

Banyard

Banyard – who teaches chess at Slade – appeared in two episodes, 'Just Desserts' and 'No Peace for the Wicked', as a disgraced dentist. He regards himself as superior to other prisoners, not a 'common criminal', an attitude which nettles fellow inmates – especially because he's serving time for 'mistreating' women after putting them under laughing gas!

Banyard was played by Eric Dodson, who was born in Peterborough in 1920 and started amateur acting while waiting for his call-up during World War II. He eventually joined the RAF in 1941 and trained in Canada in coastal command before spending the rest of the war flying bombers and, in 1944, serving in Yugoslavia as a liaison officer.

When he was demobbed he returned to acting, initially in rep in Edinburgh. After spending several years working the repertory circuit, he made his West End debut in *The Young Elizabeth* in the early 1950s.

He also appeared in various films, including *Night Train for Inverness* (1960), *Sentenced for Life* (1960), *The Dock Brief* (1962), *Battle of Britain* (1969), *The Mirror Crack'd* (1980), with Elizabeth Taylor, and *The Walter Ego* (1991).

On television, he was seen as the head porter in *Jekyll and Hyde*, Sir Gerald in *Suspicion*, Reverend Johns in *Poldark*, a magistrate in *Lovejoy*, Sir Robert in *Grace and Favour*, Sir Edward in *Press Gang*, and as a village headman in *Doctor Who*. He also appeared in *The Sweeney, The Saint, The Avengers, Fresh Fields, Rumpole of the Bailey, All Creatures Great and Small, It Ain't Half Hot, Mum* and *'Allo, 'Allo*.

A long illness prevented Eric from working for the last five years of his life, and he died in January 2000.

Crusher

The almighty Crusher is one of Harry Grout's henchmen, and he's summoned whenever some muscle is required.

John Dair was topping the bill as a singer at London's Lyceum when he was offered the chance to play Crusher in the series. 'A gentleman called Cliff Castle from the BBC asked me one night if I'd ever thought of doing television. I thought he was referring to my voice, but a week later he phoned and asked if I fancied doing a bit on *Porridge*. I initially appeared in the episode 'The Harder They Fall', the first television job I ever had.'

Unfortunately the costume department at the Beeb couldn't find a prison suit big enough to fit John's large frame. 'I used to wear a boiler suit. After finishing the boxing-match scenes on location, I noticed Ronnie Barker and the director looking at me; I thought they were going to throw me off because I didn't have a prison suit, but they asked if I'd come back on Sunday to do some filming in front of the audience. From there, I returned to appear in several other episodes.'

John, who's now seventy, saw his character as a 'heavy' and thus his presence his most important feature. 'I must have done all right, because I then became Crusher. And in the film I was known as Samson, who had a head-case of a mate – a psychopath called Delilah. It was a fantastic time, working on *Porridge*.'

Thanks to the exposure he received on the sitcom, John Dair never looked back. He went on to appear on numerous shows, including *The Ken Dodd Show, The Morecambe and Wise Show, Jack the Ripper, Our Friends in the North* – in which he played Charlie Dawson – and an episode of *The Lenny Henry Show*, as Father Christmas. On the big screen, he appeared as Big John in 1983's *Yellowbeard*, Vinnie Ricorso in *Batman* (1989), the Fat Man in *Sweet Nothing* (1990), Derek in *Hear My Song* (1991) and Macleish in *Loch Ness* (1995).

Born in Dundee, John drove bulldozers and mobile cranes on building sites before turning to singing. At a club one evening, he happened to mention that he could sing better than the entertainer could and was invited on stage to prove it. He sang two songs and before the night was out received various invites to sing in local clubs. He travelled the country before working at the Strand for four years.

John no longer sings professionally and concentrates on acting instead; he's also been seen in commercials, including a recent one for Wall's sausages.

Dylan

Dylan – real name Melvin Bottomley – is a hippie who in 'A Day Out' joins the working party assigned the task of helping the local council dig drainage ditches. Described by Fletch as 'lazy', Dylan was thrown out of art school for drawing on the walls and is one of Slade's eccentrics – he wears an earring, his hair is long and he tiedyes his uniform.

Philip Jackson enjoyed the experience of appearing as Dylan in *Porridge*, but avoids watching the episode like the plague. 'It's not a pleasant experience, watching myself; I look very inexperienced in the episode, like I'm on automatic pilot. And, of course, in hindsight you always notice things you'd have done differently, given the chance to do the job again.'

Born in Retford, Nottinghamshire, in 1948, Philip gained a BA in drama from Bristol University. He'd acted as a child at school and youth clubs, but when he embarked on his degree course he envisaged becoming a director rather than an actor. However, further forays on the stage during his student days saw him head for an acting career, beginning at the Liverpool Playhouse as a soldier in *Coriolanus*. Philip remained at Liverpool for eighteen months before striking lucky and working with The Royal Court.

Philip was appearing in *Blooming Youth* for the BBC when Syd Lotterby saw him. Shortly afterwards, he was offered the role of Dylan. His extensive small-screen CV includes appearances in *Coronation Street, Murder Most Horrid, Hamish Macbeth, Heartbeat, Coming Home, Last of the Summer Wine* (as Gordon), *Touching Evil* and *The Last Salute*, as Leonard Spanwick. He's also worked on several films.

Philip last worked in the theatre seven years ago, and nowadays the medium of television dominates his time. He recently played Robert in the series *Black Cab* and Chief Inspector Japp in episodes of *Poirot*.

Evans

Evans is first mentioned by Mackay in 'New Faces, Old Hands', but is not actually seen until the second episode in series one, 'The Hustler'. Mackay informs the Governor that Evans had to be isolated for attempting to eat electric light-bulbs upon discovering he couldn't get any razor blades, so you can imagine Fletch's reaction when he discovers he's got to share a cell with him! The Welshman is rarely seen without his cap or obligatory fag clinging to his lower lip – even during regular visits to the psychiatrist.

Ray Dunbobbin, who during his career saw success as both writer and actor, played Evans. Born in Canada, Ray moved to Liverpool with his British parents as a boy. He completed his education in the city and upon leaving school furthered his interest in art by working in a couple of Liverpool's art studios.

By this point in his life, Ray had developed an enthusiasm for acting and spent much of his spare time performing with a local amateur dramatics society. During a performance one evening, he was spotted and offered a chance to double for film actor Sam Kydd for a picture being shot at nearby Birkenhead. Ray went on to appear in numerous other films as well as establishing himself on television – often playing older characters. He was seen as a photographer in *Bergerac*, as Mr Boswell in five series of *The Liver Birds*, in *Doctor Who, Last of the Summer Wine, I Didn't Know You Cared* and *Hallelujah!* But people will probably remember him most for the six and a half years he spent playing Ralph Hardwicke in *Brookside*.

His busy career saw him appear in more than 500 radio and TV programmes. However, there were many other facets to Ray's career: alongside his acting, he became a successful scriptwriter for radio, stage and television (he scripted several episodes of *Z Cars* as well as drama and suspense plays for the BBC and Spanish television) and was a professional after-dinner speaker. For a while, Ray worked for a leading spoken-word cassette-company, abridging novels and acting as narrator.

A multitalented performer, Ray died of a heart attack in 1998.

Gay Gordon

Gay Gordon, who wears his hair in curlers, is first seen in 'Just Desserts'. Little is known about the prison poof other than that he's an oddball character with whom you wouldn't want to be stuck in a lift!

Playing the effeminate inmate was Felix Bowness. Born in Harwell and an amateur-boxing champion in his late teens, Felix has been in the entertainment business for more than four decades performing in variety shows around the country. A veteran warm-up man, he won a talent contest in Reading that led to him turning semi-pro. Then, while working in cabaret, he was spotted by a BBC producer and given a small part in radio.

With great tenacity, Felix kept plugging away, eventually making his TV debut as a stand-up comic before moving into comedy roles in shows like *Dad's Army* (in which he played three different parts).

Felix is perhaps best known for his role as jockey Fred Quilley in *Hi-De-Hi!*, and has worked frequently for the writing partnership of Jimmy Perry and David Croft: he was a customer in *Are You Being Served?*, a grocer in *You Rang,*

M'Lord?, and appeared in the earlier series *Hugh and I*. He played a relief guard in the series *Oh, Doctor Beeching!*, as well as warming up the audiences prior to recordings.

Harry Grout

Harry Grout is the Godfather of Slade Prison. He leads a comparatively cushy life as he moves towards his release; while everyone else works, he's in charge of the prison's swimming pool – even though there isn't one. Grouty is a highly influential figure – partly due to his bully-boy tactics – who served time at Parkhurst where he owned a pigeon, thus enabling him to keep in touch with his bookies. While those around him endure their Spartan lifestyle, he lives in relative luxury thanks to his radio and cigars, the company of his pet budgie (Seymour), and his pull with the warders, who bend over backwards to help him.

Harry was played by Peter Vaughan, who started his career as an ASM in repertory theatre. Born in Wem, Shropshire, in 1924, Peter has worked extensively in the theatre and on screen. His film credits include: *Sapphire, Village of the Damned, Smokescreen* and, more recently, *Remains of the Day*. His television portfolio, meanwhile, covers shows such as *The Pallisers, The Persuaders, The Sweeney, The Adventurer, Randall and Hopkirk (Deceased), Crane, Man in a Suitcase, Adam Adamant Lives!, Citizen Smith, Great Expectations, Chancer, The Return of Sherlock Holmes, Murder Most Horrid, Lovejoy* and *Our Friends in the North* (playing Felix Hutchinson).

Harris

Greasy-haired Harris is an overgrown Teddy Boy who can't be trusted around Slade Prison. His slimy nature means he's not the most popular character behind bars, especially as he's serving time for trying to snatch an old-age pensioner's handbag (though he failed because the brave-hearted lady hit

PORRIDGE

him with her bag before pinning him down until the police
arrived). As Fletch states: he's all 'wind and water'. Harris is
an annoying moaner whose nose is put out of joint when he's
relegated to pig-swilling upon Judge Rawley's arrival at Slade
Prison.

The late Ronald Lacey, who played Harris, was born in
Harrow in 1935. His early ambition was to become a professional sportsman, but he opted for acting instead and trained
at a London drama school. After several years of repertory
work, he made his movie debut in 1961's *The Boys*, playing
Billy Herne.

The sixties also saw the start of his television career, with
early appearances including episodes of *The Avengers* (1961),
Gideon's Way (1965), *Out of the Unknown* (1965), *Randall
and Hopkirk (Deceased)* (1969), *Department S* (1969) and
several episodes as Ryland in *Jason King* (1971).

By the time his life was tragically cut short in 1991 by
bowel cancer, Ronald, who also ran a theatrical agency, had
built up an impressive list of credits encompassing the whole
industry, including a spell on Broadway in *Chips With
Everything*.

Other films he was seen in include: *Doctor in Distress,
The Comedy Man, Catch Us If You Can, Dance of the
Vampires, Say Hello to Yesterday, The Prince and the Pauper,
The Death Angel* and *Yellowbeard*. While on the box he also
appeared in shows like *The Sweeney, Blake's 7, Bergerac,
Boon, Face to Face, Whatever Happened to the Likely Lads?*
and *Minder on the Orient Express*.

Cyril Heslop

The brainless Cyril Heslop, who's also done bird at Shepton
Mallet, arrives at Slade Prison the same time as Fletch and
Godber. Aged forty-one, prisoner 8995 is on his third stretch
of porridge, this time serving three years for robbery. Heslop
is as thick as two short planks, is married to Iris and comes
from Kent. He's seen in three episodes: 'New Faces, Old

Hands', 'The Hustler' and 'Men without Women', when he admits that his wife's sister, Gwendoline, who lives in Sidcup, attacked him in her kitchen and they ended up in bed.

Cast as Cyril Heslop was veteran actor Brian Glover. Born in Sheffield in 1934, Brian worked as a teacher and professional wrestler before turning to acting. A busy career saw this distinctive thespian appear in a host of shows, on stage and screen. Included in his television work are roles in *The Sweeney, Raffles, Target, Hazell* and *Doctor Who*. He also played Mr Dawson in *All Creatures Great and Small*, Mr Rottweiler in *Bottom*, Ken Farley in *The Bill*, and parts in *Don't Ask Me, The Secret Army, Return of the Saint* and *Minder* as well as Magersfontein Lugg in the 1989 series *Campion*.

On the big screen, Brian – who died in 1997 – worked on more than twenty films, including *Kes, O Lucky Man!, Brannigan, Trial by Combat, The First Great Train Robbery, An American Werewolf in London, Britannia Hospital, The Company of Wolves, Leon the Pig Farmer* and *Prince of Jutland*.

Ives

Ives, the man who everybody grew to hate, was an untrustworthy know-all who infuriated his fellow prisoners. A scouser serving time for fraud, he's a lifelong cheat.

When Liverpudlian actor Ken Jones began playing Ives, life couldn't have been busier: he was also appearing as Rex in Eric Chappell's office comedy *The Squirrels* with Patsy Rowlands and Bernard Hepton. 'I used to do *Porridge* in the morning and *The Squirrels* in the afternoon. I played Ives for a few episodes in series two but became so busy I had to reluctantly give up *Porridge*.' Having to leave the sitcom saddened Ken. 'It's not often you come across quality material so I would've liked to have stayed, but it just wasn't feasible.'

Ken feels every episode of Clement and La Frenais' sitcom was like a 'little play'. 'They were beautifully constructed and the actual situation was fantastic: if you get a closed environment like a prison and an anarchist like Fletcher trying to break the system, there's wonderful conflict. The scripts were well written.'

Ken was born in Liverpool in 1930 and left school at fourteen, joining the building trade. He eventually also ran an amateur theatre in the city for four years, together with his wife, actress Sheila Fay, who was then working as a teacher. Some years later, they decided to try their luck as professionals and joined RADA together, graduating in 1960.

Ken's career got off to a flying start when he went straight into the West End as well as appearing in the first episode of *Z Cars* (in which he went on to play a semi-regular character, Felix Smithers, a police photographer). Alongside his small-screen career Ken continued to work a great deal in rep, including a spell with Joan Littlewood's Theatre Workshop. His TV credits include *United!*, *The Planemakers*, *Hunter's Walk*, *Go for Gold*, *The Liver Birds*, *Emmerdale Farm*, *Coronation Street*, *Watching*, *Goodnight Sweetheart*, *Peak Practice* and *The Detectives*.

Ken, who now lives in West Wales, continues to work and was recently seen in *Casualty* and other television projects.

Jackdaw

The wimpy Jackdaw acts as a runner for Grouty, and appeared in 'The Harder They Fall'.

Cyril Shaps played Jackdaw, the man who tells Fletch he's wanted by Harry Grout. Born in London in 1923, Cyril worked for the London County Council's ambulance service as a clerk for five years upon leaving school. When World War II broke out, he spent five years with the Service and Educational Corps. Before he returned to civvy street in 1947, Cyril – who had always wanted to be an actor – helped prepare soldiers for demob by teaching music and drama appreciation.

When he finally left the army he won a scholarship to RADA; after graduating, he secured his first post in rep at Guildford followed by a spell in the West End. For two years he worked on Holland's radio network where his range of duties was varied, including reporting, producing and announcing. He returned to England and struggled on the job front until the chance to join the BBC's own repertory company came along.

He gradually established himself on radio and television, appearing in various shows, such as *Z Cars* and *Doctor Who*. His first film role was in 1950's *Cario Road*, and other productions he worked on include: *The Silent Enemy; Danger Within; Passport to Shame; Never Let Go; Return of a Stranger; To Sir, With Love; The Odessa File; Operation Daybreak* and *The Spy Who Loved Me*. Cyril is still busy in the profession.

Reggie Jarvis

Mancunian Reggie Jarvis appeared in the closing episode, 'Final Stretch'. Nicknamed The Red Menace (he's a Manchester United supporter), the aggressive inmate has a foul temper – as exemplified by his smashing the prison television because he couldn't get a decent picture while watching his favourite programme, *The Magic Roundabout*. Within the same episode we also see him brawling with Godber, so it's clear he's the sort of guy worth avoiding at all costs.

Jarvis was played by busy character-actor David Daker, who has appeared in shows such as *Z Cars* (as P.C. Owen Culshaw), *Doctor Who, UFO, Strangers* (as Roy Stevens), *Juliet Bravo, Sorry!, Casualty, The Bill, Midsomer Murders, The Fallen Curtain, Crown Prosecutor* (as Ben Campbell), *Boon* and *The Woman in Black*.

Keegan

Keegan, who's seen in 'The Desperate Hours', is to be
released shortly. Convicted for murdering his wife with
poison, it seems odd that he's been allocated a job in the
kitchen at Slade. When we get to see Keegan, he's become a
trusty and serves the Governor his daily cuppas. However,
Mr Venables can't ever come to terms with a murderer
serving his tea and removes him from his duties – even
though Mackay classes Keegan a 'model prisoner'.

Reading-born Ken Wynne played Keegan in the 1976
Christmas episode. Ken's father was a goods manager with
Great Western Railways, which meant frequent relocations;
despite those, most of his childhood was spent in Banbury.

He started acting with the Banbury County School and
quickly reached the conclusion that he never wanted to do
anything else with his life. Upon completing national
service in the army, Ken set about realising his ambitions
and was soon offered his first professional job at Stratford-
upon-Avon in 1946, a venue he returned to many times
during his career. His association with the Royal
Shakespeare Company extended to a tour of Australia in
1953.

Ken has appeared in most of the West End theatres and
has spent much of his acting life on the stage. He has never-
theless found time to grace the small screen in many
programmes, including several episodes of *Dixon of Dock
Green* – playing a policeman's nark – as the eccentric Mr
Deacon in *The Fall and Rise of Reginald Perrin*, Reg
Partridge in *Lovejoy*, Fenner in *The Sweeney*, Greasy Spriggs
in *The Bounder*, the churlish farmer Dennis Pratt in *All
Creatures Great and Small*, and as Ernie Mears in
EastEnders.

His film credits, meanwhile, include *Decline and Fall of a
Birdwatcher*, *Up Pompeii*, *The Alf Garnett Saga*, *Galileo* and
The Mystery of Edwin Drood.

Lukewarm

Lukewarm, who works in the kitchen, originates from Middlesbrough and is described by Fletch as being 'lilac'. Within three months of Lukewarm's release, we hear from Fletcher that he's back in trouble after stealing a lady's handbag – though he claimed it was his own. A keen knitter, Lukewarm shares a cell with old-man Blanco, while his life outside is shared with Trevor, a watch repairer from Southport.

Oldham-born Christopher Biggins had no doubts about how to play Lukewarm. 'He was obviously an iron hoof – which is a wonderful term for poof – but none of us wanted him to be a mincing queen, so it was played, basically, a bit like me. For example, I used to do knitting so I suggested the character should knit, which helped make him a little fey.'

Lukewarm was one of the memorable inmates, and Christopher enjoyed being associated with the show. 'When we finished the first series, Ronnie gave the regulars a silver tankard with "Slade Prison, 1974" and our names inscribed on it. It was fantastic fun: not only was I working with a brilliant script, which is so important, but we also had Ronnie Barker who was generous to a fault. He's not a comedian, he's a comic actor of genius; and if he felt one of his lines was better said by me or somebody else, they would have it.

'It will always be a classic and its success is also due to Syd Lotterby, who managed to assemble the most wonderful cast. We had a lot of laughs doing it, and it was one of those jobs you enjoyed going to work for. There wasn't one dud performance in the whole of the series, and I'm very proud to have been involved.'

Christopher, who's also a director, grew up in Salisbury and attended elocution lessons while at school. His teacher introduced him to the theatre, and he joined the local rep. He had initially intended to stay just two weeks, but remained for two years – by the end of which time he'd earned his Equity card. Wishing to receive formal training, Christopher attended Bristol Old Vic Theatre School before joining Derby Rep. Not much later he made his West End debut in *The Owl and the Pussycat Went to Sea*, playing Head Jumbly.

His first role on TV was playing a thief in *Paul Temple*, but other credits include Podge in Clement and La Frenais' *Whatever Happened to the Likely Lads?*, Adam Painting in *Rentaghost*, Brian Reeves in the BBC sitcom *Watch This Space*, Nero in *I, Claudius*, a student in *Some Mothers Do 'Ave 'Em*, and work on *Upstairs, Downstairs, Five's Company, Poldark, Jackanory, Kidnapped* and *Surprise, Surprise*.

He's also appeared in a handful of films, including *Eskimo Nell, The Rocky Horror Picture Show, Applause* and *The Tempest*, and remains busy in the theatre, recently appearing in *School for Scandal* and in the musical *Guys and Dolls*, playing Nathan Detroit. In addition to all that, he's a regular in pantos, many of which he directs.

Christopher will always remember his time on *Porridge*. 'The most memorable episode was "Men without Women", with Fletcher drafting a letter for his fellow prisoners. When the audience suddenly realised the character called Trevor was Lukewarm's boyfriend, there was an almighty roar. It was probably the biggest laugh I've ever heard in a studio.'

McLaren

Scottish-born McLaren was brought up in an orphanage and since the age of fourteen has been in and out of care homes and prison. His early years were spent in Greenock, where a policeman had found him abandoned in an alley, protected from the elements by nothing more than a copy of the *Glasgow Herald*. He never knew his father and was unwanted by his mother, so no one was surprised when he drifted into crime. An aggressive, outspoken prisoner with a chip the size of Ben Nevis on his shoulder, he's serving a three-year sentence. McLaren works as a hospital orderly.

Tony Osoba was playing a manservant in *Churchill's People* when the offer to play McLaren came along. The character first appeared in 'Ways and Means', the penultimate episode in series one, and at the time Tony believed the role was a one-off. 'It was a great part because the character featured quite strongly. In the episode, McLaren, who was always hot-headed, winds up on the roof. Fletch comes up with one of his schemes and manages to talk McLaren down, but it was all engineered so that they both come out smelling of roses! I enjoyed the role but, at that point, there was no talk of the character becoming a regular.'

That was remedied when a second series was commissioned and McLaren became a fixture of the show. Tony was impressed with Clement and La Frenais' scripts. 'Most people probably thought that a comedy in prison was a most unlikely setting – and it probably took all the skill those guys possessed to make it succeed. I don't think too many people could have pulled it off; but their writing was so brilliant they ended up making the audience feel sympathetic towards the prisoners, even though they were being punished for their own wrongdoing. The sympathy was directed towards the inmates, not poor old Mackay and Barrowclough.'

The experience of recording episodes of *Porridge* was a happy one, as Tony recalls. 'The actors were given leeway to develop their characters, which is always pleasing, and the scripts were beautifully written: I can't remember any other show I've done where the scripts were tinkered with less. The atmosphere was such that actors were allowed to voice their opinion. Dick and Ian were often around for the read-throughs, but they never sat there as if they were protecting their precious baby – they were always prepared to listen to what others had to say.'

Tony particularly enjoyed working alongside Ronnie Barker, someone he regards as 'very generous'. 'He was the leading man, but if he saw moments where another character was doing something and it was funny, he would be the first to suggest dropping some of his own lines in order to incorporate it; obviously he was comfortable in his own abilities.'

Tony doesn't feel there was a weak episode in the entire series. 'There were some very funny episodes, then others which touched on people's feelings and sensitivities; Dick and Ian were able to couple these elements together without being maudlin or over-sentimental. I was delighted to be involved in the series, and always remember the utter disappointment if a script arrived and I wasn't in it. It's a bit of a cliché but I did get up and look forward to the day ahead because it was a joy being part of the programme.'

Tony also found the experience educational, learning a great deal about his craft from those around him. 'To be with actors of Ronnie, Richard, Fulton and Brian's calibre was wonderful. If you had anything about you, you couldn't help but observe and learn from these people – it was a superb schooling. I also owe a huge debt to Syd Lotterby. He would always encourage you and never make you feel small; if you had an idea, for example, which didn't work out, he'd never scoff.'

When the series came to an end in 1977, Tony – who went on to appear in the first episode of *Going Straight* – was very disappointed. 'It was a sad day, knowing we weren't doing any more, because it was a joy to work on. Everyone was given their fair share of lines and scenes; maybe there was an episode in which you didn't feature much, but then you'd get several nice scenes in the next. The rehearsals were good fun, and you found yourself going to work with a spring in your step, knowing you'd have a good day.'

If Glasgow-born Tony had pursued his childhood ambitions, he'd be employed as a car designer. 'By the time I was ten I could name every car on the road; I loved everything about them and would happily have lived and eaten my meals in a car. When I was thinking about going to university, I wrote to the car manufacturers to find out the best degree to study but soon discovered that no one could guarantee I'd ever be employed as a designer. I naïvely thought I'd be taken on as a designer and be creating these wonderful cars in just a few years. So I finished my A levels and made a sudden decision to become an actor.'

Tony trained at the Royal Scottish Academy of Music and Drama, during which time he was offered small parts in theatre and television. Upon graduating, he joined a Richmond-based theatre company, touring schools, before moving on to mainstream theatre, including spells working abroad and with the Royal Shakespeare Company.

Alongside his developing stage career, Tony was being cast for various television roles, with his first substantial feature part being Lawrence in *Churchill's People*. Among his 200-plus television credits are three series as Detective Constable Jarvis in *Dempsey and Makepeace*, parts in *The Professionals, Brookside, Bergerac, Minder, Doctor Who*, the role of Peter Ingram in *Coronation Street*, Barrett in *The Bureaucracy of Love* and Detective Superintendent Garrett in *The Bill*. Though he has continued to work in the theatre, including a couple of years spent with the Young Vic and various theatrical assignments in the States, since the eighties most of his work has been on the small screen.

Navy Rum

The loud-mouthed Navy Rum is one of the prisoners selected to help dig drainage ditches for the local council. Plastered in tattoos and with his long hair and beard, he cuts a rather daunting figure. Before turning to crime, he worked as a stoker on the tankers sailing the Persian Gulf. While he's been behind bars, he's served time at various prisons, including a spell with Fletcher at Maidstone.

Paul Angelis, who played Navy Rum, was offered the role after bumping into Ian La Frenais outside a London Tube station. 'We got talking and he told me he was filming *Porridge*. He asked if I'd be keen to play a character whom he described as looking like the bearded sailor on Players' cigarette packets.'

Paul accepted and headed for the location filming near Merthyr Tydfil, sporting a stick-on beard. 'It didn't stop raining, which meant we had to be careful because I had tattoos drawn all over me and they would have probably run if they'd got wet!'

Paul enjoyed playing Navy Rum so much he wished the character had developed into a regular. 'It was one of the most enjoyable jobs of my career, and it was lovely to watch Ronnie Barker at work.' But, alas, Navy Rum wasn't seen again.

Paul is a Liverpudlian who left school and began a career in merchant banking. He remained in the industry six years before auditioning for the Royal Scottish Academy of Music and Drama. After winning a full scholarship he joined the Academy in 1963, graduating two years later. He moved to London and earned his Equity card touring with a children's theatre company. A couple of fringe productions followed before Paul broke into television and went on to make early appearances in a number of shows. These included *Z Cars* (he was seen in 150 episodes as P.C. Bannerman), *Theatre 625*, *Callan*, *The Sweeney*, *The Liver Birds* (as Polly James' boyfriend), *George and Mildred*, *Robin's Nest*, *Juliet Bravo*, *Bergerac* and *Honey Lane*. More recent TV credits include: *Boon*, *Casualty* and *The Bill*, ten episodes of *Coronation Street* as Alf Roberts' chauffeur, a policeman in *EastEnders* and Reg Titley in the 1999 series *The Grimleys*.

On the big screen, he provided voices for the Beatles' movie *Yellow Submarine* and appeared in *Otley*, *Battle of Britain* and 1981's *For Your Eyes Only*.

Paul has also written for more than thirty years, including a food programme for TSW and several shows for BBC radio. He's currently working on a novel.

Norris

'Nasty' Norris makes his only appearance in 'Happy Release', sharing the prison's infirmary with Blanco and Fletch while having his in-growing toenail removed prior to his release. When Fletch discovers the obnoxious Norris has diddled the aged Blanco out of all of his worldly goods, he ensures

Norris gets his comeuppance when he leaves Slade Prison. Fletcher devises a plan and tricks Norris into digging up a football pitch (which in reality was Loftus Road, home of Queen's Park Rangers) in search of some loot. His actions result in him being arrested again.

Actor Colin Farrell feels he has lots to thank Norris for, because playing the part helped him to overcome his dislike for recording comedy in front of a live audience. 'I hadn't done a lot of work with a live audience before *Porridge*, partly because I hated it.' Colin regarded it as an 'awful medium' and after some early experiences vowed never to do it again.

'Then I met Sydney Lotterby and was offered Nasty Norris.' Although he held reservations about the type of work, he couldn't resist playing the character. 'I'm glad I accepted the part, because I learned so much from it such as how to stay within the context of the scene, as well as not thinking about the audience unless you were considering their response to a potentially funny line. It's no good ploughing on with the dialogue if the audience are laughing at an earlier line; you have to wait for the laughter to subside.'

Prior to his taking up acting, for London-born Colin it had looked as though a musical career beckoned: he was playing instruments at seven, and belonged to the London School Symphony Orchestra by eleven. But by the time he started national service in the army, Colin's attention had already veered towards acting. He'd studied for several terms at RADA, and completed his course after giving up his uniform.

After beginning his professional career in weekly rep at Worthing, he got a lucky break by joining the original cast of *Chips with Everything* at the Royal Court in 1962, later transferring to the West End. Colin worked in theatre five years before making his television debut in a production for the BBC's *The Wednesday Play*.

Throughout the sixties and seventies, he remained busy on the small screen, appearing in shows like *Dixon of Dock Green*, *Armchair Theatre*, *Play for Today*, *Softly Softly* and

No Hiding Place. In recent years, he was seen in six series of
In Loving Memory, and in *Heartbeat, The Bill* and
Midsomer Murders. On the big screen, meanwhile, his career
has included pictures such as *Oh! What a Lovely War,*
Gandhi and *A Bridge Too Far,* playing Corporal Hancock.

Nowadays, Colin spends most time in the theatre; such
work has included a spell with the Royal Shakespeare
Company and six years touring the world with the English
Shakespeare Company.

Rawley

Stephen Rawley, who's married to Marjorie, is sentenced to
three years after being indicted for bribery and corruption.
He is a friend of the Governor's: they served in the Guards
together at Winchester, belong to the same club and socialise
frequently. It's rumoured that their amity is the reason
Rawley is given a cosy job in Central Records – something
that irks Fletcher, whose anger is fuelled by that fact that his
new cellmate was the judge who sentenced him.

Rawley arrives on the scene in 'Poetic Justice' and by the
end of the following episode, 'Rough Justice', sees his appeal
accepted. Rawley's weakness had been a younger woman: a
nineteen-year-old go-go dancer he met at his regimental
reunion when she was assisting the magician. When she
became increasingly demanding, his troubles began.

Veteran actor Maurice Denham was called in to play the
disgraced judge, just one of hundreds of roles he's performed
on stage, screen and radio during his extensive career. Born in
1909, Maurice made his name as sundry comic characters in
the 1940s radio shows *ITMA* and *Much-Binding-in-the-Marsh*
before kicking off his busy film career with *Home and School,*
Daybreak, Fame is the Spur and *The Man Within.* Other
credits include: *Dear Murderer, London Belongs to Me,*
Landfall, Don't Ever Leave Me, No Highway, Street Corner,
Carrington VC, Doctor at Sea, Sink the Bismarck!, Two-Way
Stretch, The Heroes of Telemark and *Danger Route.*

Scrounger

Scrounger helps make up the party given a day out digging drainage ditches on the moors. His knowledge of such tasks – he worked for a road gang on the motorways – may be the reason he's selected for the job. While touring the country's roadways before reverting to crime, he lived in a caravan with his wife and two children.

Johnny Wade was cast as Scrounger in the episode 'A Day Out', but it wasn't the first time he'd worked alongside Ronnie Barker, having already appeared in *The Two Ronnies* and the sixties show *Frost Over England*. Although he associates the part of Scrounger with several wet days filming in Wales, he enjoyed the experience nonetheless. 'It was good fun. The writing was superb and the characterisations perfect, especially Mackay,' says Johnny. 'I think Fulton had every drill-sergeant down to a tee, what with the sarcasm and the chin stuck out! The show had a lot going for it, particularly the rapport between Barker and Beckinsale.'

Born in Bethnal Green, Johnny started his working life as a singer after winning several talent contests. His days were spent running a market stall, selling sweets, while in the evenings he was busy working initially in cabaret and then with a band. Then he earned his television break, as a singer in the sixties soap-drama *Compact*, and played Stan Millet for three years before moving on to hit musicals, including *Guys and Dolls* and *South Pacific*, touring the world for more than three years. He's also worked at the Royal Court.

Johnny has remained busy on the box, appearing in *Z Cars*, *Coronation Street* (playing a lorry driver), *United* and four series as Roger in Yorkshire TV's *You're Only Young Twice*. Recent work has seen him appear in *EastEnders* as a drunken chauffeur, as well as in the second series of *Sunburn*, filmed in Portugal.

Spider

The creeping Spider looks after Grouty by fetching, carrying and running errands for him. He's seen in 'A Storm in a Teacup'.

Spider was played by John Moore, whose television work includes appearances in *The Avengers*, in 1961, as Ted Watson in a 1980 episode of *Juliet Bravo*, and as Joe in *Bergerac* a year later. On the big screen, he was seen in several films, such as *Countess Dracula* (1971), *The Frozen Dead, Captain Nemo and the Underwater City* and *Tess*, in 1979.

Spraggon

Spraggon, who was seen in 'A Test of Character', longs to be a writer, though his bad grammar, inability to spell and penchant for brutal language leave a lot to be desired. His cousin Ernie was a notorious tearaway and Spraggon longs to gain as much publicity as he did. Nicknamed Spraggs, his manuscripts are checked by Barrowclough in the episode while the education officer is unavailable.

Alun Armstrong, who played Spraggon, was born in Annfield Plain in 1946. He's worked on stage and screen, with his television appearances including *Whatever Happened to the Likely Lads?, The Stars Look Down, Sharing Time, This Is David Lander, Breaking Rank, Inspector Morse, Goodbye Cruel World* (as Gerald Faulkner), Uncle Teddy in *The Life and Times of Henry Pratt* and Austin Donohue in *Our Friends in the North*.

His film credits include: *A Bridge Too Far, Get Carter, The Fourteen, The French Lieutenant's Woman, White Roses, Split Second* and *Patriot Games*.

Tolly

Tolly, who's married to Norma, is one of the prisoners in 'Men without Women' who takes Fletcher's advice and sends his wife a letter – drafted by Fletch.

Tolly was played by actor Emlyn Price, who has also appeared in television shows such as *Bergerac, Remington Steele, The Bill, Boon, The Cabbage Patch, Rock Follies* (as Derek Huggin), *By the Sword Divided* (playing Corporal Veazey), *Roll Over Beethoven* and, more recently, as a policeman in 1995's *Cynthia Payne's House of Cyn* and as Neil Copeland in *Surgical Spirit*.

Tulip

Tulip appeared briefly in 'The Desperate Hours' as a fellow inmate given the disputable privilege of sampling Fletch's wine in the prison toilet. We learn nothing more about the character during the series.

Michael Redfern's appearance as Tulip in an episode of *Porridge* was just one of a myriad of shows he's appeared in. Born in Isleworth, Middlesex, early television work included Rufus Pargeter in *The Newcomers*, appearances in *George and Mildred*, as a policeman in *Robin's Nest*, and in *The Professionals* and *Agony*. Other small-screen credits include: *Never the Twain, United!, Hi-De-Hi!, The Gentle Touch, Minder, Terry and June, Sorry!, The 19th Hole*, Mr Cooper in *Bottom, The Bill, The Detectives* and *Hope and Glory*.

Reg Urwin

Reg Urwin, who'd worked for some time in the machine shop, replaces Keegan as the trusty tasked with serving the Governor his daily cup of tea. An unstable character, Urwin has been recommended three times for psychiatric treatment in the last two years. He even tried committing suicide once: intending to steal a tin of luncheon meat in a supermarket, he suddenly wondered what his world had come to. Depressed with his lot in society, he put his head down and charged towards the glass doors.

Urwin takes advantage of his new lofty position and takes Barrowclough hostage in the Governor's office, demanding ten grand and a helicopter. It's down to Fletcher to save the day.

Dudley Sutton, who played Reg Urwin, boasts a lengthy list of credits, particularly on both small and big screen. On television, he's worked on numerous productions, including *The Avengers, Department S, The Baron, The Saint, Dempsey and Makepeace, Boon, Bergerac, Armchair Theatre, Shine on Harvey Moon, The Beiderbecke Affair* (as Mr Carter), *Lovejoy*, playing Tinker, and as a tramp in *Emmerdale Farm*.

Meanwhile, his film work has included *Go to Blazes, Rotten to the Core, One More Time, Diamonds on Wheels*, McClaren in *The Pink Panther Strikes Again, The Big Sleep, George and Mildred* (playing Jacko), *Chain Reaction* and *Orlando*, as King James I.

Warren

Bunny Warren is dyslexic and relies upon fellow inmates to read his letters from home, including those from his wife, Elaine, who lives in Bolton and was responsible for coining his nickname, Bunny. Prior to life behind bars, Bunny worked in his father-in-law's ironmongery in Bolton. Although not the brightest of guys, he's always high-spirited, a rare thing at Slade.

When we first meet Warren, he's served ten months of his sentence, and blames dyslexia for his plight: he claims he had a tough break – he couldn't read the sign saying 'Burglar Alarm' and got caught!

Playing the doltish Bunny Warren was Mancunian actor Sam Kelly. Turning his hand to such a dull-witted character posed no problems. 'Syd Lotterby had used me before in an episode of *The Liver Birds* in a similar role, so when the part of Warren, a rather simple-minded chap from Bolton, came up he asked me to play that as well.'

Sam didn't need anyone to tell him how to play Warren; it was evident from the writing. 'The scripts were brilliant and just reading them brought the characters alive; there's been hardly anything that's reached the level of those scripts since.'

But in retrospect he admits he'd have played the character differently. 'I hadn't done an enormous amount of television at that time. Now I would have made my performance more subtle and less broad as a piece of acting.'

Sam enjoyed his days at Slade Prison and rates it among the highlights of his comedy career. 'It was clear from day one that the scripts were second to none, and in Ronnie I was working with a genius – I learned a lot from him. He was extremely generous: he knew he was the star of the show and consequently could afford to be generous towards other actors to make the show better.'

A few years later, Sam worked with Barker again, this time in *The Two Ronnies* stage show touring the country, including a spell at the Palladium and Down Under. 'My main function was to play Bunny Warren in a scene specially written for the show. It was only twenty minutes long but I enjoyed it.'

It doesn't surprise Sam that the sitcom continues to attract large audiences whenever it's repeated. 'It was based on characters rather than jokes and worked well; but its setting is also timeless; and until they demolish Victorian prisons they'll be able to carry on showing it, which is very nice for my bank manager,' he says, smiling.

Born in 1943, Sam trained at LAMDA after working for three years in the civil service in Liverpool. He graduated from drama school in 1967 and was soon spotted uttering one line as a newspaper reporter in an episode of *Emergency – Ward 10*.

Four years of rep work around the UK followed, including spells at Liverpool, Sheffield and Lincoln. 'I became an actor because I wanted to work in the theatre, and for me television work subsidises the theatre work. Then every now and again you get a little gem on TV which makes you realise what fun it can be.'

On the small screen, Sam's credits include a series of *The Dave Allen Show, The Dick Emery Show*, playing Bob Challis in *Coronation Street*, Mr Snagsby in *Bleak House*, Norman in two series of *Now and Then*, Dr Geering in three series of *'Allo, 'Allo*, Grunge in two series of *Haggard* and Sam in three series of *On the Up*.

Sam, who's also appeared in a handful of films, including two *Carry Ons* and the *Porridge* movie, remains a busy actor: he's recently completed a ten-part series of Carlton's sitcom *Barbara*, and there's another television project on the horizon as well as his annual stint in panto.

Blanco

Sixty-three-year-old Blanco Webb is a bespectacled old-timer who served seventeen years before receiving a pardon, in 'Happy Release', for a crime he insisted he didn't commit. Back in 1959, he was found guilty of killing his wife and hiding her body in a fridge, although he always stated her lover was responsible. He shared a cell with Lukewarm at Slade Prison and was a cheating Monopoly player. And Godber described him as being kind and gentle – but that was before he'd discovered that Blanco murdered his wife's lover.

Blanco has no family and leaves his friends behind at Slade for a life of loneliness. Reflecting on a past that saw him turn to stealing when he couldn't find employment, he's spent over half his life doing porridge.

Blanco was played by David Jason, regarded as one of the country's finest comedy actors. Forever busy on screen, David's glittering career has included such classic parts as the over-aged delivery boy Granville in four series of Roy Clarke's

Open All Hours, Pop Larkin in three series of *The Darling Buds of May* and Detective Inspector Jack Frost in *A Touch of Frost*. Considered by many to be his best performance, however, was the role of Del Trotter, the cheery wheeler-dealer in the long-running sitcom *Only Fools and Horses*.

Born in London in 1940, the son of a fish porter at Billingsgate Fish Market, David gained his first taste of acting as a fourteen-year-old in a school play. When he left school the following year, though, he followed his parents' advice and took a trade. He was initially a garage mechanic and then, after a year, switched professions and began training as an electrician; his evenings, meanwhile, were occupied performing with local amateur productions.

By the mid-sixties, David had turned professional and followed his brother, Arthur, into the world of greasepaint and footlights. Appearing at Bromley Rep in a production of Noël Coward's *South Sea Bubble* was the start of an award-winning career spanning more than three decades.

David made his television debut in 1967's children's comedy *Do Not Adjust Your Set*, alongside Michael Palin, Eric Idle and Terry Jones. He combined stage and television work for years, with appearances in *Crossroads* and in *Hark at Barker*, with Ronnie Barker, with whom he'd work so successfully years later.

Williams

Williams is a dour Welshman whose general mien makes you wonder if he should be residing in a mental institution rather than Slade Prison. A bit of an oddball, he claims to possess a large sexual appetite – compensating, perhaps, for his years of deprivation at a choir school.

Philip Madoc, who was cast as Williams, was born in Merthyr Tydfil. After working as an interpreter in German, he entered the industry in the 1960s, studying at RADA. He worked for a while in rep before moving into TV, one of his first appearances being in the 1956 production *The Count of*

Monte Cristo. Other TV work includes: Detective Chief
Superintendent Tate in *Target*, Fison in *A Very British Coup*,
and roles in *The Avengers* and *Doctor Who*. He also
appeared as Angel Martes in 'Get Me Out of Here!', an
episode of *The Champions*, as Rawlins in a *Randall &
Hopkirk (Deceased)* episode titled 'Never Trust a Ghost' in
1968, and an episode of *Man in a Suitcase*.

Philip has also made more than thirty films, including *The
Quiller Memorandum, Daleks: Invasion Earth 2150AD* and
Operation Daybreak, while recent years have been dominated
by theatre work including many classical roles. His own TV
detective series, *A Mind to Kill*, in which he plays the lead,
has been sold all over the world.

The Unseen Lags

During the series, Fletcher and the others frequently referred
to unseen inmates, such as SMUTTY GARLAND – a.k.a. Slade's
king of porn – in E-wing and TOMMY MCCREADIE, who was
planning an escape route back to the arms of his nervy wife,
a raver who's being sleeping with a limbo dancer. In 'The
Hustler' we also hear about NIFTY SMALL, who's in love with
Gruesome Glenda – a female social worker who visits the
prison on Tuesdays.

In 'A Night In', we learn that MIGHTY JOE BANKS was
Godber's previous cellmate. Fletch describes him as a 'head-
case' because he set light to his own and Godber's mattresses.
He was also the ringleader during a riot (that saw him throw
a screw off the top landing), which led to his transfer to
another prison.

In Series Two, Ives talks to Fletcher about RONNIE
ARKWRIGHT, who tried strangling his wife on visiting day
when she told him it was her last visit because she was off
to live with a Maltese 'ponce' in Morecambe. CORKSCREW
CARTER, a former solicitor before opting for a career
behind bars, is mentioned by Fletch in 'Happy Release'.
The non-speaking SID, meanwhile, plays draughts with
Fletch in the early scenes of 'The Harder They Fall', while

we discover BILLY MOFFAT is a rival to Grouty because he's running an unauthorised book for the boxing match. Other unseen inmates linked to the boxing event are NESBITT, Godber's opponent in the match, BIG MAC, favourite for the heavyweight bout ever since he put four warders in hospital after his jigsaw was knocked over, and LARRY, who's Godber's silent sparring partner.

In 'No Peace for the Wicked', Warren wants to play table tennis with MINI COOPER but can't because they haven't got a ball, while LUGLESS DOUGLAS sends them off to Fletch to get one.

We hear about TOMMY SLOCOMBE's tunnel in 'No Way Out': while prisoners sing carols at full volume, Tommy digs frantically in his search for freedom. A despicable bloke, his brother-in-law is a London villain and a friend of Harry Grout. His father, meanwhile, is Billy 'the ponce' Slocombe who escaped from Brixton in 1972, ending up on a sun-drenched Caribbean island where he's now chief of police! Helping with his escape is INKY STEPHENS, the finest forger in the country, who prepared his passport. Before the episode is out, the doctor mentions DONALDSON – who's serving five years for grand larceny and embezzlement.

ARSENIC RIGGS, who's serving time for poisoning, comes from Newcastle-under-Lyme and Fletch discusses him with Mackay in 'Poetic Justice', while in 'Rough Justice', CHARLIE GILL, who's also known by Fletch, got caught trying to escape because, being deaf, he didn't hear the dog chasing him.

In 'Pardon Me', there's reason to celebrate when the popular Blanco is awarded parole. Other prisoners whose cases are heard at the same time are GIBSON, in for car theft, whose appeal is declined, and MAC BROWN, serving time for manslaughter, who's delighted to be heading home when his case is surprisingly accepted.

We hear that a prisoner called GOMEZ passed his Spanish O level the previous year in 'A Test of Character', while in the final episode, 'Final Stretch', with Godber once again out in the wide world, Fletch's new cellmate is a Sunderland lad called NICHOLSON.

THE STAFF OF SLADE PRISON

Mr Appleton

Mr Appleton, a prison officer who works in Slade's kitchen, is seen in 'The Hustler'.

The character was played by the late Graham Ashley, who was also seen in shows such as *Doctor Who*, back in 1963, *Doctor in the House* (as a policeman), and as D.S. Tommy Hughes in the long-running police series *Dixon of Dock Green*. He appeared in various films, including *Track the Man Down*, *Man Accused*, *The Tell-Tale Heart*, *The Fast Kill*, *Alfie Darling*, *Adventures of a Taxi Driver* and 1977's *Star Wars*.

Chief Prison Officer Barrett

Chief Prison Officer Barrett made his sole appearance in a scene during 'A Day Out'. When Mr Mackay fears the worst and thinks the working party has gone missing, he apprises the Chief of the grave situation. It's clear that Mackay reports to the character, although we never hear from him again.

The Chief was played by Arnold Peters. Born in London in 1925, Arnold – who's the voice behind Jack Woolley in the long-running radio series *The Archers* – joined a dance band as a schoolboy until being called up to the RAF during the Second World War. Upon returning to civvy street, he became a professional actor and entertainer, with his first job being on radio's Children's Hour, in a programme called *Hastings of Bengal*.

Offers of work were plentiful and he joined the BBC Repertory Company in Birmingham. As well as radio and theatre work, Arnold is also a busy screen actor. His television appearances include: *Citizen Smith, Please, Sir!, The Siege of Golden Hill, Shoulder to Shoulder, United!, The Tomorrow People* and, in 1998, the BBC series, *Prince Among Men.*

Arnold has had a long-standing interest in English folk music and plays in a folk dance band.

Mr Bayliss

Mr Bayliss is Slade Prison's PT instructor and is seen in 'The Harder They Fall', training the prisoners for the forthcoming boxing tournament.

Bayliss was played by Roy Sampson, whose other credits include playing a policeman in *The Sweeney*, Harry Johnstone in an episode of *Doctor Finlay's Casebook*, Dougie Allen in 1991's *Advocates I* and the foreman of the jury in the 1992 film *Under Suspicion.*

Mr Birchwood

Mr Birchwood works as a prison officer at Slade and was seen in 'Just Desserts'.

John Rudling was a Londoner who qualified as a draughtsman before making his mark as a dependable character actor, beginning with the RSC. He moved on to work at the Players' Theatre, London, before touring with ENSA.

Repertory work as both actor and director kept him busy until film and television work came his way. His occasional big-screen appearances included the Ealing comedies *The Ladykillers, The Man in the White Suit* and *The Titfield Thunderbolt.*

On TV he's best remembered as Brabinger, the aged butler in *To the Manor Born*, but during the sitcom's run he suffered a heart attack. John died in 1983 from respiratory complications.

Mr Collinson

Mr Collinson was first seen in 'A Night In' as the prison officer who enters Fletch and Godber's cell. A sour-faced individual, Collinson is certainly not the life and soul of the officers' Christmas party.

Paul McDowell had already worked with Ronnie Barker on *The Two Ronnies* and *The Frost Report* before donning the prison officer's uniform in *Porridge*. Paul was given the freedom to develop his character's style. 'Mr Collinson was a very repressed sort of guy, someone who didn't get much out of life. He had a very sour outlook on humanity in general,' says Paul, smiling. 'He's probably married and miserable because of it, and if he'd had children, which was unlikely, they wouldn't have turned out very well.'

A successful writer himself, Paul can recognise when he's handed a decent script, and there was no doubting the quality of Clement and La Frenais' work. 'The writing was superb,' he says. 'It was a beautiful job, not a spare line, and it holds up so well even today. And the combination of Ronnie and Richard was just magic.'

Paul, who was born in London, left school and trained to be a painter at Chelsea Art College. During his student days, he formed a band, The Temperance Seven, and went on to enjoy success with six hit singles, including 'You're Driving Me Crazy', which went to number one in 1961. When Paul tired of the band, he left and worked at The Establishment, a satirical club in London, as a writer/actor, which introduced him to the world of acting.

Upon leaving the club, he worked in the United States for five years with an improvisational group, The Second City, before returning to England and writing for *The Frost Report*. His first small-screen appearance as an actor was in the second series of *The World of Beachcomber*, with Spike Milligan. On the box, he's worked predominantly in comedy, including many series with Dave Allen, *The Good Life*, *Only Fools and Horses* and four series of LWT's sitcom *The Two of Us*, playing Nicholas Lyndhurst's father, Colin Phillips. He was frequently cast as a policeman.

He's also made several films, including, in the role of a Scottish laird, *The Thirty-nine Steps*, with Robert Powell, and as a postman, 1980's *Rough Cut*.

Nowadays, Paul spends most of his time writing or teaching t'ai chi around the world; he's also had a novel published and hopes it will shortly be adapted for the screen.

Mrs Heskith

Mrs Heskith, the Governor's secretary, is seen in 'Disturbing the Peace'.

Madge Hindle was born in Blackburn in 1938 and spent her early years in amateur theatre. The role of Mrs Heskith was just one of many appearances she's made on the box. She made her debut in *On the Margin*, a drama series written by Alan Bennett, but it was her appearance as Lily in *Nearest and Dearest* that made her a household name. She went on to appear in sitcoms such as *Open All Hours* and *The Cuckoo Waltz* before spending four years behind the counter of the corner shop as Renee Bradshaw in *Coronation Street*.

Her more recent work has included playing Mrs Chadwick in *The Bright Side*, Mrs Shurer in *Lost Empires*, Elaine Dodswell in *The Rector's Wife*, and she appeared in *Anorak of Fire* and as Doreen in the 1999 series *Barbara*.

Dorothy Jamieson

Dorothy Jamieson takes over as the Governor's secretary from Mrs Heskith, and is seen in 'The Desperate Hours'. During the episode we discover she's been having an affair with Mr Barrowclough, although he tries dismissing the matter by claiming it's only a peccadillo.

Mrs Jamieson was played by Jane Wenham, who has made several film appearances, including roles in the 1950s' productions *The Teckman Mystery, An Inspector Calls* and *Make Me An Offer*. Her small-screen roles include those of Luciana in *The Comedy of Errors*, Portia in *The Spread of the Eagle*, Mrs Brittain in *The Testament of Youth*, Dolly Partridge in *Nanny* and Sophie in *Anastasia: The Mystery of Anna*.

Medical Officer

Slade Prison's Medical Officer wasn't in the best of health when he made his only appearance in 'New Faces, Old Hands'. Coughing and spluttering, he's tasked with inspecting the three new arrivals: Heslop, Godber and Fletcher. By the time we get to 'Happy Release' it's a different incumbent examining Fletch.

John Bennett, who played the spluttering medical officer in 'New Faces, Old Hands', has appeared in a host of productions during his career. His more recent credits include Idas in *Jason and the Argonauts*, the stranger in *Mulberry*, and the Corcyran Representative in *The War That Never Ends*. He's also been seen in several recent films, such as *Bridge of Dragons, The Fifth Element, Last Fair Deal* and *Priest*.

Other TV credits include *Jonathan Creek, Heartbeat, Cadfael, Hunter, Bergerac, The Professionals, Blake's 7, Survivors, The Avengers* and *Danger Man*.

Tottenham-born Terence Soall played the medical officer in 'Happy Release'. Upon leaving school, a career in acting was not what he pursued – he decided to become a journalist, and worked in Fleet Street for an international news service.

Whilst serving with the RAF in Gibraltar in 1942, he joined a theatre group and played his first role as a rejected lover. He enjoyed his experiences so much that upon returning to home shores in 1946 he gave himself five weeks to find a job in the theatre, else he'd return to the world of print. Good fortune was on his side, and the West Riding Theatre Company offered him employment.

After six months with the company he found himself touring Italy and Austria entertaining the troops. Shortly following his return to the UK, he had made his West End debut and appeared on TV. His small-screen appearances include *Coronation Street, Z Cars, Stand Up, Nigel Barton, The Master, Anna Karenina* and *Oliver Twist*. He's also appeared in several films.

Terence's busy career has covered all strands of the profession, including fourteen years directing at a drama school in Birmingham, but he'll always have a soft spot for his one-off role in *Porridge*. 'It was an enchanting show,' he enthuses. 'The two leading actors were wonderful; in fact, Richard Beckinsale was one of the most charming men you could ever meet.

'When I arrived for rehearsals, this young man [Richard] came bounding up to me and said: "You're Terence Soall, aren't you? I've seen a lot of your work." He was a lovely man.'

Doctor

The Prison Doctor is proud of his infirmary's low admission figures, and won't allow anyone into his ward unless they're literally dying on their feet.

Graham Crowden played the doc at Slade Prison, just one of many characters he's brought to life during an extensive career. In the fifties and sixties he was seen on TV in shows like *Destination Downing Street* and *Harpers West One*. He went on to work on numerous other programmes, including *Star Maidens, Raffles, The Guardians, Callan, The Adventures of Don Quick, Fraud Squad* and *Danger Man*. More recent work has seen him appear in *Don Quixote* and *The 10th Kingdom*, both in 2000.

Prison Officer

We never get to know the name of the Prison Officer who opens the prison gates to let Barrowclough and Fletcher in

during 'The Hustler', but he was played by actor John Quarmby, who received £50 for the day's filming.

John, who's now seventy-three and has been acting for more than fifty years, was born in Liverpool. After two years' national service in the RAF, he joined RADA in 1949. Repertory work dominated the first twenty years of his career, although he began appearing on TV from 1956.

His small-screen credits include: *Callan, Doomwatch, Van der Valk, 1990, Fawlty Towers* (as Mr Carnegie in 'Basil the Rat'), *Juliet Bravo, The Comic Strip Presents, The Scarlet Pimpernel, The Invisible Man, The Importance of Being Earnest, Vanity Fair, Great Expectations* and, in 1999, the mini series *Oliver Twist*.

He's also appeared in several movies, such as *Black Beauty* and *Restoration*.

Vicar

When the Prison Vicar comes calling on Fletcher during 'No Peace for the Wicked', he doesn't realise he's just one of a number of people who've disrupted Fletch's plans for a quiet afternoon. The vicar pays the price when Fletch throws him over the balcony, an act that earns him three days in isolation, something Fletch regards as bliss!

Playing the vicar was Solihull-born Tony Aitken, who started acting at his boarding school in Hereford. After training as an English and drama teacher at St Mary's University College, he taught around the Richmond area while looking for acting jobs.

His first appointment came at Hornchurch Rep, followed by two seasons at the Bristol Old Vic, by which time he'd also started being offered small parts on TV. Early small-screen appearances include *New Scotland Yard, Z Cars* and *Upstairs, Downstairs*.

Tony settled in London and while he continued working on the stage, he became more active in television comedy shows. His credits include *Agony, Married Love*, several series of *End of Part One* during the seventies, *The Lenny Henry Show, Blackadder II, Hot Metal, Open All Hours* and *No. 73* in the eighties, and more recently, *Barbara, They Never Slept, Sharpe's Justice, Keeping Up Appearances, The Bill, EastEnders* and *Doctors*.

As well as acting, Tony also runs his own voiceover recording studio.

Geoffrey Venables

Geoffrey Venables, who's married to Muriel, is the prison's weak-kneed Governor who seems more interested in the well-being of his tropical fish than the running of the prison. His passion for the natural world sees him serving on the local committee of the RSPCA, as well as opening a prison farm. He's a negative-thinking character with an ingrained resistance to fresh attitudes and ideas, especially if they're put forward by prisoners.

The Governor was played by the late Michael Barrington, who'd known Ronnie Barker for years and appeared in *The Two Ronnies* on occasions. His widow, Barbara, knows her husband enjoyed playing the Governor. 'You've got to enjoy comedy, otherwise you can't do it. He tried watching the episodes whenever possible, but was a very busy man: he did a lot of plays in the West End and went to Broadway for a while.'

As well as leading a busy theatrical life, including an eighteen-month spell at the National Theatre in *Coriolanus*, Michael, who also made the occasional film, appeared in plenty of TV shows – usually in cameo roles. His credits include *Private Schulz* for BBC2 in 1981, but he made his debut in an early episode of *Maigret*.

Michael was born in Shropshire in 1924 and, after his parents died when he was sixteen, he had to fend for himself. He wanted to train as a vet but the war disrupted his plans; after working at a munitions factory for a while he joined the Royal Engineers and served in Egypt and Greece. When he was finally demobbed he decided to try his luck as an actor and attended the Birmingham School of Drama. After graduating he entered the repertory circuit and appeared at venues such as Coventry, Birmingham and Nottingham, before making his London debut at the Vaudeville Theatre in *Salad Days*, playing three roles. Stage roles were sandwiched between television and film parts, including the 1971 picture *Follow Me*.

'For the last twelve years of his life, Michael continued to act like mad despite being an ill man,' admits Barbara. 'It was a terrible wasting disease of the lungs and he needed a lung transplant, but it was too late.' Michael died in 1988 aged sixty-four.

Mr Wainwright

Mr Wainwright, whose nickname was Napper, is an unpopular prison officer seen in 'Disturbing the Peace'. His time at Slade is short-lived because his belligerent manner causes uproar in the prison, so he's swiftly moved on to pastures new. Fletcher knows Wainwright from his days at Brixton, so when he arrives to cover for Mackay, who's attending a course, Fletch is far from pleased.

Wainwright was played by the late Peter Jeffrey, who was born in Bristol in 1929 and educated at Harrow and Pembroke College before graduating from RADA. He worked in repertory theatres up and down the country – including a season at Bristol's Old Vic – before becoming a familiar face on the small screen. His TV credits included playing Philip II of Spain in BBC's 1971 classic *Elizabeth R*, Mr Peabody in *Jewel in the Crown*, Colonel Bernwood in *Lipstick on Your Collar*, *The Planemakers*, *Triangle*, *Rising Damp*, *Lovejoy*, *The Detectives* and *One by One*.

His notable stage work included being a member of the Royal Shakespeare Company for more than thirty years, while on the big screen he was seen in several pictures, such as *Becket* (1964), *The Odessa File* (1974), *Midnight Express* (1978) and *Britannia Hospital* (1982). Peter died in 2000.

The Unseen Staff

One of the first unseen members of the prison's staff we hear about in the scripts is GRUESOME GLENDA, whose name pops up in 'The Hustler'. She's the female social worker who visits on Tuesdays. Well-known for her bicycle and brogues, we don't need to see her to realise what she's like because Fletch sums her up nicely, commenting: 'You'd be hard-pushed having an erotic fantasy about her.'

A member of staff mentioned several times but never seen was MR GILLESPIE, the welfare officer. His name is first uttered in 'Ways and Means', when we learn he recently graduated from university. Prior to joining Slade Prison, he worked at Welwyn Garden City; and he becomes a little distressed in his new place of work when prisoners head for the worldly-wise Fletcher for advice instead of him.

In 'Just Desserts', Mr Barrowclough mentions a prison officer called MR MALONE, who discovered Fletcher's missing tin of pineapple chunks during a routine security check at the prison. He's never heard of again.

Fletcher talks about a MR PRINGLE in 'Heartbreak Hotel' because he slipped on some orange peel, fell down the stairs and consequently suffers from a bad back. And, later, in 'A Test of Character', Fletch mentions MR KINGSLEY, Slade's education officer.

WHAT THE AUDIENCE THOUGHT

One method the BBC employed to monitor public opinion of its shows was to conduct audience surveys after selected episodes. Such reports were completed for several episodes of *Porridge*, and make interesting reading. Those who took part in the survey became known as members of the BBC viewing panel and, after watching all or part of the selected episodes, expressed their views about the show via a questionnaire.

What follows are extracts from the research reports:

The Harder They Fall

'This had been a consistently funny show that did credit to all concerned, the star and supporting cast being often praised among many warm comments; indeed, several thought it situation comedy . . . in "a rare top class".'

'A small number wondered "if it is correct to laugh about prison life", especially if portrayed as too soft, and, when sometimes "too crude", there was also some feeling that the series did "social good" by making "pertinent points" about certain problems and "increasing understanding" of prison life.'

The Desperate Hours

'Although felt by a few to be less than vintage *Porridge*, depending more on situation than verbal humour and tending to drag a bit at times, the programme clearly delighted most of those reporting and raised hopes for the return of a series widely held to be one of the best-written and most amusing in recent years.'

'The dialogue was excellent, some of Fletcher's almost throw-away lines being quite brilliant, viewers felt, and the situations well thought-out; two or three commented particularly on the assurance with which the plot changed direction from its light-hearted opening to the hostage sequence – still funny, but with an underlying seriousness.'

'While there was little scope as regards setting, etc., the production was usually commended, those reporting finding the prison background very convincing.'

Poetic Justice

'Whilst some disliked the confrontation between Fletcher and the judge who committed him, considering the situation "contrived" and the resulting conversations "too philosophical" to be really amusing, the large majority thoroughly approved of this "unconventional" plot, some particularly welcoming the opportunities it offered for an inclusion of a more "reflective and serious" element in the comedy.' 'Widely recognised as extremely well written, this was felt by most viewers to be another "hilarious programme" in one of the best and most intelligent comedies on television, very few actually disliking it to any degree.'

'The response to Ronnie Barker's portrayal of Fletcher was overwhelmingly appreciative. For many his "natural and outstanding" talent as a comedian "made the programme", and it was felt to be a measure of his ability that all the complexity of Fletcher's character was conveyed in such a manner that it served to make him at once credible and hilarious. Richard Beckinsale . . . was thought by most to be an excellent foil for Ronnie Barker, but was also praised in his own right.'

'Apart from a few criticisms that the pace and settings "lacked variation", the production was considered professional and "faultless" by most viewers.
Creating . . . an "almost frighteningly genuine" and authentic prison atmosphere, the setting, costumes, etc. were all applauded. Overall, a smooth-flowing and realistic production of an excellently performed and written comedy.'

Final Stretch

'The sample expressed themselves delighted with yet another witty, funny and extremely entertaining episode in which humour and sentiment were skilfully blended and which provided an excellent finale to the series.'

'Viewers were also loud in their praise for the performance of, among others, Fulton Mackay, Brian Wilde and, particularly, Richard Beckinsale . . . As one wrote: "Although it is Fletcher's Cockney wit which gives the show its appeal, undoubtedly the other actors who portray the warders, the Governor and the other prisoners made it a punishment *not* to watch *Porridge*."'

Audience Figures

PILOT (First shown on BBC2) **PRISONER AND ESCORT** 1.4 million

PORRIDGE

(All episodes shown on BBC1)

SERIES ONE

1 NEW FACES, OLD HANDS 16.1 million

2 THE HUSTLER 13.8 million

3 A NIGHT IN 13 million

4 A DAY OUT 15.2 million

5 WAYS AND MEANS 15 million

6 MEN WITHOUT WOMEN 12.1 million

SERIES TWO

1 JUST DESSERTS 14.3 million

2 HEARTBREAK HOTEL 14.4 million

3 DISTURBING THE PEACE 16.2 million

4 HAPPY RELEASE 16.2 million

5 THE HARDER THEY FALL 16.4 million

6 NO PEACE FOR THE WICKED 16.8 million

SERIES THREE

1 A STORM IN A TEACUP 15.4 million

2 POETIC JUSTICE 15.6 million

3 ROUGH JUSTICE 15.7 million

4 PARDON ME 15.4 million

5 A TEST OF CHARACTER 15.2 million

6 FINAL STRETCH 15.7 million

CHRISTMAS SPECIALS

NO WAY OUT 18.5 million

THE DESPERATE HOURS 20.8 million

GOING STRAIGHT (All episodes shown on BBC1)

1 GOING HOME 13.8 million

2 GOING TO BE ALRIGHT 14.8 million

3 GOING SOUR 12.6 million

4 GOING TO WORK 14.1 million

5. GOING, GOING, GONE 15.6 million

6 GOING OFF THE RAILS 13.3 million

First broadcast on British Television: 📺 **Friday 31 December 1982**
BBC1, 9.15 p.m.

CAST

Norman Fletcher....	**Ronnie Barker**
Lennie Godber....	**Richard Beckinsale**
Mr Mackay....	**Fulton Mackay**
Mr Barrowclough....	**Brian Wilde**
Grouty....	**Peter Vaughan**
Bainbridge....	**Julian Holloway**
The Governor....	**Geoffrey Bayldon**
Beal....	**Christopher Godwin**
Oakes....	**Barrie Rutter**
Rudge....	**Daniel Peacock**
Warren....	**Sam Kelly**
Ives....	**Ken Jones**
Banyard....	**Philip Locke**
Dines....	**Gorden Kaye**
McMillan....	**Oliver Smith**
Armstrong....	**Andrew Dunford**
Wellings....	**Steven Steen**
Simkin....	**Ivan Steward**
Small....	**Derek James**
Urquhart....	**Karl Howman**
Callaghan....	**Rod Culbertson**
Lotterby....	**Zoot Money**
Cooper....	**Derek Deadman**
Atkinson....	**Robert Putt**
Whalley....	**Allan Warren**
Whittakar....	**Stewart Harwood**
McLaren....	**Tony Osoba**
Hedley....	**John Barrett**
Morgan....	**Paul Barber**
Hayward....	**Sebastian Abineri**
Samson....	**John Dair**
Delilah....	**Barry James**
Jacko....	**Jackie Pallo Jnr.**
Tinkler....	**Robert Lee**
Cox....	**Robert Hamilton**
Miller....	**Charles Pemberton**
Lassiter....	**Colin Rix**
Collinson....	**Paul McDowell**
Medical Officer....	**Michael O'Hagan**
Chalky....	**Paul Luty**
Weatherman....	**Duncan Preston**
Alf....	**Bunny May**
Sheila....	**Elizabeth Knight**
PC Townsend....	**Nicholas McArdle**
Old Lady....	**Jean Campbell Dallas**
Old Man....	**Bill Kerry**

Production Team

Screenplay by . . . . **Dick Clement and Ian La Frenais**
Producers . . . . **Allan McKeown and Ian La Frenais**
Director . . . . **Dick Clement**
Production Manager . . . . **David Wimbury**
Second Unit Director . . . . **Ian La Frenais**
Assistant Directors . . . . **Richard Hoult and Peter Kohn**
Director of Photography . . . . **Bob Huke, BSC**
Camera Operator . . . . **Freddie Cooper**
Follow Focus . . . . **Peter Biddle**
Script Supervisor . . . . **Jane Buck**
Editor . . . **Alan Jones**
Art Director . . . . **Tim Gleeson**
Music Supervisor . . . . **Terry Oates**
(Song 'Free Inside' written by Lem Lubin and Ian La Frenais, sung by Joe Brown)
Wardrobe Master . . . . **Daryl Bristow**
Make-up . . . . **Sarah Monzani**
Hairdresser . . . . **Wendy O'Halloran**
Sound Editor . . . . **Jim Roddan**
Sound Recordist . . . . **Clive Winter**
Boom Operator . . . . **Ken Weston**
Dubbing Editor . . . . **Jim Roddan**
Dubbing Mixer . . . . **Paul Carr**
First Assistant Editor . . . . **Dina Eaton**
Technical Adviser . . . . **George Flanagan**
Production Assistant . . . . **Lindsay Sterne**
Casting . . . . **Esta Charkham**
Production Accountant . . . . **Mike Smith**
Assistants to the Producers . . . . **Georgie Dyer and Robert Vehon**
Props Buyer . . . . **Jill Quertier**
Construction Manager . . . . **Tony Graysmark**
Property Master . . . . **Jack Towns**
Craft Services . . . . **Sylvie Weston**
Stills . . . . **Albert Clarke**
Publicity . . . . **Sue D'Arcy**
Processing by . . . . **Rank Film Laboratories Ltd**
Filmed with . . . . **Panavision Equipment**
Lights by . . . . **Lee Electric (Lighting) Ltd**
Costumes supplied by . . . . **Bermans and Nathans Ltd**
Titles by . . . . **GSE Ltd.**

Certificate: . . . . **A**
Distributor: . . . . **ITC**
Production Company: **Black Lion Films (A Witzend Production)**
Length: . . . . **8,425 feet, 93 minutes duration**

Read All About It!

The movie's release received plenty of attention from the British media, but, in line with most of the examples within this genre, the conversion from small to big screen didn't impress the majority of critics, as the following reviews reveal.

'The plot is undernourished . . . and the good lines few and far between'

John Coleman, *New Statesman*, 27 July 1979

'The plot is no more substantial than might sustain one TV episode (but it's 90 minutes instead of 30)'

Valerie Jenkins, *Evening Standard*, 19 July 1979

'There is a lot of merriment to be savoured yet the film never loses sight of the grim realities of prison life that lurk beneath.'

Ian Christie, *Daily Express*, 21 July 1979

'The Dick Clement and Ian La Frenais TV series makes a happy transference to the big screen, with a fair number of predictable prison jokes, an authentic setting . . . and a truly hilarious football-match climax.'

Margaret Hintman, *Daily Mail*, 20 July 1979

'*Porridge* suffers . . . from the total lack of ambition that generally afflicts British television spin-offs . . . But, considering it was accomplished in less than a month and with a strictly limited budget, Dick Clement's film is very professional.'

Derek Malcolm, *Guardian*, 19 July 1979

THE FILM

Fletcher and Godber are already doing porridge when three
new faces arrive at Slade Prison: Beale, an arrogant warder,
Rudge, a sullen first offender serving two years, and Oakes,
an incorrigible long-termer who's halfway through a twelve-
year stretch for armed robbery.

Fletch attempts to show Rudge the ropes and demonstrate
how, with a little effort, he can adjust to life inside. Oakes,
meanwhile, knows the score only too well and soon teams up
with Harry Grout, the prison's self-appointed Godfather;
after he promises to swell his bank account with a fat, juicy
lump sum, Grouty agrees to orchestrate his escape.

To help execute the plan, the unfortunate Fletcher is
dragged into the affair. He's tasked with persuading the
prison officials to organise a football match against a
showbiz eleven, a way to divert the warders' attention. While
the match is in progress, Oakes will escape via the visiting
team's coach.

The plot goes virtually to plan and Oakes is soon heading
north; the trouble is that he ends up taking Fletch and

Godber with him. Keen not to tarnish their records, they leave Oakes and try sneaking back into Slade Prison underground, resurfacing through a manhole cover in the storeroom behind the Prison Officers' Club.

The 1970s saw a vogue for making movies out of successful television sitcoms. From *On the Buses* and *Bless This House to Are You Being Served?* and *Man About the House*, hardly a show was spared. Sadly, most offerings were flimsy versions of the small-screen originals, lacking the pace and intensity that made their respective shows successful in the first place. Most of the film plots left a lot to be desired, resembling over-stretched episodes, agonisingly spread over ninety minutes. But there were exceptions and – though many of the reviewers in the British press didn't appear to think so – *Porridge*, written by the Dick Clement and Ian La Frenais partnership, stood out from the crowd.

Dick acknowledges the challenge involved in writing sitcom-based films, and indeed has his own reservations about this one. 'You've got to pace it differently and ensure you have a story that sustains the greater length of screen time. I liked the film, but its weakness was that we didn't quite get the big laugh I wanted at the end – when Fletch and Godber returned to prison. The biggest laugh is the sequence where the new screw's bicycle is stolen but that's in the middle of the film – it's a shame. In hindsight, the scene should have been a bigger sequence, towards the end of the film.'

By the time the idea to make a film of *Porridge* arose, Dick and Ian had already formed a production company with Allan McKeown, whom they'd known for years and who, alongside La Frenais, went on to produce the picture. 'We all started working together in the early 1970s and, just before I moved to America, in 1976, we started a company, initially making television commercials,' says Allan.

At the company's inception, one of the first decisions the threesome faced was what to call it – never an easy task, and it was Dick Clement's then wife, Jenny, who inadvertently solved the problem, as Allan explains. 'We couldn't think of anything until Jenny stared at the three of us, looking rather bemused, and said: "What a hapless group you are, you look like you're at your wits' end." We suddenly thought, "What a great name for a company."' So the company was christened Witzend Productions; and when Dick and Ian moved to the States in the mid-1970s, they set up office in California.

It was when plans for an American series fell through that the time seemed right to consider making a film of *Porridge*. Allan – who's married to actress Tracey Ullman – had the job of securing a deal for the big-screen adaptation. 'I always told Dick and Ian that if they decided to make a movie of the show, I felt confident I could get the project financed.'

When a deal couldn't be struck with Columbia, Allan met executives at ITC, among them Lew Grade. The British film company snapped up the chance to transfer Clement and La Frenais' runaway success to the big screen, and assigned the project to its low-cost production wing, Black Lion Films. One of the things Allan admired about Lew Grade was his decisiveness. 'He'd listen to your pitch, then make a decision – there was none of this. "I'll get back to you next week". He was the greatest guy.'

Grade delighted Allan with his decision, then announced the size of the budget. 'He said: "The only thing is, you've

got to make it for £250,000." I agreed and we discussed the deal: we were to be fifty-fifty partners. But a couple of weeks later, Lew phoned and said: "We'll have to amend the deal because I can't let you be partners as far as television is concerned; there's no problem on the cinema side but I've got to keep television to myself." I agreed but with hindsight that was probably a mistake, because the film has been repeated on TV endlessly. However, I was green in those days and it taught me a lesson.' Allan nonetheless has no real regrets and enjoyed making the film.

Dick Clement, meanwhile, relished the chance of directing the picture. 'Everyone we spoke to, including Ronnie Barker, was interested, so we sat down here in California and wrote a script very quickly, then cut it down to size.'

As with its small-screen forerunner, locations would play a vital part in the film, and thus Allan couldn't believe his luck when a friend mentioned that Chelmsford Prison was temporarily empty. Other than the occasional scene – such as the escape sequence, which was shot in Buckinghamshire, and a glimpse of prison gates at Maidstone – the entire film was set in prison, so the chance of filming in a *real* jail was too good to ignore. Allan sought permission. 'There had been a fire inside one of the wings, so all the prisoners were moved out while the prison was refurbished. Fortunately parts of the prison remained intact and didn't need decorating; it was these areas I wanted to borrow.'

A meeting was convened with a Home Office official, and proceedings couldn't have started better when Allan discovered the head of the Prison Service was an ardent fan of the sitcom. 'The great thing about *Porridge* was that everywhere you went people had such incredibly strong feelings for the series and the characters. Luckily, we were granted permission, a lease was drawn up and, I think, I became the first person to lease out one of Britain's prisons.'

The agreement allowed the film crew to utilise the prison's hospital, workshop, a wing and the grounds; with the help of a production designer who built some interior sets, everything was soon in place. 'I visited other prisons with the designer and came away with ideas that we implemented. We didn't have a very good kitchen, so we built our own set.'

'We also built our own cell,' adds Dick Clement, 'which we used for pick-up shots. I filmed as much as possible in real cells, but when I needed to move walls around I used the constructed cell because it gave us more freedom.'

Once the final scene was in the can, it was time to pack up. This period of clearing up usually takes up to a week, but Allan remembers the mass exodus of crew desperate to leave the prison far behind. 'It can take days for everyone to clear up, especially for the electricians to remove all the wiring. After a month in prison they couldn't get out fast enough and the place was empty within a day! It was a grim location, and the weather had been very cold.'

Dick Clement concurs with Allan. 'It was a bitterly cold winter and a horrendous shoot because we had to film at weekends and fairly unsociable hours; I remember shooting for thirteen consecutive days. Whatever the budget of a movie, that's a savage schedule.'

With editing complete, the film was premièred in London before its distribution around the British Isles and abroad, including in the European and Commonwealth countries where the sitcom had become a hit. Allan McKeown was satisfied with how the film fared upon its release. 'Whenever you make a film based on a television series there is always a problem inasmuch as the TV series, by its very nature, is repetitive; you know it's on every week for half an hour and it's in little short bursts. Turning it into a ninety-minute film means there's a different dynamic, and it's fair to say that in the film there are parts where you expect it to finish and it doesn't – it goes on. Like in most movies, there's padding, but overall I think it worked well.'

Although Ronnie Barker agrees with Allan, he admits that the genre isn't his favourite medium. 'With films there's lots of stopping and starting which makes it disjointed: one minute you're working on an early scene, then you jump to another at the end of the film; it wasn't as enjoyable as the situation comedy, it suits a half-hour slot better.'

Fortunately, many of the lags imprisoned with Fletcher in Slade Prison during the sitcom's run were available for the film, and the appearance of familiar faces in supporting roles was important in its overall success. Tony Osoba once again played McLaren, but he was disappointed when the filming schedule was hit by inclement weather and he had to leave the production early, resulting in his character playing a reduced role to that originally intended. 'It was a bittersweet experience for me. I was contracted to the film for four weeks, after which I had to go off and play Hamish in the television series *Charles Endell Esquire*. Unfortunately, the weather was atrocious and filming kept being postponed. Part of the movie involved a football match, but day after day it was impossible to film because of snow. Dick Clement tried shooting a scene here and there, but we got further behind in the schedule and by the end of my contracted time I'd only shot a fraction of what I was supposed to do. Eventually, I had to leave and a lot of my intended lines were given to other characters.'

Appearing as Warren, as he had in the series, was Sam Kelly, who enjoyed the job but with hindsight doesn't feel that the concept worked as well on the big screen. 'To me, it seemed as if the production team felt they had to reintroduce all the characters – perhaps for potential foreign markets – and that took up too much time. But it was fun to do, even though it meant spending time at Chelmsford jail.'

Establishing among its audience an understanding of the film's plot and characters was a deliberate act, as Ian La Frenais explains. 'Being that we were now working in a different medium, we couldn't take it for granted that everyone knew the series; we had to cater for those people who'd never seen the show on television – that obviously took a little while.'

When Allan McKeown considers the question of whether he would have tackled anything differently, given the chance, he concedes that he wouldn't have agreed to the deal offered by Lew Grade. 'I'd have paid for the film myself, owned the negative, and gone on to make plenty of money out of it – but then, I didn't have a quarter of a million pounds. So, at the time, we were thankful to Lew for putting up the cash.'

THE REAL PORRIDGE

HM Prison Chelmsford

Back in 1979, Rannoch Daly was Assistant Governor at
Chelmsford Prison when Dick Clement, Ian La Frenais,
Ronnie Barker et al came to film the *Porridge* movie at his
prison. It's a period he remembers clearly.

I'd been home from my work as an Assistant Governor at
Chelmsford Prison for a couple of hours on the evening of
20 March 1978 when I heard a shriek from my wife in the
living room in response to a television newsflash. The prison
was on fire. I lived about three miles away in Great Baddow.
I grasped the scale of the incident a few moments later when
I tried to drive to the prison. The police had cordoned off
the whole town of Chelmsford and I had to negotiate my
way through their roadblocks. On arrival I found twenty fire
appliances in attendance.

The prison staff had managed to rescue all 217 prisoners out of their cells and into workshops, the staff
canteen and prison hospital. By working throughout the
night, the fire service brought the blaze under control, the
police organised secure transport and the prison staff
escorted the prisoners to Wandsworth and Pentonville
prisons in London. The last prisoner to depart had, in fact,
been on home leave the previous week with his family.
He'd returned to the prison, as instructed, by 1100 hrs on
21 March – and read accounts of the fire in the morning
newspaper while travelling by train from London, courtesy
of British Rail. He arrived back at Chelmsford Prison just
in time to catch the last bus out. By midday he was headed
back to London: to Wandsworth Prison, courtesy of the
Metropolitan Police.

The staff settled down to what we thought would be an
uneventful two years working in other prisons until
Chelmsford was rebuilt. The Governor, Bill Guinan, moved

to Prison Service HQ and I remained behind as 'Acting Governor' of an empty prison, the envy of many colleagues!

Towards the end of 1979, an enterprising film producer called Allan McKeown telephoned the Home Office with a request he thought was unlikely to elicit a positive response. His company was called Witzend Productions so a certain tongue-in-cheek approach was, perhaps, *de rigueur*. Nothing ventured, nothing gained; he asked the Home Office if they could provide him with an empty prison in which to film *Porridge*.

To his surprise, they sent him to Chelmsford, just up the A12 from his mother's house in Hainault. In December he arrived to meet us with the assistant producer, David Wimbury, and director, Dick Clement. They wore immaculate suits and talked big business. It was clear from their initial tour of the prison that they thought it was the right location, but it was clear also that they needed the endorsement of Dick Clement's writing partner, Ian La Frenais. He came along the following week.

A deal was struck with the Home Office full of indemnity clauses, security conditions, access regulations and all sorts of other technicalities that only David Wimbury understood. As soon as it was signed, the team returned to prepare for filming. The immaculate suits had gone. In their place were trainers, jeans, jumpers and leather jackets and a new phase of Witzend Productions.

As can be seen in the film, it was winter: January 1980. Filming lasted about six weeks. For the stars and crew there seemed to be some nervousness about meeting 'real' prison staff in a real prison. For the staff and their families there was the buzz that accompanies the making of a film and the prospect of autographs. For me, there was the fact that most prison staff wear uniforms that make their identity obvious but the Assistant Governor doesn't. There were usually dozens of film people around, occasionally hundreds. I decided that I would advertise my presence among them by wearing some distinctive cold-weather clothing: my Strathclyde University scarf and a woollen ski hat. I think I was also trying to demonstrate that I didn't fall into the script image of a prison governor. Having now learned a little more about the skills of scriptwriters, I think I may have been lucky not to end up as the punch line to one of their jokes.

On more than one occasion there was a 'meet the stars' session in the prison for staff and their families. Ronnie Barker, Fulton Mackay, Richard Beckinsale and the others were mobbed as they patiently signed autographs, shook hands, posed for photographs, joked, laughed and entertained.

I discovered later that for each of them this celebrity business was actually hard work. Ronnie Barker was not naturally ebullient and jocular. He was a rather serious man for whom being a comic actor was a craft and a profession. On one evening my wife and I joined Ronnie, Allan McKeown, Dick Clement and their partners for dinner at their hotel. They all showed a keen interest in prison life, which was very frustrating, as I wanted to talk about how they made films. Some of this interest was politeness towards their guest; some of it seemed to be the natural curiosity about a closed world that I have observed in most people; and some of it seemed to be a professional interest in the work that I was doing and they were portraying.

Ronnie Barker's conversation homed in on relationships between staff and prisoners and it seemed to me that he and Dick Clement were paying rather more attention to the answers than is often the case with dinner companions.

I learned during this film production that the script often changes during shooting and that the first task each day is to check for and learn any 'pink pages' – script amendments. I discovered this quite early in the filming, when Allan McKeown presented to me a souvenir copy of the screenplay signed by himself, Dick Clement and Ian La Frenais. I was sufficiently star-struck that I spent the evening going through every word. Ian asked next day, 'Have you read it?' I told him I had, so he was keen to know what I thought of it. Friends who know me well will not be surprised to discover that I started telling one of our best television writers about the three points where I thought the text could be improved. However, they will be very surprised indeed to learn that later in the day jokes were beginning to circulate in the team about the 'Governor's pink pages'. Ian had incorporated two of my suggestions in script amendments. I allow myself a small smile of satisfaction when I hear them spoken in the film; but I notice even more the third point, where he did not accept my advice and where, as a consequence, Godber speaks a slight inaccuracy in his account of Scottish football!

Having discovered the script I then discovered filming: watching Ronnie Barker and his colleagues work a scene through from start to finish. The scene was in a dressing room during the football match when Fletcher is bringing an 'injured' player off the field [Oakes – played by Barrie Rutter]. The 'injury' turns out to be the prelude to an escape in the visiting football team's bus [driven by Gorden Kaye]. All that was being filmed was a few seconds as Fletcher and Oakes moved from the door to the bench and said a few words – something about an 'early bath'.

The scene was played through several times and, although it had looked pretty rough the first few times, I soon realised that there was an intentional 'layering' process at work. The basics were approached first (the traverse across the room, co-ordinating the movement of the two actors) before the words in the script were added and the sequence was run through several more times. All this then had to be practised in some detail with the sound recorder checking his levels and the lighting and the cameraman getting his requirements in place. Only after this had been done several times was an attempt made at getting the whole sequence down on film – 'Lights, Camera, Action!'

At this point it became apparent how much the players, Barker in particular, had been holding in reserve. It came across as a very simple scene. However, the complexity of the presentation and the extent to which it had had to be built up, layer upon layer, had been completely obscured by the apparently natural manner of the finished product as it appeared on the screen; art from artifice.

The filming attracted the attention of the newspapers and the local radio and television journalists. The *Chelmsford Weekly News* was kept busy, and the *Observer* sent Robin Lustig. *Woman's Own* did a feature article. There were a few minutes on BBC Television's teatime news and magazine programme, *Nationwide*. They broadcast me saying that 'compared to a real prison, both Godber and Fletcher were too old. Fletcher was too smart to keep coming back to prison in his forties and Godber, at twenty-four, was well past the age of the first-timer: most prisoners were aged seventeen to twenty-six and first came to prison in their teens.'

Richard Beckinsale approached me the next day in a quiet moment between takes. He'd seen the *Nationwide* snippet. What I had said had struck him. This was a fact that he'd not come across before. He was about thirty and had a wife and daughter. By his age most prisoners were already played out. He was perturbed. However, he also told me an amusing anecdote against himself as a performer. He'd recently been starring in a comedy in a West End theatre. One scene required him to disappear behind a shop counter looking for something and, a few seconds later, to bang his head on the underside of the counter coming back up. He repeated this night after night, getting a bigger and bigger bruise on the back of his head, until he worked out that if he used a hidden piece of wood to bang under the counter he could get just as big a laugh with no bruise. The real joke was that he was doing this gag seven shows a week but the length of time it took him to work out that he could use the wood instead of his head was eight months.

Sadly, a few months later Richard died of a heart attack. There was an awards programme of some sort on television a few days after his death. Ronnie Barker was there. He was ashen and dumbstruck.

On a quiet night, when he had little filming the following day, I invited Fulton Mackay to dinner at home with my wife, Evelyn, and our daughter, Lhosa, as a break from the hotel. He accepted. Mr Mackay and Fulton

Mackay shared a name and an appearance but had little else in common. In contrast with his screen persona, Fulton's conversation was littered with cultured references to writers, poets and, particularly, painters. Almost everything he saw or spoke of was expressed in terms of a picture or an artist. Although Evelyn's parents live in Scotland, her mother, Margaret, is German. When we asked Fulton to autograph a card to her, he thought for a few moments and then proceeded to inscribe the card in German – complete with a quotation from Schiller.

His *coup de theatre* came in his conversation with Lhosa, then aged two years and three months. At that age she was quite unselfconscious and also full of the new world of words. Among her repertoire was her full name and address; our precaution should she ever seem lost. Fulton spoke with her at some length and seemed very impressed with this, getting her to repeat her name and address more than once and congratulating her on 'learning her lines'. The next day we discovered that Fulton had been learning his lines as well. He sent a large bunch of flowers to Evelyn, correctly addressed as he had memorised from Lhosa.

Fulton invited us to come and see him later in a play he was about to rehearse at the Donmar Warehouse, called 'The Hang of the Gaol'. He said he would meet us outside the theatre thirty minutes before the start of the performance. We were five minutes late, having been detained elsewhere by Allan McKeown, and Fulton was beginning to fret because we were eating into the time he'd put aside for 'getting into the character'.

The play was set in a prison that had been destroyed by fire. As I understood it from Fulton, the author had seen a newspaper reference to the fire at Chelmsford Prison and used that as the inspiration for the play. Fulton played the Inspector of Prisons who'd been sent to inquire. There were a number of suspects, a few twists and turns in the plot and, in the end, it turned out that the person who had started the fire was the Governor. However, from the Home Office point of view, it just would not do to have a governor burning down his own prison so the Inspector was told to pin it on someone else. Needless to say it didn't take Fulton too long to find a prisoner who was delighted to take the credit for the destruction of the gaol.

After filming at the prison there were some scenes to shoot in the studio and there was the editing to do in the cutting room. A few weeks later, Allan McKeown invited Evelyn and me to join the cast at a preview theatre in Soho to see the finished product. We entered a nearby pub for a pre-show drink and were greeted by Gorden Kaye, Julian Holloway – who'd played the celebrity football-team manager – and the musician Zoot Money. The minor character he played was a prisoner called Lotterby, which seemed to be a tribute to the TV series producer, Sydney Lotterby.

In the version of the film eventually released, the song sung over the opening sequences is by Joe Brown. In the version I saw that day in Soho it was Ian Dury singing 'Hit Me with Your Rhythm Stick'.

A singular distinction befell Senior Officer George Flanagan. George had been at Chelmsford for many years but he was not quite as fit as he had once been, and he had lost any initial enthusiasm for working away from home in other prisons. We gave him the job of day-to-day liaison with the film crew as their guide and mentor. As his reward the crew gave him his place in history with his appearance in the credits as a 'Technical Adviser'; the only member of Chelmsford prison staff with his name on the film. However, he's not the only one to appear in the film. Behind the closing credits we see an officer and a prison dog patrolling into the evening. They were not actors; they were real.

To say thank you and farewell to Chelmsford once the film was ready for release, Allan McKeown hired a local cinema to give a private preview for staff and their families.

A REFLECTION OF REAL LIFE?

The film revolves around an escape. A gun is smuggled into the prison by a bus driver. The bus belongs to a visiting 'celebrity' football team. A prisoner called Oakes then escapes in the bus using the gun to force Fletcher and Godber to accompany him. The whole escapade turns out to be a scam set up by genial 'Harry Grout', the Mr Big among the prisoners (played by Peter Vaughan – magnificent years later in *Our Friends Up North*). After some curious adventures Fletcher and Godber manage to smuggle themselves back into the prison in the same bus. There are numerous other story lines (e.g. the new officer – Christopher Godwin) and sub-plots (e.g. Mackay's teeth) but the escape is the central event. Oakes gets away. Mr Mackay is outwitted. The Governor is embarrassed. Fletcher is in the thick of it but remains unscathed. The prisoners have a good laugh, so do the audience.

Of course, in real life, a gun in a prison is not funny. The staff would be scared but so would the prisoners, with the possible exception of the one carrying the gun. How do the writers make it funny? Do real prison staff and real prisoners find it funny? Yes, they do.

The attitude of most prison staff and prisoners to most prison settings in films and television is that they are overly simplistic (e.g. *Escape from Alcatraz, Prisoner: Cell Block H*). The key fact about imprisonment for most viewers or members of the public is that they have no personal experience of imprisonment and draw their assumptions from their knowledge that prison necessarily involves loss of liberty. This is then assumed to be the overpowering single element in prison life, with the prisoners and the staff always wholeheartedly antagonistic towards each other. In any fictional portrait of imprisonment a riot or an escape is to be expected.

The key insight of *Porridge* is that, once a person has been imprisoned and has to make a life within that imprisonment, their whole range of human emotions, relations and imagination come into play. The same is true of the staff. They vary in their character. They have to find a *modus vivendi* with the prisoners. To varying degrees they bring their life outside the prison into work with them. Fletcher bestrides this world because he understands the need of each party for the other. He knows the extent to which the staff have to settle for something less than total mastery of the situation and the prisoners can find some space in which to exercise some choices of their own. The prisoners can have 'little victories' and the staff can accept 'little defeats'.

That doesn't mean that everything the viewer sees in episodes of *Porridge* is a literal representation of what happens in real prisons in Britain. Neither art nor theatre nor film work is like that. The best analogy I can think of is with a political cartoon. The drawings of the participants are not accurate; rather they simplify and exaggerate recognisable features so that the viewer sees instantly who is portrayed. The drawing will also convey elements of character or mood.

Because of this richness of understanding on the part of the writers, *Porridge* is itself able to enter into the cultural world of the prison. One can see *Porridge* on television in a prison with the prisoners watching the television and the staff supposedly watching the prisoners. But the staff will quite probably also be watching the television, and the prisoners – some of them – will be watching the staff. When they each catch the other's eye it will be impossible to tell whether they are smiling at Fletcher or at Mackay; or at their recognition of themselves in these roles in real life; or at their recognition of the other party or at the other party's recognition of them. Mostly they are smiling because they each know that the dynamics they are watching on television are a true reflection of the dynamics they are experiencing in their own life and work in the prison. The most reassuring thing they can discover is that their perception is shared with their opposite numbers.

Despite its artificiality, *Porridge* is at least as accurate a reflection of its world as are the best cartoons. Mackay,

Barrowclough and the Governor, Fletcher, Godber and the rest all ring true. Prison staff enjoy them. Prisoners enjoy them. Those who know nothing of prisons enjoy them. But, in addition, they learn much more about prisons through the characters in *Porridge* than they could learn from any other source.

Here's what real-life prison officers thought about *Porridge*.

Sixty-seven-year-old George Forder spent thirty-four years in the prison service before his retirement twelve years ago. His career included working at the notorious Manchester prison Strangeways and, for seven years, at Parkhurst. He believes the humour of *Porridge* was very realistic.

Humour played a big part in the daily life of a prison. Without it long-term inmates wouldn't survive the system, nor indeed would many of the staff. It lightened the load and made the days bearable for both prisoners and staff. The humour of *Porridge*, although manufactured, was very true to life. Fletcher-types existed: they were often serving long sentences and would go to just about any length to frustrate the system, or to get what they wanted. They soon knew the weak and strong points of staff; we also got to know them in the same manner.

We had to protect the weaker, less able types. I remember one prisoner who was constantly being set upon and bullied by others on the same landing. We decided the only way to deal with the situation was to relocate him. So he moved in with one of the more aggressive inmates, who'd been told that the only way to guarantee a favourable hearing at the parole board was to ensure this chap didn't come to harm – it worked perfectly.

'The characters in *Porridge*, although rather extreme, are very accurately drawn. I've known all these types during my service, including the Mackays and the Barrowcloughs – though much has changed since I retired.

As for all the privileges bestowed upon Grouty, the bigwig among the prisoners at Slade, George recollects a time at Parkhurst when long-term inmates were allowed to keep caged birds, usually budgies, in their cells.

One of the routines rigidly adhered to was the Chief Officer's rounds. He would walk round the wings in the evening, not speaking other than to tick someone off, and then return to his office. One Chief Officer had the nickname 'Curlyboots' because the toes of his boots curled upwards.

An orderly – an inmate who looked after the requirements of staff by making tea, running errands, etc. – had a budgie which was a superb talker. It would fly around the wing in the evening, chatting away. One phrase it had been taught was: 'Look out – here comes Curlyboots!' Staff tended to congregate in the tea room, which wasn't really allowed because they should have been patrolling the landings. When the tea room was full, the bird would sit outside and screech at the top of its voice: 'Look out – here comes Curlyboots!' The room cleared in seconds, with staff running in all directions.

George recalls another incident that could easily have been lifted from the pages of a *Porridge* script. Two prisoners had escaped by cutting a hole through barbed wire; while one headed for a nearby forest, the other was found sitting on the pitched roof of the building, merrily throwing slates.

The whole place was surrounded by staff as the Governor and Chief Officer arrived on the scene – not unlike Mr Mackay and Mr Venables, the Governor of Slade Prison in the sitcom. A ladder appeared and was erected to reach the guttering of the building. I must give the Governor his due because he was first up the ladder, although he came very close to getting a slate on his head!

'Come along now, John,' said the Governor as another slate whizzed by. 'This is no way to behave; come down and let's talk about your problem.'

At that moment, another voice was heard saying: 'I'll get him down for you, Governor.' It was a prisoner whose face had appeared at a cell window. The Governor agreed to let him try, and ordered the Chief Officer to get the prisoner. The Chief, who was already on the red side of pink because of the situation, turned brilliant red and came very close to bursting a blood vessel.

'Governor, we have enough problems here already without adding to them,' protested the Chief Officer. But the Governor would have none of it: if the prisoner felt he could talk his fellow inmate down, it was worth a try.

So out the prisoner came and, after scaling the ladder, it wasn't long before he was sat up on the roof as well, shouting: 'Now try and talk me down!' By now, steam was coming out of the Chief's ears. The idea of getting the fire engine out and hosing them off was suggested, and by this time any suggestion would have been acceptable.

Being a fire officer, I went off to get the engine with some helpers. It was nothing more than an engine on a trailer, which pressurised the water from the hydrant. It had never been used in anger and from test runs I found it to be such a noisy, shaky thing that I wondered how it all kept together. We arrived back at the scene to find more slates missing and another ladder placed against the other wall for whoever was to direct the jet of water from the hose. The engine started without difficulty and the shaking and rattling began. The hoses were attached and an officer scaled the ladder with the hose. All was ready, and 'Switch on!' came the request.

When the water came gushing out the hose, the two prisoners took shelter behind the tall air-vents on the roof, but it wasn't long before one of the prisoners had had enough and asked to be let down. The other inmate, meanwhile, stuck it out and a hole had to be cut in the roof from inside to allow an officer access and eventually get the prisoner down.

Overall, *Porridge* was very true to life in prisons prior to the Mountbatten Report. There were plenty of schemers, fixers and twisters like Fletcher. They involved themselves in all sorts of activities that formed the 'underworld' of prison life. Many of these activities, although quite harmless, were against the rules, but blind eyes were cast.

There were the Mackays, whose attempts to bring life back within the rules were often frustrated – but that didn't stop them trying.

Garry Morton has been a prison officer for eight years. His father has just retired from the profession after completing thirty-five years' service, and his brother works in the profession too. All are keen fans of the sitcom.

Prison officers love the programme, and it's the only show that has ever shown the industry in a good light, of sorts; it's certainly the nearest thing to the actual job.

Many programmes are made in support of the police, hospitals, fire brigade and ambulance service, and they're all shown as heroes of society. I've always felt that we're the forgotten public service – and if there's anything that makes a prison officer proud about the job he or she loves, it's every time *Porridge* is on TV.

Even today, new recruits look upon it as a symbol of everything that's good about the job; and, although it's out of date in many respects, it's still a good reference. In *Porridge* there's no scandal or deep-rooted bad feeling, which every other programme about prison seems to show with enthusiasm.

Of course, the hero for us is Mr Mackay: he's the person everyone wants to be in a comical kind of way. Anyone who makes a mistake or looks concerned about anything is referred to as Mr Barrowclough.

I can remember a few years ago, when I worked at Brixton – which Fletcher always goes on about – we hung a photo of Mr Mackay in our landing office. One of the officers faked a signature on it with the comment, 'To all my friends at Brixton – bang 'em up!' Everyone loved it, including the prisoners – a few of them wanted a copy to put in their cells.

For the next few months, whenever there was a picture of Mackay or Fletcher in a paper or magazine, no matter how small, it was quickly torn out and displayed in various cells.

Peter Hunt is fifty-one and has worked in the prison service for more than twenty-eight years. He remembers being told when he started his career that *Porridge* provided an accurate picture of life within prison.

When I joined, back in 1974, I spent eight weeks at a training school near Bristol. While there, my principal officer told us that *Porridge* was starting and that he'd had a preview of it: if anyone wanted to know what prison was like, it was best to watch it. Because – although it was a comedy and certain aspects were over-emphasised in order to lift the comedy – it was basically a true reflection of prison life at that time. He also told us that we'd see every type of character in *Porridge* during our service – and he was right.

For a while, I worked in borstals and was probably more of a disciplinarian at that point, but I found myself working with a chap who was an ex-priest and like Barrowclough in many ways. When we were on duty together it worked well, because I could tell the inmates to sit down and be quiet, but if anyone had a problem, my colleague would take them to one side and have a chat; we complemented each other.

You get people who write dramas about prisons and they take dramatic licence by putting everything in to the scripts that could possibly go wrong, including riots. But anyone who knows anything about prisons knows that riots rarely happen.

With *Porridge*, although you had to allow for the stretching of the characters and the incidents in order to create funny scenes, I could relate to what they were focusing on – often the mundane little incidents, which happen frequently. In the days the sitcom was written, the toilet paper issued to prisoners was old, stiff, shiny stuff, and they often tried pinching the softer stuff issued to staff. Exploring incidents such as that is why the programme was much more realistic than anything else written about the prison service.

Chris Muzzal is a health-care officer at a prison in Surrey who's worked in the service for nineteen years.

We all know an officer like Mackay and a prisoner like Fletcher, and the humour is spot-on. The respect – with the undertones of dislike and disgust – shown by Fletcher to the 'screws' could not be closer.

Some of the incidents I've experienced during my time in the job would have made ideal scenes in the show. When I was working in the youth custody system, I had to escort two inmates to court. They were cuffed together, but still decided to do a runner after stepping out of the van. Unfortunately, ten yards down the road they encountered a lamppost and ran either side of it, resulting in them meeting nose to nose the other side. When we had stopped laughing, they were treated for a broken nose and a lump on the forehead.

I also remember a time when an officer was escorting a vanload of staff and prisoners to another prison. In those days – pre-1981 – a prison van was affectionately known as a 'Pixie', a shortened form of the term 'prisoners in transit' or PITX.

On this occasion, for a laugh, when an officer stopped the van for a call of nature, the other officers drove off. The stranded officer, thinking the prisoners may have stolen the van and taken the officers hostage, flagged down a passing police car and excitedly began babbling about 'the pixie that just left without him'.

Only a phone call to the Governor from a police cell saved him from a short stay in a mental institution!

PORRIDGE GOES ABROAD

Often when a successful British television series is adapted for
the American market, much of the richness and vitality is lost
in translation. Style of humour differs between the cultures;
and, far too often, rather than trying out the original version,
television companies set out to remodel the show's fabric to
suit the different audience. Or that's the intention. More
usually than not, the finished product fails to deliver the
goods, is a wan shadow of its predecessor and swiftly disappears into oblivion, never to be heard of again.

Dick Clement and Ian La Frenais have experienced their fair
share of adaptations for the US market, with varying degrees
of success. *Porridge* was just one of their shows to receive the
treatment. Titled *On the Rocks*, the series was set in the
fictional Alamesa Minimum Security Prison and screened on
ABC, running to twenty-two episodes shown between 1975
and 1976. Most of the action took place in Hector Fuentes'
cell, which he shared with his friend DeMott, the optimist
Cleaver, and young offender Nicky Palik. Patrolling the prison
was the tough disciplinarian Mr Gibson, America's answer to
Mr Mackay. The show was recorded in front of a live audience and contained location scenes at a real Californian prison.
And, during 1975, it was the subject of complaints when the
National Association for Justice asked ABC to abandon the
series, believing it portrayed prison-life as too comfortable.

Producing *On the Rocks* was John Rich, who first heard
about Clement and La Frenais when Warner Brothers sent
him a script based on their sitcom *Thick as Thieves*. He was
asked to make a pilot for the US market. 'The script had been
written by an American and was about three people living
together, yet there was a terrible flaw in it, and I told Warner
Brothers so. When they asked what I meant, I replied: "These
people are not related in any way: where's the conflict?"'

John – who directed *The Dick Van Dyke Show* and
produced and directed *All in the Family*, the hugely successful
US version of *Till Death Us Do Part* – asked to see Clement
and La Frenais' original script to check if an integral element

had been excluded from the American version. 'As soon as I received it everything became clear: two of the characters were married – only a small detail that had been left out!' says John, laughing. Though he ultimately declined the offer to make the pilot, he liked Dick and Ian's style of writing and decided to find out more about their work. Via their London agents, he spoke to both of them; after seeing some copies of *Porridge* scripts, he confirmed he could make an American version. 'I knew there would be some doubters because at the time it would be cutting edge material over here. I eventually met Dick and Ian and was instantly charmed because they're very nice people; of course they were attracted to me because I said I'd give them something they weren't used to getting in England. When they asked what it was, I replied, "Money!"' says John, with a smile.

'As far as money for writers is concerned, there's no comparison between the British and American markets, and Dick and Ian had been working for a pittance in British television. There's a lot to be said for the medium in Britain: writers can generate what they like, even if it's just a one-off, while in America it's a different animal and you've got to be prepared to write the same show for years. But the compensation is the money.'

John agreed to make Clement and La Frenais equal partners in the American production and they set to work converting their successful British sitcom. 'I helped Americanise the scripts and, although we made a mistake with the casting and found no equal for the Cockney lag, we mounted a sensible production and were on for twenty-two weeks. We could have stayed on if we'd wanted, but after discussions, Dick, Ian and I knew it hadn't worked out like we'd originally intended.' Despite the programme being generally well received, none of the partners were pleased with the results. 'We did something unheard of in American television and turned down an offer to carry on for a second year,' explains John. 'The writing was wonderful, and most of the casting was successful, but we made a mistake with the lead part – even though the audience didn't necessarily share our views. Overall, we did the right thing to call it a day.'

Dick and Ian were disappointed. 'The plots translated quite well,' explains Ian. 'We really felt it could work, and saw it opening up all sorts of possibilities. But everyone was terrified it was going to be too gritty for the American market, and it ended up being a poor version of the original.

'We worked our socks off with the scripts, but the trouble was we never had a Ronnie Barker. During the course of the week, all the rewriting was making the scripts more suitable for a gang show, cushioning the actor who played the main role.'

'We were very naïve, really,' suggests Dick. 'We came over to America and were offered a deal to make a pilot, and then felt we'd go on to write the American version of *Porridge*. In hindsight, it was a naïve attitude to presume such a thing because most pilots don't get made; that we succeeded with this one was against all the odds.

'The only problem was that it wasn't very good. We stayed with it for a year, wrote twenty-three episodes, including two rewrites – and I must admit it felt like being in the trenches. It was much harder work than in Britain because we never really found an American actor who could play Fletch the way we wanted. It was amazing that we were kept on the air, and we attribute that to the tenacity of John Rich, the director.

'It just seemed as if all the subtlety and nuances of the British series had been lost; we just knew it wasn't any good. I remember being in the studio until one o'clock in the morning doing retakes. In the end, the show was made in the cutting room, which wasn't the way we'd worked before, so we weren't happy one little bit.'

Dick and Ian yearned for their home comforts. 'We longed for the simplicity of the Beeb, where you'd do the show and be in the bar by nine-thirty, before going home with the satisfaction of knowing you had another one in the can. It was so painless and this was such a tortuous process.'

John Rich has always enjoyed collaborating with Dick and Ian. 'They can do no wrong as far as I'm concerned,' he enthuses. 'They're prolific, clever and very witty; their lines are delightful because they understand comedy and how human beings act. When I'm looking for writers, I like people who aren't afraid to say something in literary English, creating a situation, comedy moment or a joke that's not necessarily understood by everybody: I call it a two per cent joke.

'If people don't understand something, it's harmless and goes straight by them. But for the small percentage of the audience who can appreciate the writing, it's rewarding. Dick and Ian reach this level and I like that. It sounds like snobbery, but I never want to write down for the masses; I'd rather have them come up to us. With *On the Rocks*, Dick, Ian and I decided that the characters would speak a patois not dissimilar to what we hear in *Porridge*; these petty felons would never speak it but the fact that they had elevated conversation made the show different.'

While he was planning the American version, John Rich had the chance to travel to London – and watched in awe as Messrs Barker and Beckinsale rehearsed an episode. 'They were magnificent and I drooled over their comic timing – I just wished we had such talent in our country!' says John. 'We have a lot of very good actors over here, obviously, but Ronnie and the rest of the cast were just wonderful; I was particularly impressed by the way they handled language with a kind of rapidity, an element I would have liked in my version.'

Despite Rich's fondness for the British version, he's certain it wouldn't have caught on with American viewers in its original form. 'The references would have been unclear to the mass audience we have, partly because of the different cultural backgrounds. There is also a difference in the style of prisons: we have very vicious prisons in America and I don't think it would work to have a show like *Porridge*, set in a more gentle form of establishment.'

On the Rocks was well received and made money for its writers, yet is rarely repeated in the States. 'It's been assigned to the hallowed halls of yesteryear,' says John Rich, smiling. 'Sometimes it's resurrected for cable channels, but here you've got to have a giant hit to earn a repeat showing. *On the Rocks* attracted a cult following but not enough to justify a repeat run. But I still have many happy memories of working with Dick and Ian.'

ON THE ROCKS

Original transmission: **Friday 11 September 1975**

Last episode shown: **17 May 1976**

All episodes were shown on Mondays, 8–8.30 p.m.

CAST

Hector Fuentes	**José Perez**
DeMott	**Hal Williams**
Cleaver	**Rick Hurst**
Nicky Palik	**Bobby Sandler**
Mr Gibson	**Mel Stewart**
Mr Sullivan	**Tom Poston**
Gabby	**Pat Cranshaw**
Baxter	**Jack Grimes**
Warden Wilbur Poindexter	**Logan Ramsey**

CASHING IN

As is the case with many successful sitcoms, *Porridge* merchandise was available to fans. In 1977, BBC Records and Tapes released two episodes on LP. The record was manufactured and distributed on the BBC's behalf by Pye and contained 'A Night In' and 'Heartbreak Hotel' (catalogue no: REB270; price: £2.99). The project was edited and co-ordinated by Sylvia Cartner, and Don Smith took the cover photos.

The theme tune for the sequel, *Going Straight*, was also released on record. With Ronnie Barker singing words penned by Clement and MacCaulay, the track hit the public domain in 1978, with EMI releasing it under catalogue number 2768.

Four novels based on *Porridge* and one on *Going Straight* have been published. The first, titled *Porridge*, was adapted from the TV series by Jonathan Marshall in 1975, and a year later BBC Books released *Another Stretch of Porridge*, adapted by Paul Victor. Paul Victor reworked more scripts in 1977 when the Beeb issued *A Further Stir of Porridge* (£3 in hardback, 70p in paperback). The final title from the BBC focusing on the sitcom was Paul Ableman's *Porridge: The Inside Story*, in 1979. The book based on *Going Straight* was adapted from the series by Paul Victor and published in 1978.

Fans of the sitcoms may be interested in tracking down 1979's *The Porridge Book of Rhyming Slang*, by Ronnie Barker (Pan Books, ISBN 0 3303 0993 5, copyright Witzend Productions). Two of Clement and La Frenais' scripts have also been published: 1983's *Television Comedy Scripts*, edited by Roy Blatchford (Longman, ISBN 0 5822 2071 8), contained the script for the *Porridge* episode 'Poetic Justice'; David Self's *Situation Comedy* (Hutchinson, ISBN 0 0914 2931 5) included the script for the *Going Straight* episode 'Going to be Alright'.

The Beeb has released a handful of videos. *A Night In* (Ref: BBCV4799) contained the episodes 'A Night In', 'The Harder They Fall' and 'A Storm in a Teacup'; *A Day Out* (Ref: BBCV5844) offered 'A Day Out', 'Ways and Means' and 'Disturbing the Peace'; and a third, *No Way Out* (Ref: BBCV6206), included 'No Way Out', 'Pardon Me' and 'A Test of Character'. More recently, the BBC marketed a four-video boxed set containing every episode of the sitcom. Issued in a presentation gift box, the set retails at £39.99.

There have been various releases of the movie on video, including that made by 4Front (Ref: 0842583); Carlton has also issued it on DVD.

GOING STRAIGHT

In March 1977, we waved goodbye to Norman Stanley Fletcher in the final episode of *Porridge*. When Fletcher is finally released from Slade Prison, he takes with him not only the nightmares of being locked up in a cell for the last few years but also a tatty bag containing his worldly possessions. Those being: a tartan penknife, one brown belt, an African shilling, a tin of corn plasters, billiard chalk, Tottenham Hotspur keyring holding two keys, a receipt from a shoe repairer's for soling and re-heeling his brown brogues, and a 1974 Ladbrokes' pocket diary. But this wasn't to be the last we'd see of the old rascal, because plans were afoot to follow his uncertain path back into society as he headed south to his Muswell Hill home.

BBC executives had invited Dick Clement and Ian La Frenais to lunch at Television Centre; the final episodes of *Porridge* had just been shown and discussions veered towards the future. 'It was a lengthy lunch and didn't finish until five, by which time a great deal of wine and brandy had been consumed,' recalls Dick. 'It was all very jolly, and in the middle of this we suddenly started talking about *Porridge*; someone asked if we'd thought about doing another series. We felt it would become repetitive if we did that, but said we were interested in seeing what happened when he got out. Everyone loved the idea and it was virtually commissioned there and then.'

The wheels were set in motion, and by February 1978 Ronnie Barker was back on the screen playing donkey-jacketed Fletcher in the first of six episodes of *Going Straight*. Joining him was his long-standing cellmate, Lennie Godber, played again by Richard Beckinsale, together with Patricia Brake as Fletch's daughter Ingrid and Nicholas Lyndhurst in an early screen outing as Fletch's dense-looking son, Raymond.

Patricia had made three appearances in *Porridge*, but the character came into her own during *Going Straight*, becoming a pivotal figure in the Fletcher household, as acknowledged by TV critics. Writing in the *Observer* in March 1978, Clive James felt Ingrid possessed a 'fluffy but compelling sexiness' and that Patricia played her 'with all the low-life zing that Cockney sparrers of stage and screen are traditionally supposed to display but never do.'

One character missing from the series was Fletcher's wife, Isobel, who left him after twenty-four years of marriage. Her absence was partly due to Ronnie Barker's wish to avoid too much domesticity within the storylines, as Dick Clement explains. 'He didn't want to suddenly get into a conventional domestic situation with wife and kids; he wanted to keep it more unique than that, which, I think, was right. That's why we wrote his wife out, leaving him no alternative but to fend for himself.'

Although the cast brought their characters alive adroitly, there was a mixed reaction to the screening of *Going Straight*: from some quarters there came the strong feeling that no sequel would ever recapture the magic and richness of its prison-based predecessor. Even though the series represented a logical progression, removing the *Porridge* characters from their familiar situation and placing them in a new environment was no easy feat; many other such attempts within the history of the small screen have ended in dismal failure. But advocates of these views hadn't accounted for the scriptwriters behind the sitcom: Dick Clement and Ian La Frenais were past masters in such affairs. They had revisited the lives of their Likely Lads, Terry Collier and Bob Ferris, and scored a huge hit with *Whatever Happened to the Likely Lads?* which many people regard as better than the original sixties series.

So a new chapter in the life of television's most popular jailbird spotlighted him trying to forge a new life against the elements of society. Says Ian La Frenais, 'For Fletcher it felt like he was walking on eggshells, especially as he was on probation. Again he was fighting the system; you had to feel his frustrations about the predicament he found himself in, and what he hadn't achieved in life. You missed all the other characters in prison, but the series wasn't any more difficult to write; in fact, it was just as enjoyable and we scripted a couple of really good episodes.'

It was clear that Clement and La Frenais' new sitcom would be hard-pushed to ascend to the heights of its predecessor. Inside prison, Fletcher was a winner, whereas outside he wrestled with the harsh realities of a life he was unaccustomed to; he couldn't find a job, and struggled to get a foothold in an unfamiliar society. Fletcher, understandably, cut a forlorn figure outside, and some loyal *Porridge* fans didn't like the way their loveable felon had turned out.

In reviewing the success of the programme, opinions varied: those involved with the actual production didn't rate it as highly as *Porridge*. Sydney Lotterby, who produced both sitcoms, views it as a mere shadow of Clement and La Frenais' study of life behind bars. 'I thought it might have worked but the sadness is that it lacked the flavour of the original series. Also, the situation was nearer a normal situation comedy and the series suffered from a lack of clear identity.' However, he realises that it is tough to judge a show against a powerhouse sitcom like *Porridge*, and is disappointed that *Going Straight* rarely gets an outing into today's bustling TV schedules. 'I think it's as good as some of the programmes going out at the moment. The first episode in particular was excellent, with Fletcher and Mackay meeting on a train.'

Fletcher struggles
with life outside
Slade Prison

It's fair to say that some fans of the original series felt slightly pained by Fletch's struggle to adjust to the big wide world outside the relative comfort of Slade Prison. As a lag, he was familiar with a system and a pattern of life; he knew how to eke out every ounce of goodness within an arid existence inside. His self-confidence, meanwhile, was boosted as his experience of bird saw him adopt almost iconic status within the prison, and he must have felt bucked by the adoration received from so many of his fellow inmates, all of whom held him in high esteem.

But once he left that world behind, and vowed never to return, he found it difficult to turn his back on the life to which he'd dedicated the lion's share of adulthood. Despite the obvious harshness of his existence behind bars, and the deprivations that go hand in hand with such, Fletcher enjoyed there a sense of security and warmth – things he struggled to find once he was out on his own. As he floundered, his status suffered and he became a lost soul, unable to claim a footing in his new environment.

Although Ronnie Barker agrees that the sequel didn't work as well as *Porridge*, he enjoyed the experience nevertheless. 'It wasn't as good, but there were some great people working on it, and we had excellent stories, too.'

Inevitably, some viewers weren't convinced about the show, either. The BBC organised an audience-research report after the screening of the opening story, 'Going Home', and discovered that a small minority echoed the views of other critics. Some claimed to have 'found it harder to adjust to Fletcher's new situation, feeling that the prison setting was ideal and that *Porridge* had a special quality of its own, which, they feared, would now be lost.'

However, much of the sample audience was more upbeat about the show. The author of the report stated that the opening story was 'warmly received by viewers', and that 'most people thought it an excellent idea that the series should be extended beyond the confines of Slade Prison.' Such a move could save the show from 'going stale and give it more scope in the form of new situations and different locations.'

Overall, the sample audience who helped conduct the survey were ardent fans of Fletcher; they were pleased to see him back on our screens – one viewer went so far as to proclaim: 'I could not imagine television without Fletcher.' Others were even quite happy to see him back inside, should circumstances dictate. The majority saw *Going Straight* as a 'logical progression' allowing Fletch the chance to set his wits against the outside world, and the fact he was able to 'transfer in this way made the series something out of the ordinary and special.'

Fans of *Porridge* had met Fletch's daughter Ingrid before, but she became a central figure in *Going Straight*

The production and acting during 'Going Home' was regarded as top notch, just like that in *Porridge*, and more than ninety per cent of people expected to watch the remainder of the series. Although no episode attracted the ratings of the most popular instalment of *Porridge* ('Desperate Hours' was watched by 20.8 million), *Going Straight* never dropped below 12 million during its six-episode run.

Without doubt, *Going Straight* is an underestimated sitcom, forever overshadowed by its big brother, something reflected by the lack of repeats on mainstream television. There are plenty of inherent qualities in *Going Straight*, from the calibre of acting and production to the sleekness of the scripts, as highlighted by Clive James in his *Observer* review. He felt that 'no other country . . . can offer a television series like *Going Straight.*' He regarded the show as the worthy successor of

Porridge and thought every line written by Clement and La Frenais 'at least twice as good as anything in the average West End play.' James acknowledged Ronnie Barker's performance, but added that, 'The secret of successful comedy is so often looked for in the wrong place. The actor's personality matters, but last and least. First and foremost comes the work at the typewriter. It is because people have thought long and hard through many drafts that Norman Fletcher or Basil Fawlty can be convincing with a single gesture.'

Like the positive views shared by the majority of viewers, the media coverage on Clement and La Frenais' new sitcom was largely encouraging, though some journalists pointed out the difficult task facing the writers. Sean Day-Lewis, writing in the *Daily Telegraph* in February 1978, felt that Fletcher's creators were 'taking a risk in setting him free from the well-defined boundaries in which he previously flourished.' After watching the opening episode, Day-Lewis remarked that it 'showed how difficult it will be to match television's funniest situation comedy.' And, though he acknowledged the versatility of Barker at the helm, he felt that: 'the outrageous candour, cynicism and cunning, the spontaneous kindliness and charm of his Fletch began to diffuse a little even in the confined space of the train taking him home.'

With Fletcher out of prison, new locations were required. While Muswell Hill was picked for Fletcher's home, a hotel in Paddington was chosen for his place of work. Mike Crisp, the production manager, found both locations. 'I was pleased to find the hotel in Paddington, which was run by a sweet little man. I told him we were making a follow-on series to *Porridge*, with Ronnie Barker as a porter in a hotel. To help convince him, I reassured him that his property wouldn't be represented in any bad light and, in the script, the guy running it is very generous because he gives Fletcher a job. Basically, I was trying to persuade him to let us use the hotel, which, eventually, he agreed to do.

'If we were going to make out the hotel was a dreadful place we'd change the name, put up different signs, and you wouldn't be able to recognise it, but that wasn't the intention, so everything remained as it was. Later, I was tasked with writing up the publicity blurb and described the place along the lines of "Fletcher takes up a new career as a hotel porter in a modest hotel close to Paddington Station". Unfortunately someone altered the text and the episode was publicised with a synopsis that read something like: "In this week's episode, Fletcher gets a job in a flea-bitten, run-down . . ." As you can imagine, the owner wasn't very happy and it took a while to sort it out.'

Sydney Lotterby assembled a production team, most of whom had worked with him on *Porridge*. One new team member was make-up designer Christine Walmesley-Cotham, whose extensive list of credits includes productions such as *Vanity Fair* and *The Buccaneers*. She'd worked with Ronnie Barker on *The Two Ronnies*, and relished the chance of doing so again. 'He's one of our finest comedy actors, but hates doing a sketch or playing a character as himself – he always needs a tiny little moustache, sideburns, a pair of glasses, something to make him different. In *Going Straight*, of course, the character had red hair.'

The hair dye was applied before each day's filming, or prior to a spell in the studio. 'We used a spray, which worked well,' recalls Christine, who even remembers the formula. 'It was three squirts of red to one squirt of brown, before being plastered with loads of Brylcreem to make it shine.'

Christine, who now works freelance after more than two decades at the BBC, regards Ronnie Barker as a 'delight to work with'. 'His sense of timing was superb, as was his overall awareness of where he was at any given time in the production.' Although Ronnie agreed to take Fletcher beyond the prison cell at Slade, he'd already decided that, once the six episodes were complete, he would leave the character behind and return to *Open All Hours*. 'It was only ever going to be one series, because I didn't want to get stuck in the character – I wanted fresh challenges. But I liked doing it, and it was lovely working with Patricia Brake and Richard Beckinsale

again. There were also other good actors, like Nigel
Hawthorne and David Swift, and, of course, Nicholas
Lyndhurst, playing my son.

'The first episode was excellent fun, because the story
involved just Fulton and me on a train, with Mr Mackay
getting more and more drunk. There's no doubt the series
could have continued but the danger was it could have
strayed further away from the original plot.'

In *Porridge*, the confinements of the prison cell induced an
intensity unsurpassed by anything the sequel had to offer, but
Going Straight was an interesting concept and deserved to be
detached from its precursor and respected as a new entity.

Dick Clement feels *Going Straight* has been neglected over
the years, but still regards it as one of his favorite pieces of
work. 'Inevitably it was different and people say it wasn't as
good as *Porridge*; maybe it wasn't – it didn't contain the
same sort of security from being inside a contained environment. Nevertheless, it still had some funny moments,
including the first episode where we also find Fulton leaving
prison. But the final episode, "Going Off the Rails", is probably the best we ever did – I'm very fond of it. It's a good
script and contains some nice textures.'

Dick is confident that were the series to be given an airing
on mainstream television now, people would view it as a
meritorious example of the sitcom genre. 'Some people were
disappointed it wasn't *Porridge* and, of course, that had been
the template, but *Going Straight* had lots going for it. Fletcher
was very much a three-dimensional character, and Ronnie's
performance as good as ever.' And just like with many of
their previous pieces of work, Clement and La Frenais focused
on the realities of life. 'He'd been inside a long time and faced
real problems when he finally got out, so we tried confronting
these predicaments. We've always done that in our scripts –
otherwise you rely on a load of jokes, which doesn't appeal to
us. People have been too harsh towards *Going Straight* and it
will always be a favourite of mine.'

The Fletcher Family

Ingrid

Fletcher's eldest daughter is the bubbly, gum-chewing blonde Ingrid, whose confident, carefree attitude towards life saw her visit her father in prison without a bra. When a shocked Fletch broached the subject, she replied, 'I don't need to, Dad. I haven't done for ages – my breasts are firm and pliant.' There's certainly no doubting her popularity with the men.

Ingrid – whose middle name is Rita – is a qualified manicurist and, though her outspokenness and tarty appearance may not be to everyone's liking, she has a heart of gold and is a hard worker. When her mother leaves home, she runs the house at 107 Alexandra Park Crescent as well as holding down a full-time job before finally marrying Lennie Godber, who's been working as a lorry driver since his release from prison.

Actress Patricia Brake was presented with an unexpected award after playing Ingrid in the *Porridge* episode 'Heartbreak Hotel'. 'It's a certificate of bralessness!' says Patricia, smiling. 'The prop boys made it for me and I hang it in my bathroom; it reads "Patricia Brake appears braless" – which I did. Even though the episode seems tame compared to today's standards, it was quite risqué at the time because no one appeared on television without a bra.'

Patricia enjoyed playing Ingrid. 'In the first *Porridge* episode I appeared in I had very little to do, but I think I made the writers laugh – from there the character grew. The scripts were wonderful and it was great working with Ronnie Barker.'

Though Ingrid became a central character when *Going Straight* was written, and even though she appeared in only a handful of *Porridge* episodes, Patricia preferred the prison-based series. '*Going Straight* didn't work so well as *Porridge*, probably because the character had so much to fight against inside. But I enjoyed them both; there aren't many decent characters written for women, so I was jolly lucky being in something as good as those two shows. You're only as good as your scripts and fortunately Dick Clement and Ian La Frenais were brilliant writers. It was classic comic writing because as well as making you laugh the scripts could make you cry.'

When she started playing Ingrid, her father went along to watch the recording at Television Centre. 'Ingrid was very tarty-looking and my father didn't recognise me – I couldn't believe it!' exclaims Patricia, who was in her twenties when she played the role. 'I was young and earnest at that time; everything was so important and I know I felt in awe most of the time.'

Born in Bath, where her father was a butcher, Patricia always wanted to be an actress. Upon leaving school at sixteen, she joined Bristol's Old Vic Drama School. Immediately after completing her two-year training, she became assistant stage-manager at Salisbury Rep. Her duties included playing every juvenile part going. 'It was a wonderful grounding, because you played an assortment of roles – you learn such a lot that way.'

After Salisbury she appeared in a fifteen-minute television series, *Home Tonight*, before performing – aged just eighteen – at Stratford as Hermia in *A Midsummer Night's Dream*. The busy start to her career continued with more small-screen offers, including a part in *The Ugliest Girl in Town*, an American production filmed in the UK. After the exposure of appearances in *Porridge* and *Going Straight*, Patricia made guest appearances in numerous comedy shows, such as Eth in *The Glums, Seconds Out*, Di in *Singles*, Cherry in *Troubles and Strife* and Central's sketch show *Mike Reid's Mates and Music*.

'I also went on to work with Ronnie Barker a lot in *The Two Ronnies*, including in the film *The Picnic*, playing the maid who disappears inside a four-poster bed at the beginning of the picnic before coming out giggling. I also did all the girls' voices. I remember Ronnie joking to me one day. He claimed I was lucky my surname began with B because he often cast me after getting tired trawling through *Spotlight* [the actors' directory] – he'd return towards the front of the book and say: "She'll do."'

Nowadays Patricia appears mostly in dramas, such as *Holby City* and *Midsomer Murders*. Her appearances in the theatre are less frequent. 'I get tired of traipsing around the country, so rarely consider anything that takes me away from home for long periods.'

Isobel

Fletcher's wife, Isobel, to whom he was married for twenty-four years, was seen just once during *Porridge*. She appeared briefly in 'Men without Women', seemingly elated upon seeing her hubby return home on compassionate leave. We then discover they had cooked up a scheme between them to effect the leave: claiming their marriage was on the rocks, Fletch soft-soaped the prison's management into allowing him time to try and patch things up with his wife; what the Governor didn't realise was that he'd pulled a similar trick while serving time at Maidstone.

The irony of Fletch's scheming is that his life is soon tainted by marital problems. When he leaves prison, he discovers that Isobel (who was manager of a dry cleaner's)

has embarked on a new life of luxury in Chingford with the affluent Reg Jessop, owner of a cardboard-box factory off London's North Circular.

Fletch and Isobel were nineteen when they tied the knot, and – except in 1955, when he was King of the Teds and had a brief fling with Gloria, a machinist from a local clothing factory – he's been devoted to his Isobel.

Isobel was played by Jone Ellis, who has been seen in numerous other shows on television over the years. Her credits include *Out of the Unknown* and *The Prisoner* during the 1960s and *Fawlty Towers* and *All Creatures Great and Small* in the seventies; *French and Saunders, Alas Smith and Jones, KYTV, An Affair in Mind* and *The Silver Chair* have followed since.

In films, she's played Brenda in 1960's *The Night of the Big Heat*, a blonde in 1967's *Quatermass and the Pit*, Bess in *Anne of the Thousand Days* and Mrs Wagstaffe in *Getting It Right*.

Marion

We never get to see Fletch's youngest daughter, Marion, but we hear plenty about her from Ingrid. She flits from job to job, beginning with one at Timothy White's, then selling shirts around the city's offices, before moving to Woolies. Fletch holds a low opinion of Marion, classing her as 'lazy'. He also dislikes her boyfriend, Ricky, whose wealth stems from running his own company, Sunset Tours, offering cheap charter flights.

By the time Fletcher returns home in *Going Straight*, Marion has been living away from home for two years, sharing a Maida Vale flat with some nurses.

Raymond

Fletcher's only son, Raymond, resides in a world of his own. When the series begins, he's just started grammar school, turning up for his first day in a uniform his father stole from a school-outfitters. But Fletch's absence during his son's form ative years has had a detrimental effect: at fourteen,

Raymond smokes thirty cigarettes a day, although there's always the possibility his habit stems from the responsibility bestowed upon him in his role as stage manager of the school play.

He may be two years older and in his final term at school when we see him for the first time in *Going Straight*, but he remains as gormless as ever. Fletcher even remarks that he needs a new battery and must have been educated in lethargy.

Nicholas Lyndhurst was seventeen when he landed the role of Raymond. Born in Emsworth, West Sussex, he attended London's Corona Drama Academy from the age of ten. He stayed eight years, paying his fees from money earned making commercials. His first television work was for BBC Schools productions, and was followed by more expansive roles: in the period drama *Anne of Avonlea*, a leading role in the BBC's adaptation of *Heidi*, and, aged fourteen, the lead in *The Prince and the Pauper*.

But his big break came in the shape of Adam Parkinson in Carla Lane's highly rated sitcom *Butterflies* in 1978. Four series were made and by the time the closing episode was transmitted, five years later, Nicholas's was a familiar face to TV viewers across the nation.

Now, in his thirties, Nicholas's impressive list of credits also includes the role of Gary Sparrow in *Goodnight Sweetheart* and, in arguably his best performance to date, playing Rodney in *Only Fools and Horses*.

GOING STRAIGHT GOING HOME

Original transmission: 📺 **Friday 24 February 1978
BBC1, 8.30 p.m.**

CAST

Norman Fletcher	**Ronnie Barker**
Mr Mackay	**Fulton Mackay**
McLaren	**Tony Osoba**
Mr Kirby	**Milton Johns**
Mr Collinson	**Paul McDowell**
Oaksie	**Timothy Bateson**
Tanner	**Norman Jones**
Scotcher	**Michael Turner**
Steward	**Bunny May**

Fletcher returns to the outside world and is determined to go straight. But just when he thinks he's free from the nightmare of Slade Prison, he bumps into Mr Mackay on the train south. They get chatting and it transpires that Mackay is travelling to the Smoke in search of a new job after twenty-five years with the prison service.

At Stafford, a couple of criminals jump on the train. They're on the run after robbing a jewellery shop and desperate to find an innocent bystander to relieve them of their loot until they're free from the pursuing police. Oaksie, one of the criminals, tells his boss to leave the bag with Fletch.

A case of mistaken identity finds Mackay lumbered with the bag of stolen property, much to Fletcher's amusement. Just when he's got the chance to land Mackay in trouble, Fletch remembers he's decided to turn over a new leaf and gets his ex-foe out of a tricky situation.

WHAT A SCENE!

Fletcher is preparing to leave prison, and chats with McLaren.

FLETCHER
D'you know, if there were two things I could take away from this prison as souvenirs, d'you know what they'd be?

MCLAREN
What?

FLETCHER
I'll give you a clue, they both belong to Mr Mackay.

Original transmission: Friday 3 March 1978
BBC1, 8.30 p.m.

CAST

Norman Fletcher. . . . **Ronnie Barker**
Lennie Godber. . . . **Richard Beckinsale**
Ingrid Fletcher. . . . **Patricia Brake**
Shirley Chapman. . . . **Rowena Cooper**
Raymond. . . . **Nicholas Lyndhurst**
Householder. . . . **Michael Stainton**
Builder. . . . **Norman Hartley**

Fletcher is resolved to keep straight but he's finding it tough
adjusting to life outside, especially as his wife, Isobel, has left
him for a life of luxury with Reg Jessop, a cardboard-box
manufacturer. Fletch has his first appointment with his
probation officer, Shirley Chapman,
who's disappointed to hear his
refusal to accept Reg Jessop's
job offer at his cardboard-
box factory. She'll have
to fix him up instead.

Short of cash, Fletch
announces to his daughter
Ingrid that a few years ago
he buried thousands of
pounds in a turnip field in
Essex. But when she learns it is
stolen money, she doesn't want
anything to do with it. Fletcher,
though, could do with an
upturn in his luck and decides
it's worth recovering; he sets
out with his spade to unearth
his fortune, only to find that
new houses have been built
on top of the site!

213

WHAT A SCENE!

Ingrid enquires as to what sort of day her dad has had.

INGRID

I said what sort of day have you had?

FLETCHER

Oh, not bad. I popped in to The White Hart for a swift half; then I had a pint and a pie in The Anchor, signed on, of course, at the labour and then I popped in The Magpie for a swift half, and then I went down to The Old Ship for a swift half en route to The Rainbow Club.

INGRID

Why did you go down The Rainbow?

FLETCHER

It's all that walking about, it made me thirsty.

Original transmission: 📺 **Friday 10 March 1978**
BBC1, 8.30 p.m.

CAST

Norman Fletcher....	**Ronnie Barker**
Ingrid....	**Patricia Brake**
Raymond....	**Nicholas Lyndhurst**
Penny....	**Roberta Tovey**
Dante....	**Freddie Earlle**
Perce....	**Ron Pember**
Arthur....	**Dave Hill**

Fletcher's a forty-five-year-old ex-lag with no money, no job and no wife, and his situation is dragging him down. He feels his prospects are as exciting as 'a wet Sunday in Merthyr Tydfil', and to make matters worse he sees nothing but an untrustworthy, cynical world around him.

While Ingrid works as a manicurist, Fletch's daily routines involve doing the shopping and stopping for a quick cuppa at Dante's Café, where he becomes a crime-stopper. As Perce, the local milkman, counts his takings, a girl tries slipping her hand into his moneybag. But Fletcher spots the incident and steps in just in time to prevent her committing the dirty deed.

Feeling the loud-mouthed degenerate's need is greater than his, he plays the Good Samaritan by giving her his cuppa and a stick of Kit-Kat. Before long, Fletch's hospitality extends to inviting her home for a hot bath and a wholesome meal.

When he discovers she's run away from home, Fletcher's altruistic tendencies take over and he tries giving her some free advice; the last thing Fletch wants is to see a girl heading for a life like his, which has involved eleven years behind bars.

Sadly, his admirable intentions appear to backfire when Penny swipes Ingrid's purse from her handbag, but a final gesture from the girl helps restore Fletch's faith in human nature.

WHAT A SCENE!

**Fletch is getting depressed about the cynical,
untrusting world he's encountered since his release.**

INGRID
Now you mustn't let things get on top of you – you never
have.

FLETCHER
I know. I didn't think it was going to be as hard as this,
that's all. I want to make myself useful, you know, I
want to have a job, but with my record.

INGRID
Now that's not true. There's over a million unemployed
in this country. There's boys what left Raymond's school
two years ago who don't know nothing else but a dole
queue.

FLETCHER
But it's this attitude of cynicism and mistrust I keep
coming up against, which in turn makes me more
cynical and that's something I've always resisted, you
know that very well, don't ya? I mean I went into the
Post Office the other day just to get a Postal Order for
my pools; they've got a four-penny Biro chained to the
wall. I mean, it still didn't write but it was chained to the
wall.

INGRID
Well that's normal these days, Dad, it's the mood of the
country.

Original transmission: 📺 **Friday 17 March 1978**
BBC1, 8.30 p.m.

CAST

Norman Fletcher	**Ronnie Barker**
Lennie Godber	**Richard Beckinsale**
Ingrid	**Patricia Brake**
Mr McEwan	**David Swift**
Shirley Chapman	**Rowena Cooper**
Pamela	**Elizabeth Cassidy**
Alfie	**Eric Francis**
Vic	**Stephen Tate**

Thanks to Mrs Chapman at the probation service, Fletch is fixed up with a job at the Dolphin Hotel, where the owner, Mr McEwan, helps ex-convicts get that all-important break upon release. For Fletch the idea of working takes some getting used to, partly because it's his first ever job – something Godber, who's dating Ingrid, finds highly amusing.

Fletch claims that he accepted the job to prove to the world – and to his family – that he could gain employment, but when he starts having second thoughts about turning up, Godber and Ingrid supply a helping hand.

WHAT A SCENE!

Godber discusses Fletch's new job.

GODBER
It must be your first legitimate job in . . . how long is it?

FLETCHER
Ever.

GODBER
(Laughs) What? Straight up, you've never had a job in your life?

FLETCHER
No, not unless you count the army.

INGRID
Which we don't because you were on the fiddle even then. D'you know, when I was a nipper all my party dresses were made out of parachute silk.

FLETCHER
You wouldn't have complained if you'd ever fallen out of a window, would you?

Original transmission: 📺 **Friday 24 March 1978**
BBC1, 8.25 p.m.

CAST

Norman Fletcher . . . . **Ronnie Barker**
Lennie Godber . . . . **Richard Beckinsale**
Ingrid . . . . **Patricia Brake**
Mr McEwan . . . . **David Swift**
Giles . . . . **Donald Morley**
Wellings . . . . **Nigel Hawthorne**
Mrs Appleby . . . . **Lally Bowers**
Raymond . . . . **Nicholas Lyndhurst**
Crowther . . . . **Peter Postlethwaite**
Nulty . . . . **Martin Milman**

It's two months since Fletch's release and he's settled into his
job as night porter at a local hotel. When a man arrives at
the hotel, Fletch recognises the face but can't place his name.
An old woman soon follows and deposits expensive jewellery
in the safe, and Fletch's memory rushes back: the mystery
man is Wellings, an ex-con with whom he served time. He's a
con man who, along with an old woman, worked the south
coast. While the old dear distracted the porter, Wellings
would rob the safe, pretend the jewellery had been stolen and
then claim off the insurance. Fletch takes matters into his
own hands – but soon gets into difficulties.

WHAT A SCENE!

Ingrid contemplates marrying Godber.

GODBER

I've got a lot in common with your dad, haven't I?

INGRID

Unfortunately, yes. That's always going to embarrass me,
that is. I mean, when we live somewhere nice people are
going to ask me how I met my husband. And I'm going to
have to say: 'He shared a cell with my dad.'

Original transmission: 📺 **Friday 7 April 1978**
BBC1, 8.30 p.m.

CAST

Norman Fletcher....	**Ronnie Barker**
Lennie Godber....	**Richard Beckinsale**
Ingrid....	**Patricia Brake**
Pybus....	**Alfred Lynch**
Police Sergeant....	**Royston Tickner**
Police Inspector....	**Robert Raglan**
Mrs Gilchrist....	**Gwyneth Owen**
Man....	**Norman Scace**
Shop Assistant....	**Val McCrimmon**
Registrar....	**Bill Horsley**
Raymond....	**Nicholas Lyndhurst**

After participating in an identity parade, Fletch meets an old acquaintance, Dave Pybus, a man with a camelhair coat, white tie and flashy motor. Dave offers to push some business Fletch's way, but he declines because he's going to go straight. In case Fletch changes his mind, Pybus leaves him his business card.

With Ingrid's wedding to Godber looming, Fletch wants to discuss arrangements – not that he's got much spare cash to help finance the event. It seems everything has been sorted, but upon discovering that his estranged wife's wealthy lover, Reg Jessop, is financing the reception at a plush establishment in Stanmore, Fletch takes umbrage.

Strapped for cash, Fletch has second thoughts about Dave Pybus' offer to earn a fast buck. Acting as lookout will bag him £500, and, although the work is on the morning of Ingrid's wedding, he'll be finished in time for the big occasion. It seems too good to refuse, but when Fletch enters a pet shop and recalls life behind bars, he pulls out of the job just in time for his daughter's nuptials.

WHAT A SCENE!

Fletch meets an old acquaintance, Dave Pybus, and over a drink they discuss their differing fortunes.

FLETCHER

To look at you, Dave, I wouldn't say you were exactly on your uppers. I mean that whistle, the car you drove us here in: automatic, two-tone, real leather upholstery, wing mirrors.

PYBUS

No, I'm thinking of changing it. Well it's coming up to 20,000. And my bloke, you know what puts the spanners to it, he says: 'Dave, best to do it now before something big goes like the gearbox.'

FLETCHER

Yes, I know what you mean, yes, I have the same problem with my bike. I've got to trade that in before the bell drops off.

PRODUCTION TEAM

ALL EPISODES WRITTEN BY
Dick Clement and Ian La Frenais

SIGNATURE TUNE WRITTEN BY
Tony Macauley and Dick Clement

FILM CAMERAMAN
Reg Pope
(all episodes except 'Going Sour')

FILM EDITOR
Bill Wright
(all episodes except 'Going Sour')

FILM SOUND
Ron Blight
(all episodes except 'Going Sour')

MAKE-UP
Christine Walmesley-Cotham

COSTUMES
Mary Husband

LIGHTING
John Dixon

SOUND
Richard Chamberlain

VIDEOTAPE EDITOR
John Turner (episodes 1–2 & 5);
Matt Boney (episode 3);
Roger Harvey (episodes 4 & 6)

PRODUCTION ASSISTANT
Mike Crisp

DESIGNER
Tim Gleeson

PRODUCER/DIRECTOR
Sydney Lotterby

222

A-Z OF PERIPHERAL CHARACTERS

APPEARING IN *PORRIDGE* AND *GOING STRAIGHT*

Only characters that have not been profiled in more depth elsewhere in the book are listed in this chapter.

Pilot (Prisoner and Escort)

The Prison Warder (Hamish Roughead) works at Brixton Prison and hands Fletcher over to Mackay and Barrowclough when he's transferred to Slade Prison.

Porridge (Series One) – A Day Out

The Landlord (Ralph Watson) works at the pub frequented by Fltecher and Mackay.

The Nurse (Peggy Mason) is a district nurse who cycles past the prisoners while they're digging their ditches.

The VICAR (Robert Gillespie) is seen in the village pub when Mackay pops in for a drink.

The Verger (John Rutland) accompanies the Vicar to the local pub before heading back to the church once he hears prisoners are working on the moors. –

Porridge (Series One) – Men without Women

Elaine (Rosalind Elliot) is Warren's beloved who is seen on visiting day.

Iris (Andonia Katsaros) is Heslop's wife, who arrives on visiting day.

Sergeant Norris (Royston Tickner) accompanies Fletcher to his home when he's granted forty-eight hours' compassionate leave after hearing his wife has, supposedly, found someone else.

Trevor (Donald Groves) is Lukewarm's partner who comes calling on visiting day. He's a watch repairer from Southport.

Norma (Susan Littler) is Tolly's wife who visits him in prison.

Porridge (Series Two) – No Peace for the Wicked

Prison Visitors (Ivor Roberts, Barbara New, Geoffrey Greenhill) are Home Office officials given a tour of the prison by Mackay.

Porridge (Series One) – No Way Out

The NURSE (Elisabeth Day) is employed at the hospital Fletch visits for a knee examination.

Sandra (Carol Hawkins) is a London girl who dresses up as a nurse in order to pass on a blank passport to Fletch while he attends hospital.

Going Straight – Going Home

Mr Kirby (Milton Johns) is the prison officer who returns Fletch's possessions upon his release. He's a miserable character: Fletcher remarks that he's never seen him smile.

Oaksie (Timothy Bateson) meets Fletcher on the train he catches upon his release. Cloth-capped Oaksie boards the train at Stafford.

Mr Scotcher (Michael Turner) is a policeman in the Flying Squad who once collared Fletcher. He boards Fletcher's train and is on the hunt for thieves who broke into a jeweller's. Believing the stolen goods are still on board, he questions Fletcher.

Steward (Bunny May) is the steward on the train Fletcher catches after being released from prison.

Mr Tanner (Norman Jones) joins the train with Oaksie at Stafford. Claims he was a major in the army – but, being as he's a criminal, it's uncertain. When he wants a bag delivered in London, because he's getting off at Watford, he confuses Mackay for Fletcher and persuades the prison officer to do the dirty deed.

Going Straight – Going to Be Alright

Householder (Michael Stainton) owns the house built on top of the money Fletcher buried a few years ago. He sees Fletch with his spade and ends up hiring him to dig a pond.

Shirley Chapman (Rowena Cooper) is Fletch's probation officer at the Muswell Hill office. They meet twice a week and she helps find him a job at the Dolphin Hotel. She's married with two kids, but her spouse, who's an aerospace engineer, is currently unemployed.

Man in Probation Office (Norman Hartley) is sitting waiting at the probation office when Fletcher arrives for his first meeting. It turns out he's a painter and decorator, there to provide a quote for giving the depressing office a fresh lick of paint.

Going Straight – Going Sour

Arthur Boyle (Dave Hill) arrives at the end of the episode to take Penny to Portsmouth and return the purse she'd pinched from Ingrid's handbag. Arthur is Penny's mother's partner.

Dante (Freddie Earlle) owns Dante's Café, where Fletch visits. States he comes from Sicily but Fletch knows better and reminds him his roots are in Stoke Newington.

Penny (Roberta Tovey) is spotted by Fletcher in the café trying to pinch money from the local milkman's moneybag. Fletch tries leading her back on to the straight and narrow with some fatherly advice. She used to live in Camberwell but when her mother moved to Portsmouth, together with her partner, Penny ran away from home. Her intention was to live with a friend, Pauline Soper, but her plans fell through. She eventually ends up moving to Pompey.

Perce (Ron Pember) is the local milkman who's counting his takings in the café when Fletcher arrives. Unknowingly, he's nearly a victim of crime when Penny tries grabbing his moneybag. Claims he's a happily married man when Fletch enquires about his rendezvous with a lady nearby.

The Policeman (not credited) pops into Dante's Café while Fletcher is there with Penny. From the girl's reaction, Fletch realises she's on the run from the police and befriends her.

Going Straight – Going to Work

Alfie (Eric Francis) is the barman at The Black Lion, Fletch's local.

Mr McEwan (David Swift) owns the Dolphin Hotel where Fletch works as a night porter. A bearded man who spent many years in Malawi, McEwan likes helping the local probation service by offering employment to convicts upon release.

Pamela (Elizabeth Cassidy) is the secretary-cum-receptionist at the Dolphin Hotel who's a little sceptical about Mr McEwan's policy of employing ex-cons.

Vic (Stephen Tate) leaves the pub just as Fletch enters.

Going Straight – Going, Going, Gone

Mrs Appleby (Lally Bowers) is staying in room 2 at the Dolphin Hotel. When she asks Fletcher to put her necklace in the safe, he thinks she's in partnership with Mr Wellings and is planning to defraud the insurance company. But he's wrong: the wealthy grey-haired old lady is genuine and has visited the hotel for years. Her son works in the theatre while her late hubby used to own a toffee company.

Cheryl (Rikki Howard) is the blonde who accompanies Giles, who mistakenly calls her Beryl, into the Dolphin Hotel.

Thomas Clifford Crowther (Peter Postlethwaite),

formerly serving with the West End Central police force, is now working with the Flying Squad. He stops to chat with Fletch just round the corner from the Dolphin Hotel.

Giles (Donald Morley) arrives at the Dolphin Hotel late one night with a young blonde called Cheryl. Smiling like a Cheshire cat, he asks for a room, claiming his car has broken down, the blonde is his wife and he's decided to stay the night, although it's clear he wants the room for a little hanky-panky.

Nulty (Martin Milman) works for Crowther in the Flying Squad. Upon spotting Fletcher, they get out of their Ford Granada to find out what he's up to. Whilst doing so their car is pinched.

Mr Wellings (Nigel Hawthorne) has room 26 at the Dolphin Hotel. He's a former conman who served time with Fletcher at Maidstone. Used to work with an old woman along the south coast in places like Bournemouth and Torquay, submitting false insurance claims. But Wellings has been straight for six years and works as a bathroom-tile salesman.

Going Straight – Going Off the Rails

Mrs Gilchrist (Gwyneth Owen) is the woman who's asked to try and identify a suspect at the identity parade, but fails to pick anyone because the person she's looking for is ginger-haired.

The Man (Norman Scacc) is a bespectacled man, standing in the identity parade, who Fletcher annoys.

The Police Inspector (Robert Raglan) ushers Mrs Gilchrist to the identity parade.

The Police Sergeant (Royston Tickner) helps co-ordinate the identity parade at the police station. He knows Fletch.

Dave Pybus (Alfred Lynch) knows Fletch from years gone by and offers him the chance to earn £500 as a lookout during a forthcoming job he's arranging.

Rather ostentatious, Pybus used to frequent Fletch's old local, The Hand and Flower, and now runs a business manufacturing party novelties, while his other work is rather less legal.

The Registrar (Bill Horsley) marries Ingrid and Godber.

The Shop Assistant (Val McCrimmon) works in a pet shop that Fletch enters pretending he's buying a dog for Ingrid's wedding present. But when all the cages start reminding him of prison, he leaves.

Porridge: The Scripts

FOREWORD

Fletcher was an easy character to play and I didn't have to think too much about it, which is fortunate. I think much of that is because there was a lot of me in Fletch; there was also plenty of my father, too. Although the character was a Cockney and I was born in Oxford, he was working class and I could relate to him.

Although he was out for everything he could get, being a wide-boy, he was a likeable chap. You always need charm in a character, even if you're playing an old tramp, and I think Fletcher possessed a lot of that.

Working on the show was such a delight, particularly as everyone worked so well together. When it came to rehearsals we'd race through them with ease. We'd often start at ten and be finished by one, simply because we all knew what we were doing. Obviously I was carrying a lot of the responsibility on my shoulders but I never received anything but total support from the rest of the team; you knew no one was going to let you down, ruin a gag or bit of timing.

I feel I owe much to *Porridge*. It was probably the best and most important show I did.

RONNIE BARKER 2002

INTRODUCTION

The first time Ian and I ever sat down to write together was in a pub in the Old Brompton Road. I don't remember any discussion about who should do the actual scribbling, but it was me. This tradition continued and when asked about it we used to answer that it was because my calligraphy was more legible than Ian's. It is, but I don't think that is the entire reason.

The essentials haven't varied much over the years. We write *together*. Other collaborators work by e-mail or split the script up and say, 'You do that scene, I'll do this one.' If it works, fine, but it's not the way we do it. We discuss everything. It starts with the story. What's the main thrust and where are the juicy scenes? Inevitably, while we're kicking ideas around, some dialogue occurs to us. I suppose we're doing a form of actors' improvisation. So we step into character and throw out a line and a response may occur and if it's any good we incorporate it when we do the actual writing.

A tape recorder might sound like a good idea for this stage of the process. I think we even bought a couple over the years but the batteries ran out, or we forgot to switch them on and then the thought of wading through all the discarded drivel in search of a forgotten gem was too daunting and time-consuming. We jot down anything we really like and then it's time to write 'Fade In'.

Everything is debated, alternatives considered, choices made. And as I'm always the one with the pen in my hand – here's the hidden agenda – I have the power to choose my version over Ian's if it is a split vote. But if he doesn't like it when he sees it on the page and raises the red flag, back it goes. Or maybe we find a compromise, another line, another word.

We switched to a computer a few years ago. Ian stared at the grey cube on the table with deep suspicion. When I started to tap the keys he was appalled. 'You're not going to do that *while we're writing*?' I certainly was, because the alternative was transcribing everything at the end of the day after he'd gone home. He grudgingly got used to it after a while, won over by the obvious advantages of instant print-outs and corrections, though it was a year before he walked round to my side of the table to take a look at the text on the screen.

Somebody once said that writing is all about re-writing. It's certainly true in our case. Bang the words down on paper then polish, edit, tighten and improve. With an original screenplay everything is carved as if from a new block of granite. Every character, every setting needs to be discovered. It's different with a television series. Once the actors have played the characters a few times, their voices are in your head.

If I wanted to conjure up Fletcher, I imagined him sitting in his cell and somebody bursting in to tell him that an asteroid was due to hit the earth in three days. I can hear his response now: 'Oh yes?'

Just two words. But spoken with the infinite scepticism of a man who believes nothing until he sees it with his own eyes. A small thing in itself but a great clue to character. He's wary, protective of what's his and determined to let no man make a sucker of him.

We wrote the first series of *Porridge* when we were rehearsing the stage musical *Billy*. It was a very happy time. One show was written on our knees in the Midland Hotel, Manchester. I'm pretty certain it was 'A Night In'. We felt it was important to do one show entirely in the cell, since prison is, after all, about being locked in. We also felt it should touch on how tough it is, especially for a young prisoner. It ended up as one of our favourite episodes, a 'two-hander' between Ronnie Barker and Richard Beckinsale, who wonderfully captured all of Lennie's fear and vulnerability.

The last series was written in California, where we were already doing the American version of the show. The writing process for Network TV was totally different, quite horrible and we never ever wanted to do it again. However, we kept it on the air for an entire season – twenty-two shows – and had run out of the original scripts. So as a matter of record, the story of the judge who sent Fletcher down turning up in Slade was originally done in America and then 'translated' back into English. It was sometimes difficult to remember if a line had originated in the American version or had already been used.

We're often asked about the differences between American humour and the English variety. The truth is, a good joke is a good joke. The real difference is to do with sociology and class in particular. Think of Shaw's *Pygmalion* or anything by Alan Ayckbourn. But when you mine for the American equivalent you run into race, a subject on which people are far more sensitive.

The last thing to say about writing *Porridge* is how painless it was. From the outset we knew we were writing for Ronnie Barker, in our view a comic genius.

Syd Lotterby did us an enormous favour when he cast Fulton Mackay and Brian Wilde for the pilot – though at the time we had no idea that it would become a series. But all three performances were firmly in our mind's eye – and ear – when we sat down to begin the series.

True, the research set us back, when we went round Wormwood Scrubs and Brixton, because we were hit by the harsh reality of life inside and how very unfunny it is. Even more reassuring, then, to picture Ronnie as Fletcher. The key was his attitude, his ability to make the very best of a bad situation and find little victories that get him through each day. He is a survivor, in the tradition of Falstaff or the Good Soldier Schweik. What would he say to that?

'Oh yes?'

DICK CLEMENT 2002

EPISODE GUIDE

THE PILOT

PRISONER AND ESCORT

Original transmission: Sunday 1 April 1973, BBC2, 8.15 p.m.
First repeat: Tuesday 7 August 1973, BBC1, 8.30 p.m.
Cast: Norman Fletcher Ronnie Barker **Mr Barrowclough** Brian Wilde
Mr Mackay Fulton Mackay **Prison Constable** Hamish Roughead

SERIES ONE

1. NEW FACES, OLD HANDS

Original transmission: Thursday 5 September 1974, BBC1, 8.30 p.m.
First repeat: Friday 21 February 1975, BBC1, 8.30 p.m.
Cast: Norman Fletcher Ronnie Barker **Mr Barrowclough** Brian Wilde
Mr Mackay Fulton Mackay **Lennie Godber** Richard Beckinsale **Cyril Heslop**
Brian Glover **Medical Officer** John Bennett **The Governor** Michael Barrington
Other prison officers Ronald Musgrove, Edward Cogdale and Keith Norrish

2. THE HUSTLER

Original transmission: Thursday 12 September 1974, BBC1, 8.30 p.m.
First repeat: Friday 28 February 1975, BBC1, 8.30 p.m.
Cast: Norman Fletcher Ronnie Barker **Mr Barrowclough** Brian Wilde
Mr Mackay Fulton Mackay **Lennie Godber** Richard Beckinsale **Heslop**
Brian Glover **Ives** Ken Jones **Lukewarm** Christopher Biggins **Evans** Ray
Dunbobbin **Mr Appleton** Graham Ashley **Prison Officer** John Quarmby

3. A NIGHT IN

Original transmission: Thursday 19 September 1974, BBC1, 8.30 p.m.
First repeat: Friday 7 March 1975, BBC1, 8.30 p.m.
Cast: Norman Fletcher Ronnie Barker **Lennie Godber** Richard Beckinsale
Prison Officer Paul McDowell

4. A DAY OUT

Original transmission: Thursday 26 September 1974, BBC1, 8.30 p.m.

First repeat: Friday 14 March 1975, BBC1, 8.30 p.m.

Cast: Norman Fletcher Ronnie Barker **Mr Mackay** Fulton Mackay
Lennie Godber Richard Beckinsale **Ives** Ken Jones **Navyrum** Paul Angelis
Dylan Philip Jackson **Scrounger** Johnny Wade **Vicar** Robert Gillespie
Verger John Rutland **Chief Prison Officer** Arnold Peters **Landlord**
Ralph Watson **Nurse** Peggy Mason

5. WAYS AND MEANS

Original transmission: Thursday 3 October 1974, BBC1, 8.30 p.m.

First repeat: Friday 21 March 1975, BBC1, 8.30 p.m.

Cast: Norman Fletcher Ronnie Barker **Mr Barrowclough** Brian Wilde
Mr Mackay Fulton Mackay **Ives** Ken Jones **The Governor** Michael
Barrington **McLaren** Tony Osoba

6. MEN WITHOUT WOMEN

Original transmission: Thursday 10 October 1974, BBC1, 8.30 p.m.

First repeat: Friday 28 March 1975, BBC1, 9.05 p.m.

Cast: Norman Fletcher Ronnie Barker **Mr Barrowclough** Brian Wilde
Mr Mackay Fulton Mackay **Warren** Sam Kelly **Cyril Heslop** Brian Glover
The Governor Michael Barrington **Lukewarm** Christopher Biggins
Sergeant Norris Royston Tickner **Tolly** Emlyn Price **Isobel** June Ellis
Ingrid Fletcher Patricia Brake **Norma** Susan Littler **Iris** Andonia Katsaros
Elaine Rosalind Elliot **Trevor** Donald Groves

SERIES TWO

1. JUST DESSERTS

Original transmission: Friday 24 October 1975, BBC1, 8.30 p.m.
First repeat: Thursday 20 May 1976, BBC1, 8 p.m.
Cast: Norman Fletcher Ronnie Barker **Mr Barrowclough** Brian Wilde
Mr Mackay Fulton Mackay **Lennie Godber** Richard Beckinsale **Ives**
Ken Jones **Warren** Sam Kelly **McLaren** Tony Osoba **Lukewarm**
Christopher Biggins **Banyard** Eric Dodson **Mr Appleton** Graham Ashley
Mr Birchwood John Rudling **Gay Gordon** Felix Bowness

2. HEARTBREAK HOTEL

Original transmission: Friday 31 October 1975, BBC1, 8.30 p.m.
First repeat: Thursday 27 May 1976, BBC1, 8 p.m.
Cast: Norman Fletcher Ronnie Barker **Mr Barrowclough** Brian Wilde
Mr Mackay Fulton Mackay **Lennie Godber** Richard Beckinsale **Ingrid**
Patricia Brake **Mrs Godber** Maggie Flint **Jackdaw** Cyril Shaps

3. DISTURBING THE PEACE

Original transmission: Friday 7 November 1975, BBC1, 8.30 p.m.
First repeat: Thursday 3 June 1976, BBC1, 7.55 p.m.
Cast: Norman Fletcher Ronnie Barker **Mr Barrowclough** Brian Wilde
Mr Mackay Fulton Mackay **Lennie Godber** Richard Beckinsale
Mr Wainwright Peter Jeffrey **Williams** Philip Madoc **Warren** Sam Kelly
McLaren Tony Osoba **The Governor** Michael Barrington **Secretary
(Mrs Heskith)** Madge Hindle

4. NO PEACE FOR THE WICKED

Original transmission: Friday 14 November 1975, BBC1, 8.30 p.m.
First repeat: Thursday 17 June 1976, BBC1, 8 p.m.
Cast: Norman Fletcher Ronnie Barker **Mr Barrowclough** Brian Wilde
Mr Mackay Fulton Mackay **Blanco** David Jason **Warren** Sam Kelly
McLaren Tony Osoba **Banyard** Eric Dodson **The Governor** Michael
Barrington **Mr Collinson** Paul McDowell **Chaplain** Tony Aitken
Prison Visitors Ivor Roberts, Barbara New and Geoffrey Greenhill

5. HAPPY RELEASE

Original transmission: Friday 21 November 1975, BBC1, 8.30 p.m.
First repeat: Thursday 24 June 1976, BBC1, 8 p.m.
Cast: Norman Fletcher Ronnie Barker **Mr Barrowclough** Brian Wilde
Mr Mackay Fulton Mackay **Lennie Godber** Richard Beckinsale
Blanco David Jason **Norris** Colin Farrell **Mr Collinson** Paul McDowell
Medical Officer Terence Soall

6. THE HARDER THEY FALL

Original transmission: Friday 28 November 1975, BBC1, 8.30 p.m.
First repeat: Thursday 1 July 1976, BBC1, 7.55 p.m.
Cast: Norman Fletcher Ronnie Barker **Mr Barrowclough** Brian Wilde
Mr Mackay Fulton Mackay **Lennie Godber** Richard Beckinsale
Harry Grout Peter Vaughan **Jackdaw** Cyril Shaps **P.T.I.** Roy Sampson

SERIES THREE

1. A STORM IN A TEACUP

Original transmission: Friday 18 February 1977, BBC1, 8.30 p.m.
First repeat: Friday 27 January 1978, BBC1, 8.30 p.m.
Cast: Norman Fletcher Ronnie Barker **Mr Barrowclough** Brian Wilde
Mr Mackay Fulton Mackay **Lennie Godber** Richard Beckinsale **Harry
Grout** Peter Vaughan **Harris** Ronald Lacey **Warren** Sam Kelly **McLaren**
Tony Osoba **Lukewarm** Christopher Biggins **Spider** John Moore
Crusher John Dair

2. POETIC JUSTICE

Original transmission: Friday 25 February 1977, BBC1, 8.30 p.m.
First repeat: Friday 13 January 1978, BBC1, 8.30 p.m.
Cast: Norman Fletcher Ronnie Barker **Mr Barrowclough** Brian Wilde
Mr Mackay Fulton Mackay **Lennie Godber** Richard Beckinsale **Rawley**
Maurice Denham **Harris** Ronald Lacey **Warren** Sam Kelly **McLaren** Tony
Osoba **The Governor** Michael Barrington **Mr Collinson** Paul McDowell

3. ROUGH JUSTICE

Original transmission: Friday 4 March 1977, BBC1, 8.30 p.m.
First repeat: Friday 20 January 1978, BBC1, 8.30 p.m.
Cast: Norman Fletcher Ronnie Barker **Mr Barrowclough** Brian Wilde
Mr Mackay Fulton Mackay **Lennie Godber** Richard Beckinsale
Rawley Maurice Denham **Harris** Ronald Lacey **Warren** Sam Kelly
McLaren Tony Osoba

4. PARDON ME

Original transmission: Friday 11 March 1977, BBC1, 8.30 p.m.
First repeat: Friday 3 February 1978, BBC1, 8.30 p.m.
Cast: Norman Fletcher Ronnie Barker **Mr Barrowclough** Brian Wilde
Mr Mackay Fulton Mackay **Lennie Godber** Richard Beckinsale
Blanco David Jason **Warren** Sam Kelly **Lukewarm** Christopher Biggins
The Governor Michael Barrington

5. A TEST OF CHARACTER

Original transmission: Friday 18 March 1977, BBC1, 8.30 p.m.
First repeat: Friday 10 February 1978, BBC1, 8.30 p.m.
Cast: Norman Fletcher Ronnie Barker **Mr Barrowclough** Brian Wilde
Mr Mackay Fulton Mackay **Lennie Godber** Richard Beckinsale
Spraggon Alun Armstrong **Warren** Sam Kelly **McLaren** Tony Osoba

6. FINAL STRETCH

Original transmission: Friday 25 March 1977, BBC1, 8.30 p.m.
First repeat: Friday 17 February 1978, BBC1, 8.30 p.m.
Cast: Norman Fletcher Ronnie Barker **Mr Barrowclough** Brian Wilde
Mr Mackay Fulton Mackay **Lennie Godber** Richard Beckinsale
Jarvis David Daker **Warren** Sam Kelly **Ingrid** Patricia Brake
Crusher John Dair

CHRISTMAS SPECIALS

NO WAY OUT

Original transmission: Wednesday 24 December 1975,
BBC1, 8.25 p.m. (40-minute episode)

First repeat: Thursday 8 July 1976, BBC1, 7.50 p.m.

Cast: Norman Fletcher Ronnie Barker

Mr Barrowclough Brian Wilde **Mr Mackay** Fulton Mackay **Lennie Godber**
Richard Beckinsale **Harry Grout** Peter Vaughan **Prison Doctor** Graham
Crowden **Warren** Sam Kelly **Lukewarm** Christopher Biggins **Sandra**
Carol Hawkins **Nurse** Elisabeth Day

THE DESPERATE HOURS

Original transmission: Friday 24 December 1976, BBC1, 8 p.m.

First repeat: Friday 1 April 1977, BBC1, 8.15 p.m.

Cast: Norman Fletcher Ronnie Barker **Mr Barrowclough** Brian Wilde
Mr Mackay Fulton Mackay **Lennie Godber** Richard Beckinsale
Reg Urwin Dudley Sutton **Warren** Sam Kelly **McLaren** Tony Osoba
The Governor Michael Barrington **Keegan** Ken Wynne **Tulip** Michael
Redfern **Mrs Jamieson** Jane Wenham

PRODUCTION TEAM

All episodes written by Dick Clement and Ian La Frenais
Producer/Director: Sydney Lotterby
Executive Producer: James Gilbert (Pilot)

Music: Max Harris
Film Cameraman: Alan Featherstone (Pilot); Len Newson (S1, episodes 1, 2, 3 and 6); Keith Taylor (S1, episodes 4 and 5); Ken Willicombe (S2, episodes 2, 3, 4 and 6); Kenneth MacMillan (S2, episode 5); John Tiley ('No Way Out'); John McGlashan (S3)
Film Editor: Geoffrey Botterill (S1, episodes 1 and 2); Ray Millichope (Pilot; S1, episodes 3, 4, 5 and 6; S2, episodes 2, 3, 4, 5 and 6; 'No Way Out'); John Dunstan (S3)
Film Sound: Ron Blight (credited on 'No Way Out')
Make-up: Penny Delamar (Pilot); Sylvia James (S1); Ann Ailes-Stevenson (S2; 'No Way Out'); Suzanne Broad ('The Desperate Hours'; S3)
Costume: Penny Lowe (Pilot); Mary Husband (S1 and S3); Betty Aldiss (S2); Susan Wheal ('No Way Out'); Robin Stubbs ('The Desperate Hours')
Lighting: Peter Smee (Pilot; S1, episodes 1, 2, 3, 4 and 6; S2, episodes 1, 2, 3 and 4; 'No Way Out'); Peter Wesson (S1, episode 5; S3); Brian Clemett (S2, episode 5); Sam Barclay ('The Desperate Hours')
Sound: Mike McCarthy (Pilot); Anthony Philpot (S1; S2; 'The Desperate Hours'); Jeff Booth ('No Way Out'); John Holmes (S3)
Production Assistant: Ray Butt (S1); Dave Perrottet (S2); Alan Bell ('No Way Out'); Mike Crisp ('The Desperate Hours' and S3)
Technical Adviser: Jonathan Marshall (credited on S1, episodes 1–4)
Designer: Tim Gleeson (Pilot; S1, episodes 1, 2, 5 and 6; S2, episode 1; 'No Way Out'; 'The Desperate Hours'; S3); David Chandler (S1, episodes 3 and 6); Gerry Scott (S1, episodes 4 and 5); John Pusey (S2, episodes 2, 3, 4, 5 and 6)

PILOT

PRISONER AND ESCORT

1. OPENING TITLES

2. STREET

*Fletcher, Mackay and a Police
Constable walk towards a parked
van. Barrowclough is sitting in the
van reading a newspaper. He sees
the men approaching and gets
out. The others reach the back
of the van.*

POLICE CONSTABLE

Right, he's all yours then. Happy New
Year, Jock.

MACKAY

Aye, escort duty on New Year's Eve.

POLICE CONSTABLE

Happy New Year, Fletcher.

*Fletcher and Mackay get into
the van.*

FLETCHER

Oh yes, very witty, very droll.

*Barrowclough gets in the van.
The constable shuts the door,
bangs on it and the van drives off.
Zoom out as we see the van
approach St Pancras station.*

MAGISTRATE (VOICEOVER)

(*Offscreen*) Norman Stanley Fletcher,

you have pleaded guilty to the charges
brought by this court, and it is now my
duty to pass sentence. You are an
habitual criminal, who accepts arrest
as an occupational hazard, and
presumably accepts imprisonment in
the same casual manner. We therefore
feel constrained to commit you to the
maximum term allowed for these
offences – we sentence you to five
years' imprisonment. Do you wish to
address the court?

3. RAILWAY CARRIAGE

*Mackay, Fletcher and Barrowclough
are sitting in first-class
compartment. The blinds into
the corridor are drawn.*

FLETCHER

Cobblers.

BARROWCLOUGH

What?

FLETCHER

What Brian Clough says about
London clubs.

MACKAY
(*Grabbing the paper*) That's my paper.

FLETCHER
Can I have a look at your *Penthouse* then?

MACKAY
Get your own.

FLETCHER
How can I get my own? We're in motion, aren't we?

MACKAY
Shoulda thought of that at the station.

FLETCHER
At the station I wasn't even permitted a Jimmy Riddle.

MACKAY
Shut your mouth.
There is a pause.

BARROWCLOUGH
You can have a look at my *Angling Times* if you like.

MACKAY
No, he can't. God Almighty, mollycoddling him already! People seem to forget what prison's for. He's paying a debt to society. Not having an all-expenses-paid holiday with privileges and magazines. You're going to prison to be punished.
There is a pause. Then Fletcher leans across to Barrowclough.

FLETCHER
I spy with my little eye something beginning with (*indicating Mackay with his head*) C.

MACKAY
You watch it, sonny.

FLETCHER
Constable?

MACKAY
Don't come it with me.

FLETCHER
I wouldn't, Mr Mackay, I wouldn't – otherwise you'd wait until the train picked up a fair bit of speed outside Hemel Hempstead and chuck me out of the window. Put it down as attempted escape.

BARROWCLOUGH
He wouldn't do that.

FLETCHER
No, I suppose not . . . he couldn't spell Hemel Hempstead, he'd wait till Rugby.

MACKAY
I'm a reasonable man. But one more allegation of brutality and I'll knock your block off . . .

BARROWCLOUGH
Look, it's a long journey ahead so . . . so let's not conduct it in an atmosphere of hostility and aggression. Why don't we all have a nice cup of tea?
He starts to get to his feet.

BARROWCLOUGH
Both take milk and sugar?

MACKAY
You sit still, I'll get them.

BARROWCLOUGH
(*Looking for money*) Well, let me pay. (*To Fletcher*) Anything you want?

FLETCHER

Thanks, mate. Tea with two sugars, and I'll have one of those individual fruit pies if they've got any . . .
Mackay slams the door shut before Fletcher finishes.

FLETCHER

He's a laugh, in' he?

BARROWCLOUGH

I suppose it's with bein' a Scotsman and being deprived of Hogmanay. I mean they do take it very seriously the Scots.

FLETCHER

Yeah, well they take any excuse for drinking seriously, don't they. Nothing social about their drinking, is there. With them it's not the case of a few friends mellowing over a glass of vino. No, no . . . they just drink to get drunk. (*Looking through a magazine*) Cor, look at 'er. Only one thing worse than a drunken Scot and that's a sober one.

BARROWCLOUGH

I'm Scots on my mother's side.

FLETCHER

Yeah, well second generation, in' it? Different fing.

BARROWCLOUGH

Anyhow, I'm a bit of all sorts. Scots, English, Irish . . . Polish –

FLETCHER

She got about a bit your mother.

BARROWCLOUGH

Oh no, I didn't mean . . .

FLETCHER

I'm pure London myself. In fact, pure North London. You go to the graveyard in Muswell Hill, it's full of Fletchers. Shall I tell you something? There's always been a Fletcher round my way, right back to . . . oh I should think Henry the Fourth Part One.

BARROWCLOUGH

Oh . . . I haven't got any heritage. I know me grandfather was an ironmonger in Accrington. But before that . . .

FLETCHER

My great-grandfather was William Wellington Fletcher. The last man in England to be hanged for horse-stealing. And Matthew Jarvis Fletcher – he was Newgate with Jack Sheppard, wun' he? That's well known.

BARROWCLOUGH

So it runs in the family, does it – crime, like?

FLETCHER

Possibly. I know there's a load of Fletchers in Australia.

BARROWCLOUGH

So you come from a rough neighbourhood?

FLETCHER

No, I told you – Muswell Hill. It's very suburban, Muswell Hill. Respectable.

BARROWCLOUGH

Broken home?

FLETCHER

Not at all. They've just celebrated their diamond wedding.

BARROWCLOUGH

Oh. I was just wondering why . . .

FLETCHER

Well, when I left school I went round the local Labour and appraised the professional opportunities open to me. Unfortunately my lack of scholastic achievement prevented me from doing the things I really fancied, such as stockbrokerin' or teaching tennis at a girls' school. And I didn't reckon working in a cardboard box factory. So I robbed this sub-post office off the North Circular.

BARROWCLOUGH

And you never looked back since, so to speak.

FLETCHER

No – nor have I ever been short of 3d. stamps.

BARROWCLOUGH

What have you gone down for this time?

FLETCHER

Aw, don't talk about it. Be a farce if it wasn't such a tragedy. Own fault, should have stuck to what I know best. Housebreaking. But I lifts this lorry. Impulse steal. You know what I mean, impulse steal. I think it's a doddle, don't I?

BARROWCLOUGH

I gather it wasn't.

FLETCHER

Yeah, you know why, though – flaming brakes failed. Criminal letting lorries on the road in that condition. And he

was overloaded. So there I was, wiv five ton on me back roarin' down bloody Archway.

BARROWCLOUGH

Wonder you weren't killed.

FLETCHER

I nearly was. Went through three back gardens, went clean through a brick wall and finished up in somebody's tool shed.

BARROWCLOUGH

Did they get you for wilful destruction of property? I mean, knocking that wall down.

FLETCHER

Yeah. And I asked for six other fences to be taken into consideration.

Barrowclough does not react to Fletcher's wit.

FLETCHER

Get it, get it?

BARROWCLOUGH

Pardon?

FLETCHER

Oh never mind.

There is a pause. He fumbles in his pocket and finds some chewing gum.

FLETCHER

Here – tell you what. Have a bit of this.

BARROWCLOUGH

You've only two bits left.

FLETCHER

Yeah . . . what made you take up this lark then?

BARROWCLOUGH

Prison service?

FLETCHER

Yeah, what made you fancy it like?

BARROWCLOUGH

I always wanted a vocation which would satisfy my desire to perform useful public service . . . and get a free house and uniform.

FLETCHER

What's it like, this nick?

BARROWCLOUGH

Oh very good. Modern you see. Experimental. With a cricket pitch and a psychiatrist.

FLETCHER

Oh yeah. Bird's bird though, in' it?

BARROWCLOUGH

Not with this one. If you took advantage of our courses, of our many occupational and/or recreational activities . . . well, you put your mind to it, you could come out an intermediate welder or an accomplished oboe player.

FLETCHER

Oh yeah.

BARROWCLOUGH

Pity you're not in longer, you could have taken up civil engineering.

FLETCHER

Oh pity. That is a pity. Pity I didn't get a ten stretch. Then I could have took my welding finals, and be a doctor of philosophy.

BARROWCLOUGH

(*Tentatively*) I'm a bit of an amateur botanist myself. So sometimes I take some of the prisoners out on the fells to explore the natural phenomena of our countryside.

At this Fletcher's eyes register interest.

FLETCHER

Out on the fells, is it?

BARROWCLOUGH

Yes, lovely views.

FLETCHER

I might put down for that. That might interest me. Natural phenomena of our countryside – how far's the nearest railway station?

BARROWCLOUGH

Oh that's the beauty of it you see, we're miles from anywhere.

FLETCHER

(*Less enthusiastically*) Oh are we.

BARROWCLOUGH

We also have an arts and crafts section. Or you could learn woodwork.

FLETCHER

Listen, squire, I don't want no courses, no reconditioning, resettlement. All I want to do is mind me own business, do my porridge and count the days till I get out.

BARROWCLOUGH

You'll change you know.

FLETCHER

What?

BARROWCLOUGH

Even the most cynical and hardened criminals have changed at this place. They've responded you see to our approach which is based not on

correction and punishment, but sympathy and understanding.
The door of the compartment slides open and an unsympathetic Mackay enters, carrying three cardboard cups.

MACKAY
I forget if you took sugar or not but it makes no difference 'cos I spilt most of yours on the way back, but what you gonna do about it?

FLETCHER
Where's this sympathy and understanding? How's he working at your nick? Blimey, he'd bring back the birch at the drop of an helmet.

MACKAY
What's he on about?

BARROWCLOUGH
Mr Mackay runs several of our group activities.

FLETCHER
Yeah. Like rock-breaking and compulsory pot-holing.

MACKAY
I'll soon have you in shape, Fletcher. I'll soon have you a shadow of your former self.

FLETCHER
I bet he's secretary to the Lord Chief Justice Goddard Appreciation Society.

MACKAY
Just keep your nose clean, lad. Just show me some respect and keep your nose clean, you'll be all right. I'm hard but fair.

FLETCHER
Like Leeds United?

MACKAY
If you like. You play ball with me, and I'll play ball with you, and you'll find me a reasonable man.

FLETCHER
Good, good . . . could I have a look at your *Penthouse* now?

MACKAY
Can you hell!

FLETCHER
You've got to admire consistency . . .
Barrowclough offers Fletcher his Angling Times.

FLETCHER
Try page twenty-four.

4. RAILWAY STATION
A train is leaving the station. As the last coach passes, Fletcher and Barrowclough are walking along the platform. They leave the station. Outside they walk to a waiting minibus.

FLETCHER
How far we got to go then?

MACKAY
About an hour and a half. Across the fells.

FLETCHER
Can I have a Johnny Riddle then?

MACKAY
You should have thought of that earlier.

FLETCHER
I did think of it earlier. There's been

nothing else on my mind for ages.
Why are you so reluctant to let me
go to the lavatory?
Mackay holds up handcuffs.
FLETCHER
Oh I see.
*Barrowclough starts undoing the
minibus doors.*
BARROWCLOUGH
You'd better let him go, we can't stop
in transit.
Mackay unlocks the handcuffs.
MACKAY
All right then, behind the bus.
FLETCHER
Thank you, Mackay.
*He goes round behind the minibus.
He looks at the petrol cap and his
expression changes. Fletcher checks
in the direction of Mackay and
Barrowclough to make sure they are
not watching and takes off the petrol
cap. Then he unzips his flies.
In the distance the minibus can
be seen driving along. Suddenly
it stalls. Mackay gets out. He
walks round to the front of the
minibus and lifts the bonnet.
Barrowclough and Fletcher
join him.*
BARROWCLOUGH
What do you reckon it is?
MACKAY
How do I know? I'm no mechanic.
FLETCHER
Plugs, is it? Or ignition?

MACKAY
Put the bracelets on him.
*Barrowclough starts to comply.
Mackay moves back to try
the starter.*
MACKAY
Don't you be thinking that fate's given
you a last chance of freedom.
FLETCHER
Don't believe in fate.
*The starter makes
unpromising noises.*
BARROWCLOUGH
Sounds like the carburettor.
FLETCHER
Have to get the bus then, won't we?
MACKAY
What bus?
FLETCHER
Hitch a lift then.
MACKAY
Who drives round here on New
Year's Eve?
BARROWCLOUGH
Who drives round here any time?
FLETCHER
Getting a bit parky, in' it?
BARROWCLOUGH
Be dark soon.
MACKAY
God Almighty!
FLETCHER
Don't you know how to fix it then?
Hasn't one of your many instructional
courses taught you how to cope with
mechanical failure?

BARROWCLOUGH

It's survival we'll need out here. Be dark soon. And they forecast snow.

MACKAY

Pull yourself together Mr Barrowclough.

FLETCHER

No need to take it out on him.

MACKAY

Look, there's one thing for it. I'm going on. Going on to the prison. Now listen to me. You do not move. You do not move from here and you do not take the bracelets off him. Right?

BARROWCLOUGH

Right, Mr Mackay.

MACKAY

(*To Fletcher*) And you behave yourself.

FLETCHER

Right, Mr Mackay.

Mackay walks off down the road. Fletcher and Barrowclough are shivering. To keep warm Fletcher flaps his arms across his chest, forgetting the handcuffs. He jerks Barrowclough.

FLETCHER

Sorry, mate.

5. MINIBUS

Outside the wind howls loudly. Barrowclough and Fletcher, still handcuffed, are sitting side by side in the minibus. Barrowclough blows on his hand, as Fletcher blows on his.

FLETCHER

By the time they find us we'll be dead

with exposure. Like Robert Taylor at the end of that picture.

BARROWCLOUGH

What picture?

FLETCHER

Western about buffalo hunting. In the deep frozen North. And he had to spend the night out in the open. Up a tree he was.

BARROWCLOUGH

Why was he up a tree?

FLETCHER

What? Well I 'spect he was avoiding marauding buffalo, driven half-crazy by the extreme cold.

BARROWCLOUGH

Oh yes, marauding buffalo . . .

FLETCHER

Driven half-crazy by the extreme cold. Much as we'll be in an hour or two. Ain't there no houses or farms near here?

BARROWCLOUGH

There's a cottage not far.

FLETCHER

Well, let's go there then.

BARROWCLOUGH

Mr Mackay says we're not to leave the van.

FLETCHER

All right – we'll die in the van.

BARROWCLOUGH

Anyway it will be all locked up, they only use it in the summer.

FLETCHER

So what?

BARROWCLOUGH

How will we get in?

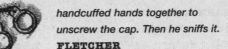

FLETCHER

Mr Barrowclough . . .

BARROWCLOUGH

Yes.

FLETCHER

I'm only a flaming housebreaker, in' I?

6. COTTAGE: LIVING ROOM

It is night time. Fletcher and Barrowclough come in from the kitchen. They walk to an old sofa and sit as near as possible to the glowing fire. They have mugs of black coffee in their outside hands, but their inside hands are still handcuffed together.

BARROWCLOUGH

I wish we had a drop of milk.

FLETCHER

It's the hot drink that counts.

BARROWCLOUGH

And you'd think they'd've had some sugar somewhere.

FLETCHER

Tell you what – try a drop of this in it.

He puts his hand in his pocket and produces a hip flask.

BARROWCLOUGH

What is it?

FLETCHER

I'm not sure –

With this he moves the two

handcuffed hands together to unscrew the cap. Then he sniffs it.

FLETCHER

Scotch.

BARROWCLOUGH

Oh no, anyway – I'm on duty.

FLETCHER

It's medicinal. Help to revive us. Take the chill out of our numbed bones.

BARROWCLOUGH

Where d'you get it?

FLETCHER

It must have accidentally fallen out the back of Mr Mackay's pocket, when he got off the van.

BARROWCLOUGH

You stole it!

FLETCHER

I didn't. I told you, it fell off the back of the van.

He drinks.

BARROWCLOUGH

Is whisky medicinal?

FLETCHER

Yeah. I always feel better after I've had a few.

BARROWCLOUGH

Oh all right then, if it's medicinal.

Fletcher pours some whisky into Barrowclough's mug.

BARROWCLOUGH

That's enough.

Fletcher takes a quick swig out of the flask before pouring some whisky into his coffee. Then he looks at his watch.

FLETCHER
Hey . . . it's New Year now, you know.
BARROWCLOUGH
Is it? Oh, all the best then.
FLETCHER
Yeah, and to you, mate.
They sip their drinks.
FLETCHER
Like *The Defiant Ones*.
BARROWCLOUGH
Beg your pardon?
FLETCHER
That was pictures an' all. *The Defiant Ones*. 'Bout these two convicts on the run, chained together like we are. Only one was black, one was white. Fact, if you had a bit of coloured blood in you, 'stead of all that Polish rubbish you've got, you could have been Sidney Poitier to my Tony Curtis.
BARROWCLOUGH
We have a Cinema Club at the prison. Only last Tuesday we showed *Irrigation in the Gobi Desert*. On the same bill with *Birds of the Farne Islands*.
FLETCHER
Standing room only, was it?
BARROWCLOUGH
No, we didn't have much of a turnout that night.
FLETCHER
I'm amazed.
BARROWCLOUGH
My wife likes the pictures. But we don't go much these days.

FLETCHER
No wonder – so bloomin' remote. Stuck in the middle of Cumberland where you going to find a cinema?
BARROWCLOUGH
That's the trouble. My wife, she feels very bad about being deprived of the excitement and amenities that a city can offer. She's always terribly unsettled every time we come back from our monthly day trip to Workington.
FLETCHER
Oh yes. I can see how the lights of Workington might turn a young girl's head.
BARROWCLOUGH
How d'you mean?
FLETCHER
Well, come on, mate. Amenities in Workington? Ain't got Christianity up here yet so you can't even go to a church social.
BARROWCLOUGH
Different for you – Londoners. My wife's always wanted to be cosmopolitan. Should have put in for a transfer to the Scrubs – or Brixton.
FLETCHER
No, if you was going to go to Brixton, mate, you'd have to be Sidney Poitier.
BARROWCLOUGH
(*Leaning back*) Too late now.
FLETCHER
So er, your old lady feels . . . deprived, does she?

BARROWCLOUGH

Well, she sees a future of frustrated ambitions stretching before her. She doesn't like what I do or where we live. So over the years she's grown bitter and unsettled, full of restless urges. Which have manifested themselves in various ways like bad temper, spots and sleeping with the postman. (*Drinks*) And there were liaisons with other men. We got to rowing all the time. Things went from bad to worse. Eventually we went to see this marriage guidance counsellor.

FLETCHER

That help, did it?

BARROWCLOUGH

It helped her! She ran off with him.

FLETCHER

Oh well, you're well out of it, aren't you, mate. You're well out of a slag like that.

BARROWCLOUGH

She's come back.

FLETCHER

Oh I see . . . well, people change.

Barrowclough moves along the sofa and lies back.

BARROWCLOUGH

I blame myself. I'm a failure. I'm only hanging on to this job by the skin of me teeth. I got so depressed I thought I'd take advantage of the prison psychiatric department. See them about my inferiority complex. Well, it's not a complex really – I am inferior.

FLETCHER

Aw come on, leave it off. Look, I don't know you very well. I can tell that you're a man of kindness, compassion and humanity. Now, you can't buy those, can you? Would you swap them for a colour telly and a penthouse in Workington? 'Course you wouldn't.

BARROWCLOUGH

I suppose not.

Fletcher empties flask into Barrowclough's mug.

FLETCHER

Here finish this. You can't go through life thinking that you should have been something else. You're doing the job you always wanted to do. You must think, this is what I am. I am what I am, and when it's all over I'll look God straight in the eye and say, I've done it my way.

BARROWCLOUGH

I've done it my way.

FLETCHER

Confidence in yourself.

BARROWCLOUGH

Confidence . . .

FLETCHER

Trust your own judgement and initiative.

BARROWCLOUGH

Initiative . . .

FLETCHER

Why don't you take these handcuffs off?

BARROWCLOUGH

(*Not hearing this*) D'you know, I've

never talked to anyone before – not
really talked.

FLETCHER

Yeah – yeah . . . why don't you take
these handcuffs off?

BARROWCLOUGH

Handcuffs?

FLETCHER

It's the circulation, in' it? Cuttin' off the
supply to my head.

BARROWCLOUGH

We have rules . . .

FLETCHER

What about judgement – initiative.
Are you going to do it their way,
or are you going to do it your way?
Confidence in yourself.

*Barrowclough thinks very hard
for a minute, then comes to
a decision.*

BARROWCLOUGH

I'm going to take them off. Yes. I am
taking them off. I am taking them off
because if I don't I'm betraying the
principles of my prison and myself in
approaching prisoners with sympathy
and understanding.

*Fletcher watches anxiously as
Barrowclough fishes for the key.*

BARROWCLOUGH

You are a criminal – habitual and
hereditary. But until we show *you* trust,
how are you going to *learn* trust?

FLETCHER

That is irrefutably true. What more
can I say?

*The handcuffs come off, and both
men rub their wrists with relief.
Barrowclough yawns, lying back
against the sofa.*

BARROWCLOUGH

Made me quite sleepy that whisky has.
Quite drowsy.

FLETCHER

Another good reason for taking them off.
We couldn't have kipped down there
like Babes in the Wood, could we?

BARROWCLOUGH

I can hardly keep me eyes open.

FLETCHER

You get your feet up, my old son.
Get a decent bit of shut-eye. I'll push
these two chairs together.

*He does so, settling in the
chairs, but in a position to
watch Barrowclough.*

BARROWCLOUGH

You know, Fletcher, I hope you do
decide to join my botany group.

FLETCHER

I'll give it serious consideration, squire.

BARROWCLOUGH

I feel a better man for tonight. More
confident. I don't feel a failure. I feel
that for once I've used my judgement,
and I'm right.

FLETCHER

Right?

BARROWCLOUGH

Right about you, Fletcher.

*Fletcher watches Barrowclough
who has fallen asleep.*

FLETCHER

Mr Barrowclough?

There is no reply. Fletcher gets up.

FLETCHER

Mr Barrowclough?

Fletcher rushes out. Barrowclough continues sleeping.

7. COUNTRYSIDE

It is night time. Fletcher escapes. He is seen running and scrambling up and down hillsides. Eventually he reaches the edge of a farm but the fierce barking of a dog forces him to change direction. As dawn breaks he is still running. As he runs past a brick wall, he notices there is a gap in it. Through it can be seen a cottage. Fletcher comes back and looks at the cottage. He decides to check it out. He runs towards the cottage.

8. COTTAGE: SCULLERY

Morning. Fletcher opens a window and climbs into the scullery. He moves one of the doors. Suddenly he

hears a cough (offscreen). He grasps a heavy bucket and moves behind the door. The door opens and Barrowclough walks in.

BARROWCLOUGH

Fletcher, are you out here?

Fletcher drops the bucket in surprise.

FLETCHER

Mr Barrowclough.

BARROWCLOUGH

What a shock you gave me. What are you doing here?

FLETCHER

That's what I'd like to know.

BARROWCLOUGH

What are you doing with that saucepan?

FLETCHER

Milk – milk . . . I've just been out to get you some milk for your coffee – thought I might find a stray cow about.

BARROWCLOUGH

You look terrible, as if you've been up all night.

FLETCHER

Couldn't sleep, could I?

BARROWCLOUGH

It was a very nice thought but all the same you shouldn't have done it. You could have got lost. People are always getting lost on these fells. Wander around in circles they do.

FLETCHER

Do they?

9. FLETCHER'S CELL

Fletcher is lying on his bunk.
Mackay walks in.

MACKAY

So – whose good behaviour last night made him the Governor's blue-eyed boy?

FLETCHER

I must be the first man to have earned remission before I even got here.

MACKAY

Don't give me any of your officious lip, Fletcher. I know you were trying to work one last night.

FLETCHER

On what do you base that supposition, Mr Mackay?

MACKAY

On the evidence of our motor mechanic's report on the van.

FLETCHER

Oh.

MACKAY

It appears that the petrol tank had more in it after our journey than before. Only what was in it certainly was not 5-star. Now I'm going to be watching you like a hawk, 'cos nobody goes over the wall at this prison.

FLETCHER

No, Mr Mackay, no one takes the petrol out of you.

Mackay goes out, passing Barrowclough who walks into the cell.

BARROWCLOUGH

What did you say to the Governor?

FLETCHER

What?

BARROWCLOUGH

What did you say to the Governor?

FLETCHER

Why – give you a rollicking, did he?

BARROWCLOUGH

Far from it. He congratulated me on my handling of the situation. He said I was a credit to the service, praised my judgement and initiative and my capacity to remain calm under crisis.

FLETCHER

That's all right then.

BARROWCLOUGH

But you must have said something.

FLETCHER

All I said was that any naughty thoughts I'd harboured of escape were quickly dispelled by the cool authority of my escort, Mr Barrowclough. A man to whom I later owed my life, owing to the fact that he forced me from the vehicle against my will, to take shelter against the elements, supporting or half-carrying my exhausted body across several miles of rough terrain. Just what anyone would say, really.

BARROWCLOUGH

Did you mean all that, Fletcher?

FLETCHER

No – p'raps I coloured the incidents of the night a little. But I see no reason why you and I shouldn't start the New Year on a good footing with the authorities.

BARROWCLOUGH

I've never been praised before.

FLETCHER

How's it feel?

BARROWCLOUGH

Wonderful. You know, Fletcher, you've done a lot for me the last twenty-four hours. You've given me strength, confidence and . . . friendship. Is there nothing I can do for you in return?

FLETCHER

Well, I expect a few things might occur to me during the ensuing months . . . in fact there is one little thing now.

BARROWCLOUGH

Yes?

FLETCHER

If you could see your way clear to bringing me some reading matter, nothing too heavy, the odd glossy nude.

BARROWCLOUGH

Certainly.

FLETCHER

And when you've got turned round p'raps you'd do something about this cell – like, shifting me to one that faces south-west 'cos I'm not going to get much sun in here, am I? Oh, and this

botany club of yours, nature walks, is it? Outside the prison?

BARROWCLOUGH

That's right.

FLETCHER

Put me down for it will you, as soon as possible.

He walks Barrowclough round the cell, discussing what he can do.

SERIES ONE

→ **EPISODE ONE: NEW FACES, OLD HANDS**

→ **EPISODE TWO: THE HUSTLER**

→ **EPISODE THREE: A NIGHT IN**

→ **EPISODE FOUR: A DAY OUT**

→ **EPISODE FIVE: WAYS AND MEANS**

→ **EPISODE SIX: MEN WITHOUT WOMEN**

MEMORIES

Sydney Lotterby (Producer/Director)
Philip Jackson (Dylan in 'A Day Out')
Tony Osoba (McLaren in the series)

SERIES ONE

EPISODE ONE: NEW FACES, OLD HANDS

1. PRISON LANDING

A key is seen going into lock.
A door opens. Mackay, the chief
Prison Officer and Barrowclough
walk through. They lock the door
and walk along the gantry, stopping
outside a cell door.

MACKAY

The three new arrivals, Mr Leach.
Heslop, Cyril, forty-one. Three years,
robbery third stretch. Thick as two
short planks – no ulcers with that one.
Godber, Leonard Arthur, twenty-three.
First offender, two years breaking and
entering. Seems somewhat naïve.
Could be corrupted. Possibly by this
one – Fletcher, Norman Stanley, forty-
two. Five years. He's the one I brought
up from Brixton. Knows the score,
done a lot of bird, water off a duck's
back. (*Stepping back from spyhole*) I'll
be watching that one.

2. RECEPTION ROOM

Weak sun is filtering through a
barred window.

MACKAY

(*Voiceover*) What a beautiful day.

The camera reveals Mackay
standing at the window looking out.

MACKAY

For the time of year, quite astonishing.
Beautiful day.

The camera now shows Fletcher,
Godber and Heslop standing in a
line on the other side of the room.

FLETCHER

Oh lovely. P'raps later on we can all go
out for a cycle ride.

MACKAY

Know what they say about New
Year's Day? "What you do on the
First Day of the Year, you do all the
year round." In the case of you
three gentlemen that's perfectly true.
(*Addressing Lennie*) You, laddy –
you Mr Godber – first time, isn't it?
You must be wondering what an
average day in prison is like. Tell
him, Fletcher.

FLETCHER
It's exactly like the day before,
Mr Mackay.
MACKAY
The voice of experience. And tell him
how the average day begins, Fletcher.
FLETCHER
Begins at 7.00 a.m. You'll be woken
by a persistent and deafening bell.
Then the screws will come round –
MACKAY
I beg your pardon.
FLETCHER
The prison officers will come round.
Offering such encouragements as
'Wakey wakey, get your socks on,
move you 'orrible creatures.' We shall
respond to this badinage with such
remarks as 'Good morning, sir, Good
Lord is that the time,' or 'Who's been
having your old lady while you've been
on night duty?'
MACKAY
Very comical, Fletcher. Eight o'clock
slop out, eight ten breakfast. Eight
fifteen return to cell, nine o'clock –
yes, Fletcher?
FLETCHER
Slop out again, Mr Mackay, followed
by work till eleven fifteen when we –
MACKAY
Exercise. Walking in pairs, five to six
yards apart, no conversing to pairs in
front or behind. This is followed by the
highlight of the day, quiet Fletcher I'm
asking Heslop.

FLETCHER
Who?
MACKAY
You've been inside Heslop, what is,
the highlight of the day?
HESLOP
Er . . . er . . . visiting hours?
MACKAY
We're in Cumberland, man. A barren
windswept fell north of the Pennines.
We are two weeks from Euston! When
you see your loved ones it'll be the
highlight of the *year*.
*Fletcher turns to an increasingly
dismayed Lennie.*
FLETCHER
Glad you came?
MACKAY
Fletcher –
FLETCHER
Sir?
MACKAY
Highlight of the day.
FLETCHER
Highlight of the day – dinner, sir.
MACKAY
Which is –
FLETCHER
Nourishing.
MACKAY
Nourishing is it not.
FLETCHER
Can't wait, sir.
MACKAY
Midday, bang up.
Lennie looks hopeful.

MACKAY

Not what you think, laddy – back to your cells. Thirteen hundred, slop out, work, tea, evening association, which means in principle that you can follow a wide range of recreational activities; which in practice means television or ping pong.

HESLOP

Telly?

FLETCHER

Yeah, but only till seven. When there's only news and kids stuff. So if you're a fan of *Z Cars*, my son, forget it. You'll have to get your kicks from the Wombles of bleedin' Wimbledon.

MACKAY

Seven thirty, slop out, supper, seven forty-five, lights out, any questions?

FLETCHER

Any point?

MACKAY

None whatsoever. At ease.

He starts to prepare for documentation.

LENNIE

So this is Colditz.

FLETCHER

Colditz! You're joking. Compared to this place Colditz was a doddle. Load of public schoolboys playing leapfrog and making tunnels. This is nick this is. We spend our day slopping out and sewing mailbags. And by seven forty-five our lights are out. Colditz that time of night,

they'd be brewing cocoa and having pillow fights.

There is a knock on the door.

Lennie takes out a cigarette.

MACKAY

(*Crossing to Lennie*) Godber, who said you could smoke – did I say you could smoke?

FLETCHER

(*Taking the cigarette*) Don't think he wants you to smoke.

LENNIE

I was trying to give 'em up anyway.

FLETCHER

I'll help you.

Barrowclough comes in with documents.

MACKAY

I'm leaving you with Mr Barrowclough. Oh one more thing. Nice to have you with us.

He leaves.

HESLOP

My wife was coming next week.

FLETCHER

What? Who said that?

HESLOP

He says once a year. My wife was coming next week. Wrote to me. Staying overnight with her cousin in Barrow-in-Furness. Not fair. Not fair if she has to stay there indefinitely.

FLETCHER

Not fair on anyone to stay in Barrow-in-Furness.

BARROWCLOUGH

Heslop.

FLETCHER

Who?

BARROWCLOUGH

Will you step up here, please.
Christian name?

HESLOP

Cyril.

BARROWCLOUGH

Date of birth?

HESLOP

1st April 1933.

He hands over his personal effects
to Barrowclough who puts them
in box.

LENNIE

What's happening now?

FLETCHER

We're about to be dehumanised. First
they give us a number, take away our
personal possessions. Then they give
us a thorough medical check-up, and
we have a bath in six inches of
lukewarm water. Watch out for the
bath-house cleaners.

LENNIE

Why?

FLETCHER

Lot of trustee poofs work the
bath-house.

He crosses the room and sits down.

LENNIE

Know all the form, don't you?

He sits down.

Been here before?

FLETCHER

Not here – all the same though.
Porridge is porridge, in' it?

LENNIE

First time for me. Don't know how I'll
get through.

FLETCHER

Cheer up. Could be worse. State
this country's in. Could be free.
Out there with no work, and a
crumbling economy. Think how
'orrible that would be. Nothing to
do but go to bed early and increase
the population.

LENNIE

Won't be doing that for a while.

FLETCHER

Oh no, course not. Shouldn't have
said that, tasteless joke.

LENNIE

I'm going to feel ever so deprived.
'Cos I had this fiancée, Denise, who
was ever so active in that direction.

FLETCHER

You'll have to drink a lot of tea.

LENNIE

What good's a cup of tea going to do?

FLETCHER

It's what they put in it.

LENNIE

What?

FLETCHER

Something which will moderate your
memories of Denise.

LENNIE

I don't drink tea.

FLETCHER

You are in trouble.

He pauses.

FLETCHER

So's the bloke you share a cell with.

LENNIE

I'll have to throw myself into my mailbags – is that what you do here?

FLETCHER

Depends. Word of advice, son. What you tell 'em today can decide how tolerable your life here's going to be. I mean, if you want to work somewhere cushy and warm, like the kitchens or the library or the Governor's office, then you got to invent yourself a new career.

LENNIE

Oh.

Heslop, now in his underclothes, moves off to wait.

BARROWCLOUGH

All right. Let's have one of you.

Fletcher and Lennie get up. Fletcher gestures to Lennie to sit down.

FLETCHER

Me, Mr Barrowclough.

He winks at Lennie.

BARROWCLOUGH

It's Fletcher, of course, isn't it?

FLETCHER

Yes, Mr Barrowclough.

BARROWCLOUGH

Christian name?

FLETCHER

Norman Stanley.

BARROWCLOUGH

Date of birth?

FLETCHER

2–2–32.

BARROWCLOUGH

Next of kin?

FLETCHER

My beloved Isobel. The little woman. Well, she ain't so little. I said to her the other day, Isobel, I'll never get over you, I'll have to get up and go round.

He laughs and turns to the others for their reaction. Heslop does not react.

BARROWCLOUGH

Address?

FLETCHER

107 Alexandria Park Crescent, N.5.

BARROWCLOUGH

Occupation?

FLETCHER

Librarian during the day.

BARROWCLOUGH

During the day?

FLETCHER

Yeah. At night I was a chef. Library or the kitchen, I don't mind.

3. PRISON GOVERNOR'S OFFICE

Inside the office there is a tropical fish tank. Venables, the Governor, is

*sprinkling food on the surface of
the water.*
*The office is furnished strictly to
Home Office specifications in terms
of furniture, filing cabinets and
cream distemper. On one wall there
is a professional diploma, and a
photograph of a younger Venables
as a policeman in Kuala Lumpur.
On his desk is a photograph of his
son, Guy, graduating at Keele
University in Geography.
Venables takes the Daily Telegraph
which is on his desk. His books
are about the law, reform,
rehabilitation and the diseases
of tropical fish. Venables looks
into the tank rather anxiously
when there is a knock at the
door, and Mackay enters,
coming to attention.*

MACKAY
Good morning, Governor.

VENABLES
Not sure if it is, Mr Mackay, not sure if
it is.

MACKAY
Oh, sir? What's wrong.

*Venables beckons him across to the
tank. Mackay registers impatience.*

VENABLES
It's my four-eyed butterfly fish.

MACKAY
Would that be one with four eyes, sir?

VENABLES
No, no, it's just called that. *Chaetodon*

Capistratus. (*Pointing him out*) There's
the little fellow, this one.

MACKAY
(*Bending down with Venables to look
at the fish*) Poorly is he, sir?

VENABLES
You noticed?

MACKAY
I assumed, from your concern.

VENABLES
Yes. I'm rather afraid, Mr Mackay that
he may have developed fin rot.

MACKAY
Oh dear, sir.

He stands up.

VENABLES
Either that or lymphocystis.

MACKAY
Oh dear, sir.

VENABLES
(*Stands up*) Contagious, you see.
Have to isolate the little fellow.

MACKAY
Much as I've had to do with Evans, sir.

Venables turns away from his fish.

VENABLES
Evans?

MACKAY
Had to isolate him again, sir.

VENABLES
What has he done now?

He crosses to the desk.

MACKAY
Been eating light bulbs, sir.

VENABLES

Light bulbs? Did he say why he was eating light bulbs?

MACKAY

Yes, sir. Said it was because he couldn't get hold of any razor blades.

Venables sits down.

VENABLES

What have you done with him?

MACKAY

Locked him in his cell, sir. Taking the precautions first of all of removing the light bulb.

VENABLES

Is the MO free?

MACKAY

He's with the new arrivals at the moment, sir. But I can hurry them through.

VENABLES

As quick as possible. This is a very urgent situation.

MACKAY

I'll get him to Evans right away, sir.

VENABLES

I don't mean Evans. I mean here.

MACKAY

Here?

VENABLES

Fin rot can be fatal, Mr Mackay.

4. MEDICAL ROOM

Inside Fletcher, Lennie and Heslop are sitting on a bench waiting for the Medical Officer.

FLETCHER

Oh, I meant to tell you – when you see the doc tell him you've got bad feet.

LENNIE

Why?

FLETCHER

'Cos then you might get your brothel creepers back. Otherwise you'll have to wear those prison-issue shoes. Guarantee you bad feet for the rest of your life, they will.

LENNIE

Oh, I see.

Heslop starts to laugh. The others look at him.

FLETCHER

It's not funny. Perfectly true.

HESLOP

No, I don't mean that. I mean that's funny about your wife being a big woman and you havin' to get up and go round.

FLETCHER

Oh. I see. Thank you. Anyhow, remember that about the feet. What religion are you?

LENNIE

C of E, I suppose.

FLETCHER

That's no good. Get no perks with C of E. Whereas if you was a Sikh you could grow your hair long. Or if you was a Muslim they'd have to send you in special grub from outside.

LENNIE

Don't like Chinese food.

FLETCHER

Muslim ain't Chinese.

LENNIE

What is Muslim food then?

FLETCHER

What? . . . Well it's . . . it's well, it's more exotic grub than the filth you'll eat here, otherwise the Muslims wouldn't eat it, would they? Or you could say you were Jewish. Yeah, say you're Jewish. Oh no, you couldn't get away with that, could you? Doctor's just going to examine you. He'd spot the evidence.

LENNIE

Evidence?

FLETCHER

With Jews it's only circumstantial. (*Explaining*) They been circumstanted.

Medical Officer enters, coughing, and walks across to the table.

MEDICAL OFFICER

Tropical fish.

FLETCHER

Pardon?

MEDICAL OFFICER

Nothing . . . I'm the (*Coughing*) Medical Officer.

FLETCHER

That's reassuring, in' it?

MEDICAL OFFICER

Now I have to give you men a stringent medical. It's important that we ascertain your medical history and state of health. (*Coughing again*) Right, Fletcher.

Fletcher limps forward. During the questioning a cursory inspection takes place, with particular attention to the armpits.

MEDICAL OFFICER

Have you ever had crabs?

FLETCHER

No – I don't eat fish.

The Medical Officer winces.

MEDICAL OFFICER

Lice?

FLETCHER

No.

MEDICAL OFFICER

VD?

FLETCHER

No.

MEDICAL OFFICER

(*Looking in Fletcher's ear*) Suffer from any illness?

FLETCHER

Bad feet.

MEDICAL OFFICER

Suffer from any illness?

FLETCHER

Bad feet.

MEDICAL OFFICER

Paid a recent visit to a doctor or hospital?

FLETCHER

Only for my bad feet.

MEDICAL OFFICER

Are you now or have you been at any time a practising homosexual?

FLETCHER

With these feet? Who'd want me?

MEDICAL OFFICER

Right – A1.

He stamps Fletcher's form.

FLETCHER

A1 – hang on, hang on. I can hardly walk.

MEDICAL OFFICER

Fletcher – everyone in this prison's trying to pull something, (*crossing to the scales*) lying about their feet or their teeth or their eyesight or their appendix. And on top of that I've got a Governor who's got fin rot.

FLETCHER

Got what rot?

MEDICAL OFFICER

Fish, tropical bloody fish.

He puts Fletcher under the height measure.

FLETCHER

Oh? Interest of his, is it?

MEDICAL OFFICER

Obsession. That and pigs.

FLETCHER

Pigs?

MEDICAL OFFICER

(*Crossing to desk*) He's started a prison farm to indulge his interest in livestock. Only it's the rest of us who have to look after it. His pigs and his fish and his favourite Jersey cow.

I'm a man of medicine not a vet. Half the pills in here are for animals. Prisoner came in here yesterday with earache and I gave him pills to dry up his milk.

He takes a spoon of medicine.

FLETCHER

You must be rushed off your feet, doc.

MEDICAL OFFICER

I cannot cope, man.

FLETCHER

Good job they ain't bad feet like mine.

MEDICAL OFFICER

You're A1. I've told you. (*Pointing to some flasks on the table*) You see those flasks? I want you to fill one.

FLETCHER

From here?

MEDICAL OFFICER

Behind the screen. Now, where's Heslop?

Heslop walks toward the Medical Officer as Fletcher takes the flask.

LENNIE

Didn't pull that one did you, Fletch?

FLETCHER

What?

LENNIE

Prison shoes for you, eh.

FLETCHER

All right, sonny Jim. Lose a few, lose a

few. But my little chat was invaluable. Know something about the Governor, don't I? That's another priority for your first day.

LENNIE

Oh. I see, yes.

FLETCHER

Know your Governor.

LENNIE

Here, Fletcher.

FLETCHER

What?

LENNIE

What's he mean by practising homosexual?

FLETCHER

One who ain't quite got it right yet. Cheers.

Goes behind the screen.

5. PRISON MESS

Barrowclough and other Prison Officers sit at a table playing cards. Fletcher, Lennie and Heslop move to another table with trays of food.

LENNIE

Will we eat with everyone else tonight?

They all sit down.

FLETCHER

Don't be in no hurry to get thrown in with the others. Bunch of criminals, they are. And don't eat too much of that stuff. Otherwise you might dull your palate for tonight's piss de resistance.

LENNIE

What's it likely to be?

FLETCHER

Likely to be lumpy, lukewarm, grey and gritty. I told you to say you was a Muslim.

HESLOP

Sheep's eyes.

FLETCHER

Yeah – what?

HESLOP

What Muslims eat. Figs. Desert. Wadis and things.

FLETCHER

Oh I see. Yeah well . . . thank you, Lawrence of Arabia.

LENNIE

Why didn't you put down Muslim?

FLETCHER

I don't need to, do I? Going to be working in the kitchens.

LENNIE

But they haven't allocated us jobs yet.

Fletcher indicates the card players.

FLETCHER

Look, that screw. Barrowclough. Tall one. Looks like Arthur Askey on stilts. Well, I got him there, ain't I? Putty. He'll see me all right.

LENNIE

How come?

FLETCHER

He brought me up from Brixton. Handcuffed we was. Well, you establish a rapport with a man what you're handcuffed to on a long trip.

LENNIE

S'pose you must do. Specially when you go to the lavatory.

FLETCHER

(*Put out slightly*) Oh, you've got a sense of humour, I see. Come in handy during the grim nightmare of your next two years.

LENNIE

Will it be that bad?

FLETCHER

Listen – the important thing is to remember who you once was. And to keep a bit of that person intact up here.

He taps his temple.

FLETCHER

Don't get bitter, or militant, or try to screw the system, 'cos it'll only screw you. Just keep your nose clean, bide your time and do your porridge.

LENNIE

I'm only here due to tragic circumstances.

FLETCHER

Which were?

LENNIE

I got caught.

FLETCHER

Oh yes, I've had a few tragedies of that nature.

LENNIE

It was my fiancée, Denise. She has this nice flat in a tower block in Smethwick. Well, it's her mam's, like. Very nice. Overlooks the M6. So

I thought I'd get her some nice things for it. So I didn't want to have far to cart 'em, like, so I did the flat next door, 'cos I knew he'd be away, like, 'cos he drives a juggernaut from West Bromwich to Brussels. Only he had a puncture outside Coventry and came home and found me and kicked me head in.

HESLOP

Ramsgate.

FLETCHER

Pardon?

HESLOP

Took the wife.

FLETCHER

Took the wife where Mr Heslop?

HESLOP

To see *Lawrence of Arabia*. It was raining see. Couldn't go on the beach at Ramsgate. Took her to the pictures.

FLETCHER

Rains a lot in Ramsgate.

HESLOP

Rained the next day.

FLETCHER

Told you it would.

HESLOP

But she'd seen the film on at the other cinema so we come home. Although we did stop for a cup of tea at her sister's in Sidcup.

FLETCHER

Why don't you put that on a postcard and send it to Tony Blackburn's magic moments.

HESLOP

What?

FLETCHER

One thing I shall miss about not sharing a cell with you two will be the cut and thrust of your intellectual conversation.

LENNIE

Won't we all be in together?

FLETCHER

No, I'm having a single cell. I like my privacy. I prefers to be alone see. Don't like sharing. Don't like dominoes or cribbage or other people's sweaty feet.

LENNIE

I'd prefer a single cell. 'Cos I want to study.

FLETCHER

Study?

LENNIE

Well, I've had an education. I've got an 'O' Level in geography.

FLETCHER

Oh, that'll come in handy that will. If there's an escape party from here you're bound to be included 'cos you'll know the way to Carlisle station.

LENNIE

Very interesting, geography. It's all part of education.

FLETCHER

Yeah, but it's not the sort of subject you can make a career out of. Only reason people learn geography is so they can teach other people geography. Ain't no use to anybody. No use

knowing the capital of Siam or what an isthmus is.

LENNIE

Well, I don't have to use geography, I can learn a trade they said.

FLETCHER

In principle; you can come out with a diploma in some glamour occupation like house-decorating or shoe repairing. Or you can become a welder. There's a riveting profession – get it, get it.

He looks at Heslop.

HESLOP

What?

FLETCHER

Oh never mind.

LENNIE

Here, won't I be able to learn a trade then?

FLETCHER

Oh yes, there are certain things you can learn inside that you can become expert at. Like how to open a safe, steal a car, forge a banknote. Bloke I was in Maidstone with – Charlie Mossop, first offender he was, by the time he come out he was a brilliant forger. But brilliant. And he only went in for reckless driving.

LENNIE

I'm fed up with crime, I want to go straight.

FLETCHER

(*Looking appalled*) How old are you, son?

LENNIE

Twenty-three.

FLETCHER

Twenty-three and you want to go straight, what sort of attitude is that? Got your whole life before you.

HESLOP

What's an isthmus?

FLETCHER

What, what? What is it now, Dr Bronowski?

HESLOP

What you said – isthmus. What's an isthmus?

FLETCHER

Oh. Well it's a thing in' it . . . a thing in geography. A geographical expression –

LENNIE

It's a strip of land joining together two larger pieces of land.

FLETCHER

Yeah, strip of land, right.

LENNIE

See, education.

FLETCHER

I'm not saying don't put down for the educational classes. Current affairs, pottery, archaeology. I'll be putting down for that. What. Hour every night in a nice warm classroom. Bit of luck you get a woman teacher. See a bit of thigh when she drops her chalk. Oh yes, I've nothing against education.

Lennie gets out a packet of cigarettes, which he offers to the others.

LENNIE

Fag?

FLETCHER

Oh ta.

Fletcher and Heslop both take one and put them straight into their pockets.

LENNIE

Oh.

FLETCHER

We're not bein' impolite, Lennie, my son. It's just that him and me we've been inside before, and you see inside, snout is like gold. You was mad to give us those.

LENNIE

But you took them.

FLETCHER

Ah yes well, learn the hard way, isn't it? Learn not to be so lavish, you're not Paul Getty. Should have just lit one and shared it.

Heslop takes Lennie's cigarette and has a puff at it, then passes it to Fletcher.

Barrowclough gets up from the card game and comes to them.

BARROWCLOUGH

Right, drink up lads, shall we?

FLETCHER

What's next on the agenda, Mr Barrowclough?

BARROWCLOUGH

Got to see the Governor, haven't we? Right. Clear the stuff up. Put that fag out.

*Fletcher pinches out the cigarette
and pockets it.*

FLETCHER
Waste not, want not.

LENNIE
Here –

FLETCHER
Learn the hard way, son. Now come
on, clear up.

*Lennie and Heslop take their
trays away. Fletcher takes
Barrowclough aside.*

FLETCHER
Did you er – get what I asked you for,
Mr Barrowclough?

BARROWCLOUGH
Well, there wasn't much in the library,
just this booklet. (*Gets it from his
pocket*) *Know your Tropical Fish*.

FLETCHER
Oh good – it's my hobby, you see.

BARROWCLOUGH
D'you know, by an extraordinary
coincidence that's the Governor's hobby.

FLETCHER
Really? Would you believe it.

BARROWCLOUGH
Likes all animals. On the local
committee of the RSPCA. Between
ourselves I often think he'd have
been better off in charge of a zoo than
a prison.

FLETCHER
Caged animals – well, we're all the
same, ain't we? Talking of cages,
you will get me one facing south,

won't you – on me own. I'm not a
sharer you see. I mean the boy,
he's all right, but he sniffs a lot.
And Heslop, he's not on my
intellectual level. Don't think he's
on anybody's level really. If the
Governor *did* open a zoo, Heslop'd
be a big attraction.

BARROWCLOUGH
Fletcher, you must understand
that I'm a Prison Officer and
you are a prisoner. You must
recognise that relationship. I am
not here to be cajoled or coerced
into doing what you want, when
you want it.

FLETCHER
Mr Barrowclough, please, of course
not. Would I ever?

*He turns and leaves. Barrowclough
is left holding Fletcher's tray.*

BARROWCLOUGH
Well, as long as that's understood.

*Barrowclough realises he has got
the tray and bangs it down on
the table.*

6. EXERCISE YARD

*Camera shows the prisoners
marching in the exercise yard.
Fletcher is marching;
Heslop is marching;
Lennie is marching.
Mackay watches Fletcher and
Barrowclough march across
the yard.*

7. GOVERNOR'S OFFICE

Venables, Mackay and Barrowclough are in the Governor's office.

MACKAY

Fetch them in, Mr Barrowclough.

Barrowclough brings in Fletcher, Lennie and Heslop.

MACKAY

Stand straight in front of the Governor. (*Pointing them out*) Heslop, Godber, Fletcher, sir.

VENABLES

Thank you, Mr Mackay. Now you men have been sent here for varying offences and varying terms of imprisonment. This is not a top-grade security prison, you are C class prisoners. However, if any of you abuses the less stringent security measures which we impose here, you will quickly find that we are on you like a ton of . . .

He breaks off noticing that Fletcher is staring in another direction.

VENABLES

Are you listening, Fletcher?

MACKAY

Face the front.

FLETCHER

I am sorry, Mr Venables, sir. I just couldn't help noticing your aquarium. Interest of mine, you see, indoor fish, tropical fish.

VENABLES

Oh really?

MACKAY

All right, Fletcher.

FLETCHER

Sorry, Mr Mackay. Sorry, sir. But something is bothering me.

VENABLES

What is bothering you, Fletcher?

FLETCHER

Well, sir, this is only a first impression but . . . I think your four-eyed butterfly fish has got a touch of fin rot.

8. FLETCHER'S CELL

There are two bunks and a chair inside the cell. Heslop is lying on the top bunk rolling a cigarette. Lennie sits on the chair, while Fletcher lies on the bottom bunk reading a copy of Farmers Weekly.

LENNIE

Crafty old nurk, aren't you, Fletcher?

FLETCHER

Hang about, I'm just finishing this on Artificial Insemination what the Governor gave me.

LENNIE

Fell for it, didn't he? He really believed your interest in fish and livestock.

FLETCHER

Ain't been a bad day. I told you this is the day what conditions how tolerable your life'll become here.

LENNIE

I think he was impressed by my 'O' Level in geography.

The cell door is unlocked and Mackay enters, carrying a pair of shoes.

MACKAY

All right, lads, on your feet. Exam results. Been a full and exciting day. Firstly Godber – your shoes, courtesy of the M.O.

He hands Lennie his shoes.

FLETCHER

How d'you work that?

LENNIE

Told him about my flat feet, didn't I?

MACKAY

Which he believes, Fletcher. Young Godber's still got some credibility. Unlike yourself. I'm afraid we're having to split this lovely threesome up. One of you're going to a sing.

FLETCHER

Oh yes – only right.

He starts to gather his things.

MACKAY

Not so fast, Fletcher.

FLETCHER

You what?

MACKAY

Get your things together, Godber.

FLETCHER

Godber – him. A cell on his own.

MACKAY

Governor thought it would be more conducive to study.

LENNIE

Oh, that's lovely. I didn't fancy sharing – no offence.

FLETCHER

You didn't fancy sharing. What about me – you leaving me here with the Brain of Britain here?

MACKAY

There'll be three of you. We're moving Evans in here.

FLETCHER

Evans! That Welsh lunatic who eats light bulbs!

MACKAY

Only when he can't get razor blades.

FLETCHER

Oh marvellous. Can I have permission to grow a beard?

MACKAY

Jobs. Kitchen – Godber.

LENNIE

Oh that'll be nice – all warm and second helpings.

MACKAY

Library – Heslop.

FLETCHER

Library! Him! He's an illiterate.

HESLOP

I read a book once. It was green.

FLETCHER

And what's he got the kitchen for. First time in, God Almighty he should be breaking rocks or something – paying his dues. This is victimisation! I'm an old hand, I should have something befitting my seniority.

MACKAY

Special duties.

FLETCHER

What?

MACKAY

Special duties. Who's the Governor's blue-eyed boy?

FLETCHER

Well, we had a bit of a rapport yes. Cementated by our common interest in all things bright and beautiful, all creatures great and small.

MACKAY

Governor said you're just the man he's been waiting for.

FLETCHER

Oh. Oh I see. All right then. (*Turning to Lennie*) Kitchens – eat your heart out, Godber. Green it was.

9. PRISON FARM

The prison Governor and Fletcher are outside in the prison farm.

GOVERNOR

Good morning, Fletcher.

FLETCHER

Morning, sir.

GOVERNOR

It always gives me great pleasure to place a man in a job which gives him real fulfilment.

FLETCHER

Fulfilment, yes, thank you, sir.

Fletcher is cleaning out the pigsty. He is surrounded by pigs.

GOVERNOR

Oh, the article in *Farmers Weekly*, did you finish it?

FLETCHER

I'm afraid I didn't, sir. Oh, I would have done, only Evans ate it.

Fletcher continues digging.

SERIES ONE

EPISODE TWO: THE HUSTLER

1. HEN HOUSE

Chickens in a coop. Offstage the voices of Fletcher and Ives can be heard.

IVES

Come on, come on. You can do it, my love.

FLETCHER

Come on gel, come on gel. Force it out. Effort! Effort!

IVES

Come on, my son.

FLETCHER

Hang about. It's a girl, you nurk. 'My son'.

IVES

How d'you know it's a girl?

FLETCHER

Hens is all girls, Ives.

IVES

Are they?

FLETCHER

Course they are. All hens are females. Your male is your cock.

IVES

Oh yes . . . here, listen, there's a hell of a lot more females than males.

FLETCHER

'Course there are. That's why your cock always looks so smug. Always knows it's there. Hence the expression, cock sure.

They resume their encouragements.

FLETCHER

Come on gel, force it out.

IVES

Mine's looking inament.

Fletches takes a quick look at Ives's bird.

FLETCHER

Nodded off, she has.

IVES

Here, listen, want to double the bet?

FLETCHER

Certainly.

IVES

Right. Done.

FLETCHER

You certainly have been.

IVES

Why?

FLETCHER

Jackpot.

An egg rolls down its little channel.

Fletcher picks it up.

FLETCHER

Thanks, gel. And thank you, Ives.

Ives disgruntledly takes out two handed-rolled snouts from his breast pocket. He is about to hand them over when he has a thought.

IVES

Listen, double or quits.

He takes the egg from Fletcher and puts both hands behind his back.

IVES

Which hand's it in? Go on, fair's fair. Double or quits.

FLETCHER

All right.

Ives holds out his hands. Fletcher thinks, then taps one.

FLETCHER

That one.

Ives shouts with delight and opens an empty hand.

IVES

Ha! We're even.

FLETCHER

Oh in that one, was it?

He squeezes Ives's other hand breaking the egg within.

IVES

(*Shaking off the sticky egg from his hand*) Oh Fletcher, not funny, not funny.

FLETCHER

Can't take a yolk some people.

VOICE OFF

(*Shouting*) Ives!

Ives picks his bucket up and leaves.

Fletcher checks that he has gone and then moves to Ives's hen.

FLETCHER

Poor old Ives, what a loser. If Elizabeth Taylor had triplets and he was one of them, he'd be the one in the middle on the bottle . . . You're not a loser are you, gel? You'd 'a won by rights, if I hadn't cut off your access.

He removes a crumpled handkerchief from the channel beneath the chicken and an egg rolls down. He goes to the door and checks then puts some eggs in a bag of grain.

FLETCHER

This, girls, is what you might call one of the perks of this job. Now with those eggs I can get myself a quarter ounce of shag, or two tubes of toothpaste, or three bars of fruit and nut, or I could take them along to E Wing and see Smutty Garland, King of the Porn. Trade 'em in for one of his dirty books. Filled with full frontal naked nubiles . . . No, I'd rather have the fruit and nut.

2. PRISON FARM

Close up of a trough. Swill is being poured into it. Pigs come over to eat. Fletcher looks at them.

FLETCHER

Gawd, you're messy. And you eat like pigs. Here, can you lot run? There's a thought, pig-racing. That would make a nice little flutter, wouldn't it? The Slade Prison Selling Plate for Pigs . . . the Royal Cheltenham Pork Cup . . . I could have a book. Become an owner, and have my own stable – sty . . . Yeah, thought appeals, thought appeals. The Bacon Handicap.
He laughs and moves away.

FLETCHER

The Bacon Handicap.
A pig looks up at Fletcher.

3. HEN HOUSE

Fletcher walks into the hen house and looks at the chickens.

FLETCHER

Hello, darlings, still trying, are you?

BARROWCLOUGH

(*Appearing*) 'Morning, Fletcher.

FLETCHER

Oh morning, Mr Barrowclough. How's things?

BARROWCLOUGH

That man Ives, what was he doing round here?

FLETCHER

What – oh he was just dropping in on his way to the silos.

BARROWCLOUGH

Wasn't taking bets, was he?

FLETCHER

Bets?

BARROWCLOUGH

It has been suspected that he's Harry Grout's runner.

FLETCHER

(*Innocently*) Runner? Mr Barrowclough. Runner?

BARROWCLOUGH

Taking bets.

FLETCHER

Oh yeah.

BARROWCLOUGH

Harry Grout's a long-term prisoner and he's not the pleasantest of men, and he seems to exert an unhealthy influence. We're fairly sure that he runs both gambling and tobacco in this prison. I – I'm telling you this Fletcher because . . . well you're a good chap and I wouldn't want you to get sucked into that circle.

FLETCHER

Don't worry. Oh Mr Barrowclough, have no fear on that score. Gambling appals me. Seen the consequences too often.

BARROWCLOUGH

It's like a plague in this prison.

FLETCHER

Not one of my vices – got too many other things to do – 'ere do you think pigs can run?

BARROWCLOUGH

Run?

FLETCHER

Could they be trained to run?

BARROWCLOUGH

Why?

FLETCHER

What! Oh I just thought it would make a change for them. The exercise.

BARROWCLOUGH

Well, it's good to see you're taking an interest in your fellow creatures.

He goes to sit down but is stopped by Fletcher.

FLETCHER

Don't sit there, Mr Barrowclough. You'll dirty your uniform. I'll get you a chair.

He moves to get a chair and then back again.

BARROWCLOUGH

I gather you're settling in, down on the farm.

FLETCHER

(*Goes to sit, realises*) Oh . . . it ain't too bad, tell the truth. When I was assigned to it, well I took offence at first, 'cos I've never been a rural man. Always had a deep mistrust of animals.

BARROWCLOUGH

I thought you told the Governor you had a keen interest in farming and livestock.

FLETCHER

(*Guiltily*) Oh, yes, that. Farming and livestock, yes. Just that I ain't so keen on the animal end of it.

BARROWCLOUGH

(*Obviously not seeing*) Oh, I see. You're very lucky to be here, you know. Normally a trusty gets a job like this. Privileged position.

FLETCHER

Don't think I don't appreciate it, Mr Barrowclough. I'm sure you had something to do with it, knowing your kind and generous nature.

BARROWCLOUGH

No, nothing to do with –

FLETCHER

(*Knowingly*) Say no more, say no more. When you going to get me a single cell then?

BARROWCLOUGH

It's not in my power, Fletcher.

FLETCHER

See, I'm not a sharer. And those two I'm in with, Heslop and Evans, well I mean there's no rapport . . . no intellectual stimulus. You know what I mean.

BARROWCLOUGH

Evans, yes, he's a strange fellow. Is he still eating light bulbs?

FLETCHER

No, he's got a taste for other things now. Ate my shaving mirror yesterday.

BARROWCLOUGH

I'm afraid there's little I can do. And it's wrong of you to ask me.

FLETCHER

What? Oh no. Wait. Please. You mustn't think – you must NOT think that I'm trying to influence you, to coerce you to . . . I can hardly bring myself to say the word . . . BRIBE you.

Barrowclough reacts.

FLETCHER

What – a prison officer what's been
specially chosen by the Home Office
for his integrity and honesty.

He has a quick look round.

FLETCHER

'Ere would a dozen eggs make
a difference?

Barrowclough looks shocked.

FLETCHER

No, of course not.

4. PRISON FARM/PRISON

*Barrowclough is seen locking up.
Fletcher is waiting for him.
Barrowclough moves to Fletcher
and they walk off together to the
prison gates. There they knock. The
door is opened by a Prison Officer
and they go in.*

FLETCHER

Lovely day for it.

PRISON OFFICER

You won't be getting it for a long time.

FLETCHER

You obviously ain't had it for a
long time.

Prison Officer reacting.

5. PRISON KITCHEN

*Lennie is washing down one of the
big hotplates. Also in the kitchen is*

*a trusty cook; he is called
Lukewarm, after his cooking.
Fletcher enters, putting down his
boxes of eggs on the working
surface. He has with him his plastic
bag of grain with the concealed
eggs. He's followed in by Prison
Officer Appleton.*

FLETCHER

There y'are, Lukewarm. Three dozen
and two.

LUKEWARM

What? What's wrong with those hens
since you took over? Shell shock?

APPLETON

Thievin' are you, Fletcher?

FLETCHER

No need for that is there, Mr Appleton,
no need for that sort of defamatory.

APPLETON

Always pilfering, the whole lot of you.

FLETCHER

(*Outraged*) Now listen, Mr Appleton,
I resent that. I may have done some
bad things in my life, wouldn't be here
if I hadn't, but I ain't a petty sneak
thief, that's not my style at all.

APPLETON

All right, all right.

*He turns away and Fletcher nimbly
picks up a packet of margarine
from the working surface and slips*

it into his pocket, as he crosses to
the table, gingerly putting down his
bag of grain.

FLETCHER

Er . . . Lennie . . . anyone er . . . left a
message here for me?

LENNIE

Yeah. Bloke come in and said Harry
Grout said permission granted.

FLETCHER

Did he? Oh, good.

LENNIE

Permission for what?

FLETCHER

Permission to hold a game.

LENNIE

What game?

FLETCHER

Keep your voice down.

LENNIE

(*Quieter*) What game?

FLETCHER

A game of chance, my son.

LENNIE

How d'you mean?

FLETCHER

Oh for gawd's sake, Godber.
A gamble. A flutter.

LENNIE

But gambling ain't allowed.

FLETCHER

'Course it ain't allowed. That's
precisely why we're doin' it.

LENNIE

Why d'you have to get permission off
this Grout?

FLETCHER

(*Pained*) Godber, son, you've been
here a week, ain't you learned
nothing? Officially this hotel is run
by a governor appointed by the
Home Office, Mr Venables. But in
practice of course we knows
different. In practice General Harry
Grout can bring this nick to a
standstill if he so wishes.

LENNIE

What d'you play for – big stakes, is it?

FLETCHER

We will do if Lukewarm can nick some
from the meat safe. We play for
anything negotiable. Snout mostly. But
it won't be for chicken feed . . . pity
really 'cos I got plenty of that.

LENNIE

I've noticed people are always
betting on something. I suppose it's
their way of generating excitement
to counter the misery of their
monotonous existence.

FLETCHER

What? Oh yes – right. It ain't just the
excitement of the game, what you win
or what you lost. It's the pleasure what
you get for doing it under their noses,
surruptitious, like.

LENNIE

There's two blokes next door to me
who've had a bet on how many bricks
there are in their cell.

FLETCHER

Oh yes. Commonplace that.

LENNIE

I can't think or study. It's driving me mad, listening to 'em. Recount after recount. Three hundred and forty-one, three hundred and forty-two . . .

FLETCHER

Blokes doing stir'll bet on anything. Two flies going up a wall, hymn numbers in the chapel. Two flies going down a wall . . . I even laid an egg on a bet today – made a bet on egg laying. There was a big game last night in D Wing. Weren't you aware of the atmosphere in the air? It was electric – the tension.

LENNIE

Tension, I noticed that. But I thought that was because Tuesday's the day that female social worker comes round.

FLETCHER

What, gruesome Glenda? Her with the brogues and the bicycle. You'd be hard pushed to have an erotic fantasy about that one.

LENNIE

I dunno. Nifty Small's in love with her. He stole her bicycle saddle.

FLETCHER

Really? Gawd the ride back must have been painful for her. He won't have that long. They'll soon find it.

LENNIE

What, under his pillow! I bet they won't.

FLETCHER

(*Instantly*) All right, you're on. How much? Two fags?

LENNIE

'Ere, 'ere, I'm not gambling. My mother said gambling will get you into trouble.

FLETCHER

Son, it may have escaped your notice but you're in prison. Your mother was too late. You is in trouble.

LENNIE

Yeah, well nevertheless I'm not gambling. I'm not counting bricks or watching flies. Gambling's one thing I'm going to resist inside.

FLETCHER

Bet you can't.

LENNIE

Oh yes I can.

FLETCHER

Bet you a bar of soap you can't.

LENNIE

I bet I can.

FLETCHER

There you are. You bet me you wouldn't bet me. So you just lost your first bet. That's a bar of soap you owe me. Work that out.

Ives walks in carrying a sack of potatoes.

APPLETON

Where are you going, Ives?

IVES

Er just er . . . got the spuds, Mr Appleton . . .

APPLETON

Get on with it, Ives.

FLETCHER

(*Walking across*) Got the spuds, Ives?

IVES

'Ere listen, Fletcher. How much do they weigh then?

FLETCHER

You know already.

IVES

'Course I don't. No scales out there.

FLETCHER

What's the bet then?

IVES

All the eggs you've got in there.

FLETCHER

You crafty nurk. Against what?

IVES

Ounce of snout.

FLETCHER

Fair enough.

IVES

Are you in, son?

LENNIE

No, I'm not.

Fletcher appraises the bag expertly then picks it up, testingly.

FLETCHER

Nearest one, eh!

IVES

Nearest one.

FLETCHER

Twenty-three pounds.

IVES

I'll say twenty-seven.

FLETCHER

Gave that a lot of thought, didn't you?

IVES

Just over twenty-seven.

Ives lifts the potatoes on to the scales. They weigh just over twenty-seven pounds.

IVES

Well I never, would you believe it?

BOTH

Just over twenty-seven.

IVES

Thank you . . . Sh-ting.

FLETCHER

You knew, didn't you?

IVES

Here listen. I ain't no cheat.

FLETCHER

What? You're in here for fraudulent conversion. It's your career that is, cheating.

IVES

Lose gracefully, come on, here listen.

FLETCHER

You're a crafty conniving gink, Ives.

IVES

Bad loser.

FLETCHER

Here you are then.

He hands over the eggs.

IVES

(*Putting them in his pockets*) Come in handy these. Owes Grout, don't I. Don't do to owe Grouty.

FLETCHER

Now naff off.

Mackay enters.

MACKAY
Morning, Mr Appleton.
*Everyone redoubles their illusion of
activity, including Appleton.*
APPLETON
Morning, Mr Mackay.
MACKAY
Fletcher! What are you doing, Ives?
IVES
Oh – I just brought the spuds,
Mr Mackay.
*Fletcher tries to leave with his bag
of grain.*
MACKAY
Where are you going, Fletcher?
FLETCHER
Pig swill.
MACKAY
Pardon!!
FLETCHER
See about the pig swill, Mr Mackay.
Little fellows need their swill this time
of day.
Fletcher starts to go.
MACKAY
(*Gesturing*) Just a minute.
FLETCHER
I've swept all that Mr Ma . . .
MACKAY
Fletcher – come here.
Fletcher goes across.
MACKAY
I'm told your chickens are on short
time. I'm told that since you arrived
at the farm egg production has
fallen drastically.

FLETCHER
Don't blame me, Mr Mackay. Perhaps
they're in a foul mood . . .
MACKAY
Don't you come it with me, Fletcher.
Now, what have we here?
FLETCHER
Crown jewels. Chicken meal,
Mr Mackay.
MACKAY
Empty it. (*To Ives*) Ives, stands still.
FLETCHER
Empty it?
MACKAY
Empty it.
FLETCHER
Make ever such a mess.
Godber walks over.
MACKAY
Godber . . . Empty it.
*Fletcher tips bag of grain on to
table. Mackay pokes about in it with
his truncheon.*
MACKAY
All right, Fletcher. But if I catch
you thieving . . .
FLETCHER
I won't.
MACKAY
Won't what?
FLETCHER
Let you catch me, Mr Mackay.
Mackay sees Ives.
MACKAY
Ives – where are you going,
horrible Ives?

IVES

'Ere listen, I'm behindhand Mr Mackay. I've got them turnips –

MACKAY

Come here, Ives.

IVES

Yes, but –

MACKAY

Come here, Ives.

Ives complies reluctantly.

MACKAY

Bit of a jackdaw yourself, aren't you, Ives? Last time we caught you in the kitchens you were trying to steal a meat cleaver.

IVES

Only to sharpen my pencil, Mr Mackay.

MACKAY

No, it was not, Mr Ives. It was used to persuade your cell-mate to part with his Pirelli calendar.

He raises Ives's hands and starts to pat his pockets.

MACKAY

Now what have we picked up today – a meat skewer?

He pats hands down Ives's body. The crunch of eggs is heard as he bangs on pockets. Ives reacts in discomfort.

MACKAY

Follow me, Mr Ives.

Mackay marches out. Ives follows walking awkwardly. He looks at Fletcher.

FLETCHER

Yolk's on you again, son.

6. PRISON LANDING

It is association hour. Ives walks past several prisoners and goes up stairs, along the gantry and towards Fletcher's cell.

7. FLETCHER'S CELL

It is a three-cell with a double-tiered bunk on one side and a single bed on the other. There is a chair beside the washbasin under the barred window, on which Fletcher is sitting cleaning his shoes. On the top bunk lies Heslop, thinking.

Evans is on the lower bunk, rolling snout.

The cell door is open. Fletcher looks under his feet as if having mislaid something.

FLETCHER

Here, Evans, you haven't eaten my shoe polish, have you?

EVANS

No, course I haven't.

FLETCHER

You sure?

EVANS

'Course I'm sure. What would I eat shoe polish for?

FLETCHER

I don't know. Maybe it was to make my shaving mirror go down easier.

Ives enters.

IVES

'Ere listen.

FLETCHER

Don't we knock, don't we knock?

IVES

No, no, 'ere listen. Word is you've got a game going.

FLETCHER

Oh say it a bit louder. Few people in E Wing didn't catch that. Why don't you bellow it from the bleedin' rooftops.

IVES

It's all right, the screws are brewing up.

FLETCHER

(*Sitting*) Subtle as an air-raid you are, Ives.

IVES

No, listen, is that gen? You got a game put together?

FLETCHER

Yup.

IVES

Grouty give the OK, did he?

FLETCHER

At a price, yeah.

IVES

When is it?

FLETCHER

Saturday afternoon. When the world is watching *Grandstand*, and the screws are playing E Wing at football.

IVES

Can I be in?

FLETCHER

Sorry, old son. Full house.

IVES

Who's in then?

FLETCHER

Myself. Mr Heslop, here. Lukewarm from the kitchen. And Mr Evans – providing he don't eat the dice.

IVES

Oh it's dice, is it?

FLETCHER

(*Rising*) What? Oh well, possibly, possibly. Said enough, said enough.

IVES

You can make room for one more.

FLETCHER

Not your sort, Ives.

IVES

'Ere listen –

FLETCHER

It's all been arranged, it's all set up, right? So naff off.

IVES

You telling me you going to set a game up? In this place. What? You ain't got a snowball's. Gambling here?

FLETCHER

Same in any nick. Question of integrity. Where there's a will there's a way.

IVES

(*Sitting*) You're so lairy, aren't you, Fletcher? Well it might have been a doddle in your last nick. But they cut off privileges here for the toss of a coin.

EVANS

I've had my privileges cut off.

FLETCHER

Oh yes, did it hurt much?

IVES

They'll have your guts for garters if they see you gambling with anything. Draughts, dominoes. Even that whatsit, that game with the wooden spelling . . .

FLETCHER

Scribble?

IVES

Scribble, that an' all. Venables comes down like the clappers he did. Ever since the Earwig Derby.

FLETCHER

The what?

IVES

The Earwig Derby.

EVANS

Earwig Derby yes, tragic that.

FLETCHER

When was this?

IVES

Last Earwig season, wasn't it. Organised by Grouty, of course. Very much on the lines of the Jockey Club. There was handicaps, eliminators, and then in September, the Grand Final – well, the Derby. Over eight yards across the Laundry floor. Whole prison was on. Then Mackay finds out, doesn't he. How we never knew.

FLETCHER

What did he do?

IVES

Put his foot down.

He starts stamping his foot down by way of illustration.

IVES

Right on top of 'em.

EVANS

No need for that, there wasn't.

Heslop belatedly joins in.

HESLOP

It's dice, is it?

FLETCHER

Oh you're with us are you, Mr Heslop?

HESLOP

You never told me it was dice.

FLETCHER

I did, I told you Saturday, only it's obviously just permutated.

IVES

Listen Fletcher, you've got no chance, no chance at all.

FLETCHER

I don't agree, I find geraniums do very well in chalky soil providing you give them a drop of moisture and you don't let the cat near them.

Barrowclough enters.

FLETCHER

Oh, here's Mr Barrowclough, well, well, what a nice surprise.

BARROWCLOUGH

Evans . . . Oh yes, Ives, up to no good?

IVES

'Ere listen.

BARROWCLOUGH

Usually are, Ives, it has to be said.

FLETCHER

It transpired that Mr Ives and I have a common interest in geraniums.

IVES

Oh yes, geraniums. Nice little fellas.
My cousin used to breed them.

FLETCHER

Grow them.

IVES

Grow them.

BARROWCLOUGH

Really? Now you know something,
I'm a bit of a horticulturalist myself.

FLETCHER

Oh really . . . oh gawd.

BARROWCLOUGH

Anyhow no time to go into that now.

FLETCHER

Oh. More's the pity.

BARROWCLOUGH

Come along Evans – time for your visit
to the psychiatrist.

IVES

'Ere listen – you still trying to work one
by eating things?

FLETCHER

Yes, he is. Playing havoc with my
personal possessions.

EVANS

Playing havoc with my digestion.
*He leaves the cell, rubbing
his stomach.*

IVES

Listen, Fletcher. Where d'you get the
dice then?

FLETCHER

Lukewarm made them in the kitchen.
Out of pastry. He baked them.

IVES

Won't they break?

FLETCHER

Not his pastry.

HESLOP

I'm very fond of geraniums.
Fletcher lies down. Ives sits down.

HESLOP

Flowers, things like that. Not that we
had a garden. My house just had a
yard. A yard with a wringer and a
bicycle in it. But the wife's sister's
house in Sidcup, that has a riot of
colour. What with his vegetables, she
never had to want for anything.

FLETCHER

Is that it?
Ives looks and nods.

FLETCHER

Comes in bursts like that. Another of
those poignant anecdotes from the
rich pageant of Mr Heslop's past, the
Patience Strong of Cell Block 11. You
can see how lucky I am to be in here
with him.

IVES

I can see why you dealt him in.

FLETCHER

First come, first served.

IVES

'Ere listen. You'll never pull it off.

FLETCHER

What you talking about?

IVES

Organise this game and get away
with it.

FLETCHER

(*Rising*) It's already organised.

IVES

But I bet you can't get away with it.

FLETCHER

Put your money where your –

IVES

Mouth is, I will do.

FLETCHER

Go on then.

IVES

How much?

FLETCHER

Try me.

IVES

A biggy.

FLETCHER

Big as you like.

IVES

How big?

FLETCHER

Try me.

IVES

Snout.

FLETCHER

Obviously.

IVES

All right then. Half a pound.

He says this as if expecting the reaction "Don't be ridiculous", but instead Fletcher agrees.

FLETCHER

Fair enough.

Fletcher's nonchalance unnerves Ives.

IVES

Did you hear me, Fletcher? I said half a pound.

FLETCHER

I heard you.

IVES

That's eight ounces.

FLETCHER

Nice one, Einstein.

IVES

Now let's get this perfectly clear – and you're a witness.

He indicates Heslop, then checks the door again.

IVES

I'm betting you half a pound of snout that you won't see your game through. You'll get found out, or busted, or whatever.

FLETCHER

You're on.

Ives looks visibly shaken at the size of the bet.

IVES

All right then. That's done then. I'll be off then.

FLETCHER

I'd lay a little of that off if I was you, my son.

Ives leaves.

HESLOP

Got a lot of bottle, Fletcher, a lot of bottle.

FLETCHER

Where there's a will there's a way. Here's my shoe polish.

HESLOP

When I was doing bird in Shepton Mallet we used to bet on the number of bricks in a cell.

FLETCHER

Oh original yes. How did you get on?

Fletcher walks to the table, then to the bed.

HESLOP

All I know is there was over thirty-seven.

FLETCHER

Oh roomy, wasn't it? When I was in Maidstone, d'you know what we had going? We only had a roulette game going that's all. With a dartboard, see. People bet on it. You could be on red or black, evens or odds, sequences or individual numbers. And your croupier was a bloke what was blindfolded and threw the dart. We used to play in association and we bribed this screw to turn a blind eye. Big game it was, mammoth.

HESLOP

Oh crafty that, roulette.

FLETCHER

Yeah . . . pity it came to such a tragic end.

HESLOP

What happened?

FLETCHER

One night the croupier got a bit careless. Now the screw turns a blind eye to everything.

9. COKE STORE

Inside the coke store Evans, Heslop, Lukewarm and Fletcher are sitting on boxes round a tea chest.

HESLOP

You sure they won't find us in here?

FLETCHER

Lukewarm here assures me they won't – he being a trusty, happens to have access to the coke store key. Cosy, ain't it?

LUKEWARM

They'll never look down here today.

FLETCHER

No – officially, as you know, we're all watching E Wing play the screws at football, a game that will occupy a lot of attention.

LUKEWARM

And the attention of the hospital as well later on, the way they go at each other.

FLETCHER

Yeah – should be quite a bloodbath, with any luck.

There are murmurs of approval and agreement.

FLETCHER

I did try to persuade Tommy Macready to put forward his escape attempt to today. 'Cos knowing Tommy he'll cock it up and the diversion would have come in very handy. However, he couldn't be swayed as he pointed out, quite rightly, state this country's in you can't rely on trains at the weekend.

HESLOP

I didn't know Tommy was going over the wall.

LUKEWARM

Oh yes, common knowledge.

EVANS

Domestic problems.

FLETCHER

Wife's got nerves or something.

LUKEWARM

Things are getting on top of her, are they?

FLETCHER

Quite the reverse. She's sleeping with a limbo dancer.

LUKEWARM

A limbo dancer? Is he black?

FLETCHER

Black and blue, I should think, knowing her. What a raver! Now then . . .

LUKEWARM

Oh, before I forget – something to nibble at for later.

He hands out packets of sandwiches.

EVANS

Ooh, lovely – I haven't had a square meal for ages.

FLETCHER

Not since my shaving mirror. Thanks, Lukewarm – you spoil us. I wish I'd had a mother like you. I might have gone straight.

LUKEWARM

Or bent.

HESLOP

Can I eat mine now?

FLETCHER

No you can't – he's like a big kid, ain't he? Soon as you get outside the front door, you want to start the picnic. Wait! Now the rules, gentlemen. One: Stakes – minimum bet, one fag. You cannot raise more than half the kitty. Two: Losers – and some of us have to lose, don't we? Divvy up within twenty-four hours – if not Mr Heslop here will come round with a reminder – just like the Post Office.

EVANS

The Post Office?

FLETCHER

Yeah, he'll stick one on you. Now we're all set. Right?

OTHERS

Right.

FLETCHER

Right.

LUKEWARM

And the game.

FLETCHER

And the game gentlemen.

He stands up and gets his shirt out from his trousers. There are snakes and ladders drawn on it.

FLETCHER

The game is snakes and ladders.

10. FILM

Mackay enters closely followed by Barrowclough.

MACKAY

I knew something was up,

Mr Barrowclough. My antennae told me. I know when there's a Big Deal at Dodge City in this place.

Mr Barrowclough shuts and locks the door.

BARROWCLOUGH

I sometimes think it's a waste of our manpower – trying to crack down on gambling – I mean, men will gamble.

Barrowclough and Mackay walk along the alley.

MACKAY

Gambling leads to debts, Mr Barrowclough. And debts lead to ill-feeling, antagonism. Lack of discipline.

BARROWCLOUGH

Did your antennae tell you where this game is taking place?

MACKAY

No, that was Ives, horrible Ives.

BARROWCLOUGH

No honour among thieves.

MACKAY

Not where there's gambling at stake, that's why it has to be stamped out.

BARROWCLOUGH

Where are they?

MACKEY

We're getting warmer.

They stop walking.

MACKAY

They're down there.

BARROWCLOUGH

What – in the boiler house?

MACKAY

In the coke store.

BARROWCLOUGH

Well, should we –

MACKAY

No, wait a moment. I've arranged for a special delivery.

He moves round the corner and gives the signal. Coal is seen going down the chute. Mackay and Barrowclough move to the doorway and wait. A door opens and Evans, Heslop, Fletcher and Lukewarm rush out covered in soot.

MACKAY

Welcome to the Black and White Minstrel Show.

They move up the alley.

11. CELL

Fletcher is collecting his things together inside the cell, when Ives puts his head round the door.

IVES

Evening, Fletcher.

Fletcher gives him no acknowledgement.

IVES

I – I heard this time the coke was on you.

FLETCHER

What? Oh yes, you're a very witty man. Full of that irrepressible Liverpudlian wit we've all heard about.

IVES

What the Governor say then?

FLETCHER

Said I'd abused his trust. Said I'd lost my privileged position on the farm. Said I'd lose my privileges for the next four weeks. Also said I was an evil influence and not the sort of man who should be sharing a cell and corrupting the likes of Heslop and Evans. So he's shifting me to a single cell.

IVES

Oh dear, how tragic. I am sorry.

FLETCHER

All right, don't give me all that. I know you grassed, Ives. As does the entire prison. As you will find out when you take your first turn round the recreation yard. I'm not saying there'll be any unpleasantness, but if I were you I'd try and borrow some shin pads from the PTI.

IVES

'Ere listen, Fletcher.

FLETCHER

Not that I bears you any ill-feeling, you 'orrible contemptuous despicable git you. No, no, you was just a pawn in my grand strategy.

IVES

Never mind about that, there's still the bet, there's still the bet – you owes me, Fletcher.

FLETCHER

That is true, that is true. And that half pound of snout may provide some consolation to you in the nightmare days that lie ahead.

Barrowclough comes in.

BARROWCLOUGH

Ready, Fletcher?

FLETCHER

Just coming, Mr Barrowclough.

IVES

'Ere listen, you take the heat off me and we'll forget about the bet. We're even. I mean you're never going to raise half a pound of snout, are you?

FLETCHER

No, there's no problem. I'll take it out me winnings.

IVES

Winnings? What winnings?

FLETCHER

Lose a few, gain a few. I was betting the whole landing half a pound of snout I'd be in a single cell by Sunday. I'm going to be rolling in it.

12. PRISON LANDING

Barrowclough and Fletcher come out of the cell and walk along the gantry. A prisoner passes Fletcher some tobacco.

They go down the stairs. Prisoners hand over tobacco to Fletcher. They go down more stairs. More prisoners give him tobacco.

SERIES ONE

EPISODE THREE: A NIGHT IN

1. PRISON

*It is association hour. Lennie goes
down stairs.*
*He walks past other prisoners on
his way to Fletcher's cell.*

2. FLETCHER'S CELL

*Lennie walks in. Fletcher is sitting
on the lower bunk writing a letter.
Lennie is a bit diffident.*

LENNIE
Oh er . . . hello, Fletch.

He is met with silence.

LENNIE
You er . . . you was expecting me? I
mean they informed you?

FLETCHER
They informed me, yes.

LENNIE
Only temporary they said.

FLETCHER
You bet your life it's only temporary.
Single cell this is, by rights.

LENNIE
Not my fault.

FLETCHER
I'm just saying.

LENNIE
Only temporary.

FLETCHER
Look, park your stuff, get out the light.
*Lennie pauses awkwardly,
indicating the lower bunk.*

LENNIE
Er . . . is this where you want me
to sleep?

FLETCHER
What?

LENNIE
Well, I presume I'm in the bottom bunk.
I mean, top bunk's status in the nick.

FLETCHER
'Course it is. You're in the bottom
bunk, yes.

LENNIE
Well, if you wouldn't mind shifting your
stuff, I could --

FLETCHER
What? Oh, all right. God Almighty.
He moves his stuff to the top bunk.

*Lennie begins to unpack his stuff
and make up his bunk.*

LENNIE

Not my fault.

FLETCHER

No no, so you keep telling me.

LENNIE

Not my fault if they have a riot on my
landing. My cell mate, Banksy, he was
one of the ringleaders, like. He set fire
to his mattress. And mine.

FLETCHER

Head case, that Banks.

LENNIE

He's being transferred.

FLETCHER

Head case.

LENNIE

He wasn't a bad bloke to share a cell
with. He was always very nice to me.
He showed me the ropes and taught
me cribbage. And he never displayed
no violence. He was the gentlest
of men.

FLETCHER

Oih . . .

*He nods to Lennie indicating that he
should go to the other washstand.*

LENNIE

(*Crossing over*) Oh . . . He found
this kitten and smuggled it into
the cell and from the way he handled
it you could see the gentle side of
his nature.

FLETCHER

You what? Before he lit his mattress

I heard he threw a screw off the
top landing.

LENNIE

Well, he weren't hurt. He hit the
safety net.

FLETCHER

That, Godber, is somewhat academic.
The point is that a fifteen-stone prison
officer was hurled from a top landing
by your cell mate, mighty Joe Banks.

LENNIE

Only because he said he couldn't
keep the kitten.

FLETCHER

Hardly an excuse, sonny Jim. Hardly
an excuse. Can't see that cutting
much ice with his parole board.

LENNIE

Where's the harm in keeping a kitten?

FLETCHER

It's not allowed, that's the point. It's
against prison procedure. Caged birds,
well yes, sometimes they'll let you keep
caged birds. Insects in a matchbox.
But you can't keep cats. And Banks
knows that, the porridge he's done.

LENNIE

It was only a little kitten.

FLETCHER

A kitten differs from a cat only in scale.
They share the same lavatorial
tendencies, they pee on your blankets.

LENNIE

Just don't see the harm.

FLETCHER

There are rules. For example, I have

certain rules in this cell here. Well, not so much rules as standards. This is my cell, in which you're a temporary resident, and as such you will honour those standards.

LENNIE
Which are?

FLETCHER
You don't rabbit, you don't snore, and you don't pick your nose.

LENNIE
I don't think I do any of them.

FLETCHER
Good, good. Then we should get on passably well.

LENNIE
Banksy never complained anyhow.

FLETCHER
Well, he wouldn't, not an animal like Banksy.

LENNIE
But I don't.
He sits down.

FLETCHER
Good good, fine fine – you're sitting on my paper.

LENNIE
Oh, sorry.
He gets up off a crumpled copy of the Sun and passes it over.

FLETCHER
Oh another thing. Newspapers. You can read the paper, but when, and only when I've finished with it.

LENNIE
All right.

FLETCHER
Right – get out of the way.
*There is a pause while Fletcher climbs up into the top bunk and settles down with his paper. His shoes are off, and there is a big hole in one of his socks.
Lennie starts to set out a few personal possessions, including a photograph of his fiancée, only inscribed "Lennie – for always, Denise". He has also got some needle and thread, a tin of shag tobacco and some papers, a tin of throat lozenges, a box of liquorice all-sorts and shaving kit.*

LENNIE
I've got some grey darning thread.

FLETCHER
(*Irritably*) What?

LENNIE
I've got some grey darning thread if you want that hole darned up.

FLETCHER
(*Politer*) What? Oh yes, thanks – yes.
He takes off his sock and hands it down to Lennie, who by his reaction registers that he had not expected to do the darning himself. He decides not to make a stand.

LENNIE
Your standards don't include sweaty feet, I notice.

FLETCHER
Man who don't sweat ain't healthy. Like a dog with a dry nose.

LENNIE

(*Getting the darning kit*) Settling in OK, are you?

FLETCHER

I'm all right, keep me pecker up. Can't grind me down. Bide your time, that's what it's all down to, bide your time.

Bells start to ring and doors start to slam, signalling lockup time. Voices are heard in the distance.

LENNIE

Unnatural in't it, men in cages.

FLETCHER

Bide your time.

LENNIE

I don't mind work. And as I'm in the kitchens I always get plenty of grub. And the screws ain't too bad, by and large . . .

A prison officer appears, gives a cursory check, then slams the door and locks it.

FLETCHER

Goodnight, sunshine . . . Charmless nurk. Oh dear, I forgot to put me shoes out to be cleaned.

Lennie walks across to the window.

LENNIE

This is the bit I can't stand though.

FLETCHER

What?

LENNIE

Lockup. It's only quarter-to-eight. Barely dark. If I was at home now I'd just be going out for the evening.

FLETCHER

That's the point you see, son. We're here to be punished, ain't we? Deprived of all our creature comforts. And the little things you've been taking for granted all these years. Like a comfy shirt, decent smoke, a night out.

LENNIE

A night out . . .

There is a pause.

FLETCHER

Look, if you're so keen we'll go out. We could find a couple of girls – two of them darlings what dance on *Top of the Pops*. Yes, Pan's People. Beautiful Babs – don't know what her name is. Arrange to meet them in some dimly lit Italiano restaurant. Then we could go on somewhere if you like. Some night club . . . dance till dawn. Then back to their luxury penthouse, and wallop. But you see I done all that last night so I'm a bit knackered. Also we'd have to get all ponced up and you'd have to darn me socks. So why don't we just have a quiet night in? All right?

LENNIE

If you say so, Fletch.

FLETCHER

That's what you've got to tell yourself. You're just having a quiet night in.

He goes back to the Sun. There is a pause.

LENNIE

(*Gloomily*) Trouble is I've got six

hundred and ninety-eight quiet nights in to go.

FLETCHER

Less than some.

Lennie looks at the picture of Denise.

LENNIE

D'you think she'll wait?

FLETCHER

(*Abstractedly*) What?

LENNIE

D'you think she'll wait?

FLETCHER

Who?

LENNIE

Denise. My fiancée.

FLETCHER

Oh yes, Denise, fiancée.

LENNIE

Well, do you?

FLETCHER

I dunno. I shouldn't think she'll wait *in* for six hundred and ninety-eight nights.

LENNIE

She is my fiancée.

FLETCHER

Yes, I know, but when she said she'd love you for ever she didn't know you were going to get put away for two years, did she?

LENNIE

I miss her so much. I can't sleep for thinking about her.

FLETCHER

Doesn't do no good that. Don't do no good lying awake at night brooding and twitching about what you ain't going to get no more. Carnal thoughts – well, best to give them the Big E, the elbow. Less you think about women the better – cor, look at that. 'Beauty Queen shocks Council. Lovely Sharon Spenser, twenty-two, shocked members of her town Council when they learned that she played the title role in the new sex-sational film *The Virgin and the Vicar.*'

LENNIE

I wonder which she played?

FLETCHER

'"Had we known," said a Council spokesman, "We would never have crowned her floral Queen." "I don't know what all the fuss is about," said Sharon, a former convent girl, whose hobbies include water ski-ing and carpentry. "I am proud of my body and what I do with it in my spare time is none of the Council's business".' She'd never get planning permission for that.

Both stare at the photograph for several seconds, their eyes glazing with obvious relish.

FLETCHER

Yes . . . yes . . . got every right to be proud of a body like that. Oh yes. Ravishing little thing, isn't she? Mischievous little mouth. Look at that mouth. Full of mischief. I bet that's been up to some mischief. Yes . . . what was I saying?

PORRIDGE – THE SCRIPTS

LENNIE

You were saying the less you think about women the better.

FLETCHER

Oh yes, yes, carnal thoughts, yes, fatal.

LENNIE

She reminds me of Denise a bit.

FLETCHER

Which bit?

LENNIE

No – Denise. My fiancée.

FLETCHER

Oh yes, the lovely Denise, yes right.

LENNIE

Not that they're similar in appearance, but they're both . . . physical. Know what I mean?

FLETCHER

You're not telling me your Denise is a star of the silver screen, are you? Albeit a grubby one in a backroom.

LENNIE

Oh no, nothing like that.

FLETCHER

Not a model, then?

LENNIE

Oh no, though I once took some provocative Polaroids of her when we were caravanning in the Gower Peninsula. I don't mean mucky, like. But she was sort of expressing herself . . . Posing, like.

He gives his impression of Denise posing provocatively on the

Gower Peninsula. Fletcher looks disapproving.

FLETCHER

Come on, son! Leave it off! What will the neighbours think?

He is aware of the spyhole in the cell door.

LENNIE

Oh sorry, Fletch.

FLETCHER

Ain't thinking of me, son. They know which side my bread's buttered . . : It's you. Harm can come to a growing lad. You're the one could drive the fairies round here into a frenzy.

LENNIE

But I'm engaged to Denise.

FLETCHER

Means naff all to them, my son. They're all engaged to each other. Denise is a thing of your past. A letter in your top pocket. A photograph under your pillow. A warm tingle in your loins.

LENNIE

In me what?

FLETCHER

Your loins.

LENNIE

What are loins?

FLETCHER

(*Exasperatedly*) Loins is . . . look, when you think of her, when you thinks of Denise in the still of the night, think of the times you once had, don't you ever get a warm tingle?

LENNIE

Oh – yes.

FLETCHER

Well, where you gets it, that's your loins.

There is a pause.

LENNIE

I thought they were my –

He lies down on the bottom bunk.

FLETCHER

Well there's lots of words for them.

LENNIE

She is a very physical girl, Denise. She was a Beauty Queen. Finalist at the Office Machinery Exhibition. Miss Duplicating, she was. And her picture was in the paper and she became a pin-up of two thousand sailors in an aircraft carrier in Gibraltar. They wrote to her and said she was the girl they'd most like to ink their rolls.

FLETCHER

That must have made you very proud, Lennie, knowing that your fiancée was the sexual fantasy of an entire aircraft carrier.

LENNIE

Oh, I didn't know her then. That was before she moved to Smethwick, before that never-to-be-forgotten day when I met her at a supermarket in the Bull Ring – oh that's in Birmingham. She was stamping 'Special Offer' on giant-sized jars of pickled onions. I came round the corner from condiments and sauces and my wire trolley went

over her foot. It was a magic moment. We both knew. I said to her straight off 'Will you meet me outside?' I said. And she said, 'All right.'

FLETCHER

God preserve us, Godber. Romance.

He gets down from his bunk.

LENNIE

How d'you mean? I told you it was beautiful.

FLETCHER

I know, son, I know. But all I'm saying is if you had your time again, you might pick a more romantic setting to meet the love of your life. 'She was stamping "Special Offer" on giant-sized pickled onions,' I mean bloody hell, it's not Romeo and Juliet, is it.

He sits down. There is a pause.

LENNIE

Was your courtship any more romantic?

FLETCHER

Well no . . . in truth it wasn't really. I'm a city boy like you. And it was after the war. I had a bit more space than you, but that was mostly bomb sites. There was the pictures – the Muswell Hill Odeon. Or the back seat of a car – if I could open one. But somehow we had more chance to improvise. Today these great cold hostile concrete blocks. No hiding place. Can't make love in a launderette.

There is a pause.

LENNIE

We did.

FLETCHER
What? Oh . . .
LENNIE
It was very quiet at the time.
FLETCHER
That's a relief to us all.
LENNIE
We had three bagfuls to do . . . and it
was bitter out.
FLETCHER
Hardly entitles you, I'd have thought.
However I don't know Birmingham.
Now, my eldest, Ingrid –
LENNIE
Ingrid?
FLETCHER
Yes, my old lady called her that after
Ingrid Bergman what was a famous
film star who was sweeping the
country at the time, but I don't
suppose you remember her, *For Whom
the Bell Tolls, Casablanca, Spellbound.*
LENNIE
Oh I think I've seen that on the telly. Is
that the one about the scientists in the
secret laboratory in Arizona and this
man drinks this substance by mistake
and turns into a werewolf and carries
off the mad doctor's niece and does
things to her in the catacombs?
FLETCHER
No.
LENNIE
Oh.
FLETCHER
No, that weren't one of Ingrid's. No,

I can say without fear of contradiction
that Ingrid was never in no catacomb
with no werewolf. My daughter Ingrid
might have been, but certainly not the
lovely Miss Bergman.
*He rises and crosses to stick up
the photograph.*
LENNIE
What were you going to say about
your daughter Ingrid?
FLETCHER
(*Sitting down*) What? Was I? Oh yes,
my point was that my eldest, was –
this is between ourselves, Godber –
she was conceived in Highgate
Cemetery. You see we weren't married
at the time. Of course we got married
when we realised young Ingrid was
on the way. But at the time we wasn't.
And we needed somewhere to
consummate the passion we felt for
each other.
LENNIE
But a cemetery!
FLETCHER
Oh yes, but a very famous and
historic cemetery.
LENNIE
Still seems a bit indecent to me.
FLETCHER
(*Indignantly*) No more indecent than
doing it in your local launderette three
bags full. Anyhow it wasn't premeditated
'cos we'd gone there to see Karl Marx's
tomb. I was politically minded at the
time, and very randy. Mind you, my

political career never got beyond
painting slogans on viaduct walls.

LENNIE

I've done that. Last thing I painted was
Lennie Godber loves Denise Shorter
on a warehouse wall.

FLETCHER

Denise Shorter?

LENNIE

My fiancée?

FLETCHER

Oh that Denise Shorter.

He gets up and gets a chair.

LENNIE

(*Hanging up photo*) I wrote to her in
association hour. Helped to pass the
time. I didn't have a class, you see.

FLETCHER

What class are you on?

LENNIE

Shoe repairing.

FLETCHER

Oh that's useful, yes. Very elevating,
yes. You're not in the shoe
repairing class are you? . . . Load of
cobblers that.

LENNIE

Just helps kill the time. Anything to
take me mind off the monotony of
this place.

FLETCHER

Listen, this ain't so bad, this nick.
Compared to Leicester, Parkhurst, high
security places like that. Got closed
circuit cameras there. Can't even go to
the lavatory without it being on television.

Not that that would worry an exhibitionist
like yourself, of course. Someone who
makes love in launderettes.

The lights go out.

LENNIE

Oh, I ain't got me things off yet.

FLETCHER

Move over, will you, son?

*He moves, then gives a yell
of pain.*

FLETCHER

Owww!

LENNIE

What's the matter?

FLETCHER

Something stuck in me foot.

LENNIE

That must be me darning needle.

FLETCHER

Well, what's it doing there?

LENNIE

I was darning your sock.

FLETCHER

Well, do it in the morning.

*Lennie, trying to help, inadvertently
steps on Fletcher's foot.*

FLETCHER

Now you're standing on me other foot.

LENNIE

Oh, I'm sorry.

He moves.

FLETCHER

You've just injured both my
feet, Godber.

LENNIE

I didn't mean –

FLETCHER

Just go to bed, son.

LENNIE

I'm not undressed yet.

FLETCHER

Just go to bed till I get into bed, then you can get out again.

Lennie complies. Fletcher climbs up on to the top bunk, muttering as he does.

FLETCHER

Not enough room to share . . . no privacy . . . bet he snores . . . he certainly rabbits.

LENNIE

D'you want a liquorice all-sort?

FLETCHER

No, I don't want a . . . liquorice all-sort.

There is a pause.

FLETCHER

How d'you get liquorice all-sorts?

LENNIE

(*Taking his shoes off*) I swopped them for a pound of marge I whipped from the kitchen.

FLETCHER

Learning, aren't you?

LENNIE

(*Taking his trousers off*) Little victories, you told me that.

FLETCHER

Shall we get some kip?

Lennie has been undressing and now gets into the lower bunk. There is a long pause.

LENNIE

Fletcher . . .

FLETCHER

(*Wearily*) Wha-at?

LENNIE

D'you know what I've found useful since I've been inside?

FLETCHER

What have you found useful, Godber?

LENNIE

I've started to do something which I haven't done since I was a kiddy.

Fletcher wonders whatever is coming next.

LENNIE

I find it helps. D'you know what I do?

FLETCHER

I shudder to think, son.

There is a pause.

LENNIE

I pray.

FLETCHER

Pray?

LENNIE

Yes, I've started saying me prayers.

FLETCHER

God preserve us.

LENNIE
That's what I keep asking him. So if you don't mind –

FLETCHER
If you must.

Lennie closes his eyes and starts praying.

LENNIE
Dear God, thank you for getting me through another day. Thank you for the letter from Denise and the liquorice all-sorts. Please look after Denise in your infinite wisdom. And the same applies to me Mum, Dad – wherever he is – and me Aunty Vi and Uncle Donald, Uncle Les and Aunty Con, me Aunty Rita in Newport Pagnall, and Cousin Rita in Walsall. And Cissie, and Stu, and Vic, and all the lads in the darts team at the Bell and Dragon.

He pauses.

LENNIE
And Norma and her husband who emigrated to Melbourne.

FLETCHER
Is this a prayer? Or a dedication on the Jimmy Young show?

There is a slight pause. We think Lennie has shut up but we are wrong.

LENNIE
And please God, look after Fletcher and forgive him for being such a bad-tempered, evil-minded, cantankerous old git.

Fletcher's face reflects his indignation.

3. PRISON

It is night. In the prison there is almost complete silence, save for a lone prison officer making his rounds on the landing and a few assorted snores.

4. CELL

Night time. A match flares as Fletcher lights up a smoke. Lennie speaks from below.

LENNIE
You awake, Fletch?

FLETCHER
No.

LENNIE
Oh.

There is a pause.

FLETCHER
Why?

LENNIE
Nor me neither.

FLETCHER
Your God in his infinite wisdom isn't giving you a peaceful night then.

LENNIE
Wasn't one of the things I asked for.

FLETCHER
That's true. He won't be getting much kip either, the list you gave him.

LENNIE
Don't be irreverent.

FLETCHER
You've changed your spots, ain't you? Day we come in, when we went through reception you didn't even

know if you was C of E, Pressed Beef or a flaming Buddhist.

LENNIE

Don't think it matters much. I just believe in God – doesn't matter which lot you support. I admit my belief's only been revived since I come in here. 'Cos I prayed when I was a kid, like. When I was up in Juvenile Court and when Villa looked like doing well in the Cup. But I became disillusioned with religion. I got probation and Villa got knocked out by Rotherham one-nothing.

FLETCHER

That's typical, in' it? Most people never give a second thought, do they? When things are going well, ticking along with scant regard for the ten commandments. Stealing, committing adultery, coveting each other's oxes. Then, wallop. In the face of adversity – (*In a cringing falsetto*) 'Please God, please help your loyal and trusted servant.' Huh!

LENNIE

You're right. But I am in the face of adversity. I hate prison, Fletch. It makes me depressed and it makes me afraid. I hate the air of defeat and the smell of disinfectant. I hate the shouting and the keys. And I hate not having a handle on the inside of that door.

He nods towards the cell door. Fletcher is not unsympathetic.

FLETCHER

(*Getting down from his bunk*) Kids like

you shouldn't be in prison, son. It's the system, see. You ain't here to be reformed or rehabilitated. You're here because of public revenge. Now it's different for me. Occupational hazard being as my occupation's breaking the law. But my family ain't gone short, most years. Three kids and my old lady. Show you their picture when it's light. Now my youngest, he just got into Grammar School.

LENNIE

Has he?

FLETCHER

Yes, lovely school. Costs a bit, you know. Books, equipment. But when my son showed up first day he was short of nothing. Rugby boots, blazer, scarf, the lot. Now he wouldn't have had all that if his dad had been a struggling clerk or a – or a shoe repairer. No. The reason he had all that was that his dad robbed a school outfitters.

LENNIE

What would your son think if he knew the truth?

FLETCHER

He'd think 'Oh so that's why the blazer's a bit big.' But he'll grow into it.

LENNIE

So you only do it for your family then?

FLETCHER

And my old lady, yes.

He gets up and goes across for some water.

FLETCHER
Twenty-four years we been together.
Married at nineteen see – too young,
'course it is, but that's Highgate
Cemetery for you.

LENNIE
You must love her very much.

FLETCHER
Yeah, well . . .

LENNIE
'Cos when you were asleep like, you
were saying things.

FLETCHER
Who me – what? Saying what?

LENNIE
Just saying her name over and over
again. 'Gloria, my love – oh Glor, Glor,
my love.'

FLETCHER
Was I?

LENNIE
Yes. I found that very moving – even
though it woke me up.

There is a long pause.

FLETCHER
Thing is . . . my old lady's called
Isobel.

LENNIE
Then who's Gloria?

FLETCHER
(*Puzzled*) You may well ask. You sure it
was Gloria?

LENNIE
Positive.

FLETCHER
Gloria. Gloria? . . . (*Remembering*) Yes,

there was a Gloria once – well, more
than once in fact – many, many times.

LENNIE
Was that before you met your Isobel?

FLETCHER
(*Confidentially*) In truth er – it wasn't,
Lennie. This was a little indiscretion
round about 1955. I remember that
'cos at the time I was King of the Teds
in Muswell Hill. And Gloria she was a
machinist – clothing factory. So I used
to go round to her place, get me evil
way and get me trousers narrowed at
the same time.

LENNIE
I could never be unfaithful to Denise.

FLETCHER
Ah now, listen, listen. Don't get no
wrong impression. This was an
indiscretion. You must imagine my
position. You can't be King of the
Teds and say at ten o'clock I've got
to go home to the wife. Not after
you've just smashed up an
Amusement Arcade.

LENNIE
So you don't make a habit of
indiscretions?

FLETCHER
'Course not. Look, Isobel's my old
lady and she knows it.

There is a pause.

LENNIE
Then who's Sharon?

FLETCHER
Sharon!!

LENNIE

After Gloria you was moaning about
a Sharon.

FLETCHER

I couldn't have been, I don't know no
Sharons – here hang about! She was
the girl in the *Sun*, weren't she?
Beauty Queen shocks Council. Yes,
yes, I was having this dream and she
was in it, comes back to me now . . .

LENNIE

(*In censure*) Carnal thoughts.

FLETCHER

Listen, Godber. No one asked you to
eavesdrop on my dreams. It's about
the only place you have any privacy
inside – your head. You want to
remember that, son. Dreams is your
escape. No locked doors in dreams.
No boundaries, no frontiers. Dreams
is freedom.

This impresses Lennie.

LENNIE

Freedom.

FLETCHER

No locked doors.

LENNIE

That's true, Fletch, that's really true.

FLETCHER

Well, I'm getting back to mine and I
suggest you do the same.

LENNIE

I will do, I will. And thank you, Fletch.

FLETCHER

(*Quite grumpily*) All right. Goodnight.
He turns over.

FLETCHER

Now, where was I . . .

LENNIE

Beauty Queen shocks Council.

FLETCHER

Oh yes . . . the way she was
performing in my dream, I can see why.

5. PRISON

*The prison is bathed in the light
of dawn. Early morning sounds can
be heard. On the prison landing
officers walking along the building,
banging their keys against
the doors and shouting their
wake-up calls.*

6. CELL

Fletcher is waking up.

FLETCHER

There's my alarm call.

*He swings himself into a
sitting position and his feet hit
Lennie's head.*

FLETCHER

Oops. Sorry, son.

LENNIE

No, no, Fletch. It's your cell. Sorry if
my head hit your foot.

He gets up.

FLETCHER

How d'you sleep then?

LENNIE

Very well since our midnight chat.

FLETCHER

Did you dream? Did you find that

freedom I promised you, that land of exotic fantasy?

LENNIE

Oh yes. It was Denise and I. We were in the launderette and we got through five bagfuls without stopping. Trouble is this bloke came in and spoilt it.

FLETCHER

Oh what a pity.

LENNIE

It was you.

FLETCHER

Couldn't have been. I was with Sharon Spencer all night up at the Hylton.

LENNIE

Fletch . . .

FLETCHER

What?

LENNIE

In the rush, moving here I well, er – I like, mislaid something.

FLETCHER

What?

LENNIE

My toothpaste.

FLETCHER

Oh yes.

LENNIE

Well, er – could I possibly have a loan of yours?

FLETCHER

Have a loan of my toothpaste?

LENNIE

Just a squeeze, like.

FLETCHER

Have a loan of my toothpaste?

LENNIE

I'll give you a liquorice all-sort.

FLETCHER

Oh!

LENNIE

(*Getting them from under his pillow*) I've got some left.

FLETCHER

Got the round one with the pink coconut? There's only one, you know.

LENNIE

Yes.

FLETCHER

All right then.

There's a slight pause.

LENNIE

Fletch.

FLETCHER

Now what? Suppose you ain't got no shaving cream.

LENNIE

No. I just wanted to thank you.

FLETCHER

Oh?

LENNIE

For helping me out. With advice, like. You know, it's like that song – 'Help me make it through the night.'

FLETCHER

What song's that?

LENNIE

Don't suppose you'd know it. More contemporary than your era. Suppose as King of the Teds your tastes were more Eddie Cochran and Conway Twitty.

FLETCHER

No. No my tastes were a bit more mellow. What was it I used to like? Kay Starr. Rosemary Clooney. And what was that song . . . (*Sings*) 'See the Pyramids along the Nile' . . . Jo Stafford.

LENNIE

Don't know him.

FLETCHER

He was a girl you nurk. Jo's a girl's name. They don't write songs like that now. Had a bit of melody in them days.

LENNIE

You're a sentimentalist at heart.

FLETCHER

(*Suspiciously*) What?

LENNIE

I know that under that gruff unpleasant exterior there's a kind man with feelings.

FLETCHER

(*Gruffly*) Yes, well --

He sits down to put his shoes on, then leaps up in pain, hitting his head on the top bunk.

FLETCHER

Bloody hell, bloody hell.

LENNIE

Oh, was it the darning needle again? *There is the sound of a door being unlocked.*

FLETCHER

I'll swing for you, Godber, I swear it. *The cell door is opened by a dour Prison Officer.*

PRISON OFFICER

What's going on here then? Did you assault this man, Godber?

LENNIE

He sat on my darning needle.

PRISON OFFICER

Is that true, Fletcher?

FLETCHER

Oh naff off. Can't you see I'm in agony?

PRISON OFFICER

Why don't you get a move on?

FLETCHER

Why don't you go home and find out who's been sleeping with your old lady while you've been on night duty?

PRISON OFFICER

(*Re-entering*) Oh that's original, Fletcher. I've been having that for the last seven years.

He leaves. Lennie and Fletcher sit down.

FLETCHER

Yeah, and so has she. *A Prison Officer can be heard unlocking another door.*

PRISON OFFICER (VOICEOVER)

(*Offscreen*) Come on, move it.

VOICE (VOICEOVER)

(*Offscreen*) Who's been sleeping with your old lady then?

Fletcher gets his boots and sits down to put them on.

LENNIE

Here you are, you can have these.

FLETCHER

What?

LENNIE

Go on – all of them. Present like.

FLETCHER

Oh, all right then. Not say no, son.

LENNIE

It's meant as a thank you. 'Cos when that door's locked I am depressed and I am afraid, and you – you know – just make it a bit more tolerable.

FLETCHER

You'll get used to it, Len. And the night's not so long, is it? It's your human spirit, see. They can't break that, those nurks. We'll be all right, you and me, son. Here, we'll go out tonight if you like.

LENNIE

With those dancers?

FLETCHER

If you like. Or I could ring Miss Sharon Spencer, eh? She'll have a big friend. Bound to. Soft lights, music, night club . . .

LENNIE

It's discos now.

He stands up.

FLETCHER

What? Oh well – as you say. Anyhow, think about it.

LENNIE

I will, I will. See how I feel. On the other hand, Fletch –

FLETCHER

Yeah.

LENNIE

If we don't feel like it, we might just have a quiet night in.

FLETCHER

Right. Right.

Fletcher picks up the pot. Lennie picks up the bucket and they move to the cell door.

Prisoners are walking along the landing with buckets etc. for slop-up. Fletcher comes out of his cell, followed by Lennie and they join the line.

1 SERIES ONE

EPISODE FOUR: A DAY OUT

1. PRISON
Prison Officers are seen knocking up prisoners.

2. FLETCHER'S CELL
Fletcher wakes up and sees that Lennie has almost finished dressing.

FLETCHER
Oh yes, what's your rush? Getting released, are you?

LENNIE
Been looking forward to today.

FLETCHER
What's so special about today? Only one good thing about a new day in here, it replaces the old one. Crossed one off, haven't we?

LENNIE
But we're going out today. Aren't we? Breath of fresh air. Trees. Walking on grass. The sounds of birds in the branches.

FLETCHER
Don't get so flaming lyrical, Wordsworth. All we're going to do is dig drains for the council. Stooped six hours over a shovel. Doing a job they'd only give to prisoners, seeing as any civilised geezer would tell 'em to stuff it.

LENNIE
I don't care what they make us do. We're going outside that's all I care. A whole day out of here.

FLETCHER
You're like a kid on a school trip, aren't you?

LENNIE
You don't fool me, Fletch. You just mask your enthusiasm, you do. But if you were that indifferent, why would you have gone to the trouble of bribing yourself on to the party?

FLETCHER
Yuh, well . . .

LENNIE
Yeah, well.

FLETCHER
Well I can't deny the thought of fresh air appeals. Get the smell of disinfectant out me nostrils. Not to mention your festering feet.

LENNIE

I change my socks every day.

FLETCHER

Pity you can't change your feet.

LENNIE

If it ain't one thing it's another . . . I don't complain about your personal habits.

FLETCHER

What personal habits? I don't have any personal habits.

LENNIE

Yes, you do.

FLETCHER

I do not!

LENNIE

You do.

FLETCHER

Like what?

LENNIE

You talk with your mouth full, you whistle out of tune, you snore, you spit . . .

FLETCHER

How dare you? I do not whistle out of tune. You've got a cheek you have, you've got a flaming nerve. This is supposed to be a single cell, this is – by rights, mine. You've got a nerve talking about my personal habits. You was dragged up in some Birmingham backstreet.

LENNIE

I had a good upbringing, I did. We may not have had much money but my mother kept us spotless.

FLETCHER

Well you ain't spotless now, are you? Your clothes are covered in gravy stains. So don't give me no stick about personal table manners.

LENNIE

Look, everybody at our table is covered in gravy stains – it's your gravy! I told you, you talk with your mouth full.

Fletcher starts cleaning his teeth.

FLETCHER

You'd better watch it, Godber. I'm warning you. I do not talk with my mouth full.

LENNIE

Look, you're doing it now, I'm covered in toothpaste.

FLETCHER

Cheeky young nurk.

LENNIE

Don't let's fall out, Fletch. We don't want to spoil things this early. Today's the big day.

FLETCHER

It ain't that big a day, son. Ain't a coach trip to Southend. Not a day at the seaside, with a trip up the pier and a big nosh up and reduced rates at the local knocking shop. We're only going across a remote Cumberland moor, to a remote Cumberland village to dig drains. Sustained by the remote possibility that the district nurse might pass by on her bicycle and give us all an exciting glimpse of stocking top.

LENNIE

A woman . . . a woman on her bicycle.

FLETCHER

Maybe, maybe.

LENNIE

No, Fletch, I can see her. Clear as day.
In her uniform, on her bicycle.

FLETCHER

District nurse, huh. Some old spinster
with brogues and bike rider's buttocks.

LENNIE

No, she's young, Fletch, honest,
young and nice looking. Well, more
than that, beautiful really. And the prim
uniform which she so proudly wears
can barely conceal the voluptuous
figure within.

FLETCHER

Oh. Voluptuous figure within, is it?

LENNIE

Yeah. Which her prim uniform
cannot conceal.

FLETCHER

Barely.

LENNIE

Her face is at once innocent
and knowing.

FLETCHER

I know them innocent faces.

LENNIE

Obviously primitive passions are
stirring deep within her breast.

FLETCHER

Oh deep one, is it?

LENNIE

Oh definitely.

FLETCHER

Here hang on, what's this gorgeous
deep-chested thigh-flashing bit
of nooky doing up this neck of
the woods?

LENNIE

(*Hesitates for only a second*) Well, you
see, she comes home to nurse her
dad what's been sick with a fatal,
tropical disease.

FLETCHER

Fatal is it, that could kill you.

LENNIE

She turned her back on the bright
lights like out of duty.

FLETCHER

Of course she did, didn't she? Could've
been a model, girl like that, cover girl,
chased by playboys and Arab princes.

LENNIE

Instead of which –

FLETCHER

Instead of which she returns to nurse
her ailing dad, trying hard to subdue
her primitive stirrings, until the day
when fate decrees she has a puncture
right next to the drain I'm digging.

LENNIE

Here, hang on, I saw her first.

FLETCHER

Naff off, Godber, age before beauty.
I'm at her side, picking her up, dusting
her down, and not failing to notice as I
do her proud, firm body. She's
sprained her perfectly formed ankle,
and I carries her over several miles of

ploughed sludge, staggering at last,
exhausted, into her lonely cottage
miles from anywhere, leaving the two
of us thrown together as night falls.

LENNIE

What about Dad, then?

FLETCHER

Oh he's dead. There's just us. Me and
her. Together. Alone. And she pours
me a drink, after slipping out of her
wet uniform. Slip, slip. Then she gets
me some grub. And I eat, and we talk.

LENNIE

There you go again, Fletch.

FLETCHER

What?

LENNIE

Talking with your mouth full.

Fletcher throws a shoe at Lennie.

3. ASSEMBLY ROOM

*Navyrum, Ives and Scrounger
are waiting.*

NAVYRUM

Hey Ives, how did you work your way
on this doddle? Bribed a lot of people
in high places.

IVES

'Ere listen –

NAVYRUM

You're not a working man. Not a bird
bones skiving little git like you.

IVES

'Ere listen –

NAVYRUM

I'm a working man. Always have been.

Stoker. Paid my dues. Tankers.
Persian Gulf. Big sweat I'll tell ye.

IVES

'Ere listen, Navyrum, I'll do my share,
don't you worry.

SCROUNGER

I had a job once, worked on a road
gang. Motorway. Naffing job that was.
Had to live on a caravan site with
the old woman and two nippers.
Always mud. Work in mud, come
home to mud.

IVES

Should feel at home today then.

*The door is unlocked and
Barrowolough brings Fletcher and
Lennie in then locks the door again.*

OTHERS

Hello, Fletch, Lennie.

LENNIE

Hello lads.

FLETCHER

Gentlemen . . . all right, Scrounger.
Here, how did this little runt fiddle his
way on this?

IVES

'Ere listen –

FLETCHER

Can't even shovel his peas he can't
without getting tennis elbow.

IVES

Don't you worry, I'll do my share.

NAVYRUM

'E's a skivin' git.

FLETCHER

That's exactly what he is Navyrum,

you're not wrong there. And how are you? D'you know young Lennie Godber, my temporary cell mate?

LENNIE

(*Nods*) Hello.

NAVYRUM

Hello, son.

Fletcher and Lennie sit down.

FLETCHER

Me and Navyrum were in Maidstone together. When he gets to know you a bit better he might let you come round one night and read his tattoos.

SCROUNGER

Who are we waiting for?

NAVYRUM

Dylan.

FLETCHER

Dylan! That long-haired anarchist nurk. We've got a right lot here, ain't we, for a hard day's work. A twelve-stone weakling and the King of the Huddersfield Hippies.

The door is unlocked and Barrowclough comes in with Dylan. Dylan acknowledges the others with a nod.

FLETCHER

Well now, Dylan, speak of the devil.

DYLAN

Listen man, my name's Melvyn, what's all this Dylan scene?

FLETCHER

Not out of malice, son, we calls you that out of affection. We calls you that 'cos you reminds us of Dylan.

DYLAN

Bob Dylan?

FLETCHER

No, that hippy rabbit on *The Magic Roundabout.*

DYLAN

I'm not a hippy.

FLETCHER

You're the nearest thing we've got to one. You wear an earring and you got chucked out of art school for writing on the walls, and you're the only one here what's tidied their prison uniform.

DYLAN

Oh man . . .

BARROWCLOUGH

I didn't know you watched *The Magic Roundabout,* Fletcher.

FLETCHER

Yes, good ain't it?

DYLAN

Magic Roundabout.

FLETCHER

All right, all right. Gives a lot of innocent people a lot of pleasure. Even gives us guilty people a lot of pleasure. Simple pleasures are very precious to us, ain't they, Scrounger?

SCROUNGER

Like this day out.

LENNIE

Oh yeah, be great to see a bit of grass, smell the flowers.

BARROWCLOUGH

Oh you'll have to join our Botany Club, you'll enjoy that. I run it in the summer. We get out on the fells exploring the natural phenomena of our countryside.

FLETCHER

Oh do you? All young Lennie and I want to explore is that young nurse, eh, son?

NAVYRUM

Nurse? What's this then? Which nurse?

LENNIE

She's mine. He commandeered my fantasy.

NAVYRUM

What we waiting for then?

BARROWCLOUGH

We're waiting for Mr Mackay.

FLETCHER

Oh dear, Scotland the brave – is he coming?

BARROWCLOUGH

Mr Mackay's in charge, yes.

NAVYRUM

Git.

DYLAN

Pig.

FLETCHER

Charmless nurk.

The door has been unlocked and Mackay enters.

MACKAY

What's going on then?

FLETCHER

Oh morning, Mr Mackay. Just voted you man of the year.

MACKAY

On your feet all of you.

They all stand.

MACKAY

None of your facetious lip, Fletcher.

FLETCHER

You'll get none of it today, Mr Mackay.

MACKAY

Now as this work party is composed of such a spineless, delinquent obstreperous rabble, let's make a few things crystal clear. There will be no skiving, no fraternising with members of the public, no kipping in the long grass, and another thing there will not be is visits to the nearest pub masquerading as Irish labourers working on a mythical motorway extension. Any questions?

FLETCHER

Yeah, I've got a question.

MACKAY

What?

FLETCHER

Is the ball and chain worn outside the wellington boot or inside?

4. PRISON

A bus approaches the prison gates. The warder opens the gate and the bus drives through and away.

5. ROAD AND DITCH

Camera shows a churchyard. Not far away a nurse is cycling up a hill. The prisoners' work party are at the roadside.

The nurse cycles past them. They come out of the ditch and react to her. She wobbles on her bicycle.

MACKAY

Quiet the lot of you.

He crosses to the ditch.

MACKAY

Just get on with it. Ives, put some effort into it.

IVES

'Ere listen, everyone picks on me. I do my share.

FLETCHER

I think you'd have us in chains, wouldn't you, Mr Mackay – if you had your way.

MACKAY

With the greatest of pleasure.

He turns to leave.

DYLAN

Pig.

Mackay turns back.

MACKAY

Did you speak, Bottomley?

DYLAN

Dig. I was just telling Fletcher to dig.

FLETCHER

Who're you calling a pig?

LENNIE

Can we sing?

MACKAY

Sing?

FLETCHER

What we got to sing about?

LENNIE

No, but it would help like. Keep our spirits up. Like the Negro slaves on the plantations in the deep South. Work songs, things like that, kept their spirits up, didn't it? We're working in a gang, just like them.

FLETCHER

If you chuck much more mud about we'll all look like 'em an' all.

NAVYRUM

Used to sing in the Gulf. Stoking. Sing opera.

He starts singing. The others join in.

FLETCHER

Oh dear.

MACKAY

Thank God for that.

FLETCHER

Thank gawd for that.

MACKAY

I'm just popping down to the village to er . . . get some part for my lawnmower.

He moves to the door of the van and addresses Barrowclough.

MACKAY

So er . . . you take charge, all right?

BARROWCLOUGH

You'll not be long, will you?

MACKAY

(*Getting into van*) You're perfectly capable, man.

BARROWCLOUGH

Ah, but you see there's a lot of them and only one of me.

MACKAY

Pull yourself together, Mr Barrowclough.

The van starts up.
In the ditch Fletcher notices the
van's departure. The group cheers.

SCROUNGER

Where's he going then?

FLETCHER

He's going after that district nurse, he
ain't so fussy as us, is he?

BARROWCLOUGH

(*Moving to the ditch*) Now listen, you
men. Let's knuckle down. My
approach may not be as rigid as Mr
Mackay's but there's work to be done
and I'm here to see it gets done, so
there'll be no shirking, no slacking and
no taking advantage of my good
nature. Right.

ALL

Right, Mr Barrowclough.

They start chatting.

6. CHURCH

Inside the church the work party
are having a smoke and taking
it easy.

LENNIE

Nice this, isn't it Fletch? Being out
I mean.

FLETCHER

Oh yes, well, makes a change. Get a
bit more exercise. Mind you I'd like
today to be a bit more to write home
about. Pub just down the road.
Wouldn't half like to be in it. Pop in the
village shop. Get some sweets, and
a *Reveille*.

LENNIE

Ain't possible, is it?

FLETCHER

It's been done.

Barrowclough comes in.

BARROWCLOUGH

Oh no – now come along men,
you've had a good long smoke
break, it's high time we got back
to it. We shouldn't be smoking in
here at all.

FLETCHER

We had to have somewhere to sit,
couldn't sit on the damp grass, could
we? 'Cos it's bad for you, very bad
for you.

BARROWCLOUGH

It's usual to sit on the earth you dig
out – form little piles.

FLETCHER

Exactly, that's what I'm worried about,
forming little piles.

BARROWCLOUGH

That's enough, Fletcher. Now we really
must knuckle down. (*Counting*) One,
two, three . . . Now, where's Ives?

FLETCHER

He's outside desecrating holy ground,
isn't he?

BARROWCLOUGH

How do you mean?

FLETCHER

Gone for a slash in the churchyard.

At that moment there is a terrible
scream and Ives comes in clutching
his trousers.

IVES
'Ere listen, help, I've been stung.

FLETCHER
Obviously the Lord's retribution, you vulgar nurk. Bee, was it?

IVES
I don't know what it was, I ain't a flaming zoologist.

LENNIE
Maybe it was a wasp. Or a hornet.

IVES
What difference does it make?

FLETCHER
Makes a lot of difference. Different degree of pain and poison.

IVES
It was a great big thing.

FLETCHER
Oh hornet, fatal.

IVES
What you mean, fatal?

FLETCHER
Listen lads, if one of us don't suck the poison out of Ives's system he's going to die.

There is a silence.

FLETCHER
You're going to die, old son.

IVES
'Ere, listen, that's not funny.

BARROWCLOUGH
Don't joke, Fletcher, the man is in some distress – it's all right, Ives, it's almost certainly just a wasp sting.

IVES
I'm dying.

FLETCHER
(*Knocks Ives*) Yes, come on again.
(*Moving to Barrowclough*)
Permission to make a suggestion, Mr Barrowclough.

BARROWCLOUGH
What?

FLETCHER
Why don't someone go down the village get some ointment or TCP. Then the only problem's getting a volunteer to rub it on. I'd be willing to go and get some.

The others cough.

BARROWCLOUGH
Go to the village?

FLETCHER
I'd be willing to take that long walk on this mission of mercy.

BARROWCLOUGH
Well, I suppose . . . if you went straight there and back.

FLETCHER
What else, Mr Barrowclough? Man's life at stake. Need money, of course. Expensive those antibiotics.

BARROWCLOUGH
All right, well here, I've only got a pound.

FLETCHER
That should cover it.

BARROWCLOUGH
Now look, Fletcher –

FLETCHER
Mr Barrowclough please, every second counts.

He goes.

7. PUB

In the pub Fletcher hands over a pound note to the landlord and takes a pint of beer.

LANDLORD

Thank you, sir. You look as if you need that one.

FLETCHER

Thanks. I do, don't I? First one I've had for ages. Well, I'm not allowed, am I? Doctor says I'm not to drink – ulcer, you see. Can't take it any more. But just occasionally I have a little sip. *He sinks back the pint in about three seconds flat and bangs the glass on the counter.*

FLETCHER

Fill it up, then.

The landlord takes the glass.

FLETCHER

Oh and six packets of crisps.

LANDLORD

With an ulcer?

FLETCHER

No – cheese and onion. Not for me, for the lads.

LANDLORD

Lads?

FLETCHER

What lads? Oh yes, what lads – oh well, we're working on the motorway, aren't we?

LANDLORD

What motorway?

FLETCHER

The . . . the *new* by-pass.

LANDLORD

But we've never heard of the new by-pass.

FLETCHER

No, it's that new, that's why you ain't heard of it. I've only just heard of it myself.

LANDLORD

But this is outrageous. This whole area's National Trust. What's the use in having a by-pass through here?

FLETCHER

Now look, mate, it's none of my doing, is it? I see your point of view, despoiling England's green and pleasant land, it worried me – that's how I got the ulcer, isn't it? *The vicar and his verger walk into the pub.*

VICAR

Good morning all.

VERGER

Did you hear the thunder? It's going to p-pelt down in a minute.

LANDLORD

Vicar, have you heard?

VICAR

Heard what?

LANDLORD

They're building a new by-pass.

VICAR

Where?

FLETCHER

Where? Ah well. Over there, isn't it? *He points vaguely in the direction of the Gents.*

VICAR

But what's the point of a by-pass? There's nothing to bypass, except for the prison, of course.

FLETCHER

What prison, eh?

LANDLORD

Six hundred bloody criminals on our doorstep.

VICAR

Now now, Frank, you mustn't pre-judge these men. They're serving their penance.

FLETCHER

Quite right, Rev. Public revenge, isn't it? Eye for an eye. Tooth for a nail.

VICAR

No, we must treat them with tolerance and compassion. I don't mean to sound pious but people must keep an open mind. My mind, like the doors of my church, is always open.

FLETCHER

Well spoken, Rev. Greater joy in heaven over a sinner what repenteth.

VICAR

Repenteth, yes indeed. I was wondering – would you like to –

FLETCHER

I would, yes. Pint, please.

VICAR

Oh fine, yes . . . would you do the

honours Frank . . . in fact I was going to ask if you'd like to bring your chums over to evensong on Sunday.

FLETCHER

Oh? What? Well . . . much as we'd like to we may not be able to get out, er across. Tell you what, we'll come if we're free – all right? Cheers.

OTHERS

Cheers.

Mackay walks in.

VICAR

Ah here's a man with a different point of view. Morning, Mr Mackay.

MACKAY

Morning Padre, sir.

LANDLORD/VERGER

Morning, Mr Mackay.

MACKAY

Morning, gentlemen. Different point of view to what?

VICAR

To our friend here.

They turn to Fletcher but he has gone.

LANDLORD

Oh, where's he vanished to?

VICAR

Oh.

MACKAY

I'll have a whisky with a pint chaser.

LANDLORD

On duty?

MACKAY

I'm only half on duty. Got a works party down the road.

VICAR

Works party?

MACKAY

They're digging ditches down Felton Bank.

VICAR

Prisoners?

MACKAY

Oh yes.

VICAR

Verger, why don't you pop down to the church?

VERGER

But it's going to pour again any minute.

VICAR

You've got your bike, pop down and lock the church door.

VERGER

But why?

VICAR

You heard what he said – there's a bunch of criminals loose in the area.

8. PUB

Verger walks out of the pub. He puts on his bicycle clips, then turns to bike but there's an empty space where his bicycle should have been.

9. ROAD

Fletcher is cycling along the road. He puts his hand in his jacket and gets out a beer mug. He drinks from it, then chucks the mug over a fence. Sheep bleat in the background. Fletcher cycles on down the road.

10. CHURCH

Inside Navyrum is showing Lennie his tattoos. The other members of the work party and Barrowclough are also present.

NAVYRUM

This one was done in Valparaiso. That's in South America. Chile. Very Catholic country, Chile. Hence the religious overtones.

LENNIE

What's her name – Doris? Doesn't sound very Chilean.

NAVYRUM

No, she weren't. She were from Bootle. Stranded there with a juggling act. What with me being from the Pool that's how we got on so well, hence the affectionate overtones.

LENNIE

'I'll always . . .'

NAVYRUM

Don't read it out loud, son – not in here.

Fletcher walks in.

FLETCHER

What you all doing in here? You was just going out when I left.

BARROWCLOUGH

We heard the thunder and Navyrum assured me we were due for a heavy storm, him having been in the Navy he knows the signs. Well, have you got the ointment?

FLETCHER

Ointment?

IVES

I'm dying – 'ere listen.

FLETCHER

Oh, about the ointment, oh yes, thing
is see the village shop it was closed,
wasn't it? Closed for lunch hour.

BARROWCLOUGH

But it's only half-past eleven.

FLETCHER

Yeah well, it's not my fault, is it? They
close for lunch earlier in the country,
don't they, 'cos they get up earlier and
they get hungry.

IVES

Oh come on, I'm in agony. I'm ablaze.

FLETCHER

Stick it in the font, then.

IVES

I might die.

FLETCHER

Anyone know the burial service?

NAVYRUM

I buried a bloke at sea once.

FLETCHER

Oh you're all right, Ives, then, there's a
reservoir up the road.

BARROWCLOUGH

Oh dear, this day's turning into a
disaster. Come on, there's not
going to be any storm. It's passed
over. We should be getting that
ditch dug.

He goes to the door.

LENNIE

You crafty nurk, Fletch, you've been
down the pub, ain't you?

SCROUNGER

You have, haven't you?

FLETCHER

Don't think I'd forget the lads, do you?

He hands out packets of crisps.

FLETCHER

Here you are, then. That'll put hair on
your legs.

BARROWCLOUGH

Is all this out of my pound, Fletcher?

FLETCHER

It was, and me and the lads are more
than grateful, aren't we?

LENNIE

Yes, Mr Barrowclough.

SCROUNGER

Thank you, Mr Barrowclough.

NAVYRUM

You're a toff, Mr Barrowclough.

FLETCHER

Eat up, lads. Now we've got all that
protein inside us we can get on with
the digging.

BARROWCLOUGH

Digging, yes, there's been precious
little done so far. Come on, lads.

SCROUNGER

Come on, Ives, you're not dead yet.

LENNIE

That's funny, this door's stuck.

FLETCHER

Let's have a look. It's not stuck,
it's locked.

11. ROAD AND DITCH

The verger is walking along the

road. *A van drives up to him and
stops. Mackay gets out.*

VERGER

Someone's stolen my bike, I bet it's
one of your lot.

MACKAY

Nonsense, my lot are hard at it. Without
my say-so they wouldn't dare move.

He moves to the ditch.

MACKAY

All right, you lot.

*He looks down and sees an empty
ditch.*

MACKAY

Oh my God, they've scarpered.

12. CHURCH

*The prisoners are locked in
the church. Barrowclough has
failed to find a way out and
joins the others.*

BARROWCLOUGH

The vestry's locked as well – there's no
other way out.

IVES

'Ere listen, we could break a window.

FLETCHER

That window's four hundred years old.
This is a church, you nurk. Have
you got no sense of reverence?
You're a Palestine, that's what you
are, a Palestine.

BARROWCLOUGH

Philistine, I think you mean.

FLETCHER

Yeah well, depends on your religion,
don't it?

DYLAN

Let's ring the bell, some cat might
hear that.

BARROWCLOUGH

They never use this bell. It's ancient,
you see, like the tower. Last time it was
heard in these parts was to warn the
villagers of marauding Scots.

FLETCHER

Marauding Scots, was it?

BARROWCLOUGH

In the sixteenth century, yes. They
came over the border, pillaging crops
and, well, ravishing the womenfolk and
all that.

FLETCHER

Oh well, that bell'll put the wind up a
few vests, won't it? Probably all flee
south with their possessions strapped
to the back of their Vauxhall Vivas.
Mind you, I reckon a few of the
womenfolk might stay. Eh? I mean, it's
been four hundred years since they
had a good ravishin'.

BARROWCLOUGH

Can't you do something? You've been
convicted for breaking and entering.

FLETCHER

Breaking and entering, yes. Entering, is
the operative word. I ain't never been
convicted for breaking out of nowhere.

LENNIE

Flippin' hell. We get one day out from nick and what happens. We get locked in.

13. FILM

Camera shows a telephone dial. A finger is dialling.

MACKAY

Chief Officer Barrett, Mackay here, sir . . . Mackay. Something has occurred, sir, to which I feel I ought to draw your attention.

Camera shows a van. Mackay and Barrett are inside it talking.

BARRETT

Just down this road, are they?

MACKAY

Not any more, sir. I still say you should put out a full scale alarm, Mr Barrett.

BARRETT

And I still say your judgement is impaired, Mr Mackay. And I am not making a fool out of Slade Prison or burdening the taxpayer with a full scale alert until I have personally verified the facts.

The van pulls up at the ditch and both men get out.

MACKAY

What did I tell you, there, what did I tell you?

The ditch is empty. The work party comes up and greets the officers.

BARROWCLOUGH

(*Standing up*) Afternoon, Mr Barrett,

sir. Mr Mackay. All present and correct, sir.

BARRETT

Pull yourself together, Mr Mackay.

Fletcher winks at Barrowclough who is looking at him.

14. CELL

Fletcher, Lennie and Mackay are in Fletcher's cell.

MACKAY

I have been dropped in it, have I not, Fletcher? I have been put upon from a great height.

FLETCHER

Oh dear, Mr Mackay. I'm sorry to hear that, Mr Mackay. Anything we can do to alleviate it, as it were?

MACKAY

When I am in it, Fletcher, I absorb it with a stiff upper lip.

FLETCHER

No choice have you, if you're up to (*Gesturing*) here in it.

MACKAY

Stand still. I absorb it with cool Celtic calm, like a man. And then I relieve my frustrations by making sure that everyone down the line below me suffers.

FLETCHER

What?

MACKAY

Suffers.

LENNIE

Hey, that's not fair.

MACKAY

Fair?

LENNIE

Why take it out on us? Nobody's fault we got locked in the church.

FLETCHER

Yeah, we might still be there now if it hadn't been for that funeral.

MACKAY

Why were you in the church to begin with if you weren't skiving? Abusing our trust. Taking advantage of Barrowclough's laxity.

FLETCHER

I didn't know Mr Barrowclough had laxity, did you, Lennie?

LENNIE

No, poor fellow. 'Cos we were miles from anywhere.

MACKAY

Godber.

LENNIE

Sir.

MACKAY

Do not imagine that you will be excluded from my spiteful resentment. Over the next few weeks you'll both suffer some terrible indignities. Your feet Fletcher, your dinky little size sevens, will not touch the floor. I harbour grudges.

He goes out.

LENNIE

He means it.

FLETCHER

Yeah well.

LENNIE

It was worth it though, weren't it, Fletch?

FLETCHER

'Course it was, my son. A day out. Pint of beer, bag of crisps. Ives in agony. All that and him being dropped in, wallop! We did all right, son.

LENNIE

You did better than most, Fletch.

FLETCHER

Yeah well, naturally.

LENNIE

I got something out the day meself.

FLETCHER

Oh yes. What?

LENNIE

Something I nicked from the church.

He produces a crumpled surplice.

LENNIE

A surplice.

FLETCHER

You stole? From the church?

LENNIE

It's the only place you can get 'em.

FLETCHER

What do you want it for anyway?

LENNIE

It'll satisfy a need I've had for some time, this will.

FLETCHER

What you talking about?

LENNIE

It's to cover me from the gravy when you talk with your mouth full.

SERIES ONE

EPISODE FIVE: WAYS AND MEANS

1. PRISON WORKROOM

Fletcher, Ives, McLaren and other prisoners are making fishing nets. Barrowclough is supervising them.

FLETCHER

Oh shame on it.

BARROWCLOUGH

What's the matter?

FLETCHER

I've just dropped a stitch. (*Sewing*) Oh f . . .

BARROWCLOUGH

Is something wrong, Fletcher?

FLETCHER

'Course something's wrong. It's the job that's wrong, in' it? Grown men spending eight hours a day sewing fishing nets. Can you think of anything more demeaning or indignified?

BARROWCLOUGH

Mailbags. It's a step up from mailbags.

MCLAREN

This isn't a job, it's a punishment.

Everyone in this room's being punished, 'cos we haven't been good little boys.

IVES

Pity you lost that cushy job on the farm, eh? Fresh air – free eggs every day.

FLETCHER

Free – more like half a dozen.

BARROWCLOUGH

I knew you were pilfering eggs.

He walks across to Fletcher.

FLETCHER

Yeah, well it's like young McLaren says. I'm being punished, in' I? What chance has a man got? When all the establishment forces are aligned against him.

BARROWCLOUGH

Now, Fletcher, you've been in prison long enough to know the score. You've broken the rules. You've upset Mr Mackay and you must accept the consequences.

FLETCHER

I thought you was going to appeal to the Governor on my behalf, Mr Barrowclough.

BARROWCLOUGH

The Governor has no time for you, Fletcher. He's very disappointed in you, just as I am.

FLETCHER

All right, Mr Barrowclough, all right. We knows society's extracting its revenge on those what never had a chance to begin with. Look at McLaren here. Never had a chance, have you, son?

McLAREN

Cowing used to it, ain't I?

BARROWCLOUGH

Yes, he's being punished just like you.

FLETCHER

Why? What did he do?

McLAREN

I spoilt the stinking soup.

FLETCHER

He spoilt the soup! And for that he has to pay the penance – well, what chance has any of us got?

BARROWCLOUGH

McLaren, that's not the whole truth as you well know. You spoilt the soup because you held a prison officer's head under it for two minutes.

McLAREN

Yeah, well . . .

BARROWCLOUGH

You tried to drown that prison officer, McLaren. It was a vicious and unprovoked attack.

FLETCHER

(*Amused*) Tried to drown him!

McLAREN

He cowing asked for it.

BARROWCLOUGH

You could have severely scalded him.

FLETCHER

Not in this nick you couldn't. Not with the lukewarm soup we get. Poisoned him possibly, yeah, could have poisoned him.

IVES

What sort of soup, was it?

McLAREN

Mixed vegetable.

FLETCHER

Mixed vegetable. Stone me. I bet he was furious. All those bits of barley and carrot up his nose.

BARROWCLOUGH

It's not funny, Fletcher. It was a vicious attack, and that's why McLaren's here. And your attitude makes it quite clear why you're here.

FLETCHER

Oh I see, yes, well. Yes, well, I see, yes, well.

McLAREN

I was provoked.

FLETCHER

I bet you were, my son.

McLAREN

He called me a black bastard.

BARROWCLOUGH

Now if that were true if he really did say that, you could have gone straight to the Governor, McLaren.

FLETCHER

Oh yeah, fat chance. I mean technically he ain't got a leg to stand on. Technically the facts as stated by the prison officer are not wholly inaccurate. Being as how he is 'a' negroid, and 'b' illegitimate.

MCLAREN

It was the way he said it.

FLETCHER

I know that. You know that. He'll probably tell the Governor that in the course of conversation he simply observed that you were non-caucasian and born out of wedlock.

BARROWCLOUGH

Now that's enough talking, all of you. Work to be done.

FLETCHER

Work! Knitting string vests for hippopotamuses. This probably won't fit me anyway. They're cunning, ain't they? 'Cos giving you a job like this, they knows that we won't cock it up. They knows we wouldn't do nothing slipshod, 'cos we'd be screwing up those brave fishermen of England, wouldn't we? Leave a few holes in here and they'd be

coming back half a ton of cod short. And the price of fish fingers would rocker. Not to mention cod pieces. Whereas of course mailbags, well – don't care if we do a sloppy job there, do we? It makes it easier for our mates that rob mail trains.

BARROWCLOUGH

Fletcher, one just has to listen to you for a matter of minutes to know your type. When you first came here I had high hopes for you, I won't pretend I didn't. It has to be said, you're surly and hostile.

FLETCHER

Yeah, well, years of prison hardens you, doesn't it? Well-known fact.

BARROWCLOUGH

But you've only been here six weeks.

FLETCHER

I'm not really hostile, I'm just resentful. Well, when I first come in here I thought between the two of us there was some sort of rapport there, you know?

BARROWCLOUGH

(*Sitting down next to Fletcher*) You mean you thought I was 'in your pocket' – is that the term for it?

FLETCHER

Terrible thing to say. What a terrible thing to say. Just 'cos I asked you one or two little favours. What a terrible thing to say! In themselves they was meaningless but they would just have made life that little bit more tolerable.

BARROWCLOUGH

Your little favours were supposed to include getting you a new cell, with a

window facing south-west, not to
mention the extra blankets and the bit
of carpet, the special soap, extra
tobacco, carpet slippers, a set of
darts, a roll of soft toilet paper and
some Kendal mint cake.

FLETCHER
All right, don't exaggerate. I said you
needn't bother with the darts if you
were pushed.

BARROWCLOUGH
Now, I haven't forgotten that you've
given me very helpful advice on . . .
domestic matters. Don't think Mrs
Barrowclough and I don't appreciate
that 'cos we do. But I'll be damned if
I'll let you treat me like some glorified
batman.

FLETCHER
I ain't just referring to your . . . marital
problems. Though one can't help
reflect that there's been some change
in your old lady's attitude . . .

BARROWCLOUGH
How can you tell that?

FLETCHER
Oh just little things. In the morning your
general demeanour. A spring in your
step. That certain smile that plays
around your lips when you comes round
in the morning ordering us to slop out.

BARROWCLOUGH
What certain smile?

FLETCHER
The smile of a man who's getting
his oats.

BARROWCLOUGH
(*Embarrassed*) Fletcher!

FLETCHER
Are you denying it?

BARROWCLOUGH
Look, I've said I'm grateful.

FLETCHER
Oh yes. Well, yes. I don't want your
gratitude, Mr Barrowclough. I've learnt
my lesson. It's them and us.

BARROWCLOUGH
Look, Fletcher –

FLETCHER
Now, if you'll excuse me, I must get
back to my knitting. Talking to you I'm
getting all behind like a cow's tail.
I might not get my full sixty pee this
week. Sixty pee a week . . . Still it's
just enough money to cover the cost of
a jar of Wintergreen Ointment. 'Cos all
my money goes on medicaments.
'Cos I've never been a well man.
Always been suspect to lumbago
and rheumatics . . . all those illnesses
what are caused by not having
enough blankets, having a cold
draughty cell facing north-east, and
walking around on concrete floors
without carpet slippers.

BARROWCLOUGH
I'll see about the extra blanket.

FLETCHER
No. No, no, no, no. I want nothing
from you or no one. Nothing,
nothing, nothing . . .
Barrowclough moves.

FLETCHER
Well, there is one thing, since you insist. One very minor thing.

BARROWCLOUGH
What thing?

FLETCHER
I want a job in the library.

2A. FLETCHER'S CELL

He is washing his blistered hands. Fletcher's cell door is open as it is association hour.

FLETCHER
Gawd Almighty. I hope the fishermen of England flaming appreciate me. I won't never play the harpsichord again. I doubt if I'll even be able to wipe me own nose.

Fletcher picks up a towel and bar of soap and leaves his cell.

2B. PRISON LANDING

As he goes out he collides with McLaren, causing him to drop a newspaper, a couple of oranges and his metal comb.

MCLAREN
Cowing hell.

FLETCHER
Sorry, son, sorry.

MCLAREN
(*Threateningly*) Can't you watch where you're cowing going, Fletcher?

FLETCHER
(*Backing off*) I've said I'm sorry, son. My fault, my fault. Won't happen again. Promise you.

MCLAREN
Watch it.

FLETCHER
I will, son. I promise. No borra, eh? I'm not a well man.

McLaren gives him another evil glance, then bends down to pick up his oranges.
As he does so his head is facing inside Fletcher's cell.

FLETCHER
I don't want no trouble with you, McLaren.

He kicks him up the backside causing him to fall on his face inside Fletcher's cell.

2C. CELL

Before McLaren can recover, Fletcher has grabbed the kid by the collar and hauled him to his feet, pushed him over the table, their faces a couple of inches apart. Fletcher speaks to him, disguising his genuine threat with a gentle, reasonable voice.

FLETCHER
Now I know you're an 'ard case, son.

We all do. We know you're full of nasty militant feelings. But if you ever speaks to me like that again, I shall twist your head round like a cork in a bottle of Beaujolais. Pull it off and give it to that poof Roland in B Block to keep his wigs on.

MCLAREN

(*Choking*) Yes, Fletch.

FLETCHER

And are we sorry?

MCLAREN

Yes we are, Fletch.

FLETCHER

Right. Don't lie about there. Got any snout?

MCLAREN

No.

FLETCHER

There's some under that pillow. Help yourself.

MCLAREN

Oh ta.

As he does so Fletcher picks up the oranges, the paper and the comb.

FLETCHER

Here you are – here's your things. Your own worst enemy, ain't you, son? *He sits down.*

MCLAREN

Oh yes?

FLETCHER

Sit down, sit down. I know things ain't easy for you. Being black with a Scottish father. I mean, it's an unfortunate mixture. It's the Scottish side what brings out all that aggression in you.

MCLAREN

Is it?

FLETCHER

Yeah, course it is. I mean, it subdues your basic West Indian personality. Which is one of exuberant high spirits. All them steel bands, and carnivals, like. Lordy Lordy bit. Someone just has to score a boundary in a test match and they have a firework display.

MCLAREN

I've never set foot in the West Indies. I was born in Greenock. Or at least found. Some copper found me up an alley wrapped in a *Glasgow Herald*.

FLETCHER

Yeah, well, I did admit, didn't I, you ain't had it easy.

MCLAREN

I never knew my father. Mam who didn't want me. Flaming orphanage, and I'm black with a Scottish accent. What you want me to be, Fletcher, happy-go-bloody-lucky?

FLETCHER

It could be worse, son, couldn't it?

MCLAREN

Could it?

FLETCHER
(*Thinks hard*) . . . No, I don't suppose it could, in all honesty. But you don't want to let that illegitimate tag worry you. Lots of famous people was illegitimate. Royalty like. And William the Conqueror . . . Lawrence of Arabia . . . Leonardo da Vinci . . . Napper Wainwright.

MCLAREN
Who's Napper Wainwright?

FLETCHER
He was a screw in Brixton . . . mind you, he was a right bastard.

MCLAREN
Never let you forget.

FLETCHER
It ain't a stigma no more. Not these days, in these liberated times. Out of fashion, marriage is. All these glamour people, these trendsetters, your pop stars and television personalities, well all their offspring's outta wedlock, isn't it? Frankly, in a few years time, illegitimates is going to be fashionable figures. Like homosexuals are at the moment. In fact, being an illegitimate black poof's about as chic as you could get.

MCLAREN
(*Rising*) I'm not a –

FLETCHER
Oh come on, I know that –

MCLAREN
If anyone suggests –

FLETCHER
'Course no one won't. See the way you fly off the handle? Own worst enemy. Come the hard man, where's it get you?

MCLAREN
Got me pride.
Sits back on the bunk.

FLETCHER
Oh yes, pride is it? Listen, we ain't even got privacy in here, and where's a man's pride when he ain't got no privacy! You have to learn to turn the other cheek. Yes sir, no sir, three bags full, sir.

MCLAREN
Makes me sick to my guts.

FLETCHER
(*Rising and sitting at the bottom of the bunk*) Look sonny Jim, sonny Jock. You're nipping along the by-pass in a restricted area, right? And the police stop you. Then you think – what have I done, what's their game? So you leaps out the car and really has a go at them. 'Cos you're not going to take no stick from some jumped-up copper who's been watching too many *Z Cars*. In other words, you come on strong. So what happens? A night in the cooler – fifty-pound fine, lose your licence for six months. And they'd only stopped you to point out your rear light was wonky.

MCLAREN

Don't see the point.

FLETCHER

The point is if you'd leapt out, all smarmy and subservient, 'What, constable, my off-side rear? My word, constable – what a blessing you boys in blue are so diligent.' And it's cost you nothing has it? Except your pride and two tickets to the Police Ball.

MCLAREN

You obviously had no reason to hate the law like me. I hate 'em all. They even open letters from my girlfriend.

FLETCHER

Oh yeah. Passionate, are they?

MCLAREN

I can't enjoy them if I feel that lot's read 'em already. It's not right.

FLETCHER

'Course it ain't right, son, but they still do it, don't they? We've all had that. I was on remand once in Brixton. I done this job – a jeweller's in Southwark. Only they got me, but they didn't get the stuff, see. I hadn't . . . you know what I mean. (*Indicating stashing it*) I'd . . . So I'm in Brixton. And I writes to my old lady, Isobel, and says how sorry I was that I got done. Then I says, 'As you may well be a bit short this winter without me providing why don't you plant your own vegetables? I suggest you dig over the back garden as soon as possible.' 'Course next morning

there's twelve police round there with shovels, the devious nurks.

MCLAREN

Typical. Did they find the stuff?

FLETCHER

'Course they didn't, it was in the bottom drawer of the wardrobe. Just my way of getting the garden turned over, see. Why let Isobel do it when you've got twelve great big nosey coppers with spades – if you'll pardon the expression.

MCLAREN

You crafty nurk.

FLETCHER

We had some beautiful broccoli with Christmas dinner. I wrote to her next and suggested she swept the chimney, but they wouldn't buy that one.

MCLAREN

I get your point. You beat them at their own game.

FLETCHER

Subtle. Certainly more subtle than immersing a screw in the soup of the day.

MCLAREN

Wait till it's pea soup next time. Drown quicker in pea soup, it's thicker. Or maybe semolina pudding.

FLETCHER

How long you in for, son?

MCLAREN

Three years.

FLETCHER

You ain't going to be out for ten, the way you're going. Remission's all that counts. Gettin' out of here. I used to be like you once. Not 'ard but lairy, you know. Knew it all. But I wants out. And your time would come that bit sooner if you learned to turn the other cheek.

MCLAREN

I'm not as bad as people make out, you know. I ain't hit a screw for three months.

FLETCHER

No, you ain't actually hit one. But apart from the soup incident, you've tripped one down a flight of stairs, locked one in the deep freeze, caught one in the goolies with a football and put an overdose of cascara in the Padre's cocoa.

MCLAREN

Got a lot of pleasure out of that.

FLETCHER

Yeah, and a lot of solitary. Not as much as the Padre got. He was shut in the bog all week.

MCLAREN

Welfare Officer wants me to see a psychiatrist. Observation like. Thinks I need psychiatric help,

FLETCHER

Would you mind that?

MCLAREN

'Course not. I'd be crazy to turn it down. Cushy, hospital. Better grub, soft bed.

FLETCHER

So when you going to see him then?

MCLAREN

I'm not. Governor wouldn't wear it, would he? Said he knew my sort, I was trying it on.

FLETCHER

Yeah, he's shrewder than we credit him for, that Venables. It's my problem, see. Trying to ingratiate myself back in his good books. I've lost a lot of ground in the credibility stakes.

MCLAREN

Well thanks, Fletch, like. It's been more use than talking to the Welfare Officer.

FLETCHER

Turn the other cheek, son.

MCLAREN

I'll try. I know you're right in principle, like.

FLETCHER

For your own good.

MCLAREN

You're straight you are, Fletcher. Bloke can trust you.

FLETCHER

Don't forget your things.

MCLAREN

Oh, thanks. Where's me orange?

FLETCHER

Dunno son – in't it outside on the floor?

MCLAREN

(*Looking*) No, it's not there.

FLETCHER

Someone's had it – bunch of criminals in here, aren't they?

MCLAREN

Oh cowing heck. All right, tata Fletch.

FLETCHER

Mind how you go.

McLaren leaves. Fletcher gets the orange out of his pocket and starts to peel it.

3. FOOTBALL PITCH

Mackay blows his whistle and leaves the shot. A fight ensues among the players.
Mackay moves to the players to separate them.
Barrowclough and Fletcher are watching.
Mackay and the players argue. He sends McLaren off.

BARROWCLOUGH

He's got a natural talent that lad, but that's the third sending off in four games – it'll mean suspension.

FLETCHER

Own worst enemy.

BARROWCLOUGH

You know that lad needs help.

FLETCHER

Yeah . . . maybe I'm the one who could help him.

Camera shows the players and Mackay again. He blows his whistle and drops the ball.
An alarm bell sounds.

4. CELL

It is association hour and the cell door is open. Fletcher is sitting on the bottom bunk reading. The alarm bell is still ringing.
Barrowclough enters and walks across to the window.

FLETCHER

If that's for me tell them I'll ring back.

BARROWCLOUGH

It's McLaren.

FLETCHER

Oh he's gone over the wall, has he?

BARROWCLOUGH

He's on the roof and he won't come down. Threatening to chuck himself over, unless we answer his demands.

FLETCHER

Oh yes.

He gets up and walks to the table.

BARROWCLOUGH
Get the prison a bad name this sort of thing. If we don't get him down it'll be on *News at Ten*.

FLETCHER
(*Sitting on the chair*) Oh yes.
Then *Panorama*. *World in Action*.
Then the six-part serial in the *Sunday Times*, taking the lid off the penal system.

BARROWCLOUGH
It upsets the men this sort of thing.

FLETCHER
They'll be banging their mugs playing the *Anvil Chorus* on the radiators. You could have a full-scale riot on your hands by tea-time – hang about. What day is it?

BARROWCLOUGH
Thursday.

FLETCHER
Oh no, they won't riot this afternoon. Good tea on a Thursday, in' it? Cauliflower cheese.

BARROWCLOUGH
Fletcher, you take nothing seriously. There's a man's life in danger, to say nothing of the reputation of Slade Prison.

FLETCHER
Oh dear, we don't want to lose our goodwill do we? Or we won't get any bookings for next season.

BARROWCLOUGH
Your flippancy is in very bad taste at a time like this.

FLETCHER
How are they trying to get him down?

BARROWCLOUGH
At the moment the Padre's trying to talk him down through a megaphone.

FLETCHER
The Padre? Is he sober? I mean, the village pub's just closed, isn't it?

BARROWCLOUGH
He's not alone. He's with the Welfare Officer, Mr Gillespie.

FLETCHER
What's he know – the lad's just out of university. Got no experience of the practical. He's probably thumbing through his textbooks now. Trying to find the chapter on Negro nutters and how to deal with them.

BARROWCLOUGH
I think you're being a bit hard on Mr Gillespie.

FLETCHER
Mr Barrowclough! Permission to see the Governor.
He is putting on his jacket.

BARROWCLOUGH
What! Not now, Fletcher. Perhaps when it's all over.

FLETCHER
It's about now that I want to talk.

About the lad. I think I might be able
to help.

BARROWCLOUGH

Help the lad?

FLETCHER

Come on then, are you going to take
me or not?

BARROWCLOUGH

Well, I will if you think it might help –
but Mr Mackay's in charge.

FLETCHER

There you are then. Anything's better
than leaving it to Mr Mackay. He'd
probably just let the lad jump . . .

Barrowclough goes.

FLETCHER

. . . and then jump on him.

5. PRISON GOVERNOR'S
OFFICE

*Fletcher and Barrowclough are
standing in front of the Governor's
desk. Mackay walks across and to
the left of Fletcher.*

VENABLES

In the circumstances I'm willing to
listen to anybody. But what makes you
think you can achieve what we can't,
Fletcher? Do you know something
we don't?

FLETCHER

I know something about what makes

the lad tick. I'm not saying you're not an
experienced man in these matters,
Mr Venables. As is Mr Mackay here and
Mr Gillespie and the Padre. But in his
mind you all represent the establishment
which only inflames his feelings of
hostility and persecution. I mean the
Padre's been out there rabbiting for two
hours, and all he's had for his trouble's a
brick up his megaphone.

VENABLES

(*To Mackay*) How is the Padre?

MACKAY

He's very upset, sir. Very upset that he
couldn't get through to the man. Very
upset also about losing two of his
front teeth.

BARROWCLOUGH

There'll be no sermon on Sunday.

VENABLES

Thank heaven for small mercies.

FLETCHER

You see, it's a question of attitude, isn't
it, sir? Last thing the lad wanted was
all that preaching and sermonising.
Same with our well-meaning intrepid
Mr Gillespie. Asked for trouble, didn't
he, going up that ladder.

VENABLES

How is Mr Gillespie?

MACKAY

As comfortable as could be
expected, sir.

BARROWCLOUGH

We must do something. We can't
leave McLaren where he is, sir.

MACKAY

Why not? Let him sweat it out.
Then tonight when that cold wind
comes whistling over the Pennines,
let him freeze it out. If we give way
to him by just one inch, we'll
establish a regrettable precedent.
We'll have prisoners crawling on
every inch of rooftop, clamouring
for extra blankets, cleaner sheets,
bigger helpings.

FLETCHER

On the other hand –

VENABLES

Yes?

FLETCHER

On the other hand, I could go up and
talk to the lad. He don't trust you lot,
right? And you can't send for friends
or family 'cos the lad ain't got none.
But maybe – and I say maybe – he
may respond to the overtures of one
of his fellow inmates.

MACKAY

Poppycock!

VENABLES

Quiet, Mr Mackay. There is a point
here, a very good point. It could be
quite dangerous, Fletcher.

FLETCHER

Yes, yes. I know. I'm aware that I'm
putting life and limb in some jeopardy.
But you try not to think about things
like that. Try to ignore the tight knot of
fear in the stomach, which I ain't had
since Kuala Lumpur.

VENABLES

Kuala Lumpur?

FLETCHER

Yes, I was there National Service.
Fighting those Malayan bandits for
Queen and Country. Jungle warfare.
Wading through swamps up to here,
rifle above your head to keep the
barrel dry. (*To Mackay*) You know
what I mean. You'd had some of that,
sir. Suddenly you're in a clearing,
there'd be nothing but the sound of
the night creatures in the
undergrowth, and Taffy Williams's
stomach rumbling. Anyway –

VENABLES

Has this any relevance to McLaren's
predicament?

FLETCHER

Oh. Only to show that I'm no stranger
to danger.

BARROWCLOUGH

Do you know I was in Singapore for
my National Service. RAF Equipment.

FLETCHER

Oh, Singapore. Doddle, Singapore.
We'd have given our eyeteeth for
Singapore. All them historical temples
and hysterical brothels.

VENABLES

Gentlemen, there's a man on the roof.

MACKAY

Sir, we cannot let a prisoner go up.
We have to deal with our own
problems, we can't leave them in the
hands of a prisoner.

FLETCHER

Oh, in that case, sir, then we might as well accept the alternative.

VENABLES

What alternative?

FLETCHER

You'll have to go up.

6. PRISON BUILDINGS

McLaren is on the rooftop waving.
Camera shows emergency vehicles and people watching, among them a fireman, a medical orderly, a warder.
Fletcher walks into shot, looks up at the roof and then at the fire engine.
Camera zooms to the ladder.
Fletcher looks at it.

MACKAY

Cold feet, eh?

FLETCHER

What me? No never. Let's get on with it.

He leaves the shot.

MACKAY

Kuala Lumpur!

Fletcher starts climbing up the ladder.
Mackay is watching him.
The fireman is working the levers on the engine as Fletcher goes up the ladder. It extends.
Fletcher looks down at the scene

below and looks horrified.
The fireman is watching him.
Fletcher reaches the roof gutter and starts to get off.

MCLAREN

Hi, Fletch. Lovely view up here.

Fletcher is panting on the edge of the roof.

MCLAREN

Hey watch out for them slates, they're a bit dodgy.

FLETCHER

Yeah, yeah.

He scrambles up on the roof.

FLETCHER

High enough, in' it?

MCLAREN

It was your idea. You said climb a roof.

FLETCHER

Did you have to pick such a high one? I'm not a bleedin' steeplejack if you are.

MCLAREN

Makes you look more of a hero. Got more dramatic impact.

FLETCHER

Don't use words like impact, will you? Not at this height.

MCLAREN

Want a bit of chewing gum?

FLETCHER

'Course I don't. Let's get down off of here.

MCLAREN

We can't go yet. You're supposed to talk me out of it. I'm a nutter, remember. We'll be up here at least an hour before I succumb to your eloquent persuasion.

FLETCHER

An hour? I've got vertigo. I'm sick. I'm dizzy.

MCLAREN

We'll go down in time for tea. It's cauliflower cheese today, isn't it?

Fletcher falls out of shot. Slates rushing past. Barrowclough reacts to Fletcher's falling.

Mackay reacts. The camera reveals Fletcher is astride the chimney pot.

MCLAREN

Hey, Fletch, where you going – it's not teatime yet.

Fletcher is perched on the edge of the roof.

7. PRISON HOSPITAL

It is a small ward with seven beds in it. Only one is occupied, by Ives. A breezy-looking Fletcher enters, pushing a trolley with books on it.

FLETCHER

Ding-dong, Fletcher calling. Your friendly mobile library!

IVES

'Ere listen –

FLETCHER

Oh, it's you Ives – how'd you work this number?

IVES

What d'you mean, I'm ill – gastro-enteritis.

FLETCHER

Oh, they're not difficult symptoms to fake. Keep running to the bog every five minutes clutching your stomach and screaming in agony.

IVES

I didn't fake nothing. I really got it.

FLETCHER

(*Looking at chart*) Oh, that's unusual. Must be some sort of record, a genuine illness in this hospital.

IVES

What about you? I heard you was in here last week.

FLETCHER

I had a few bruises, but they say I can still have children.

IVES

I heard it was shock. They told me you couldn't stop shaking for two days.

FLETCHER

All right, Ives – wouldn't you be shaking after an heroic ascent like that?

IVES

Your descent weren't so heroic. The kid had to bring you down on his back.

FLETCHER

Look, don't needle me, Ives. Otherwise you won't be getting anything worth reading off here at all. I shall be palming you off with *Lamb's Tales from Shakespeare* without benefit of mint sauce.

IVES

'Ere listen –

FLETCHER

No, you listen to me, Ives. That little rooftop caper was all set up, it was all arranged between McLaren and me. He went up there so I could rescue him.

IVES

Oh yeah.

FLETCHER

All right, I didn't expect to get a dizzy turn like I did. But at least I goes up a hero and he comes down one. As a result of which I have leapfrogged my way back into the Governor's good books. My slate is clean and all my misdemeanours is writ off. And here I am – assistant librarian. And the kid McLaren, who they've decided to treat with sympathy and understanding . . .

IVES

Yeah, I've seen him – hospital orderly – cushy number. 'Ere listen, what about a decent book – know what I mean.

FLETCHER

You mean something a bit risqué.

IVES

Won't be risky, I won't tell anyone.

FLETCHER

Risqué means dirty, you nurk.

IVES

Oh dirty, yes. That's what I mean, yes.

FLETCHER

Well, I could offer you this one – it's all about the sex-starved lady pygmies of the Malaysian jungle.

IVES

What's it called?

FLETCHER

Little Women.

IVES

Little Women.

FLETCHER

It's an erotic classic. Don't you remember that trial at the Old Bailey?

IVES

Er, vaguely like. 'Ere, what's it doing in the prison library?

FLETCHER

Library? What? I nicked that from the Governor's private bookshelf. It was concealed next to the tropical fish year book for 1973. Here listen to this . . .

He opens the book and starts reading.

FLETCHER

'She come out of the clearing her flimsy shift soaked by the sudden monsoon. Through it Gilbert could discern the firm contours of her proud young Malaysian body. She stood there unashamed staring him straight in the kneecap. She was everything that he had imagined on that long train ride from Kuala

Lumpur. He gazed in awe at her half-naked uptilted perfectly formed –'
He shuts the book.

IVES

'Ere listen, perfectly formed what, perfectly formed what?

FLETCHER

I'll give you a clue. There was two of them, and they went up and down when she ran, and I don't mean her eyebrows. Now if you was to borrow this torrid saga of Malaysian love rites, well it could be yours for only two snouts, couldn't it?

IVES

Done.

FLETCHER

In advance.

IVES

Done.

FLETCHER

You certainly have been.
He wheels the trolley off.
As he does so, McLaren comes up with another trolley and they bump into each other.

McLAREN

Just watch it, you clumsy nurk.

FLETCHER

Hey, hey, hey. Have we learnt nothing? Where did that ever get us?

McLAREN

Oh . . . sorry, Mr Fletcher.

FLETCHER

That's all right, Mr McLaren. And how's things in the medical world?

McLAREN

Cushy, Mr Fletcher. And the library?

FLETCHER

A doddle, Mr McLaren.

McLAREN

Did you get me *The Godfather*?

FLETCHER

Did you get me the Wintergreen Ointment?
McLaren hands Fletcher the ointment and Fletcher hands McLaren the book.

SERIES ONE

EPISODE SIX: MEN WITHOUT WOMEN

1. PRISON

Camera shows the prison warder.
Then zooms to Warren who is
sweeping. He looks and sees
Fletcher planting flowers.
Warren glances at the warder, then
moves towards Fletcher.

WARREN

'Ere, Fletch . . .

FLETCHER

Naff off. I'm thinking.

WARREN

Thinking?

FLETCHER

Yes – thinking. I realise, Warren, that to
you and the rest of that lot, thinking is
an alien pastime. But some of us –
more endowed with a bit of grey matter
where it matters, namely up here,
preserve our identity and sanity in this
place by thinking.

WARREN

But what are you thinking?

FLETCHER

At the moment I'm thinking 'Why
won't this bloke Warren naff off and
leave me alone?'

WARREN

Look, Fletch, I realise you're a
man of . . .

FLETCHER

Intellect.

WARREN

Intellect, yes –

FLETCHER

And erudition.

WARREN

That an' all, Fletch, if you say so. But
that was why I wanted to have a word,
see. I got this letter . . .

He produces a letter.

FLETCHER

(*Taking letter*) Oh yes. Yes. From a
woman, I would assess.

WARREN

That's right. How can you tell?

FLETCHER

It's in the handwriting, isn't it?
The warder is approaching. Fletcher
drops the letter and starts to dig.

The warder walks past.
Warren reacts to letter being buried.
Fletcher stops digging after warder
has passed and bends down to pick
up the letter. He sniffs at it.

FLETCHER

Female handwriting, in' it? And judging
by the stationery and the perfume, a
woman of little sophistication or class.
He hands the letter back to Warren.

WARREN

That's right, it's from the wife.

FLETCHER

Oh, I don't mean to infer –

WARREN

No, you're a clever bloke, Fletch.
That's why I wanted your help, really.

FLETCHER

Oh, I see another one. My counsel is
it? Advice to the lovelorn. Now you
want me to assess the situation and
compose an appropriate response.

WARREN

No, it's simpler than that . . . Just want
you to read it to me . . .

2. ASSOCIATION ROOM

Fletcher is sitting at a table with
Warren, Heslop, Lukewarm and Tolly.
He has Warren's letter in front
of him.

FLETCHER

Now, this letter of Warren's – it's very,
very typical. It's your classic wives' letter
after you've done eight months to a
year – that sort of period. I mean wives
make all those marital vows, but you
have to be around to make sure they
do love, honour and obey, don't you?

TOLLY

Yuh.

WARREN

Right.

HESLOP

Yes.

LUKEWARM

How true.

FLETCHER

You see, after a while a wife gets restless
urges. So having got restless, chances
are they weaken and gets naughty.
Warren thumps his fist against
the table.

WARREN

I'll kill her. I'll throttle her.

FLETCHER

Yes . . . that is one solution, but what
we're looking for here is something a
little more constructive. Besides, you're
in here and she's in Bolton.

WARREN

It's visiting day next week.

FLETCHER

Yes, yes, we know. But if you was to
strangle your wife on visiting day
there's a good chance you'd lose half
your remission.

WARREN
I'm just saying.
LUKEWARM
Ooh, he's so impulsive.
WARREN
I'm just saying.
TOLLY
Leave it off, Warren. Leave it to Fletch, he knows, doesn't he?
FLETCHER
Thank you, Tolly, for the vote of confidence. Now, where was I?
LUKEWARM
Just getting to the naughty bit.
FLETCHER
Oh yes. Now having got naughty she gets guilty. So in my reply that I've written out here I have sought to achieve subtlety with strength. An obvious display of affection but carrying beneath it a hint of menace.
The others murmur. Fletcher starts reading.
FLETCHER
'My darling – I realise these are difficult times for you. Here we are, men without women – and you are women without men with all your attendant frustrations' – nice phrase that, isn't it?
They murmur assent.
LUKEWARM
Well chosen.
FLETCHER
Got it out of the *Reader's Digest*. 'I realise my love, that it is a lot to ask, to ask you to wait for me. But I will be

upset, dearest one, if I hear about you having a nibble of something you shouldn't. In other words, dear heart, I have friends on the outside, who have friends who have friends. And any word of hanky panky will be followed by swift and merciless retribution. I hope the weather is nice and you are feeling well in yourself. Yours etc.' – blah, blah, blah.
LUKEWARM
Subtlety with strength, oh yes.
TOLLY
Very good, Fletch. I told you, Warren, Fletch knows.
HESLOP
My wife's sister lives in Sidcup. And sometimes we stay there, or drop in for a cuppa when we bin to the coast.
The others exchange looks.
HESLOP
(*Leaning forward*) Anyhow, once we was there, and while my wife was upstairs powdering her nose prior to going to see *Paint Your Wagon* by the Sidcup Operatic, her sister touched me.
There is an expectant pause, but Heslop fails to go on.
FLETCHER
Where, where?
HESLOP
In the kitchen. She got very . . . heated. Had me pressed up against the Aga.
FLETCHER
'Spect you got fairly heated then didn't you, up against the Aga?

HESLOP

She was saying how she'd always fancied me, she knew it was wrong, being as she was the wife's sister, but she couldn't control her true feelings no longer. I had to say 'Now listen Gwendolyn' – that was her name, see – I said, 'Listen, Gwendolyn, this is no way to behave. It's not right, it isn't decent and what happened must never happen again.'

WARREN

But nothing did happen.

FLETCHER

All you did was give her a lecture.

HESLOP

That was an hour later when we were getting out of bed.

FLETCHER

Look, look, what point is it you're making, Einstein? You're on a different time scale to all the rest of us. His head's about twenty minutes slow. Now then, I'd done copies of this letter . . . (*Starts distributing them*) . . . there's one for each of you. You just have to write 'em out in your own handwriting. I'll do yours Warren for a small fee, as you can't write. And of course you must fill in the names of your loved ones. (*To Heslop*) My beloved Iris . . . (*To Tolly*) My darling Norma . . . (*To Lukewarm*) My dearest Trevor. Now post these sharp 'cos we want them to read these before they comes up visiting day. So that they can be duly humble and apprehensive.

HESLOP

There's no evidence that my Iris has strayed from the straight and narrow.

FLETCHER

What? Oh well, post it in any case. A stitch in time saves a hole in the trousers.

HESLOP

Oh right, I'll post it then.

FLETCHER

No sense leaving these things to the last minute.

A bell sounds.

FLETCHER

Now gentlemen, haven't we forgotten something?

WARREN

Oh yes, fair's fair. Cough up, lads.

They all produce little tins of tobacco and hand over a hand-rolled cigarette.

TOLLY

You got no problem on this score then, Fletch? Marriage, like?

FLETCHER

No, no. I been married a bit longer than you lad, ain't I? And she knows her place.

LUKEWARM

Doesn't she get upset that you keep going inside all the time?

FLETCHER

I don't keep going inside all the time.

LUKEWARM

You are fairly consistent. And she's got a home and three kids to run – I don't know how she does it, I don't know how she does it.

FLETCHER

Oh, I'm not saying it ain't hard, obviously. A few weeks ago she had to build a new coal bunker. That's a terrible job for a woman, isn't it?

LUKEWARM

You mean she had to mix all the cement and all that?

FLETCHER

Oh no, no, no, that was all right. Her mother came over and did that.

BARROWCLOUGH

Come on now, lads . . . Well, Fletcher, have you employed yourself usefully this evening?

FLETCHER

Just giving the lads the benefit of my experience, Mr Barrowclough.

BARROWCLOUGH

I've heard that your opinion is sought in this prison. Mr Gillespie, the Welfare Officer, he was saying he's running out of customers.

FLETCHER

Yeah, well, Welfare Officers – like the Padre, they're not to be trusted.

BARROWCLOUGH

I think you're being a bit harsh on a very well-meaning body of men and women.

FLETCHER

I ain't saying they ain't well-intentioned. But the lads, you know, they bring me their problems, they know I speak their language.

He sits down.

FLETCHER

By the way, how's things with your old lady?

BARROWCLOUGH

What? Oh well . . . difficult, you know, Fletcher, she's been a bit better since you and I had that chat, but well, things could be easier. She's not an easy woman to live with, my wife.

FLETCHER

No, no . . . not still the postman, is it?

BARROWCLOUGH

Oh no – heaven forbid. He's in the sorting office in Carlisle now.

FLETCHER

Sorted him out, did they?

BARROWCLOUGH

Pardon?

FLETCHER

Nothing, nothing. Shouldn't joke at your expense.

BARROWCLOUGH

No, no. Well, I'm afraid I'll have to ask you to . . .

Fletcher picks up chair.

FLETCHER

Yeah, I know. Time I turned in.

BARROWCLOUGH

I hate this part of the job you know, Fletcher. Shutting men up, caging them in.

FLETCHER

Yes – it is a shame. Just when the good telly's starting an' all. All we ever see's the flaming news. And *Town and Around*. Fat lot of interest to us that is. Locked in here.

BARROWCLOUGH

No. I've never got used to bolting those doors. I think of you in that little cell . . . and I think of me going out of here, and going home, to my house. To my wife, who's waiting for me. *He stops as if something's occurred to him.*

FLETCHER

(*Rising*) What's wrong, Mr Barrowclough?

BARROWCLOUGH

I sometimes wish I was in here with you lot . . .

3. PRISON LANDING

The cell doors are open, leaving the prisoners free to fraternise within their own landing. Prisoners with towels and slop buckets are moving among themselves. Camera follows Warren as he walks along the corridor and enters a cell.

4. FLETCHER'S CELL

Fletcher is on his bunk reading when Warren enters with a slop bucket.

WARREN

Fletch . . . Would you do the honours? *He produces another letter and hands it over.*

FLETCHER

What read this you mean? All right . . . (*Sniffing the letter*) . . . the wife?

WARREN

(*Sitting*) Yeah, knows her perfume anywhere.

FLETCHER

Not surprised, Warren. It's very distinctive. Should think it kills ninety-nine per cent of all known germs.

WARREN

Don't you like it – should I tell her to change it?

FLETCHER

No, no, my son. You're safe from other men as long as she wears this. *He starts to read.*

FLETCHER

'My dear Bunny'. Bunny?

WARREN

Yes, Bunny Warren.

FLETCHER

Oh – Bunny Warren. 'I got your letter, for which many thanks. It's wonderful that already prison has taught you to write and spell proper. Who knows what you may come out . . .' – what's this word? Oh . . . 'qualified as'. It was the k-w that fooled me . . . 'Now

Bunny, about this other thing. I don't
know where you've got these doubts
from. I spend my nights watching the
box on which is placed your picture
which I cut out the *Manchester
Evening News*. It is the one of you
resisting arrest, but I have cut off the
two policemen. I've left the Alsatian on
as I know how fond you are of
animals. I did go out Sunday I admit,
but only to see your mother who has
had to go into Salford again with her
feet.' How she usually go in then – on
her hands and knees?

WARREN

No, no, what she means is er – she's
had to go back to chiropodist like.
She's always had these feet, you see.

FLETCHER

Has she? The same ones? Oh.
Anyhow . . . 'Never mind the expense,
I am coming up visiting day, to put
your mind at rest.'

Warren gives a thumbs up sign.

FLETCHER

'I will get Saturday morning off at the
laundry. I miss you and I think of us
when you were at home and you used
to take my . . .'

He breaks off.

WARREN

What – used to what?

FLETCHER

Oh well, this last bit's a bit intimate,
Warren, I don't think I should read it
aloud in front of me. Personal, isn't it?

WARREN

What is it? What's she say?

FLETCHER

Er . . . well, how can I say it?
Well, the gist of it is . . . she
missed your er – no. Put it
another way . . . which you obviously
did. No, it's just that . . . well,
she regrets that you're not home
providing for her.

WARREN

Oh. Oh good. Anything else?

FLETCHER

Anything else would be a bit of an
anti-climax. It just says 'I wish you
were here. Oh well, I must stop and
get on my lover . . . Oh, must stop
and get on, my lover . . . See you
Sat. Elaine.'

WARREN

Oh. Yes, she's a good girl Elaine. No
problems there – what you think, Fletch?

FLETCHER

It's a nice letter, Warren. Heartfelt. You
can tell. And coming up Saturday,
isn't she?

WARREN

Aye. And so is Heslop's missus. All the
way from Kent. And Tolly's wife. You're
a clever lad, Fletch.

FLETCHER

Yeah, well.

WARREN

Your ole lady coming, is she?

FLETCHER

She'll be here.

WARREN

You had a letter like?

FLETCHER

No, I ain't actually but . . . she'll be here.

WARREN

I think Lukewarm's fella's coming
up as well.

FLETCHER

Is he now? 'Course Lukewarm's got a
different sort of problem from the rest
of you. His Trevor's the insecure one
there, isn't he? I mean there's six
hundred men in here. So whereas
you're all worried what your wives are
up to on the outside, Trevor's worried
what Lukewarm's up to on the inside.
Mackay walks in.

WARREN

Morning, Mr Mackay. See you, Fletch.
And thanks again, mate.
He leaves.

MACKAY

Thanks? What was all that about?

FLETCHER

Bit of advice . . . Matter of the heart,
Mr Mackay. Between him and me.

MACKAY

Tell me, Fletcher, is it true that this
is the office of Slade Prison's
Miss Lonelyhearts?
He laughs.

FLETCHER

That why you're here then, is it?
Problems of that nature.

MACKAY

I do not have problems of that nature.

FLETCHER

Oh come on, Mr Mackay, all screws,
beg your pardon, all prison officers
have problems in that area. I mean
matrimonially you and me are very
similar. 'Cos while we're in here we
can't be too sure what our old ladies
are getting up to, can we? No difference.

MACKAY

There is a major difference, Fletcher.
Your wives are criminals' wives.
They belong to the criminal classes
with all their inherent traits of
slovenliness and promiscuity. Our
wives are the wives of uniformed men,
used to a life of service and duty,
decency and moral fibre. My house
reflects my wife.

FLETCHER

Big, is it?

MACKAY

It's spotless. And when I get home of
an evening my uniform for the next
day has been cleaned and pressed,
the jacket with its buttons gleaming,
the trousers with razor sharp creases
and the shirt crisply laundered.

FLETCHER

Oh yes? So what's that prove? Your
old lady's having it away with the bloke
from the dry cleaners.

MACKAY

I refuse to rise to your bait. It's obvious that your cynicism derives from some bitter personal experience of your own.

FLETCHER

No, no, no, no. Nothing wrong with my marriage. No doubts about my Isobel. My wife and I have always got on very well.

MACKAY

You've spent half your married life in prison, man.

FLETCHER

Absence makes the heart grow fonder in our case. Bet your old lady wouldn't mind a break from all that ironing and cleaning.

He sits on the bed.

MACKAY

My wife has never had any desire other than to be by my side. Before Prison Service you know, Fletcher, I was in the Army. I was a drill sergeant in the Argyll and Sutherland Highlanders.

FLETCHER

I'd never have guessed that!

MACKAY

And even though I was posted to some far-flung places, Marie would always be with me.

FLETCHER

I bet she was. Brassing up, polishing, blancoing. Female batman. I can just see you coming in of an evening off the parade ground – 'Marie, Stand by your ironing board!!!'

MACKAY

Seventeen years of domestic contentment.

He starts to go.

FLETCHER

Er – Mr Mackay – drill sergeant, was it?

MACKAY

That's right, Fletcher, drill sergeant.

FLETCHER

Do everything by numbers, did you?

Mackay returns.

MACKAY

I am not rising to your bait, Fletcher, and it's naïve of you to assume that I would.

Finally he leaves.

FLETCHER

Even with your old lady. Numbers is it. 'Marie, I am about to make passionate love to you – stand by your bed. Wait for it! Wait for it! Knickers down – two three!'

An enraged Mackay re-enters, pointing his truncheon at Fletcher threateningly.

MACKAY

I'll have you, Fletcher!

FLETCHER

Don't you hit me!

5. COUNTRY ROAD/COACH

A coach is seen travelling along a country road. Inside are Elaine, Iris, Norma and Ingrid talking.

NORMA

Couldn't be much farther this place, could it?

INGRID

I've had to come from London. Had to be at Euston by eight. And there was no buffet on the train.

NORMA

Never is, is there? Or if there is, it's only yesterday's sausage rolls.

ELAINE

I've only come from Bolton. But it's taken me all morning to get here. Change at Manchester. Change at Carlisle. Least when he was in Strangeways I only had a bus ride.

NORMA

It's us that suffers chuck. Us that has to cope with no money and a family to run, and no man around the house.

IRIS

They thinks you've got a man about the house. I've come all the way from Kent because of his suspicious mind. I had this letter.

ELAINE

Me an' all.

NORMA

Me too.

IRIS

Yeah but what a nerve – listen to this.

She gets her letter out and starts reading.

IRIS

'I realise my luv that it is a lot to ask, to ask you to wait for me. But I will be upset dearest one, if I hear about you having a nibble of something you shouldn't.'

The other wives get their letters out. Trevor also produces his letter. The bus arrives at the prison gates, they open and the bus drives in.

6. VISITING ROOM

Heslop, Warren, Lukewarm and Tolly are jostling at a window to catch a glimpse of the arriving visitors.

HESLOP

There's my girl, there she is.

WARREN

Can see my Elaine.

HESLOP

Look at the little darlings. Don't you want to have a look, Fletch?

FLETCHER

See her soon enough, won't I? I know what she looks like.

BARROWCLOUGH

Come on now, sit down, let's have some order.

The prisoners move away from the window and take up their seats.

TOLLY

Did the trick then, Fletch?

FLETCHER

Yeah, well.

HESLOP

Kent's a long way, you know.

LUKEWARM

Trevor's come all the way from Southport. He'll have had to close the shop. He's a watch repairer.

WARREN

I did a watch repairer's once.

FLETCHER

Yeah and now you're doing time for it.
Did you get that, Mr Barrowclough?

BARROWCLOUGH

Oh yes, very funny, Fletcher, very funny.
Nice to see you all in such good spirits.

WARREN

I'm sure I can smell Elaine's perfume.

FLETCHER

No, that's the sheep dip from the
prison farm, that is.

There is a knock on the door.
Barrowclough unlocks it. The wives
walk in and join their husbands.
Ingrid moves to Fletcher.

FLETCHER

Ingrid!

INGRID

Hello, Dad.

FLETCHER

Where's your mother?

Others are immediately captivated
by this.

FLETCHER

I said, where's your mother?

INGRID

She couldn't come, Dad.

FLETCHER

Not ill, is she?

INGRID

No, she –

FLETCHER

She, what?

INGRID

She's found another man, Dad.

7. GOVERNOR'S OFFICE

VENABLES

(*Crossing to his desk and sitting down*)
Morose you say, Mr Barrowclough.

BARROWCLOUGH

I have the Welfare Officer's report here,
sir. Mr Gillespie feels that psychologically
Fletcher is overcompensating for the
traumatic shock of –

VENABLES

Oh, don't spout that university clap trap
at me. Young Gillespie – what does he
know? These lads come in here with no
experience of life. How can they have?
Not two minutes ago they were in rag
parades, blowing clarinets and throwing
flour bags at old ladies.

BARROWCLOUGH

I think you're being a bit harsh on a
very well-meaning body of men, sir. Mr
Gillespie has done work in the field, sir.

VENABLES

In Welwyn Garden City! Hardly a walk
on the wild side. What is it?
Compassionate parole?

BARROWCLOUGH

Just forty-eight hours to help him sort
out his problems. They have been
married twenty-four years.

VENABLES

Alright – wheel him in then.

Barrowclough walks across to the door and opens it to admit a melancholy Fletcher who stands in front of the Governor's desk.

VENABLES

Now, Fletcher, as we all know . . . you've had this domestic . . . well, I suppose, crisis isn't too strong a word, is it?

FLETCHER

My wife's scarpered. Yes, I think crisis is a very good word.

BARROWCLOUGH

She hasn't actually left you yet, Fletcher.

FLETCHER

She's about to.

VENABLES

What do we know about the other man?

FLETCHER

Well apparently, from what I 'licited from my eldest, he's a heating engineer – see we was getting new central heating installed. So obviously he was round there quite a while . . . younger man, bit of patter, from what I heard, new Capri in mustard yellow with wing mirrors.

VENABLES

Younger man, was it?

FLETCHER

Yeah, with wing mirrors, bound to turn a woman's head.

VENABLES

It couldn't just be an infatuation?

FLETCHER

Not according to my eldest, Ingrid. She knows the score, my girl. She says they're planning a new life together in Hemel Hempstead.

BARROWCLOUGH

Oh I know Hemel Hempstead. Pass through it on the train – it looks nice there.

Venables and Fletcher look at him.

VENABLES

Yes, yes . . . well now the Welfare Officer seems to think it would help if we gave compassionate parole.

FLETCHER

Parole – what get out, like?

VENABLES

Not so much get out as go out. For forty-eight hours only. You could go on Friday. Report to the local police on arrival, but otherwise the weekend would be your own.

FLETCHER

I see . . . well, no harm in trying, get a decent Sunday dinner I suppose.

VENABLES

Now, Fletcher, if that's your attitude –

FLETCHER

No, no, Governor, I'm sorry. My flippancy was only masking my deep wounds. If you see fit, sir. I shall go. For the sake of my marriage and your trust in me I'll go. I wonder if Spurs are playing at home?

8. POLICE STATION

Camera shows sign outside the police station. Then Fletcher and Sergeant Norris come out. They

*walk round a corner and carry on
up the street.*

FLETCHER

Look I've checked in – you know where
I live, you don't have to walk me home.

SGT NORRIS

I don't mind, Fletch. Breath of fresh air.

FLETCHER

I'm going home to see my old lady. It's
personal, matters of a personal nature.
That's the reason for my parole.

SGT NORRIS

It's the personal nature that concerns
me Fletch. Want you to greet your wife
with sympathy and understanding.
Don't want you to force her head
through the mangle.

9. FLETCHER'S HOUSE: HALLWAY AND STUDIO

*Ingrid opens the front door to see
Fletcher and the Sergeant.*

INGRID

Hello, Dad.

FLETCHER

Hello, love. Your mother in, is she?

INGRID

In there.

FLETCHER

You know Sergeant Norris, don't you?

INGRID

Met him in court.

SGT NORRIS

Only stopping a minute, love.

*They file through into the living room.
Isobel is waiting, standing in front of*

*the fireplace, composed and
assured. She is an attractive woman
in her forties, dressed neatly.*

FLETCHER

Isobel . . .

ISOBEL

Norman . . .

FLETCHER

I got this compassionate parole.

ISOBEL

So they told us.

FLETCHER

Yeah well . . .

ISOBEL

There's no need for you to stay
Sergeant Norris. Thank you.

SGT NORRIS

I just thought that –

ISOBEL

Yes, well, there's no need for worries
on that score is there, so if you'll
excuse us?

*Fletcher and Isobel greet each
other with warmth and affection.
They hug each other.*

ISOBEL

Hello, Norman!

FLETCHER

Hello, my love.

ISOBEL

It worked then?

FLETCHER

Like a flaming charm.

ISOBEL

I knew it would. It worked in
Maidstone. Knew it would again.

FLETCHER

Like a flaming charm. 'She's found another man . . .'

ISOBEL

Ingrid, go and get your dad's slippers and put the kettle on.

FLETCHER

And don't be in too much of an hurry to come back, neither. Your mother and I have got a lot to make up.

INGRID

It's just like when I was a kid – if you give me some money I'll go to the pictures.

FLETCHER

It's worth it. (*Goes to get money then stops*) Hang on – that's how her brother was born. Puddle off.

10. STREET

On the street is parked a car. A man is washing his car.

11. LIVING ROOM

Fletcher, shoes off, feet up, is reading a Sunday paper. Isobel comes in with grip and carrier bag.

ISOBEL

You'll have to move I'm afraid, love.

FLETCHER

Won't take long to get to Euston on a Sunday.

ISOBEL

Did Sergeant Norris say he'd drive you there? I've given you some apples. And a banana. And some tangerines – what a price they are. But you need the fruit, it's good for your complexion. You should get shaved, love. Norris'll be here soon.

Fletcher gets to his feet and turns off the TV set.

FLETCHER

Yeah, I suppose so.

ISOBEL

It's been lovely having you, Norman.

FLETCHER

Done me a power of good, Isobel. See you and the kids. Colour telly, home cooking . . . Spurs winning at home, and soft lavatory paper.

ISOBEL

It's all here when you come out. Just bide your time, love.

FLETCHER

Tell you one thing, gel. I ain't going back in again after this stretch.

ISOBEL

You've said that before.

FLETCHER

I mean it. I've had me fill of porridge. It's full of kids these days. Talk about a generation gap. Father figure, I am. No, it's been a mug's game my life. And seein' and seein' the kids, and realising I'm missing them growing up . . . and all the things this weekend gave me. I tell you . . . the best things in life ain't free . . . but the best thing in life is bein' free.

ISOBEL

Oh Norman, you say lovely things,
what made you think of that?

FLETCHER

I didn't . . . Randolph Scott said it just
before you came in.

12. OUTSIDE PRISON

*The minibus carrying Fletcher
approaches the prison gates and
drives through.*

13. ASSOCIATION ROOM

*Prisoners are carrying on with their
activities. Fletcher and
Barrowclough enter the area.
Lukewarm sees Fletcher and nudges
Heslop. They all see Fletcher.*

WARREN

Er . . . you all right, Fletch?

FLETCHER

What?

WARREN

No, Fletch, listen – me and the lads
just wanted to say – we're sorry.
I mean I know we laughed about it last
week but, you know – well, look, the
fact that you're not so clever after all,
just makes you more human like the
rest of us.

FLETCHER

Oh yeah. Let me ask you something
Warren – what you done – this
weekend?

WARREN

What? Well –

FLETCHER

I'll tell you. Same as you did last
weekend. Had a freezing shower,
cleaned your shoes, washed your
vest, had your dinner, had another
freezing shower, spent the evening
lying on your bunk picking your nose.
Some of us was in the pub, some of
us was eating roast beef, or watching
Spurs play at home, or having a sing-
song with their friends and relatives.
(*Crossing to behind Heslop*) Or lying in
a big crisp bed with their crisp old
lady. (*To Heslop*) Have a banana.

He crosses to his cell.
*Mackay and Barrowclough are
walking along.*

MACKAY

All right, let's have you – come on.

BARROWCLOUGH

You can see the difference in Fletcher.
I think Mr Venables sending him home
has made him realise what he's missing.
It's suddenly dawned on him that he's
been on a mug's game all these years.

MACKAY

Oh yes. He's had the cockiness
knocked out of him. We've seen the
last of his lairy insolence. You can't
beat the system, Mr Barrowclough.
*They reach Fletcher's cell door and
Mackay flicks open the eyepiece.
Fletcher is sitting on the lower
bunk, looking depressed. He looks
up: gives an evil grin and thrusts up
two fingers in a vulgar gesture.*

1 MEMORIES

Sydney Lotterby (Producer/Director)

'As soon as I saw the pilot script, "Prisoner and Escort", I knew I wanted to direct it. It was such a good script and just pleading to be done. It revealed the essence of Dick and Ian's writing: they don't write jokes, they write situations and explore the personalities of the characters, which is why they're such good writers. The humour in their scripts comes from the situations they put their characters into. With *Porridge*, their work was very accurate and seemed to reveal how a prisoner felt – it was almost as if they'd experienced prison life themselves!

'Despite the quality of the pilot script, however, I doubted whether the idea for a prison-based sitcom gave enough scope for an entire series, it was too confined – that is until I received the scripts for the first series.

'A director's job is easy when you have quality scripts; there are no problems with the dialogue or the situations, all you have to do is make sure that both you and the actors interpret the script accurately and without ostentation, and the end result will be perfect.'

Philip Jackson (Dylan in 'A Day Out')

'*Porridge* was one of my first TV jobs. Syd Lotterby had seen me in a *Play for Today* called *Blooming Youth*, an improvised film about students. He obviously thought I was the man to play Dylan, the Huddersfield hippie; mainly, I suspect, because of my extraordinary hairstyle! It was the first time I was ever offered a job with no interview or audition.

'Rehearsals in London were hilarious, then much bonding was made in the hotel bar when we filmed the outside scenes in South Wales. During frequent stoppages for the bad weather, Ronnie played poker with the crew, taking care not to win! The studio was my first experience of recording in front of a live audience, and I found it incredibly nerve-wracking. Just before we began, I saw Ronnie in the wings and even he looked petrified, but as soon as he went on, the panic disappeared from his face and you never for a second could have believed he was nervous.

'The initial scene with Richard and Ronnie was a bit edgy at first, and Ronnie did a deliberate cock-up halfway through, which relaxed the audience and actors alike. He was brilliant at gauging the atmosphere at any one time and constantly came up with ideas to relieve any tension. If an actor (me, for example) had a good line that didn't get a laugh, he was always able in some way to do something funny and make it look as if it wasn't you who'd messed it up. This was a total comedic instinct on display and I learned a great deal from watching him. Several of his lines came from larking about, ad-libbing in rehearsal, and the best ones stayed in. I remember the line about cheese and onion crisps in the pub came from such a moment.

'Looking back after nearly thirty years, I think there was a great sense that we were involved in something special. The show has lived on and my amazing hairstyle is still on regular display!'

Tony Osoba (McLaren in the series)
'Although transmitted fifth out of the six episodes of series one, "Ways and Means" was actually the last to be recorded and I recall joining a team which had been together for several weeks and who had all got to know each other well. However, I was made very welcome and soon felt at ease, thus dispelling the natural nervousness that I had been experiencing in the lead up to rehearsals.

'A week or two before, I had been invited to attend a casting to meet Ronnie Barker and Sydney Lotterby at the BBC rehearsal block in west London. I later discovered that a television director I'd recently worked with had recommended me and I shall be eternally grateful to Mike Vardy for that. When I learned that I had been offered the part, I was consumed with excitement and nerves in equal measure and couldn't wait to start work.

'As I say, I was quickly made to feel at home by the cast and crew and filming at the various locations passed all too quickly as I revelled in playing the rather hotheaded prisoner, McLaren, wonderfully written by Dick Clement and Ian La Frenais. Among the many kindnesses, I recall the reassurance and humour shown to me by Ray Butt, the PA, who later received great acclaim as a comedy producer/director in his own right.

'The scene on the roof which ends with Fletcher sliding down the tiles and straddling a drainpipe is one that always brings tears to people's eyes: tears of sympathy as well as laughter. Two roofs were used during the shooting of the scene: a school roof in Ealing for the close-ups and the roof of a psychiatric hospital near Watford for the longer shots. As we filmed in the hospital there would be many people milling around the grounds – crew and technicians, cast, patients and hospital staff; it was difficult telling who was who at times! I remember standing talking to a female member of the crew and a hospital doctor. We chatted for several minutes and then the doctor suddenly pulled the woman's skirt up before running off. It turned out, of course, that the "doctor" was actually a patient.

'In the studio, I was new to the tricky technique of playing television comedy in front of a live audience, but adapted fairly well under the sure but gentle guidance of Ronnie and Syd. However, I was mortified at one point when, during a break in recording, a voice from the audience called out: "Where's my orange?" It was a tag line from a part of the show that we hadn't arrived at yet. Ronnie looked startled and whispered under his breath: "How do they know that?" I didn't have the nerve to tell him that I had recognised the voice as that of my sister Trish. She and my mother were in the audience that evening and a few days earlier I had proudly been showing them the script and discussing my role, including that tag line. Fortunately, as ever in the studio, time was pressing and we could no longer dwell on the possible identity of the mystery caller!

'The evening was a success and I was delighted when the character of McLaren was incorporated into the subsequent series. I owe a great deal to *Porridge* and this episode in particular.'

Patricia Brake (Ingrid in the series)
'In September 1972 I starred in a *Play for Today* purely because I happened to be in the right late stage of pregnancy with my daughter Hannah. My part in *The Bouncing Boy* was arduous and when I had a really early call the make-up artist Ann Ailes, as she was then, came to my home. We became good friends and it was a great piece of luck that she then went on to work on *Porridge* and recommended me to Syd Lotterby. Luckily, I had already appeared in a sit-com called *Second Time Around*, playing the young wife, so I had a little experience of recording with an audience.

'In my first episode, *Men Without Women*, I had to say, "Hullo, Dad" several times which seemed to make Ian and Dick laugh, and thankfully they wrote me into more episodes where I had a great deal more to do. Ronnie was a delight to work with and I learnt a great deal from him. Always generous, he often made sure that the camera was on me for a particular moment during a scene together, very unusual in this business, and the way he could develop and add to an already very funny script was simply pure genius. In *Heartbreak Hotel* I appeared not wearing a bra, very risqué in 1975, and hanging on my bathroom wall now is a certificate made by the props department commemorating this momentous occasion. Later on I was cast several times in *The Two Ronnies*. Ronnie B said it was simply because my surname began with a B, and when he'd been through *Spotlight*, the actors directory, several times and got back to me he said, "She'll do." Now, many years later, I'm so proud to have been a part of *Porridge* and watch the repeats with delight, and I'm still rather secretly pleased that Clive James fancied me.'

2 SERIES TWO

MEMORIES

Sam Kelly (Warren in the series)
Tony Osoba (McLaren in the series)
Philip Madoc (Williams in 'Disturbing the Peace')

SERIES TWO

EPISODE ONE: JUST DESSERTS

1. FLETCHER'S CELL

Fletcher is searching anxiously among his meagre possessions. He is obviously angry at losing whatever it is he cannot find. He goes to Lennie's bed and looks under the pillow. He looks at the picture of Denise and replaces it.

An air of resolution comes over his face. And he goes out of the cell. Fletcher walks along the catwalk and down the stairs into the association area.

He goes up to the table where Lukewarm, Banyard and Warren are sitting.

Ives is next to them at a table alone reading the paper.

They all greet him with 'Good mornings, etc.'

FLETCHER

Never mind the good mornings.

WARREN

What's up, Fletch?

FLETCHER

What's up, I'll tell you what's up. Are you listening, Ives?

Ives looks up from his reading.

IVES

(*Putting the paper down*) Oh sorry – yes.

FLETCHER

I don't know how to tell you this, gentlemen, but . . . there is a thief among us.

The others look at each other.

WARREN

There's nigh on six hundred people in this prison and I should think two-thirds of them are in for stealing something.

FLETCHER

That was stealing on the outside, Warren. Against civilians. That's work, that is. Making a living. Skullduggery. But the theft to which I'm referring has been perpetrated within these walls. Which is despicable. A crime which offends the dignity of any normal law-abiding criminal.

BANYARD

What is the nature of this alleged offence?

FLETCHER

There's nothing alleged about it,

Mr Banyard. Someone has crept into my cell and lifted a two-pound tin of pineapple chunks.

IVES

(*Impressed*) Pineapple chunks?

FLETCHER

Keep your voice down. We are discussing contraband after all.

IVES

(*Quieter*) Pineapple chunks?

FLETCHER

Correct. One tin of chunks, pineapple. Thickly cut chunks of delicious pineapple, soaked in a heavy syrup, from the sunkissed shores of Honolulu.

LUKEWARM

Mmmm, lovely.

FLETCHER

(*Sharply*) I trust the look on your face doesn't convey a pleasant memory, Lukewarm?

LUKEWARM

'Course not, Fletch. I haven't had your chunks.

BANYARD

Have you any idea who took them?

FLETCHER

I was hoping that our little chat might throw some light on the matter. 'Cos I can tell you, I'm extremely dischuffed about this. Luxuries are few and far between in this neck of the woods. I'd been looking forward to that, I had. Particularly partial to tinned pineapple. Very fond of all tinned fruits but particularly tinned pineapple. In the

absence of tinned pears, that is. Bad enough if I'd had some snout nicked, or a new razor blade. Or even money, God forbid. But never my tin of pineapple chunks.

WARREN

When did you discover they was missing, Fletch?

FLETCHER

Just now, you nurk! I was going to have some of them after my Sunday lunch. For dessert. To supplement your wretched cuisine, Lukewarm.

LUKEWARM

I do the best I can with the materials provided.

IVES

'Ere listen, I had something whipped last week.

The others laugh.

IVES

No, honest, listen. You remember visiting day when Ronnie Arkwright's old lady said she weren't coming back no more, 'cos she was going to live with a Maltese ponce in Morecambe. And Ronnie went berserk and attempted to strangle her until restrained by that Scottish screw with the harelip.

FLETCHER

You paint a pretty picture, Ives, go on. They could use you on *Jackanory*.

IVES

Well, during the commotion my missis slipped me a jar of her mother's homemade gooseberry preserve. Now, 'ere listen . . . on the Tuesday, I'd had most of it, and d'you know I was only out the cell for half an hour, but in that time some scroat whipped the rest. While I was in the Hobby Shop making me Bugs Bunny Money Bank.

FLETCHER

(*Sarcastically*) Oh yes. Well, now we're getting somewhere, aren't we? We've narrowed the trail down. The net is closing in. We know the thief has a sweet tooth.

Banyard seems bored with the proceedings and gets up as if to go.

BANYARD

Look, any speculation you have about who took your pineapple chunks, I hardly think applies to me.

FLETCHER

Oh yes, Mr Banyard. Would you mind reseating yourself and elaborating on that if you would.

BANYARD

Well, unlike the rest of you, I'm not a common criminal.

FLETCHER

Has it escaped your attention that you're doing porridge and have been for eighteen months now?

BANYARD

You know what I mean. I'm a professional man, a dentist, and consequently –

FLETCHER

Just let's get the record straight. You

was a dentist. It's been some time now since they struck you off their list. Following those regrettable incidents with the laughing gas. You may not consider yourself a criminal but to the ladies in question it certainly weren't no laughing matter.

LUKEWARM

He is a good dentist though. He did a lovely job on my bridge when the old one fell in the soup.

FLETCHER

I'm not questioning his dental ability. Just making the point that he can't set himself above the rest of us.

The others react with indignation.

IVES

'Ere listen.

FLETCHER

No, you 'ere listen. Pass the word round, right? I'm going for me shower now to stretch me legs, an' wash 'em an' all. Then I'm going to chapel to contemplate the errors of my ways and make peace with my bookmaker. If, when I come back my tin of pineapple has not been returned, we'll have to open a full scale enquiry. A thing like this can spread. If we can't live 'ere together and trust one another then where are we?

There is a murmur of reluctant agreement and Fletcher leaves.

WARREN

Quite right.

He goes to get some Polos.

WARREN

Here – who's pinched my Polos?

Fletcher enters his cell, and gestures for the others to follow.

The prisoners troop in. They include Banyard, Ives, Lukewarm and Warren, and about five others. The cumulative effect is a bit like the cabin scene in Night at the Opera. As they walk in Fletcher is saying:

FLETCHER

Come on in, make yourselves as comfortable as possible . . .

WARREN

(*Enjoying himself*) Pass right down the cell, please.

FLETCHER

This is not a laughing matter, Bunny.

WARREN

Sorry, Fletch.

FLETCHER

Who's keeping an eye open?

IVES

Gay Gordon. He's at the end of the landing.

FLETCHER

Bit conspicuous, isn't she? She's got her hair in curlers.

LUKEWARM

Nifty's at the other end.

BANYARD

I take it that the pineapple chunks have not been returned?

FLETCHER

No, they haven't. Now I've established when the crime was committed, and each of you lot had the MMO. Means, motives and opportunity.

BANYARD

(*Very Agatha Christie*) Are you saying that the thief is one of us . . . here in this very room?

FLETCHER

That's exactly what I am saying, Monsieur Poirot, yes.

They all look at each other uneasily.

FLETCHER

You lot were all on this landing before bang-up last night.

WARREN

Weren't you?

FLETCHER

Not all the time. At one stage I went over to see genial Harry Grout, didn't I, to negotiate the tobacco concession.

McLaren enters with difficulty.

MCLAREN

Kangaroo court aye, heard about it.

FLETCHER

Ah, McLaren, can we make room for McLaren, budge up.

It is difficult, but they manage it.

MCLAREN

No reason to exclude me you know, Fletch. All in this together. Finger of suspicion points at everyone. Just like to mention, of course, that if anyone points it at me, I'll clobber 'em.

FLETCHER

Good of you to be so reasonable, McLaren. Now just to recap, I've established that the crime was perpetrated during the fifteen minutes before bang-up last night.

MCLAREN

I was in the gym, working on me weights.

LUKEWARM

I was playing ping pong. With these two and Gay Gordon. Mixed doubles.

BANYARD

I was teaching Atlas chess.

WARREN

I was watching telly – (*To another*) Well you were as well, weren't you? And Crabs.

FLETCHER

Oh hello, Crabs, I didn't see you there. We don't need sworn statements from everybody.

BANYARD

Nevertheless, we should adhere to the fundamental principles on which our legal system was founded.

FLETCHER

You mean that every man is innocent until proven guilty.

BANYARD

Quite.

FLETCHER

True, true. On the other hand it's nearly lunch and there is amongst us one who is notorious for this kind of petty two-faced gittery, so I suggests we grab hold of Ives now and extract a swift confession.

All eyes turn to Ives.

IVES

'Ere listen . . .

MCLAREN

I'll extract the confession.

He gets Ives in a headlock.

IVES

'Ere listen, it wasn't me, straight up. I was in the Hobby Room. Making me toys, honest.

MCLAREN

Oh wait. That's true, that is. Saw him meself. On the way back from the gym. Making a big fluffy panda he was. He's good. Have you seen his Bugs Bunny Money Bank?

FLETCHER

No, is he doing it now?

MCLAREN

I think you're barking up the wrong tree, Fletch.

IVES

(*Hoarsely*) Could you let me go?

MCLAREN

Fletch?

FLETCHER

Yeah. Let him go, let him go.

McLaren does so.

FLETCHER

So we still live with the knowledge that there's a thief among us.

BANYARD

Where d'you get the pineapple in the first place?

FLETCHER

Stole it from the kitchen, didn't I?

A head peeps round the door. It is Gay Gordon.
GORDON
Mackay . . .
He disappears.
FLETCHER
(*Quietly*) All right, lads – we all know what we're here for. The initial gathering of the newly formed Slade Prison Cowboy Club. All together now . . .
He conducts them and they sing.
ALL
Home, home on the range . . .
Where the deer and the antelope play,
Where seldom is heard –
MACKAY
Quiet the lot of you, you horrible rabble!
Mackay arrives.
FLETCHER
(*Speaking*) A discouraging word?
MACKAY
What is going on here?
FLETCHER
Oh Mr Mackay. It's Mr Mackay, pardners.
ALL
Howdy, Mr Mackay.
MCLAREN
How.
MACKAY
I said, what is going on here?
FLETCHER
Cowboy Club, sir.
MACKAY
The what?

FLETCHER
Friends of the West. Kindred spirits, brought together by a mutual love and interest in those far-off days of the new frontier. We plan to meet, sing the songs –
MACKAY
Poppycock! This is an unlawful assembly, Fletcher. Prison regulations clearly state that no more than three prisoners will at any time congregate in a cell.
FLETCHER
Ah there, Mr Mackay, you have the advantage over me. Try as I might I have been unable to obtain a copy of the current Home Office Regulations.
MACKAY
Get on your feet the lot of you. There are only two rules in this prison. One: you do not write on the walls. Two: you will obey all rules. Back to your cells, the lot of you.
FLETCHER
All right lads, you'd better mosey along.
They start to troop out.
WARREN
See you later, Fletch. I'll bring round me Gene Autry songbook.
LUKEWARM
Adios, amigos . . .
Fletcher and Mackay are left alone.
FLETCHER
Well . . . highlight of the week coming up, Sunday lunch – can I offer you a sherry?

MACKAY

There is a growing current of insubordination and laxity in this prison. A definite rise in insolence. And pilfering.

FLETCHER

Pilfering, yes. Me and some of the lads have noticed that.

MACKAY

I'm not referring to petty sneak thieving amongst yourselves. That's to be expected amongst incorrigible criminals. I'm referring to thefts of prison property. Mark my words, Fletcher – it will not be tolerated.

Lennie enters in his kitchen whites and small chef's hat and spots Mackay.

LENNIE

Oh.

MACKAY

Ah yes, Godber. What are you up to?

LENNIE

Off work, sir. Been up since six this morning.

FLETCHER

Yes the lad's tired, sir. So if you'll excuse us –

MACKAY

This is a very unfortunate combination.

FLETCHER

Oh yes, how's that?

MACKAY

Godber with his opportunities to steal from the kitchen. And you with your distribution network.

LENNIE

Here, I don't steal, I resent that!

MACKAY

Oh you resent that, do you, Godber? Butter wouldn't melt in your mouth.

FLETCHER

That's a good idea, how much could you get in your mouth?

LENNIE

Don't make waves, Fletch.

Mackay starts to search Lennie.

LENNIE

No, I want to say. This is not on, Mr Mackay. (*As Mackay searches him*) All right, I'm inside, I have done wrong, and I've got that stigma to bear. But I'm paying my penance, I'm paying my dues.

MACKAY

What makes you think you're any different from anyone else?

LENNIE

Certain circumstances brought me here. Environment. Lack of parental guidance. Times were tough, I did go off the rails but I did have a few decent qualities underneath and I've learnt my lesson. Now I won't grass and I won't cheat and I will not steal.

MACKAY

Hmmm. All right, sonny Jim, we'll say no more . . . for the present.

Mackay goes.

FLETCHER

Well said, son. You even impressed

Mackay with your eloquence and
obvious sincerity.

LENNIE
Should think so. Suspicious old scroat.

FLETCHER
Good thing you were clean though.

LENNIE
Good job he didn't look under me hat.
*He takes it off, revealing half a
pound of marge perched on the
top of his head.*

3. PRISON
*Camera shows the prison in the
early evening, after lock-up but
before lights out.*

3A. CELL
*It is night time. Fletcher is cleaning
his teeth in his underclothes,
Lennie is looking for something
under his bed.*

LENNIE
Fletch?

FLETCHER
Whah?

LENNIE
Can I have a loan of your black
boot polish?

FLETCHER
(*Spitting*) Why?

LENNIE
Why? Why do you think? Me mascara's
run out.

FLETCHER
Don't be cheeky, young Godber.

LENNIE
I just want to clean me shoes.

FLETCHER
Borrow someone else's.

LENNIE
It's after lock-up.

FLETCHER
Then you should have thought of
that earlier.

LENNIE
Aren't you going to give me a measly
bit of shoe polish?

FLETCHER
No. I think that in the light of certain
events, it would be better if in the
future what one has one keeps.

LENNIE
I notice you didn't say this till after I
shared my margarine with you.

FLETCHER
I've done enough for you, Godber.
Boot polish, snout, toothpaste – the
first night you moved in here I give you
my toothpaste.

LENNIE
You give me one squeeze.

FLETCHER
On three successive nights! That adds
up to a lot of toothpaste.

LENNIE
Your squeezes don't.

FLETCHER
That weren't no ordinary toothpaste,
neither. That had hexochloroform in

the stripes. I got that special to match
my pyjamas.

Lennie starts to darn his socks.

LENNIE

I gave you liquorice all-sorts for that
toothpaste. Fair exchange is no robbery.

FLETCHER

When you were at death's door last
month with your inflamed bronchs,
who gave you a TCP throat lozenge?

LENNIE

Yeah. Lozenge. Singular.

FLETCHER

Who saved you all those matchsticks
when you wanted to make a model of
the *Cutty Sark*?

LENNIE

And who sat on it?

FLETCHER

Well, it was a pointless exercise. You
need a ten stretch to finish the *Cutty
Sark* in matchsticks. You should have
used chair legs like I told you.

LENNIE

Who stole nails for you from carpentry
classes so you could stick your pin-ups
on the wall? And who gave you half his
mother's home-made shortbread?

FLETCHER

Home-made shortbread, yeah. I used
that to hammer the nails in with.

LENNIE

You ungrateful nurk.

FLETCHER

Who loaned you their darning
wool then?

LENNIE

You did. And who's darning whose
socks then?

FLETCHER

Oh. Oh are they my socks?

LENNIE

'Course they are. I don't go through
my socks.

FLETCHER

Oh I didn't realise . . .

LENNIE

Apparently.

FLETCHER

Yeah well. Ta very much then.

LENNIE

(*Sulkily*) My pleasure.

FLETCHER

Go on then, here's me shoe polish.
Don't take too much.

*Lennie takes a small smear on
his brush.*

LENNIE

You told me when I moved in here that
our best protection against those
nurks out there was mutual interest.
Team spirit.

FLETCHER

Yes, but my trust has been
misplaced, hasn't it, as that missing
tin of pineapple has proved. I was
careless enough to forget that this
is a jungle in here. You can't trust
no one.

LENNIE

Here! Are you including me in
that remark?

FLETCHER
What remark was that?

LENNIE
About not trusting anybody.

FLETCHER
Look after number one, that's what it's all about.

LENNIE
That's not answering my question.

FLETCHER
What question's that then?

LENNIE
Do you think I nicked your chunks?

Fletcher is deliberately vague and evasive.

FLETCHER
Who knows who took them?

LENNIE
Fletcher, don't evade me. This is a very critical point in our relationship.

FLETCHER
Never mind that. You just darn your socks . . . my socks.

LENNIE
No. No. I want an answer. I respect you, Fletch. I owe you a lot, and I'm not talking about stripey toothpaste. I've never pretend to be cool or off-hand about doing stir. It bleeding petrified me. But you made it tolerable. You taught me the right approach. In me head. I get by now. Just, but I get by. I'm grateful, very grateful. And do you think I'd repay that by stealing your tin of naffing pineapple chunks . . . not even me favourite fruit.

FLETCHER
(*Pacifying him*) Here, here, here . . . it never entered my head, Lennie. If there's one person I know didn't take them it's you.

LENNIE
Yeah well.

FLETCHER
Of course. You and me. Oppoes, ain't we?

LENNIE
I dunno.

FLETCHER
You know we are. Living like this, like caged animals we're bound to get the needle sometimes. But I trust you. Implicit. I know you didn't take my pineapple.

LENNIE
How can you be sure?

FLETCHER
'Cos I know you. I know the type of person you are.

There is a pause while Lennie digests this.

FLETCHER
'Sides, when you were in the shower I went through all your gear!

4A. CORRIDOR
Camera shows Barrowclough walking along a corridor towards library door.

4B. LIBRARY

To describe this as a library is an overstatement. It is a small dusty room, full of old books with broken spines and grubby paperbacks. There is a locked door with a meshed grille at the back of the room. A chipped table has an old filing cabinet on it. There is also a very ancient typewriter behind which sits Fletcher, tapping out index cards as he catalogues new books. Barrowclough unlocks the door and walks in. Fletcher looks up.

FLETCHER
Ah, morning, Mr Barrowclough.

BARROWCLOUGH
Fletcher . . .

FLETCHER
Have a nice weekend then, did you?

BARROWCLOUGH
Not especially.

FLETCHER
Least the weather kept nice.

BARROWCLOUGH
Did it? The sun rarely shines in my household.

FLETCHER
You should put another window in.

BARROWCLOUGH
I wasn't referring to the architecture.

FLETCHER
Oh dear.

BARROWCLOUGH
But I haven't come to discuss my domestic situation . . .

FLETCHER
Your problems are my problems.

BARROWCLOUGH
I'm aware of that. I'm aware that's true at times. And that's why I've been lenient with you, Fletcher.

FLETCHER
Lenient?

BARROWCLOUGH
I haven't had a chance to talk to you since I went off duty for the weekend, but on Saturday afternoon when you were all out watching the football match, Mr Malone and I were detailed by Mr Mackay to do an RSC.

FLETCHER
A what?

BARROWCLOUGH
A random security check.

FLETCHER
Oh yes. The vocabulary varies from nick to nick. In practice it's the same thing though, isn't it? Burgling, a despicable infringement of civil liberties.

BARROWCLOUGH
The practice is justified though, Fletcher, when one finds stolen tins of pineapple chunks.

There is a long pause. Then Fletcher makes a game try.

FLETCHER
Where?

BARROWCLOUGH
Don't play games with me, Fletcher.

It was in your cell as you well know, and by rights I should have reported it.

FLETCHER
(*With a glimmer of hope*) You didn't then?

BARROWCLOUGH
No. As it happened, Mr Malone's attention was distracted. He was in the showers at the time, taking up the tiles looking for a missing hatchet. Fletcher, if I had reported that find you would have lost this job, had loss of privileges and probably solitary confinement.

FLETCHER
(*Contritely*) Well, what can I say, Mr Barrowclough?

BARROWCLOUGH
You can promise me to keep your nose clean. I reckoned I possibly owed you a favour, and the consequences would have been a bit severe. But that's wiped the slate clean. Now we're all square, right?

FLETCHER
Right, sir.

BARROWCLOUGH
You know this is a very cushy number here. This is a better job than most *trusties* have got.

FLETCHER
It's not all that easy. I've got a very complicated index to complete.

BARROWCLOUGH
Yes and you've been doing it for five weeks.

FLETCHER
I want to avoid mistakes, don't I?

BARROWCLOUGH
You want to avoid finishing it. 'Cos then you've got to decorate the room, which is why you were put in here in the first place.

FLETCHER
Waiting for the paint, sir.

BARROWCLOUGH
Where is it?

FLETCHER
Stolen, sir.

BARROWCLOUGH
What is happening to this prison?

FLETCHER
Strong criminal element in here, sir.

BARROWCLOUGH
There's just too much petty pilfering going on. Mr Mackay is on my back to stamp it out. I've let you off the hook, Fletcher. And in return I expect to see a sharp decrease on your block.

FLETCHER
Rest assured, sir.

Barrowclough seems satisfied with this.

FLETCHER
By the way . . . the tin of pineapple, did you manage to return it to the food store?

Barrowclough now looks slightly uncomfortable.

BARROWCLOUGH
Not exactly. I took it home and the wife did gammon steak Hawaii.

FLETCHER

Oh very nice, very nice. Gammon steak Hawaii. So the pineapple has been consumed!

BARROWCLOUGH

I hadn't intended to. But the wife found it and . . . insisted that we ate it. I could do very little about it.

FLETCHER

Only eat it.

BARROWCLOUGH

Under protest.

FLETCHER

On top of gammon. Well now we have quite a different situation here, don't we? I mean, if I did commit the alleged offence – which in the absence of evidence is somewhat difficult to prove – you are unquestionably an accessory before, after and during the facts. You're a felon same as me.

BARROWCLOUGH

I am aware of the situation. I would suggest that we purchase another tin of pineapple, and replace it in the food store.

FLETCHER

What do you mean we? I can't just troll down the village store at will.

BARROWCLOUGH

Oh no. I realise that, Fletcher. I shall get it. You shall pay for it.

5. KITCHEN

It is mid-morning, before lunch. There is a bustle of activity. Huge cauldrons of soup are bubbling. Several prisoners are going about their various tasks under the watchful eye of a Prison Officer. Lennie brings over a tray of Cornish pasties to a hotplate by which Lukewarm is standing. He talks to him quietly.

LENNIE

Hey, Lukewarm. Make a bit of a commotion in a minute, will you?

LUKEWARM

What for? You're not going to escape, are you? It's a good lunch today. We've got jelly.

Lennie looks around to make sure no one's in earshot.

LENNIE

I'm going to whip Fletch a tin of pineapple.

LUKEWARM

What for?

LENNIE

Surprise, like.

LUKEWARM

Bit dodgy. There's only one tin left.

LENNIE

Well . . .

He moves across the kitchen towards the store cupboard. Then turns and nods at Lukewarm. Lukewarm looks sadly at the tray of pastries.

LUKEWARM

(*To self*) They came out lovely an' all.

He drops them on the floor.
The Prison Officer comes over
to Lukewarm.

PO

What's all this, Lewis? Get all this
mess cleared up at once!

While the hubbub is going on Lennie
goes into the store cupboard.
Warren goes past the cupboard with
a laundry basket. A hand drops a tin
into it. Lennie comes out and reacts
with pleasure, but then reacts again
in alarm. Mr Birchwood, the civilian
catering administrator, walks across
to the cupboard and goes in.

BIRCHWOOD

Good morning, Mr Appleton.

APPLETON

Morning, Mr Birchwood.

Warren and Lennie exchange
anxious glances as he goes into
the cupboard. Birchwood comes
out of the cupboard and
confronts Appleton.

BIRCHWOOD

Mr Appleton – there's a tin of
pineapple chunks missing.

APPLETON

All right . . . (*Turns to a prisoner*) You –
fetch Mr Mackay from the Mess Hall.

The prisoner goes.

APPLETON

Everyone stay just where they are.
(*To Lennie*) You, where you are off to?

LENNIE

I've forgotten where I was.

He moves back. Appleton starts
to search them.

APPLETON

Come on, arms up.

LUKEWARM

Come on, Mr Appleton, we haven't
got time for all this – I've got a whole
trayful of pasties to get ready.

APPLETON

They'll have to wait, won't they?

LUKEWARM

They can't wait, they have to do
twenty-five minutes on Regulo 6.

They continue talking as
Barrowclough enters and crosses
over to the store cupboard. He looks
very shifty and nervous. He opens
the door and puts the tin back on the
shelf. He comes out of the cupboard
and moves away. Mackay comes
into the kitchen.

MACKAY

All right, what's going on here?

APPLETON

Pilfering we think, sir.

BIRCHWOOD

Tin of pineapple chunks, sir. There was
a tin in that cupboard half an hour ago.
I'm sure of that.

MACKAY

Who was last seen in that vicinity?

APPLETON

(*Indicating Lennie*) Godber was there
a minute ago.

MACKAY

Oh, was he? Well, that makes
sense. Your come-uppance is well
overdue, Godber.

*As Mackay speaks, he
approaches Lennie.*

MACKAY

Why is your hat standing to
attention, Godber?

He prods it with his stick.

LENNIE

Ow, Mr Mackay.

*Mackay removes the hat. Naturally
there is nothing underneath it.
Mackay is disappointed.*

MACKAY

All right. Now just stand there. All of you.
Very well, Mr Birchwood. Where was
the crime perpetrated?

BIRCHWOOD

From this cupboard, Mr Mackay.

He leads Mackay to it.

BIRCHWOOD

I saw straight off, 'cos there was only
the one tin there.

*He opens the cupboard door.
Mackay goes in and comes out
with a tin of pineapple. He hands
it to Birchwood.*

MACKAY

Is this the one that's missing?

BIRCHWOOD

(*Looking at it*) That's the one,
yes, sir.

MACKAY

Pull yourself together, Mr Birchwood.

*Lennie reacts with relief. Warren is
on his knees praying.*

6. CELL

*Lennie is alone in the cell finishing
a shave.*

WARREN

Here . . .

*Warren produces the tin of pineapple
chunks from under his jacket, and
hands it to Lennie who quickly hides
it under his pillow.*

WARREN

(*Wanting reassuring*) Now, listen.
Tell me. There were two tins there,
weren't there?

LENNIE

Just the one.

WARREN

Then I was right. It were a miracle.

LENNIE

Apparently. No other explanation.

WARREN

Scares you a bit though, doesn't it?

LENNIE

I don't pretend to understand.

WARREN

'The Miracle of Slade Prison'. I tell you
something, Len, I was brought up a
Catholic – not a very good one. But after
this – well. Makes you think, doesn't it?

LENNIE

God moves in a mysterious way. His
wonders to perform.

WARREN

See you in church.

He goes. Lennie takes the tin from under his pillow. He gets a label with 'surprise, surprise!' written on it in large letters and ties it round the tin. He looks at Fletcher's bunk. There is a towel on it. With a grin he places it under Fletcher's towel.

He moves away quickly on hearing Fletcher enter. Fletcher is not in the best of moods.

LENNIE
'Lo, Fletch.

FLETCHER
Oh yes . . .

LENNIE
What's the matter?

FLETCHER
What's the matter, some new paint's arrived.

LENNIE
So?

FLETCHER
So, it means I've got to decorate that library, doesn't it?

LENNIE
Can't you get rid of it, like all the other consignments?

FLETCHER
No – not a chance. There's not a screw left who hasn't got a gleaming front fence.

LENNIE
(Happily) Well never mind, life could be worse.

FLETCHER
Oh yes?

Fletcher picks up his towel, but still looking at Lennie, not noticing the tin.

Lennie starts to snigger. In pleasurable anticipation of Fletcher's discovery.

FLETCHER
What's got into you, Godber?

He throws his towel on the tin again.

LENNIE
You'll find out soon enough.

Mackay enters.

FLETCHER
Oh that's all we need, isn't it?

MACKAY
Haven't come to see you, Fletcher.

FLETCHER
What a shame, sir.

MACKAY
Came to see Godber. Now laddie, don't want you developing a chip. Don't want you to think I'm picking on you. I have a job to do. And whatever else I am, I'm firm but fair. I want you to know that I treat you all with equal contempt.

LENNIE
I appreciate that, Mr Mackay.

FLETCHER
What's all this about?

LENNIE
He thought I'd been pilfering again.

FLETCHER
Oh, did he? Well that should come as no surprise to you, son. They think

→ 153 ←

we're all at it, don't they? Think we're all thieves in here. We're under continual harassment. Suspicion. Sneaking around, poking through our belongings, with any justification whatsoever. Now if you'll excuse me I'm going for a shower.

LENNIE

No.

FLETCHER

You what?

LENNIE

You don't need to, Fletch. You're so . . . clean.

FLETCHER

What's got into you, Godber? (*To Mackay*) You lot are warping this lad's mind.

Fletcher picks up towel and moves towards the door. The tin of pineapple is left uncovered. Mackay sees it.

MACKAY

Fletcher . . .

Lennie winces. Fletcher comes back.

FLETCHER

What?

MACKAY

What is that?

FLETCHER

What's what?

He looks to where Mackay is pointing.

FLETCHER

Bloody hell!

MACKAY

Come along with me, Fletcher.

FLETCHER

Now, listen.

MACKAY

You won't need your towel.

FLETCHER

It's a plant.

MACKAY

Oh no, it's not, it's a tin of pineapple. Come along with me.

FLETCHER

I've been framed.

Mackay leaves. Fletcher follows, picking up his shirt.

Lennie moves across to get the tin. Takes off the label and makes for the door. Camera shows Mackay, followed by Fletcher, walking along the catwalk.

Lennie comes out of the cell with the tin.

LENNIE

Anyone got a tin opener?

Fletcher reacts then moves on.

SERIES TWO

EPISODE TWO: HEARTBREAK HOTEL

1. FLETCHER'S CELL
A small transistor radio is on in the cell.
From it comes the voice of a DJ with romantic mood music playing in the background. Lennie is sitting on his bed, darning his socks and listening intently.

DJ
Here's a request from Brigit in Dundee for a boy, she only knows him as Ricky but he has blue eyes, dark curly hair and looks a bit like David Essex. Brigit is sixteen and works in product control in a cake factory and her job is to spot flawed almonds.
Fletcher comes into the cell as the DJ gives the last fascinating piece of irrelevant detail.

DJ
Brigit was on a coach trip to the Ayrshire coast last summer and met Ricky briefly at a dance. All she knows is that he's from Glasgow.
Fletcher turns off the radio and takes over from the DJ.

FLETCHER
She knows he's from Glasgow and his hobbies include getting drunk and beating up lavatory attendants.

LENNIE
Here, I was listening to that.

FLETCHER
Yeah, well, I'm not. Teenage sentimental slush.

LENNIE
I have to sit through your *Gardeners' Question Time* and *Friday Night is Music Night*.

FLETCHER
All right, all right. And I sit through *Rosko's Round Table* but I draw the line at David 'Diddy' Hamilton. The wireless is never off in this nick.

LENNIE
Well, the screws think it makes us work harder. They're piping Tony Blackburn through to the kitchens now.

FLETCHER
They're doing that 'cos they believe we're in prison to be punished.

LENNIE
I wanted to hear that bit. 'Cos that was their special request slot. That was their 'Hello Young Lovers' corner.

FLETCHER
Oh yes?

LENNIE
And I'd written in, like. For a record.
For Denise.

FLETCHER
Denise?

LENNIE
My fiancée.

FLETCHER
Oh yes, that Denise, of
course, yes.

LENNIE
Just wanted to convey my undying
feelings of affection and devotion.
'Everlasting Love' that was the record
I asked for.

FLETCHER
You should have asked for 'My Ding-
a-Ling'.

LENNIE
I been listening all week, but it ain't
been on yet. Not fair. You'd think my
needs were greater than an almond
sorter's from Dundee.

FLETCHER
Hang about. Did you write this on
prison notepaper?

LENNIE
Yes. If you remember I gave you me
last sheet of Basildon Bond.

FLETCHER
That's it then.

LENNIE
Why? Are they biased
against prisoners?

FLETCHER
P'raps not officially. But I don't
recall ever having heard a prisoner's
request on the air. Forces yes.
Aircraft carriers or ack-ack batteries,
but never heard nothing from no
one from the *nick*.

LENNIE
It's a disgrace. We have a rotten
enough life in here without having our
requests refused. That's discrimination
that is. And five five and a halfpenny
stamps up the spout.

FLETCHER
You can see it from their point of view.
The public what pay their radio licence
faithful every year. Take offence,
wouldn't they? Sitting down to Sunday
lunch with their beloved *Family
Favourites*. Suddenly they read out a
card with a Parkhurst postmark. Says
could Tommy 'Mad Dog' Hollister
please have 'Clair de Lune'.

Mackay enters.

MACKAY
'Clair de Lune'?

FLETCHER
Oh. Yeah, it's French, Mr Mackay.
French for 'By the light of the
silvery moon'.

MACKAY
I thought for a moment, Fletcher, you
were having a cultural conversation.

LENNIE
P'raps you could tell us the ruling,
Mr Mackay.

MACKAY

The ruling, Godber?

FLETCHER

Miss Lonelyloins here, lovelorn Lennie,
he wants to know whether the BBC
plays prisoners' requests?

MACKAY

No. The answer to that is no,
on the grounds that it caused
embarrassment.

LENNIE

Embarrassment?

MACKAY

To the prisoners' families. The family
might have excused his absence by
telling the neighbours that the felon in
question was abroad, or working on a
North Sea oil rig.

LENNIE

Oh I see.

MACKAY

No doubt your wife, Fletcher, has
told your friends that you're on
a five-year safari.

He laughs.

FLETCHER

(*Reading paper*) No, no. She tells them
I'm doing missionary work in Scotland.

MACKAY

No, Godber. The practice was also
open to abuse. There was nothing to
stop prisoners sending messages in
code across our airways.

FLETCHER

Ah, that's a point – yeah, that's a
point. Listen to some heartwarming
Christmas message from some poor
lag. To his beloved wife and family and
little Tiny Tim. Could he please hear
Harry Secombe with 'The Impossible
Dream'. Translated what he really
meant was 'Nobby, have the ladder
round the back of E Wing, Boxing Day
– and bring me a mince pie.'

LENNIE

Oh it's a good idea, that.

MACKAY

It's an abuse of privilege, Godber.
Which is why I'm here.

FLETCHER

Oh, I thought it was a social call.

MACKAY

Six rolls of soft toilet paper have
disappeared from the Governor's
closet – the Governor's own personal
water closet.

FLETCHER

Oh dear. Would you Adam and Eve it?
What next?

MACKAY

Knowing you, Fletcher, probably
the seat.

Lennie laughs.

FLETCHER

Don't look at me.

LENNIE

Nor me. It's writing paper I'm short of.

MACKAY

It's not right. We've had to give the
Governor standard prison issue tissue.

LENNIE

That's rough.

FLETCHER

Not half, it ain't. That'll wipe the smile off his face.

They both laugh.

MACKAY

Fortune has given you two privileged positions in this prison. You would be foolish to jeopardise them by any infraction of the rules . . . I'll say no more.

He leaves. They call after him.

FLETCHER

Thank you, Mr Mackay.

LENNIE

Yes, thanks for the advice.

FLETCHER

To which we'll pay great heed . . . now naff off.

LENNIE

Always picking on us, isn't he?

FLETCHER

Well, that's his devious suspicious mind, the nosy nurk. Care for a glass of toilet roll?

He tips up the jug, revealing a pink roll of soft toilet tissue.

LENNIE

Eh, you've got one!

FLETCHER

Yeah. I had six.

LENNIE

Where's the other five?

FLETCHER

I traded them, didn't I?

LENNIE

Who to?

FLETCHER

There are a few inmates with some refinement in this nick. Bottom landing, call at the end, there's some embezzlers in there. Mr Banyard, the unfrocked dentist. Well those middle-class white-collar felons . . . leapt at 'em, didn't they?

LENNIE

What d'you get?

FLETCHER

Well, they owe me, don't they? Lot of nice middle-class merchandise. I'm promised a cricket sweater, a pair of Hush Puppies and a box of after-dinner mints.

Fletcher sits down, retrieves his socks and bundles them up.

LENNIE

Hey.

FLETCHER

What?

LENNIE

Share and share alike.

FLETCHER

Yes. What!!

LENNIE

Rule of the house, isn't it?

FLETCHER

Share my toilet roll?

LENNIE

Only fair.

FLETCHER

Share my toilet roll!!! Godber.

LENNIE

Only fair.

He sits glowering.

LENNIE

Look at all them darned socks.

FLETCHER

All right then.

He picks up the toilet roll and tears off one piece, handing it to Lennie.

FLETCHER

Mind how you go.

2. VISITING

A door is unlocked and wives, sweethearts, mothers, a few dads and brothers are ushered in under the watching eye of Mackay. The camera picks out Ingrid, Fletcher's daughter, and an older woman soon to be revealed as Mrs Godber, Lennie's mother. They move to their respective prisoners, who greet them at their individual tables. Fletcher and Lennie are sitting at adjacent tables.

INGRID

Hello, Dad.

FLETCHER

Hello, Ingrid, love.

LENNIE

Hello, Mum.

MRS GODBER

Hello, son.

Fletcher registers Lennie's visitor and Lennie makes the introductions.

LENNIE

Oh er – this is me mum, Fletch.

MRS GODBER

Hello, Mr Fletcher.

FLETCHER

Oh, pleasure's mine, Mrs Godber. Got a fine lad there. This is my eldest, Ingrid.

INGRID

Hello.

MACKAY

(*Calling out*) Sit down, Fletcher! And you, Godber! This is not a royal garden party.

He laughs. They sit down, muttering at Mackay.

Ingrid and Fletcher lean in closely towards each other and speak intimately.

INGRID

Who's he then?

FLETCHER

That's Mr Mackay. Charmless Celtic nurk.

INGRID

And who's the boy?

FLETCHER

Oh that's Lennie. Lennie Godber, my temporary cell-mate. He's from Birmingham but he's got an 'O' Level in geography.

INGRID

Oh.

FLETCHER

Well, you have to find your way round Birmingham. Well, how's your mother then?

INGRID

Oh fine, Dad. Sends her love and everything.

FLETCHER

How's your sister?

INGRID

Oh, Marion's fine. Got a new job.

FLETCHER

Gawd, does she never
keep a job for more than
three weeks?

INGRID

It's the bosses she has trouble with.
They molest her, she alleges.

FLETCHER

Well, that's her. Skirt right up to her
expectations. Where is she now?

INGRID

Timothy White's.

FLETCHER

Oh. Oh, that's better.
Shouldn't get molested there.
All qualified pharmacists,
aren't they?

INGRID

Her flat fell through.

FLETCHER

What flat's this?

INGRID

The one behind Olympia that she
shared with six other people.

FLETCHER

Six? Fell through to the flat below I
should think.

INGRID

No, the rent went up so she's home
again, pro tem.

FLETCHER

And how's young Raymond?

INGRID

Oh, Raymond won the mile in the
school sports.

FLETCHER

Oh, did he? Wish I had, I might not be
in here now.

INGRID

And he came in second in the high
jump. And he's swimming for the
school. And he's stage manager in
the play.

FLETCHER

Why isn't he in it? Last year he was
Yum Yum in the *Mikado*.

INGRID

His voice has gone.

FLETCHER

Oh.

INGRID

Well, he's on thirty a day.

FLETCHER

Thirty a day, that's shocking. At
fourteen! What a waste of money.

INGRID

He does save the coupons, Dad. He
wants to buy himself an aqualung.

FLETCHER

He'll need one if he sticks to thirty a day.

INGRID

Wants to go skin diving in St Ives.

FLETCHER

I notice all his achievements are extra-
curricular. Isn't there anything he
fancies inside the classroom?

INGRID

Mostly the girls, Dad.

FLETCHER

(*Speaking as a parent*) Here, here! Tell him to watch that, to curb his appetites. Don't want him getting no girl into trouble.

INGRID

If you hadn't I wouldn't be here.

FLETCHER

Ingrid, there's no need for coarse remarks of that nature. I can't believe my ears when I talk to kids today.

INGRID

There's nothing wrong, Dad. You and Mum have proved that your love wasn't just a passing infatuation. Silver wedding.

FLETCHER

Nevertheless, I don't want my adolescent love life held up as a yardstick to young Raymond. He's only fourteen. When what happened happened to your mother and me we was mature responsible sixteen-year-olds. We had something behind us. We was in Highgate Cemetery – it was the tomb of Karl Marx. Your mother had a steady job in Gamages hardware department. And I had my plastering diploma from Borstal.

INGRID

Yes, Dad.

FLETCHER

Speaking of Highgate Cemetery, how's your love life? Not still that Eddie Risley, is it?

Her look shows that it is.

FLETCHER

I warned you enough about him, gel. He's a crook is Eddie Risley.

INGRID

Oh he's straight, Dad. Just he's a tough businessman. It's not fair what people keep saying about him. They tell you he'd sell his own mother.

FLETCHER

I heard that on very good authority.

INGRID

Who from?

FLETCHER

The two blokes who bought his mother.

INGRID

It's no use talking to you about Eddie. You got a blind spot about him.

FLETCHER

So have you, my gel. He's giving you a bad time. Isn't he?

INGRID

I just don't know where I am with him.

FLETCHER

You do pick them, Ingrid. You're a bonny girl with a lovely nature. You could have anyone, you could. And you're not getting any younger, you know. You're twenty-four, girl. Has to be said.

INGRID

That's not old.

FLETCHER

It is for a teenager, and a spinster.

INGRID

Oh Dad . . . things have changed since your day. Girls want to be . . .

well, lots of girls don't want to be tied
down so quick. They feel there's
alternatives to marriage.

FLETCHER
Not in Muswell Hill, they don't.
Nothing's changed there.

INGRID
They've twinned the Odeon.

FLETCHER
I'm talking about standards. Moral
standards. All these social
commentators – they don't know
Britain. They all live within a stone's
throw of each other in NW1. They ain't
never been north of Hampstead or
south of Sloane Square. But in the real
world – Birmingham, Bristol, Muswell
Hill – the fundamentals haven't changed
– here, are you wearing a bra?

INGRID
I don't need to, Dad.

FLETCHER
You what?

INGRID
I haven't done for years. My breasts
are firm and pliant.

FLETCHER
(Whispering) Ingrid, please. This ain't
San Tropay you know, this is Slade
bleedin' Prison. There's six hundred
men in here would go berserk at a
glimpse of shin, never mind
unfettered knockers.
It's Ingrid's turn to be embarrassed.

INGRID
Dad!

FLETCHER
I'm sorry, gel, but it has to be said.
You're very naïve in certain ways.
Very naïve about the effect your
body has on the shackled male.

INGRID
Dad, you're naïve in certain
ways. I shouldn't think anyone's
even noticed.
*They look round. The camera
reveals that all the male heads,
Lennie's included, are focused
firmly on Ingrid's unfettered
womanhood.*

3. LANDING
*It is night time. There is the sound
of snores and coughs.*

3A. CELL
*Lennie is asleep. Suddenly his bunk
is shaken.*

FLETCHER
Godber . . . Godber! . . . GODBER!!
*Lennie opens his eyes, trying to
emerge from a deep sleep.*

LENNIE
What, what, what???!!!

FLETCHER
Are you awake?

LENNIE
I am now . . . what's the matter?

FLETCHER
Got any snout?

LENNIE
No. Would you believe it?

FLETCHER
(*Grumpily*) I'd believe it, you inconsiderate nurk.

LENNIE
I thought you'd given it up.

FLETCHER
I feel like starting again.
There is a pause. Fletcher gets out off the bunk and lowers himself to the floor. He looks uncharacteristically worried and preoccupied.

FLETCHER
Mind your head.

LENNIE
Me mum brought me some Maltesers.

FLETCHER
No, thanks.

LENNIE
And some of her Parkin cake.

FLETCHER
No, thanks. If you ain't got no snout, naff off back to sleep.

LENNIE
Oh thanks very much, you bad-tempered old scroat. What's wrong with you anyway?

FLETCHER
Things on my mind, ain't there?

LENNIE
Like what?

FLETCHER
My business.

LENNIE
Oh come on, Fletch. Might as well talk it out. I mean, you woke me up.

FLETCHER
Get depressed at times that's all. Stinking stir.
He kicks the table.

LENNIE
That's not like you, Fletch.

FLETCHER
A father's place is at home, with his kids – giving them affection, parental guidance. I got three of 'em, you know.

LENNIE
Yes, I know.

FLETCHER
Fourteen, nineteen and twenty-four.

LENNIE
Quite a gap between each.

FLETCHER
Circumstances dictated that.

LENNIE
How?

FLETCHER
Kept going in prison for five years, didn't I?

LENNIE
Oh.

FLETCHER
The two youngest – well, that's a terrible age the teens, in' it? You expect trouble. But Ingrid, my eldest, you'd think she'd have learnt some lessons by now.

LENNIE
She looked a nice girl to me. She had lovely –

FLETCHER
(*Quickly*) I know what she's got lovely,

Godber. It's her father you're talking to, be very careful!

LENNIE
(*Calming him*) Eyes, I was going to say. Eyes. Big and blue.

FLETCHER
(*Mollified*) Oh.

LENNIE
Nice smile too which seemed to indicate a nice disposition and a warm and generous nature.

FLETCHER
Yes, yes. True, true. That's all right then.

LENNIE
(*Carefully*) Fletch, I hope you don't mind but I couldn't help overhearing a bit of what you was saying – well, most of us did.

FLETCHER
Oh yes?

LENNIE
Doesn't sound good enough for her, that Eddie Risley, if you ask me.

FLETCHER
He ain't. He used to say he was in the motor trade – know what he did? Forged car log books. Not that she'd believe it.

LENNIE
How could you be sure?

FLETCHER
'Cos I bought two off him.

There is a pause.

FLETCHER
They weren't much cop. He'd spelt Citroën with an S . . .

LENNIE
Well, with a bit of luck he'll get rumbled sooner or later and sent away. Give her a chance to find someone new. I should think your Marion awakening to the possibilities of her sex, she'll settle down at Timothy White's. And I wouldn't worry too much about your Raymond either. I was on thirty a day when I was fourteen. Oh, and by the way, congratulations on your silver wedding.

FLETCHER
Godber, did you earwig all my conversation? Couldn't you have talked to your poor old mum? It's a long shlep from Birmingham.

LENNIE
She doesn't have much to say for herself does Mum. She's a canny old soul but she only gives me a catalogue of family ailments.

FLETCHER
What about news of the lovely Denise?

LENNIE
She don't talk about Denise 'cos she don't approve of her.

FLETCHER
Why?

LENNIE
'Cos she uses green nail varnish and doesn't wear a bra.

FLETCHER
Sounds as if she and my Ingrid have got a lot in common.

There is a pause.

LENNIE

Your Ingrid's got nicer knockers.

4. ASSOCIATION AREA

Fletcher is playing draughts. As he makes a move, Barrowclough shouts from the landing above.

BARROWCLOUGH

Fletcher . . . could I have a word.

Fletcher calls out from the table.

FLETCHER

I'm playing draughts, ain't I?

BARROWCLOUGH

It is rather important. Wouldn't ask otherwise.

FLETCHER

So's this important . . .

He makes a move. The other player makes a move and takes four of Fletcher's men.

FLETCHER

Still, if duty calls, better abandon this game, Cecil. Call it a draw. Half each.

He gets up and takes half the board with him. He walks to the stairs.

4A. CELL

Barrowclough walks in, followed by Fletcher.

BARROWCLOUGH

I'm sorry to interrupt you in association hour.

FLETCHER

'S all right. Only draughts.

BARROWCLOUGH

Not your game as a rule, is it?

FLETCHER

What else is left? Only news on the telly and someone's trod on the ping pong ball.

BARROWCLOUGH

Oh, I am sorry. Anyhow I wanted a quiet word.

FLETCHER

I'm all ears.

BARROWCLOUGH

Do you know where Godber is?

FLETCHER

He'll be at one of his poxy evening classes. What is it today, Tuesday? Tuesday – woodwork.

BARROWCLOUGH

He's up in front of the Governor.

FLETCHER

What? The kid? What's he done?

BARROWCLOUGH

He attacked another prisoner. At work, in the kitchens. He attacked Jackdaw with a soup ladle.

FLETCHER

I don't believe it.

BARROWCLOUGH

It's true. A severe and unprovoked attack the officer said.

FLETCHER

I don't believe it. I know Jackdaw gets on your wick, he gets on all our wicks but young Lennie's a passive lad, he wouldn't hurt a fly.

BARROWCLOUGH

That's why I came to you. I thought

you might be able to shed some light on the matter.

FLETCHER
I dunno. He was his usual self this morning. And at lunch he was quite cheerful. Mind you, one of your colleagues, Mr Pringle, did slip on some orange peel and fall down some stairs hurting his back – so we were all quite cheerful.

BARROWCLOUGH
Fletcher, you must be serious. Godber's in trouble. It's so irrational. I mean I like that lad, I think he's got a lot of promise.

FLETCHER
Well, that's prison, isn't it? The system. Already turning a nice quiet lad into a violent criminal. You're sitting on a volcano which at any time might erupt in an explosion of desperate violence and mayhem.

BARROWCLOUGH
Fletcher – you've got your finger on the pulse. What can we do to avert it?

FLETCHER
There's only one thing which might help to postpone the inevitable holocaust.

BARROWCLOUGH
What? What?

FLETCHER
You'll have to indent for some new ping pong balls.

4B. FILM
A warder unlocks the gate. Lennie enters and walks along the catwalk
and past Barrowclough into Fletcher's cell.

4C. CELL
Lennie goes to the bed and takes off his jacket. Fletcher watches him for a moment.

FLETCHER
Well then . . .?

LENNIE
Well then what?

FLETCHER
I heard.

LENNIE
Heard what?

FLETCHER
I heard you hit Jackdaw with a ladle.

LENNIE
Heard right then, didn't you?

FLETCHER
(*Fishing*) I'm sure you had your reasons.

LENNIE
Yes, I did.

Fletcher waits but nothing else is forthcoming.

FLETCHER
Ain't you going to the cooler then?

LENNIE
No. I'm not.

FLETCHER
Well, you're a lucky lad then, aren't you?

LENNIE
Lucky, am I?

FLETCHER
Assault! Ladling a fellow prisoner. Automatic cooler offence, ladling.

LENNIE

(*Staccato*) Governor gave me a severe reprimand and loss of privileges. Would have got cooler. But accepted my mitigating circumstances.

FLETCHER

Oh . . . mitigating circumstances. Well, you must have had . . .

There is a pause.

FLETCHER

Don't have to tell me.

He gets off his bunk.

FLETCHER

Don't have to tell me what drove a normal affable lad like yourself to the pitch where he suddenly launches himself on another prisoner with a deadly weapon, to wit a ladle.

LENNIE

I won't then. Rather not.

FLETCHER

I see.

There is a pause.

FLETCHER

Doesn't occur to you that your hitherto blameless record is due in no small part to yours truly. I'm just the bloke who showed you the ropes, helped you get by, kept you on the rails, loaned you his soft toilet paper.

LENNIE

I'm not ungrateful, Fletch, honest. Every time I go to the bog, I'm not ungrateful.

FLETCHER

Godber, having eavesdropped into

every aspect of my private life, don't you think I'm entitled to know a bit of yours!

Lennie sighs then says reluctantly.

LENNIE

I had some news. Which upset me. Jackdaw thought it was a joke. Kept taking the mick. Wouldn't leave it off. So I hit him. While the balance of my mind was disturbed.

FLETCHER

News?

LENNIE

Yeah.

There is a pause.

FLETCHER

(*Sitting by Lennie*) What news?

Lennie takes a letter out of his pocket and hands it to Fletcher, who opens it.

FLETCHER

Oh, I see, it's a 'Dear John' letter, ain't it?

LENNIE

Yeah – Dear Lennie, in my case.

FLETCHER

Naturally, yours, no longer for ever, Denise, eh?

LENNIE

'S right.

FLETCHER

Dear, dear. So it's the demise of Denise then?

LENNIE

Not funny, Fletch.

FLETCHER

Was I making a joke?

LENNIE

Not what I call a joke, no.

FLETCHER

Don't you think I haven't seen this happen many, many times? Only natural. You could say inevitable. Least your Denise has been honest enough to write a letter. 'Cos they're all at it like knives while we're in here.

LENNIE

Came out of the blue though this, Fletch. No hint of it a fortnight ago in her last letter. Her only concern then was whether we should have a canary or a budgerigar.

FLETCHER

In your future life together?

LENNIE

Yes.

FLETCHER

Well, that's one decision you don't have to make.

LENNIE

No.

There is a pause.

FLETCHER

I know it's now academic, but speaking personally, from personal experience, I would say I would always without doubt plump for the budgerigar.

LENNIE

Oh, why?

FLETCHER

Budgies is friendlier. And they're very prone to draughts, canaries – it's the angle of the tail.

LENNIE

Oh.

FLETCHER

I speak from experience as I say. We had a canary once . . . surly little bleeder he was.

LENNIE

Yes, well as you say, it's a bit academic now, Fletch.

FLETCHER

So your Denise . . . has . . . er . . . she er . . . I mean er, there's another man is there, presumably?

Lennie nods.

FLETCHER

D'you know him?

LENNIE

His name's Kenneth – he's in the Merchant Navy. Third engineer, qualified. No contest, is there?

He gets up, walks across the cell and sits down again.

FLETCHER

Oh well, Jack the lad, isn't he? The blue-eyed boy with his navy blue uniform and the gold braid. Oh well, the sun shines out of his pot-hole. It's all temporary, son, all temporary. When he goes back to sea – sailor beware then. You'll be out with Denise, he'll be in the Persian Gulf. That's when you resume your rightful position, in her affections that is. I tell you, this is only a temporary setback.

LENNIE

I don't think so, Fletch.

FLETCHER

No sweat.

LENNIE

She's married him.

FLETCHER

She done what!

LENNIE

Last Saturday, Smethwick Registry Office. She thought it was my right to know.

FLETCHER

Married!

LENNIE

Apparently it kept fine for them and the Cross Keys did them proud. Pâté and ham salad.

FLETCHER

(*Rising and walking across*) Pâté and ham salad. Well, I'm appalled. Words fail me. I'm speechless. Nothing will surprise me any more. *Jackdaw comes in with his arm in a sling and his head bandaged.*

FLETCHER

Jackdaw!

JACKDAW

Now look 'ere . . .

FLETCHER

God preserve us, Jackdaw, what do you look like?

JACKDAW

All right, all right.

FLETCHER

You been driving golf balls in your cell again.

JACKDAW

Ask him!

LENNIE

(*Walking over to Jackdaw*) I'm sorry, Jackdaw, straight up. There was no call for that.

JACKDAW

What d'you get?

LENNIE

Didn't get the cooler. Deserved it.

JACKDAW

'Ere listen, no hard feelings.

LENNIE

That's good of you, Jackdaw. 'Cos you're entitled.

FLETCHER

Yes, very commendable, Jackdaw. Why don't you shake on it?

JACKDAW

I'd sooner not.

He indicates his bandaged right arm.

JACKDAW

I just come in to say that I realise that you er . . . you er . . . that there were –

FLETCHER

The circumstances was mitigating.

JACKDAW

That's it. As you say, Fletch. That I bear no grudges, 'cos obviously you've suffered a great emotional upheaval. And it'll take some time to get over. Thing like this does, doesn't it, like? But as soon as you're back to normal and my wrist is better I'll er –

He points to his head.

JACKDAW

I'll get you for this!!

5. VISITING ROOM

Ingrid is sitting in the same seat as before, facing Fletcher.

INGRID

Mum's definitely coming up next month. She would have come today only the doctor expressly forbade it. Said she'd be a fool to herself.

FLETCHER

It's nothing serious though?

INGRID

Just something going round he says.

There is a pause. Then comes the news.

INGRID

Marion ain't with Timothy White's no longer.

FLETCHER

(*With heavy sarcasm*) Dispensed with her services, did they?

INGRID

It wasn't molestation this time. But she got a job selling shirts. She shows them round the offices.

FLETCHER

Well, make a change from showing her knickers round the office.

INGRID

And she's found a flat in Maida Vale, which she's sharing with some nurses. And what you'll be most glad to hear is that Eddie and me have split up.

FLETCHER

Not before time, gel. That's a relief to us all.

A voice can be heard from their right. The camera reveals Lennie, sitting opposite his mum again.

LENNIE

Yes, we was worried about that liaison.

FLETCHER

(*Indignantly*) Do you mind, Godber! I'm sorry Mrs Godber, no offence, but I've warned the lad about this before. Ain't you got any news from your home front?

MRS GODBER

I'm sorry, it's my fault. I can never think of what to say to him. It's like visiting people in hospital.

FLETCHER

Force yourself.

Mackay bears down on them.

MACKAY

Here, here, here, here! You all know the procedure. Conversations will be confined to the relative or friend opposite the prisoner in question. There will be no fractricide.

FLETCHER

That's what I was telling him, Mr Mackay. (*Then pointedly to Lennie*) So if you'll excuse us, Godber.

LENNIE

Sorry, Fletch. Sorry miss.

He smiles at Ingrid, who smiles back.

INGRID

That's all right.

FLETCHER

So anyhow, you give Eddie the elbow then? Good for you, girl. Just listen to your old dad in future.

INGRID

I do, Dad. Ain't you noticed how much more discreet I am today?

FLETCHER

How d'you mean?

INGRID

Well, last time I was here I obviously embarrassed you in front of your friends. Well, this time, I ain't given you no cause, have I?

FLETCHER

Ain't you? I don't get you, girl.

INGRID

Oh Dad . . . look – I'm wearing a bra. *She pulls up her sweater to reveal a black bra. The entire room is goggle-eyed and sick with lust.*

6. CELL

Lennie is folding a letter into an envelope and then licks and seals it. Fletcher enters, taking something furtively from his pocket.

FLETCHER

Look at that.

It is a ping pong ball.

LENNIE

What?

FLETCHER

New ping pong ball. Two star.

LENNIE

But you don't play.

FLETCHER

(With an expression that says, will he never learn) I don't play. But all you other nurks do, don't you? There's a severe scarcity of ping pong balls in this nick. I'll get a quarter-pound of snout for this.

LENNIE

Oh. *(Seriously)* Fletch – can I ask you something?

FLETCHER

(Looking for a hiding place) Feel free.

LENNIE

You know when I was very down the other day. After Denise's letter.

FLETCHER

Yes.

LENNIE

When I was worried about the stigma of being an ex-con . . .

FLETCHER

Yes . . .

LENNIE

Well, will it be a problem for me? I mean, will I be able to work me way back into society?

FLETCHER

That depends, son. Depends on the breaks.

LENNIE

Have there been any problems for you? When you get out?

FLETCHER

Not for me, no. I've never had to worry about no references, no testimonials. 'Cos I've always gone straight, straight back into crime. It's different with you,

Lennie – you're young, you're healthy, you've got an honest face.

LENNIE
Is that enough?

FLETCHER
Yes, yes. Character. That's what I can read. And you've got it, son. You're a good lad.

LENNIE
So you think, if someone really cared for me, a girl, like . . . she'd overlook my past misdemeanours?

FLETCHER
Certainly. If she's any sort of human being of course she would. Like anybody would. Lennie, my son, you have to learn to believe in yourself. I believe in you.

LENNIE
Do you, Fletch?

FLETCHER
'Course I do.

Lennie is cheered by this.

LENNIE
Oh good. I'm going to send this then.

He holds up the letter.

LENNIE
Would you give it to your mucker Barrowclough? To post in the village.

FLETCHER
(*Reading the address*) BBC . . .?

LENNIE
It's on plain notepaper, so they won't know it's from a prisoner.

FLETCHER
'Hello Young Lovers Corner.' Oh gawd.

Is all this soul-searching for the benefit of that slag Denise?

LENNIE
No, not her.

FLETCHER
Well who?

LENNIE
Ingrid.

FLETCHER
(*Quietly*) My Ingrid . . .

LENNIE
(*Quoting his letter*) Yeah . . . 'Our eyes met across a crowded room . . .'

FLETCHER
My daughter Ingrid!

LENNIE
'And though we didn't know each other, we both knew . . .'

FLETCHER
(*Exploding*) You think I'd let my beloved Ingrid take up with the likes of you! A bleeding juvenile delinquent from the backstreets of Birmingham! *He raises his fist, about to bring it down on Lennie.*

LENNIE
(*Urgently*) Fletch, be careful, be careful.

FLETCHER
(*Checked*) What?

Lennie unclenches Fletcher's fist.

LENNIE
You've crushed your ping-pong ball!

SERIES TWO

EPISODE THREE: DISTURBING THE PEACE

1. LIBRARY
Fletcher is stacking the old books on to a trolley when the door is unlocked and Barrowclough enters.

BARROWCLOUGH
Right, Fletcher, you'd better get on your rounds, hospital and Governor.

FLETCHER
Just picking something out special for the Governor, Mr Barrowclough. Got a good one for his wife an' all. 'A Perilous Odyssey of Love and Anguish Set in Turbulent Tuscany'. Very torrid according to the write-up.

BARROWCLOUGH
Not too torrid, is it?

FLETCHER
Have no fear. It's done in very good taste. They always put the lights out.

BARROWCLOUGH
Come on then, let's get along.
He is trying to rush Fletcher. Fletcher produces a paper.

FLETCHER
Oh, just before we go, could you sign this, Mr Barrowclough? Requisition for new books. I know

how busy you are so don't trouble to read it, just sign at the bottom where I've indicated.
Fletcher has placed the paper in front of him, but Barrowclough hesitates.

BARROWCLOUGH
Just have a quick glance through . . .

FLETCHER
(*Disapprovingly*) Well, we are a bit behindhand, I mean, chop chop.
Barrowclough, however, insists on checking the list, then frowns.

BARROWCLOUGH
There's several here quite unsuitable, not suitable at all. Look at this . . .

FLETCHER
What?

BARROWCLOUGH
(*Shocked*) The Great Escape . . . Nudes of the Naughty Nineties . . . A History of Erotica.

FLETCHER
I couldn't find it on the map.

BARROWCLOUGH
I can't let these through, Flotcher. They're mostly sexual or subversive.

He scratches them out.

FLETCHER

Oh, leave *Voodoo Woman*. It's a classic, that.

BARROWCLOUGH

You've got a very privileged job in this library, Fletcher. Take care you don't lose it.

He gives the list back to Fletcher, who, disgruntled, looks at what has survived the censor's pen.

FLETCHER

I see you've allowed the Enid Blyton Omnibus. The lads'll be chuffed about that.

BARROWCLOUGH

There is a limit.

FLETCHER

Yes, yes, I can appreciate your point of view. There's always two sides, isn't there? Sort of thing I want to bring out in my forthcoming book.

BARROWCLOUGH

Book!

FLETCHER

Well, working in the library has rekindled my literary aspirations. So I'm working on this book, see. On prison life. From the man within, like.

BARROWCLOUGH

(*Not keen*) Prison life.

FLETCHER

Ah, but don't worry, I'm very objective. I haven't overlooked the difficult task which confronts you brave boys in blue and I've sought to shed light on your problems as much as the ones faced by my fellow felons.

BARROWCLOUGH

(*Reassured*) Oh good, good. What are you going to call your book, Fletcher?

FLETCHER

Don't Let the Bastards Grind You Down. *Fletcher exits, pushing his trolley.*

2. GOVERNOR'S OFFICE

Mr Venables is sitting at his desk going through the mail with his secretary, Mrs Heskith. She is in her latish thirties, a local lady wearing sensible shoes.

VENABLES

Is this all the mail then, Mrs Heskith?

MRS HESKITH

Yes, Mr Venables. The Home Office have confirmed the dates of Mr Mackay's promotion course.

Venables picks up the relevant letter, studying it doubtfully for a moment.

VENABLES

What? Yes, yes . . . it's difficult enough running a prison without losing someone of Mr Mackay's calibre.

MRS HESKITH

Don't forget Tuesday is the magistrates' inspection.

VENABLES

Oh is it? We'd better put on a bit of a

show for them. We'll have a roast, and get out the tinned pears . . . with cream.

MRS HESKITH

Cream?

VENABLES

Well, you know . . . Carnation milk or whatever it is.

MRS HESKITH

Right, I'll get along then.

She goes to the door and bumps into Fletcher who enters, pushing his little trolleyload of books.

FLETCHER

Oh good morning, Mrs Heskith, what a rare treat.

She gives him a coy smile and tries to edge round his trolley, a little flustered.

MRS HESKITH

Oh yes, good morning, Fletcher.

FLETCHER

What a lovely cardigan. Goes with your eyes, two of your best features if I may say so, tho' I expect you've been told many times before –

VENABLES

Fletcher, what is it?

FLETCHER

Oh. Morning, sir.

VENABLES

Thank you, Mrs Heskith. You'd better go and get me that release form to sign. *She leaves. Fletcher gives her a quick appraisal as she goes.*

FLETCHER

(*Sotto voce*) Well I would, if you wouldn't.

VENABLES

What is it, Fletcher?

FLETCHER

Books, sir. New consignment, sir. You always like to have first pick of a new consignment.

VENABLES

It's not a question of first pick. I like to look them over to ensure there's nothing unsuitable for the men.

FLETCHER

I found one book you wanted, sir. *He gives him a book.*

VENABLES

(*Puzzled*) Tom Brown's Schooldays.

FLETCHER

The title's irrelevant, sir. Point is it's exactly three-quarters of an inch thick, which is just what you said you wanted to prop up your wobbly bookcase.

VENABLES

Oh splendid, Fletcher. Thank you. *Venables bends down to prop up the desk with the book, withdrawing a telephone directory. Fletcher automatically takes the opportunity to pocket what he can: a rubber, a pencil sharpener, a felt pen, two cigarettes from an open packet and a paper clip. He also cranes his head to read the letter about Mackay, showing more than a passing interest in it. Then he straightens himself up, just as Venables is also doing so.*

VENABLES

Yes, that's much better. Much better.
Well, Fletcher, cut along.

Mrs Heskith re-enters with a release
form for signature. Fletcher again
watches her, as he makes to go.

MRS HESKITH

The release form, sir.

VENABLES

Oh good . . . where's my pen?

Not surprisingly, he cannot find it on
the desk.

FLETCHER

Oh . . . borrow mine, sir.

He produces Venables's pen.

VENABLES

Oh, thank you, Fletcher.

He takes it and signs the form,
handing it back to Mrs Heskith and
pocketing the pen.
Meanwhile Fletcher is looking at
her, causing her some slight
embarrassment.

VENABLES

Go on then, Fletcher.

FLETCHER

Yes sir, it's just –

VENABLES

What, what?

FLETCHER

My pen, sir.

VENABLES

Oh I'm terribly sorry.

He hands it back.

FLETCHER

They all look alike, don't they, sir?

3. ASSOCIATION AREA

It is evening, association time.
Mackay walks around the men.

3A. CELL

Fletcher is emptying his pockets
and putting the items on the table.

LENNIE

Is that it, then?

FLETCHER

Yes – apart from a very interesting bit of
information. I always learn something
when I go in the Governor's office.

LENNIE

Like what?

FLETCHER

Well . . . apart from the fact that
there's something simmering between
him and Mrs Heskith – which we'll
bear in mind for future reference,
won't we – I also saw a memo on
Venables's desk. Upside down of
course, but years of being in the nick
have taught me to read memos
upside down.

LENNIE

What did it say?

FLETCHER

'Eciffo emoh, laitnedifnoc'.

LENNIE

What the hell's that mean?

FLETCHER

'Home Office, Confidential', backwards.

LENNIE

What was it about then?

FLETCHER

Something to do with Mackay's going on a course.

LENNIE

When, where, what course?

FLETCHER

Naff off, you nurk, I only had four seconds. But I reckon it must be something to do with promotion or transfer.

LENNIE

He ain't let on, like.

FLETCHER

He don't know yet, only me and the Governor knows so far.

MACKAY

(*Offscreen*) Come on, you men!

LENNIE

Aren't those his dulcet tones now, on the landing? Shall we ask him?

FLETCHER

No, no, no. We've got a situation here which I can turn to my advantage.

MACKAY

(*Offscreen*) Get your hair cut.

FLETCHER

(*Getting paper*) No time like the present – pretend you're listening.
Fletcher reads the paper. Lennie gets on his bunk.

FLETCHER

I see here, Godber, that with Saturn

passing through your opposite sign of Cancer, this may be an exhausting and turbulent month for you. Must be moving you out the kitchens on to dustbins.

MACKAY

Seeking solace in the stars now, are we?

FLETCHER

Oh evening, Mr Mackay. If you'll excuse me – 'As Uranus is one of the most powerful and unpredictable planets – future events will be likewise unpredictable.'

MACKAY

I should have thought all your futures were somewhat predictable – hm, hm, hm . . . Now if your stars were true they would say, 'Little change for the next four years. No opportunities for travel, and absolutely no prospect of romance on the horizon.'

FLETCHER

Only a question of scale. When you're deprived of romance as what we are, a chance brush with the Governor's secretary is like a naughty weekend in Boulogne with a teenage nymphomaniac, see it's only a question of scale.

LENNIE

When's your birthday, Mr Mackay?

MACKAY

April the twenty-fifth.

FLETCHER

(*Looking in the paper*) Oh yes, Taurus.

Not the subtlest of signs. The bull.
Here we are. 'Endeavours you have
been hoping for come to fruition.'
Oh look at this . . . 'A favourable
time for a move and seeking
opportunities elsewhere.'

MACKAY
Poppycock.

FLETCHER
No, they're rarely wrong. You must be
moving on, Mr Mackay.

LENNIE
Holiday?

MACKAY
Not till August.

LENNIE
Your retirement's not due just yet, is it?

MACKAY
Don't be insolent, Godber.

FLETCHER
Well, it's very clear in the stars, very
clear. A move is clearly indicated.

MACKAY
Out of the question.

FLETCHER
Want a bet?

MACKAY
You'd wager on this nonsense?

FLETCHER
When it's as clear as this I would.
Doesn't do to deride what you don't
know. The paranormal, the psychic.
Take my Uncle Godfrey. Walked
under a ladder one day. Laughed
about it he did. Walked under it.
Purposely, like. And d'you know,

over the next forty-three years he lost
all his teeth.

MACKAY
You'd lose your shirt betting on this
astronomical nonsense.

FLETCHER
It's not nonsense. I'll bet you
anything that within a few days
you'll be leaving your familiar
surroundings.

MACKAY
Step outside, Fletcher.

FLETCHER
What have I said now?

MACKAY
Step outside.

*Fletcher gets up, passes Mackay
and goes out. Mackay follows him
out of the cell.*

MACKAY
You have the nerve to offer to bet
with a prison officer? In front of
young Godber.

FLETCHER
Oh, I never thought, Mr Mackay.

MACKAY
What are you trying to do, disillusion
the boy?

FLETCHER
Sorry, Mr Mackay.

MACKAY
How much then?

FLETCHER
A quid?

MACKAY
You're on.

4. PRISON GATES

Camera shows a minibus. Mackay approaches it, shakes hands with Venables and gets in. Cheering is heard from prisoners on work detail.

5. ASSOCIATION AREA

It is night time. Fletcher is at a table with McLaren, Warren and Williams, who are playing draughts. Fletcher himself is reading the Sun. The mood is relaxed.

WARREN

Eh, did he pay up, Fletch?

FLETCHER

Certainly. With all the ill-grace you'd expect from that charmless Celtic nurk.

They grin in satisfaction.

MCLAREN

Twos up with that paper, eh?

FLETCHER

When I've finished.

WARREN

You've had it long enough. Are there some nice birds in it?

FLETCHER

I ain't looking at birds, am I? I'm reading the editorial. I'm not like you lot. All you want out a paper is horses and nudes. Some of us is a bit curious about what's going on in the world. I like to keep abreast.

Lennie joins them at the table, wearing his kitchen whites.

LENNIE

Yes, he does. Got breasts pasted all over our cell.

Fletcher looks at him.

FLETCHER

What!

The others chuckle.

WILLIAMS

I'm not a breast man myself.

FLETCHER

I beg your pardon, Mr Williams?

WILLIAMS

My initial interest is always awakened by the leg.

FLETCHER

Just one of them?

MCLAREN

I hear you're a bit of a ladies' man on the outside, Williams.

WILLIAMS

I've had my moments. I have a large sexual appetite, see. Probably compensating for those years of deprivation in the Bridge End Choral School. Consequentially I suffer more than most in prison.

Fletcher finishes reading the paper, which is grabbed by McLaren.

FLETCHER

Well listen, from what I just been reading I think we're better off in here. This country's on the verge of economic ruin. This once great nation is hovering on the brink of the abyss.

MCLAREN
That's the bosses' fault.

FLETCHER
It's not the bosses, Vanessa, it's the average man. The people who'd rather draw National Assistance than take a job. People who won't do a decent day's work for a decent day's wages . . . people much like ourselves.

WARREN
My Elaine says she doesn't know where it's going to stop.

FLETCHER
What?

WARREN
Prices, like. No one's got any money.

LENNIE
By the time you lot get out of here, there'll be no one worth robbing.

FLETCHER
By then Britain should be reaping the benefits of North Sea oil. Can tell the A-rabs to stuff it and can we please buy London back.

MCLAREN
Scottish oil. Don't forget that. Scottish oil.

FLETCHER
Oh, listen to the Scottish Nationalist, all of a sudden. Well, well, would you believe it. A dusky Rob Roy. What tartan do you wear, the Black Watch?

MCLAREN
Naff off, Fletcher.

FLETCHER
All right so it's Scottish oil. It's English expertise what'll get it out.

LENNIE
Texan.

FLETCHER
(*Exasperated*) I don't know why I get drawn into these pointless arguments with you nurks. The only point I was trying so painstakingly to make is that we're better off inside.

WARREN
He's not wrong, I've known worse stir.

WILLIAMS
Me an' all.

FLETCHER
Right. And with Mackay gone . . . happy days are here again. Chance to work a few things, in't there?

WILLIAMS
True. Old Barrowclough don't exactly rule with a rod of iron, does he?

FLETCHER
We can start having a flutter again. What about frog racing? We could revive that. Get them from the farm.

WILLIAMS
Should I tell you something about frogs? Which is a fact. Like me, the frog has an exceptional sexual appetite. When the frog and his mate, mate, he's at it for twenty-eight days non-stop.

LENNIE
Twenty-eight days.

WILLIAMS
Non-stop.

FLETCHER

No wonder his eyes bulge out.

Barrowclough enters through the gates with Wainwright.

FLETCHER

Oh gawd.

WARREN

What's up, Fletch?

FLETCHER

Happy days. Life of Riley. I think they're over.

LENNIE

What you talking about?

FLETCHER

You heard me mention a screw in Brixton, Napper Wainwright. Right bastard.

LENNIE

Yeah, why?

FLETCHER

He's just walked in the door, that's why.

They all turn to see Wainwright and Barrowclough walking behind one of the other tables to the guarded curiosity of the prisoners sitting at it.

WARREN

He looks a right one.

MCLAREN

You don't suppose he's Mackay's replacement?

FLETCHER

That's exactly what I am supposing.

LENNIE

Living legend, isn't he, in the Prison Service?

FLETCHER

Not only that, he's got promotion. Stripes, isn't it? Well, lads . . . let's hope success has mellowed him.

As if for an answer, we hear Wainwright bawl out an unfortunate prisoner, in a voice which reveals him as a Londoner.

WAINWRIGHT

(*Rapidly*) Something to say to me, have you? Have you? Well my name's Wainwright. You address me as 'Mr Wainwright' or 'Sir'. Now button your lip!

FLETCHER

It has!

WARREN

He's coming over.

Wainwright approaches them.

WAINWRIGHT

Norman Stanley Fletcher, on your feet. I knew our paths would cross again, my son. The day you left Brixton I said to you, 'This is not goodbye, Fletcher, this is merely au-revoyer.'

FLETCHER

I have to admit you did, Mr Wainwright, and I said to you, 'Why don't you . . .' That is, I gave you certain advice regarding the Warders' Comfort Offertory Box.

WAINWRIGHT

I haven't forgotten what you said!

FLETCHER

And did you manage it?

Wainwright's narrowed eyes promise future retribution.

WAINWRIGHT

It doesn't pay to come it with me, Fletcher. You remember me.

He widens his audience to include the rest of the group at the table.

WAINWRIGHT

I have this mean streak, see. I know it's despicable but I'm prejudiced.

MCLAREN

That'll make a nice change.

WAINWRIGHT

Sonny Jim, I'm not just prejudiced against you lot . . . *I'm* prejudiced against – (*Rapid-fire*) liberals, longhairs, pill-heads, winos, queens, slags, squealers, pikeys and grease-balls. Are you in there, sonny?

He has suddenly switched his attention to Lennie.

FLETCHER

Isn't everybody?

WAINWRIGHT

Quiet, Fletcher, I was talking to the boy. I said, are you in there?

Lennie thinks seriously about it, then speaks with some relief.

LENNIE

I don't think so, I'm Church of England.

Wainwright's look once more promises further retribution. The others snigger.

WAINWRIGHT

We've only just met, and already he's given me a grudge to bear.

Barrowclough comes over to join Wainwright.

BARROWCLOUGH

Oh, I see you men have been getting acquainted with Mr Wainwright.

CHORUS

(*Not thrilled*) Yes, yes . . .

FLETCHER

Some of us have had that dubious privilege earlier in our careers.

BARROWCLOUGH

Oh really?

WAINWRIGHT

(*Indicating Fletcher*) This one passed through Brixton on a couple of brief but memorable occasions.

BARROWCLOUGH

Oh well, it's nice to bump into old faces, old . . .

FLETCHER

Adversaries.

BARROWCLOUGH

No no, that's not the word, Fletcher. I keep telling these men, Mr Wainwright, that our role is to help them . . . to encourage them in a programme of self-improvement and rehabilitation. To prepare them for going back into society.

WAINWRIGHT

Our role, Mr Barrowclough, is to keep them away from society. Our role is to keep these scheming bastards locked in.

He strides away.

BARROWCLOUGH

Yes, well I . . . I expect he's a bit tired after the long journey.

He goes after Wainwright.

MCLAREN

Spoke too soon, Fletch.

WILLIAMS

(*Singing*) Happy days are here again . . .

They all join in.

WAINWRIGHT

(*Offscreen*) Quiet!

The singing stops abruptly.

6. CANTEEN

Wainwright comes in, surveys the scene, then walks along behind the line of men being served. Lennie is dishing out potatoes. As Wainwright gets level with Lennie some potato drops on Wainwright's shoe. He indicates for Lennie to come to him. Lennie does so. He wipes the potato off Wainwright's shoe, then goes back to serving again.

6A. ASSOCIATION

A group of prisoners is watching a boxing match on television. Camera shows a hand which switches the set off. It is Wainwright, who says:

WAINWRIGHT

Beddy byes . . .

6B. CORRIDOR

Fletcher and other prisoners are washing the floor. Camera shows feet as they walk over floor leaving marks.

FLETCHER

Oh Mr Wainwright, now look what you've done.

Wainwright walks back to Fletcher.

FLETCHER

Have to do it all again now.

He gets a cloth from the bucket and throws it on the floor. It splashes Wainwright's boot. Fletcher washes the floor. Wainwright moves and steps on his hand.

7. CELL

Fletcher is unbandaging his hand. Lennie is building a model.

LENNIE

What a swine, stepping on your hand like that.

FLETCHER

Be fair. Complete accident. His foot slipped. He was aiming for my head.

LENNIE

What are we going to do about it, Fletch?

FLETCHER

I'll have a word with Warren and McLaren, they're dab hands at sabotage.

LENNIE
Your stars didn't predict this, did they?

FLETCHER
Yes, well, that's all a load of cobblers isn't it? . . .

Barrowclough appears at the cell door.

BARROWCLOUGH
Mind if I come in?

FLETCHER
All right, wipe your feet.

Barrowclough enters.

LENNIE
You look a bit bushed, Mr Barrowclough.

BARROWCLOUGH
Well, I am. It's that Mr Wainwright. He's been through this prison like a dose of salts. He's reorganised the entire duty roster.

FLETCHER
Oh, tough titty. Any idea how many curtailments we've suffered? No fraternising in the exercise yard. Shorter telly hours. And he's only commandeered our ping-pong table for your bleeding mess.

BARROWCLOUGH
Only until our billiard table's been recovered.

FLETCHER
Oh yes, well . . .

BARROWCLOUGH
Well, it's your fault it needed recovering.

FLETCHER
Our fault?

BARROWCLOUGH
Some prisoner certainly tampered with it.

FLETCHER
Can you prove that?

BARROWCLOUGH
We can at least surmise it. When Nosher Garrett went over the wall he was picked up in Blackpool wearing a green baize suit.

FLETCHER
Look, I'm not being drawn into any more pointless arguments.

BARROWCLOUGH
No . . . well, I really came to say cheerio, 'cos you won't be seeing so much of me in the future. He's got me down for a transfer to the farm.

LENNIE
What?

BARROWCLOUGH
Says I should just be in charge of trusties. Says I'm not really suited to a cell block. Where I'm at the mercy of infractious and recalcitrant prisoners like yourself, Fletcher – no offence you understand, these are his words, not mine.

FLETCHER
Look, Mr Barrowclough, we've got to prevent this.

He gets up and goes across to Barrowclough.

FLETCHER
Trouble is you see, if truth be told,

your humanity is mistaken by them
nurks as mollycoddling.

BARROWCLOUGH
I've only tried to be fair and
encourage them –

FLETCHER
'Course you have. I knows that, and
you know that. But you'll have to
change your ways. If you don't want
to spend the rest of your life down
the farm, knee deep in cow dung in
charge of trusty udder-pullers.

BARROWCLOUGH
Change my ways?

FLETCHER
Yeah. Don't let people take advantage.
Come on strong. Wield the big stick.

LENNIE
Put on a bit of a show, like.
You know . . . Mean, moody
and magnificent.

There is a pause.

BARROWCLOUGH
Oh, I don't know.

8. CANTEEN

*Camera shows food, trays, men
being served. A Prison Officer is
walking up the line of prisoners.
Lennie, who is serving, looks at
McLaren. McLaren looks at
Fletcher. Fletcher gets up and goes.
He looks at the clock. Fletcher
nods. Warren receives nod and
nods the other way. McLaren
receives nod and turns to Lennie.*

MCLAREN
Hey you. I'm talking to you.

LENNIE
Me?

Heads turn.

MCLAREN
Yes you, Fanny Craddock . . . there's a
caterpillar on my plate.

LENNIE
Well a caterpillar don't eat much.

MCLAREN
You what?

*He leans across the counter and
grabs Lennie.*

LENNIE
Ease up, Mac, it's only a make-
believe riot.

MCLAREN
I know kid, but I have to make it
look authentic.

LENNIE
But you're strangling me.

MCLAREN
I know, but nothing personal, you
understand. This food's no fit for
swine. We've had enough, lads.

Warren gets up.

WARREN
We want a riot.

*Camera shows tables being turned
up, food being upset, plates
dropped, Lennie with peas over his
head thrown by McLaren. A Prison
Officer blows his whistle and is
showered with potatoes.
Alarm bells start ringing.*

Prison warders come running.
There is the noise of cell doors
being slammed. The warders run
along the catwalk.
Camera shows Wainwright's head
as he comes into view. The door
is unlocked and he goes into
the canteen.
The prisoners stop.
Wainwright starts to speak but food
is thrown at him and he finally
backs out.

9. GOVERNOR'S OFFICE

Camera shows a tray with a
glass of water and two pink pills.
Mrs Heskith gives it to Venables.

VENABLES

Thank you, Mrs Heskith.

He gulps the pills down.

MRS HESKITH

You're only supposed to take two
before retiring.

VENABLES

If we don't put a stop to this riot, that
may be tomorrow.

Mrs Heskith leans over the desk.
Fletcher comes in at that moment,
pulling his trolley load of books.

FLETCHER

Oops! Oopsadaisy! Sorry.

VENABLES

What on earth do you want, Fletcher?

FLETCHER

Another load of new books, sir.

VENABLES

At a time like this!

FLETCHER

Oh yes, well I wasn't to know, was I . . .

VENABLES

I'm referring to the riot!

FLETCHER

Oh, the riot, yes. Another nasty
situation, sir.

VENABLES

It is indeed. At the moment there's a
systematic and wilful destruction of
furniture and crockery. They're knee
deep in plates in there.

FLETCHER

Like a Greek restaurant on New
Year's Eve.

VENABLES

Don't be flippant, Fletcher. I'd've
thought Mr Wainwright would have
been the ideal man for this situation,
but he seemed to make matters worse.

FLETCHER

If truth were told, sir, it's Mr Wainwright
what aggravated the situation now in
the first place. Now that's just between
me, you, Mrs Heskith and the bedpost.

MRS HESKITH

I'll just get this typed up then.

VENABLES

I suppose I'll have to go down
there myself.

FLETCHER

No offence, sir, but there's only one man in this prison who could quell that riot. Only one man who could confront that ugly vicious mob and defuse the powder keg of emotion.

VENABLES

Who? Who?

10. FARM

Barrowclough is supervising the prisoners working on the pig farm. He turns.

BARROWCLOUGH

Me, what do you mean me?

11. CANTEEN

Riot is still going on.
McLaren is shouting 'Load, aim, fire!' Food is being thrown. The firing party throws potatoes. Barrowclough goes to the canteen door. A PO unlocks it and Barrowclough walks in. The door is shut behind him. Barrowclough walks into the canteen. The prisoners stop.

BARROWCLOUGH

Now we . . . why don't we all put those things down?

The prisoners do so.

BARROWCLOUGH

This mess will all have to be cleared up, you know.

They start to clear up.

BARROWCLOUGH

Not yet though . . . In the meantime, why don't we all file back to our cells in an orderly fashion.

The prisoners start to file out of the canteen. As Lennie passes Barrowclough he stops.

LENNIE

Mean, moody, magnificent!

11A. YARD/LANDING

Camera shows Warren and McLaren being marched across the yard. They enter through the gate on to the prison landing and walk along the catwalk. The prisoners congratulate them.

12. CELL

Fletcher and Lennie are in their cell.

FLETCHER

(*Speaking through the door*) Well done, lads.

LENNIE

Congratulations.

Warren and McLaren walk in.

MCLAREN

Worth it, wasn't it?

FLETCHER

Well worth it, my son.

MCLAREN

Barrowclough's back on the landing, then?

FLETCHER

Yes and Wainwright's back in Brixton, where he belongs. Loss of face, wasn't it? Had to leave, bloke like that.

MCLAREN

So happy days are here again, eh?

FLETCHER

Normal service has been resumed.

They all laugh.

Meanwhile Mackay has entered the association area and is looking around, when he hears laughter from Fletcher's cell. He walks to it and goes in. Fletcher catches his eye at last.

Mackay looks.

FLETCHER

Oh . . . Mr Mackay, what a nice surprise. Nice surprise, isn't it, lads?

McLaren and Warren leave.

MACKAY

I thought it might be, Fletcher. I think some of you wrongly assumed that I had left, gone for good, but as you see nothing could be further from the truth. Only I'm somewhat disturbed to hear what's been happening in my absence. So now, we're going to have a new regime here. Based not on leniency and laxity but discipline, hard work, and blind unquestioning obedience. Feet will not touch the ground, and lives will be made a misery – I'm BACK and I'M IN CHARGE HERE.

Mackay leaves.

Fletcher and Lennie look at each other.

Mackay is walking along the catwalk when suddenly he hears Fletcher and Lennie singing 'For he's a jolly good fellow'. The camera shows Fletcher and Lennie singing in their cell. Gradually other prisoners are heard joining in the singing.

SERIES TWO

EPISODE FOUR: NO PEACE FOR THE WICKED

1. ASSOCIATION AREA

Fletcher walks along the catwalk with a mug of tea and a magazine towards his cell. McLaren is fixing his boots. Then he moves off upstairs towards Fletcher's cell.

1A. FLETCHER'S CELL

Fletcher comes into his cell with the mug of tea and magazine. He is singing to himself.

FLETCHER
Born free . . .
Till somebody shopped me
Now I'm doing solitree.

McLaren walks in.

MCLAREN
Got any chewing gum, Fletch?

FLETCHER
(*Chewing*) No, never use it.

MCLAREN
Aw come on, you mean old scroat.

Fletcher reluctantly scoops a piece of gum out of his pocket, tears it in half and hands it over.

FLETCHER
Here you are – don't eat it all at once.

MCLAREN
Ta. Going to watch the game?

FLETCHER
Naff off.

MCLAREN
Be a guid game.

FLETCHER
What, A and B Wing, that bloodbath.

MCLAREN
If we win we win the trophy.

FLETCHER
What trophy?

MCLAREN
It's a silver cup.

FLETCHER
Correction. It was a silver cup. It disappeared from the Governor's office on Tuesday night.

MCLAREN
Who'd have done that?

FLETCHER
I can't be sure but I've narrowed it down to six hundred suspects.

MCLAREN
Never see that again. Be melted down by now.

FLETCHER

Just have to play for the honour
of the wing, won't you?

MCLAREN

You should cheer us on, Fletch.
It's your wing.

FLETCHER

It's not my wing. I just happen to be
incarcerated in this wing. At Her
Majesty's pleasure. It's not your wing
neither, is it? I'm surprised at you
coming the Tom Brown's schooldays
bit. Tom Black's schooldays, yes.

MCLAREN

I'm not. When I'm out there I'm
playing for Morton. Against Celtic at
Hampden. And we stuff them.

FLETCHER

I've got better things to do than watch
people being stuffed at football.

MCLAREN

Got visitors?

FLETCHER

No.

MCLAREN

Got a card game going?

FLETCHER

No.

MCLAREN

Just watching the box, are you?

FLETCHER

No. Three times wrong in a row.

MCLAREN

What you doing then?

FLETCHER

I'm going fox-hunting, aren't I?

MCLAREN

No, seriously – you ought to do
something. You've got five years,
Fletch. If you don't do anything your
stretch will be endless.

FLETCHER

Here listen to me, sonny Jock.
Don't tell me how to survive in here.
I was doing time when you was
running around stealing mangoes on
the plantation.

MCLAREN

What do you mean, plantation? I
was brought up in a Greenock
housing estate!

FLETCHER

All right, when you were
stealing mangoes on a Greenock
housing estate.

He gets up on his bunk.

MCLAREN

It's a beautiful day out there as well.

FLETCHER

It's a beautiful day in here as well –
d'you know why? 'Cos all you lot are
out there. That's what I like about the
weekend. You're playing football,
others are gambling away their hard-
earned money, some of them are
indulging in their pathetic hobbies.
And I ends up with some peace and
quiet. Go on then – enjoy your game.
Take no prisoners.

*McLaren goes. Fletcher gets off his
bunk and walks across the cell,
humming to himself.*

FLETCHER

'I believe for every drop of rain
that falls . . .'

Warren walks in.

Fletcher notices him.

FLETCHER

Oh – what do you want?

WARREN

Me and Mini Cooper want to go and
play ping-pong.

FLETCHER

Don't let me stop yer.

WARREN

Er well . . . there aren't any balls, like.
And Lugless Douglas said you had one.

FLETCHER

Who told Lugless?

WARREN

He just heard.

FLETCHER

He just what?

WARREN

Is it true?

FLETCHER

I've got one hidden – yes.

WARREN

Would you lend us it then?

FLETCHER

Lease. Let us discuss the possibility of
leasing you the ball, Bunny. Then we
might have some basis for negotiation.

WARREN

How much is it then?

FLETCHER

One snout . . .

Warren starts to get one.

FLETCHER

Ah, ah, ah . . . per hour. Minimum
three hours.

WARREN

You're a hard man, Fletch.

FLETCHER

No. I'm not hard I'm just taking
advantage of something which
happened to bounce my way. If you
was dealing with Harry Grout's
syndicate you'd have to leave your
wristwatch as a deposit against the
ball being trod on. And if you didn't
return the ball your wristwatch would
get trod on . . . ad infinitum.

WARREN

All right, Fletch, you're on.

He hands over the snout.

FLETCHER

What's this then?

WARREN

It's good shag, honest.

FLETCHER

All right . . .

He puts it away.

WARREN

Where's the ball then?

FLETCHER

Oh yes.

He gets the ball.

WARREN

It's a funny colour.

FLETCHER

I got it off McLaren.

WARREN

D'you want a game yourself later?

FLETCHER
Certainly not. Don't do you no good exercise.

WARREN
Helps to pass the time.

FLETCHER
I don't need any help to pass the time, thank you.

Warren leaves.

FLETCHER
Next?

Banyard puts his head round the door.

BANYARD
Erm, Fletcher . . .

FLETCHER
(*With a look saying what is it now!*)
Yes?

BANYARD
Erm . . . a few of us have formed a drama group.

FLETCHER
(*Unenthusiastically*) Oh yes.

BANYARD
Well, I was wondering – do you have any theatrical inclinations?

FLETCHER
No.

BANYARD
You don't necessarily have to act. You could be prompter or work the lights or operate the wind machine.

FLETCHER
(*Getting on to bunk*) The wind machine, what you want one of those for, just

enlist Ives, he's a walking wind machine he is.

BANYARD
We want to do some contemporary plays, we thought we'd start with a thriller, *Wait Until Dark*, d'you remember that one? They made a film of it with Audrey Hepburn.

FLETCHER
I don't think I could slim down in time.

BANYARD
Oh there's no shortage of Audrey Hepburns, it's prompters and lighting men we need.

FLETCHER
I don't really go for the theatre much. Now if you was getting up a concert party, well . . . could maybe help you out there. Singing. 'Cos in the old days I was always round the pubs in North London you know, like the Angel, Walthamstow, Friday nights. 'Ladzangenelmen . . . let's have a big hand for Frankie Fletcher.' 'Course it's Norman really, but Frankie sounded better, was more showbiz, know what I mean? What was the one we used to do? I say 'we' 'cos I was backed by Ted Prendergast and the Organaires. You remember Ted Prendergast?

BANYARD
I don't think so.

FLETCHER
You should do. He was on *Workers' Playtime* once. A cardboard factory in Letchworth.

BANYARD

No, I would have remembered.

FLETCHER

Yes – I suppose you would. We used to do – (*Singing*) See the pyramids along the Nile
Watch the sunrise on a tropic isle . . .

BANYARD

No, we're not doing a concert party.

FLETCHER

Oh well then, naff off Sir Lawrence, leave me be, eh.

BANYARD

I just thought it might relieve the boredom.

FLETCHER

The boredom will be relieved as soon as you leave this room.

BANYARD

Oh charming . . .

He starts to go.

FLETCHER

Give my love to Miss Hepburn.

Fletcher settles back on his bunk and opens Penthouse.

FLETCHER

(*Singing*) Time on my hands . . .

He opens the centrefold and looks at the girl.

FLETCHER

You in my arms . . .

He glances towards the door where a large wooden mule can be seen peering round. Fletcher looks away, then looks back again.

FLETCHER

What are you looking at?

The mule is still there.

FLETCHER

All right then, I give up.

Blanco comes in through the doorway.

FLETCHER

Hello, Blanco.

BLANCO

Hello, Fletch.

FLETCHER

Would you mind explaining?

BLANCO

(*Wheeling mule in*) It's my Muffin. It's Muffin the Mule. You know him what's on television.

FLETCHER

Muffin the Mule on television. When was the last time you watched television?

BLANCO

Some time back. I've been too busy making him.

FLETCHER

Well, he's very lovely. Is there any particular reason why you bring him round here though?

BLANCO

Just finished him. I wanted you to be the first one to see him. Taken me nigh on fifteen year.

FLETCHER

Fifteen years – has it? Still worth it though, isn't it?

BLANCO

D'you know now it's done . . . I'm at a bit of a loose end.

FLETCHER

Yes, well I expect you are, Blanco. You could always study – improve your mind.

BLANCO

I tried that once – I got a book out of the library, on memory training. Studied it for months. Then I had to pack it in.

FLETCHER

Why?

BLANCO

I forgot where I left the book.

FLETCHER

Oh dear. Here, try smoking yourself to death instead.

BLANCO

Bless you, Fletcher. I was making it for my three-year-old niece. She's grown up a bit, works as an air hostess. Never thought it would take this long.

FLETCHER

Time flies when you're having fun.

BLANCO

Oh. Aye. Can I borrow your magazine?

FLETCHER

No, you can't.

BLANCO

After you've finished with it.

FLETCHER

No, you can't.

BLANCO

See, now that I've finished Muffin I want to catch up on me reading.

FLETCHER

You should start with something a little less controversial, you know what your blood pressure's like. Try the *Radio Times*. Tell you what, will you settle for a Jaffa cake?

BLANCO

Have you got some?

FLETCHER

No. But let's see what providence will provide. Just get me boots on. (*To the mule*) Come on, Muffin, walkies . . .

2. ASSOCIATION AREA

Fletcher goes out of the cell followed by Blanco with the mule. They walk along the catwalk and arrive at a cubby-hole door. Fletcher knocks.

COLLINSON

(*Offscreen*) Come in.

Fletcher goes in.

3. CUBBY-HOLE (OFFICER'S ROOM)

Inside the cubby-hole is a desk with papers on it.

*On the wall is a 'switchboard'
referring to each cell on the landing
with lights that illuminate when a bell
is rung from the cell. There are keys
on the wall, some faded regulations,
a single-bar electric fire. A youngish
Prison Officer, Collinson, sits at the
desk. He has a mug of tea, and on
the desk a packet of Jaffa cakes.
He is not the friendliest of men.*

COLLINSON
What is it?

FLETCHER
(*Quietly*) Mr Collinson, sorry to
disturb you – I can see you're busy –
not take a minute . . . It's just old
Blanco. He's finished his wooden
mule, and er, he'd like you to
see it, know what I mean. Not
take a minute.

COLLINSON
Oh. Oh, all right . . .

*He gets up, squeezes past
Fletcher, who eyes the Jaffa cakes
on the desk.*

4. ASSOCIATION AREA

*Collinson comes out of his cubby-
hole. Blanco is waiting there.*

COLLINSON
Oh yes . . . this is the mule is it, Blanco?

BLANCO
Yes, sir, fifteen years.

COLLINSON
Oh well, it's worth it, you don't often
see craftsmanship of that quality.

BLANCO
Thank you, sir, nice of you to say so.

COLLINSON
All right then, off you go,
Blanco, then.

BLANCO
Yes, sir.

FLETCHER
Very kind of you, Mr Collinson.
I mean a word from someone like
yourself – you don't know how
we appreciate that.

COLLINSON
All right then.

*He returns to the cubby-hole.
Outside Fletcher gives Blanco
a biscuit.*

BLANCO
You're a lad, Fletch.

FLETCHER
Yeah, well, say no more.

BLANCO
Sorry if I disturbed you.

FLETCHER
Any time for you.

BLANCO
I think I'll nip down and
watch *Grandstand*.

He picks up the mule.

FLETCHER
Oh yeah, while you're down there put
the word round, I'm incommunicado.

BLANCO
You're in the where?

FLETCHER
I don't want to be disturbed.

BLANCO

We'll tell 'em.

He moves off down the stairs.

5. CELL

Fletcher enters his cell and walks to the bed. He climbs on to the top bunk and settles down with his magazine. He has an 'Alone at last' expression. After a moment we hear someone clearing his throat.

FLETCHER

Yes?

Barrowclough is in the doorway.

BARROWCLOUGH

Oh Fletcher . . .

FLETCHER

Mr Barrowclough – on your way out would you lock me in so's I can get some privacy?

BARROWCLOUGH

On a lovely afternoon like this? I thought you'd be out in the yard, or in the hobby shop. Seems such a waste to be stuck in here.

FLETCHER

It's not a waste to me. I like to spend my Saturday afternoons in my cell. With my feet up and a bit of reading matter. I don't want to play games, or do exercises. Nor do I want to carve

toys, take saxophone lessons, form an amateur dramatic group, or watch *The Blue Lamp* on BBC2, a film glamourising that despicable bunch what put me here in the first place.

BARROWCLOUGH

It's a damn sight better than lying on your bunk reading that lewd lascivious rubbish. If a man puts his mind to it a man can better himself in here. There's a lot more opportunities now than when I first joined the service. Spraggon, you know him in E Block, Spraggon has made a six-foot space rocket out of milk bottle tops.

FLETCHER

Really.

BARROWCLOUGH

It's a work of art. Belongs to a museum. He used three colours. The nose cone's in red, homogenised, the bulk of it's made out of ordinary silver top, and the Governor's gold tops provided a nice motif round the centre.

FLETCHER

Well, he'll never get it off the ground.

BARROWCLOUGH

There's Rafferty having his watercolours exhibited in a Carlisle art gallery. Not to mention all the professional qualifications that vocational training has given people in this prison. Brickies, plasterers. Even the Tooley brothers left here with a diploma in welding.

FLETCHER

Yes and what did they do with it, soon

as they got out? Welded their way into Barclays Bank in Blackburn High Street.

BARROWCLOUGH

Yes – well – the point I'm trying to make is that we at least gave them the opportunity to do something legitimate with their lives.

FLETCHER

And the point I'm trying to make is that they'll just abuse the opportunity. They're felons, Mr Barrowclough. You get a bloke in here. Teach him how to use a printing press. What's he do when he goes out? Does he join the *Northern Echo*, does he fairycakes. He stays at home and forges premium bonds – only sensible.

BARROWCLOUGH

I won't accept your cynicism. I just don't like seeing a fully grown man with a good brain – 'cos you're not stupid, Fletcher – wasting his time. You should do something whatever it is.

FLETCHER

Oh – is that the lecture over? Is that what you come in to say, Mr Barrowclough?

BARROWCLOUGH

I didn't come in to lecture you.

FLETCHER

No, well, we never did discover the purpose of your visit, you never said.

BARROWCLOUGH

Didn't I . . . I don't know – (*Thinks*) Oh well, I just dropped by 'cos I had nothing better to do.

FLETCHER

Would you believe it, would you Adam and Eve it? Your lives are emptier than ours.

BARROWCLOUGH

They are not! I have my allotment.

FLETCHER

Your allotment – listen, Mr Barrowclough, if the system wants to do something really constructive for us chaps, give us more freedom, better grub. Give us conjugal visits.

BARROWCLOUGH

Give you what?

FLETCHER

Conjugals. From the Latin, *conjugo*, meaning to have it off.

BARROWCLOUGH

We can't do that –

FLETCHER

With our old ladies! All above board, Bristol fashion. It's what some prisons do, have special quarters. Where wives come up, and we spend the whole weekend . . . manifesting our long-felt wants.

BARROWCLOUGH

I don't know of any prisons where they -

FLETCHER

Maybe not here. But certainly abroad. Certainly Holland, and America, where they have more enlightened penal systems.

BARROWCLOUGH

They just allow the wives to visit, and they spend the whole weekend . . .

FLETCHER

Conjugating, yeah.

BARROWCLOUGH

That's more than I'm allowed at home.

Barrowclough moves off, shaking his head.

FLETCHER

Mr Barrowclough.

Barrowclough stops in the doorway.

FLETCHER

Here you are, Mr Barrowclough, your needs are greater than mine.

He offers Barrowclough the magazine.

BARROWCLOUGH

Certainly not, Fletcher.

He leaves.

FLETCHER

(*Spreading out the centrefold*) Well, my little treasure. Alone at last.

6. ASSOCIATION AREA

Mackay unlocks the door and three visitors enter the association area. Mackay closes it again.

MACKAY

This is a typical cell block.

WOMAN

Why do you have the nets?

MACKAY

Suicide, ma'am. The prevention of.

WOMAN

Do you have many instances of that?

MACKAY

Certainly not, ma'am. It's against the rules.

OLDER MAN

I suppose it's also useful if any of these chaps get violent and take it into their heads to throw each other over the edge.

MACKAY

If they get violent, sir, they generally throw us over the edge.

YOUNGER MAN

Do you have a bad record of violence in this prison?

MACKAY

Oh no, sir. That's because we at Slade Prison encourage a wide range of activities. This helps the men express themselves in various ways, releasing much of the pent-up aggression endemic to the incarcerated male.

WOMAN

Is that what most of them are doing now?

MACKAY

Absolutely. You will notice how at the weekend every prisoner has seized the opportunity to enjoy the extensive facilities which we provide.

Mackay looks into Fletcher's cell and then looks back again.

MACKAY

There are always some exceptions, of course.

WOMAN
Could we have a look in a cell?

MACKAY
Certainly, ma'am . . .
He ushers them into Fletcher's cell.

7. CELL
The three visitors and Mackay enter Fletcher's cell. He is still lying on his bunk reading.

OLDER MAN
Is this man sick?

MACKAY
Are you sick, Fletcher?

FLETCHER
I'm sick of interruptions.

WOMAN
Oh please, this fellow's probably trying to relax.

FLETCHER
Oh be my guest.

OLDER MAN
Please don't get up.

MACKAY
This is a typical cell.

WOMAN
Single or double?

MACKAY
Double, ma'am, as indicated by the presence of the two bunks. Prisoners are, of course, allowed to personalise their cells. You notice the radio, the matches. And, of course, they're allowed to decorate their lockers with mementoes of family and home.
He opens the cupboard door and is faced by several photographs of nudes.

FLETCHER
Those two are the wife, and that's the wife's sister.

MACKAY
Perhaps you would like to see the recreation room.

OLDER MAN
Yes, we are rather disturbing this man's privacy.

FLETCHER
Privacy! Precious little of that in here.

MACKAY
Fletcher!

YOUNGER MAN
No, no, please, let the man speak.

FLETCHER
Well, have you noticed any signs of privacy on your rounds? Seen a door without a peephole? Seen a shower curtain or a cubicle door in the latrines? Very hard, you know, to retain a vestige of human dignity when you're sitting on the bog and a whole football team clatters past on their way to the showers.

WOMAN
Yes – well –

FLETCHER
Yes well – notice the way Mr Mackay

barged in here. Never so much of a by my leave or kiss my foot. Paid no more regard to me than he did the washbasin – in fact less.

MACKAY

Privacy is one of the privileges you forfeit when you transgress the law. This is not a hotel. They do forget that they're in here to be punished.

FLETCHER

Oh yes. Eye for an eye. Tooth for a nail.

OLDER MAN

You sound as if you're a Londoner.

FLETCHER

I am, sir, yes. It's the accent.

OLDER MAN

Long way from home up here. What's a Londoner doing in this neck of the woods?

FLETCHER

This particular Londoner is doing five years. What are you doing?

MACKAY

Fletcher!

OLDER MAN

No, no, fair question. Well, Fletcher, we're all attached to the Home Office in one capacity or another. And it's through these visits that we learn more about our penal system. And only by seeing things for ourselves and talking to people like yourself are we able to make recommendation for change and reform.

FLETCHER

Change yes . . . well, if you can supply

a new coat of paint, give us an improved supply of ping-pong balls. But reform, save yourselves the bother.

MACKAY

I don't think this particular prisoner's opinion is particularly instructive.

FLETCHER

Oh, isn't it? Let me tell you I've been in more nicks than he has. So whose opinion is more instructive?

WOMAN

I would value it.

FLETCHER

I bet you would – oh, I see. Well, obviously we can't have total amnesty. Got to keep a few hard cases locked away so we can walk the streets at night. But you should do with the rest of us what they do in Scandinavia. Make us work off our debt to society. On farms, building sites, factories, hospitals.

WOMAN

That's one school of thought, of course.

OLDER MAN

You know despite what this man says about rehabilitation, I think his attitude proves the contrary.

MACKAY

You what?

OLDER MAN

Now this system of working off your sentence, I can see it working with men like you.

YOUNGER MAN

If you had a choice, what area would you choose to work in?

FLETCHER

Well, if I had the choice I'd probably choose the building site.

WOMAN

The fresh air?

FLETCHER

Yes . . . but mostly 'cos I could nick meself a fortune.

He goes back to reading the magazine.

FLETCHER

(*Reading*) Cor look at her!

OLDER MAN

The recreation room next is it, Mr Mackay?

Mackay ushers the visitors out.

MACKAY

Hopeless case, sir. Classic recidivist.

YOUNGER MAN

Bit of a surly character.

OLDER MAN

Yes, but articulate.

MACKAY

Like a lorry.

They leave.

FLETCHER

(*Getting off his bunk*) Is there anybody else?

8. ASSOCIATION AREA

Fletcher comes out of his cell and stands on the catwalk. He looks around for any more interruptions, then goes back inside the cell.

9. CELL

Fletcher enters his cell. He swings straight up on top of his bunk and settles himself down, bashing his pillows and lying on his side. There is a pause. Then Warren's voice can be heard.

WARREN

'Scuse me, Fletch –

FLETCHER

What!!

He leaps straight up in the air, falls off his bunk and lands face to face with Warren.

WARREN

Were you asleep?

FLETCHER

Sleep, what chance have I had to sleep?!! More chance of having a sleep at Waterloo in the rush hour! What's wrong with you nurks in here? Can't you see when a man wants to be left alone?

WARREN

I'm sorry, it's just . . . your ball's got a crack in it.

Fletcher has to think about this for a moment.

FLETCHER

Pardon?

Warren holds up the ball.

WARREN

Cracked.

FLETCHER

(*Menacingly*) Better than having no balls at all.

WARREN

Spoilt the game though –

FLETCHER

I'll have it back then.

WARREN

I'll have the fag back then.

FLETCHER

You will not. You should have examined the merchandise when the transaction was transacted.

WARREN

That's not fair, Fletch.

FLETCHER

Fair? Since when was life ever fair? Is it fair that I should suffer this continual bombardment of people who don't know how to occupy their own time and minds? Saturday afternoon provides a few sacred hours when one can enjoy one's own company. It's not much to ask. It don't last long. Only till teatime when we traipse across to have that hideous mixture masquerading as cottage pie. When will you blokes learn that surviving in stir is a state of mind? It's an attitude. It's learning to live with yourself.

WARREN

(*Sniffing*) Sorry, Fletch.

Fletcher turns away, then softens his attitude to another approach.

FLETCHER

I like you, Warren. Believe me there are many times when I crave your company. I love those action-packed anecdotes of yours of the days when you worked in your father-in-law's ironmonger's in Bury.

WARREN

Bolton.

FLETCHER

Bolton, yes, even better. I was only too eager to look at your snaps the other day. Of your wife's day trip to Lake Windermere.

Warren reaches towards his top pocket.

WARREN

Oh, I've got some more.

Fletcher turns away and grasps the edge of the top bunk to prevent himself from grasping Warren's neck.

FLETCHER

God, give me strength.

WARREN

They didn't come out too well, I expect it was the rain.

FLETCHER

(*Controlling himself*) Just . . . just put them on the table, Warren, and they'll help to while away my evening.

WARREN

Oh, fine, right.

He does so.

WARREN

I'll be off then, Fletch, I'll not disturb you no more.

FLETCHER

Promise?

WARREN

Yeah.

FLETCHER

Here – d'you promise?

WARREN

I promise.

Warren goes. Fletcher laughs. Puts the photos down but drops them. Goes down on his knees to pick them up.

FLETCHER

Dear God, you might think it's a bit of a liberty me asking you favours, but on the other hand there is more joy in heaven when a sinner repenteth. Isn't that right, sir? It's only a small thing I ask . . . keep these nurks off my back, can't you? 'Cos if anyone else walks through that door I might not be answerable for the consequences. Know what I mean, God?

The Chaplain appears at the doorway.

CHAPLAIN

Ah, Fletcher . . . I'd been meaning to have a bit of a chat for some time.

Fletcher rises and moves towards the Chaplain.

10. GOVERNOR'S OFFICE

The office is empty. Then camera shows the door opening and Mackay's voice can be heard.

MACKAY

Left, right, left, right, left, right . . .

Fletcher is marched in by Mackay.

MACKAY

Halt. Face the front. Stand still. For the chop, you know that. No exit. If ever I have any doubts about the system it's people like you that reassure me. Because in the final analysis, in the final analysis, your criminal character will always show through like ink on blotting paper.

VENABLES

(*Offscreen*) They're in there already, are they?

Venables enters. He is wearing a football scarf, which he removes.

VENABLES

Mr Mackay.

MACKAY

Yes sir, Fletcher, sir. Sorry to fetch you from the game.

VENABLES

Not at all. This is a serious matter, a desperately serious matter. These Home Office visitors, they weren't around when the incident took place?

MACKAY

No, sir. Fortunately I had them in the woodwork room at the time.

VENABLES

Thank heavens for that, 'cos we must hush up a thing like this.

MACKAY

Face the front.

VENABLES

Did anyone witness it?

MACKAY

Only old Blanco Webb, sir. And Mr Collinson heard the scream.

VENABLES

Fletcher, what got into you?

Fletcher shrugs.

MACKAY

Face the front.

VENABLES

I'm talking to you, Fletcher.

FLETCHER

Everyone's talking to me, sir. End of my tether, see. Think I'm losing my mind, sir. Possibly I should have psychiatric observation in the hospital, sir.

VENABLES

Psychiatric observation . . . well, I don't know . . .

MACKAY

No, you don't. Sir – an unprovoked attack. And even Slade Prison, which has had its share of violence, has never known a chaplain thrown off a balcony.

FLETCHER

I knew the safety net was there, sir.

VENABLES

That's hardly the point. The chaplain was shattered.

FLETCHER

He'll bounce back, sir. He did a bit.

VENABLES

Don't be insolent, Fletcher. I have no alternative but to give you the maximum period of solitary confinement. Then we'll have to discuss the matter further.

FLETCHER

Yes, sir.

VENABLES

You've only yourself to blame. You have a very regrettable attitude, Fletcher. Perhaps you'll dwell on that over the next three days in isolation.

FLETCHER

Three days is it, sir?

VENABLES

Yes, it certainly is. All right, wheel him out.

FLETCHER

Could I just ask one thing, sir?

VENABLES

What?

FLETCHER

Couldn't make it a fortnight, could you?

Mackay marches him off.

SERIES TWO

EPISODE FIVE: HAPPY RELEASE

1. MEDICAL OFFICER'S ROOM

The Medical Officer is examining a prisoner. Mackay enters.

MACKAY

Is it true about Fletcher, sir?

MO

What? Oh morning, Mr Mackay.

MACKAY

Is it true about Fletcher, Doctor?

MO

Oh yes, I'm afraid it is.

MACKAY

Oh – definite?

MO

Yes, we had him down at Carlisle General, they verified it.

MACKAY

Where is he now?

MO

He's back here. We've just got him to bed.

MACKAY

No possibility of a mistake?

MO

No, no. The X-rays are positive.

MACKAY

In other words there's nothing we can do about it?

MO

Nothing.

MACKAY

Fletcher of all people.

MO

That's the way it is.

MACKAY

How long would you say?

MO

Three weeks. Maybe a month.

MACKAY

I had him down for the drainage detail you know . . . and now he gets three cushy weeks on his back with a broken ankle, there's no justice.

Mackay starts to go.

MO

I said it could even be a month.

2. HOSPITAL WARD

Fletcher is in bed with his plastered leg in traction. Screens surround his bed.
Next to him is the old lag, Blanco, who is asleep. Opposite is Norris, another prisoner.
A prison orderly removes the screens from around Fletcher.

FLETCHER
Thank you, Charlie. I'll do the same for you one day.

Mackay enters.

FLETCHER
Oh, Mr Mackay, how kind. I don't think it's official visiting hours, you know.

MACKAY
You're a lucky man, Fletcher.

FLETCHER
No grapes then?

MACKAY
I just wanted to verify with my own eyes that you weren't malingering.

FLETCHER
No, no. My foot is broken. You can see the plaster. The evidence is irrefootable.

Fletcher laughs at his own joke.

FLETCHER
Did you hear that Blanco, oh you're asleep.

MACKAY
I won't pretend your indisposition isn't very frustrating, Fletcher.

FLETCHER
Not to me, it isn't. Better grub in here.

Better beds an' all. Got me own cushion here.

MACKAY
Since you lost your soft number in the library I was all ready to make your life a misery.

FLETCHER
I gathered that when you sent me up that twenty-foot ladder to clean pigeon droppings out the guttering.

MACKAY
Wouldn't surprise me if you fell intentionally.

FLETCHER
No, no, it's just poetic justice. You was out to victimise me, and all you've done is give me a passport to comfort and seclusion. Mind you, I do have to put up with that scroat Norris for the next few days.

NORRIS
Oh yeah, well it cuts two ways, don't it?

FLETCHER
Shut your face, Norris, or I'll hit you with me frying pan.

NORRIS
Violence now, eh?

MACKAY
Quiet, both of you.

BLANCO
(*Waking up*) What is it?

FLETCHER
Ssh, it's all right.

MACKAY
And you.

NORRIS

He started it. He's been at me all afternoon, Mr Mackay.

MACKAY

That's one thing I can't blame Fletcher for, Norris. You're not the pleasantest of men. In fact you're a horrible creature.

NORRIS

Here! I done my bird! I'm being released in two days.

MACKAY

Yes, and you're skiving to the last.

NORRIS

I've had surgery. Ingrown toenail.

MACKAY

I know the kind of surgery I would give you had I my way.

FLETCHER

Couldn't have waited till you got out, could you? Had to burden our overworked prison medical service.

MACKAY

Which is exactly what you're doing, Fletcher.

FLETCHER

Yeah, well we know whose fault that is, don't we?

MACKAY

Four weeks. Maximum. I can bide my time. I'll soon have you up on your foot.

FLETCHER

Not before it's mended.

MACKAY

You're in discomfort, are you?

FLETCHER

Well, nothing to speak of.

MACKAY

Oh come on, Fletcher, it's giving you hell, admit it.

He pulls the traction.

FLETCHER

No.

MACKAY

Not even the odd twinge?

FLETCHER

No, no. Not now the plaster is on.

MACKAY

There's no justice. (*Lets traction go*)

He lets traction go, shakes his head and leaves.

FLETCHER

And the next object is, a thwarted screw, a thwarted screw . . .

NORRIS

I'm in pain.

FLETCHER

Pardon?

NORRIS

I'm in pain.

FLETCHER

Good.

NORRIS

I've had surgery.

FLETCHER

I've had X-rays.

NORRIS

X-rays isn't surgery.

FLETCHER

Surgery. Ingrown toenail.

NORRIS

I haven't slept for days with the pain. Shadow of my former self I am.

FLETCHER

Well, your former self wasn't much to begin with, Norris.

NORRIS

Naff off.

FLETCHER

Soon as my broken foot's better I'm going to use it to stand on your ingrowing toenail.

NORRIS

Have to hurry, won't you? I'm out of here Thursday!

The door is unlocked by a Prison officer.

Lennie is admitted, wearing kitchen whites and pushing a food trolley.

LENNIE

Meals on wheels.

FLETCHER

Oh, look at this. Look at this, Blanco. What's on the menu then, Lennie? Apart from yesterday's gravy stains.

LENNIE

Braised steak and carrots, mashed potatoes, bananas and custard.

Starts to serve.

FLETCHER

Oh good – what's for afters?

LENNIE

Tomato soup.

FLETCHER

Hear that Blanco? Bananas and custard.

BLANCO

I've got no appetite.

FLETCHER

You've got to eat, Blanco. Keep your strength up. If you don't eat you will be ill – oh you are ill, aren't you?

NORRIS

If he won't have it, I'll have it.

FLETCHER

You will not! You leave it by his bedside, Lennie. Anything he don't fancy now he can have later . . . or I'll have it.

LENNIE

How are you then, Fletch?

FLETCHER

All right – surviving. How's yourself?

LENNIE

Not as comfy as you are. Look at those crisp, clean sheets.

FLETCHER

Yeah well – give us some more carrots.

NORRIS

Don't leave me short.

LENNIE

Shut up, Norris. Here you are, Blanco. I'll just put this here then. He don't look too chipper, does he?

FLETCHER

He's all right. Just a bit depressed that's all.

LENNIE

Looks at death's door to me.

FLETCHER

Shut up – gawd, you youngsters. Don't have much tact, do you? You don't make remarks about death's

door to people. Not in hospital.
Specially when they're at death's door.

BLANCO

(*Laughing weakly*) Ha ha . . . that's a
good one, Fletch.

FLETCHER

Well, you've got to laugh, ain't you?

LENNIE

(*Serving Norris but addressing
Fletcher*) You're cheery enough.

FLETCHER

Can't complain. Life of Riley, in' it? And I
had a nice day out, Lennie. Went down
to Carlisle General and got plastered.

Lennie laughs.

FLETCHER

And there was some lovely nurses
there – kept popping their heads
round the door. Giggling like. 'Cos
there I was, a convict. Mister Menace
– handcuffed to a wheelchair.

LENNIE

Sort of like Ironside – only bent.

FLETCHER

Well yeah . . . it was my air of villainy
what titillated them. 'Course some have
bigger titillations than others. (*Lowering
voice*) I was in this cubicle with this
ravishing West Indian sister . . .

*A Prison Officer appears at
the doorway.*

PRISON OFFICER

Come on lad, you've had long
enough fiddling around with that.

FLETCHER

That's what she said.

LENNIE

Oh can I just hear the end of this . . .

PRISON OFFICER

No you can't, come along.

LENNIE

Tell me tomorrow then, Fletch.

FLETCHER

It'll keep.

Lennie starts to wheel trolley away.

LENNIE

Sleep well.

FLETCHER

And you. Look after yourself.

LENNIE

I will. Nice change having a cell to
meself. It don't half smell fresh in there
without your feet.

NORRIS

How do you think we feel?

LENNIE

Shut up, Norris.

He leaves.

FLETCHER

I should think you'll be glad to get
out of here on Thursday, Norris, it'll
give you a better opportunity to be
more revolting to a larger number
of people.

BLANCO

I'll certainly be glad to see the back of
him. You know I never had much.
Possessions like. But in the last three
days before you came in here he's
had 'em all.

FLETCHER

How d'you mean?

BLANCO

He's had me wireless. And me silver snuff holder. Real silver, Fletch. Antique. I kept me snout in it. He had all the snout an' all.

FLETCHER

(*To Norris*) Is this true?

NORRIS

Fair and square.

BLANCO

And me musical box which plays 'Waltzing Matilda' when you open the lid.

FLETCHER

What'd he do, he just took 'em? Well, he's going to put 'em right back I tell you that, Blanco.

NORRIS

Fair and square. Cards, wasn't it?

FLETCHER

Oh dear, oh dear, Blanco. You don't play cards with him.

BLANCO

Brag, nine-card brag.

NORRIS

Fair and square.

FLETCHER

You'll give those back, Norris.

NORRIS

Will I . . . heck.

He goes.

FLETCHER

Don't worry, Blanco, me old son, I'll get them back for you.

BLANCO

It doesn't matter, Fletch. What do I need with a 'Waltzing Matilda' music box where I'm going?

FLETCHER

You ain't going nowhere, mate, you've got another two years to do.

BLANCO

I'm going out of here sooner than that.

FLETCHER

You're too old to escape, Blanco. You'll never get over the wall. You been watching too much of that *Colditz*, you have.

BLANCO

I'm going out of here in a wooden overcoat.

FLETCHER

Oh come on, Blanco – dear me, what kind of talk's that?

BLANCO

No, me time's about up, Fletch. I'm not going to last the distance. Tired heart the doctor says. Tired everything more like. I come in here to die.

FLETCHER

No, you didn't. You come in here yes-ter-die. Get it, get it?

BLANCO

(*With a wan smile*) Oh Fletch, they were cracking that when even I was at school.

FLETCHER

Well, that raised a smile.

BLANCO

You don't have to gee me up, lad. I'm not afraid. It's time I went to that great cell block in the sky.

FLETCHER

Rubbish. Bloke like you ain't ready for celestial porridge yet awhile. You're not old. You look old but that's prison. Prison puts years on a man's physical appearance. Got to remember you're only twenty-nine.

BLANCO

(*Smiling*) Sixty-three.

FLETCHER

Sixty-three, you're not past it at sixty-three. Most of the government's older than that.

BLANCO

And look at the state this country's in. Mind you it weren't much better when I were a lad. Depression. Hard times. No work. Took to stealing. Such a waste. Spent nigh on half me life in one nick or another. Lost all me family. Mostly through neglect. Mine. That's why I'm resigned to passing on. Well, more than that, relieved.

FLETCHER

Come off it, there's years of wear left in you yet. Charlie Chaplin become a father nigh on eighty. Winston Churchill was at least your age when he had his finest hour. As was my Uncle Wilfred.

BLANCO

What did he do?

FLETCHER

When he was seventy he married this gorgeous young dental assistant. 'Course it killed him. But you should

have seen the smirk on his face in the coffin.

BLANCO

Died with his boots off, did he?

FLETCHER

Yeah – and his teeth out. Couldn't get the coffin lid down for three days. State of mind, age. You're as young as you feel. For instance, this old boy goes to the doctor, see. The doctor says, 'What's wrong then?' And the old boy says, 'Well it's the wife and I – we ain't getting any pleasure out of sex any more.' The doc like, he's a bit taken aback. He says, 'How old are you?' 'Eighty.' 'And the wife?' 'Seventy-nine.' He says, 'Well, when d'you first notice this?' And the old boy says, 'Last night . . . then again this morning.'

They laugh.

BLANCO

I heard that at school an' all.

3. HOSPITAL WING

The camera shows the exterior of the hospital wing at night.

3A. HOSPITAL WARD

It is night time. The room is lit by a dim hospital night light and some moonlight through the barred window. Blanco is coughing, unable

to sleep. Norris is sound asleep,
snoring lightly.
Fletcher is asleep but moves
restlessly in his bed. Blanco
coughs again.

BLANCO
(*Quietly*) Fletch . . . Fletch!

FLETCHER
Mmmmh?

BLANCO
Want to talk to you.

FLETCHER
Whassamatter?

BLANCO
Wanted to tell you something –
important, like . . . while he's asleep.
He indicates Norris.

BLANCO
He is asleep, isn't he?

There is an answering snore
from Norris.

FLETCHER
Unless he snores when he's
awake, yes.

BLANCO
Well, you see, I've got something
of value.

FLETCHER
How do you mean?

BLANCO
Well, you see, I've got no family – I
told you that. And the few things I've
got – well, Norris has got them now,
since the nine-card brag. But I still got
one thing of value. And I'd like to
bequeath it.

FLETCHER
You're getting morbid again.

BLANCO
I'm not. I'm being practical. 'Cos if owt
happened to me, no one would know
about my legacy.

FLETCHER
Listen, if you want to make a will, it's
no good talking to me, Blanco. You
want a solicitor, we got one on our
landing. He'll see you right. Straight
as a die, he is.

BLANCO
What's his name?

FLETCHER
Corkscrew Carter. Nice bloke.

BLANCO
My legacy is not the sort I
can legalise.

FLETCHER
Why not?

BLANCO
It's ill-gotten gains. Buried somewhere
in Leeds.

FLETCHER
Oh, ill-gotten gains, is it? Oh, I see.

BLANCO
Shall I tell you about it?

FLETCHER
Not now.

BLANCO
Well it was like this. There were three
of us. And we done this wages van
on the way to a fridge factory near
Otley. Don't you remember reading
about it?

FLETCHER

I don't Blanco, no.

BLANCO

It were in *Yorkshire Post*.

FLETCHER

If it didn't make the *Muswell Hill Examiner* or *Titbits* I wouldn't have seen it.

BLANCO

I s'pose not. Anyway it were an untidy job. Lot of things went wrong.

FLETCHER

You wouldn't be here if they hadn't.

BLANCO

The other two lads were brothers, Jack Brackett and Harry erm . . .

FLETCHER

Brackett, was it?

BLANCO

That's right. Did you know him?

FLETCHER

No, no. Only through his brother.

BLANCO

Oh, 'cos their escape were in *Yorkshire Post*. They got away in a fishing boat from Bridlington –

FLETCHER

Will this take long, Blanco – only my foot's gone to sleep, and I'd like to catch it up.

BLANCO

Not that the Bracketts knew where I'd put loot in any case.

FLETCHER

Blanco – fascinating as it is to stroll down felony lane with you –

BLANCO

I'm the one who's got the map. I'm the one who knows where it's buried.

FLETCHER

Oh gawd, it's bleeding Treasure Island now, is it?

BLANCO

Eight thousand quid.

FLETCHER

(*Eyes widen*) How much?

Norris's eyes open but he remains still.

BLANCO

Eight thousand quid.

FLETCHER

Eight big ones?

BLANCO

Maybe nine. Used notes. Didn't have time to count 'em. According to *Yorkshire Post* it were fifteen, but that were the thieving company, trying to diddle Lloyds.

FLETCHER

Now listen, me old son. I obviously never realised the magnitude of your legacy.

BLANCO

The map's yours, Fletch.

He gives him the map.

FLETCHER

I don't know what to say. Words fail me. I shall use the money wisely, Blanco, rest assured. Let me ask you one question. If you don't snuff it – which we all hope and pray for, that you won't that is – then on your

release you'll presumably want your
map back.

BLANCO

Oh . . . oh well, if I did last the
distance I suppose so, yes.

FLETCHER

And you'd trust me to give it to you?

BLANCO

Of course I would, Fletch.

FLETCHER

D'you know, Blanco, in all my life I
don't think anyone's ever shown me
trust like that . . . probation officers,
Borstal principals, judges. And yet
here you are – a man who ain't known
me long, or in great intimacy,
entrusting me with everything he's got
in the world.

BLANCO

I am that, Fletch.

There's a pause.

FLETCHER

You must be bleeding barmy.

4. HOSPITAL WARD

*Later that night, on his rounds,
Barrowclough looks through the
glass panel on the ward door, which
adjoins the medical room. He moves
off. Fletcher is fast asleep, as is
Blanco in the next bed. Norris
appears at Fletcher's bed. He is
searching Fletcher's possessions.*

*He checks the pockets of Fletcher's
hospital issue robe. Nothing.*

*Norris freezes as Fletcher rolls over,
but he now has his back to Norris,
who pushes a cautions hand under
the pillows. Fletcher moves again
restlessly, rolling on to his back,
thus trapping Norris's hand. Norris
hesitates a moment, looking down
at the sleeping Fletcher. Then he
carefully slips his hand into the
breast pocket of his pyjamas.
Again nothing.*

*More gingerly than ever, Norris now
starts to search under the sheets.
His hand moves lower in the bed.
Fletcher opens an eye, at first unsure
what is going on. Then:*

FLETCHER

Help!!

*Norris, as if stung, leaps back and
scurries across the room.*

FLETCHER

Help – what the hell's going on here?
Who was that? Was that you, Norris?

*Norris slides back in bed and starts
snoring before his head has even
hit the pillow.*

FLETCHER

Norris, was that you?

BLANCO

(*Waking*) What's going on –
what's happening?

FLETCHER

I'm not sure, Blanco. I think I've just
been molested.

The door is unlocked and the lights go on. Barrowclough enters, wearing his most anxious expression.

BARROWCLOUGH

What is it? What was all that noise, what is it?

FLETCHER

Oh, Mr Barrowclough, thank God It's you!

BARROWCLOUGH

Why, Fletcher? Whatever's happening – what's going on?

NORRIS

(*Feigning waking*) What's happening? What going on?

FLETCHER

Don't give me that parrot fashion, Norris, you despicable nurk!

BARROWCLOUGH

Will you answer my question, Fletcher?

FLETCHER

I was awoken, Mr Barrowclough. Woken by a foreign hand.

BARROWCLOUGH

A foreign hand?

FLETCHER

Well, you know what I mean, Norris was over here, sir.

BARROWCLOUGH

What were you up to – stealing?

NORRIS

I haven't been up to anything.

FLETCHER

Don't give me that, you were over here rummaging In my pyjamas.

BARROWCLOUGH

Have you got any valuables here, Fletcher?

FLETCHER

Only what I always keep in my pyjamas.

BLANCO

He could have been after your lemon barley water.

FLETCHER

What – in my pyjamas? Funny shaped bottle.

BARROWCLOUGH

What have you got to say for yourself, Norris?

NORRIS

What's he got that I'd want to nick? One orange and a pair of smelly slippers.

FLETCHER

You've just put yourself right in it there. I got those slippers off Mr Barrowclough. Present they were. My first week in here.

BARROWCLOUGH

Yes well, we don't need to go into that now. They were second hand, and I happened to be finished with them.

FLETCHER

Nevertheless I appreciated and grew to love those, Mr Barrowclough. And I wouldn't like to see them falling into the wrong hands – or in this case, feet.

NORRIS

I don't want your tatty old slippers.

BARROWCLOUGH

They are not tally. They cost thirty-two and six in the old currency.

He looks at Norris's table.

BARROWCLOUGH

You go out of this prison in two days' time, Norris. You must be ruddy mad to risk losing remission by going back to your nasty little habits.

NORRIS

Why d'you take his word for it?

BARROWCLOUGH

Fletcher's not the sort of person who's likely to scream out in the middle of the night over nothing. Though for the life of me I can't think what there is to steal. You're not hiding anything are you, Fletcher?

FLETCHER

Hiding?

He looks at Blanco.

BARROWCLOUGH

You're not hiding a bottle of surgical alcohol?

FLETCHER

Hide? No, sir.

Barrowclough tugs at Fletcher's blankets.

FLETCHER

Gerroff.

BARROWCLOUGH

Fletcher!

Fletcher reluctantly releases his grip on the blankets. Blanco reacts anxiously. Barrowclough pulls back the blankets. While he makes

a cursory inspection of the pillows and sheets, Fletcher is moaning bitterly.

FLETCHER

Isn't it marvellous? Eh, Blanco? Marvellous, isn't it? The suspicion, the mistrust. Even in our sick beds, racked with pain we're still subject to these indignities.

BARROWCLOUGH

This won't take a moment, Fletcher, I just want to get to the bottom of this.

FLETCHER

Yes, you're well on your way an' all!

He pulls the blankets back and examines underneath the bed, looking inside the slippers.

BARROWCLOUGH

I thought for once I'd have some peace and quiet on this shift. But there's never a moment when one of you isn't up to something.

He picks up the slippers.

BARROWCLOUGH

Oh, you've broken the pom-poms.

Sudden thought strikes him.

BARROWCLOUGH

My God.

FLETCHER

Where are you going now?

BARROWCLOUGH

It just occurred to me that this whole farce has all the classic elements of a diversionary tactic. When I get back I'll probably find that the rest of the wing has tunnelled their way to freedom.

He starts to go.

FLETCHER

'Ere.

BARROWCLOUGH

What?

FLETCHER

Lights out.

Barrowclough leaves.

FLETCHER

He's left that door unlocked. It's not good enough is it – a burglar could walk straight in here.

5. PRISON

Camera shows the prison in the morning.

5A. HOSPITAL WARD

Lennie is serving breakfast.

LENNIE

Here you are, Blanco. Nice bit of marmalade here.

FLETCHER

What's the news from the outside world?

LENNIE

Mackay's in an ever so rotten mood. Villa drew. At home. Weather forecast said winds moderate to light. (*Giving food to Fletcher*) The hot water's working again. If you're quick. And it's cauliflower cheese for your supper tonight.

FLETCHER

Dear, oh dear. That's the trouble with being cooped up in hospital. You miss it all – don't you?

LENNIE

I only give the highlights. I missed out the boring bits.

FLETCHER

Well, when you come back later, can you bring me a newspaper – the *Sun*. And something to read. I've finished these two books . . . Oh er . . .

He looks to see if Norris is watching but he is eating his breakfast.

FLETCHER

Would you make sure these books go back to my cell?

He gets the map from his plastered leg and puts it inside a book. He hands it to Lennie, winking at him.

FLETCHER

I don't want those thieving nurks on the landing getting at them.

PRISON OFFICER

Come on, Godber.

LENNIE

Oh naffing hell. See you then, Fletch.

FLETCHER

Yes, drive carefully.

Lennie wheels the trolley away.

FLETCHER

(*To Blanco*) How's your tomato then, Blanco?

BLANCO

Had worse. But not much.

NORRIS
I'll have his.

FLETCHER
You'll have it all down your front if you're not careful.

NORRIS
Listen you two, I'd like a word. I'll come straight to the point. I was awake last night. I heard.

FLETCHER
Heard – heard what?

NORRIS
About the map.

FLETCHER
Don't know what he's talking about, do you Blanco? What map's this then?

NORRIS
Come on, Fletch, don't pee around. Listen, you could cut me in.

FLETCHER
I don't know what you're talking about.

NORRIS
You know what I'm talking about. The map, the gelt – the buried gelt, in Leeds.

BLANCO
Why should we cut you in?

NORRIS
Ah see – there is a map, isn't there?

FLETCHER
All right, then, all right, there is a map. But why should we cut you in?

NORRIS
I'm going out tomorrow.

FLETCHER
So.

NORRIS
Well, Blanco ain't out for two years, and you're not for three. Anything could happen. They could find it . . . or, or build a multi-storey car park on top of it. So I could keep it safe, couldn't I? Put it in a building society. Invest it, like.

FLETCHER
I know what you'd invest it in, Norris. You'd invest it in a brighter future for your despicable self. By the time we come out there wouldn't be a penny left. You'd squander it in a vulgar orgy of wining and dining northern tarts in northern night clubs.

BLANCO
Yeah. That's what I'd planned to do with it.

FLETCHER
You're entitled, Blanco. It's your money.

NORRIS
It won't be if he snuffs it, will it? You're going to cop it.

FLETCHER
I happens to be his chosen benefactor. And you happen to be someone he can't bear the sight of. You're only the bloke what cheated him out of his most treasured possessions. His snuff box and his radio, and his little Matilda what goes round. Tell you what though, Norris, if you can find the map you're welcome to a share.

BLANCO
Here, Fletch.

FLETCHER

Go on then, straight up. I mean I ain't been able to leave this room, have I? Not with this plaster.

NORRIS

That's a deal, is it?

FLETCHER

Have to find it first.

NORRIS

I know where you hid it.

FLETCHER

You ain't that clever, Norris.

Norris lunges at Fletcher's plaster and tries to pull it off. Fletcher yells in agony.

6. LANDING

Norris, now fully dressed, makes his way up the steps towards the upper landing through the bustle of association hour.

6A. CELL

It is night time. Lennie is lying on the upper bunk, reading a paper, when Norris enters.

NORRIS

'Ere, Godber.

LENNIE

Oh hello, Norris. Come to say your goodbyes, have you?

NORRIS

No, it's just that er – Fletch said when he give you those books, did he leave a bit of paper in it? By mistake, like.

LENNIE

Why?

NORRIS

He just wanted it. I said I'd take it over to him.

LENNIE

(*Suspiciously*) Bit of paper, like?

NORRIS

Yeah, quite meaningless.

LENNIE

Why's he want it then?

NORRIS

I dunno, it's meaningless –

He sees the two books on a chair and grabs them. There is nothing in them.

LENNIE

Meaningless, is it?

NORRIS

Was there a bit of paper in here?

LENNIE

Could be.

Norris tries another tack.

NORRIS

Look, Godber – I mean, Lennie – how d'you like to make some money? I mean real money. On the outside.

LENNIE

Not much use to me as I'm on the inside, is it?

NORRIS

All right. I've got gear on the inside. And my back wages.

LENNIE

What for – a meaningless bit of paper?

NORRIS

Ask no questions, son.

Lennie swings down from his bunk.

LENNIE

No questions about the fact that this is behind my mate's back. This, obviously, whatever it is, belongs to Fletch.

NORRIS

Never mind about Fletch. He only worries about number one. Look I'm offering you all my back pay. And my snout.

LENNIE

Fletch's my cellie. My mate.

NORRIS

(*Producing goods one by one*) I've got a silver snuff holder. Antique. Worth a lot of money.

LENNIE

He's been good to me, Fletch.

NORRIS

And a music box. Plays 'Waltzing Matilda'.

LENNIE

Contrary to popular belief in here, we're not all without scruples. Fletcher's shown me friendship. You can't buy that. Without him I'd've gone under in here.

NORRIS

There's a radio as well. Japanese.

LENNIE

All right, then, done.

Norris grins in satisfaction.

7. PRISON GATES

Camera shows the prison gates. Norris walks out with a carrier bag and parcel and to a waiting minibus. He gets in and the minibus drives off.

8. HOSPITAL WARD

Lennie wheels the lunch trolley into the ward.

FLETCHER

(*Indignantly*) Oh here he comes! The Judas Iscariot of Slade Prison.

BLANCO

Don't know how he dares show his face.

FLETCHER

Judas. You betrayed us, didn't you, Godber – you betrayed us to that evil Norris.

LENNIE

(*Unfazed*) Yes, I did.

FLETCHER

Thank God for that – how did it go?

LENNIE

Like a charm.

FLETCHER

(*To Blanco*) Like a charm – D'you hear that – like a charm.

They all laugh.

Lennie picks up the cover on one of the trays.

LENNIE

What have we here? One radio.

One snuff holder. And one Australian music box.

He puts them on Blanco's bedside table.

FLETCHER
There you are, Blanco, with all thy worldly goods we thee endow.

BLANCO
(*Chuffed*) Oh lads, lads.

FLETCHER
(*To Lennie*) What did you do with Norris's snout?

LENNIE
There was so much there wasn't room for it! And I've stashed the back pay.

FLETCHER
Split it three ways, fair enough?

LENNIE
When d'you cook this up, Fletch?

FLETCHER
That first afternoon when Norris was having his bath.

LENNIE
Lovely idea. He really thought you *had* some money buried.

FLETCHER
It's him. Lovely bit of acting. He had me going, he did in the small hours. 'Course we knew Norris would be earwigging. Person like that always does.

BLANCO
D'you think he'll go straight there?

FLETCHER
Oh gawd yes, the best is yet to come.

LENNIE
Should think he'll be in Leeds by midday.

FLETCHER
Yes. Then he'll go to an ironmonger's and buy a shovel – 'course he'll lie low this afternoon. Won't go there till everyone's gone home. (*To Blanco*) Here we'll listen to your wireless tonight. Might hear something on the nine o'clock news.

They all laugh.

9. FIELD

A man is walking along. He stops, looks at a map, turns and walks on. Further along he stops walking, puts the map away and starts to dig. Lights start coming on. The sign 'Leeds United' can be seen. It is a floodlit football ground. A guard with a dog is walking towards Norris.

10. HOSPITAL WARD

Fletcher and Blanco are listening to the radio.

ANNOUNCER
(*Voiceover*) Later a man was detained at Leeds Police headquarters, charged with trespass and causing wilful damage to the property of Leeds United Football Club. He is being remanded . . .

SERIES TWO

EPISODE SIX: THE HARDER THEY FALL

1. ASSOCIATION AREA 1.

Lennie is seen walking through the association area and going upstairs. A prisoner at a table speaks to him.

PRISONER

Hey, Len, heard you made the team.

LENNIE

Yeah, well . . .

He carries on up the stairs. At the top he meets Barrowclough.

BARROWCLOUGH

The champ, is it?

LENNIE

Not yet.

BARROWCLOUGH

Double rations then.

LENNIE

If I want 'em.

BARROWCLOUGH

I thought that was the whole point in boxing. Getting a double ration chit.

LENNIE

Well, you see, if I have double rations of Slade Prison's food I won't be a middle-weight, I'll be an overweight.

BARROWCLOUGH

I trust you're not complaining about the food, Godber?

LENNIE

No complaints, sir.

BARROWCLOUGH

It's a jolly sight better than a lot of people get in their own homes. And I speak from experience. Of prison food, that is.

LENNIE

Yes, sir. I mean it's not much to look at, but then neither is ready-mixed concrete, and that doesn't taste very nice either.

BARROWCLOUGH

Well, that's all right then . . . I'm glad to hear you're taking a sensible . . . *Lennie has gone.*

BARROWCLOUGH

Pardon?

2. CELL

It is evening. Fletcher has just finished a game of draughts with another prisoner. They pack up.

FLETCHER

Cheerio – thanks for the game.

The prisoner goes, passing Lennie on his way in. Lennie is wearing a tracksuit.

LENNIE

'Lo, Fletch.

FLETCHER

Oh gawd, the athlete.

LENNIE

Nothing wrong with that. Keep in shape. Better than draughts. You could do with losing a few pounds, Fletch.

FLETCHER

Thanks to draughts, I just won two pounds, ain't I?

LENNIE

You cheat at draughts.

FLETCHER

Here, you watch your tongue, or I'll knock your block off.

LENNIE

Oh no, you won't, Fletch . . .

He starts to shadow box at Fletcher.

LENNIE

Made the boxing team, didn't I . . .

He starts slapping Fletcher's face in an irritating manner.

LENNIE

Didn't I, didn't I . . . Come on, Fletch, where's your guard?

FLETCHER

He's outside, want me to call him in? Naff off, sit down, will you? Boxing now, is it?

Lennie nods.

FLETCHER

Gawd, Godber, you've taken every niffing course in this prison. Arts and Crafts, 'O' Levels, Pottery, Spanish. What are you going to do with Spanish, become an interpreter, are you?

LENNIE

Si, si, Señor.

FLETCHER

That's it, is it? Six weeks of concentrated study and what have we got – 'Si, si, Señor!'

LENNIE

No, listen . . . No tiene vaca, pero tiene uno burro.

FLETCHER

Go on then, I'll buy it.

LENNIE

I haven't got a cow, but I have got a donkey.

FLETCHER

Oh that'll come in handy, that's extremely useful, that is. On your first Spanish holiday, pick up a shy little señorita, she starts whispering sweet nothings up your nose and what do you say? 'Well, I haven't got a cow, darling, but I have got a donkey.'

LENNIE

Vaya con Dios – that's Spanish.

FLETCHER

People like you from Birmingham would be better off learning English. I hope this boxing lark won't last long. 'Cos you do bring a terrible smell of sweat and liniment into my room.

LENNIE

Takes away the smell of your aftershave. Seriously though, Fletch, I'm dead chuffed at making the boxing squad. Big match next week.

FLETCHER

You're only boxing for our wing.

LENNIE

I know but . . .

FLETCHER

Against another wing.

LENNIE

Even so.

FLETCHER

Hardly Madison Square Garden, is it?

LENNIE

It's a start, Fletch. I'm going to work at this. It's the great working-class escape, sport. That and rock and roll.

FLETCHER

No doubt you'll get round to that sooner or later.

LENNIE

I've got all the credentials to be a fighter. Deprived childhood, terrible background. Mr Hopkins, the PTI, says I've got natural ability.

FLETCHER

If you show all the flair in the ring that you show for Spanish, my son, you ain't half due a clobbering.

LENNIE

Que sera, sera . . .

FLETCHER

Kiss her what?

Jackdaw comes in.

JACKDAW

Hey, Fletch, Grouty wants to see you.

FLETCHER

Pardon?

JACKDAW

Grouty. Wants a word.

FLETCHER

Are you running for Harry Grout, now, Jackdaw?

JACKDAW

I'm one of his firm.

FLETCHER

He must be scraping the barrel.

JACKDAW

Watch it.

FLETCHER

Oh hark at him. Now that he's under the protective wing of genial Harry Grout he's full of bravado, isn't he?

JACKDAW

Well are you coming then?

FLETCHER

I might stroll across in due course, yeah.

JACKDAW

I'm supposed to take you with me.

FLETCHER

I'm a bit heavy to lift, Jackdaw. Tell you what, you scurry back,

I know the way. Tell Harry I want
to change me socks and cut me
toenails, all right?

JACKDAW
On your head be it.

He leaves.

LENNIE
Was that wise?

FLETCHER
Yeah – he's all right Harry. I know he has
a long past of mayhem and violence,
but this is the last year of a long, long
stretch. He ain't going to come the
heavy and cock up his release at this
stage, is he?

LENNIE
S'pose not.

FLETCHER
He's happy being the tobacco baron,
and running all the rackets.

LENNIE
Wonder what he wants to see
you for?

FLETCHER
Maybe he wants a slice of my
draughts action.

They laugh.

FLETCHER
Now where's me clippers?

LENNIE
Oh Fletch, you're not going to cut
your toenails in here.

FLETCHER
Well I ain't going to grow them
indefinitely, and I'm not tall enough to
get me feet out the window.

LENNIE
All right, but you always cut 'em on
my bunk.

*He walks over to the table and
sits down.*

FLETCHER
Oh I'm sorry if it offends your sense of
Birmingham propriety. I hope you're
going to take a shower to wash that
liniment off. Smells like a Turkish
wrestler's jock strap in here.

LENNIE
Yes well, you've travelled Fletch, you
know these things.

*Mackay comes in and walks across
to Lennie.*

MACKAY
Hello, Godber. No, sit down. I'm told
congratulations are in order.

LENNIE
Oh, the boxing. Thank you, Mr
Mackay, yes.

MACKAY
Fine outlet, boxing. The noble art.
Teaches you discipline, dedication and
team spirit. Oh yes. I was no slouch
myself at your age. I once boxed for
Midlothian Boys.

FLETCHER
Who against, Lanarkshire Girls?

MACKAY
In the Army I boxed for the battalion.

LENNIE
Did you, Mr Mackay?

MACKAY
First Battalion. Argyle and Sutherland

Highlanders. Great regiment, great tradition. A regiment I was proud to serve.

FLETCHER

A regiment which is now defunct. Despite all those nurks who put stickers in their car windows.

MACKAY

I expect you were in the Ordnance Corps, Fletcher. Something which kept you well out of the line of fire. Probably served your time embezzling stores in some cushy posting like Shoeburyness. *He laughs.*

FLETCHER

Well, you're wrong there. I did active service. Malaya. Kuala Lumpur. That's where I did my embezzling. And I wasn't in no Ordnance Corps. I was in the RASC.

LENNIE

What's that stand for?

FLETCHER

Run Away Someone's Coming. *He laughs.*

MACKAY

National Service would have done you good, Godber. The Army's good to its boxers.

FLETCHER

I don't reckon boxing's such a noble art at all.

MACKAY

No?

FLETCHER

I had a friend once – haven't told you this before, have I? He was a light-heavy. Good strong, boy. Won a few fights. Suddenly thought he was the bee's knees. Fast cars, easy women. Classic story of too much, too soon. He just blew up. He got into debt and ended up in one of those travelling booths. Four fights a night, seven night a week. Well the body can't take that punishment. His brain went soft, his reflexes went. You know – punchy. Just became like a vegetable – an incoherent non-thinking zombie.

MACKAY

What became of him?

FLETCHER

He joined the prison service as a Warder. Doing very well. *Mackay knows he's been had. He goes.*

3. LANDING

It is evening. Fletcher moves up on to the landing. He passes a Prison Officer on the stairs and gives a polite nod.

3A. GROUT'S CELL

It is evening. Grout's cell is extremely well furnished. It is a single cell with a quilted counterpane on the bed; an expensive radio and record player; a lamp made from an old

*Chianti bottle; and several framed
pictures of friends and well-known
sporting personalities. He also has
chintzy curtains, a rug, a magazine
rack and a budgie in a cage. Harry
Grout himself is a heavy-set man;
an affable East London villain
though one should be aware of a
sense of power when he chooses to
switch off the charm. He is listening
to the radio on stereo headphones
when Fletcher enters. Harry looks
up and sees him, indicating that he
should wait a moment till he has
finished listening.*

*Fletcher enters the cell, looks around,
touches the birdcage and waits.*

GROUTY

Archers. Never miss.

FLETCHER

They still on, are they?

GROUT

Doris is in a bit of a state. She's got
Dutch Elm disease.

FLETCHER

Oh dear, poor Doris.

GROUT

Don't you follow *The Archers*?

FLETCHER

I don't, Grouty. Not for some years.
Not since Grace copped it when I was
in Shepton Mallet. That's nice.

Grout is putting on a dressing gown.

FLETCHER

I like the radio, mind. *Gardeners'
Question Time* and *Desert Island Discs*.

GROUT

I like a good play meself. And a *Book
at Bedtime*, never miss that.

FLETCHER

I like that. But of course they don't
allow us the wireless that late.

GROUT

Don't they? No one's ever told me.

FLETCHER

Don't suppose anyone's ever dared.
Nice place you got here.

GROUT

Do you like it?

FLETCHER

All the creature comforts. Like the lamp.

GROUT

Memento. Of Alassio. That's in Italy
that is.

FLETCHER

Wasn't it Alassio that they extradited
you from?

GROUT

That's right. I came back handcuffed to
Scotcher of the Yard on Alitalia. I paid
the extra and moved us both up into
first class. Bit of a perk for him, he's
never been south of Worthing before.
Bought the Chianti for me, duty free,
and got him a bottle of Sambuca.

FLETCHER

In the light of your subsequent
sentence, it might have been better if
you'd given the judge the Sambuca.

GROUT

I offered him five hundred quid, what
more could I do?

FLETCHER

Oh I suppose not . . .

Jackdaw enters with a tray of cocoa.

GROUT

Yes, come in, Jackdaw. Cocoa, Fletch?

FLETCHER

Oh, don't mind if I do.

GROUT

Sugar?

Hands Fletcher a two-pound bag.

FLETCHER

Thank you.

JACKDAW

(*Holding up a packet of bird seed*)
Should I feed Seymour, Harry?

GROUT

Yeah, go on.

Fletcher looks round.

FLETCHER

Seymour? Oh your feathered friend.
Very nice.

GROUT

He's company of an evening. When
I was in Parkhurst I had a pigeon.

FLETCHER

Oh like the Birdman of Alcatraz.

GROUT

Not really, no.

FLETCHER

No, not really I suppose. Took a
bit more room though, didn't he?
A pigeon.

GROUT

Just a bit, yeah. On the other hand
how else could I keep in touch with
the bookmakers?

FLETCHER

Oh I see – yeah.

He pauses.

GROUT

Brought me in a few bob.

FLETCHER

Yeah, must have done. What
did you do with it when you had
to leave?

GROUT

I ate it.

FLETCHER

Oh very nice. I should watch your step
if I were you, Jackdaw.

JACKDAW

Will we – that be all then, Harry?

GROUT

Probably, but hang about . . . oh
and Jackdaw?

JACKDAW

Yes, Harry?

GROUT

We're in conference so do the
minding, right?

JACKDAW

Yes, Harry.

He withdraws.

GROUT

Do you want a Bath Oliver?

FLETCHER

You got a bath in here an' all?

Grout offers him a biscuit.

FLETCHER

Oh, biscuit.

GROUT

With your cocoa?

FLETCHER

No thanks, Grouty. Got to watch the weight, you know what I mean.

He spoons four heaped spoonfuls of sugar into his cocoa.

GROUT

Well then; Fletch . . .

FLETCHER

Well then, Grouty . . .

GROUT

They're going to have this boxing match, aren't they?

FLETCHER

So I hear. Inter prison championships or something.

GROUT

Well then – money to be made.

FLETCHER

You mean a flutter?

GROUT

Sport means competition, don't it? Which means there's a winner and a loser. Which is all right providing you're on the winner.

FLETCHER

Forgive me for saying this, Grouty, but do you need the funds? I mean if you want money all you have to do is go to people and they give it to you.

GROUT

Where's the fun in that? We're talking about sport, my son. The speculation, the excitement, the tension, the thrill of the outcome.

FLETCHER

Oh the thrill of the outcome, yes.

GROUT

That's what I enjoy.

FLETCHER

Yeah, yeah.

GROUT

That's why I want you to fix the fight.

FLETCHER

You what?

GROUT

Well that's putting it a bit strong. What I mean is what I want you to do is to feed me certain information so that I get all my thrill of speculation and excitement from knowing that I'm on a certainty.

FLETCHER

Feed you what information, Harry? There's seven fights. Wing against wing.

GROUT

I know that, but as they all have to train in the same gymnasium, it just needs someone with an experienced eye to run over the form. Someone like yourself. As you know, in this nick I have a bit of a rival. Namely the presumptuous upstart, Billy Moffatt.

FLETCHER

That nurk, Moffatt. No contest, Harry.

GROUT

Nevertheless he's running a book. Without my seal of approval. So I'd like to take him to the cleaners.

FLETCHER

Yes, I sees your point, Harry, but you know me, I'm a loner. I sees myself as

the Randolph Scott of Slade Prison.
I don't like being responsible to nobody,
not even someone as distinguished
as yourself. So I think really the best
thing is for me to say straight off, very
adamantly, that I decline this flattering
invitation. Thanks for the cocoa.

*He starts towards the doorway.
There is a very large prisoner
standing there.*

GROUT
You disappoint me, Fletch.

*Fletcher changes his mind and
returns to Grout.*

FLETCHER
When do I start?

4. GYM

*Lennie is sparring with Larry in the
ring. The PTI is watching them.
Fletcher walks into the gym.*

REFEREE
What are you on, Fletcher? Charity
walk, is it?

FLETCHER
You know me, Mr Bayliss. I'm not a
man what gets involved in the
recreational pastime of this prison.
When all around me's a frenzy of
activity, I'm happy to be on my bunk
whittling. But I was lying there, you
know, and I was thinking about the
honour of the wing, and I realised that
it would be a crime if I didn't offer you
the benefit of my experience.

Mackay approaches.

MACKAY
What experience is this, Fletcher?

FLETCHER
Oh hello, Mr Mackay. My experience
of ringcraft, the noble art. Just telling
Mr Bayliss how my know-how is at
his disposal.

MACKAY
Well, we don't know what to say,
do we, lads? We're overwhelmed.
All right then, Fletcher. In the ring.

FLETCHER
In the ring? What d'you mean, in
the ring?

MACKAY
Show the lads a thing or two.

FLETCHER
I'm offering you my advice.
My expertise.

MACKAY
Have to show the lads a thing or two.
Show 'em the old magic's still there.
How else will they believe in you?

He starts putting gloves on Fletcher.

FLETCHER
The England Squad believe in Don
Revie, but he don't get on the park
and kick a ball around. Angelo Lundee
– he don't spar with Ali. Stays in the
corner, muttering words of advice and
minding the gumshield.

MACKAY
He wants to work for the squad, lads,
he has to show willing, doesn't he?

*The prisoners agree. Fletcher
is trapped.*

REFEREE

Go on then, Fletch, out you come, Larry.

Larry gets out of the ring. Fletcher climbs in. Fletcher walks up to Lennie who pushes his gloves forward in the prematch gesture.

FLETCHER

Now just go easy, sonny. Don't make me lose my rag. Hey, watch it.

LENNIE

Keep your guard up, Fletcher.

REFEREE

Seconds out.

He rings the bell.

FLETCHER

Fire drill, oh – back to the cells everyone.

He walks to the ropes.

MACKAY

Fletcher.

FLETCHER

Oh sir, sorry, sir. Yes, sir.

He returns to Lennie and starts ducking round him. Lennie just stands there in amazement. Finally he takes one punch at Fletcher. Fletcher falls to the ground.

5. UTILITY ROOM

It is evening. Jackdaw, followed by Fletcher, comes down the corridor and up to the door. He unlocks it. Grout is sitting on an old deckchair, smoking a cigar, when Jackdaw ushers Fletcher into the utility room.

GROUT

Come in, Fletch. How are you?

FLETCHER

I'll live, I suppose.

JACKDAW

Should I er – ?

GROUT

Yeah, keep an eye.

Jackdaw withdraws. Fletcher looks around him with some distaste.

FLETCHER

Preferred your other place.

GROUT

The less you and I are seen together the better. So what's the form then?

FLETCHER

Well there's not much to choose between any of the matchings, Grouty. Anybody's guess who'll win the flyweight, since they're both equally stupid and cowardly. Question of which one bursts into tears first. I think Big Mac's a certainty in the heavyweight.

GROUT

Well we all know that.

FLETCHER

The other certainty, I must say, is young Godber. 'Course being his second, I've been able to give a bit extra, y'know – phuh phuh.

GROUT

Yes, I heard from other quarters, he's well favoured. Good strong boy.

FLETCHER

And his opponent, young Nesbitt – he just hasn't got it. No contact.

GROUT

Well that's the one then.

FLETCHER

You won't get very good odds
on Godber.

GROUT

No, but I will on Nesbitt.

*Fletcher realises instantly the
implications of this.*

FLETCHER

Oh now, Harry . . .

GROUT

Tell the lad to make it look good. And
then go down in the second.

FLETCHER

Oh Grouty, please! Not the lad. It
means a lot to him.

GROUT

Means a lot to me, Fletch. Billy Moffatt
will be on your boy.

FLETCHER

But why him? Why not nobble
Big Mac? Get even better odds on
his opponent.

GROUT

Don't be daft. Where's the credibility
in Big Mac going down? He put
four screws in the hospital last
year when someone knocked his
jigsaw over. Can you see Hermigton
beating him?

FLETCHER

David beat Goliath.

GROUT

With a sling full of shot, not a
left hook.

FLETCHER

Put some shot in his glove?

GROUT

No, no, it's got to be Godber.

FLETCHER

But, Grouty, I'm not sure the lad will
do it. He's young, he's idealistic.
He's still got his scruples.

GROUT

If he don't do what I ask, he may not
have them much longer.

6. FLETCHER'S CELL

*Lennie is doing press-ups on the cell
floor when Fletcher enters, diffidently
and watches him for a moment.*

FLETCHER

Oh, anyone we know?

LENNIE

Just a minute, Fletch . . . twenty-four
. . . twenty-five . . .

*He collapses, then staggers on to
his bunk.*

LENNIE

Twenty-five, Fletch.

FLETCHER

That's very commendable.

He gives Lennie a mug of tea.

LENNIE

Thank you. And I did twenty pull-ups
on the wall bars before I left the gym.

FLETCHER

Twenty? Really?

LENNIE

Pull-ups. Yes.

Fletcher looks at Lennie panting on the bed for a minute and then shakes his head.

FLETCHER

Is it worth it?

LENNIE

How d'you mean?

FLETCHER

All these press-ups, and pull-ups. All these deep breathing exercises. And this weight-lifting. It's a bit daft in' it? I mean it's just punishment.

LENNIE

It's for the boxing, Fletch.

FLETCHER

I know, Len, I know. That's my worry, you see.

LENNIE

Why?

FLETCHER

My concern, my very genuine concern is that you're neglecting your pottery classes. And all those other arts and crafts activities in which you indulged so diligently. And what's happened to your elementary plumbing – that's gone down the drain an' all. You see there's no future in boxing. It's a mug's game. Snout?

He offers him some.

LENNIE

No, I'd better not.

He pats his chest.

FLETCHER

Suit yourself. Oh here, that reminds me. I got you some chocolate – your favourite, fruit and nut.

He gives it to him.

LENNIE

Oh that's ever so kind, Fletch. I'll save it till after the fight.

FLETCHER

Suit yourself.

LENNIE

You all right, Fletch?

FLETCHER

What do you mean, am I all right?

LENNIE

Well, the snout, the tea and the chocolate. It's not you, normally you're so mean.

FLETCHER

What do you mean – mean?

LENNIE

(*Standing up*) I was wondering if my right cross had done some permanent brain damage. I think you ought to go to the MO and have your bumps felt.

He laughs.

FLETCHER

(*Walking over to Lennie*) Now you listen to me, Godber, you listen to me. Just shut your mouth and hear me out, you cocky young scroat.

LENNIE

(*Sitting down*) That's better. That's the old Fletch.

FLETCHER

(*Crossing to Lennie*) No, it isn't. It isn't

your old Fletch you see before you but a very troubled man.

LENNIE

Oh?

Fletcher paces the floor for a few moments, then says.

FLETCHER

I'm a cynical old so-and-so . . . well, I don't have to tell you. It's 'cos I've seen it all. You on the other hand haven't seen anything. That's what gives you your naïve charm I suppose. You ain't had all the idealism ground out of you. Yet! But I have to ask you – well *tell* you – what someone has asked me – well *told* me – they were wondering – well they was insisting – if you could see your way clear – not that you have very much choice . . . I don't know how to say this, kid . . .

LENNIE

What is it you're trying to say, Fletch?

Fletcher looks him in the eye.

FLETCHER

Tomorrow night's not going to be your night, Lennie.

LENNIE

How?

FLETCHER

(*Taking a deep breath*) Harry Grout wants you to take a dive in the second.

Lennie stares at him blankly.

FLETCHER

Don't look at me in that way, son. You're shocked, of course you are . . . and me . . . I'm ashamed.

There is a pause before Lennie says, quietly.

LENNIE

I can't do that, Fletch.

FLETCHER

I knew you'd say that, Len . . . and I respect you for it. But you have to see the position I'm in.

LENNIE

I appreciate that, Fletch. But I just can't do it.

FLETCHER

But it means nothing! What does it mean after all! It's a wing against a wing. It's meaningless!

LENNIE

I know that.

FLETCHER

Then why can't you do this? For me!

LENNIE

I've already promised Billy Moffatt to take a dive in the first.

Fletcher is outraged.

FLETCHER

You've what! You're going to take a dive –

LENNIE

Keep your voice down, Fletch.

FLETCHER

(*Voice down*) You're taking a dive for Moffatt?

LENNIE

Yes.

FLETCHER

I don't pretend to understand the younger generation. I really don't.

Would you mind telling me why?

LENNIE

They asked me first.

FLETCHER

Oh, they asked you first. So you're in the market for corruption, are you? Case of the biggest bidder, is it?

LENNIE

Oh come on, Fletch! You know the score. I may be innocent and naïve but I'm not bloody daft. I'm au fait with the realities inside. I'd rather be clobbered in the ring than out of it. It's the easy way out – no skin off my nose.

FLETCHER

It's me that's going to get skinned! And not just off the nose neither.

LENNIE

'Spose you want your fruit and nut back.

FLETCHER

I most certainly do.

He takes it and starts eating it.

FLETCHER

You've disappointed me you have. You could have been a contender, you could.

LENNIE

But you just said . . .

FLETCHER

Never mind what I just said, you forget what I just said, it's none of your business what I just said! Things have changed between you and me. I'm disappointed, bitterly disappointed in you. I've never been so let down since

my son Raymond broke into his school one night and had a prior peep at the exam papers.

LENNIE

Did he?

FLETCHER

Yes he did, and he still didn't pass.

7. UTILITY ROOM

It is night time. Grout is still sitting in the same chair. He is talking to Fletcher.

GROUT

Well, I don't know what to make of youngsters today. No moral fibre.

FLETCHER

They won't be told.

GROUT

Poses a problem though, don't it?

FLETCHER

Now wait a minute, Grouty. Godber's still going to lose. We're all on Nesbitt to win, so there's no conflict of interests, is there?

GROUT

There's no odds neither. All the big money in this nick's on Nesbitt – wouldn't even get evens.

FLETCHER

Why don't we just withdraw gracefully from this one, Harry? It's getting ever so complicated. Why don't you just go back to demanding money with menaces?

GROUT

That doesn't satisfy my sporting

instincts, I told you before, I like the excitement, the old adrenalin. Only one thing for it. If they've nobbled Godber we've to make sure that he wins.

FLETCHER
How?

GROUT
You nobble Nesbitt.

Fletcher looks in pain.

8. GYM

Prisoners are coming in to take their seats. Grout and Jackdaw are among them. Grout looks at Moffatt.

9. CHANGING ROOM

The boxers are getting ready for the fight. Fletcher and Lennie come in.

LENNIE
What's up, Fletch?

FLETCH
I want a word.

LENNIE
What?

FLETCHER
The fix is on.

LENNIE
Well I know that, don't I? I'm going down in the first.

FLETCHER
Yeah, well don't hang about, 'cos so is Nesbitt.

LENNIE
Is he?

FLETCHER
Which is serious for all three of us. If you win, you're in trouble with Moffatt. If Nesbitt wins he's in trouble with Grouty. And whoever wins I'm in trouble with both of them. One of us is going to suffer, and it's going to be me twice. It ain't the customs of the fight I'm worried about, it's the outcome of the outcome.

LENNIE
Whatever it is it's going to be serious.

FLETCHER
That much is certain, my son. In fact the only element of speculation in this fight is which one of you hits the flaming canvas first.

LENNIE
What are we going to do?

10. GYM

The boxers enter with their seconds and climb into the ring. The Referee calls the boxers over to him.

REFEREE
All right, lads, let's have a good fight. If you go down take a mandatory count of eight, you break when I say break and you fight fair, right?

THE BOXERS
The boxers touch gloves and return to their respective corners.

FLETCHER

(*Putting gumshield in Lennie's mouth*)
Go in and may the best man lose.
Nesbitt in his corner is also getting
his gumshield.
The bell rings.

VOICE

(*Offscreen*) Seconds out, round one.
Grout and Moffat are watching the
fight when both boxers go down.
Lennie is on the floor apparently
knocked out. The referee starts to
count. Fletcher, relieved, counts
with him.
Grout leaves, as do Moffat and the
other prisoners.

11. FLETCHER'S CELL

It is night time. Lennie is on his
bunk. Fletcher is brought into the
cell by a Warder.

FLETCHER

Thanks very much, James. I'm
sorry I don't seem to have any
small change.
The Warder goes and slams the
door shut.

FLETCHER

(*To Lennie*) Are you all right?

LENNIE

'Course I am. Hardly touched me.
What did Grouty say?

FLETCHER

Couldn't say anything, could he?

LENNIE

He didn't suspect?

FLETCHER

He's all right. Bets were void, weren't
they? So he didn't gain anything – on
the other hand he didn't lose anything.
Nor did he lose any prestige to that
Billy Moffat.

LENNIE

A great idea. Nobody won, and none
of us lost.

FLETCHER

Er yeah . . . well, that's not exactly true.

LENNIE

How d'you mean?

FLETCHER

There was somebody who came out
of this ahead.

LENNIE

You?

FLETCHER

Confidentially, I made quite a bit of
money off of that bent warder who
works in the bakery.

LENNIE

How?

FLETCHER

I was the only bloke in this nick what
bet on a draw. Chocolate?

MEMORIES

Sam Kelly (Warren in the series)

'Can you imagine the joy in speaking the lines and working with those actors for someone who had hardly set foot in a television studio in 1975? That was me playing the illiterate Bunny Warren, a man who was inside because he couldn't read the sign that said "burglar alarm". And who better to be inside with than the brilliant Mr Barker. Don't mistake Ronnie for a comedian, he's a great actor with the skill and generosity that made newcomers like me gain in confidence with each episode, and the knowledge that with good actors around him the show would work and that he would shine. And shine he did! Norman Fletcher is without doubt one of the greatest creations in the history of television.

'Syd Lotterby had used me previously in an episode of *The Liver Birds* and in a one-off sitcom playing, of all things, Cilla Black's boyfriend. To have crossed his mind when casting *Porridge* has helped my career to take off in all directions, both in television and the theatre. Innumerable sitcoms later I give thanks to Syd.

'What do I remember of a fantastic couple of years? The hilarious weekly read-throughs (I deliberately didn't read the scripts beforehand); the rehearsals with Ronnie putting in his little looks, double takes and the odd extra line; Fulton Mackay fussing around on his way towards that marvellous performance. I watched relentlessly, instinctively knowing that I was learning all the time. I watched everyone: Beckinsale, Osoba, Biggins, Ken Jones. I learned things from actors far less experienced than I, and now that Ronnie has retired I can safely say that I stole some of his expressions and "takes" and shamelessly use them to this day.

'Favourite moments are many: Philip Madoc on the mating habits of spiders; Lukewarm knitting while waiting for a visit from his boyfriend; Fletcher wangling a weekend at home in his big bed with his big wife; the food riot (which nearly brought Ealing Studios out on strike); the two episodes with the legendary Maurice Denham as a bent judge; great visiting actors such as Ronald Lacey, Dudley Sutton, Madge Hindle, Patricia Brake and Peter Jeffrey. And a great comic coup was the fey governor who couldn't cope with anything, least of all Norman Stanley Fletcher.

'*Porridge* worked because it was truthful. Despite the laugh, jokes and hilarious characters there was no doubt that these men were in prison. Acting is about being truthful, nothing else, and we were blessed with two writers who knew that and who could write in no other way.'

Tony Osoba (McLaren in the series)

' "Disturbing the Peace" is one of my favourite episodes and I vividly recall filming the riot scene on the set at Ealing film studios. The *Porridge* sets were always quite superb – testimony to the brilliance of the designers Tim Gleeson, John Pusey, David Chandler and Gerry Scott. Many people were convinced that we shot the series in a real prison.

'I think the writing beautifully sets up the character of Napper Wainwright and his relationship with Fletcher. The late Peter Jeffrey captured the essence of Wainwright magnificently and later I was privileged to enjoy hooking and slicing my way round the golf course in the company of this delightful man.

'Meanwhile, back at the riot, can you imagine turning a group of thirty people loose in a canteen scene and encouraging them to chuck the food around? What we'd all have given for that to have happened at school dinners! And nobody telling you off. To make sure everything was suitably messy we were supplied with appropriate victuals: vats of mashed potatoes, tureens of mushy peas, etc.

'The downside to all of this delinquent fun was that we ran out of time whilst filming the scene and had to return the following day to complete it. Continuity meant that the costumes couldn't be washed and the set had to remain exactly as it had been left. Even now I recall with nauseous clarity climbing into my costume, still wet in patches with the congealing mushy peas, cracking in other places with hardened mashed potato and squelching around the set, slipping and sliding on unspeakable concoctions formed from our previous day's efforts. And as to the smell, well I won't even begin to describe that. Ah, all in the name of art! Fond memories.'

Philip Madoc (Williams in 'Disturbing the Peace')
'The first sight of Machu Picchu, the approach through the Sik and entry into Petra, the advent of sliced bread – could these moments in my life compare with the phone call from Ronnie Barker inviting me to be in *Porridge*? Comparisons are odorous [sic] and the jury is still out – but I can certainly say – without fear of contradiction, that the week spent with Ronnie and that splendid cast made upon me the most indelible of impressions. Ronnie, Richard, Fulton and Brian were perfect and we worked with an impeccable script. In Mr Williams I had the most interesting of parts.

'*Porridge* has always seemed to me to be underpinned with truth, subtlety and delicacy, and Sydney Lotterby was most clearly in tune with it all. I would love to have developed my character in other episodes, but Sydney later told me – unsolicited – that he had himself found the character fascinating, had tried to get hold of the writers (Dick Clement and Ian La Frenais) to suggest that they might like to extend Mr Williams's lease, but they were in America at the time and he failed to contact them. Nevertheless it was an experience just to be in this one episode, "Disturbing the Peace", and I know that whenever it still appears, it continues to provoke much laughter and is sheer enjoyment.'

SERIES THREE

MEMORIES

Colin Farrell (Norris in 'Happy Release')
Christopher Biggins (Lukewarm in the series)
Cyril Shaps (Jackdaw in 'The Harder They Fall')

SERIES THREE

EPISODE ONE: A STORM IN A TEACUP

1. FLETCHER'S CELL

Fletcher sits at the table reading a tatty paperback. He has a mug of tea. Warren walks in, eating an apple.

WARREN

What are you reading, Fletch?

FLETCHER

A book.

WARREN

No, I meant what sort of book?

FLETCHER

A paperback sort of book, lots of bits of paper all stuck together down the left-hand side.

WARREN

Is it a good book?

FLETCHER

I won't know that till I've finished it, will I? Which will be some time if I get these continual interruptions.

WARREN

I'd read books, if I could read.

Fletcher, for the first time, looks up, then looks back to his book.

WARREN

Is it a dirty book?

FLETCHER

Yes, filthy. Coming back from lunch, I dropped it in a puddle.

McLaren approaches.

MCLAREN

Reading a book, Fletch?

FLETCHER

No, I'm ironing.

McLaren peers over his shoulder, reading.

FLETCHER

Don't do that. Read over my shoulder. Can't stand that. Height of bad manners, that.

McLaren lowers his head to read cover.

MCLAREN

Mandingo . . . what's that about then?

FLETCHER

Curiously enough, it's about your lot. Slaves in the Deep South.

MCLAREN

Scots, are they?

FLETCHER

Blacks, sonny Jock, blacks. Your – ancestors. Toiling in the cotton fields.

MCLAREN

My ancestors are from the West Indies. Or at least half of them.

FLETCHER

All the same. Slaves an' that. This lot picked cotton. Your lot picked bananas. Comes down to the same difference. A load of blacks toiling in the fields under a boiling sun picking something.

WARREN

I thought slaves were in Roman times. In galleys, rowing like.

FLETCHER

Well yes, them, Warren, them was your galley slaves.

WARREN

But they was white. I know they was 'cause I've seen all them films. Set in Roman times. And they always had slaves in them. And Rosanna Podesta. Oh and Steve Reeves. Did you see Jason and the Golden Fleas?

FLETCHER

Jason and the Golden Fleece – fleece would be the word you had in mind, Warren – if you had a mind to have it in, that is.

WARREN

Oh what was that other one – I loved it at the time. Oh yes! Jason and the Astronauts.

MCLAREN

You dim nurk, Warren. You're thinking of Jason and the Juggernauts. I know that because . . .

FLETCHER

(*Interrupting*) Gawd! Listen Philip Jenkinson, if you'll excuse me I think this is where I came in. I remember it was that bit in the picture where Rod Steiger hit Sidney Poitier over the head with a cup of tea 'cos he wouldn't let him read (*Standing up*) his book in peace.

MCLAREN

(*Standing up*) Sorry, Fletch – we're just going.

FLETCHER

No, carry on – you might as well stay and see the shoot out at the end. With any luck, Jason there might get his argonauts blown off.

Fletcher leaves with his mug of tea and his book.

WARREN

That's funny. I didn't think they had guns then.

MCLAREN

When?

WARREN

In the days of Kirk Douglas.

2. ASSOCIATION AREA

Fletcher walks down the stairs with his book and his mug of tea. He goes to the table where Lukewarm is sitting. He looks at Lukewarm and then sits opposite him and starts to read.

LUKEWARM

Reading a book, Fletch?

FLETCHER

Oh gawd, don't you start. Just carry on with your balaclava, there might be another war. In fact, there will be if I don't finish this book.

He takes a sip of tea and puts the mug down.

MACKAY

(*Offscreen*) Harris!

Mackay walks up.

MACKAY

Stand where you are – stand still!

HARRIS

Me, Mr Mackay?

MACKAY

Yes, you. Don't move.

Lukewarm and Fletcher look up at Mackay.

MACKAY

You've been to the medical room.

HARRIS

Yes, sir. Just had me dressing changed like.

MACKAY

The orderly thinks you may have palmed some pills.

HARRIS

Not me, sir.

Mackay starts to search Harris. Fletcher looks up.

FLETCHER

Never a dull moment.

He takes a sip of tea, puts the mug down and goes back to reading. Mackay is still searching Harris who looks down.

Pills drop out of Harris's trouser leg and he kicks them over the edge. Pills drop down splashing Fletcher.

FLETCHER

Who did that?

LUKEWARM

Did what?

FLETCHER

Bleeding sparrows in our roof again? Anything on my face?

Mackay finishes searching Harris.

MACKAY

Come with me, Harris.

HARRIS

'Ere listen, I'm clean. You got no right. This is harassment.

MACKAY

(*Walking away*) I'll harass you, Harris – I'm going to strip you down.

LUKEWARM

Ooh, some girls have all the luck.

He turns away. Mackay looks for the voice. Then he indicates to Harris to come and marches him off.

LUKEWARM

He'd whip anything, him. Don't know what he wants with pills.

FLETCHER

(*Getting up as he speaks*) Oh come on. You know the racket in here. Always someone who wants to be picked up or zonked out. Inside same as outside, in' it? Can't see it meself. Not my cup of tea, drugs. *He walks off with his mug of tea and his book.*

3. CELL

Lennie is still in his chef's outfit, washing, when Fletcher enters, carrying his mug of tea and his book.

LENNIE

'Lo, Fletch.

FLETCHER

Oh, they've gone, have they?

LENNIE

Who?

FLETCHER

Warren and McLaren – the black and white minstrels.

LENNIE

Oh yeah. Hey, I did the lunches on my own today – did you like it?

FLETCHER

Tell me something – what was the name of that pudding?

LENNIE

Tapioca.

FLETCHER

Oh, tapioca was it?

He sits down.

FLETCHER

D'you think you could sneak a dollop back here?

LENNIE

P'raps. Liked it that much, did you?

FLETCHER

No, but I need something to stick down the sole of my shoe with.

LENNIE

I'll ignore that. Can't bait me. Tapioca off a duck's back.

Fletcher takes a sip of tea.

FLETCHER

Tea's cold now.

LENNIE

(*Crossing to his bunk*) Tapioca off za duck's back.

He laughs.

LENNIE

What was the kerfuffle? I heard Mackay nabbed Harris.

FLETCHER

Oh that. Thought he'd been pinching pills from the MO's.

LENNIE

(*Removing trousers*) Had he?

FLETCHER

Probably. Didn't find nothing. Must have stashed 'em.

LENNIE

Wonder where?

FLETCHER

Why?

LENNIE

Wouldn't mind them dropping into my hands. Windfall that.

FLETCHER

You don't even knows what they was.

LENNIE

Wouldn't matter to the blokes in here. Currency.

FLETCHER

Oh I see, you'd sell them, would you? You'd take on the might of genial Harry Grout.

Lennie thinks.

LENNIE

No, p'raps not. I'd have 'em myself.

FLETCHER

Drug addict!

LENNIE

Oh come on, Fletch. Your generation has a lot of prejudice about drugs. It's fear through ignorance.

FLETCHER

My generation's sensible enough to know that drugs don't do no one no good no how. They're anathema to me, they are.

LENNIE

There's even drugs for that.

FLETCHER

What?

LENNIE

Anathema.

FLETCHER

Anathema is an expression, not an ailment.

LENNIE

I know, I was only making a joke.

FLETCHER

Godber, you have used up your joke ration for the month with that tapioca pudding.

4. LANDING

Harris comes out of Mackay's office, thinking.
He climbs up stairs and walks along the landing.
Arm comes out from a cell and pulls him inside.

5. GROUT'S CELL

Crusher has pulled Harris into the cell and he swings him round to face Grouty, who is sitting in his chair with a tray on which are the remains of his lunch.

HARRIS

Oh, hello, Mr Grout, sir.

GROUT

Thank you, Crusher. Would you take the tray away.

CRUSHER

Yes, sir.

He picks up the tray and hands it to Spider.

SPIDER

Didn't you like your tapioca?

GROUT

Oh that's what it was.

SPIDER

Want me to open a box of those crystallised fruits?

GROUT

No, I mustn't.

Patting stomach.

SPIDER

Tins of mandarins then? They ain't fattening.

GROUT

I didn't know we had any.

SPIDER

We hadn't but young Tomkiss had a food parcel, didn't he, Crusher?

CRUSHER

(*Laughing*) Yeah . . .

GROUT

And he gave us some?

SPIDER

In a manner of speaking. I know you likes a mandarin.

GROUT

I'll have 'em for me tea. On your way.

Spider leaves, followed by Crusher. Grout crosses to the right of Harris, picks up a napkin ring and puts his napkin into it.

HARRIS

Mandarins eh – rare treat.

GROUT

Harris.

HARRIS

Yes, sir.

GROUT

What did Mackay just do to you?

HARRIS

Frisked me over.

GROUT

Why?

HARRIS

Dunno.

GROUT

Must have had a reason.

HARRIS

Oh well, he alleged I took some pills from the MO's.

GROUT

Had you?

HARRIS

'Course not.

GROUT

Dangerous things to do. Dangerous things, drugs. If they get taken injudiciously, they can be harmful. Leads to addiction. Seen it happen too often.

HARRIS

Oh I see. Well, that's a good reason for me not to whip pills, isn't it?

GROUT

Oh I agree.

HARRIS

I didn't honest.

GROUT

Harris, you're a born tea leaf. It's force of habit. Whip now – think later. That's your motto.

HARRIS

Honest – I only went in there to get me bandage changed.

GROUT

(*Moving closer*) I see. By the way, how is the arm?

HARRIS

Oh well. It's coming on quite nicely –

He screams as Grout pulls at the arm.

6. FLETCHER'S CELL

Fletcher is on the top bunk reading. Lennie is standing.
They are both startled by the scream.

LENNIE

What was that?

FLETCHER

I dunno. Someone's gone on hunger strike and they're force-feeding him your tapioca.

LENNIE

(*Going to the door*) No, but it was a terrible scream. Bloodcurdling.

FLETCHER

Probably one of your drug addict friends taking the cold chicken cure.

LENNIE

Cold turkey.

FLETCHER

Yeah, well they use chicken in here, don't they?

LENNIE

(*Returning to the bunk*)
You just don't understand, Fletch.
Fear through ignorance.

FLETCHER

(*Sitting up*) Listen, I'm not ignorant. I'm just more aware of the abuse than you seem to be. I've seen it happen. Saw some of my comrades in arms got addicted to morphine.

LENNIE

When was this?

FLETCHER

Comrades in arms. Wasn't in the launderette – when I was in the Army.

LENNIE

Why did they have morphine?

FLETCHER

To ease the pain of the gunshot wounds.

LENNIE

Where was you stationed, a rifle range?

FLETCHER

You're an impudent nurk, you are, Godber. While you were safely sleeping in your Smethwick crib, some of us was doing our bit for Queen and country. In the steaming Malayan jungle at the height of the terror.

LENNIE

You told me you was in the stores.

FLETCHER

In Kuala Lumpur.

LENNIE

There wasn't any fighting in Kuala Lumpur.

FLETCHER

There was in the stores. Anyway, I'm not talking about that. I'm talking about when I lay wounded in hospital.

LENNIE

You told me that an' all – four days with a septic toenail, wasn't it?

FLETCHER

(*Getting off his bunk*) Oh, it's easy for you, isn't it? Not being there in the heat of it. You heard that scream just now. When I was in hospital that would go on all night.

LENNIE

It's your own fault – you should have left the nurses alone, shouldn't you?

FLETCHER

Oh shut up. (*Looking at his mug*) I must wash this out.

He crosses to the washbasin. Grout walks in. Crusher stands in the doorway.

FLETCHER

Oh hello, Crusher – hello, Grouty.

GROUT

Hello, Fletch.

LENNIE

Hello, Grouty.

GROUT

Goodbye, Godber.

Lennie leaves. Crusher also leaves and shuts the door.

FLETCHER

What's up then, Grouty?

He puts the mug down on the table.

GROUT

Oh – I just er had a word with Harris.

FLETCHER

Oh, I heard you, yes.

GROUT

He whipped some pills.

FLETCHER

Comes as no surprise.

GROUT

Said that when Mackay frisked him, he dropped them over the landing.

FLETCHER

Really?

GROUT

Immediately under which there were only two people at the time.

FLETCHER

Yeah, that's right, me and Lukewarm.

GROUT

Well, Lukewarm wouldn't, would he – I mean anything for a quiet life, him. As long as he's got his knitting.

FLETCHER

Just a minute – wouldn't what?

GROUT

Take advantage.

He sits down.

FLETCHER

Take advantage?

GROUT

Of a windfall. Have a chair, Fletcher.

FLETCHER

Oh – thank you very much.

GROUT

See, this is the problem, Fletch. I want those pills back where they belong.

FLETCHER
In your pocket?
GROUT
Dear me no. In the MO's office.
FLETCHER
Oh I see. I didn't know you shared my views on the evils of drugs, Grouty.
GROUT
It's not that exactly. It's just that despicable pilfering of this nature could mess up my own pill-peddling operation.
FLETCHER
Oh I didn't know about that.
GROUT
(*Gets out a cigar*) Very few people do. That's one of its virtues. Now unless those pills are returned, Mackay is going to ask the MO to take an inventory to establish what's missing. And if that happens they're going to find that there's more pills missing than they ever imagined.
FLETCHER
Oh dear me, yes. Couldn't you replace them from stock?
GROUT
I haven't got any stock. I don't keep 'em. I peddle them.
FLETCHER
Yes, I see your point.
GROUT
Well then, we've got an hour.
FLETCHER
Oh, we've got an hour have we? Oh I see, yes.

GROUT
Yes. Fortunately tho MO's over in the married quarters for an hour or so lancing Mrs Barrowclough's boil.
FLETCHER
Now Grouty, you and me know each other. I give you my solemn word – you know it's sacrosanct – that I ain't got the pills.
GROUT
The point is you're one of the few people in this nick in a position to acquire some *more* pills.
FLETCHER
How?
GROUT
Come on! You work the admin block. The Governor, secretaries, typists. Doesn't matter what sort of pills they are. As long as they're back in the MO's office – then I'll get the word to Mackay it's taken care of.

FLETCHER
Yeah, well that will solve it. Even supposing I can do what you suggest – what am I looking for?
GROUT
Pills is pills, Fletch. Aspirin, allergy pills, slimming pills.

FLETCHER

Here – those typists are all on the pill.
They're all ravers over there.

GROUT

Now steady on Fletch, there are limits.
If you whip those and the MO issues
them to some poor bloke with
toothache, what then?

FLETCHER

Stop his teeth getting pregnant,
won't it.

He laughs. Grouty does not react.

FLETCHER

It's a serious matter, isn't it?
(*Looking away*) Well, I can't guarantee
anything, Grouty. But of course I'll do
the best I can.

GROUT

(*Rising*) I'm sure you will, Fletch.

*He walks to the door, then
turns back.*

GROUT

Oh, if there's any codeine while
you're there, get a couple for Harris.
Apparently his arm's playing him up.

He leaves. Fletcher is furious.
He gets up and goes to the window.

LENNIE

(*Entering*) What were that about?

FLETCHER

Grouty wants me to whip some
pills for him.

LENNIE

Why?

FLETCHER

To replace the pills Harris whipped.

LENNIE

Well, where are the pills Harris whipped?

FLETCHER

Precisely. Where are the peppers that
Peter Piper picked? If we knew that,
sonny Jim, there'd be no problem,
would there?

LENNIE

(*Sitting by the table*) Barrowclough
has pills.

FLETCHER

Does he?

LENNIE

All sorts. Nerve pills, indigestion pills.
And he's a vitamin freak. He takes so
many of 'em, I should think when he
makes love he rattles.

FLETCHER

Don't think he'll be having a rattle for
some time – apparently his old lady
has a boil.

He sits down.

LENNIE

Depends where the boil is.

FLETCHER

The boil is in a very nasty place.

LENNIE

Where?

FLETCHER

Married quarters.

LENNIE

Ooh, nasty.

FLETCHER

And what is more, it is being attended
to by the MO which Is why we've still
got fifty minutes.

LENNIE

We?

FLETCHER

Oh come on, Godber, you're
supposed to be my mate, aren't you?

LENNIE

I'm your mate,
Fletch. Always have
been, always will be
I hope.

FLETCHER

(*Rising*) Then help
me get some pills!

LENNIE

I would do but for one thing.

FLETCHER

What?

LENNIE

You told me not to have anything to do
with drugs.

*Fletcher raises his arm as if
to backhand Lennie, when
Barrowclough comes in.*

BARROWCLOUGH

Fletcher?

Fletcher freezes, arm still raised.

FLETCHER

What?

BARROWCLOUGH

Raised arms.

Fletcher looks round for one.

FLETCHER

Raised arm, sir – where?

BARROWCLOUGH

(*Pointing*) There.

Fletcher sees it.

FLETCHER

Oh that. That is not a raised arm, sir.
That is a flexed arm. It's me muscles –
can't clench, you see.

He demonstrates.

FLETCHER

Muscular stress. It's due to me nervous
condition. I wish I had something for
nerves. A pill or something.

BARROWCLOUGH

I have pills for my nerves.

FLETCHER

Really – what an unbelievable
coincidence! Are you telling me you
have something which can alleviate
the suffering?

BARROWCLOUGH

Well, I don't carry them around with me.

Fletcher lowers his arm immediately.

FLETCHER

Oh don't you. No, I noticed you
weren't rattling.

He sits down.

BARROWCLOUGH

They're prescribed, you see.
They're only mild tranquillisers,
but they help me cope with the
horrors of life.

FLETCHER

Yes. How is Mrs Barrowclough?

BARROWCLOUGH

Not too good, I'm afraid. As you know,
she's not the easiest of women to live
with at the best of times, but now that
she can't sit down . . .

FLETCHER

Oh, we thought that's where it was.

BARROWCLOUGH

What?

FLETCHER

The boil.

BARROWCLOUGH

How did you know about my wife's boil?

FLETCHER

Oh – it just leaked out.

BARROWCLOUGH

We're hoping a hot poultice will help.

FLETCHER

You want to slap a dollop of Godber's tapioca pudding on it. That would make her sit up and take notice.

BARROWCLOUGH

Oh, that's what it was.

LENNIE

I'd like to see you lot do any better.

FLETCHER

Well, of course, a lot of these blemishes is caused by lack of vitamins.

LENNIE

Oh, I don't think so. I think a boil's more to do with the bloodstream.

FLETCHER

Shut your face, Godber. When I want a second opinion I'll go to Harley Street.

BARROWCLOUGH

I've always been a great believer in vitamins. I think that's why I have such a good complexion.

FLETCHER

(*Standing up*) Yes, that's what I need you know. 'Cos my nerves is caused by vitamin deficiency. You haven't got any to spare, have you, Mr Barrowclough?

BARROWCLOUGH

I'll bring you some in the morning.

FLETCHER

Oh – too late then, don't bother.

BARROWCLOUGH

Well, it's never too late to improve your health.

FLETCHER

By tomorrow morning my health might be a lot worse. Got anything for broken kneecaps?

BARROWCLOUGH

I don't think I follow.

FLETCHER

I shan't be able to either with broken kneecaps.

LENNIE

(*Mumbling to himself*) I do me best with the ingredients provided. Chef said my raspberry blancmange was the finest he'd ever tasted.

They look at him.

FLETCHER

No seriously, Mr Barrowclough, the main problem with my nerves and my lack of vitamins is the terrible indigestion it brings on.

BARROWCLOUGH

Oh, really?

FLETCHER

Yes, terrible.

BARROWCLOUGH

Oh I can help you there.

He produces a packet of Alka-Seltzer from his pocket.

BARROWCLOUGH

Have you got a mug, or something?

He picks up Fletcher's mug and goes to the washbasin to rinse it when Fletcher interrupts him.

FLETCHER

(*Holding two tablets*) No, don't bother. They're too big.

BARROWCLOUGH

What on earth do you mean, too big?

FLETCHER

Oh well . . . I mean my condition's too chronic for anything as big as that. I even get indigestion if I eat Rennies too quickly.

BARROWCLOUGH

I must say you seem to be in pretty poor physical shape, Fletcher.

FLETCHER

Oh, I can put up with it. The thing that really gets me is the blinding headaches.

BARROWCLOUGH

(*Taking the tablets back*) Then I suggest you go on sick parade tomorrow. Get a couple of codeine from the MO.

He leaves. Fletcher follows him to the door.

FLETCHER

That was no flaming help, was it?

(*To Lennie*) And nor was you!

LENNIE

Not talking to you.

FLETCHER

Pardon?

LENNIE

Not talking to you.

FLETCHER

Just proved yourself wrong. Why do you think you aren't talking to me?

LENNIE

Had enough of your derogatory remarks about my culinary prowess.

FLETCHER

Has your culinary prowess got any relevance to the urgent matter at hand? No, it has not. When Grouty asks you a favour it is with the clear understanding that the favour will be done. If it isn't, he takes it as a personal affront and sends round his big henchmen to mete out retribution – from Crusher with love.

LENNIE

That'll solve your problem then – you'll end up in the hospital. No shortage of pills there.

Harris walks in.

HARRIS

'Lo, Fletch.

FLETCHER

You've got a bleeding nerve, Harris.

HARRIS

What?

FLETCHER
Showing your face round here.

HARRIS
Why?

FLETCHER
Cause of all the trouble, ain't you?

HARRIS
All right, all right I took 'em. But I
haven't got 'em now.

FLETCHER
Well, what are you doing here then?

HARRIS
I heard you'd got a bit of a problem.
You've got to find some pills and I
think I know where I can lay me hands
on some.

FLETCHER
(*Getting up*) Well flaming 'eck, Harris,
why didn't you tell Grouty this in the
first place?

HARRIS
Wouldn't dare. See, er . . . today
wasn't the first day I nicked some.
But I never knew about Grouty's
racket. And if he knew I'd taken
some before – ooh dear me –
too dire to contemplate, isn't it?

LENNIE
What sort of pills have you
been taking?

HARRIS
Anything. Always a market in here,
isn't there? Uppers, downers,
twisters, benders.

FLETCHER
Let me get this straight. What you're
saying is you've still got a previous
theft intact, have you?

HARRIS
Could be.

FLETCHER
So you give 'em to me, and I get
them to Grouty pretending I got
them elsewhere.

HARRIS
'Sright. I think it's a very noble gesture
on my part, don't you? Get us both
out the clarts, right?

FLETCHER
Yes, yes, very noble, Harris. Let's have
'em then.

HARRIS
No, no, hold your horses.

FLETCHER
What?

HARRIS
Depends, doesn't it?

FLETCHER
Depends on what?

HARRIS
How much?

FLETCHER
How much!!!

HARRIS
Fair do's. Give you a fair price an' all.

FLETCHER

Words fail me.

He walks to the window.

LENNIE

Has it occurred to you, Harris, that there's more at stake in life than a quick quid? Such as comradeship, honour, and chivalry?

HARRIS

No.

FLETCHER

Don't try to appeal to his better nature, son, 'cause he ain't got none. There's only one language the Harrises of this world understand and that's the one I intend to use in future negotiations.

HARRIS

What's that, Fletch?

Fletcher moves toward him.

HARRIS

No, no, Fletch . . .

7. LANDING

Several prisoners are in the association area.

Barrowclough is walking along the landing. As he passes two prisoners there is a loud scream.

Barrowclough looks around.

The prisoners do not react.

Barrowclough moves on.

8. GROUT'S CELL

Grout is on his own when there is a polite knock.

GROUT

Come in.

Fletcher enters.

GROUT

Oh, it's you, Fletch.

Fletcher puts a small packet in front of Grout.

FLETCHER

There you are, then.

GROUT

Already.

FLETCHER

Yeah, well, you said it was a matter of some urgency. But just for the record, those aren't the original pills. I did not steal them. I had to get those using all my ingenuity.

GROUT

(*Significantly*) Yes, I heard you.

FLETCHER

I just hope that this puts me at the bottom of your 'favours to be done by' list.

GROUT

Certainly, Fletch.

FLETCHER

What a lunch hour. Didn't even have time to finish my cup of tea. And now I've got to get back to work.

GROUT

(*Lying on the bed*) Yes, well, no peace for the wicked.

FLETCHER

Don't you have work to go to, Grouty?

GROUT

No, I'm on light duties, Fletch. They put me in charge of the swimming pool.

FLETCHER

That's nice, we ain't got one.

GROUT

I know.

FLETCHER

Oh – clerical error, was it?

GROUT

Something like that – which is why time hangs so heavy on my hands.

FLETCHER

Oh dear me. What a shame. Well I'd best be off then. Don't want to interrupt your boredom.

He walks towards the door.

FLETCHER

Aren't those crystallised fruits over there?

GROUT

Yes.

FLETCHER

My favourite them.

GROUT

Really, mine too. Pass them over will you?

Fletcher picks up the box. Grout has opened his pyjama case and is putting the pills inside.

GROUT

Any idea what these pills are?

FLETCHER

(*Walking to Grout*) Well, you said yourself a pill is a pill.

GROUT

No, but you got to be careful with drugs. These could be highly dangerous.

FLETCHER

Well – yes, yes – best be on the safe side. Try 'em out in the Governor's cup of tea.

Grout takes the box of fruits, but Fletcher, unnoticed holds back one fruit. When Grout is not looking, Fletcher puts it in his mouth and leaves.

9. FLETCHER'S CELL

Lennie is lying on Fletcher's top bunk, reading Fletcher's grubby paperback, when the master himself enters, not in the best of moods.

FLETCHER

What are you doing on my bunk, Godber?

LENNIE

More light up here.

FLETCHER

Yeah, to read *my* book by. Give it here.

He grabs it from him.

LENNIE

I only borrowed it.

He is swinging himself round on the bunk.

FLETCHER

Lost my place, in't you?

LENNIE

(*Getting off the bunk*) That's a good scene, that is. Where the plantation owner gets hold of the nubile young slave girl behind the cotton gin –

FLETCHER

Here, shut up, will you! I haven't got that far yet. Blimey, you got that far! You've had a hard afternoon, in't you?

LENNIE

I'm entitled. Up at four, me. No joke, you know, frying five hundred eggs at dawn.

FLETCHER

You want to make one vast omelette and let 'em get on with it. You could have tidied up a bit. I mean, look at this place. Haven't even washed the mugs out.

He swishes his tea into the sink, then reacts in surprise.

FLETCHER

'Ere, what's this?

LENNIE

What's what?

FLETCHER

Look.

He holds up a small packet of pills and moves to the table. Lennie joins him.

LENNIE

Where's that come from?

FLETCHER

It was in the tea.

LENNIE

Open it then, have a look.

FLETCHER

You know what these are, don't you? These are the original pills Harris got rid of. What are they?

LENNIE

(*Picks up two*) Can't be sure. Could be amphetamines. Or maybe Bennies.

FLETCHER

Whose?

LENNIE

Benzedrine. How did they get in your tea?

FLETCHER

They must have fallen from above.

LENNIE

Oh – Bennies from heaven.

FLETCHER

What?

LENNIE

Joke.

FLETCHER

Do me a favour.

LENNIE

It's funny though, isn't it? When you think of all the trouble you went to and they was under your nose all the time.

FLETCHER

Whole thing was a storm in a teacup.

LENNIE

What?

FLETCHER

Another joke. And better than yours.

MACKAY

(*Offscreen*) Move you men!

Fletcher puts his mug down.

FLETCHER

Mackay.

He crosses to the door.

LENNIE

(*Indicating pills*) Get rid of those.

Fletcher returns to the table.

LENNIE

He'll find 'em.

FLETCHER

Where?

MACKAY

(*Offscreen*) Don't lounge around the landing.

FLETCHER

Naffing hell.

LENNIE

Swallow them?

FLETCHER

Swallow them?

They grab some pills and start to swallow them.

Mackay looks in suspiciously.

MACKAY

What's wrong with you two?

FLETCHER

Nothing, Mr Mackay.

MACKAY

I can always tell when a man is acting suspiciously. Got something to hide.

He walks in.

MACKAY

Fletcher?

FLETCHER

No, sir.

Mackay goes over to Lennie.

MACKAY

Godber?

LENNIE

No, sir.

The container that held the pills appears to pass to Fletcher's hand. Mackay's head whips round. He points to Fletcher's hand.

MACKAY

All right, Fletcher.

He lifts Fletcher's right hand and taps it. Fletcher opens it but there are no pills in it. Mackay grabs the left hand which reveals the pills.

MACKAY

What's this?

FLETCHER

What's what?

MACKAY

I repeat what's this?

FLETCHER

Oh it's a thing, sir.

MACKAY

A thing that looks like a container for pills.

He opens it.

LENNIE

Just a couple, like – for Fletcher's . . .

FLETCHER/LENNIE

Nerves – indigestion.

FLETCHER/LENNIE

Indigestion – nerves.

FLETCHER

I gets the indigestion on account of my nerves, and visa versa.

MACKAY

Pills are a dirty word in this prison. Nearly caught Harris this morning.

FLETCHER

Oh well, a man like Harris, sir.

MACKAY

Since the doctor told me what was missing, I'd like to think the wretched fellow ate the whole lot of them.

Fletcher and Lennie exchange glances. Mackay walks away.

FLETCHER

'Scuse me, Mr Mackay. Out of idle curiosity – what was they then?

MACKAY

They were the MO's own pills. Well not exactly his . . . (*Crossing to Fletcher*)

They were for his spaniel's bad breath. Carry on.

He goes out. Fletcher and Lennie look at each other.

LENNIE

How d'you feel, Fletch?

FLETCHER

Rough . . . ruff.

SERIES THREE

EPISODE TWO: POETIC JUSTICE

1. LANDING

Harris and Lennie are carrying a bed, supervised by Barrowclough. They start to go upstairs.

LENNIE

Fletch won't like this you know, Mr Barrowclough.

HARRIS

He naffing won't. Didn't like you moving in here, never mind a third.

BARROWCLOUGH

Fletcher will have no choice in the matter. We're running a prison not a hotel. Prisons are very overcrowded this time of year.

LENNIE

Not surprising really. It's bitter out.

They walk along the landing and into Fletcher's cell with the bed, followed by Barrowclough.

BARROWCLOUGH

Take it in and lean it up against the wall.

Fletcher is crossing the bridge, singing.

FLETCHER

Some enchanted evening,
You may see a stranger . . .

VOICE

Shut up.

FLETCHER

Naff off!
You may see a stranger,
Across a crowded room . . .

He is making his way to his cell.

2. FLETCHER'S CELL

Fletcher walks in.

FLETCHER

Hello, what's this here?
A stranger in a crowded room.

BARROWCLOUGH

I'm just off, Fletcher.

FLETCHER

Oh no you're not.

BARROWCLOUGH

Pardon?

FLETCHER

What is that?

BARROWCLOUGH

What is what?

FLETCHER

That bed – what is it?

BARROWCLOUGH

It's a bed.

FLETCHER

What is that bed doing across my already overcrowded cell?

BARROWCLOUGH

Well . . .

FLETCHER

And why is Harris here? I hope there's no connection between that bed and 'orrible Harris.

HARRIS

'Ere, I only brung it 'ere.

FLETCHER

Oh good, then you can just brung it out again.

BARROWCLOUGH

Fletcher, an alarming rise in crime rates in this country has caused an extra burden on an already overworked penal system.

FLETCHER

Oh yes?

BARROWCLOUGH

That in turn has meant that prisons have had to stretch their already limited resources to try and accommodate the extra influx of convicted felons.

FLETCHER

Oh yes I see, of course.

BARROWCLOUGH

Well, as long as you appreciate our difficult position.

FLETCHER

I do yes. We've all got to make the best of a difficult situation. Now shift that bed out of here.

BARROWCLOUGH

Fletcher, a new arrival is moving in here and that's that, so you may as well accept it as a fait accompli.

He leaves. Fletcher crosses to the door.

HARRIS

I'll be off too then, Fletch. Bit crowded in here. I hope the three of you will be very happy.

FLETCHER

Naff off, Harris.

HARRIS

Naff off yourself, Fletch. With knobs on.

He leaves. Fletcher closes the door.

LENNIE

I'm afraid the whole rhythm of our lives is in some jeopardy, Fletch.

FLETCHER

Flaming outrage. Where's my shirt?

He goes to his bunk.

FLETCHER

What's the word then?

LENNIE

Well I had a word with Davey Greener who works in reception. He says there's three come in today. And one of them's a bit of a mystery. Name's Rawley. He was never documented.

FLETCHER

How d'you mean?

LENNIE

The screw just whipped him off some place. No documentation, no mug shots.

FLETCHER

Really?

LENNIE

I think they whipped him straight up to the Guvnor.

FLETCHER

Maybe he's a celebrity. Maybe a rock star on a drug bust and they took him off for a press conference.

LENNIE

He was no rock star. Kind of small and bald and flat-footed.

FLETCHER

Might be Elton John.

LENNIE

No, no, he walked like a pregnant duck.

FLETCHER

'Ere, 'ere, stop that.

LENNIE

Stop what?

FLETCHER

That. Drawing attention to people's physical peculiarities. I've noticed that about you recently. I was saying to Jacky, young people today are always taking the mick out of folk because they're too tall or too fat or walk with bow legs.

LENNIE

Who's Jacky?

FLETCHER

You know – bloke in the hobby shop. Fat guy with ears like jug handles.

3. GOVERNOR'S OFFICE

Prison Officer Collinson at the door.
Rawley walks in.

COLLINSON

All right, Rawley, step in front of the Governor. Stand still, straighten up. Rawley, sir.

GOVERNOR

Thank you, Mr Collinson, that will be all.

COLLINSON

Excuse me, sir – you want me to leave you alone? With a prisoner?

GOVERNOR

(*Standing up*) It will be all right I think in this case.

COLLINSON

If you say so, sir.

He leaves. They wait for him to go.

GOVERNOR
Steven . . .

RAWLEY
Hello, Geoffrey.

GOVERNOR
I thought we should have a little
chat before we document you.
But . . . what can I say?

RAWLEY
Perhaps the less said, the better.

GOVERNOR
Tragic . . . how's Marjorie taking
all of this? .

RAWLEY
As well as can be expected. And how
are you, Geoffrey?

GOVERNOR
Oh I'm all right.

RAWLEY
And – Muriel?

GOVERNOR
Busy as ever. She has her committees,
I have my prison.

Offers Rawley a cigarette.

RAWLEY
Haven't seen you both for such a
long time.

GOVERNOR
You must come round for dinner.
Oh no, of course, you won't be
able to. Silly me.

RAWLEY
Not unless my appeal comes
through, no.

GOVERNOR
This whole thing is most embarrassing
for me.

He sits down.

RAWLEY
It's a little worse than that for me.
The entire fabric of my life has collapsed.

GOVERNOR
Yes, but see it from my point of view.
We were at Winchester together.
In the Guards together. We're in
the same Club.

RAWLEY
We won't be for much longer – they've
asked for my resignation.

GOVERNOR
Nevertheless, our relationship is going
to create a bit of a problem.

RAWLEY
Is there any reason why people should
become aware of it?

GOVERNOR
Perhaps not. There isn't anyone from
the old school here, thank God.

RAWLEY
There's everything else though –
officers, Clubmen, Rotarians. In the
shower an embezzler came up to me
and gave me a Masonic handshake.

GOVERNOR

There you are, you see.

RAWLEY

I don't want to plead special treatment of course, but couldn't you separate me in a single cell with a few books?

GOVERNOR

Fatal. Can't have secrets in here. Cause speculation. Resentment. Best thing is to slip you into a cell with other men.

RAWLEY

But I'd be with a bunch of common criminals.

GOVERNOR

With due respect, Steven, since the verdict you are a common criminal.

There is a knock at the door.

GOVERNOR

Come in.

Mackay enters.

MACKAY

You sent for me, sir.

GOVERNOR

Ah Mr Mackay, I want to discuss a delicate situation with you. Please close the door.

Mackay shuts the door.

GOVERNOR

This is an old friend of mine, Steven Rawley, who will be with us for a while.

MACKAY

(*Shaking hands*) How do you do, sir? Will you be staying for lunch?

RAWLEY

If my appeal fails, I'll be staying for three years.

Mackay starts to laugh, then checks himself.

4. ASSOCIATION AREA

Fletcher is sitting at a table with Lennie, Warren and McLaren. Mackay walks through the gates with Rawley. Rawley is not in prison uniform.

LENNIE

Hey, that's him – the mystery man. Him with Mackay.

MACKAY

All right, you men. This is Rawley who's moving in with Fletcher and Godber. I don't know what you've heard about him already, but I want you to treat him just like any other prisoner – understand?

ALL

Yes, Mr Mackay.

MACKAY

Carry on.

He leaves.

RAWLEY

Good afternoon.

LENNIE

Afternoon. I'm Godber . . . you're in with us.

RAWLEY

Oh.

Fletcher has been staring at Rawley in amazement.

FLETCHER

God preserve us!

RAWLEY

I'm sorry?

LENNIE

Oh, this is Fletch. He's in with
us an' all.

RAWLEY

Really.

FLETCHER

You don't remember me, do you?

RAWLEY

Your face is vaguely familiar, but I
can't quite . . .

FLETCHER

Middlesex Assizes? Three years ago?

WARREN

Oh, did you two do a job together
or something?

FLETCHER

Do a job? He's the judge who bleeding
sent me here!

*Rawley peers at Fletcher anxiously.
The others stare at Rawley.*

FLETCHER

The Honourable Judge Steven Rawley!
In person! How are the mighty fallen!

RAWLEY

I'm sorry, I still don't recall you . . .

FLETCHER

Why should you? I am merely one of
a thousand faces who come before
you, while you weigh our lives in the
balance of what you call justice!

RAWLEY

(*Instantly*) It's Fletcher, isn't it?

FLETCHER

Oh, you remember now?

RAWLEY

I remember your rhetoric. I remember
your endless protestations of innocence.

FLETCHER

Which you were deaf to.

LENNIE

But you were guilty, Fletch. You've told
us that.

FLETCHER

That is beside the point, Godber.

RAWLEY

It did seem relevant when
I passed sentence.

FLETCHER

The point is the man was not fit
to sentence me, as his presence
here indicates.

WARREN

He's still a judge. Or he were at
the time.

MCLAREN

Yeah, but obviously a bent one.
When you're sent up it's one thing
knowing it's by an upright pillar of
society. But Fletcher's been sent
down by a fellow con.

FLETCHER

Thank you, Jock. He is the same as
me. How d'you think I feel being sent
down by a crook like me?

LENNIE

A judge inside!

MCLAREN

What d'they bust you for then?

RAWLEY
Bust?

MCLAREN
What were the charges against you?

RAWLEY
I was indicted on three counts for corruption at common law – party to a criminal conspiracy; forgery of legal documents under the Forgery Acts of 1913–48; and accepting an illicit –

FLETCHER
(*Joining in with Rawley*) – payment as an officer of the crown.

FLETCHER
That's bribery and corruption, don't camouflage it behind that legal mumbo jumbo.

RAWLEY
I have no wish to camouflage anything. As I instructed my counsel, 'Let light be shed on this whole sorry affair. Let's bring it out into the open, let there be no half truths or evasions.'

LENNIE
Well, that's refreshingly honest. So you're saying you're guilty then.

RAWLEY
I refuse to discuss the matter, pending my appeal.

MCLAREN
You're bound to get off. Old school tie, top lawyers.

RAWLEY
If they were that good, I'd be out on bail now.

FLETCHER
Listen, it's a token stretch. Most of what you call us common folk never get the chance of bail. Some blokes are inside for months pending appeal.

LENNIE
The same law sent him down what sent us down, Fletcher.

FLETCHER
What are you saying, Godber?

LENNIE
What I'm saying is, I think his presence here is very reassuring. It's a vindication of our legal system. It proves that no one is beyond the reach of the law.

FLETCHER
I just ask myself for every one of his kind they nobble, how many's getting away with it? The bloke who sent him up is probably worse than he is.

MCLAREN
Hear, hear!

FLETCHER
Why, do you know him?

RAWLEY
(*Making an emotional appeal*)
Don't you think I have a conscience? Can you imagine what it's been like, to live a lie'?

FLETCHER

'Course we can, we're criminals.
does it all the time.

Barrowclough walks in.

BARROWCLOUGH

(*Approaching the table*) How are you
lads improving the sunshine hour?

*Rawley stands, pauses, then sits
down again.*

FLETCHER

We was just getting acquainted with
our learned friend.

BARROWCLOUGH

Oh you know who he is then?

FLETCHER

We met professionally, so to speak.

BARROWCLOUGH

I see. Well you men must treat Rawley
no different from any other prisoner.

MCLAREN

We will if you will.

BARROWCLOUGH

What's that supposed to
mean, McLaren?

MCLAREN

Dinna show no favours.

BARROWCLOUGH

Rawley will get no favours from me.
Whatever you were before, you're just
a number now. A statistic. A set of
fingerprints. A mug shot, like the
rest of these men. You'll pay your
dues the same way they do – is
that understood?

RAWLEY

Yes.

BARROWCLOUGH

Yes, what?

LENNIE

(*Prompting*) Yes, Mr Barrowclough.

RAWLEY

Yes, Mr Barrowclough.

BARROWCLOUGH

That's better. Now we must see about
getting you a job. Could you come this
way please, your honour.

*The others react as Barrowclough
leads Rawley away.*

5. CELL

*It is night time. Lennie is in his
pyjamas and is making up Rawley's
bed when Fletcher comes in from
the showers.*

FLETCHER

What are you doing, Godber?

LENNIE

Oh, just making his bed up.
He couldn't do it himself.

FLETCHER

Well, I suggest you let him bleeding
learn. Either that, or roll your trousers
up and wear a little frilly apron.

LENNIE

Oh come on Fletch, go easy on him.
He's lonely, he's afraid. Just like I was,
me first night.

FLETCHER

He's the enemy within. Within my cell, what's more.

LENNIE

No, he ain't, Fletch. He *was* a judge. But now he's a con like the rest of us.

FLETCHER

Don't you believe it. He's the establishment, he is. And I don't fancy the establishment breathing down my neck all day and all night. I mean you must admit it's a bit unusual, Godber.

LENNIE

What is?

FLETCHER

Well, when a judge sentences you to five years, you don't expect him to come in with you.

Rawley comes in, having just returned from the showers.

RAWLEY

Oh you've made my bed up, Godber, that's most kind.

FLETCHER

Ovaltine or Horlicks, is it?

RAWLEY

Excuse me?

FLETCHER

And what colour do you want your brown shoes polished?

LENNIE

Leave it off, Fletch.

FLETCHER

Where you been – having a nightcap with the Chief Warders?

RAWLEY

Look, I have no influence in here. If I had I'd be in a single cell with a few books instead of sharing with people like . . .

FLETCHER

Go on say it, people (*Crossing to the table*) like us, say it. Listen, let me tell you something about people like us. We don't make no alibis. We deserve to be here. But compared to you lot, there's something very honest about our dishonesty. Some people like us had no way of getting things, except to take them. People like you, you had it all, but you wanted more.

LENNIE

Look, he's a criminal now. Are you saying that right is only open to the poor? Don't you think the rich have a right to be criminals as well?

FLETCHER

They better not try it. The unions will be on to them straight away.

LENNIE

Don't be stupid.

FLETCHER

I'm not being stupid. You're being stupid.

LENNIE

I'm not being stupid.

FLETCHER

Well one of us is being stupid.

FLETCHER/LENNIE TOGETHER

Well, it's not me.

LENNIE

I'm just annoyed 'cause you're so inconsistent, Fletch.

FLETCHER

I'm not inconsistent.

LENNIE

Don't start that again. You are, you're inconsistent in your attitude. Inside is not out there. Inside's another world it is. We're all equal. We only have one enemy, that's the screws. And we only have one purpose in life, that's screwing the system.

RAWLEY

(*Sitting down on the bed*) Godber is right. I know we've always been on opposite sides of the fence. You're the sort of people I'd normally cross the street to avoid. But the fence is down now.

FLETCHER

I still think the gulf between us is immeasurably wide. I mean him and me, and most of the lads in here, we come from the same background, ran the same streets. They're a little different from your streets. Your streets have rich kids riding round on bicycles waving tennis racquets. Rows of elm trees and hand-carved privet hedges. Don't have no problems on your streets.

RAWLEY

Yes we do. I had to spend fifteen hundred pounds last year on Dutch Elm disease.

FLETCHER

Yeah? And I bet you went to a private doctor with it though, didn't you?

RAWLEY

Look, I know you're bound to feel cynical, I understand your attitude, but we all have one thing in common – we're in trouble.

LENNIE

He's right, Fletch.

FLETCHER

I'm just clearing the air, letting you know my feelings.

RAWLEY

I shall do my best to be as unobtrusive as possible.

FLETCHER

Unobtrusive, I see yes. Well get yourself a hammock then.

He crosses to the bunk.

FLETCHER

Shift your barrow.

Lennie moves. Fletcher climbs on to the top bunk.

LENNIE

He's a miserable old scroat. Listen, rules of the house. Top bunk's his. Seniority, like. No one reads the paper till he's through with it. It's best to speak only when spoken to, and his is the toothpaste with the marked tube.

RAWLEY

I have my own toilet requisites.

FLETCHER

Just as well.

LENNIE

Never borrow anything of Fletcher's without express permission

FLETCHER

I am not mean, Godber, if that's what you're saying. It's just that I never give anybody anything. What one has one keeps.

LENNIE

Oh come on, Fletch. You are mean.

FLETCHER

No, I'm not. Thrifty perhaps. Frugal.

LENNIE

He unwraps Bounty Bars under water so I can't hear he's got one.

RAWLEY

I'll be only too willing to share any of the few things they've allowed me.

FLETCHER

Bribery and corruption, he's at it again!

RAWLEY

I only meant . . .

FLETCHER

Just get yourself to bye-byes, Judge Jeffreys.

RAWLEY

Well, let me say that whatever rules you make, I will go along with them.

LENNIE

Oh we're very democratic in here – Fletcher decides and we agree.

6. LANDING

Camera shows Prison Officers locking up.

6A. CELL

It is night time. Fletcher is on the top bunk. Lennie is lying on his bunk. Rawley is sitting reading in his bed. A Prison Officer looks in and closes and locks the door.

LENNIE

(*To Rawley*) Want some snout?

RAWLEY

Oh I don't, thank you. Only very occasionally.

LENNIE

Currency in here, snout.

RAWLEY

Really?

He looks very depressed.

LENNIE

You all right?

RAWLEY

Since that door slammed shut, I've realised what prison is all about.

LENNIE

I know the feeling. This is my first stretch, you know. But stir's a state of mind and survival's in your own head. His Highness taught me that. (*Jerking a thumb upwards to Fletcher*) It's only the first twelve months that are the worst . . . ha, ha, ha . . .

He registers that his joke has gone down like a lead balloon.

LENNIE

. . . Sorry.

RAWLEY

Don't feel sorry for me.

LENNIE

Oh, but I do. I mean, you've had so much more to lose than the rest of us. Position, respect. It's the classic story of a man who had it all and blew it all away in a moment of weakness.

FLETCHER

This is life, not *Peyton Place*.

RAWLEY

My weakness was a younger woman. An avaricious, grasping nineteen-year-old go-go dancer.

LENNIE

Oh, the younger woman, yes, typical.

RAWLEY

Yes, one sees it happen so many times to colleagues. What is it, some middle-aged madness that affects us all? She was a sweet young thing when I first met her. Then over the years she demanded more and more. Trinkets, trips abroad, a car, a maisonette in South Kensington.

FLETCHER

I was wrong, this is *Peyton Place*.

LENNIE

How did you meet her?

The lights go out.

RAWLEY

Oh.

LENNIE

Half-past ten.

Rawley looks at his watch.

LENNIE

How did you meet her?

RAWLEY

At our regional reunion.

FLETCHER

Oh, nice. She was in your regiment, was she?

RAWLEY

She was part of the cabaret. She was assisting a magician called the Great Alfredo. While he was making cockatoos disappear, my eyes never left Sandra's long shapely legs.

LENNIE

Long and shapely, were they?

FLETCHER

Look, where are those legs now? One glimpse of a young thigh through a fishnet stocking and look at you.

LENNIE

Well, human weakness takes many forms. Desire, greed, lust – we're all here for different reasons, aren't we?

FLETCHER

With respect, Godber, we're all here for the same reason – we got caught.

7. LANDING

Barrowclough is on the upper landing.

BARROWCLOUGH

B 3–76 all correct.

MACKAY

B 3 unlock.

A Prison Officer is in the association area.

PO

B 1–83 all correct.

MACKAY

B 1 unlock.

A Prison Officer is on the landing by the stairs.

PO

B 2–96 all correct.

MACKAY

B 2 unlock.

Barrowclough and the two Prison Officers are opening up.

7A. CELL

It is morning. Fletcher is brushing his teeth. He looks at the range of toiletries on the judge's table.

FLETCHER

You can tell we have the upper echelons in here. Have you seen these toiletries? Mustang talc for men, Rave D'Amour shaving cream by Jean Marie of Paris, and exhibit C, a badger's hair shaving brush. My God, no wonder you never see a badger these days.

LENNIE

(*Cleaning teeth*) Nocturnal animal, the badger.

FLETCHER

Pardon, Godber?

LENNIE

Nocturnal. Only comes out at night.

FLETCHER

'Course they do. They've learnt their lesson, haven't they? If they comes out during the day, people keep making shaving brushes out of them.

RAWLEY

You're more than welcome to use any of my things.

FLETCHER

No, thank you. And you better not, if you know what's good for you.

RAWLEY

Why?

FLETCHER

Any idea what effect Mustang will have on the fairies in here? They'd all come up from the bottom of the garden.

The door is unlocked and Mackay walks in.

MACKAY

Good morning, Rawley. How did you sleep?

FLETCHER

(*Poking his head round the door*) Oh listen to this. Oh dear! All this time I been inside, you never asked me how I slept.

MACKAY

I know how you sleep, Fletcher.
You sleep soundly because you have
no conscience, no shame, no guilt.

FLETCHER

True.

He returns to the washbasin.

RAWLEY

All the things which explain my
sleepless night.

MACKAY

You'll have the weekend to settle in.
Saturday today, you will stop work
at noon. Then the rest of the day
is your own.

LENNIE

I'll take you to the football match
if you like.

RAWLEY

I'm quite prepared to work on. Help kill
time, that sort of thing.

FLETCHER

'Ere – if you wants to be one of
us now, you knocks off when we
knocks off.

MACKAY

Typical prison mentality.

FLETCHER

No. Just a working-class mentality.

MACKAY

You see yourself as working
class, Fletcher?

FLETCHER

I always used to. Till I went to
Glasgow one time. Then I realised
I was middle class.

MACKAY

Fletcher!

RAWLEY

All I meant was I rather enjoyed the
work you assigned me to.

FLETCHER

'Course you do. Central Records.
Privilege, that is.

MACKAY

No, it's not, Fletcher.

FLETCHER

You'll have to admit it's one of the
cushiest numbers in this nick.

MACKAY

That's perfectly true, but that does not
mean it's a privilege.

FLETCHER

No, but which would you rather do,
Mackay? Central Records or Latrine
duty? Can't sit and read the paper in
there, can you? Well you can, but it
gets very repetitive. 'Now wash your
hands, now wash your hands, now
wash your hands.' One day inside,
he scores a job must trusties don't get.

MACKAY

He's an educated man. Isn't it logical
we should give him a job which
requires a clerical aptitude?

FLETCHER

If you don't mind my saying, so,
Mr Mackay, leave it off. Since when
has logic had anything to do with
job allocation round here? Who was
making our raspberry blancmange in
the canteen yesterday? Riggs – and
he's in here for poisoning.

LENNIE

Is he really?

FLETCHER

Certainly. Cause célèbre he was in
his home town of Newcastle-under-
Lyme. In fact, all his in-laws are under
lime now.

LENNIE

Is that why they call him Arsenic Riggs?

FLETCHER

No, that's 'cos he once sat on a razor
blade, you nurk.

LENNIE

He didn't, did he?

FLETCHER

Oh God preserve us.

MACKAY

I'm sorry, Rawley, that you're forced to
share a cell with riff-raff.

RAWLEY

No, they've been most kind
and considerate.

MACKAY

I hope so. Because I'm aware of the
situation, Fletcher, between you and
ex-Justice Rawley. But there will
be no malice. No vindictiveness.
No grudges borne from bitter memory.

FLETCHER

Grudge? How could I bear a grudge?
What has this man ever done to me –
except rob me of five years of my life.

8. ASSOCIATION AREA/LANDING

*Camera shows a dartboard and
a prisoner about to throw a dart,
when Rawley enters the cell block.
Rawley looks around and then
moves along the landing.
Harris tries to block his way.
Rawley tries to get past him.
He attempts to go upstairs but
the way is blocked by another
hefty prisoner.
Finally Rawley manages to get to
his cell and goes in. Fletcher is
at the table reading. He looks
up at Rawley.
McLaren, Harris and the other
prisoner follow Rawley into the cell.
Fletcher shuts his book, picks it up
as he stands up and leaves.*

9. ANOTHER CELL

*A prisoner is sitting on a bed
as Rawley comes in followed
by McLaren, Harris and the
other prisoner.*

RAWLEY

Good afternoon.

McLaren shoves the prisoner out of his cell.

RAWLEY

Seems rather quiet.

He turns to face McLaren.

MCLAREN

Oh it is. (*Taking Rawley's mug*) Everyone's at a game or visiting their loved ones. That's why we chose this moment.

RAWLEY

Moment for what?

HARRIS

Lots of blokes in here got something to settle with you. Blokes with long memories and even longer stretches.

MCLAREN

Doing you a good turn. Get it over with all at once.

He nods to the prisoner who closes the door.

MCLAREN

Then you won't have to live your life with one eye cocked over your left shoulder wondering when it's going to happen. 'Cause it's going to happen now.

Rawley tries to get up but is pushed back.

MCLAREN

Dinna fret looking for screws, there's not one in sight.

HARRIS

What do you think we are, naffing amateurs?

Rawley stands and struggles to go. Fletcher enters.

FLETCHER

Hello, hello, what's this? *Gunfight at the OK Corral*, is it?

MCLAREN

Fletcher, he's got it coming. Now you'd be the prime suspect, so we're doing you a favour. Get yourself across the yard and out of harm's way.

FLETCHER

Are you about to inflict damage on my cellmate?

HARRIS

On your what?

FLETCHER

On my cellmate. The bloke with which I share a cell.

MCLAREN

He's no friend of yours.

FLETCHER

He don't have to be a friend. But he's one of us now, and we looks after our own, don't we?

MCLAREN

What are you saying, Fletch?

FLETCHER

I'm saying if you takes him on, you takes me on an' all. Don't be misled by this bulky torso. It conceals a man of steel. On your way, Judge.

RAWLEY

On my way where?

FLETCHER

Out the yard. Go and watch the football, you need the fresh air.

Rawley pauses.

FLETCHER

Don't worry, the word'll go round. No one will touch a hair of your head.

Rawley goes.

HARRIS

Naffin 'ell, is that it?

MCLAREN

If Fletch says so, that's it. But I'd love to know why. What are you doing siding with the establishment?

FLETCHER

You knows me better than that. It's just that I uses my head. (*Holding book up*) What's this?

HARRIS

What's what?

FLETCHER

No, not what's what – *Who's Who*. I been looking up Rawley. Cross-referenced with our dear Governor. D'you know what – they only went to the same school, only went in the same regiment, belong to the same Club. They're lifelong bleedin' oppoes, those two.

HARRIS

That makes it worse!

FLETCHER

Does it? Do we quench our appetite for blood, or do we agree that what this cell block has always lacked, is a lifelong friend of the Governor? Think about it.

He drops book on Harris's toe.

10. LANDING

The Prison Officers are locking up.

10A. CELL

It is night time. Lennie Is on his bunk. Rawley is sitting in his bed. Fletcher gives Rawley a mug of tea.

RAWLEY

Thank you.

FLETCHER

Comfy, your honour? Want another pillow?

He walks over to Lennie's bunk and takes his pillow. He goes back to Rawley's bed.

RAWLEY

(*Propping pillow under him*) Oh, thank you.

FLETCHER

Extra blanket?

RAWLEY

No, thank you, I'm warm enough.

LENNIE

If you're scared of the cockroaches, we can take turns watching out for them.

RAWLEY

You're most kind. And let me say again, Fletcher, how much I appreciate what you did for me.

FLETCHER

A man in here has a right to prove himself.

LENNIE

Here – I said that first.

FLETCHER

Yeah. Well, it's hardly original, is it?

RAWLEY

You more than anyone, Fletcher, had every right to despise me.

FLETCHER

No point in that, your worship. No, let's just sit here and reminisce about happier times. Tell us about you and the Governor for example. That should while away a few hours.

RAWLEY

Myself and the Governor?

FLETCHER

Yes, well didn't I hear something somewhere that you once knew each other, was it?

He offers a biscuit.

RAWLEY

(*Taking biscuit*) Known each other for years.

LENNIE

Really, what a coincidence.

RAWLEY

I hope this doesn't explain your change of attitude, Fletcher.

FLETCHER

What?

RAWLEY

I trust you're not hoping to profit from my past relationship with Geo . . . the Governor. Because I must warn you that anything I know about him is in the strictest confidence.

FLETCHER

Oh, is it?

(He gets up and removes the pillow).

FLETCHER

I'll have me pillow back then.

He throws the pillow at Lennie and starts undressing.

RAWLEY

Fletcher. I am grateful. I do appreciate what you did for me today.

FLETCHER

Not all that grateful obviously.

RAWLEY

Shake?

FLETCHER

What?

RAWLEY

Shake.

FLETCHER

Shake what?

RAWLEY

Hands. No hard feelings, that sort
of thing.

FLETCHER

Why should I have any hard feelings?
You're only the bloke that put me
in here.

RAWLEY

Fletcher, I had no choice.

FLETCHER

'Course you did. Several. Could have
rejected the jury's verdict. Ordered a
retrial. Given me a suspended
sentence. Bound me over.

RAWLEY

Not in the face of the evidence.

LENNIE

And not with your record, Fletch.

FLETCHER

I suppose so.

LENNIE

You were guilty – you said so yourself.

FLETCHER

Yes, you're right. And seeing him in
here has made me realise what a big
mistake I made. My one regret is that
I didn't know then what I know now.

RAWLEY

Oh, that's reassuring.

FLETCHER

What is?

RAWLEY

Remorse.

FLETCHER

Remorse! It's nothing to do with
remorse! It's just that if I'd known you
was crooked I could have slipped you
a few bob!

SERIES THREE

EPISODE THREE: ROUGH JUSTICE

1. FLETCHER'S CELL
Fletcher is writing a letter.
Warren comes in tentatively.

FLETCHER
What d'you want, Warren?

WARREN
How did you know it was me?

FLETCHER
Rear-view mirror. What d'you want?

WARREN
I need a letter written. Home, like.

FLETCHER
Warren, how long you been inside?

WARREN
Nigh on ten months now.

FLETCHER
Don't you think you could have taken advantage of the educational facilities and got rid of your illiteracy?

WARREN
I'm not illiterate, Fletch.

FLETCHER
Forgive me, I thought that was the word what described someone who can't read or write.

WARREN
I'm not illiterate. I suffer from dyslexia.
Fletcher looks puzzled.

WARREN
You don't know what it means,
do you?

FLETCHER
Dyslexia? Well, it's obviously some sort of acid stomach, isn't it? Though why that should stop you reading or writing, I can't imagine.

WARREN
You're wrong. Dyslexia is word blindness, like. I can't make out words when they're written down. They all get jumbled up in my head.

FLETCHER
Yeah, well there's plenty of room, ain't there?

WARREN
Tragic really. If they'd diagnosed it when I were a lad, I wouldn't be in here now.

FLETCHER

Oh here we go. The customary alibi.
The hard luck story.

WARREN

It's true in my case. I had a real
tough break. You see, I couldn't
read the sign.

FLETCHER

What sign was this?

WARREN

The one that said, 'Warning –
Burglar Alarm'.

Fletcher laughs.

FLETCHER

Pardon my laughing. That's much the
same excuse as Charlie Gill – he's that
burglar in B Wing.

WARREN

How?

FLETCHER

He's deaf, he didn't hear the dog.

WARREN

I didn't know he were short of hearing.

FLETCHER

That ain't all he's short of since that
Airedale got him.

WARREN

I'll come back later I think.

FLETCHER

No, hang about.

He walks over to Warren.

FLETCHER

I'll do it for you. Usual rates. Half a
snout a page.

WARREN

No, I weren't going to ask you.

FLETCHER

What?

WARREN

I were going to ask your new celly,
Judge Rawley.

FLETCHER

Why?

WARREN

Take advantage, like. He's a judge.
Educated man. Oxford. Public school.

FLETCHER

Oh I see – suddenly bowled over
by his worship's academic pedigree,
you've dispensed with my literary
services, have you?

WARREN

No offence, like. I just thought he has
to be the best person for the job.

FLETCHER

Here – letter writing is an art. A gift.
What sort of love letter is he going to
write? 'My dear Elaine, I am in receipt
of your letter of the 6th inst., wherebeit
I, the undersigned, hereforward to be
referred to as the third party, etc. etc.'
What do you want to do, woo her or
sue her?

WARREN

Well, I just thought –

FLETCHER

You just thought wrong as usual.
Letter writing is a creative art,
endowed to a few of us. I mean,
how many of you nurks in here have
my poetic turn of phrase? For example,
here's what I'm writing to my nearest
and dearest – just read that. Oh you
can't, can you, I'll read it. (*Reading*)
'My Darling, Though we have been
driven apart by cruel fate, and an
inexcusable misdirection of a jury by a
biased judge, who is now sharing a cell
with me, I know that our love transcends
these grey, grim walls that have driven
us apart. You are with me in my heart
and this knowledge helps me to wring
a few drops of comfort from the limp,
damp towel of life. Kiss the baby for
me, your own Norman . . .'

WARREN

Oh yes, that's beautiful, Fletch.

FLETCHER

Yeah, well.

WARREN

I'm sorry, Fletch. Will you do a letter
for me? When you've got a moment?

FLETCHER

When I've got a moment, yes. But first
I've got to finish this, get it sent off.
Then after that I've got to write to
the wife.

*He goes back to the table and sits
down. Rawley comes in.*

RAWLEY

Oh, good afternoon, Warren.

WARREN

Oh, hello, Judge – your Honour.

He bows.

FLETCHER

Don't call him that. Don't smarm up
to him. He is not a judge. He is a
former judge, an ex-judge. He has
been de-benched. De-wigged.

WARREN

He's pending appeal, and you
never know . . .

RAWLEY

Oh, Warren, that matter you raised
with me in the canteen. I'll give it a
little thought and speak to you about
it later.

WARREN

Oh thank you, Judge. See you, Fletch.

He goes.

FLETCHER

Oh – has he been raising things in the
canteen again? What little matter was
this then?

RAWLEY

Oh, just a legal matter.
Something to do with his sister's
tenancy of her council house.

FLETCHER

Oh, I see. Setting up shop, are we?

RAWLEY

Excuse me?

FLETCHER

Judge Rawley, QC, is now open
for business. What you charging then?

RAWLEY

I'm not charging anything.

FLETCHER

Well, that's daft to start with. If you have any expertise in here which is in demand, then it's saleable. Rule of the house. It's expected. And any philanthropic notions will be taken as a sign of weakness.

RAWLEY

Oh, I didn't realise . . .

FLETCHER

No, well, you ain't got the acumen. I'll work out your fees, we'll split 'em fifty-fifty.

RAWLEY

I have no intention . . .

FLETCHER

You will do.

RAWLEY

I will not.

FLETCHER

Early days. We could clean up. I mean, there's six hundred blokes in here, all of whom has a legal gripe of one sort of another. We do have an ex-solicitor across the block, but he only knows about mortgages and there's not a lot of call for that in here. One thing we are sure of is that we're always gonna have a roof over our head – albeit with a few slates missing here and there. I tell you where we could score heavy. All the poofs in here are getting a movement together. You know, 'Equal Rights for Homosexuals'. You're the perfect man to represent them. Queen's Counsel, ain't you?

RAWLEY

I am not hawking my legal expertise to the highest bidder.

FLETCHER

No need to. I do the hawking. You just dispense.

RAWLEY

Out of the question. I would be mad to engage in anything of that nature, until I hear the result of my appeal. Within a month I could be back on the bench. One has to preserve some sort of integrity.

FLETCHER

Oh integrity is it? I love your high moral tone, despite the disgrace you've wrought on your profession. Do get it into your head, you're now inside. Another world. It's a jungle in here. And you just happen to be fortunate enough to be sharing a cage with King Kong.

2. LANDING

Harris walks along the landing. He goes past two prisoners who sniff the air as he walks by.

2A. CELL

Lennie is making a model aeroplane. He looks up, sniffing the air. Harris walks in.

LENNIE

Is that you?

HARRIS

Me what?

LENNIE

That pong.

HARRIS

There's a reason for this pong.

LENNIE

Well I hope so, Harris. Is it curable?

HARRIS

They've moved me back on the naffing farm, haven't they?

LENNIE

Nice job, farm. Lots of exercise. Fresh air.

HARRIS

Fresh air? I'm swilling out the flaming pigs. You know why, don't you?

LENNIE

Well, they try to fit people into their most appropriate function. You and pigs, that makes sense.

HARRIS

Watch your lip, Godber.

LENNIE

(*Tries to watch lip*) Can't see it from here.

HARRIS

I'll tell you why I'm on the farm. 'Cause they've been rejigging jobs round here. To accommodate your naffing VIP.

LENNIE

Judge Rawley?

HARRIS

That's him. And he only went straight into a clerk's job. Trusty's by right.

LENNIE

Has its advantages though, the farm. Don't you get outside trips, like?

HARRIS

Oh yes. Only today I went for a trip in the back of a pig truck that hadn't been cleaned for three weeks, slipping about inside. We picked up six new pigs and clipped back just in time for supper.

LENNIE

Couldn't you have had a bath?

HARRIS

This is what I smell like after a bath. Oh and I'm forgetting the highlight of the day – I caught a glimpse of a woman.

LENNIE

A female woman, really? What was she like?

HARRIS

Well, porridge does strange things to a man. It's the first time I've been turned on by a fifteen-stone pig breeder.

Fletcher and Warren walk in.

FLETCHER

What are you on, Harris?

HARRIS

Social call.

FLETCHER

(*Sniffing*) Dear me, what's that smell?

HARRIS

Put me back on the pig farm, didn't they?

FLETCHER

Yeah. I heard the pigs held a protest march. Least it takes away the smell of Godber's aeroplane glue.

WARREN

I quite like the smell, Harris. Reminds me of home.

FLETCHER

Born on a farm, was you?

WARREN

No.

Fletcher looks at Warren and shakes his head.

FLETCHER

Clear off, Harris, go on. It's beginning to smell like a Turkish restaurant on a Monday morning in here.

HARRIS

If this cell stinks, it's because of His Worship. Don't know how you stomach a bloke like that.

FLETCHER

We know what we can stomach. Naff off, Harris.

HARRIS

We'll have him you know. In the end we'll have him.

He leaves.

FLETCHER

Charmless nurk!

LENNIE

Hey, has he whipped my Aerofix? (*Searching for it*) Oh no, here it is.

FLETCHER

You're always leaving that around, Godber. I come back last week from the shower and sat on it unbenknownst. I had to be prised out me underpants – talk about a stiff upper lip.

WARREN

Come on then, Fletch, let's have me letter.

FLETCHER

Let's see the snout first, then.

Warren gives him a cigarette.

FLETCHER

Cor – who rolls yours? Twiggy?

He walks across to get an envelope from under his pillow.

WARREN

Is it good?

FLETCHER

Fantastic, my son.

WARREN

Long as Elaine will like it.

FLETCHER

Without question. You see, last night on the box they was showing an old Rita Hayworth film. *Fire Down Below* it was called. Which is exactly what your Elaine will feel when she reads this.

LENNIE
Let's have a look.

*Warren walks over to give Lennie
the letter.*

WARREN
Will you read it for me, please?

LENNIE
Who was Rita Hayworth?

FLETCHER
(*Sitting on the bed*) Gawd, Godber,
you are ignorant.

LENNIE
No, I'm just young.

FLETCHER
Well, you missed out, my son.
Your generation – what have you got?
Television – Joan Bakewell and Janet
Street Porter.

LENNIE
No, since the Olympics,
my sexual fantasies are mostly
East European gymnasts.

FLETCHER
I'm talking about women, my son.
Your Rhonda Flemings, your Virginia
Mayos. And at the top of that glorious
pile of pulchritude was always . . .
my Rita.

LENNIE
(*Peering at the letter*) Your favourite,
was she?

FLETCHER
Still is.

LENNIE
Is that why you've put Dear Rita
instead of Elaine?

FLETCHER
I haven't, have I? Give it to me.

He takes the letter.

FLETCHER
Where's me pen?

*He gets the pen and changes
the letter.*

WARREN
'Ere, that's not going to look too nice.
She'll think I've got a Rita on me mind.
She'll get jealous.

FLETCHER
Not now she won't.

He sits down next to Warren.

FLETCHER
I've crossed it out and put Errol Flynn.
Do you want me to read it to you?

WARREN
Yes, please.

FLETCHER
Dear Errol Flynn –

*They all laugh. Rawley comes in
carrying a towel and washing things.*

RAWLEY
Fletch – oh good evening, Warren.

WARREN
Good evening.

RAWLEY
Fletch, I just bumped into that
middle-aged Teddy Boy – what's
his name?

LENNIE

Harris.

RAWLEY

Yes, very abusive.

FLETCHER

Don't you worry about Harris. He's all wind and water. You know what he's in for, don't you? Snatching an old-age pensioner's handbag.

WARREN

He never!

FLETCHER

At least he tried to. She pinned him down till the cops arrived. She kept hitting him over the head with the handbag.

WARREN

And that subdued him?

FLETCHER

Not half – it had a brick in it. She was just on her way to do a smash and grab.

WARREN

Oh blimey.

RAWLEY

Well, he was most abusive.

FLETCHER

Take no notice of Harris.

RAWLEY

But he threatened me.

LENNIE

Don't you worry, your Honour. If anyone comes on strong, you know we'll always back you up.

FLETCHER

Yeah, we'll see you all right.

RAWLEY

You already have. And I would like to say how grateful I am to you. You men have every right to despise me. Especially you, Fletch, since I sent you here in the first place. But you have shown me only kindness and compassion. I feel a bond with you men – I know it has been forged in adversity, but I think it will remain with me for the rest of my life.

FLETCHER

'Ere leave it off, Judge. Go on like this, you're going to make us forget our scruples and start liking you.

RAWLEY

No, I mean this. Who'd have thought a few months ago that I could so much as talk to you? Now I find that I respect – more than that – I trust you.

LENNIE

You mean that?

RAWLEY

Most sincerely.

He turns to pick up the towel.
His expression changes.

RAWLEY

Just a moment.

There is a pause.

RAWLEY

Which one of you stole my watch?

FLETCHER

You what?

RAWLEY

My watch. It was there when I went to the showers, it's not there now.

LENNIE

'Ere – hold your horses.
What's happened to this most
sincere trust you felt for us?

RAWLEY

That was before one of you
stole my watch.

FLETCHER

(*Standing up*) We don't rip each
other off. We're mates, oppoes.
We have a code.

RAWLEY

But I'm still an outsider.

FLETCHER

That's true. Give him his watch, Len.

LENNIE

That's not funny, Fletch. I'm no
petty sneak thief. Give him his
watch, Warren.

WARREN

Pardon? I haven't got his naffing
watch. I only come in here for me
letter, which I haven't had read yet.

LENNIE

See what you've done, Judge. Stirred
up mistrust among people who trust
each other implicitly. Go on, Fletch,
give him his watch.

FLETCHER

(*Waving the letter*) Talk to me like that,
Godber! You watch it, my son, or I'll
darken your outlook.

WARREN

(*Snatching the letter*) Don't scrunch it.

RAWLEY

I'm sorry, I'm sorry. I was being
stupidly hasty. One should never make
accusations without firm evidence.

WARREN

Never bothered the law in my
home town.

FLETCHER

What's that supposed to mean?

RAWLEY

But I swear to you, my watch was
there when I went to take my shower.

FLETCHER

Harris. Harris – how long was he here
before I came in?

LENNIE

Long enough. He could have palmed it
when I was glueing this aileron on.

WARREN

Come on then. (*Starting to go*) Let's
gerr'after that nurk.

FLETCHER

Hold on, hold on, you know the crafty
git will have stashed it by now.
*A bell rings. It is the prelude to
lock-up.*

LENNIE

Lock-up. Timed his exit well an' all.
Can't go nowhere now.

WARREN

I'll have to be off home, Fletch.
Should I not say nowt?

FLETCHER

Yeah, shtum, Warren. Me and
Judge will have words regarding
the possibility of further procedure.

3. PRISON

*It is night time. Prison Officers are
on their rounds.*

3A. CELL

*It is night time. Rawley and Lennie
are in bed. Fletcher is standing by
the window.*

RAWLEY

We cannot take the law into our own
hands. I shall report the theft to the
proper channels.

FLETCHER

Listen, we ain't going to set upon
Harris. We're going to conduct a
civilised investigation. We're all familiar
with the working of the law, and we're
fortunate in this instance to have a
guest Judge.

RAWLEY

What?

FLETCHER

Yes, one thing is certain, you do knows
your law.

RAWLEY

You mean, you want me to preside at
a hearing?

FLETCHER

At a trial, my son.

RAWLEY

But do we have
enough to go on?

LENNIE

Yes. Harris's reputation.

RAWLEY

I know he's objectionable, but is
he a known thief?

FLETCHER

You should know better than to ask
questions like that. We might tell you
things which would prejudice your
impartiality, know what I mean.
He gets up on his bunk.

LENNIE

Innocent till proven guilty, like.

RAWLEY

Of course, of course. Least I know
about Harris the better.

FLETCHER

'Sright. Why should you want to
know about him? A despicable
nurk like that what would sell his
Granny's Wintergreen.
He sees Rawley's look of dismay.

FLETCHER

Oh sorry, let that be stricken from the
record, your Honour.

LENNIE

Are you going to prosecute, Fletch?

FLETCHER

Certainly. Should be interesting, see
the other side of the fence, like.

RAWLEY

But do you know enough about
legal procedure?

FLETCHER

Been up enough, ain't I? Look, when
you chooses your living breaking the
law, it pays to know the laws you're
breaking. And I've had enough first-
hand experience with counsels.
Clever men, most of them. Although my
last one weren't too bright, as my
presence in this nick indicates.

RAWLEY

As the presiding Judge at your trial,
Fletcher, I thought your counsel argued
eloquently against – impossible odds.
Lennie laughs.

FLETCHER

(*Lifting up the mattress*) Godber!
Listen, my counsel, Spence, that's him,
he was a loser going in. And I ain't
referring to the evidence. I'm talking
about his attitude. He sent me this
letter when I was on remand in Brixton.
Listen I'll read it to you 'cos I kept it.
He gets it off the top of his cupboard.

FLETCHER

And you know what the pompous git
says – I couldn't believe it. This was
written to me while I was on remand in
Brixton. 'Dear Mr Fletcher – '

LENNIE

It's good this.

FLETCHER

'I should like you to know that myself
and my staff shall dispose ourselves
with the utmost vigour and dedication
in refuting the charges against you.
Investigators will pursue a tenacious
enquiry into unearthing evidence and
testimony. Researchers will work into
the night assembling and collating the
facts at our disposal, on which I shall
marshal a defence which has left no
stone unturned, no avenue unexplored
and which will culminate in your
honourable and justifiable release.
In the meantime, please proceed
with your escape plan.'

4. BOILER ROOM

*A table and chairs have been
positioned to make a court room.*

RAWLEY

This is most irregular, I cannot
say I'm happy about these
proceedings, Fletcher.

FLETCHER

Yeah, well happiness is relative, isn't it?
I mean this is nick, who's happy –
know what I mean?

WARREN

Hey up – here comes the accused.
He moves down the stairs.

FLETCHER

Under escort, is he?

WARREN
Yeah. Black Jock's got him in a half-nelson.

FLETCHER
All right your Honour, sit down. Court is convened.

A protesting Harris is propelled in by McLaren.

HARRIS
Here, here, what's going on then? You got no flaming right . . .

FLETCHER
Silence in court.

HARRIS
You what?

FLETCHER
Listen, Harris, we are here to pursue the course of justice and find you guilty.

RAWLEY
Fletcher, please. None of us heard that. Well, if we did it's stricken from our minds.

HARRIS
What is?

MCLAREN
The fact that you're guilty.

HARRIS
Guilty – guilty of what? Now listen, I'm . . .

FLETCHER
No you listen, Harris – shut up. A watch has disappeared from our flowery dell and you are the prime suspect.

HARRIS
Why me?

FLETCHER
Because otherwise it's us three and we're above suspicion. Right?

HARRIS
No, it's not flaming right.

MCLAREN
Shut up.

RAWLEY
I must protest these –

FLETCHER
Just stay out of this for the moment, your Honour, d'you mind? Thank you. Now, Harris, let me put your mind at rest. You shall get a fair trial. We have a qualified Judge with a long though slightly blemished record. We have an eye-witness.

HARRIS
Who?

LENNIE
Me.

FLETCHER
And I am going to prosecute you. But to ensure absolute fair play, you will be defended.

HARRIS
Oh.

FLETCHER
By Warren.

HARRIS
By Warren!

WARREN
What's wrong with that?

HARRIS

He's flaming
illiterate, he is.

MCLAREN

Shut up.

HARRIS

Naffing hell –
doesn't a man have a right to speak?

MCLAREN

In your case, only when spoken to.

FLETCHER

If you're innocent, Harris, what you in
such a state about, then?

HARRIS

Wouldn't you get into a state if Warren
was defending you?

WARREN

Here, Harris, I didn't volunteer for
this job, I don't like you.

HARRIS

(*To Rawley*) Do you hear this, do you
hear this?

FLETCHER

It's all right, Harris, he don't have to
like you to defend you. You think any
of our counsels liked us?

LENNIE

That's a good point, that is.

FLETCHER

Right, Harris, how do you plead . . .?

RAWLEY

Excuse me, Fletcher.

FLETCHER

What?

RAWLEY

Excuse me . . .

FLETCHER

Oh yes, be my guest.

RAWLEY

All right then, Harris, how do you
plead? Guilty or Not Guilty?

HARRIS

Not Guilty.

FLETCHER

I see – a liar as well as a thief.

WARREN

(*Rising*) Objection.

RAWLEY

All right then, Warren, go on. What is
your objection?

WARREN

Er – I don't know.

He sits down again.

HARRIS

Flaming heck. You were objecting
to the fact that I was called a liar
and a thief!

WARREN

No, I wasn't. We all know you're a liar
and a thief, Harris.

RAWLEY

That remark will be struck from
the record.

FLETCHER

This is all getting out of hand. I'd like
to call my first and only witness,
Leonard Arthur Godber. Take the
stand, would you please.

Lennie moves forward.

LENNIE

I swear to tell the truth, the whole . . .

FLETCHER

Never mind all that, we've got about ten minutes before the screws tumble us. Just tell us about the events of last night, Mr Godber.

LENNIE

Well Mr Rawley took his watch off prior to going to the showers. At the time I was in our cell utilising my spare time in a constructive manner, i.e. making a model of a Flying Fortress.

RAWLEY

(*Writing*) Not so fast, Mr Godber.

Lennie looks at Fletcher.

FLETCHER

Hurry up, then.

LENNIE

Harris come in. Then Mr Fletcher and the defending counsel entered the room telling the accused to naff off.

HARRIS

Which I did.

LENNIE

Which he promptly did. Shortly afterwards the watch was found not to be there and has not been seen since.

RAWLEY

Counsel for the Defence – that's you, Warren.

Warren looks.

RAWLEY

Do you wish to cross-examine this witness.

WARREN

Pardon?

RAWLEY

Do you wish to ask him any questions?

WARREN

No, I were there, I know what happened.

Lennie goes back and sits down.

HARRIS

Flamin' heck – they're all in it together – this isn't justice.

MCLAREN

I've warned you.

RAWLEY

Let him speak. He has that right.

HARRIS

Thank you, Judge. Now you know as well as me that this is a mockery. They all know that this is flaming hearsay. No one can prove nowt. Like where's your evidence?

McLaren drags Harris back.

RAWLEY

Please, please. I have to agree with him. One man's word against another does not constitute legal evidence. This case would not stand up in a court of law, upon which these proceedings are supposedly modelling themselves. In the absence of evidence, there is no prima facie case and I am forced to dismiss the accused.

HARRIS

Thank you, your Honour.

FLETCHER

Now hang about, Judge – whose side are you on?

RAWLEY

I'm sorry, Fletcher, you insisted on a proper enquiry.

MCLAREN

Judge – your Honour – would a signed confession help?

RAWLEY

Do we have one?

MCLAREN

I could soon get one.

HARRIS

He's threatening me.

RAWLEY

Please, please, I must protest.

FLETCHER

You've had your go, Judge, it's best you stay out of this, know what I mean? McLaren, please. Now then, Harris, we don't want no unpleasantness. So wherever you stashed the watch, go git it out. All right? If you traded it, go trade it back. We just wants that watch back. If not, the consequences to your good self are too dire to contemplate.

HARRIS

Have I definitely been found Not Guilty?

FLETCHER

Yes.

HARRIS

All right – I'll go and get it.

He hurries off.

FLETCHER

See what I mean?

5. CELL

It is night time. Lennie is putting the finishing touches to his model when Fletcher comes in.

FLETCHER

Aye, aye.

LENNIE

Evening, Fletch. Look, almost finished.

FLETCHER

Oh yes, very good. How you going to get it in the bottle then?

LENNIE

Going to hang it on the ceiling. When I was a kid I had planes all over me bedroom. Me dad made them – from the war, like. Hurricanes, Spitfires, Messerschmitts. That's how I know what shape a Flying Fortress was. Me dad told me.

FLETCHER

Pity he didn't tell you about what shape Rita Hayworth and Rhonda Fleming was an' all.

LENNIE

No, he didn't talk much about women.

FLETCHER

Didn't he? Was he all right your dad? Not one of them, was he?

LENNIE

My dad – he didn't know they existed in them days.

FLETCHER

Oh yes. Your poofter just wasn't so blatant then. In my father's day they used to horsewhip them, you know. Now they've become fashionable. What worries me is they might make it compulsory.

LENNIE

Hey, seen the Judge?

FLETCHER

No, but I heard he had a call to see the Governor.

LENNIE

What'll that be about?

FLETCHER

Have to ask him, won't we?

LENNIE

Here, you don't think he'll blow the gaff do you? About our Kangaroo court?

FLETCHER

Nah. He's learned we takes care of our own. He'll respect that.

LENNIE

Specially since Harris gave him his watch back.

Rawley walks in.

RAWLEY

Hello, Fletch – Lennie.

LENNIE

Hello, your Honour.

RAWLEY

I'm glad you're both here because I want to thank you, and tell you that I now realise a lot of what you say is true. There are grave abuses of justice. There is often one law for the poor and oppressed, and another law for the rich and powerful. And the poor usually suffer while the rich get off with clever lawyers. I shall remember that lesson when I leave here.

FLETCHER

Which won't be for some time though, will it?

RAWLEY

Oh no. I'm going out tonight.

LENNIE

You're what – going out?

RAWLEY

Yes.

FLETCHER

Your appeal came through?

RAWLEY

Certainly. I'm rich and powerful. I have clever lawyers.

He goes. Fletcher and Lennie react. Fletcher sits on the table.

6. PRISON LANDING

Barrowclough comes out of Fletcher's cell followed by two prisoners carrying a bed.
As they walk along the landing they pass Judge Rawley, now in civilian clothes.
Barrowclough stops and says goodbye to him.
The Judge then moves along the landing. He looks down to the association area and sees Fletcher.
He turns and starts to go downstairs.

6A. ASSOCIATION AREA

It is night time.
The prisoners are reading and
playing cards, including Fletcher,
Lennie, Warren and McLaren.
The chatter fades away as
Rawley approaches. He is now
accompanied by Mackay.

MACKAY

All right, you men! Fletcher, Godber –
the Governor has kindly allowed
Mr Rawley to bid you a fond farewell.

FLETCHER

Oh, it's Mister now, is it?

MACKAY

Certainly. If the appeal court judges say
his nose is clean, that's good enough
for me. They are, after all, men of the
highest integrity, in the land.

FLETCHER

What are you talking about? He's *one*
of them!

MACKAY

Precisely. And he's innocent.
Which proves my point.

FLETCHER

(*Confused – thinks*) Just a minute.

LENNIE

Get out of that. You can't, can you?
Fletcher glares at him, defeated.

MACKAY

(*To Rawley*) As brief as possible,
if you wouldn't mind my laud –
the van is waiting.
He moves away from the group.

RAWLEY

(*A little uncomfortable, clears his*
throat) Er, gentlemen, it's just that I
wanted to say goodbye – and to thank
you once more; and to promise you
something. Whatever I can do to
improve the system, I shall do. This has
been a frightening experience for me
. . . but thanks to you men, a
rewarding one.
There is a moment's silence.
Their attitude is not clear.

FLETCHER

(*Gets up and shakes hands*) Listen,
you got a break. No one holds that
against anybody.
There is a murmur of agreement
with Fletcher's sentiments.
Lennie and Warren shake
Rawley's hand. Others give him
a clap on the shoulder and make
'no hard feelings' sounds.

LENNIE

(*Shaking hands*) You behave yourself
now. Don't want to see you back,
do we?

RAWLEY

Thank you, thank you . . .
He shakes hands with Warren and
McLaren.

RAWLEY

Bunny . . . Jock . . . Oh,
one more thing. Fletcher I'd
like you to have this.
He offers his watch.

FLETCHER

No, I don't want your watch. No need for that. 'Sides, only reason they allow watches in this nick is to remind us how slowly the time passes.

RAWLEY

But perhaps you could trade it. It's valuable.

FLETCHER

(*Taking it*) Oh, ta very much then.

He sits down.

MACKAY

(*Adopting the tone he reserves for visitors*) Time's up, Mr Rawley – mustn't keep the van-driver waiting, must we? He'll be wanting his tea.

RAWLEY

Once again then, goodbye . . . my friends.

He turns to leave.

LENNIE

Here, Judge. When we get out, we'll come and look you up.

FLETCHER

Yeah, talk about old times, re-establish our friendship, meet your family . . . Bring our wives round to meet *your* wife.

There is a chorus of agreement from the lads.

RAWLEY

(*His face registering the awful truth*) You will? Oh. That will be . . . awfully nice . . .

He goes.

MCLAREN

Off he goes – free as a bird.

FLETCHER

And free to go and find himself a bird, an' all.

LENNIE

While we remain behind to carry on vegetating.

FLETCHER

True, Lennie, true. But I like to think we've all learnt a little from his visit, albeit short. I think we may all have gained something as a result.

LENNIE

You have – you've gained his wristwatch.

WARREN

Needn't have bothered with that trial. Waste of time.

FLETCHER

Not in my case, Bunny. As Lennie so rightly remarks, in my case I have gained time – in the shape of this genuine gold-plated, fourteen-jewelled gents wristwatch, in full working . . . just a minute.

He rattles it to his ear. Then, with a deft movement, opens the back to the watch.

FLETCHER

Where's that Harris, I'll murder him – it's got no bleeding works in it.

He gets up and throws the watch.

SERIES THREE

EPISODE FOUR: PARDON ME

1. ASSOCIATION AREA

Prisoners are sitting at tables, reading, playing cards, etc. Fletcher and Blanco are playing Monopoly. Fletcher has just rolled the dice and picks up a 'Chance' card. He laughs . . .

FLETCHER

Would you Adam and Eve it – 'Go to Jail, Go directly to Jail. Do not pass go, do not collect . . .'

BLANCO

(Putting card at the bottom of pile) I know the flaming words. Just get on with it.

FLETCHER

All right, all right, then.

BLANCO

I could recite every card on the whole flaming board if I wanted. Been playing every day for donkey's years.

FLETCHER

(Giving him the shaker) No need to be so grumpy though, Blanco, is there? Go on, your toss.

Blanco tosses and makes his move.

FLETCHER

Four and three. Seven.

BLANCO

I know, I can count. I may be old but I've still got all my faculties.

He accidentally, on purpose, flicks a hotel on to the floor.

BLANCO

Oh, I've lost a hotel – reach me it, will you, Fletch?

FLETCHER

Leave it off, Blanco. I mean, none of us was born yesterday. I know that ploy of old.

BLANCO

Ploy?

FLETCHER

While I'm down there picking up your hotel you help yourself. I lose Bond Street and Kings Cross in the process.

BLANCO

That's a lie. Listen, Fletch, I'm not like

you lot. You take cheating as a way
of life. But I'm an older man with an
older man's sense of values, and if you
don't give a rats about my sciatic
nerve, I'll get the hotel meself!

FLETCHER

Hey, hey, hang on. I'm sorry, Blanco,
honest, I'm sorry. You're right, we're all
so corrupt in here, we forget there's
the odd honest soul.

BLANCO

Yes, you do.

FLETCHER

I'll find it for you.

*He bends down to look for
the hotel.*

*Blanco adds two more
properties to his street.*

FLETCHER

I don't see it.

BLANCO

Oh look, it's only there.

*He bends down to retrieve
the hotel from beneath his feet.
Fletcher swiftly helps himself to
some more money from the bank.
Blanco straightens up.*

BLANCO

Now, let's have no more talk of
cheating, let's just get on
with the game.

FLETCHER

Right, my son.

BLANCO

Your toss.

Fletcher throws.

FLETCHER

Odd number – three. I'm staying
in the nick.

BLANCO

My go.

FLETCHER

Come on then, seven and you'll land
on my hotels.

Blanco throws.

BLANCO

Ten! Missed you.

*With glee he moves on to 'Chance'.
Fletcher eyes Barrowclough
approaching.*

FLETCHER

Watch it, watch it, Barra.

*Blanco turns to look. Fatally, as
Fletcher takes a 'Chance' card from
his pocket and puts it on top of the
pack. Blanco turns back and goes
to pick up the card.*

FLETCHER

No, no, that's your Raquel Welch –
Community Chest. Come on, get on
with it, this one's the Chance pile.
Pick up your card.

Blanco does so.

BLANCO

'Go back three spaces.'

*Fletcher counts back, moving
Blanco's piece on to Vine Street.*

FLETCHER

Oh dear, one, two, three – that's Vine Street with hotels. Ten hundred pounds.

BLANCO

What!?

FLETCHER

Ten hundred pounds, but I'll accept one thousand pounds, thank you very much.

BLANCO

Oh, me back.

FLETCHER

Never mind your back, just give us the money.

Barrowclough approaches Lennie who is sitting reading.

BARROWCLOUGH

Are they still playing?

LENNIE

Four days now. Could make the *Guinness Book of Records*.

BARROWCLOUGH

They're cheating each other into a stalemate, that's why.

He walks across to Blanco.

BARROWCLOUGH

All right, you two. I think it's well nigh time you wrapped up this marathon. Lock-up in five minutes.

LENNIE

There's other people in here would like to use that board. You do tend to monopolise that game. Gerrit?

BARROWCLOUGH

What? Oh I see, yes, very witty, Godber.

LENNIE

I thought so.

BARROWCLOUGH

Very sharp.

LENNIE

Quick as a flash, really. Do you know what's brown, lives in the ocean and attacks young mermaids?

BARROWCLOUGH

No, I can't say I do, Godber.

LENNIE

Jack the Kipper.

FLETCHER

Do you hear this? Palace of Varieties, isn't it?

BARROWCLOUGH

(*Thinking*) Jack the Kipper . . .

He resumes his round.

FLETCHER

Come on then, we'd better write all this down.

He and Blanco start wrapping up the game, making a plan of where they have got to. Lukewarm approaches them.

LUKEWARM

Oh, here you are. Now come on, you're a very naughty old person. You promised me you were going to wash your work shirt – so you'd look presentable for the Parole Board.

BLANCO

I'm going to, aren't I? In a minute.

FLETCHER

Come off it, Lukewarm. Seventeen-year stretch, you think the Parole Board's going to be swayed by a clean shirt? It's his clean record that counts.

LUKEWARM

Silly to jeopardise it for the sake of a drop of soap and water though, isn't it?

BLANCO

Look, I've got two on Piccadilly.

He turns to Lukewarm.

BLANCO

I'll come in a minute.

LUKEWARM

See you do. I'm going to get the tea now. I've got your mug.

He leaves.

BLANCO

Worse than me daughter, nagging.

FLETCHER

I though he was your daughter.

BLANCO

Still, he does keep the cell spotless.

FLETCHER

Well, you soon won't have to worry about that. You're on your way out, ain't you?

BLANCO

No – nothing's certain. Nothing's definite.

FLETCHER

'Course it is. A doddle. A mere formality. Even Mr Barrowclough would bet on that, and you know how middle of the road he is on every flaming issue. If you ask for a yes or no, he says, 'It depends what you mean by yes or no.'

BARROWCLOUGH

What was that, Fletcher?

FLETCHER

I was saying, sir, you are unwilling to commit yourself on issues. Like to hedge your bets, sit on the fence, know what I mean?

BARROWCLOUGH

I do not. I'm as positive in my opinions as the next man!

FLETCHER

Oh well then, you'd agree Old Blanco's release is a formality this time round?

BARROWCLOUGH

Oh . . . well, I wouldn't like to say. I mean, one has to consider both sides.

FLETCHER

Oh – you sure you're not sure, are you?

BARROWCLOUGH

Oh positive.

He goes.

FLETCHER

Naffin' heck.

LENNIE

It's a disgrace he hasn't been free and clear years before now.

FLETCHER

You're on your way, Pop. Even genial Harry Grout's giving odds on.

BLANCO

I won't bank on nowt, Fletch.
Too accustomed to disappointment.

FLETCHER

You know what your trouble's been? Always insisting you was innocent. You see that's where you make your mistake. For the Parole Board, it's better to be guilty and ashamed than innocent and defiant.

BLANCO

That's true. You have to show them how you've reformed.

FLETCHER

Right. In other words, you have to prove you've changed. That you ain't as despicable as what you once was. That's why parole's a piece of cake if you once was an alcoholic or a junkie, or dressed up in women's clothes.

LENNIE

So what about a bloke like me who only had the one lapse into petty crime. Who otherwise came from a decent home and had an 'O' Level in geography. What are my chances?

FLETCHER

I think your best bet is to buy yourself a cocktail dress and matching handbag. Naff all!

2. PRISON

It is night time. Prison Officers are on the prowl.

2A. FLETCHER'S CELL

It is night time. Fletcher and Lennie are lying in their beds.

LENNIE

Fletch?

FLETCHER

Huh?

LENNIE

Fletcher, do you think Blanco's a cert for parole this time?

FLETCHER

Need the beds, don't they?

LENNIE

What was he originally sent up for?

FLETCHER

Now, son, been inside long enough to know you don't ask that. Take people for what they are, not what they was.

LENNIE

I know that, Fletch, but come on.

Nothing you could say about Blanco
would put me off the old boy. He's one
of the nicest human beings in here.
He's kind and gentle and helpful.
Don't make no difference to me
what he's done.

FLETCHER
He done his wife.

LENNIE
What?

FLETCHER
Done her in. Locked her in a
deep freeze.

LENNIE
And we knock around with a
bloodthirsty old scroat like that?

FLETCHER
See! That's why you don't ask.

LENNIE
I'm sorry, I'm sorry. That was an
irrational outburst. Any roads . . . long
time ago, wasn't it?

FLETCHER
Oh you mean it's okay to refrigerate
your old lady as long as it's way back
in 1959?

LENNIE
I mean, he's obviously changed.
Had time to repent, like.

FLETCHER
The point is that he's never repented.
Always claimed he never done it.
Said she had a lover, and that it
was the lover who killed her.

LENNIE
And was it?

FLETCHER
It's very probable 'cos he disappeared
very smartish – he never hung around
long enough to be asked.

LENNIE
'Spose there's no way of ever knowing
now. So long ago.

FLETCHER
Right. And a wife can't testify against
her old man, so there's no point calling
on the wonders of modern science.

LENNIE
How do you mean?

FLETCHER
No point defrosting her and asking
what really happened. Cor it's like an
icebox in here.

3. CELL
*Fletcher is sitting at the table doing
a crossword. Lennie enters.*

LENNIE
Here.

FLETCHER
What?

LENNIE
Know summat you don't for once.

FLETCHER
That'll be the day.
*Lennie looks over Fletcher's
right shoulder.*

LENNIE

Well, I know thirteen across for a start.

FLETCHER

(*Irritably*) Look, Godber, if you wouldn't mind. Height of bad manners, that is.

LENNIE

Anyhow, it's Rook. 'Type of Bird'. R blank blank K. Rook.

FLETCHER

Not necessarily.

LENNIE

R blank blank K! What else could it be but Rook?

FLETCHER

It could just be – Rilk.

LENNIE

Rilk?

FLETCHER

Yes, Rilk.

LENNIE

No such bird.

FLETCHER

That is where you are wrong. See, Godber, you're not as smart as you thought you was.

LENNIE

What's a flaming Rilk, then?

FLETCHER

The Rilk is a migratory bird from the Baltic shores of North Finland. Its most distinguishable feature is that it flies backwards to keep the snow out of its eyes . . . ask me another, Magnus?

LENNIE

I bet it's Rook.

FLETCHER

Too obvious, Rook. Look it's R I L K – Rilk. So what's this piece of knowledge you're aching to tell me?

LENNIE

Oh yes. First Parole Board results are through.

FLETCHER

And?

LENNIE

They've turned down Gibson who's in for car theft – and okayed Mal Brown who's in for manslaughter. I mean, that's barmy, isn't it?

FLETCHER

Not really. Just reflects society's current sense of values.

LENNIE

How d'you mean?

FLETCHER

Takes only one minute to create a life. Takes ten to make a car. And about five minutes for it to fall to pieces. *He walks across to the door and sees Blanco and Lukewarm approaching along the landing.*

FLETCHER

Hey up, Nat Mills and Bobbie.

LUKEWARM

Well the old devil did it this time.

FLETCHER

What – worked his parole?

LUKEWARM

Yes – sailed through. It was that clean
shirt that did it.

FLETCHER

Told you, didn't I? Doddle. Come on in.

They all go into the cell.

FLETCHER

He did it, Len. Sit down, Blanco.
We're all very glad for you, ain't
we, Len?

BLANCO

Ta, Fletch.

LUKEWARM

Surprise, surprise.

Produces some Jaffa cakes.
Lukewarm and Fletcher stand.
Blanco and Lennie sit.

LENNIE

Been a few changes, though.
Since 1959.

FLETCHER

I flogged a hot car in 1959.
Ford Zodiac it was. Two-tone Ford
Zodiac with wing mirrors. Took the
wife to Butlins on the proceeds.
We won a bronze medal in the
'Tea for Two' cha-cha.

LENNIE

I were in Junior School in 1959.
Sitting next to Ann Podmore.
She was left-handed.

FLETCHER

Bet you got on the right side
of her then.

BLANCO

I remember 1959 only as the year

I were sent away for something I
didn't do.

FLETCHER

Here, listen mate, you're casting a
gloom on the whole proceedings.
I mean, we're only trying to be festive,
which does befit, dunnit?

BLANCO

Reckon?

FLETCHER

And here, now you're going out,
you can level with your mates.
Was you innocent all this time?

BLANCO

I was that. Listen, Fletch, I know you'd
like to think I've been screwing
the system all this time. But truth is,
system's screwed me for seventeen
years. That's why I've come to
a decision.

FLETCHER

Decision?

BLANCO

Aye. For all these years, I've stood
me ground. Claiming me innocence.
If I accept parole you know what I'm
doing, don't you? Admitting me guilt.

FLETCHER

(*Leaning towards Blanco*) Blanco,
parole wipes the slate clean. It says
you're free and clear.

BLANCO

It's not a pardon. It says you've done your bird for what they sent you up for in the first place. That's not good enough.

He stands up.

BLANCO

It says we'll let you out now and don't be a bad lad again. Well, I were never the bad lad they said I were in the first place. So they can take their parole – and SHOVE IT!

He turns on his heel and leaves them.

4. PRISON ALLOTMENT

Camera shows a spade digging. Fletcher and Blanco are in the prison allotment.

FLETCHER

You haven't, have you?

BLANCO

I have.

FLETCHER

Told 'em to stuff it?

BLANCO

Aye.

FLETCHER

What did Guv'nor say, then?

BLANCO

Put the wind up his clappers, I know that.

FLETCHER

You could be on the streets now, you know. Free. Queueing up at the Labour Exchange. Standing in the rain waiting for a bus. Couldn't you?

BLANCO

Waited long enough. Bit longer won't make no difference. Fetch me the scraper, will you?

FLETCHER

Rhubarb's coming on a treat.

BLANCO

Can't wait to get your hands on my rhubarb, can you? Thought I'd bequeath that if I got out, did you? In lieu of Monopoly debts?

FLETCHER

Don't be daft.

BLANCO

And me strawberries. Well, I'm still here, right? And this is still my allotment.

FLETCHER

We'd've looked after it, you know that. Till you came back inside.

BLANCO

Reckon you would.Just like life, prison. Makes plans and do naff all about it. Look at this place.I were going to do so much. Caulies, I thought. And spring onions, and big ripe runner beans.

Maybe even raspberries and goosegogs
. . . never got round to it. In all that time.

FLETCHER

Didn't one Governor once let you
grow grapes?

BLANCO

Aye, one time. I read all about vines.
Knew I could grow grapes here, even
in this neck of the woods. I did an' all.
Bloody marvel, it were. Seeing those
ripe juicy beauties, up here . . . then
they made me pack it in.

FLETCHER

Why?

BLANCO

Grapes make wine, don't they?

FLETCHER

Do they? Always used potato peelings
and anti-freeze myself.

BLANCO

Didn't tumble till we'd got about a
dozen bottles put down.

FLETCHER

Nice drop, was it?

BLANCO

In the wine stakes, I don't suppose
it was a classic. But to a man who
hadn't had a drink for eleven years –
Chateau Slade were the finest drop
I ever supped . . .

FLETCHER

If you weren't such a stubborn old
mule, you could be out there now
supping champagne.

BLANCO

Got me pride.

FLETCHER

Freedom's pride.

BLANCO

Want both, Fletch.

FLETCHER

Have to see what we can do then.
Fletcher walks away.

5. ASSOCIATION AREA

Barrowclough comes down stairs.
He walks along the area and is
surprised to find Fletcher, Lennie
and Lukewarm sitting there.

BARROWCLOUGH

Saturday, and you're all indoors!

FLETCHER

Crow, sir.

BARROWCLOUGH

I beg your pardon?

FLETCHER

These are the central headquarters of
our campaign – Crow . . . C–R–O–W.

BARROWCLOUGH

Which stands for what?

FLETCHER

The Campaign for the Release of
Old Webb. You know – Blanco.
We wanted to make it the Campaign
for the Release and Pardon of Old
Webb, but that would've spelt Crapow

– which sounds a bit rude when
you're petitioning the Home Office.

BARROWCLOUGH

The Home Office?

FLETCHER

Well, eventually the Home Office.
The Governor first.

LENNIE

See, Old Blanco doesn't want to go out
free and guilty. So we have to make
sure he goes out free and innocent.

LUKEWARM

Which is what Crow is all about.

LENNIE

Already got three hundred signatures.

BARROWCLOUGH

But what are you petitioning for?

FLETCHER

There's two ways we can spring him.
First, we can demand a retrial.

BARROWCLOUGH

After all this time! I should think the
Judge, the jury and most of the
witnesses are nearly all dead by now.

FLETCHER

Yeah, well that may be to the old boy's
advantage, know what I mean?
Secondly, the Governor has the right to
request a pardon from the Home Office,

under Sub-section twenty-three,
Part three, Paragraph D, Penal Code
(*Giving Barrowclough the book*) as
amended by the Act of 1972.

BARROWCLOUGH

Really?

FLETCHER

Oh yes, well-known fact that is.
But we're going for the retrial.
That's what this petition's all about.

***Warren comes in with a sheet of
paper in his hand.***

WARREN

Hey, look at this, Fletch. I've done
the mailbag room and got sixty-
three signatures.

He sits down.

LUKEWARM

Oh, lovely.

LENNIE

Give 'em here, Warren.

He takes the sheet.

BARROWCLOUGH

Just a minute. Sixty-three? There's only
forty fellows work in the mailbag room.

FLETCHER

Just goes to show the strength of their
feelings, don't it?

BARROWCLOUGH

There are twenty-three Xs on this
sheet, Warren.

WARREN

Lot of folk in this nick can't write.

BARROWCLOUGH

How can you be sure that these Xs are
the genuine article?

FLETCHER

Don't be daft, Mr Barrowclough.
Look at the difference in the handwriting.
Look here – one bloke's spelt X with
a Y. I'll cross him off.

BARROWCLOUGH

Well, I have to say it's a praiseworthy
effort. My only fear is the Governor's
attitude. He has an automatic
resistance to any notion proposed
by you lot.

FLETCHER

You could maybe help us there,
Mr Barrowclough, sir. Add some
weight to our pitch, like.

LENNIE

Give us the credibility we apparently lack.

BARROWCLOUGH

How?

FLETCHER

Well, you're a humanitarian, ain'tcha?
You're no hardnose.

WARREN

You've played fair with us.

LENNIE

Always have done.

LUKEWARM

Always seen our point of view.

FLETCHER

Your example has brought reason and
compassion into a world where too
often only violence prevails.

ALL

Yes.

BARROWCLOUGH

Well, as you know, I consider you men
are in here to be helped, not punished.
I try to understand, not condemn.
I respect your rights and if you have a
just cause, I'll back it to the hilt.

FLETCHER

Never doubted it, sir, so would you just
add your Monica here.

He offers Barrowclough the sheet.

BARROWCLOUGH

What?

LENNIE

Just cause, sir.

FLETCHER

Here's a pen.

LENNIE

Here, that's my pen.

He takes it.

LENNIE

That's where it went.

FLETCHER

Shut up.

He takes the pen back.

FLETCHER

Here you are, Mr Barrowclough.

BARROWCLOUGH

Oh no, you don't. No blinking fear.
I'm up for promotion next month.
I'm not jeopardising that by being party
to a prisoners' conspiracy!

He goes.

LUKEWARM

Well, I never.

LENNIE

Hardly the humanitarian we reckoned, is he?

FLETCHER

No, but give him his dues, he's smarter than we thought.

LENNIE

Pity, though. Get his signature and a few more screws might've followed.

FLETCHER

No bother.

He reaches for the pen and starts to write.

FLETCHER

H.J. Barrowclough . . .

WARREN

Can you really forge Barra's signature?

FLETCHER

'Course I can. How d'you think we got the new requisition for ping pong balls last week?

LENNIE

You'll be for it if they trace it back to you, Fletch.

FLETCHER

They're more likely to trace it back to you, it's your pen.

He puts the pen in front of Lennie.

6. GOVERNOR'S OFFICE

The Governor and Mackay are standing by the desk.

MACKAY

It means trouble, sir, with a capital T. We've got to stamp it out from the word go.

GOVERNOR

All right, they'd better come in.

MACKAY

(*Walking over to the door*) All right, Mr Barrowclough, wheel 'em in.

Barrowclough enters with Fletcher, Lennie, Warren and Lukewarm.

BARROWCLOUGH

Left, right, left. Left, right, left.

MACKAY

Stand still in front of the Governor.

BARROWCLOUGH

The petitioners, sir.

GOVERNOR

Now listen, you men, I'm not in favour of prisoners' pressure groups.

BARROWCLOUGH

They have the right, Governor, under sub-section thirteen which clearly states that in the event of –

GOVERNOR

Don't spout the Penal Code at me, Barrowclough.

FLETCHER

Let us say straight off, sir, how much we appreciate you seeing us. May I present, sir, for your perusal and consideration (*Placing petition on the desk*) our petition for the retrial of Old Man Blanco, sir.

The Governor looks at the sheets of signatures.

GOVERNOR

Do we have this many men here?

LENNIE

The petition, sir, is a sincere expression of the feeling in Slade Prison. And the fact they have responded in this way is a tribute to your enlightened administration.

GOVERNOR

Is it?

FLETCHER

Oh most certainly, sir. All them blokes out there, burly felons, putting their names to a piece of paper. In, as the lad puts it, a less enlightened administration, they'd have torn the place apart by now.

MACKAY

Is that a threat, Fletcher!

FLETCHER

Not a threat, sir. Observation. Based on several years of first-hand experience of the mood of the incarcerated male.

GOVERNOR

The mood is this strong?

FLETCHER

Growing stronger every minute . . . and uglier, sir. Present company excepted of course.

MACKAY

Sir, what is the point of this? The authorities have been compassionate enough to offer Webb a parole. He should accept it and be grateful for it.

FLETCHER

Not enough, Mr Mackay. Had to clear his name, see?

MACKAY

Then the man's a stubborn old fool.

BARROWCLOUGH

No, no, no. Stubborn, but not foolish. Something quite heroic about all this.

He trails off catching Mackay's incensed look.

BARROWCLOUGH

But, as you say, the man's a fool.

GOVERNOR

The case was too long ago, Fletcher, for a re-trial.

FLETCHER

There's ways and means, sir. This petition's only the first step in making this a national issue.

GOVERNOR

National?

LENNIE

We want to make Old Blanco a national hero. We want to touch the conscience of the nation. We want the spotlight of the mass media on the old fella.

GOVERNOR

Mass media!

FLETCHER

Yeah, make him a corse celebre . . .
Get him on the telly, in the papers.
You might be a celebrity yourself,
Governor. Might get on the *Michael
Parkinson Show* – or if the worst
came to the worst, Esther Rantzen.

MACKAY

There's no way in the world that
this petition could escalate into a
national issue.

FLETCHER

Oh in itself, no, Mr Mackay, you're
right of course. That's why we need
the hunger strike.

GOVERNOR

Hunger strike – what hunger strike?

FLETCHER

Old Blanco's. But don't worry, Gov,
a man of his age and his state,
shouldn't last more than a week.
*There is a moment's silence while
this is digested.*

GOVERNOR

All right, you can leave this here.

FLETCHER

I think we should discuss this further.

MACKAY

On your way . . . Fletcher.

GOVERNOR

Yes, get back to your cells.

FLETCHER

Sir.
*Barrowclough escorts the prisoners
out of the office, closing the door
behind them.*

GOVERNOR

A hunger strike . . .

MACKAY

Typical of Fletcher's devious mentality,
sir. Turning the old man into some kind
of martyr.

GOVERNOR

The last thing a prison needs,
Mr Mackay, is a martyr . . .

7. LANDING

*A Prison Officer unlocks the gates.
Fletcher and Lennie come into view.*

LENNIE

What you think, Fletch?

FLETCH

Keep 'em crossed, son.

LENNIE

Did seem to cause a bit of panic, like.

FLETCHER

Which was the intended effect.
They'll just have to scratch around
for an alternative now, won't they?

LENNIE

Pardon?

FLETCHER

They'll have to scratch around for an alternative.

He moves on.

LENNIE

No – pardon.

FLETCHER

Granted.

He goes.

8. GOVERNOR'S OFFICE

The Governor is sitting at his desk. Mackay is still standing. There is a tentative knock on the door.

GOVERNOR

Yes?

Barrowclough walks in.

BARROWCLOUGH

Could I just have one more word, sir?

MACKAY

Have you left those men out there without an escort?

BARROWCLOUGH

No, no, Mr Collinson's taking them back to their cells.

MACKAY

Just as well – last week we lost a typewriter.

He checks the outer office.

GOVERNOR

What is it, Mr Barrowclough?

BARROWCLOUGH

(*Crossing over to the desk*) There might be a solution to this problem, sir. Which I'm sure you're aware of, given your knowledge of the Penal Code.

The Governor looks at Mackay for help but Mackay looks equally puzzled.

GOVERNOR

Er . . . refresh my memory, Mr Barrowclough.

BARROWCLOUGH

Sub-section twenty-three, part three, paragraph D.

GOVERNOR

Ah! Yes . . . yes . . . good old sub-section twenty-three, paragraph G.

BARROWCLOUGH

D, sir, paragraph D.

GOVERNOR

D, yes! Of course. Er, jog my memory again, will you, Mr Barrowclough?

BARROWCLOUGH

Well, as you know, sir, under special circumstances the Governor of a prison has the right, if his discretion feels it's warranted –

GOVERNOR

Yes?

BARROWCLOUGH

To request the Home Office for a prisoner's pardon.

GOVERNOR

A pardon?

BARROWCLOUGH

That's right, sir.

MACKAY

A pardon?

GOVERNOR

It would certainly put paid to the news of a hunger strike being splashed across the newspapers.

BARROWCLOUGH

Well, all round, by and large, it does seem a good idea.

GOVERNOR

Yes, well I'm paid to come up with ideas in situations like this. I'll submit a recommendation to the Home Office. Can we get rid of all this nonsense –

He starts to push aside the petition when something catches his eye.

GOVERNOR

Just a minute . . . your signature's on this thing, Mr Barrowclough.

BARROWCLOUGH

(*Looking for his spectacles*) Oh no, sir, some mistake, sir.

Mackay picks up the petition.

MACKAY

Look man – look at that. Is that not your signature?

BARROWCLOUGH

(*Takes the petition*) Must be a forgery, sir.

He looks at it.

BARROWCLOUGH

No, that is my signature. I must have signed it.

9. CELL

Fletcher is in his cell when Lennie walks in with an envelope.

LENNIE

So miracles do happen, then. Off out today, is he?

FLETCHER

Yes, free pardon. 'Course they're all claiming credit for it. The Governor's happily going round saying he thought of it; Barrowclough's miserable because he thinks he thought of it. Funny thing is, *we* know who really did think of it, don't we?

LENNIE

Yes, me.

FLETCHER

What you talking about, Godber?

LENNIE

Only joking.

FLETCHER

Joking – I've not got over that Jack the Kipper yet.

LENNIE

Hello – Lukewarm.

Lukewarm enters.

LUKEWARM

Gentlemen, may I present the best-dressed man in Slade Prison.

He stands aside and Blanco enters, dressed in a seventeen-year-old light grey suit now a mite too large for him.

FLETCHER

Oh yes. Very elegant. Where d'you nick that – War on Want?

BLANCO

I think it were Fifty Shilling Tailor's.

FLETCHER

You were robbed.

BLANCO

January Sale, 1959.

LENNIE

Back in fashion then.

FLETCHER

I think in '59 I wore Italian pin stripes. And a shirt with a Billy Eckstein collar.

LENNIE

I wore short grey flannel shorts.

FLETCHER

All right.

BLANCO

I wore this suit to my wife's funeral.

FLETCHER

Hardly black, is it?

BLANCO

Couldn't afford another suit. Only just finished paying for that damn freezer. Terrible to think she finished up inside it. Mind you I suppose it were fitting in a way, 'cos all her life she were a cold woman.

Barrowclough puts his head round the cell door.

BARROWCLOUGH

Don't be long, Mr Webb. Bus is waiting.

He goes.

FLETCHER

Thank you.

BLANCO

By gum, d'you know how good that sounds? Mr Webb.

FLETCHER

When you goes out there, hold your head up high, my son.

BLANCO

I will that, Fletch.

There is a pause.

BLANCO

I'm not very good, you know, at expressing gratitude. But I know what you done . . . and I'll not forget it.

He shakes Fletcher's hand.

FLETCHER

You're going out now. All that matters.

LENNIE

Got a lot of living to make up for. Don't waste your time nattering with the likes of us.

BLANCO

I don't want much from life.

FLETCHER

I know, but it's good to know that justice has been done – albeit a bit late. This pardon's for your family name, for your children and your grandchildren. That's why we done it. So's you can walk out of here and look any man in the face without shame or guilt. Life's taken a lot from you, me old mate, but all you need back from it is your pride, right?

BLANCO

Right, Fletch.

LENNIE

Tarra, Blanco. Keep your nose clean.

BLANCO

So long – same to you, son.

FLETCHER

Oh and one more thing, of course.

BLANCO

What?

FLETCHER

You sue the Government for every penny they've got.

BLANCO

Too bloody true, I will.

LUKEWARM

(*Stands up and gives him cigarettes*)

Ta, ta Blanco – I'll miss you.

BLANCO

Thanks for looking after me. I'll try and get that scented notepaper that you want.

FLETCHER

Here listen – We knows you didn't do in your old lady, which means

some other bloke did. And you paid the penance. But don't you go out there harbouring thoughts of revenge.

BLANCO

I know him what did it. It were the wife's lover. But don't you worry, I shan't waste my time looking for him – he's dead.

FLETCHER

Oh that's all right then.

BLANCO

That I do know. It were me that killed him. Cheerio.

He leaves. The others exchange looks of consternation.

SERIES THREE

EPISODE FIVE: A TEST OF CHARACTER

1. STUDIO
FLETCHER'S CELL

It is night time. Lennie is sitting at the table studying, textbooks in front of him. He is deep in concentration. Fletcher walks in singing.

FLETCHER

There's just one place for me
Near you
And forever I'll be
Near you –

He crosses the cell and puts his towel on the end of his bunk.

FLETCHER

Times when we're apart
I can't hear my heart.

LENNIE

Naff off, Fletch.

FLETCHER

(*Still singing*) Say you'll never stray
More than just one bunk away.

LENNIE

Naff off, Fletch.

FLETCHER

I beg your pardon, Godber?

LENNIE

You heard.

FLETCHER

Shall I tell you something?
Prison's coarsened you, my lad.

LENNIE

Yeah well, it's hardly finishing school, is it?

FLETCHER

Nevertheless when you first come in here, you did retain some vestiges of old world courtesy – such as respect for your elders.

LENNIE

When I first come in here, you taught me the value of peace and quiet. I'm in accordance with that now.

FLETCHER

Meaning?

LENNIE

Meaning – Do not disturb.

FLETCHER

Suit yourself. Not another word.

LENNIE

Thanks, Fletch.

He goes back to his books. There is a pause.

FLETCHER

(*Putting a shirt on*) No, not another word. Not a single, solitary word will emit from my lips forthwith . . . forthwith my lips are sealed, sealed are forthwith my lips . . . I have sealed forth my lips with . . .

LENNIE

Fletch!!

FLETCHER

What?

LENNIE

You weren't going to say nowt.

FLETCHER

I'm not, am I? Honest. Schtum, right. With a capital Scht.

Lennie goes back to reading. A few moments later, Fletcher goes over to him, cupping his hands.

FLETCHER

Here, Len.

LENNIE

Oh, naffin' heck!

FLETCHER

No, no, this won't take a minute.

LENNIE

What?

Fletcher holds his hands in front of Lennie.

FLETCHER

Guess what I've got in my hand.

LENNIE

I don't care, Fletch, go away, won't you?

FLETCHER

No, it's a good one this. Have a guess. What have I got in my hands? Go on then.

LENNIE

Okay. A cockroach.

FLETCHER

No.

LENNIE

I give up.

FLETCHER

You've got two more guesses.

LENNIE

A walnut.

FLETCHER

A walnut! Where could I get a walnut?

LENNIE

All right – it's a naffin' giraffe with a harelip wearing purple Y-fronts!

Fletcher looks at Lennie and then opens his cupped palms ever so slightly, peering. He sniffs.

FLETCHER

You've been peeping!

LENNIE

Oh God, give me strength!

FLETCHER

Didn't you like that – I thought it was funny. Maybe I told it wrong. Let's try it again.

LENNIE

Fletcher, naff off! I've asked you nicely. I have an exam and I need to study.

FLETCHER

I have no objection to that. Just go and do it somewhere else, right?

LENNIE

Where, for instance?

FLETCHER

Education Room for one. That would seem the most appropriate.

LENNIE

There's a lecture in there tonight. The Accident Prevention Officer is speaking on Industrial safety.

FLETCHER

That's been cancelled.

LENNIE

Has it?

FLETCHER

Yeah. On his way here the Accident Prevention Officer fell off his bike. He's in Carlisle General now.

LENNIE

I wish you were.

FLETCHER

Listen, Godber – there are two people to a cell you know. And it's very

unsettling for a social misfit like me to have someone sat here who wants to better himself.

LENNIE

Yeah, well when I get out of here I may have another 'O' Level. What will you have to show for it? Just another stretch done!

Mackay appears.

MACKAY

Oh yes, oh yes.

FLETCHER

(*Getting on his bunk*) The Town Crier.

MACKAY

What's going on here? A heated exchange, is it? Raised voices.

FLETCHER

Oh here it is, Mother Superior.

MACKAY

Watch your lip, Fletcher.

FLETCHER

My lips are sealed, sir. Forthwith my lips are sealed.

LENNIE

If only that were true.

MACKAY

What's the problem?

He walks across to Lennie.

MACKAY

Godber?

LENNIE

I'm trying to study, Mr Mackay.
You're always encouraging education,
rehabilitation – only there's nowhere in
this naffing nick conducive to it.

MACKAY

I'm afraid that won't cut much ice with
an ageing recidivist like Fletcher.

FLETCHER

Ageing what?

MACKAY

Recidivist. A person who pays his
penance for performing a crime,
goes out and straight off performs
another one.

FLETCHER

Oh – you means a professional.

MACKAY

No – I mean an habitual criminal.
Something which you may not have
been if you'd stuck in to your
education like laddo here.

FLETCHER

Yeah, well I never finished school,
did I? Never got as far as exams.
What was it called – School
Certificate in them days.

MACKAY

I can imagine.

FLETCHER

Always playing truant.

MACKAY

Oh yes.

FLETCHER

Well it was the war. We was always on
the bomb sites, collecting shrapnel and
that. Learning about sex in the air-raid
shelters during their off-peak hours.
So eventually they sent me to a
special school with other kids who
were always playing truant. But we
never learned nothing.

MACKAY

And why not?

FLETCHER

No one ever turned up for school.

MACKAY

See me, I had to leave school at
fourteen. Help bring a living wage into
the house. Hard times in those days in
the Lanarkshire coalfields. My father
was an unemployed miner but there
were still eight children to provide for.

FLETCHER

Eight kids eh? He wasn't unemployed
the whole of the time then?

MACKAY

Did I hear you correctly, Fletcher?

FLETCHER

No you didn't, sir.

MACKAY

Let me tell you something, not one
of our family neglected education.
Not one. Even under the most difficult
circumstances like Godber here.
I've had to pass exams, you know.
(*Picking a book up*) *The Aspects of*

the Reformation. What's the subject you're studying, Godber?

LENNIE
History. 'O' Level like. Already got one 'O' Level before I come inside. Geography.

MACKAY
That's the spirit, laddie. You stick in. And I'm telling you, Fletcher, no I'm ordering you – you do nothing to hinder this lad's concentration, otherwise get out.

FLETCHER
I just come in from work – I'm entitled.

MACKAY
You're entitled to nothing in here except to obey the sound of my voice. When's the exam, son?

LENNIE
Two days' time.

MACKAY
Right, so make yourself scarce, Fletcher. Is that clear!
He exits.

FLETCHER
(*Calling after him*) All right, all right, I'll go out for the evening! Give us the keys, I'll let meself in. So. Can't stay in me own flowery dell in case it upsets his nibs' concentration here.

LENNIE
You can if you're quiet. It's not much to ask, Fletch. Means a lot to me, this exam does.

FLETCHER
History, is it?

LENNIE
Yes.

FLETCHER
History and geography, huh!

LENNIE
What d'you mean, huh?

FLETCHER
Well they got no application have they in real life?

LENNIE
The point is not what exam I get, the point is that I got an exam. That's what's going to impress any future employer. That I had enough diligence and application to pass an exam even under the most adverse circumstances imaginable.

FLETCHER
It's not easy studying in the nick.

LENNIE
All I'm saying is, it's worth a try and I'm trying.

FLETCHER
Oh well, far be it for me, et cetera.
He settles back with a satsuma.
Lennie studies his books.
Fletcher looks at him, there
is a pause.

FLETCHER
Quiet enough for you, then?

LENNIE

Thank you.

FLETCHER

You won't know I'm here.

A few moments of rare silence,
then Warren comes in.

WARREN

Evening, lads.

LENNIE

Oh gawd.

FLETCHER

Ssshhh.

WARREN

What's up?

LENNIE

Naffin' heck.

FLETCHER

I didn't ask him round!

LENNIE

It's impossible.

WARREN

What's up?

FLETCHER

Seat of learning in here, this is.
Professor Godber's studying for his NBG.

WARREN

Oh he's always at that lark, is Len.

LENNIE

(*Slamming the book shut*) Cobblers
to it. I give up.

He goes across to his bunk.

WARREN

I know knowledge.

FLETCHER

You know knowledge? You can't
even read.

WARREN

Maybe not, but I get it from the telly.
Schools programmes, *University
Challenge*, *Sale of the Century*. I learn
things and I digest them with my
memory. Shall I give you an example?

FLETCHER

No.

WARREN

Right. Apparently. Are you listening,
Fletch? If every Chinaman in China
jumped up and down – at the same
moment, like – it would cause a tidal
wave which would engulf America.

FLETCHER

Really.

WARREN

Straight up. (*Doubtfully*) Or is
it Australia?

FLETCHER

Hey – that could be used as a secret
weapon. They could hold the threat of
that one over President Carter's head.
One jump up and down all at the same
time and whoosh! World domination.

WARREN

Yeah.

He pauses.

WARREN

But they wouldn't though, would they?

FLETCHER

Well, they might you know, knowing the Chinese. If anyone could pull it off they could. 'Cos they're regimented. Do everything by numbers. Look at the menu in a Chinese Restaurant. Never work in England.

WARREN

We could, if we put our minds to it.

FLETCHER

Not a snowball's. The British working man wouldn't demean himself by jumping in the air, in case he spilt his tea.

WARREN

Still, that is knowledge, isn't it?

FLETCHER

Oh yes. May I enquire where you got this fascinating piece of information, Warren?

WARREN

Someone read it to me once from a magazine in this chiropodist's waiting room.

FLETCHER

Oh dear. What was wrong with you – toothache?

WARREN

No, I was there with me feet, you see.

FLETCHER

Naturally.

WARREN

I've always had these feet, like. It's a good chiropodist, though. They're very quick.

FLETCHER

Do they do them while you wait?

WARREN

Eh?

FLETCHER

I mean – or do they say leave 'em with us, they'll be ready Thursday. Soled and heeled.

WARREN

Get off – you're pulling my leg, Fletch.

FLETCHER

I wouldn't dare. Your foot might come off.

WARREN

No, listen, I've got some more knowledge. Even better. It's about planets.

FLETCHER

Oh planets – that'll be nice. Even better! You should write all this down, Len.

LENNIE

I've chucked the towel in.

WARREN

Now, does anyone have a football?

LENNIE

No, we ain't gotta football.

WARREN

Never mind, we can use something else. Can I borrow one of your satsumas, Fletch?

FLETCHER

My satsumas?

WARREN

And I've got my ping-pong ball.

FLETCHER

What's all this about, Bunny?

WARREN

I'll show you, I'll show you.

Fletcher gives him a satsuma.

FLETCHER

I want that back. Unbruised.

WARREN

Yes.

*He takes the chamber pot and
places it on the shelf.*

WARREN

Now, we don't have a football but
we can use this Jerry to be the sun.
'Course it should be round like a
football 'cos the sun's round.

FLETCHER

That wouldn't be any good if it was
round, would it?

WARREN

Why not?

FLETCHER

You wouldn't be able to sit on it.
You'd keep rolling off.

LENNIE

Just let him get on with it.

FLETCHER

It's all in the sun tomorrow –
that's true. Get on with it.

WARREN

So pretend the Jerry's a football but
it's really the sun.

FLETCHER

I am, I am.

WARREN

Now this ping-pong ball is supposed
to be the planet Mercury, and that
goes right here. Excuse me, Fletch.
Because it's nearest the sun.

FLETCHER

I'll get a chair in the shade then.

He moves over and sits down.

WARREN

Now – one, two, three, four
(*Pacing steps out*)
Bumps into Fletcher.

WARREN

Oh, excuse me, Fletch, you're sitting
where the Earth goes.

FLETCHER

(*Getting up*) Am I – oh dear. Have I got
any on my trousers?

WARREN

Now this satsuma is the planet Earth,
and that goes here. Now.

LENNIE

You left out Venus.

WARREN

You what?

LENNIE

Venus comes between Mercury and
the Earth.

FLETCHER

(*Stamping foot*) Yeah, about here.

WARREN

Oh, that's right. And Venus is smaller than the Earth so we need something smaller than a satsuma.

LENNIE

Your brain.

WARREN

Fletch, you got a prune?

FLETCHER

Curiously enough I'm fresh out of prunes. They got all wrinkled, so I chucked 'em out. Why don't you skip Venus?

WARREN

If you like. (*Pointing to the three objects*) sun . . . Mercury . . . skip Venus . . . Earth. Now, on this scale, not counting the sun, how far away from this cell where we are would the nearest star be? Lennie?

LENNIE

Is this one of these trick questions?

WARREN

No, no.

LENNIE

(*Getting up*) 'Cos if it is I'll stuff you, Warren.

WARREN

No it's not – straight up.

LENNIE

All right. Let's get this straight.
That's the sun, Mercury, Earth.
On that scale . . .

WARREN

On that scale.

LENNIE

Where would the nearest star be . . .

LENNIE/WARREN TOGETHER

. . . to where we are now.

WARREN

That's right.

LENNIE

I would imagine, er yes, I would reckon, like, well, let's see, then . . .
I'll say the recreation yard.

WARREN

Wrong. Fletch?

FLETCHER

Recreation yard must be wrong. Got to be the Married Quarters, hasn't it? Thereabouts.

WARREN

You're wrong as well.

FLETCHER

Not by much I bet.

WARREN

Johannesburg!

FLETCHER

Never – never in a thousand years.

WARREN

It is. The nearest star would be in
Johannesburg . . . (*Doubt sets in*)
Or is it Australia?

Lennie walks to the table and picks
up his books.

LENNIE

I don't believe it, I just don't believe
it. You lot will drive me round the
ruddy twist.

WARREN

What's wrong, that's learning that is.

LENNIE

Oh yes, and what have I learned today
then? The sun is a chamberpot which
is really a football, and America will
drown given the unlikely probability
that six hundred million Chinese jump
up and down in unison!

He throws the ping pong ball and
gets out.

WARREN

What have I said?

FLETCHER

(*Moving chamber pot*) Finished with
the sun have you?

WARREN

It's the exam, is it? The strain, like?

FLETCHER

Won't open no doors though.

WARREN

History?

FLETCHER

At this point in time, yeah – it happens
to be history. You know what he's like.
Been through every course in this nick
like a dose of salts.

WARREN

He gets discouraged so easy.
Look how quick he jacked in
elementary Spanish.

FLETCHER

Yeah, elementary it was an' all.
After four weeks all he knew was
the Spanish for 'bread' and 'donkey'.
That's not going to get you far in
Spain, is it? Unless you want to live
on donkey sandwiches.

WARREN

I think he gives things in 'cos you
undermine his confidence.

FLETCHER

Oh it's my fault, is it?

WARREN

Yes. It's tough enough to study inside,
but you distract him.

FLETCHER

Hold your horses, Bunny. If Godber
passes that exam it will be due in no
small part to yours truly.

WARREN

How?

FLETCHER

How? I've been tutoring him, in' I?
Up all night sometimes. Learning
him about the Second World War,
as told by someone what lived
through it – me.

WARREN

Is he studying World War II then?

FLETCHER

Does it matter? A war is a war, it's
all history, in' it?

WARREN

Just saying, Fletch – thing like this
exam means a lot to young Len.
To himself like. And if he puts a lot of
store on this exam, then fails – well –

FLETCHER

What – could turn him a bit sour,
you mean?

WARREN

Shatter his confidence, like. He'll think
stuff it – go back to thieving.

FLETCHER

Well then let us agree that you and
I and the lads should unite in the
rehabilitation of Lennie Godber.

WARREN

If we can.

FLETCHER

Before he takes this exam we'll go
over the questions with him. Make sure
he passes so he can pursue a life of
honesty and integrity.

WARREN

But how can we go over
the questions?

FLETCHER

There's only one way – you and me
have got to go down the Education
Room and nick the exam papers.

2. EDUCATION ROOM

*Like all prison rooms, it is furnished
with only the basic essentials. It has
some desks and some shelves lined
with textbooks. A wall displays a
prospectus of educational
programmes, and Ministry of Labour
courses, prison rehabilitation
schemes and the like. On another
wall there is a map of the world.
Off this room is a small, private
office with a desk, a filing cabinet
and a duplicating machine.
Barrowclough and a prisoner
(Spraggon) are in the main room.
Spraggon is sitting at a desk.*

BARROWCLOUGH

This, er, manuscript of yours, Spraggon.

SPRAGGON

Always wanted to write. Always felt
I had it in me. Literary bent, like.

BARROWCLOUGH

Yes, well, it's very interesting . . . brutal, but interesting.

SPRAGGON

It would mean a lot to me. If I become a writer. Nobody in my family's ever been famous, except for me cousin Ernie.

BARROWCLOUGH

Your cousin Ernie Spraggon was a notorious tearaway.

SPRAGGON

Still famous, though, wasn't he? He got into the top ten.

BARROWCLOUGH

(*Horrified*) Top ten most wanted men, yes!

SPRAGGON

Made a name for himself, but. Couldn't go in a post office without seeing a photo of our Ernie.

BARROWCLOUGH

(*Walking over to Spraggon*) Look, er, writing could be your escape – if you'll pardon the expression – and I would be the last one to discourage that. But I think we should start with some grammatical essentials. For example, on page one, the first paragraph – there's a 'k' in knuckleduster. And also in kneecaps.

SPRAGGON

Kneecaps?

BARROWCLOUGH

Yes, the ones you break with a cricket bat at the top of page two.

SPRAGGON

Look, I know I ain't put much grammar in there. I know my spelling leaves a lot to be desired, like, but I didn't want to interrupt me stream of self-conscious, did I? See, I write with me gut.

BARROWCLOUGH

Yes, I noticed that.

3. ASSOCIATION AREA

The camera shows the association area.
McLaren, Warren and Fletcher are walking along the landing and down the stairs. They are all carrying balls. They pass Mackay at the bottom of the stairs.

MACKAY

What have you men got there?

FLETCHER

Balls, Mr Mackay.

MACKAY

Why the different sizes?

FLETCHER

That's life, sir.

They start to go. A prisoner near Mackay laughs.

MACKAY

What are you grinning at Sowerby? Get your hair cut. You too, Jones.

Jones is completely bald. He reacts. Mackay reacts and starts to go.

4. EDUCATION ROOM

The door opens and Fletcher enters,
followed by Warren and McLaren.
They are carrying a football, a tennis
ball and a ping-pong ball.

FLETCHER

Oh 'scuse me. Hello, Spraggs,
not disturbing you, am I?

SPRAGGON

No, you're all right.

FLETCHER

Wouldn't want to interrupt the literary
flow. I've heard about your aspirations
in that direction. All very glad to
hear you're going to lay down the
sword and pick up the pen. As are
lot of battered nightwatchmen
round your way.

BARROWCLOUGH

What is it, Fletcher? What do you
men want?

FLETCHER

Looking for the Education Officer, sir.
The one with the brains, you know.

BARROWCLOUGH

Mr Kingsley's taking a class. I'm just
helping him out with some of his more
bru – er basic pupils.

MCLAREN

We want you to settle an argument.

WARREN

An intellectual argument.

BARROWCLOUGH

Can't it wait? I'm dealing with Spraggon.

FLETCHER

Spraggs is used to waiting.
Been waiting parole for four years.

BARROWCLOUGH

All right, what is it then?

FLETCHER

Well, me and the lads was sitting
around our cell as one does discussing
the wonders of the universe.

BARROWCLOUGH

You were what?

FLETCHER

Yeah, this great and wondrous
galaxy what still enthralls man
with its magnitude and mystery.
Anyway, Warren has a theory what
me and McLaren are disputing.

BARROWCLOUGH

What theory?

FLETCHER

Now, must get this right. I'll show you,
Mr Barrowclough. You see this football,
well it represents the sun.

He puts it on the desk.

WARREN

It hasn't got a handle, like the Jerry,
but at least it's round.

FLETCHER

Now don't confuse things, Warren.
This ping-pong ball represents the
planet Mercury and goes here.

He places it on Spraggon's desk.

FLETCHER

We're going to skip Venus 'cos we ain't got a prune. Follow? Now this is the Earth. (*Holding up ball*) It doesn't bruise easily like a satsuma. It also bounces. That's gravity. McLaren, show us where this goes.

MCLAREN

There's not enough room in here, Fletch.

FLETCHER

Oh. Could you step in the corridor, Mr Barrowclough. Galaxy won't fit in this room it seems.

BARROWCLOUGH

Well it will, if you will just adjust the proportions.

FLETCHER

No – it has to be on this scale.

BARROWCLOUGH

Excuse me, Spraggon. I think I can see what they're trying to do. It does seem silly not to . . .

Going out of the room.

SPRAGGON

Yeah, go on, like.

Barrowclough is followed by Fletcher and McLaren. Warren quickly goes through to the inner office and tries the filing cabinet. It is locked. He returns to Spraggon.

WARREN

Hey, Spraggs, where does the Education Officer keep the keys?

SPRAGGON

Keys for what?

WARREN

Filing cabinet through there.

SPRAGGON

Hey, hey, hey. He's my tutor, old Kingsley. And Barra. They may be the screws, but they're okay. Before I met them I didn't know a semicolon from an apostrophe. When me book's published, I might dedicate it to Barra 'cos he trusts me, and you're asking me to betray that trust, right? Well, naff off!

WARREN

Tell us where the keys are and there's an ounce of snout in it for you.

SPRAGGON

In that drawer.

Warren goes quickly to desk, then freezes as Barrowclough re-enters, followed anxiously by Fletcher.

FLETCHER

Listen, we don't need to go back in there . . .

BARROWCLOUGH

If a job's worth doing it's worth doing well. I've got just the thing.

He opens a desk drawer and takes out two large red apples.

BARROWCLOUGH

There we are – just the thing we need.

(*As he passes Spraggon*) Jupiter and Saturn.

They leave the room again.
Warren quickly gets the keys from the drawer and goes into the inner office. He unlocks the filing cabinet, rifles through the documents inside until he finds a sealed official envelope. He takes it out and closes the filing cabinet. He returns the keys to the desk and puts the envelope in his pocket as the others return.

BARROWCLOUGH
I know Alpha Centauri is the nearest star. Astrology is a bit of a hobby of mine.
Fletcher looks at Warren who nods OK.

FLETCHER
Really, yeah, well . . .

BARROWCLOUGH
Now on this scale, let's see. I wouldn't have thought it was Johannesburg.

FLETCHER
Yeah, well you know where to find us if you work it out – let's face it we can't get away.

BARROWCLOUGH
Just a minute – could I have my –
Fletcher and McLaren simultaneously take large bites out of the apples.

BARROWCLOUGH
– Oh well, never mind.

MCLAREN
Sorry to take your valuable time, Mr Barrowclough.

FLETCHER
Much appreciated.
Fletcher goes out followed by Warren and McLaren. When they have left, Barrowclough shakes his head disappointedly.

BARROWCLOUGH
Do you know I think that they enacted that whole, elaborate charade . . . simply to steal my apples.

5. CELL

Lennie is studying when Fletcher enters, smug in the knowledge of his secret. He is followed by Warren, equally smug.

FLETCHER
Still hard at it, are we?

LENNIE
(*Groans*) Trying, yes.

FLETCHER
Know what they says. All work and no play makes Jack a dull beanstalk.

LENNIE
D'as a favour, Fletch.

FLETCHER
(*Winks at Warren*) Already have, my son.

LENNIE
All right, you left the cell for half an hour. But did you have to come back so soon?

FLETCHER
Knew you'd miss me, little flower.
Knew you'd be worried if I didn't come
back before nightfall.

LENNIE
Where've you been?

FLETCHER
Down the Education Room.

LENNIE
(*Surprised*) What for?

FLETCHER
Thought we'd enrol in something,
didn't we, Warren?

LENNIE
(*More surprised*) For what?

FLETCHER
Trigonometry.

WARREN
What's that?

FLETCHER
Gawd, thick as two short planks.

LENNIE
Go on then, tell him.

FLETCHER
Tell him what?

LENNIE
What trigonometry is.

FLETCHER
Well, if he doesn't know by now –

LENNIE
– then it's time someone told him,
isn't it. Go on?

FLETCHER
Don't come it with me in that sarky
tone, Godber.

LENNIE
Look, Fletch. I will be the first person
in this nick to admit I owe you a lot.
But one of the reasons I so desperately
want to pass this exam tomorrow is
so's I have a chance of not ending
up like you.

FLETCHER
I'll have to think about that a minute.
It's an insult, isn't it?

WARREN
Ungrateful, that's what. If he only
knew . . .

LENNIE
(*Back to book*) Knew what?

WARREN
Knew how much Fletch cares.

FLETCHER
(*Grieved*) No, no, don't bother him.

LENNIE
Cares about what?

WARREN
Cares about you, that's what.

FLETCHER
(*Never appreciated*) One day
perhaps . . .

WARREN
No, you tell him, Fletch. Tell him what
you just done for the benefit of his nibs
here at great personal risk to yourself.

FLETCHER
You played your small part, Warren.
And McLaren. Though it makes
you wonder why we took such
terrible risks.

LENNIE

(*Leaving book*) What terrible risks? On my behalf? Listen, the only thing I ask you to do on my behalf is give me half a flaming chance to pass the exam!

FLETCHER

Which is precisely what we have done, Godber!

WARREN

We're only going to make sure you passes it, aren't we?

LENNIE

How?

FLETCHER

By going over the questions with you so you can prepare the appropriate answers.

LENNIE

(*Patiently*) In that case, it would be useful to have the appropriate questions.

FLETCHER

You've got 'em.

From inside his jacket he has taken the envelope and throws it in front of Lennie.

LENNIE

(*Picks it up curiously*) What's this?

FLETCHER

(*Airily*) Tomorrow's exam paper. Now shift yourself 'cos we gotta get it back where it come from.

LENNIE

(*Not taking it in*) The exam paper?

WARREN

(*Chuffed*) Yeah, we did it, didn't we?

Lennie hurls the envelope down as if he was scalded.

LENNIE

No!

He stands up. Fletcher and Warren exchange puzzled looks.

FLETCHER

What do you mean – no?

LENNIE

I mean NO. I don't want to cheat. I want to pass this exam honestly!

FLETCHER

Well, of course you do. But honesty is only something you can afford once you made it. And passing this exam is going to help you make it.

LENNIE

Don't you understand? I've cheated all me life. For the first time in my life I want to do something straight.

FLETCHER

Look – once you've passed this exam, no one's going to know *how* you passed it.

LENNIE

I will. Look, if I fail, I fail. But I'm not going to pass through cheating.

Fletcher decides to use the persuasive rationale.

FLETCHER

Len, Len. No, no, listen, will you? Lennie, my son, cheating isn't a crime.

He says this as if it were an obvious, irrefutable truth. Lennie looks at him as if to say – what are you talking about?

FLETCHER

'Course it isn't. Cheating is – getting away with it. World of difference. I mean, everyone cheats.

WARREN

(*Going to sit beside Lennie*) Listen, Len, you know when you play draughts with Fletch and he says he thinks one fell on the floor and could you pick it up, so you bend down only when you straighten up you find the board's rearranged – that's all cheating is.

FLETCHER

That's right.

WARREN

Oh, so you admit it?

FLETCHER

Name of the game, isn't it? Getting away with it. It's not what you do in life – it's what you get caught doing.

WARREN

And if you don't get caught . . .

FLETCHER

You're away, ain'tcha? Home and dry.

LENNIE

No.

FLETCHER

Listen, Godber, you watch your favourite television programme – *Kojak* – Telly Savalas, you think he's such a great actor. Well you know why he's always opening filing cabinets and looking at his shirt cuffs? Eh? 'Cos his lines are written all over the place.

WARREN

(*Rising*) And that's cheating.

FLETCHER

Right. But who gives a rat's? Listen, son, cheating is only another word for conning. Putting one over. And if that was a crime, the whole country would be doing porridge. I tell you what would be a crime. You turning down this golden opportunity we are handing you.

WARREN

We took a big risk to get that for you, Len.

LENNIE

All right, I appreciate your efforts. You want my thanks – thanks. But I'll do it my way.

He lays down the envelope, stands, walks to his bunk and lies down.

FLETCHER

If you do it your way, you ain't honest, you're dumb. 'Cos if you do it your way – you'll fail.

LENNIE

There comes a point in everyone's life

when the only person you're cheating is yourself. It's like cheating at patience.

WARREN

Fletcher does that an' all.

FLETCHER

Come on, Warren, what's the use? Let's leave him.

He and Warren make to leave the cell. Fletcher pauses.

FLETCHER

You're at the crossroads of life, Godber. You make your own breaks, son, 'cos when you get out there, people are going to give you precious few. You can go up for a job one day with all the qualifications in the world and get pipped by some nurk who's never passed an exam in his life. But he's got the right accent, plays for the local rugby club and he ain't never been in no nick!

Fletcher throws the envelope to the floor, turns and leaves the cell with Warren.

Lennie sits at the table looking at the envelope lying there. He wrestles with his conscience. Then he glances back to the open cell door. He picks up the envelope, pauses for a moment, then slowly opens the flap.

At that moment, Warren peers into the cell through a crack in the door. He smiles.

6. ASSOCIATION AREA

Prisoners are sitting around playing cards, draughts, etc. Fletcher and Warren are sitting at a table.

WARREN

Lennie should be out of his exam soon.

FLETCHER

Yeah, I wonder how he got on? Mind you, you must never let him know that you know.

WARREN

'Course not. Guvnor will be pleased when he passes 'cos Slade Prison's got a terrible academic record, Fletch.

FLETCHER

Oh I don't know. Chap got his 'O' Level in Spanish last year – what's his name – Gomez. Hey here he comes.

Lennie comes down to them.

FLETCHER

Hello then, son. How did the exam go?

LENNIE

Some questions were a bit tough, but it weren't as bad as I thought it were going to be.

FLETCHER

No, I'll bet it wasn't.

LENNIE

I think my essay was pretty fair.
Me spelling's a bit dodgy like, but they
can't have any complaints about the
factual content and that's what counts
most, isn't it?

FLETCHER

Oh yes, that's what counts.
Anyhow, asides from your essay,
what about the more technical
questions then? The dates?

LENNIE

I'll just keep me fingers crossed. But I
will admit to being quietly confident.

FLETCHER

Quietly confident, say no more.

LENNIE

I'll tell you one thing, though. Pass or
fail, at least I have the satisfaction of
knowing I did it on me own.

FLETCHER

You what?

LENNIE

I did it on me own efforts.

WARREN

Your own efforts!!

FLETCHER

Er, Godber, would you like to rephrase
that? Bearing in mind that some of us
may know a little more than what you
thinks we do.

LENNIE

I'm just saying I did it my way. With no
help from no one.

FLETCHER

Listen, Godber, there are many sorts
of crime and we're all here for most
of them. But the one thing I can't
abide is hypocrisy!

WARREN

That's the worst offence of all in my
book an' all.

LENNIE

So?

FLETCHER

So cut out the holier-than-thou
attitude, Godber, you steaming
hypocrite. He saw you through the
crack in the door – Warren saw you
look at those papers.

LENNIE

Yeah I clocked them, but it didn't make
no difference.

FLETCHER

How can you say that!

LENNIE

Who actually lifted them?

WARREN

Me.

LENNIE

Next time, pick someone who
can read.

FLETCHER

What?

LENNIE

You nicked the Biology papers.

SERIES THREE

EPISODE SIX: FINAL STRETCH

1. VISITING ROOM

*Barrowclough is walking down
the rows of visitors and prisoners.
Ingrid is visiting Fletcher; Mrs Godber,
Lennie and Jarvis (a tough
unpleasant-looking inmate) is
being visited by his brother.*

INGRID

I know it's only Feb, but if you book
your holiday now it's ever so cheap.
So me and Barbara, you don't know
Barbara, she's my friend at work –
we fancy going to Rimini. That's on
the Adriatic. We thought Italy because
your money goes much further there.
That's 'cos the lira's the only
European currency what's as
bad off as the pound.

*Fletcher has been listening with little
interest. He casts dubious looks at
Barrowclough, who seems to be
hovering nearby.*

INGRID

It's either Rimini or Portofino – which is
supposed to be rather smart. I believe
Rex Harrison goes there.

FLETCHER

Anyhow, the riot is set for Tuesday,
we're going to barricade ourselves in
with half a dozen screws as hostages
with which we can bargain for better
living conditions.

*Barrowclough has heard this. As he
was meant to. He takes the bait,
whipping round on Fletcher.*

FLETCHER

(*Got him*) I knew he was earwigging.

INGRID

What?

FLETCHER

Listening to every word he was, of our
supposedly private conversation.

BARROWCLOUGH

I was doing no such thing, Fletcher.

FLETCHER

Yes, you were, Mr Barrowclough.
Shouldn't be allowed, hovering.

BARROWCLOUGH

It wouldn't be necessary if we could

trust you people not to pass each other contraband.

FLETCHER
Oh I see, it's contraband now, is it? Hear that!

He has a packet of cigarettes in front of him.

FLETCHER
Here, check this. She's brung me half a pound of hashish in there, she has.

With this, he throws the packet across the table towards Barrowclough, but it falls on the floor.

BARROWCLOUGH
There's no need to take that attitude, Fletcher.

He bends to pick up the packet. As he does so, the entire row of visitors flick contraband across the table to their loved ones. It disappears instantly – just before Barrowclough straightens up, handing over the packet.

BARROWCLOUGH
Here you are – now just carry on.

INGRID
Where was I?

BARROWCLOUGH
Rimini or Portofino.

He moves on.

INGRID
Oh yes, well we was thinking of May before it gets too touristy –

FLETCHER
Listen, girl, has it not occurred to you that it's a bit tactless in front of your old dad. This conversation about foreign climes.

INGRID
Oh.

FLETCHER
I mean you know –

INGRID
(*Sympathetically*) You've passed the halfway mark, Dad. Less to do than's already done. With parole, only another year – just under.

FLETCHER
Oh, is that all – that's nothing, just a mere bagatelle, isn't it?

INGRID
Getting rough, is it?

FLETCHER
Oh you know me, I'll survive. It's just every time I see you or Marion or Raymond I realise you're all grown up a bit more. Without me.

INGRID
I grew up before you come in, Dad.

FLETCHER
Oh you had. Grew up too soon, you did. You somehow bypassed puberty.

INGRID
No, I didn't. You bypassed my puberty by going into Maidstone.

FLETCHER

Nevertheless it has to be said, you
was wearing a 36D in Junior School.

INGRID

Not my fault, that's nature.

FLETCHER

All right, all right put 'em away.
forewent my parental responsibilities
during your most formative years.
Same with young Marion.

INGRID

Oh she'll be all right. Don't you worry,
Marion will always end up on her own
two feet.

FLETCHER

If she ever gets herself off her back.

Ingrid looks shocked.

FLETCHER

No, no, I didn't mean that to sound like
it did. I mean, she's a lazy little so-and-
so, that's all. She still work at Woolies?

INGRID

She don't need to, Dad. 'Cos her
boyfriend Ricky's ever so well off.
He's got three cars. He gave her
one for Christmas.

FLETCHER

I'll bet he did. Did she get a present
as well?

INGRID

Dad!

FLETCHER

Well . . .

INGRID

If she marries Ricky, she'll want
for nothing.

FLETCHER

If. What's he do, this Ricky?

INGRID

He runs these cheap charter
aeroplane trips.

FLETCHER

What's it called? Gullible's Travels?

INGRID

No – Sunset Tours. It was him what
put me and Barbara on to Rimini.

FLETCHER

What I'm trying to say is, his three cars
was bought from the deposits scraped
together by the likes of you.

INGRID

Dad! I hate to hear you talk like this.
You never give no one the benefit of
the doubt. You're getting so cynical in
your old age.

FLETCHER

Listen, it ain't no bed of roses in here.

INGRID

You've got nothing to bleat about.
You chose to live outside the law,
so you accept the consequences.
What was it you told young Lennie?
If you can't do the time, don't do
the crime!

FLETCHER

How d'you know I told young
Godber that?

INGRID

He told me in one of his letters.

She turns to look at Lennie and waves. Lennie waves back.

FLETCHER

Oh – so you've been keeping in touch, have you?

INGRID

Only pen pals.

FLETCHER

Yeah well, but he's going out next week, isn't he? Won't need no stamps on your letters then, will you?

INGRID

Subject to his parole board.

FLETCHER

Oh he'll smarm his way past that lot with his naïve charm, his boyish smile and his one flaming 'O' Level in geography. Probably get lost as soon as he's outside the gates.

INGRID

That's why you're so grumpy! He's going out and you're going to miss him.

FLETCHER

Miss him? That's not the point. His going out reminds me that I ain't going out. I'm staying in. While he's out I'll still be in, won't I?

INGRID

Won't be too long, Dad. Tell you what,

soon as your release date is set I'll get in touch with Ricky and he can book you some lovely holiday in the sun.

FLETCHER

Yeah, well after Marion and you, why not me and your mam? Then apart from young Raymond he'll have done the whole family.

2. PRISON YARD

Barrowclough comes out followed by several prisoners. They file out and walk away.

Jarvis calls out to Godber.

JARVIS

Godber!

Godber waits until Jarvis catches him up. They walk along together. Barrowclough is watching the prisoners. More prisoners come out of the door, including Fletcher. The prisoners are walking away. Godber and Jarvis start fighting. Barrowclough is locking the door when he notices the fight.

BARROWCLOUGH

Stop that – just a minute!

Fletcher is walking along. He spots the fight.

Barrowclough runs to break up the fight.

3. MACKAY'S OFFICE

Lennie and Jarvis are standing side by side in front of Mackay. Barrowclough is in attendance.

MACKAY

What's all this about then?

LENNIE

What's all what about, Mr Mackay?

MACKAY

Brawling in the yard.

LENNIE

Weren't brawling, sir.

JARVIS

Just fooling around. Playful high spirits, sir.

LENNIE

We were just re-enacting a big momont from last Sunday's football on the telly. The bit where Peter Shilton dived at Charlie George's feet.

MACKAY

I don't recall Charlie George smashing a dustbin lid over Peter Shilton's skull. Not even in the action replay.

LENNIE

He would have done if he'd had one handy.

MACKAY

Don't be funny with me, Godber.

LENNIE

Not trying to be, sir.

MACKAY

You were brawling.

LENNIE

Wasn't sir, honest. Got me parole board next week. Daft to jeopardise that, wouldn't I?

MACKAY

You would indeed, sonny.

JARVIS

Len's my mate, sir. Him and me are like that.

He holds up two crossed fingers.

MACKAY

(*Questioningly*) Mr Barrowclough?

BARROWCLOUGH

(*Uncertain*) Well, I was some distance away, but it did seem to be a vicious altercation.

LENNIE

Oh, from a way's away it could easily have been misconstrued. If you'd been close up you could have seen we were smiling.

He smiles briefly by way of demonstration.

JARVIS

Straight up, sir.

MACKAY

You're no stranger to violence, Jarvis. Your only interest in football was supervising violence at the Stretford End. It's no coincidence that since your imprisonment football hooliganism has declined.

JARVIS

Didn't know no better then, sir.
But thanks to people like Len . . .

LENNIE

It's true, sir. Look . . .

He turns to Jarvis and says,
challengingly.

LENNIE

Manchester United are rubbish
compared to Villa.

JARVIS

(*Evenly*) You could be right, Len.

LENNIE

Doesn't that prove it, sir?

Mackay looks towards
Barrowclough, as if to say
can you believe these two?

LENNIE

I admit we got a bit boisterous
in the yard.

JARVIS

That's true. But to me, sir, Len's family.

LENNIE

(*Touched*) D'you mean that, Jarvis?

JARVIS

Cross me heart.

LENNIE

Well, I'm touched. You don't know
what that means to me.

MACKAY

I'm in two minds, Mr Barrowclough.
Should I give them solitary confinement
or announce their engagement?

4. ASSOCIATION AREA

BARROWCLOUGH

Back to your cells. And think
yourselves damned lucky!

LENNIE/JARVIS TOGETHER

Thank you, Mr Barrowclough.

They walk along the landing.
Barrowclough watches them and
then walks off.
Jarvis and Lennie are walking along.

LENNIE

Got out of that then.

JARVIS

Bloody did.

LENNIE

Did well in there, us.
Abbott and Costello.

JARVIS

Morecambe and Wise.

LENNIE

We were daft though. Having a go in
front of the screws.

JARVIS

Should have found somewhere private.

LENNIE

We will do. (*Stopping*) 'Cos I'm going to punch your lights out, musclehead! *He goes.*

5. FLETCHER'S CELL

It is night time.

FLETCHER

(*Appalled*) I thought I knew you, Godber.

LENNIE

If someone provokes you, what you s'posed to do, back off?

FLETCHER

If you're up for parole next Monday, most certainly, yes.

LENNIE

He made certain remarks.

FLETCHER

What remarks?

LENNIE

Never you mind. Suffice to say I found them insulting and offensive.

FLETCHER

If my release was in the balance here, ain't an insult in the world that would prevent me from turning the other cheek.

LENNIE

Have to draw the line somewhere.

FLETCHER

Wrong. You could bring in the question of the virtue of my old woman; call me a poof; even tell me I molest goats – water off a duck's back to me – or in this case, off a goat's back.

LENNIE

P'raps you haven't the same pride as what I do.

FLETCHER

Oh, it's the old pride stakes, is it? The old self-respect.

LENNIE

It matters.

FLETCHER

Self-respect is something you preserve on the outside. No such thing inside – you forfeited that when you were sent down. Anyhow, people's opinion in here matters naff all.

LENNIE

Not doing it for them. Doing it for me.

FLETCHER

I was talking to my daughter today.

LENNIE

Ingrid?

FLETCHER

Yeah, your pen pal. She says, you know, I don't give anyone the benefit of the doubt. Thinks I'm cynical. She's probably right. I just thought someone like you could just about make it out there but . . .

LENNIE

But what?

FLETCHER

You obviously ain't got the bottle.

LENNIE

If I hadn't got no bottle, would I be taking on Jarvis?

FLETCHER

That ain't bottle, that's stupidity. Tell you what does take bottle in life – knowing when to turn the other cheek. Like Gary Cooper in *High Noon*, Alan Ladd in *Shane*, or . . . Gregory Peck in *The Big Country*, Glenn Ford in *The Fastest Gun Alive*.

LENNIE

I've seen those pictures.

FLETCHER

Then you know what I mean.

LENNIE

Just answer me one question.

FLETCHER

Gladly.

LENNIE

How come all them films ended in the worst fights you ever seen? Teeth and whiskers all over the place.

FLETCHER

I'll tell you why, sonny Jim. Because Hollywood had to pander to the public's insatiable thirst for senseless violence.

LENNIE

No, you're wrong. Those films raised a moral question which had to be answered by the last reel. A man has to do . . .

FLETCHER

(*Joining him*) . . .what a man has to do – yes, yes, oh blimey it's Batman, is it?

LENNIE

There is a basic truth there though.

FLETCHER

Let me ask you one question.

LENNIE

Go on.

FLETCHER

(*Going over to Lennie*) Would Gary Cooper and all them others have done what they done had they been up for parole next Monday? And would they have walked into the final shoot-out so willingly had they known their adversary was Reggie, the Red Menace, Jarvis? You see, there's two sorts of violence inside. One that's born out of frustration and despair, and one that comes from the likes of Reggie Jarvis. A man full of Mancunian macho 'cos he's got five years to do and nothing to lose. You've got everything to lose. Unless freedom ain't everything. Then, well . . .

LENNIE

Listen, Fletch, I appreciate your concern but it's just something I have to do.

FLETCHER

I'll make one final appeal to your sense, Godber. Then I'll wash my hands of it.

LENNIE

Go on then.

FLETCHER

There are three good reasons why you shouldn't take on Jarvis. A – you could jeopardise your parole; and B – it offends civilised sensibilities.

LENNIE

What about C?

FLETCHER

C – it's obvious, ain't it? C – he'll bleedin' murder you!

6. RECREATION ROOM

A few prisoners are playing cards or smoking. The TV is off. Fletcher sits playing dominoes with Warren.

FLETCHER

Knock.

He puts a matchstick in the kitty.

WARREN

Four–five.

FLETCHER

Knock.

WARREN

Double five.

FLETCHER

(*With rising irritability*) Knock.

WARREN

Five–one.

Barrowclough comes in.

BARROWCLOUGH

Excuse me, Fletcher.

FLETCHER

Oh dear me, interruption – void game. *He throws all his dominoes on the table and withdraws his matchsticks.*

WARREN

I only had one to play.

FLETCHER

Well, that's hard luck, me old son. But we can hardly continue playing when Mr Barrowclough has something to say, can we?

BARROWCLOUGH

There was no need to break up your game, Fletcher.

WARREN

See!

FLETCHER

(*Pity!*) Too late now. Showed me hand, ain't I?

Warren disgustedly throws his remaining domino in. Barrowclough examines their respective hands.

BARROWCLOUGH

Oh, you'd have beaten him hollow there, Warren.

FLETCHER

(*Mixing the dominoes*) Matter of opinion. So what's the problem then?

BARROWCLOUGH

Just a word in your ear.

Fletcher indicates Warren.

FLETCHER

Oh. Try this one – it's further away from *him*.

BARROWCLOUGH

Oh, Warren's all right, he's a friend.

FLETCHER
Friend of whose?

BARROWCLOUGH
Godber's.

FLETCHER
What *about* Godber?

BARROWCLOUGH
Him and Jarvis –

FLETCHER
What about Jarvis?

BARROWCLOUGH
You know.

FLETCHER
Do I?

BARROWCLOUGH
You were there – after visiting –
in the yard.

FLETCHER
Was I? Where was this then?

BARROWCLOUGH
I must say, you're not much of a
conversationalist, Fletcher.

FLETCHER
What's you on about,
Mr Barrowclough?

BARROWCLOUGH
(*Darkly*) Something's brewing.

FLETCHER
Oh good. Two sugars.

BARROWCLOUGH
You know very well what I mean.

FLETCHER
Do I? Oh good.

BARROWCLOUGH
I'll say no more.

FLETCHER
Yes, I think you've said enough.

BARROWCLOUGH
As long as we understand each other.

FLETCHER
Perfectly, Mr Barrowclough.

BARROWCLOUGH
Good.
*He goes off. Fletcher starts to select
dominoes for a new game.*

WARREN
What were all that about?

FLETCHER
Godber and Jarvis had a barney in the
yard. The screws know about it – want
it stopped before it goes any further.
If it does, bad for all of us, specially
the lad. My down, double six.

WARREN
I didn't hear him say all that.

FLETCHER
Read between the lines, son. Your go.

WARREN
(*Peering at his dominoes*) Would you
believe it – I'm knocking.

FLETCHER

In the kitty. Six–two.

Lennie approaches.

WARREN

Oh, look, look, it's Lennie.

LENNIE

Hello, Fletch, Warren.

He sits down.

FLETCHER

Never mind him – have you got a two?

WARREN

No, but it's a void game, isn't it? Interruption, like.

He tries to gather the dominoes but Fletcher stops him.

FLETCHER

Naff off.

WARREN

That's what you did when Barra came up.

FLETCHER

Barra's a screw – different, ain't it?

LENNIE

What did he want?

FLETCHER

The topic was senseless violence, the prevention of.

LENNIE

If he wants to stop that, he should get the telly fixed. It's been bust for a week.

WARREN

Jarvis broke that.

FLETCHER

Only because he couldn't get a good picture of his favourite programme – *The Magic Roundabout*. I tried to tell

him – I said if Florence and Zebedee appear a little blurred, you fix it by adjusting the fine tuner with a delicate twist of the wrist. You don't chuck the set against the wall – mind you, that usually does the trick.

Jarvis enters. Only Warren notices.

WARREN

Change the subject, change the subject.

FLETCHER

What's wrong with you? Got a sore throat?

WARREN

I said change the subject.

FLETCHER

Yeah – and I saw your lips move.

Warren tries to warn them about Jarvis with a subtle indication of head but Jarvis is already upon them. He thumps the TV set twice.

FLETCHER

Are you knocking again?

JARVIS

Godber . . .

LENNIE

Hello, Jarvis.

JARVIS

Score to settle, right?

LENNIE

Any time.

JARVIS

Up to you.

LENNIE

Ready when you are.

JARVIS

What's wrong with now?

LENNIE

Why not? Telly's broke.

(*Getting up*) Nothing else to do.

WARREN

I think I'll go t' lavatory.

He starts to leave.

FLETCHER

(*Getting up*) You sit down – nothing's going to happen so just hold your horses. Or hold whatever you have to hold.

JARVIS

None of your business, Fletch.

FLETCHER

It's everyone's business, Jarvis.

He goes over to them.

FLETCHER

A happy nick is a placid nick. Cause a rumpus, you naff it up for all of us.

JARVIS

Listen, my gripe's with him. But I'll stuff the both of you if you want.

Fletcher, backs off to beside the TV set.

FLETCHER

Shut your face, toilet mouth.

WARREN

That's reminds me (*Getting up*) I really do have to go to the lavatory.

JARVIS

I'm going to have you for that.

Everyone in the room reacts to the tension. Jarvis walks up to Fletcher. Fletcher quickly picks up the TV set which he holds threateningly above his head. Mackay comes in.

MACKAY

(*Offscreen*) Everybody freeze! What's going on here?

FLETCHER

Oh we was just trying to fix the telly, Mr Mackay.

MACKAY

With the set above your head?

FLETCHER

Yeah, I was just trying the vertical hold.

WARREN

(*Amazed*) Hey, look – we got a picture.

Sure enough, to everyone's astonishment, the set starts to work. All the prisoners, except Fletcher, immediately sit down, cross their legs and start watching the programme. Mackay turns up the sound. Then walks off as they all sit enjoying the TV.

7. CELL

Fletcher is in his cell darning his socks when Warren walks in.

WARREN

Fletch.

FLETCHER

What are you doing? I told you to tag Godber. To never let him out of your sight.

WARREN

That's what I've come to tell you. It's all right, he's on duty. And Jarvis is in the yard with some of his cronies.

FLETCHER

Well, we'd better tail Godber when he comes out of the cookhouse. It's the weekend now. This is when it's going to happen, in' it?

WARREN

I had 'opes you'd've talked Len out of it. If anyone could, you could.

FLETCHER

Well, I ain't. Which is a testimony to his pigheadedness.

WARREN

Maybe we should look on the bright side. Maybe the fight won't be tumbled. And maybe Len'll do all right. I mean, he knows a bit. He made the boxing squad.

FLETCHER

The boxing squad. Oh yes, the noble art. The Queensbury Rules, the fairplay and the gumshield, and all that rubbish. While Lennie is still shaking hands Jarvis will have fractured his groin with his No. 9 prison issue boot, won't he?

WARREN

Could we nobble him? Drugs like?

FLETCHER

There is some animal tranquilliser on the farm. How much do you need to tranquillise an animal like Jarvis? Not to mention the problem of who goes and

sticks a hypodermic in his backside without him noticing. No, there's only one thing for it, you know – I'll have to take on Jarvis myself.

WARREN

You? (*Laughs*) D'you think you can put Jarvis out of action?

FLETCHER

No, you nurk. But it's Saturday morning now, ain't it? If I fight him and we're discovered, it's automatically the cooler for forty-eight hours and he won't come out till after Len's been up for his parole Monday morning.

WARREN

But hang on, if you're discovered you'll go to the cooler an' all.

FLETCHER

Yeah, well.

WARREN

You're going to blot your copy book.

FLETCHER

Yeah, well. Few weeks' remission won't do me any harm. But listen, I'm going to need your help Warren, 'cos I wouldn't last two minutes with Jarvis. The moment anything happens, you fetch the screws and you move like greased lightning. Right?

WARREN

Hey, wait a minute, Fletch. If I tip off the screws that makes me a snitch.

FLETCHER

If you don't tip them off, son, that makes me a corpse.

8. PRISON YARD

*A group of prisoners are playing
pitch and toss, including Jarvis.
The Prison Officers are chatting.
Fletcher and Warren come round
the corner of the building and
see Jarvis.
They look at him, then at a
Prison Officer.
Fletcher is walking across the yard
and he sees a group approaching.
When he reaches them he speaks.*

FLETCHER
Jarvis!

JARVIS
Oh hello, Fletch. You want in?

FLETCHER
You what?

JARVIS
Want to join in, like?

FLETCHER
Jarvis? I thought you and me had
some unfinished business. From the
television room, remember?

JARVIS
Oh that, don't be daft.

FLETCHER
I mean what I said, Jarvis.

JARVIS
No, you didn't. I know what you were
doing – trying to protect the kid.
*Jarvis turns back to the game.
Fletcher moves into Jarvis.*

FLETCHER
Jarvis!

JARVIS
What?

FLETCHER
You know when I called you
toilet mouth?

JARVIS
Yeah.

FLETCHER
I ain't taking it back.

JARVIS
Well, you're right, me old mate.
My language is a bit colourful.
Me wife's always on at me about it.
I try you know, but I can do sod all
about it.
*He returns to the game.
Fletcher turns and starts to move
away. But an idea strikes him and
he turns back. Fletcher returns to
Jarvis and taps him on the shoulder.*

FLETCHER
Jarvis.

JARVIS
Now what?

FLETCHER
Talking about your wife . . .

JARVIS
What about my wife?

FLETCHER

You're luckier than most of us. I mean, when a bloke's doing a long stretch, you know, his old lady's out looking for nooky, in' she?

JARVIS

Speak for yourself.

FLETCHER

I am. That's why I'm saying you're luckier than most. I 'eard your old lady's only been unfaithful to you twice.

JARVIS

Twice?

FLETCHER

Once with the milkman and once with the Household Cavalry.

Jarvis thinks, then laughs.

JARVIS

Huh, huh, huh – good one that, Fletch.

FLETCHER

Oh gawd.

He turns and starts to leave.
Crusher walks past Jarvis who calls out to him.

JARVIS

Here, Crusher.

CRUSHER

What?

JARVIS

Listen to this.

He laughs at the group and turns back to Crusher.

JARVIS

I heard that your old lady's only been unfaithful to you twice.

Crusher says nothing.

JARVIS

Once with the milkman and once with the Household Cavalry.

The camera shows the back of Jarvis's head and Crusher's fist punching it. Jarvis falls backwards. Suddenly the whole group starts fighting. Prison Officers start running about blowing whistles. The fight rages on. Fletcher walks off.

FLETCHER

All right then, I owe you one.

The Prison Officers run up to the group and break the fight up.

9. CELL

Fletcher is busying himself with his back to the cell door, when Lennie walks in.
He has a smile on his face and is about to enjoy imparting some news when Fletcher, without turning around, says.

FLETCHER

Congratulations.

LENNIE

(*Taken aback*) What?

FLETCHER

Congratulations. On getting your parole.

LENNIE

I was just about to tell you that.

FLETCHER

Well, I knows, don't I?

LENNIE

How?

FLETCHER

It pays me to, don't it?

LENNIE

But I only left the board an hour ago.

FLETCHER

Son, son. I works the admin block, don't I?

LENNIE

Oh yes, of course.

FLETCHER

(*Walking over to Lennie*)

Anyhow, well done.

They shake hands.

FLETCHER

Tomorrow morning then.

LENNIE

Yeah, I'd better get packed up. It's only when you move that you realise how much stuff you got.

FLETCHER

Yeah.

LENNIE

'Ere, the Governor was ever so nice about it. He let me ring my mum.

FLETCHER

I know.

LENNIE

How?

FLETCHER

I listened in on the extension.

LENNIE

Fletch!

FLETCHER

I wanted to share in your elation.

LENNIE

Oh I see.

FLETCHER

She was chuffed. Your mum.

LENNIE

Quite emotional really. For her. Wish I could tell me dad . . . if I only knew where the old bastard was.

FLETCHER

Well look at it another way. Your dad's absence meant he never knew you went in in the first place.

LENNIE

I suppose so. Come in handy today, he did.

FLETCHER

How?

LENNIE

Well I told the parole board that I thought my father's desertion was a contributory factor towards my temporary diversion from the straight and narrow. Not in so many words though.

FLETCHER

You're learning, ain't you?

LENNIE

(*Sitting*) Thanks to you, Fletch.

FLETCHER

Yeah, well.

LENNIE

If it hadn't been for you, I'd've messed this parole up, you know.

FLETCHER

True.

LENNIE

I mean, the fact that you risked solitary confinement and loss of your own remission . . . well, I mean . . . well, that's real friendship.

FLETCHER

Look, there was no way I was going to let you jeopardise your parole, son.

LENNIE

I realise that now. But I never realised it meant so much to you.

FLETCHER

'Course it did. I had three to one on you getting out.

Lennie thinks about this, then decides not to believe it.

LENNIE

You don't fool me, Fletch. You did that out of the kindness of your heart.

FLETCHER

If you believe that, then you are a stupid sentimental nurk.

LENNIE

No I'm not.

FLETCHER

Well, you're certainly stupid. As your behaviour over the Jarvis affair demonstrated only too clearly.

LENNIE

I promise you, Fletch, I did have a reason for reacting like I did. Jarvis came up to me and made an obscene remark.

FLETCHER

(*Putting envelope down*) Did that affront your Brummagen sensibilities then?

LENNIE

Yes, it did. 'Cos the remark concerned what he'd like to do to your daughter Ingrid.

FLETCHER

What?

LENNIE

To put it delicately, he indicated his carnal desires towards her, then reckoned that he fancied his chances, on account of her sexual proclivities.

FLETCHER

(*Licking envelope*) Well, she's always had those. Ever since she was thirteen. So – you was defending my family's honour, was it?

LENNIE

Seemed a good reason – I owe a lot to you, Fletch. I'd've never made the distance without you.

FLETCHER

(*Sitting*) Look, don't make me out to be no hero.

LENNIE

I wasn't. Father figure maybe.

FLETCHER

I ain't been no great shakes as a dad. 'Fact I ain't been no great shakes as anything.

LENNIE

You have to me. And I won't let you down, Fletch. I ain't coming back.

FLETCHER

Oh we all say that. But you'd better mean it, Godber. You've got your life before you. Out the last twenty years I've spent eleven of 'em doing porridge. That ain't life, that's marking time. I'm not moaning. What's done's done. But it's a terrible waste.

LENNIE

I won't be back. Given the breaks.

FLETCHER

Make the breaks. No alibis. No ifs and buts. You can make it. You're not stupid, and you're not evil. You're a good lad. Well, nuff said. Hope you're leaving me your snout.

LENNIE

Only right.

He gives Fletcher the tobacco from his box.

FLETCHER

Chocolate?

LENNIE

Fruit and nut.

He hands Fletcher the chocolate.

FLETCHER

(*Looking in box*) Other bit. (*Lennie gives him it*) And first thing you do when you go out, you do for me.

LENNIE

What?

FLETCHER

As soon as you get off the train at New Street, Birmingham, you go straight into a pub and order a pint of best bitter and drink to your old mate.

LENNIE

I'm not going to Birmingham. I was thinking of Rimini actually, with a friend. We thought May 'cos it's not so touristy then. Or perhaps Portofino . . .

10. CELL

Fletcher is lying on his bunk reading a newspaper.

10A. PRISON LANDING

Mackay comes upstairs. He pauses and then looks around, moves on. Mackay walks along the landing and stops outside Fletcher's cell. He goes in.

10B. CELL

Mackay enters.

MACKAY

Fletcher?

FLETCHER

Good afternoon, sir.

MACKAY

Good afternoon, sir?

FLETCHER

Your title, in' it, sir?

MACKAY

True. I did not expect to hear it so readily from your lips.

FLETCHER

Why make waves, eh? Only ten months to do if I keep my nose clean.

MACKAY

Throwing in the towel, are we Fletcher?

FLETCHER

I just want to get home.

MACKAY

(*Moving nearer*) I've noticed a certain change in your attitude since laddo's release. Our customary ill-feeling seems to be missing. You seem to have lost a lot of that brash Cockney lairyness. Or are you just acknowledging that the system always wins.

FLETCHER

Nobody wins, Mr Mackay. That's what's so tragic.

MACKAY

Normally I would have hesitated about pulling a sprog in here, Fletcher.

FLETCHER

Oh yes. Got some company coming in, have I?

MACKAY

In the past you have not been the healthiest of influences on first-time offenders. But now I don't think I have too much to fear. (*Crossing to the window*) Got a young lad called Nicholson moving in.

FLETCHER

Not a Scot, is he? I mean, we do draw the line somewhere.

MACKAY

(*Turning to Fletcher*) No, he's from Sunderland.

FLETCHER

Dangerously near.

MACKAY

He's a tearaway. Lashes out. Doesn't think. I have a feeling that the new quiescent Fletcher might be just what he needs.

FLETCHER

Whatever you think, Mr Mackay.

MACKAY

(*Moving nearer*) So you'll keep an eye on him?

FLETCHER

Be difficult to ignore him in a room this size.

MACKAY

No, but perhaps you'll show him the ropes, show him what you've learnt.

He walks towards the door.

FLETCHER

What have I learnt, Mr Mackay?

MACKAY

(*Crossing over to Fletcher*) That there's no point to bucking the system.

FLETCHER

Oh yes. Glad to, Mr Mackay. Sir. I'll watch out for him. I shall simply tell him three things. Bide your time (*Holds up one fingers*), keep your nose clean . . . (*Two fingers*) and don't let the bastards grind you down . . .

Fletcher puts up the third finger.

MEMORIES

Colin Farrell (Norris in 'Happy Release')

'Before being cast in "Happy Release", the fifth episode in series two, I had performed very little in front of a live TV audience. At that time I was mainly a theatre person and, in classical or modern works, considered that comedy was probably my forte. Faced with a live audience in a TV studio, however, I felt a complete plonker.

'I hated it. Should I time my lines in reaction to the audience, or totally ignore them? Should I compromise my angle to the camera in order to give the studio audience a better view? None of the stagecraft – or such camera craft as I possessed at that time – learned over the previous dozen or so years, seemed to apply and after two or three unhappy experiences, I made up my mind that TV comedy shows involving anybody other than the technicians and my fellow actors on the studio floor, were simply not my bag. Then along came Sydney Lotterby with an offer that I would have been mad to refuse.

'Nasty Norris was a character that leapt off the page at me. Instinctively, I knew how I would play him, and heard his whining tone of voice from the moment I read the first words. It was a peach. What's more, I would get the chance to work with the likes of Ronnie Barker and the wonderful Fulton Mackay, not to mention Sydney Lotterby – one of the very best of our TV comedy directors.

'Much of the action takes place in the prison sick ward because Fletcher has broken his leg. My character is across the ward complaining of an ingrowing toenail. In rehearsals, I was amazed to find that the old man in the bed opposite was being played by a friendly young chap much the same age as myself. It was, of course, David Jason. David used to come in hours before the rest of the cast to be fitted with layers of latex wrinkles and make-up, topped with a convincing grey wig. He was unrecognisable.

'Whoever had the courage and imagination to cast him in that role deserves a medal. His was a semi-regular character in the series and it gave him a marvellous kick-start to a highly successful career; but it would never happen today. Nowadays you are expected to turn up to a casting session looking exactly like the character you might be playing, and I can't imagine David would fancy travelling up to White City covered in latex!

'I think "Happy Release" must be the most repeated episode of the whole series; in fact, I've come to rely on it to pay off my overdraft at least once a year, and I need hardly say that I learned more about playing TV comedy from Ronnie and Sydney and the rest of that fantastic team, in a few short days, than almost any time before or since, so when the offer came to go into Yorkshire Television's *In Loving Memory*, where Dame Thora Hird continued my education, I felt equal to the task.'

Christopher Biggins (Lukewarm in the series)
'In 1974 I was a young actor – twenty-six years old, in fact, and terribly starstruck. When I went to visit Syd Lotterby, the director and producer of a new sitcom set in prison, I had no idea that it was written by Dick Clement and Ian La Frenais, and starred my all-time favourite comedy actor, Ronnie Barker.

'When my agent, Gillian Coffey, rang and told me I had got the part of - Lukewarm, I was over the moon; I immediately rang my parents who were thrilled. So I suddenly became part of history by being involved in one of the most popular and, thank God, most repeated sitcoms ever.

'My first day was nerve-racking and yet so exciting. Ronnie was enchanting, as were the rest of the cast, and after the read-through one knew we were on to something rather special. Ronnie was incredibly generous and if during rehearsals he felt one of his lines was better off said by another actor, he would give it over with no complaints. It was so good to work with a star who was considering the whole product; it was a lesson I took on and, hopefully, have always tried to repeat in my career. I have come across the opposite in other stars I've worked with – not everyone's like Ronnie.

'One of my fondest memories was in the episode "Men Without Women". Fletcher wrote a letter on behalf of all the inmates to their respective wives telling them of their love of the fairer sex. When the wives were travelling to the prison on the bus, one of the wives started reading out aloud the contents of the letter, when suddenly all the women realised that their letters were the same. But one of the biggest laughs in a studio I've ever heard was when Lukewarm's boyfriend brought out the same letter – it was a moment of comic genius.

'After the first series had been completed, Ronnie gave all the regulars a silver tankard with the inscription, "Slade Prison 1974" together with our character's name; he gave mine an initial so it read "Lukewarm. P". I will always treasure it.

'I remember vividly the day word reached me of the tragic death of Ronnie's co-star, the multi-talented Richard Beckinsale. I was making a film, *The Tempest*, directed by Derek Jarman, on the northeast coast. It was bitterly cold and I was having a rest in my room late one afternoon when the telephone rang: it was a journalist from the *News of the World* asking whether I'd like to comment on the death of Richard. I was stunned and devastated; what a world star he would have been if he hadn't died so young, and how proud he would have been of his daughter, Kate.

'I, in turn, am very proud to be associated with one of the most glorious television sitcoms ever, starring two huge stars and a cast you would give your eye teeth to work with, written by two literary geniuses and held together by a brilliant producer. Nearly thirty years on nothing comes near its brilliance. Thank you, Syd.'

Cyril Shaps (Jackdaw in 'The Harder They Fall')
'My memories of *Porridge* are of rehearsals which demonstrated how inventive Ronnie Barker was throughout. His improvisations, his brilliant technique and, above all, his constant good humour were an inspiration.

'We shared a love of gardening and, in particular, rockeries. I mentioned this to him and he said he would like to see mine, which was in full bloom at the time. I invited him to tea after the day's rehearsal and he agreed immediately. We had a very happy session together.'

CHRISTMAS SPECIAL

NO WAY OUT

1. ASSOCIATION AREA

The camera shows a fairy on top of a Christmas tree. Lennie walks in to the association area with two mugs of cocoa. He hears prisoners singing carols.
Lennie walks round the catwalk and stops to watch the choir. One of the singers is Lukewarm. He looks up and notices Lennie. Lennie leaves.

1A. FLETCHER'S CELL

Fletcher is pasting a newspaper cutting of a topless girl on to a piece of card, on which he has written 'Merry Xmas'. Lennie enters.

LENNIE
What's that – you making a Christmas card?

FLETCHER
Yes – it's for my brother George. I cut it out the paper.

LENNIE
Not very seasonal, is it?

FLETCHER
It is for George – he's only allowed it once a year.

LENNIE
Can you hear the carols?

FLETCHER
Yeah – shut the door, will you?

LENNIE
Don't you like it?

FLETCHER
They've been at it for two hours – and they only know four carols. And the words of one of them are a bit suspect. Shepherds washed their socks by night!

LENNIE
Don't you find it rather moving? All those blokes, some of them real tearaways, united in a common exultation of this great occasion.

FLETCHER
Don't be daft. They're singing, my son, to drown the noise of Tommy Slocombe's tunnelling.

LENNIE
Tunnelling?

FLETCHER
That's the great occasion round here. Not the coming of our Lord, the going of Tommy Slocombe.

LENNIE

Nobody ever tells me nothing.

FLETCHER

It wasn't thought an event suitable for publication. It's a secret between Tommy, six baritones, twelve tenors and soprano.

LENNIE

Have we got a soprano?

FLETCHER

Oh there's lots of sopranos in here, my son. And a few of those baritones need watching an' all. Don't let those deep gruff voices fool you. 'Come over 'ere, son.'

LENNIE

Where is the tunnel?

FLETCHER

Where's the choir?

LENNIE

Just outside cell twenty-eight.

FLETCHER

About three feet under cell twenty-nine then. Give us a biscuit.

LENNIE

Well, I like the singing. At least it brings an air of festivity into our otherwise monotonous existence. There's ever such a lot to look forward to – there's the carol service, and the concert coming up. And the tree.

FLETCHER

Useful, the tree.

LENNIE

Useful?

FLETCHER

For stashing Christmas contraband. All those dingly danglies hide a multitude of sins. And even that Christmas fairy on the top has got two ounces of tobacco shoved up her tutu.

LENNIE

No wonder she looks uncomfortable. Where did that come from?

FLETCHER

The Governor's office. It was his present for Mr Mackay. Welsh George made a nifty switch when he was in there doing the floors.

LENNIE

He must have left something to take its place.

FLETCHER

He did. An identical gift-wrapped box, which Mr Mackay will doubtless open on Christmas Day.

LENNIE

What's in it?

FLETCHER

Well, I'll tell you one thing – if he uses it for putty all his windows will fall out.

He gets up.

LENNIE

What's Christmas like inside, Fletch?

FLETCHER

Slightly less 'orrible than any other day.

I mean, the Governor don't dress up
as Santa Claus and give us all bottles
of after-shave, you know.

LENNIE

But we get turkey, don't we – do we,
do we get turkey?

FLETCHER

They call it turkey, but not seeing it
carved we don't know, do we? If it
is, the one we had in our block
last year must have been a funny
shape. Twenty-eight legs and
no breast. Like Lulu and the
Young Generation.

He sits down.

LENNIE

Hey, that's good – can I use that in my
after-dinner speech? By the by, we get
pudding as well, don't we? Xmas
pudding like, with cream?

FLETCHER

Oh yes – that artificial whipped
cream. You'd be better off shaving
with that though. And, of course,
the wheeler-dealers make
a few bob at Xmas time. Slade
Prison's Mister Big, genial Harry
Grout, has granted a few franchises.
Young Terry Maidment is making
himself a fortune, flogging mistletoe
to the poofters.

LENNIE

Just like the outside then.
People have forgotten the real
meaning of Christmas. It's just a
commercial exercise.

FLETCHER

What do you expect? Goodwill to all
men – what? From Mackay? As much
chance of getting that as you have
finding a partridge up a pear tree.

LENNIE

Still the actual day should be a bit
brighter though, shouldn't it?

FLETCHER

Won't be this year.

LENNIE

Why not?

FLETCHER

Because of that flaming tunnel. That
tunnel spells disaster for us all. That
Tommy Slocombe's only chosen to
make his break on Christmas Eve.
Dear, dear never get through the traffic.

LENNIE

(*With a smile*) Oh – he's only
got six more digging days to Christmas
then.

FLETCHER

It's not funny, sonny Jim. We're all
going to be implicated in this escape.
Whether we like it or not.

He gets up.

LENNIE

But Slocombe's such a despicable
nurk. I don't see why anyone would lift
a finger for him.

FLETCHER

It so happens young Slocombe is the
brother-in-law of a big villain in the
smoke. A man who is also a colleague
of genial Harry Grout. Now he's

obviously got the word to Harry – 'Get
our kid away for Christmas.' So Harry's
running this caper. Which means if any
of us are asked to assist we are in no
position to refuse. Otherwise, one
morning we might find something else
hanging on the Xmas tree. Us.

LENNIE
I'm not going down no tunnel, I suffer
from claustrophobia.

FLETCHER
Do you?

LENNIE
It dates back to the time when I was
stuck in a chimney for
two hours.

FLETCHER
Oh dear, how was that?

LENNIE
I was going to turn over this big house
in Sutton Coldfield. The chimney was
my only means of access.

FLETCHER
Oh yeah, and you got stuck,
did you?

LENNIE
Yes, it was terrifying. What made it
worse was my intended victims came
home from the pictures, and saw my
legs sticking out of the fireplace.
I managed to run off though.

FLETCHER
Did they give the police a description?

LENNIE
Yeah, luckily I was covered in soot.
They're still looking for a tall, blue-eyed
Negro in a black suit.

FLETCHER
Yeah – well that might excuse you
tunnelling duties. But when
Slocombe's well out of it we'll all be
well in it. You, just as much
as anybody else. The point is,
it's disturbing the equilibrium of
prison life.

LENNIE
The equilibrium?

FLETCHER
Yeah, them and us, it'll tilt the balance
of power which exists between the law
and the villain. With this escape we
shall have pushed the system too far.

LENNIE
There's nothing we can do though, is
there? I mean, what can we do?

FLETCHER
I know what I'm going to do. I intend
to be well out of it.

LENNIE
How?

FLETCHER
I'm going away for Christmas.

LENNIE
Where to, Majorca?

FLETCHER
No – everyone goes to Majorca,
don't they? No, I thought I'd try

the prison hospital this year for a
change. A, because it's the nearest
thing to a holiday in here, and B,
because I shall be far removed from
any retaliations by the screws over this
escape fiasco.

LENNIE
You'll never get in the infirmary, not
with that doctor. What's supposed to
be wrong with you?

FLETCHER
It's my knee, isn't it?

LENNIE
I never knew there was anything wrong
with your knee.

FLETCHER
No, well I've been keeping it up
my sleeve. Or more precisely, my
trouser leg.

LENNIE
What's the matter with it?

FLETCHER
Cartilage. I've lived with the pain
for years. But recently, being on
my feet all day in the damp weather,
it has escalated the pain to an
unbearable degree.

LENNIE
Which knee is it?

FLETCHER
Eh?

LENNIE
Which knee is it?

FLETCHER
This one . . . or is it this one?

2. PRISON CLINIC

DOCTOR
Am I hurting you?

WARREN
(*Happily*) Yup.

DOCTOR
Sorry.

WARREN
You got your job to do.

DOCTOR
It's a pretty bad burn.

WARREN
(*Still happily*) Yeah, I know.

The Doctor looks up at Warren.

DOCTOR
What are you so pleased about?

WARREN
Well, Doc, if you're going to hurt
yourself in here, might as well make
sure it's nothing trivial. I mean there's
no way I can go back to work with this
hand, is there?

DOCTOR
I'm reluctantly forced to admit there
isn't.

WARREN
I think I could just about make it to the
infirmary though, if somebody opens
the door for me.

DOCTOR
(*Resolutely*) You're not going to the
infirmary. You're confined to your cell
for three days.

WARREN
You can't manage in a cell on your
own with your hand tied up like this.

I know it seems silly to lie in the infirmary with a bandaged hand. But, on the other hand . . .

DOCTOR
Neither of your hands is going to find its way into the sick-bay, is that understood?

WARREN
You don't like people getting in your infirmary, do you?

DOCTOR
And mess up all those crisp white sheets, certainly not. Next! (*To Warren*) Now just hold this dressing in place for a few moments, then I'll get you bandaged up.

Fletcher enters, limping and wincing. Just the quickest of looks from the Doctor, then –

DOCTOR
Out of here, Fletcher.

FLETCHER
I got my white card.

DOCTOR
Out, out, out.

FLETCHER
I'm sick!

DOCTOR
Out!

FLETCHER
I'm entitled.

DOCTOR
Years of medical practice have enabled me to tell at a glance if a man's sick or not. You're a perfect specimen of manhood, Fletcher.

FLETCHER
It's not that I've come about, it's my knee.

DOCTOR
What's wrong with your knee?

FLETCHER
Just ask me to stand on one leg.

DOCTOR
What?

FLETCHER
Ask me to stand on one leg.

WARREN
Go on, ask him. No harm in that.

The Doctor's curiosity gets the better of him.

DOCTOR
All right, stand on one leg.

Fletcher raises a leg and then collapses on the floor as the other one buckles beneath him. He looks at the Doctor accusingly.

FLETCHER
And you call yourself a doctor!

DOCTOR
Get up, Fletcher.

FLETCHER
I don't know if I can.

He raises himself with difficulty, keeping the weight off one foot.

DOCTOR
Sit in the chair. What is it?

FLETCHER
I'll show you.

Dramatically and carefully he rolls up his trouser leg. The Doctor watches. Warren cranes forward to

*see. Fletcher uncovers a knee . . .
a perfectly normal knee . . . and
gestures towards it.*

FLETCHER

There then!

DOCTOR

There what?

FLETCHER

It's a knee.

DOCTOR

I know it's a knee, Fletcher. I learned
that in medical school.

FLETCHER

But you didn't learn about this kind of
knee. You see the old trouble has
flared up again.

DOCTOR

What old trouble? Laziness?

FLETCHER

Cartilage. And before you say anything,
it's all on my medical records.

He points towards a filing cabinet.

FLETCHER

You check your files, you'll see I have
an official history of knee trouble.

DOCTOR

I don't believe you.

FLETCHER

Have to check though, won't you?

*The Doctor turns towards the file
shaking his head.*

DOCTOR

I don't know why I'm doing this.

FLETCHER

You're doing it because you know that
there's one chance in a million that one

day one of us will be telling the truth.
*The Doctor opens the filing
cabinet and first of all removes a
Christmas cake.*

FLETCHER

What's that then?

DOCTOR

It's a Christmas cake. I get one
every year.

FLETCHER

What for?

DOCTOR

The patients in the infirmary.

WARREN

But you never *allow* any patients in
your infirmary.

DOCTOR

That's true. I always take it home for
the wife.

*The Doctor goes through the files as
Fletcher turns to Warren.*

FLETCHER

Hey, that's a turn-up for the book, ain't
it – in prison.

WARREN

What?

FLETCHER

A file with a cake in it – get it, get it?

WARREN

Oh, yes. You're a very witty
man, Fletch.

FLETCHER

Here, are you a mason?

The Doctor has found Fletcher's record and is reading it.

DOCTOR

My God, it's true – Maidstone Jail 1967. Cartilage.

WARREN

Very common with footballers that. That and groin strain.

FLETCHER

Little chance of groin strain in here.

DOCTOR

All right, I accept you have an official record of surgery on your left knee. But this was years ago.

FLETCHER

Yeah, and I've lived with the pain ever since. Now I don't complain, do I, Bunny?

WARREN

No, he don't complain. Even though we've seen him crawl in from work some days like a wounded bloodhound on his hands and knee.

FLETCHER

(*Heroically*) Please – I'm not after sympathy.

DOCTOR

What is it you are after?

FLETCHER

Well . . . every so often, when the pain becomes unbearable, I have to lie down with my leg up – just for a week or two.

DOCTOR

(*Playing along*) You think a week in the infirmary would do the trick?

FLETCHER

Maybe a week.

DOCTOR

Let me tell you something, Fletcher. Of all the penal institutions in the north of England, my infirmary has the lowest record of admissions. Donaldson, who's doing a five stretch for grand larceny and embezzlement, has more chance of getting a Barclaycard than you have of getting in my infirmary.

FLETCHER

On your head be it.

The Doctor makes up his mind. He starts to fill out a form.

DOCTOR

Fletcher, I know you, and I know you're going to make an issue out of this, and waste a lot of my valuable time with your stupid nonsense, so here's what I'm going to do. I'm going to cut it out before it goes any further.

FLETCHER

Amputate? Now, hang on . . .

WARREN

That should get you in the infirmary.

DOCTOR

I'm sending you to a civilian hospital. For X-ray and specialist examination. You'll be there and back in a day. Then the matter will be irrevocably closed.

Fletcher realises he is losing the battle.

FLETCHER

Why waste the taxpayers' money? I tell you, I know my knee. All I need is to rest up for a day or two.

DOCTOR

(*Giving Fletcher the card*) On your way, Fletcher. You're a liar and a malingerer.

FLETCHER

Harsh words, Doctor. In this season of peace and goodwill to all men. I hope your conscience pricks you, that's all.

DOCTOR

You can say a little prayer for me on Christmas morning. Next.

FLETCHER

Yeah, I will. You don't mind if I say it standing up, do you? I can't kneel down, I've got a bad knee.

He walks across to leave and shakes Warren's hand.

FLETCHER

All the best.

WARREN

Aaaagh!

3. CELL

Fletcher is in his cell. Lennie walks in. In the distance we hear the choir, now singing 'O Come All Ye Faithful'.

LENNIE

Hey, Fletch –

FLETCHER

Shut the door!

LENNIE

Harry Grout's coming to see you.

FLETCHER

(*Surprised*) What?

LENNIE

Straight up. Grouty. On his way.

FLETCHER

What did I tell you? Gawd blimey, I knew it. This will be some little favour pertaining to Slocombo's moonlight flit – hello, Harry!

Fletcher's change of expression is explained by Grout's arrival.

GROUT

Hello, Fletcher.

FLETCHER

This is a rare privilege. You don't often drop in on people. Usually you get people to drop in on you. And if they don't you get other people to drop things on them.

Lennie laughs.

GROUT

You always were a bit of a joker, Fletch.

FLETCHER

Yes, I was. Up to now. What brings you to my humble abode, Grouty?

GROUT

I wanted to get out of my cell just for a while.

FLETCHER

Change of air?

GROUT

No, a couple of warders are putting up my Christmas decorations.

Lennie laughs. Grout takes a coin from his pocket and flicks it to Lennie.

GROUT

There you are, son. Go to the pictures or something.

Lennie gets the point.

LENNIE

Oh – thank you.

He goes.

GROUT

Shut the door.

Door crashes heavily.

GROUT

Sit down, Fletch.

FLETCHER

(*Sitting down*) Oh, thank you very much. Like the smell of a nice cigar. Wish I had something festive to offer you, Grouty.

GROUT

Not in the festive mood, Fletch. There's a tunnel being dug. You've heard, I suppose?

FLETCHER

Only when they leave off singing.

GROUT

Slocombe's a relative of friends of mine on the outside, and they want him sprung.

FLETCHER

Oh, isn't his dad Billy the Ponce

Slocombe? Yes, the one that got out of Brixton in '72. Where did he end up?

GROUT

Apparently he emerged on some Caribbean Island where the authorities took advantage of his criminal experience.

FLETCHER

How?

GROUT

Made him Chief of Police.

FLETCHER

Well, he did have a bit of style, the old man.

GROUT

Trouble is, it's beholden to me to accomplish the disappearance of his idiot offspring.

FLETCHER

Delicate, Grouty.

GROUT

Extremely.

FLETCHER

If only I could help in some way.

GROUT

You can, my son.

FLETCHER

Oh gawd.

GROUT

You're having a little day trip tomorrow, aren't you?

FLETCHER

Only to get my knee X-rayed.

GROUT

Still you'll be on the outside. And
we have friends on the outside
who could take advantage of that.

FLETCHER

How?

GROUT

There'll be a package. Someone.
Somewhere. Sometime. No sweat.

FLETCHER

I'll be under escort, Grouty. I'm not just
getting the bus down there and doing
a bit of last minute Christmas
shopping at the same time, you know.

GROUT

It's only a small package. A blank
passport. Inky Stevens needs one to
give Slocombe a more acceptable
identity.

FLETCHER

Wouldn't it be safer for him to
pick up his new passport on
the outside?

GROUT

Normally, yes. But the finest forger in
the country's Inky Stevens, and he's on
the inside, isn't he?

FLETCHER

Yes, yes . . .

GROUTY

I won't be ungrateful, Fletch.

He stands up.

FLETCHER

Oh good.

GROUT

Be something extra in your Christmas
stocking for this. Besides your bad
knee, that is.

*He laughs at his own joke. When he
opens the door, the choir can be
heard again. They are now halfway
through 'God Rest Ye Merry
Gentlemen'.*

Grout reacts with pleasure.

GROUT

Oh, I like this one.

He joins in.

GROUT

'Great tidings of comfort and joy,
comfort and joy . . .'

*He gestures to Fletcher to join him.
Fletcher does so, his expression
conveying anything but comfort
and joy.*

FLETCHER

'Great tidings of comfort and joy . . .'

4. PRISON YARD

*Barrowclough and Mackay walk up
to a waiting minibus and
Barrowclough gets in.
Fletcher approaches with
a warder.*

MACKAY

Haven't you forgotten
something, Fletcher?

FLETCHER

What?

MACKAY

Your limp – ha, ha . . .

FLETCHER

Oh, yes, mock the afflicted.

MACKAY

You're not sick, as the X-rays will soon prove.

FLETCHER

Well look, let's call the whole thing off then. Seriously. I can live with pain a few years longer. Hospitals is busy enough this time of year. Yeah, I'll just hobble back to my cell.

He turns and limps away.

MACKAY

Get in, Fletcher. Mr Barrowclough has his Christmas shopping to finish.

Fletcher gets in the bus and Mackay shuts the door. The bus starts to move.

5. HOSPITAL BUILDING

The camera shows the sign 'X-ray', then the hospital building.

FLETCHER

(*Voiceover*) All right, doc, you're the expert. I can take it. Give it to me straight . . .

DOCTOR

(*Voiceover*) (*Gravely*) I am afraid I have bad news for you, Mr Fletcher.

FLETCHER

(*Voiceover*) You have?

DOCTOR

(*Voiceover*) Yes . . . you have a perfectly healthy knee.

6. HOSPITAL ANTE-ROOM

It is a bare room, with a few tables, chairs and magazines. Fletcher and Barrowclough are sitting on chairs with cups of coffee. On the chair beside Barrowclough are several gift-wrapped packages. The camera shows a young Nurse holding up an X-ray photograph of a healthy knee.

NURSE

You've really got quite an attractive knee, Mr Fletcher.

FLETCHER

Not as attractive as yours, nurse. Yeah, I bet *they're* going to have a happy Christmas, ain't they?

BARROWCLOUGH

Now, that will do, Fletcher. You're old enough to be the girl's father.

FLETCHER

No, impossible, I never been round this way before.

NURSE

The main thing is, it's a healthy knee.

FLETCHER

Those X-rays prove nothing, you cannot photograph pain.

NURSE

When did your knee trouble start?

BARROWCLOUGH

Two days ago, when he thought he'd wangle the infirmary for Christmas.

FLETCHER

No, it does not. Goes back ten years.

As the Nurse leaves Hospital Porter passes by pushing a trolley. Another girl, dressed in civilian clothes but wearing a hospital white coat over them comes up to the men.

SANDRA

Can I get you gentlemen some more coffee?

FLETCHER

No, no, let's just get back to where we come from.

BARROWCLOUGH

(*Rising*) Well, I'd like another cup of coffee. It's all milk, isn't it? I only get half and half at home.

FLETCHER

Half and half?

BARROWCLOUGH

Milk and water.

FLETCHER

Oh yeah.

BARROWCLOUGH

If it's not too much trouble, Miss. Very sweet of you to ask.

SANDRA

(*To Fletcher*) You sure you don't fancy some?

FLETCHER

Not coffee, no thank you.

She gives them a dazzling smile and leaves.

BARROWCLOUGH

Charming girl.

He sits down.

FLETCHER

Look at you. Chapel hat pegs, ain't it? More sex-starved than me. How much longer are we going to sit around this draughty corridor, then?

BARROWCLOUGH

What's the matter with you, Fletcher? You seem very ill at ease. Relax. Enjoy yourself, it's Christmas. Have a biscuit.

FLETCHER

It's your attitude that's unsettling me. 'Have a biscuit' – God Almighty. Next thing we know we'll have Mr Mackay tucking us up in bed at night.

BARROWCLOUGH

Now, Fletcher! Mr Mackay's no different from anyone else. Outside the grey grim walls of our institution you'll find that he can be an amiable man.

FLETCHER

(*Incredulously*) Amiable?

BARROWCLOUGH

On Tuesday he stroked a dog. He did. I saw it with my own eyes. The Governor's boxer.

FLETCHER

What happened?

BARROWCLOUGH

It bit him.

FLETCHER

(*Amused*) Oh dear.

BARROWCLOUGH

Oh yes. He had to have an injection in case he caught rabies.

FLETCHER

What, the dog did – yes, he would.

BARROWCLOUGH

It's nothing to laugh at.

FLETCHER

Depends on your sense of humour, doesn't it? Look, I'm like the Governor's dog, ain't I? Conditioned to mistrust in an atmosphere of mutual contempt. I'm relaxed when we get back to the nick, you lock me up and we go back to hurling insults at each other.

BARROWCLOUGH

You're spoiling my day out, Fletcher.

FLETCHER

Oh, forgive me.

BARROWCLOUGH

Don't you think I sometimes get as sick of Slade Prison as you do? Today's been a break for me.

FLETCHER

Why? What would you have been doing today back at the prison, Mr Barrowclough?

BARROWCLOUGH

I was off duty today. I just volunteered for this trip.

FLETCHER

You could have stayed at home. Spent the day with your lady wife.

BARROWCLOUGH

That's really why I volunteered.

Sandra returns carrying a tray with coffee. Barrowclough is instantly on his feet.

BARROWCLOUGH

Here, let me take that.

SANDRA

I brought an extra cup just in case.

FLETCHER

Ta very much.

BARROWCLOUGH

You must forgive our friend here. He's a little morose. Not his usual self.

SANDRA

May I say something to your friend here?

BARROWCLOUGH

Certainly, my dear, by all means. The young lady wishes to address you, Fletcher.

SANDRA

It's just that . . . well, we're all very well aware in here of . . . what you are. And we realise it can't be a very happy time of year for you. So – with your permission (*To Barrowclough*) the radiologists and me have just got a little something here.

She produces a package the size of a large, stiff Christmas card.

SANDRA

It's not very much but I think it's the thought that counts.

BARROWCLOUGH

What a very nice thought. Isn't that nice, Fletcher?

Fletcher gets up and takes the package.

FLETCHER

Oh . . . oh, very nice of you, Miss. I can't say I'm not touched. In fact I'm deeply moved. Should I open it now?

SANDRA

(*Grabbing his arm*) No!! Not before Christmas Day.

She winks at Fletcher.

FLETCHER

Oh yes. Yes, of course.

SANDRA

Spoil the surprise, wouldn't it?

FLETCHER

(*Nervously*) Oh yes . . . oh no . . . Oh.

7. CELL

It is night time. Inside Fletcher's cell Grout is tearing open the envelope which contains a Christmas card and inside that a passport.

GROUT

Well done, my son.

FLETCHER

Give me palpitations I can tell you. Right under Barrowclough's nose!

Fortunately he was put off his guard by the day out, her legs and a couple of large Johnny Walkers.

GROUT

Smart bird that Sandra.

FLETCHER

Who is she, does she work there?

GROUT

'Course not. Come up from the smoke. All it took was a bit of nerve and a white coat.

FLETCHER

My nerve nearly went.

GROUT

Not you, Fletch, you're a dab hand. I'm only sorry your knee got a clean bill of health, Fletch. But p'raps I could do you a favour in that direction.

FLETCHER

How?

GROUT

Couple of my lads could have a go at it. Damage it beyond medical dispute.

FLETCHER

Er, I think I'll pass on that one, Grouty. Much as I appreciate your kind consideration.

GROUT

Please yourself. I just thought I'd mention it, because you see I would like to elicit the help of you and the lad a little further.

FLETCHER

Ain't I done my bit, Grouty?

GROUT

You see, it's the tunnel.

FLETCHER

Hang on a bit. The kid's got claustrophobia. And look at the size of me. A ferret I ain't.

GROUT

Nothing physical. Just want you to join the choir. They've come up against a very stoney bit, and we need all the fortissimo we can get.

FLETCHER

Oh, my pleasure, Grouty. Enjoy a good sing. Used to do a lot of it down in Maidstone when we worked on the prison farm. Church hymns mostly. Favourite one with the boys was 'We plough the fields and scatter'. A lot of 'em did, an' all. Right, that's everything then, is it?

GROUT

Not quite. Just one tiny thing.

FLETCHER

Oh, please, Harry, aren't I doing my share? Smuggling, singing . . .

GROUT

It's essential to the success of our venture.

FLETCHER

Well?

GROUT

We need a bicycle.

FLETCHER

Oh certainly, what colour?

8. PRISON LANDING

Barrowclough waits for Warren, then walks along the catwalk behind him. Lukewarm sees Barrowclough and moves to the radiator. He taps it. The radiator answers (it replies to taps). Lukewarm moves towards the tables and starts singing 'The First Noel'. Other prisoners start to join in.Barrowclough and Warren walk round the catwalk as the men are singing. As he sings, Lukewarm is watching Barrowclough.

9. CELL

Fletcher and Lennie are about to leave the cell when Warren and Barrowclough walk in.

FLETCHER

What's this, Mr Barrowclough? Lunchtime, in' it?

BARROWCLOUGH

Lunch can wait. I have something very serious to say to you three.

LENNIE

Why us three?

BARROWCLOUGH

Because it was you three who were in

the yard today when I arrived at work –
you three who involved me in a
pointless discussion on the outcome
of the Cup Final in 1962. That's why
I'm asking you three one pertinent
question . . . Where-is-my-bicycle?!!
*There is a pause while the three
prisoners look at each other in
outraged innocence.*

FLETCHER
What bicycle was this, then?

BARROWCLOUGH
The one I cycled to work on.

LENNIE
You got a bicycle, then?

BARROWCLOUGH
I've had one for a month or so. Ever
since the medical officer advised me to
take more exercise.

WARREN
I had a bike once.

BARROWCLOUGH
So did I! And I want to know what's
become of it.

*Lennie frowns as if trying to
understand.*

LENNIE
Let me get this straight, Mr
Barrowclough. You are saying that
prior to our conversation you were
the owner of a bicycle?

BARROWCLOUGH
That's right, yes.

LENNIE
And that since our conversation you are
the former owner of a bicycle?

BARROWCLOUGH
That's what I'm saying, yes.
*Fletcher sits down at the table. He
tries hard to get to the nub of
the matter.*

FLETCHER
Let me get this straight,
Mr Barrowclough. You are saying that
you arrived at work as a cyclist and
you'll be leaving as a pedestrian?

BARROWCLOUGH
Yes, yes, yes!

FLETCHER
Are you assuming there's a connection
between our discussion on the '62
Cup Final and the disappearance of
your alleged bicycle?

BARROWCLOUGH
There's nothing alleged about it. Green
it was.

WARREN
When did you last see your bicycle?

BARROWCLOUGH
When I got off it.

FLETCHER
You sure you had it with you when you
got off it?

*Barrowclough produces his
cycle clips.*

BARROWCLOUGH
Why do you think I wear these?

WARREN

To stop things falling out of
your trousers?

LENNIE

If we were talking to you, how could
we have palmed your bike?

BARROWCLOUGH

It was a well-known diversionary tactic.

FLETCHER

If you ask me, lads, this whole thing
sounds very dodgy.

BARROWCLOUGH

Dodgy?

FLETCHER

It has all the classic elements of an
insurance swindle.

BARROWCLOUGH

How dare you!

FLETCHER

(*Rising*) How dare you accuse us of
being bicycle thieves.

LENNIE

I saw that film. It was a beautiful
example of early Italian neo-realism.

BARROWCLOUGH

You're as impossible as ever. I thought
at this time of year . . . oh well, that's
just my naïve trust in human nature.
I should have known better. Warren –
follow me.

WARREN

Where to?

BARROWCLOUGH

Back to your cell. I'm going to
conduct a thorough search. And
if I find anything resembling a

bicycle pump in your trousers, you're
for it!

Fletcher reacts as they exit.

10. MACKAY'S OFFICE

*It is a tiny office with a gas fire,
racks of keys and a grubby
calendar. Barrowclough, clipboard
in hand, faces Mackay who is sitting
behind his desk.*

MACKAY

Pull yourself together, Barrowclough.
It's your own fault. You should never
turn your back on them, not for a
minute.

BARROWCLOUGH

I've always thought that the best way
to encourage trust was to show them
trust.

MACKAY

They're criminals, man.

BARROWCLOUGH

They're also human beings.

MACKAY

All right – but criminal human beings.
And they too often take advantage of
your lack of control. You lack
discipline. You're gullible.

BARROWCLOUGH

I sometimes give the men the benefit
of the doubt.

MACKAY

Never do that! It's rule one! Any time a
prisoner makes a request, a prison
officer must ask himself – 'What is he up
to?' Even the simplest request must be

treated with deep mistrust and suspicion. A prisoner ties his shoelace – question! What is he concealing in his sock?

BARROWCLOUGH

I know all that of course – but I never thought they'd steal a bicycle. They can't conceal that in their sock.

MACKAY

Oh come on, man! You know what these people are like! Did we ever find any trace of our billiard table?

BARROWCLOUGH

We found the red ball.

MACKAY

They'll have dismantled your bike in an instant. If we have as much luck as we did with the billiard table, maybe you'll get back your rear light.

BARROWCLOUGH

It seems so pointless.

MACKAY

There's always a point. My antennae tell me there's something going on. Think – have they asked you anything, any seemingly innocent favours?

BARROWCLOUGH

No, no, no. Well, they asked me one thing, but it was completely innocent.

MACKAY

(*Suspiciously*) What?

BARROWCLOUGH

They asked me to help with their choir at the carol service. There can't be any harm in that.

MACKAY

And you trusted them? Haven't I just told you – once you turn your back on them, you're finished.

BARROWCLOUGH

Oh, I won't do. I'll be conducting.

MACKAY

I think I'll conduct a little enquiry. Who's running this Glee Club?

They exit.

11. ASSOCIATION AREA

The prisoners' choir, including Fletcher, Lennie, Warren and Lukewarm, are grouped round singing.

CHOIR

'Good King Wencelas looked out
On the feast of Stephen
When the snow lay round about,
Deep and crisp and even.
Brightly shone the moon that night. . .'
Mackay and Barrowclough come from the office doorway and along the catwalk.

CHOIR

'Though the frost was cruel.'

MACKAY

Silence.

FLETCHER

'When a Scotsman came in
sight, hollering . . .'

MACKAY

That will do, Fletcher.

*Lukewarm looks towards radiator
from which can be heard 'clink, clink,
clink'. Lukewarm starts to move
towards the radiator.*

MACKAY

Stand still.

Lukewarm freezes.

*Mackay walks to the centre
of the room.*

MACKAY

What's that noise?

FLETCHER

Central heating, sir.

*Mackay moves to the radiator and
kicks it twice.*

The radiator replies.

FLETCHER

Oh – didn't know you was a plumber,
Mr Mackay. Think you've mended it.

MACKAY

All right – come on, back to your cells.

WARREN

We need more rehearsal, don't we?

MACKAY

There won't be any more.

LENNIE

Christmas, isn't it?

MACKAY

You've forfeited your right
to Christmas.

LENNIE

How?

MACKAY

Through a series of incidents,
culminating in the disappearance of Mr
Barrowclough's bicycle.

He walks among the prisoners.

MACKAY

I can't prove anything of course, but
don't think that technicality will affect
my judgement in the least. You were
put in here to keep crime off the
streets. But I'm not having you
bringing it into my prison. You will be
advised to remember that we have a
solitary confinement area, with which
you will become only too familiar if you
continue to practise the contemptible
habits which brought you here in the
first place. Clear? Right – back to your
cells the lot of you. Move!

*Prisoners file past Barrowclough
and Mackay.*

FLETCHER

I suppose you realise you've stifled at
birth what could have been the start of
a religious revival in here.

MACKAY

Out, Fletcher.

*Lukewarm stops to shake
Barrowclough's hand.*

LUKEWARM

In spite of all, Merry Christmas, sir. (*Taking his hand again*) And a very happy Christmas to Mrs Barrowclough.

BARROWCLOUGH

Right, now come on – move it along . . . (*Hesitantly*) Lukewarm . . .

MACKAY

(*To Barrowclough*) That is the only attitude they respect. The only attitude that will wipe out this wave of insubordination and petty theft.

BARROWCLOUGH

I suppose you're right . . . d'you think you could countersign my report?

He hands Mackay the clipboard.

MACKAY

Very well . . . (*Feeling for his pen*) That's funny, I seem to have mislaid my pen. (*Feeling other pocket*) Where's my wallet . . . Mr Barrowclough, I've been mugged!

BARROWCLOUGH

But that's not possible, sir. We've only been here a minute. We came in here at . . . (*Automatically checks his watch*) . . . Where's my watch!

12. CELL

Lennie is making a paper chain, when an indignant Fletcher enters.

FLETCHER

It's on the bulletin board, it's official.

LENNIE

What is?

FLETCHER

Christmas is cancelled. It says on the board, 'There'll be no Xmas Eve, Xmas Day or Boxing Day. Just the 24th, 25th and 26th December.'

LENNIE

Oh well, no point in finishing this chain.

He puts down the paper chain.

FLETCHER

I told you, didn't I?

LENNIE

About the equilibrium being disturbed?

FLETCHER

Disturbed, it's upside down, my son. Marvellous, isn't it? Tick along all year, keeping your nose clean, and through sheer intimidation we all get dropped in the yuletide clarts. And then that bleeding Lukewarm, talk about daylight robbery!

LENNIE

Not his fault, Fletch, be fair. He was under Grouty's instructions like the rest of us. They needed Mackay's wallet to keep topping up the getaway car.

FLETCHER

They didn't need Barrowclough's Timex though, did they? Force of flaming habit that was. The whole thing's been a mockery. Ill-conceived, badly organised and doomed to fail –

Grout enters, Fletcher does not miss a beat.

FLETCHER

– oh hello, Grouty. I was just saying what a shame your brilliant strategy should come to naught.

GROUT

Know what they say, the best-laid plans . . .

LENNIE

Should I – er, go to the pictures?

GROUT

No, sit down, sonny – no secrets now. Bad business. My friends in the smoke are bound to bear malice.

FLETCHER

Oh no – they'd never be so heartless, Grouty.

GROUT

Why not? I would.

LENNIE

Excuse me, Mr Grout, but couldn't you reactivate the tunnel at a later date?

GROUT

No, it was off course anyhow. He's an idiot that Slocombe. He nearly come up in the laundry last week.

FLETCHER

So the tunnel's now defunct then?

GROUT

Except for storing contraband, yes.

FLETCHER

I have a glimmer of an idea, Grouty. Which may solve all our problems.

GROUT

Oh yes?

FLETCHER

If the screws was to find that tunnel, it would do two things. One, it would tilt the balance of power back in their favour, 'cos they'd be chuffed at their own perspicacity. And two, they'd think that was the intended escape route.

LENNIE

But it was.

FLETCHER

It was, but it ain't now. It's a red herring. Then while the screws are still full of self-congratulatory ardour, you get Tommy away in a dustcart or something. That should please your pals in London.

GROUT

Here, here, you have had a thought, haven't you, Fletch.

FLETCHER

Save your face, Grouty.

GROUT

That it would.

LENNIE

It'll appear to be a perfectly executed plan.

GROUT

You're not wrong, son. Tip the Governor off?

FLETCHER

No – I think Mackay should find it. In fact if you give me the blueprints I might arrange for him to drop right in it.

13. PRISON YARD

Mackay is walking down the steps to the prison yard.

MACKAY

Fletcher, I'm told you wanted a word with me.

Fletcher moves to the foot of the steps.

FLETCHER

Just a seemingly innocent stroll, Mr Mackay. Away from prying ears. Know what I mean.

MACKAY

Oh yes.

They move away together.

FLETCHER

I know you see me in the role of adversary, Mr Mackay, but we're both old hands at this game – there's you and us. But we both know that neither of us must push the other too far.

MACKAY

That's true.

FLETCHER

Thereby we maintain a tolerable rhythm of life. We must season our mutual contempt with mutual respect.

MACKAY

What are you getting at, Fletcher?

They stop.

FLETCHER

Over this way, Mr Mackay, don't want to get too near the eavesdropping nurks.

They move on.

MACKAY

You were about to say?

FLETCHER

I was about to say I don't like to see your authority undermined.

Mackay stops.

MACKAY

And?

FLETCHER

Nothing specific. I just wanted to articulate these views. Can we go a bit further?

MACKAY

If there's any point.

FLETCHER

It would be a step in the right direction.

They move on again.

MACKAY

I wish you could be a little more specific, Fletcher.

FLETCHER

Oh I've gone far enough.

He stops and stamps his feet.

FLETCHER

Getting a bit parky, isn't it?

MACKAY

I'm a very busy man, Fletcher. I didn't come out here to discuss the weather.

FLETCHER

Nor did I, Mr Mackay.

MACKAY

I don't think this conversation's having any useful purpose at all.

FLETCHER

Well, hang about and we might discover something to your advantage.

MACKAY

Fletcher, I think you're trying to divert my attention. I'm not falling for it.

FLETCHER

No, you're not, are you?

Mackay turns and moves away.

FLETCHER

I'm only trying to explain my position.

He moves and falls through a gaping hole.

Mackay turns and walks back to the hole. He looks down in amazement.

14. PRISON INFIRMARY

Fletcher is lying in bed with his knee bandaged up, eating his Christmas lunch.

The door is unlocked by a prison officer and Lennie enters, carrying a box of cigars and a package.

LENNIE

Morning, Fletch.

FLETCHER

Morning, my son.

LENNIE

They've reinstated Christmas.

FLETCHER

I know, I'm eating it.

LENNIE

Here you are. Merry Christmas.

FLETCHER

Cuban cigars!

LENNIE

They're from Grouty.

FLETCHER

Where did he get these?

LENNIE

Some things we never know, Fletch. Where did B Block get their goose? That's one from me. Bit mundane after cigars, but I knitted them myself.

Fletcher finishes unwrapping the package.

FLETCHER

Oh very nice . . . I'll wear the other one when I get the bandages off.

LENNIE

They're mittens. Grouty says he's very sorry that his directions were eighteen inches out, but that's typical of Slocombe's prowess as a surveyor.

FLETCHER

I'm not bothered. What I set out to do's all come to roost, in' it?

LENNIE

Ensconced in the hospital, right. The screws are so chuffed with finding the tunnel – you should see them out there wha-hey . . .

Mackay walks in.

MACKAY

Compliments of the
season, Fletcher.

LENNIE

See what I mean?

MACKAY

Pardon?

LENNIE

Nothing.

MACKAY

All right, Godber, cut along. Don't want
to miss your Christmas lunch.

LENNIE

See you, Fletch.

FLETCHER

In due course, son.

LENNIE

Yeah. I'll send you a get-well-
slowly card.

Mackay laughs. Lennie leaves.

FLETCHER

Well, Mr Mackay, you look a little . . .
flushed – is that the word?

MACKAY

Just been to the Governor's sherry
party. Everyone was in high spirits.
Except the doctor . . . you've got
his cake.

Fletcher reacts.

Mackay holds up a package.

MACKAY

Look at this – a present from the
Governor. Pipe tobacco, I imagine.

FLETCHER

I'd open that when you get home
if I was you, when you're on
your own.

MACKAY

Oh, I will.

FLETCHER

Yeah, I shall look forward to that.

MACKAY

Fletcher, I wanted to say that
I appreciate what you were up to
in the yard.

FLETCHER

Oh?

MACKAY

(*Laughing*) All right, Fletcher. Just
between you and me.

FLETCHER

I don't know what you're inferring, Mr
Mackay.

MACKAY

Of course you don't, officially. But as
you said we're both old hands at the
game. Like to ask you just one
question. What became of the soil that
was excavated from the tunnel?

FLETCHER

No, wait a moment. Whatever you're
assuming about our relationship,
do not assume that you have a
new informer in your back pocket.
There's you and us, and I'm still
on the side of us.

MACKAY

It's a harmless question, for future reference. I just want to know how they disposed of the soil.

FLETCHER

Can't help you.

Mackay produces a bottle of Scotch.

MACKAY

Scotland's finest.

FLETCHER

With a couple of nips out of it, I see.

MACKAY

Still an unexpected treat.

FLETCHER

Bribe, is it?

MACKAY

Christmas present.

Fletcher looks at the bottle.

MACKAY

Come along, Fletcher. Just between you and me.

FLETCHER

Is that door closed?

MACKAY

And there's no one out there.

FLETCHER

Christmas present.

MACKAY

Christmas present.

FLETCHER

You want to know where they put the soil?

MACKAY

Simple as that.

FLETCHER

I'll tell you then.

MACKAY

I thought you might.

FLETCHER

They dug another tunnel and put it down there.

Mackay laughs with satisfaction and starts to go. Then he realises he has been done. He looks back to Fletcher who is about to have a drink.

FLETCHER

Happy Christmas.

He drinks.

CHRISTMAS SPECIAL

CHRISTMAS TRAILER

FLETCHER'S CELL

Lennie and Fletcher are sitting at the table.

LENNIE

I'm looking forward to it. There's the carol service, and the concert coming up. And the tree.

FLETCHER

Useful, the tree.

LENNIE

Useful?

FLETCHER

For stashing Xmas contraband. Even the fairy on the top has got two ounces of tobacco stuffed up her skirt.

Barrowclough enters.

FLETCHER

Hello, Mr B., what brings you here?

BARROWCLOUGH

Important message from the Governor. Christmas is cancelled.

FLETCHER

You what?

LENNIE

You what?

Mackay enters behind Barrowclough.

MACKAY

Oh yes. It's official. There will be no Xmas Eve, Xmas Day, or Boxing Day. Just the 24th, 25th and 26th December.

LENNIE

He can't do that – it's traditional.

BARROWCLOUGH

He's done it.

MACKAY

It's on the bulletin board. It's just not going to *happen*.

He chuckles.

MACKAY ·

Carry on!

He and Barrowclough continue on their rounds.

FLETCHER

That's rubbish, that is. Take no notice. We shall be here, shan't we, Lennie?

LENNIE

Yeah.

FLETCHER

I mean – where can we go?

CHRISTMAS SPECIAL

THE DESPERATE HOURS

1. ASSOCIATION AREA

*Camera shows the well area
and the prisoners. A warder
walks across.
McLaren and Tulip are watching.
The warder walks past a prisoner,
who watches and then nods to
McLaren. He receives the nod, in
turn nods to Tulip and moves away.
Tulip is sitting reading a newspaper.
He receives the nod and, in turn,
nods to the prisoner at the end of
the table. The prisoner receives the
nod. He then nods to Warren.
Warren receives the nod and
leaves. McLaren comes to the gates
and nods.
Fletcher receives the nod and
shakes his head. The camera
reveals that he is standing outside
the door marked 'WC'. The door
opens and Mackay comes out. He
reacts to Fletcher and then leaves.
Fletcher then nods, gets a label from
his pocket and sticks on the door
'Gentlemen only'. He then goes in.
McLaren, Warder unlocking gate.
Warren joins McLaren*

*and they walk through the
gate and depart.
McLaren and Warren go in through
the WC door.*

2. SHOWER ROOM

*Fletcher and Tulip are near the sink.
Lennie is near the second cubicle.
McLaren and Warren walk in.*

FLETCHER

McLaren, Warren . . . I have gathered
you here as representatives of your
respective cell blocks.

WARREN

What's this all about, Fletch?

FLETCHER

A minute, please. As you know, the
festive season is almost upon us.

MCLAREN

With all the high spirits and jollity which
that entails.

FLETCHER

Now come on, Jock, that's the wrong
attitude going in, that is. Let me ask you
all what is the real meaning of
Christmas? Aside from the shepherds
and the swaddling an' that. What
comes to mind then?

LENNIE

Chestnuts roasting on an open fire.

FLETCHER

What? Oh yes, very good.

MCLAREN

What about Mackay roasting on an open fire?

FLETCHER

No, that's Guy Fawkes night.

WARREN

Crackers. Holly.

LENNIE

Treetops glistening and children listening –

FLETCHER

That will do, Godber. You can leave out the Perry Como. I'm talking about what the likes of us associate with Christmas. Aside from robbing a postman.

They look at each other.

TULIP

What?

FLETCHER

Drink.

WARREN

Drink?

FLETCHER

Drink, yes. That's what everyone does at Christmas, gets drunk. Bombed. Plastered. Elephant's trunk. Legless. Brahms and Liszt as the proverbial newt.

LENNIE

(*To McLaren*) I've never understood the derivation of that expression myself.

Are newts known to be heavy drinkers?

FLETCHER

(*Irritated by the interruption*) Time is somewhat precious. We are running a security risk. Time is somewhat precious.

LENNIE

Sorry, Fletch, I was just saying . . .

FLETCHER

Yuh, well.

TULIP

What are we here for, Fletch?

FLETCHER

Wine tasting.

TULIP

Wine tasting?

FLETCHER

Yes, unbeknownst to all and sundry and out of charity to our fellow inmates, young Godber and me have been fermenting illicit liquor since last July. We done this so it would reach its peak maturity at this festive season.

MCLAREN

Fletch, you're a marvel, you're a naffing marvel, you know that?

FLETCHER

Yuh, well.

LENNIE

I helped him as well.

WARREN

And are you dishing this stuff out, like?

FLETCHER

I knew I shouldn't have used that word,

charity, Warren. This is a business transaction. You are here to obtain a free sample – sip – and place an order for your fellow felons. Godber . . .

Lennie moves to the second cubicle, stands on the toilet bowl and takes from the cistern two bottles of colourless fluid.

FLETCHER

We are offering two selections. We have five-star in the white bottle and the two-star in the blue bottle.

PRISONER

(*Putting his head round the door*) Oi!

Tulip, Fletcher, Warren and McLaren rush to the urinals. Lennie goes to the second cubicle and sits down. The warder enters and walks round looking at them. He leaves. The prisoners return to their original places and the conversation continues.

FLETCHER

Now as I was saying, the two-star is the Vin Ordinaire, though let me tell you it ain't that ordinaire. The five-star is our special reserve, we'll sample that first.

Lennie is carefully pouring some of the five-star into a bottle cap.

LENNIE

I'd like to warn you gentlemen, that this should be sipped delicately, like a fine liqueur. It should not be smashed down the throat by the mugful, all right.

Lennie passes the cap first to Tulip.

He takes a cautious sip and passes it to Warren.

He sips and passes it to McLaren who also sips for a moment. Then they react with anguished gasps.

FLETCHER

I thought they'd like it, Len.

WARREN

You ought to have washed the bottle out first.

MCLAREN

Fletcher, are you sure this stuff is fit for human consumption?

FLETCHER

No, I'm not. That's why you three nurks is testing it for me.

TULIP

This stuff's evil, Fletcher.

FLETCHER

Don't forget it's got another week to mature. Lennie, the two-star. I should warn you gentlemen that this one isn't quite so smooth. Be careful otherwise not only will you lose the flavour and the bouquet, you will probably lose your power of speech as well.

Lennie has given them the cap of the two-star. Warren holds it. They sniff it cautiously.

MCLAREN

(*Sniffing it*) Smells like embrocation.

FLETCHER

There is a hint of that, yes.

TULIP

You could poison the whole prison, Fletcher.

FLETCHER

It's not very easy to get the right ingredients in here you know. I got the potato peelings, and the orange pips. No bother. But normally I would never have used boot polish.

There are howls of protest from the others.

FLETCHER

Only a joke, only a joke.

WARREN

(*With the cap near his lips*)
You sure?

FLETCHER

'Course I am.

Warren drinks.

FLETCHER

It was anti-freeze.

Warren splutters it out.

3. PRISON GOVERNOR'S OFFICE

Venables is checking the morning mail when there is a knock at the door.

VENABLES

Come in.

A trusty enters carrying a tray of coffee and biscuits. He is a small, inoffensive man named Keegan with a Yorkshire accent.

KEEGAN

Morning, Guv'nor.

VENABLES

Morning, er, er . . .

KEEGAN

Keegan, sir . . .

VENABLES

You're new aren't you, Keegan?

KEEGAN

I'm not new to prison, sir, I'm just a new trusty. Mr Mackay's Christmas box 'cause I'm going out soon, like.

VENABLES

Good, good. Well, don't fall back into your old ways.

KEEGAN

No chance of that, sir. Not since t' wife passed away.

VENABLES

Oh I'm sorry. When was this?

KEEGAN

A few weeks before I came inside.

VENABLES

Poor woman, what happened?

KEEGAN

I murdered her.

Venables is slightly taken aback.

VENABLES

Well, see that it doesn't happen again.

Keegan leaves as Mackay comes in.

MACKAY

Morning, sir.

VENABLES

Close the door, Mr Mackay.

MACKAY

Sir?

Closes the door.

VENABLES

This new trusty – what's his name . . . Keegan?

MACKAY

No complaints, I hope, sir.

VENABLES

The man's a murderer.

MACKAY

Oh. Yes, sir. But crime of passion. Crime passionelle – that's French. Not a criminal type. His sort of murderer makes a model prisoner. Do their porridge, no bother, full remission. According to Home Office figures, seventy-five per cent . . .

VENABLES

I'm not interested in statistics, Mr Mackay. Just don't want my morning coffee served to me by a wife murderer. All right?

MACKAY

Very good, sir.

Venables crosses to the desk.

MACKAY

Replace him, sir.

VENABLES

Now to the business in hand. I have always found Christmas to be a very difficult time.

MACKAY

Yes, sir. So open to abuse. Contraband, bartering, smuggling. There isn't a Christmas cake comes inside that isn't laced with marijuana.

VENABLES

What are we doing about that?

MACKAY

I've taken precautions, sir. I've put Mr Barrowclough on to sampling all food parcels.

VENABLES

Has he anything to report?

MACKAY

He's still too stoned to tell me, sir.

VENABLES

What about drink?

MACKAY

Always a problem, sir. They're so ingenious at hiding it, as you know, sir. I remember once they concealed it in a fire extinguisher. A fact we only discovered because a fire broke out in the education room. It was only a small fire, but after we used that particular extinguisher, it became a raging inferno.

VENABLES

Disgraceful. Well, as you know, Mr Mackay, I am a staunch teetotaller, and I am strongly opposed to drinking, legal or illegal.

MACKAY

Yes, sir.

VENABLES

So let us be especially vigilant this Christmas and hope that we get through it with a minimum of incident.

MACKAY

I'll drink to that, sir.

VENABLES

Hardly an appropriate remark, Mr Mackay.

MACKAY

Sorry, sir.

VENABLES

All right, carry on.

Mackay starts to go.

VENABLES

Oh, and you'll see about replacing er . . .

MACKAY

Keegan, sir. Yes, sir.

VENABLES

(*Drinking his coffee*) Incidentally, how did he kill his poor wife?

MACKAY

Poison, sir.

Venables looks at his coffee cup with grave misgivings.

4. ASSOCIATION AREA

As the gate is unlocked by the warder, two prisoners come out and Fletcher and Lennie go in. They stop.

FLETCHER

Hello, hello,

Camera reveals a Prison Officer searching through the bedclothes in Fletcher's cell.

FLETCHER

I think we've got burglars.

LENNIE

Who hasn't?

They move on.

4A. FLETCHER'S CELL

Fletcher and Lennie enter to discover Barrowclough in the process of turning over their cell.

FLETCHER

(*Indignantly*) What's this then?

BARROWCLOUGH

You're not being singled out, Fletcher, we're doing the whole block.

LENNIE

Harassment. Despicable infringement of civil liberties.

FLETCHER

If you told us what you was looking for, we might be able to save you all this bother.

BARROWCLOUGH

Drink.

FLETCHER

Drink? You mean alcohol? The demon rum, mother's ruin?

BARROWCLOUGH

That's what I mean, yes.

FLETCHER

I'm a strict teetotaller, Mr Barrowclough.

BARROWCLOUGH

(*Sceptically*) Really, Fletcher.

He walks across the cell.

FLETCHER

(*Following him*) Oh yes. Never touch
tea, never have. I tell you something,
the pathetic state of this country today
has got more to do with tea
than alcohol.

BARROWCLOUGH

How?

FLETCHER

Because we invented the tea break,
that's where the rot set in.

BARROWCLOUGH

You're in no position to point the finger,
Fletcher, when you've never done an
honest day's work in your life.

FLETCHER

Oh that's very nice. He's added slander
now to breaking and entering.

LENNIE

They've been turning us over all week.
D'you know what they did last night?
They come in the Hobby Shop where
we was making soft toys for orphan
children. I saw Mr Barrowclough
with me own eyes, disembowelling
my panda.

BARROWCLOUGH

Don't you think I felt bad about that?
Just as I felt bad about sampling your
food parcels.

FLETCHER

I heard you felt pretty good
afterwards, though. (*To Lennie*)
They found him standing in a
bucket of sand and singing the
'Desert Song'.

BARROWCLOUGH

(*Embarrassed*) Yes, well, I suggest you
men get this cell tidied up.

*He leaves. Fletcher raises his
voice for the departing
Barrowclough's benefit.*

FLETCHER

Oh very nice, exit the red shadow.
(*Crossing to the door*) That's charming,
ain't it? You don't find nothing, but no
apologies, no retraction. As you say,
Len, a total infringement of civil liberties.
An unjustifiable act of mistrust
and suspicion.

LENNIE

They didn't find nowt, though.

FLETCHER

'Course not, we hid it too well. Shut
the door and fetch your mug.

*Lennie does so. Fletcher, plays
barman, fetching a mug and putting
a towel across his arm. He moves to
the right of his bunk.*

FLETCHER

Good evening, sir. And what will it be?

LENNIE

The usual.

FLETCHER

Care for a drink first?

LENNIE

Why not.

FLETCHER

Large one?

LENNIE

Mind your own business.

FLETCHER

Thank you.

He unscrews screw from bedstead and pours from it into the mug. Lennie puts a finger over the hole.

LENNIE

Have one yourself.

FLETCHER

(*Taking drink*) Oh thank you, sir. When.

Lennie puts his finger back over the hole.

They drink.

FLETCHER

(*Putting screw back on*) Prisoners one, system nil.

Mackay enters.

MACKAY

Not necessarily, Fletcher.

FLETCHER

Oh my gawd . . . time gentlemen please. Haven't you got no cells to go to?

5. GOVERNOR'S OUTER OFFICE

Mrs Jamieson, the Governor's secretary, sits at her desk. Barrowclough is sitting on a bench, waiting to see Venables. He is holding a cake. Mackay opens the

door and marches Fletcher and Lennie in.

MACKAY

Left, right, halt, face the front. Good morning, Mrs Jamieson, Mr Barrowclough . . .

MRS JAMIESON

Good morning, Mr Mackay.

FLETCHER

Good morning, Mrs Jamieson – you're looking very . . .

MACKAY

Quiet, Fletcher. Is the Governor in?

BARROWCLOUGH

I'm waiting to see him, he's indisposed.

He indicates the corridor.

FLETCHER

In the where?

MRS JAMIESON

He's not feeling too well. Ever since he sampled the Christmas pudding.

LENNIE

(*Offended*) Here, I made that. Nothing wrong with it.

FLETCHER

That's what you said about your Hungarian gluelash.

MACKAY

The word Fletcher is 'goulash'.

FLETCHER

I chose the word advisedly,
Mr Mackay. Seeing as most of us were
stuck in the bog.

Venables walks in. He looks wan
and pale and walks cautiously
towards his office.

MACKAY

Attention.

FLETCHER

Bless you.

MACKAY

Morning, Governor.

VENABLES

Morning, Mr Mackay.

MACKAY

Not too good I hear, sir. Sorry to
hear it.

VENABLES

Not too good at all. That prisoner we
replaced, Keegan – you didn't put him
in the kitchen, did you?

MACKAY

No, sir.

VENABLES

I wondered if he was extracting
some terrible revenge. I'd better
have some more of that vile
stuff, Mrs Jamieson. Right,
Mr Barrowclough, you can
come through, but I warn you,
I've not got long.

He goes through into his office,
followed by Barrowclough.
Mrs J. gets a bottle of medicine and
starts to pour it into a glass.

FLETCHER

(*To Lennie*) See what you done?
A stricken Governor. What sort of
Christmas is he going to have then?

MACKAY

What sort of Christmas are you two
going to have?

FLETCHER

Chuffed, aren't you?

MACKAY

Your own fault, Fletcher. You know the
penalties for brewing illicit hooch.

FLETCHER

Wasn't illicit hooch. It was a
health drink.

MACKAY

Poppycock!

FLETCHER

No, it is not poppycock. We couldn't
get the poppies. Mind you in here
there's no shortage of . . .

MACKAY

Fletcher!

FLETCHER

Just saying, health drink. Me and four
hundred of the lads saved up a wine
gum each. Then we crushed them in a
press in the woodwork shop. The
resultant extract is a remedy for all
known ills.

LENNIE

You should give the Governor some,
Mrs Jamieson.

MACKAY

I think the Governor's sick enough.

Mrs J. stands up, crosses to the

door and goes into the office.
All look at her legs appraisingly.
Mackay notices Fletcher
and Lennie.

MACKAY

Stop it, you two.

LENNIE

I've always been attracted to older
women. When I was a lad, I always
wanted to be seduced by my aunty
Pauline. She was very sophisticated.
Worked in a dress shop in Smethwick
and wore Evening in Paris behind
her ears.

FLETCHER

Oh, behind the ears, yes, sure sign.

LENNIE

I nearly was once.

FLETCHER

What?

LENNIE

Seduced. I went round her house and
the radio was on and she said,
'Lennie, it's time you learned how to
do the foxtrot.' Well, even at the naïve
age of fourteen, I thought to myself,
'Foxtrot? In the middle of the day?
Yum, yum.'

Mackay, despite himself, is
fascinated by the story. Fletcher
notices this.

FLETCHER

Should you go on in front of Mr
Mackay? Edinburgh Presbyterian you
know. Sex is only allowed when Hearts
beat Celtic.

MACKAY

I am not interested in Godber's carnal
reminiscences.

He walks over and sits down.

FLETCHER

Well I am, so what happened, Len?

LENNIE

Nothing.

FLETCHER

What?

LENNIE

Nothing happened. I mean, she held
me very close like, but for an hour we
just danced round the living room floor
accompanied by the Northern Dance
Orchestra.

FLETCHER

Big room, is it? Godber, your stories
have a habit of tailing off like that. You
are the master of the anti-climax.

LENNIE

I can't half foxtrot though.

Mrs Jamieson returns and sits
at her desk. There is a knock on
the door.

MACKAY

Come in.

The door opens and a trusty enters
carrying a tray with coffee and
biscuits. It is Reg Urwin. He seems a
little disconcerted to see the room
so full.

URWIN

Oh . . . hello, lads.

FLETCHER

Hello, Reg.

Urwin indicates his left arm.

FLETCHER

Something wrong with your arm?

Urwin indicates the red band.

FLETCHER

Oh, trusty now, are we?

URWIN

Er, yes. Replaced Keegan, thanks to Mr Mackay.

MACKAY

If a man keeps his nose clean, I don't forget.

URWIN

Should I come back later?

MACKAY

(*Rising*) Not at all, lad – don't be thick. Take the Governor his coffee. Chop, chop.

Urwin goes through into the other office.

6. GOVERNOR'S OFFICE

Barrowclough is standing by the desk while Venables signs papers. Urwin moves towards the desk with the coffee.

URWIN

Your coffee, sir.

VENABLES

Oh, thank you, er . . .

URWIN

Urwin, sir. With a 'U'. I'm the new trusty.

VENABLES

That's a privileged position, Urwin.

URWIN

I know it is, sir. That's why I've been so well behaved the last few months. So that I could get this job. So that I could get ahead with my plan.

But a look of anguish has crossed over Venables' face.

VENABLES

(*Standing*) I'm afraid your plan will have to wait, Urwin.

He makes a dash for the door.

7. OUTER OFFICE

Fletcher and Lennie react with interest as Venables dashes through.

MRS JAMIESON

Oh, Mr Venables – have you got time to sign . . .

VENABLES

No!

He leaves. Then he comes back.

VENABLES

I'll take it with me.

FLETCHER

Pity it wasn't in triplicate.

Venables goes.

8. GOVERNOR'S OFFICE

Barrowclough and a puzzled Urwin wait.

URWIN

Where's he gone?

He moves to the door.

BARROWCLOUGH

It's just that he has a bit of an upset tummy.

URWIN

Yes, but he was instrumental in my plan, he was.

BARROWCLOUGH

What plan is this, Urwin?

URWIN

(*Distractedly*) I suppose a screw's just as good. Yeah, I don't see why not.

BARROWCLOUGH

I said, what is your plan?

URWIN

I want to get out of here.

BARROWCLOUGH

That's what we all want, Urwin.

URWIN

Yes, but you don't want me to get out as soon as what I do. That's why I'm taking you hostage.

He produces a home-made gun from his pocket and points it at Barrowclough's back. Barrowclough turns and stares incredulously.

URWIN

It's a gun. And it works. And it's loaded.

BARROWCLOUGH

Now just a moment, er . . .

URWIN

Urwin. With a 'U'.

BARROWCLOUGH

Urwin, why don't you put that gun down?

URWIN

What, so you can pick it up?

BARROWCLOUGH

You should think very carefully about what you're doing.

URWIN

Oh I have done. Now here's what I'd like you to do. First, would you draw them blinds. Second off, would you get me an 'elicopter.

Barrowclough stares at him in astonishment.

URWIN

Well go on.

Barrowclough walks across to the window.

9. OUTER OFFICE

Mackay, Fletcher and Lennie are waiting.

FLETCHER

Listen, the Governor's obviously got other things on his mind, why don't we all come back in the New Year, Mr Mackay, round about April.

MACKAY

Fletcher, I'm in no hurry. I've waited long enough for this moment.

FLETCHER

Well, in that case, let's take a seat.

They move to the bench.

MACKAY

Fletcher – how dare you?

LENNIE

I don't mind waiting. It's almost worth getting busted these days, just for a glimpse of Mrs Jamieson's lovely . . .

MACKAY

Godber.

LENNIE

Smile.

MACKAY

(*Crossing to Mrs J.*) I apologise for these two.

MRS JAMIESON

That's all right, Mr Mackay, working in prison I've learnt to turn the other cheek.

LENNIE

And a very attractive cheek, too.

The connecting door opens and a pale-looking Barrowclough pokes his head through.

BARROWCLOUGH

Eh, Mrs Jamieson, I want to get in touch with the nearest RAF station.

MRS JAMIESON

I don't know where that is.

BARROWCLOUGH

Well, the Fleet Air Arm or Air Sea Rescue. Anyone who can get me a helicopter.

FLETCHER

My word, you're being a bit lavish with your Christmas presents, aren't you, Mr Barrowclough?

BARROWCLOUGH

What?

FLETCHER

You'll need a lot of coloured paper to wrap that up.

MACKAY

Quiet, Fletcher. Is there a problem, Mr Barrowclough?

BARROWCLOUGH

Yes, Mr Mackay, something's come up.

MACKAY

Come up?

BARROWCLOUGH

Yes, I'm being held at gunpoint by Urwin here.

He gestures over his shoulder.

MACKAY

You're what?

Urwin appears behind Barrowclough, brandishing the gun.

URWIN

It's true, look.

Mrs Jamieson gives a little scream.

URWIN

Don't panic, missis. Just get on the blower.

FLETCHER

Here, Reg, you gone off your rocker?

URWIN

Shut up, Fletch.

FLETCHER

As you say, my son.

Mackay decides the time has come for him to take charge.

MACKAY

All right, Urwin. Give me that gun.

He starts to move.

URWIN

You make a move and Barrowclough gets it.

Mackay advances slowly.

MACKAY

I said, give me that gun.

BARROWCLOUGH

Shut up, Mackay! This is no time for stupid heroics.

MACKAY

We can't let these people intimidate us.

BARROWCLOUGH

That's all very well for you to say, but it's my head the gun is pointing at.

URWIN

You just naff off, Mackay. I've got two hostages, him and her, so put the word out right?

Mackay looks at Mrs Jamieson, then at Barrowclough.

BARROWCLOUGH

Go on man, do as he says.

Mackay moves reluctantly towards the door.

MACKAY

Very well. Don't panic, Mrs Jamieson,

soon have you out of this. And don't you panic, Mr Barrowclough.

FLETCHER

(*Crossing to the centre of the room*)

Mr Mackay?

MACKAY

Yes?

FLETCHER

Can we panic?

MACKAY

You two come along with me.

Fletcher and Lennie move quickly to the door.

URWIN

No – they stay. I can use them. Now naff off, Mackay.

Mackay leaves.

Mrs Jamieson looks up from the phone directory.

MRS JAMIESON

I've found the number for RAF Topcliff.

URWIN

Get them then.

She starts to dial. Fletcher and Lennie exchange glances.

FLETCHER

Listen, Reg, you don't really need us. We're only littering up the place. We'll just be getting back to our cells if it's all the same to you. Busy day ahead.

URWIN

No, I need you two. Lock that door, Godber.

Lennie locks the door.

URWIN

Now both of you, move that filing cabinet up against it.

They start to move towards the cabinet.

MRS JAMIESON

I have them on the line, Mr Barrowclough.

BARROWCLOUGH

Er . . . should I . . . talk to them in there?

He indicates the inner office.

URWIN

Yeah, go on.

Barrowclough goes through into the other office. Urwin stays in the doorway covering both rooms.

LENNIE

Er . . . is that all you wanted us for, Reg. To move the cabinet?

URWIN

Yeah.

LENNIE

Oh well . . . we'll be getting off then.

FLETCHER

Yeah, give us a hand to shift this, Len.

They start moving the cabinet but Urwin stops them.

URWIN

Hey, hey! Think I'm crackers or something?

FLETCHER

Possibly, Reg. Your behaviour ain't exactly that of a rational man.

URWIN

I know what I'm doing. Give me that key.

Lennie gives him the key. He goes to the doorway.

URWIN

We'll just sit tight and wait.

There is a pause.

MRS JAMIESON

I have a dental appointment in half an hour.

URWIN

Then you'll have to bleedin' cancel it.

10. INNER OFFICE

Barrowclough is standing at the desk, talking on the phone. Urwin watches him.

BARROWCLOUGH

Hello? Yes, this is Prison Officer Barrowclough from Slade Prison . . . well, thank you Flight Sergeant, but don't you think I ought to speak to the Commanding Officer . . . yes, I know there's only two shopping days left till Christmas, but there is some urgency here.

Urwin crosses to the desk and grabs the phone from Barrowclough.

URWIN

Here. This is Reg Urwin. I'm in charge.

I've got the gun. Listen, I'm holding a man and a woman as hostage. I don't care how you do it, but I want a chopper here in half an hour. And wait a minute –

Fletcher and Lennie are standing in the doorway listening.

URWIN

– I also want ten thousand quid in used notes. Otherwise I'm not responsible for my actions.

He puts the phone down and turns to Barrowclough.

URWIN

That's the way to talk to those people. If they ring back and they're still stalling, make believe I'm going to kill you.

BARROWCLOUGH

I'll try to remember that.

11. OUTER OFFICE

Lennie is standing by the window. Mrs Jamieson gets up from her desk and goes to the cabinet. She opens a drawer.

LENNIE

Bearing up?

MRS JAMIESON

Pardon?

LENNIE

Under the strain, like.

MRS JAMIESON

Oh I'm keeping myself busy.

Both move towards the desk.

MRS JAMIESON

Doing some of those jobs one's always putting off. Helps keep my mind occupied otherwise I might go to pieces.

LENNIE

Not you, Mrs Jamieson.

He sits on the edge of the desk.

LENNIE

I think you're holding up extremely well. Typically British, if I may say so. Stiff upper lip. Calm under crisis, that sort of thing.

MRS JAMIESON

That's sweet of you to say so.

LENNIE

To be quite honest, it doesn't surprise me. I've always admired you, Mrs Jamieson. From afar, like.

MRS JAMIESON

Oh why?

LENNIE

You remind me of my aunty Pauline.

Fletcher comes through into the room and reacts to Lennie's line.

FLETCHER

(*At door*) Oh yes. Do I really?

LENNIE

(*Crossing to the bench and sitting down*) Oh, I was just –

FLETCHER

(*Walking over to Lennie*) I know just what you was justing. (*Quietly to Lennie*) You horny little beast.

MRS JAMIESON

He was trying to keep my spirits up.

There is a knock at the door.

FLETCHER

Come in. Oh, of course, you can't, can you? Give us a hand to shift this, Lennie.

Urwin comes to the doorway.

URWIN

'Ere, wait a minute, wait a minute, who is it?

FLETCHER

Wait a minute, wait a minute, who is it?

MACKAY

(*Offscreen*) It's Mr Mackay. I've brought the coffee you asked for.

FLETCHER

(*To Urwin*) It's Mr Mackay with the coffee we asked for.

URWIN

All right, let him in. But watch it.

FLETCHER

All right, you can come in. But watch it.

They move the filing cabinet away from the door and open the door.

Mackay is there with a tray of coffee mugs. He passes it through and Mrs Jamieson takes it.

MACKAY

Is everything all right in there, Fletcher?

URWIN

Everything's all right, so naff off, Mackay.

Mrs Jamieson takes the tray to the inner office.

MACKAY

I can't believe a thing like this is happening in my prison. And at Christmastime.

FLETCHER

All right for you lot out there. Just remember it's us what are going through this terrifying ordeal.

URWIN

That'll do, Fletch. Lock the door, give me the key and put the cabinet back.

FLETCHER

Mr Mackay, one last thing. Could you do me a favour?

MACKAY

What, Fletcher?

FLETCHER

I left my socks soaking in the basin, could you wring them out for me?

Mackay glares and closes the door.

Fletcher locks it and gives the key to Urwin. They start moving the cabinet back.

12. INNER OFFICE

Barrowclough and Mrs Jamieson are serving the coffee.

BARROWCLOUGH
Here we are, Urwin.

Urwin crosses to the desk, sits down and puts his feet up.

URWIN
Ta.

He takes the coffee. Fletcher and Lennie walk in.

BARROWCLOUGH
Fletcher, Godber, help yourself to sugar.

FLETCHER
(*Picking mug up*) Well, I must say this is nice, very nice. Never thought I'd be served coffee by a screw.

LENNIE
(*Crossing from the desk to the chair*) In the Governor's office, too.

BARROWCLOUGH
Barriers tend to come down in situations like this.

FLETCHER
You don't mind if I sit then.

BARROWCLOUGH/URWIN (TOGETHER)
No, that's all right.

BARROWCLOUGH
Urwin?

URWIN
Go ahead.

Fletcher sits down. Lennie invites Mrs Jamieson to sit and then does so himself on the arm of the chair. Barrowclough remains standing.

FLETCHER
Thanks, Reg. Here's to you. Wherever you ends up.

LENNIE
Where will you go, Reg?

URWIN
Somewhere a long way away where they don't ask too many questions and don't care who I am as long as I can pay for it.

LENNIE
Oh you mean somewhere corrupt where they turn a blind eye if you grease their palm.

FLETCHER
Isle of Wight?

URWIN
I was thinking of South America or Mexico, somewhere like that.

FLETCHER
Oh yeah, funny country Mexico. Very . . . Mexican. Apparently all the dogs limp.

MRS JAMIESON
I didn't know that.

FLETCHER
Oh yes, well-known fact. It's something to do with the food.

LENNIE
Food?

FLETCHER

Bloke gets up in the morning,
contemplates his hideous breakfast
and kicks the dog.

URWIN

Really? And I'd always rather fancied
Mexico.

FLETCHER

Contrary to travel brochure myth,
they're not a happy people you know.
I suppose any country which has
tequila as its national drink is bent on
self-destruction.

Urwin finishes his coffee.

URWIN

I appreciate your advice, Fletch.
Maybe I'll think of somewhere else.

BARROWCLOUGH

You won't be going
anywhere, Urwin.

He picks up Urwin's mug.

URWIN

What?

BARROWCLOUGH

Don't you think we have well-
rehearsed precautions for emergencies
like this? Don't you worry, Mrs
Jamieson, you and I will not be going
South of the Border down Mexico way.

URWIN

What you on about?

BARROWCLOUGH

Didn't it puzzle you that I was being so
polite, handing out the coffee? That
was because one of those mugs was
laced with a powerful tranquilliser which

acts very swiftly, and in a few
moments, Urwin, in a few moments
you will be happily asleep in the
land of nod.

*There is a loud snore from Fletcher
who is now fast asleep, an empty
mug of coffee in his hand.*

13. ASSOCIATION AREA/LANDING

*Camera shows feet walking on the
landing. A senior Police Officer is
marching along. He meets up with
the Governor. They cross the
bridge together and walk along the
landing, round a corner and in
through a door.*

14A. MACKAY'S OFFICE

*Mackay is brewing tea as Venables
enters with the Senior Police Officer.*

VENABLES

Any word yet?

MACKAY

Not yet, no, sir. But everything's
under control. The rest of the prison
is quiet – all in the cells locked up.
Cup of tea, sir?

VENABLES

No, no. So they've no idea what's
going on?

MACKAY

(*Crossing to desk*) They know
something's up. They probably think
someone's gone over the wall.

VENABLES

As long as we keep the lid on
this thing.

MACKAY

(*Looking at his watch*) That stuff should
have worked by now. I put enough in
to knock out a rhinoceros.

VENABLES

I still can't believe that this is
happening here. Where did he get the
gun?

MACKAY

Probably made it. He's spent a lot of
time in the machine shop has Urwin,
and now one can see why.

The phone rings.

MACKAY

Aha!

He picks up the receiver.

MACKAY

Everything all right, Barrowclough . . .

His expression changes.

MACKAY

I see . . . yes, Urwin. Mr Urwin. Very
well. I'll remember that.

He puts the phone down.

VENABLES

What's happened?

MACKAY

Urwin says thank you for the coffee, it
perked him up. Fletcher on the other
hand is sleeping like a rhinoceros.

14B. INNER OFFICE

*Fletcher's head is on one side,
facing a stuffed trout which is
mounted on the wall. He is
still asleep.*

*The phone rings in the
outer office.*

MRS JAMIESON

Hello . . . Just one moment.

Urwin moves to the door.

URWIN

Is that for me?

MRS JAMIESON

(*At her desk*) I'm afraid not.

She walks to the door.

MRS JAMIESON

It's your wife, Mr Barrowclough.

BARROWCLOUGH

Oh dear. How does she sound?

MRS JAMIESON

Same as usual.

BARROWCLOUGH

Oh dear. (*To Urwin*) May I?

URWIN

Be my guest.

*Barrowclough goes across to the
phone.*

BARROWCLOUGH

Perhaps she hasn't heard yet.

He stands at the desk and picks up the phone.

BARROWCLOUGH

Hello, dear . . . what? No, I haven't forgotten but I think I should tell you there's a chance I may be late this evening . . . Now just a minute, Alice . . . Alice, if you'd give me a moment to explain . . . I know I've been late three times this week already, but I'm being held at gunpoint as a hostage . . . I *know* we're supposed to be going round to Mrs Wainwright's at eight . . . yes, yes, it's rude and inconsiderate, but I may be going abroad in a helicopter . . . Alice, I don't believe you've heard a word . . . at gunpoint, yes! There's Mrs Jamieson, two prisoners and myself . . .

He sits down and turns away.

BARROWCLOUGH

What do you mean, 'Oh is that woman with you!' . . .

Mrs Jamieson goes back to the outer office.

BARROWCLOUGH

Well, of course she's going too, neither of us has much say in the matter. Of *course* I'm not glad! Alice, this is pointless. I'll try and call again, but if I don't I suggest you watch the six o'clock news.

He replaces the phone and is suddenly aware that Lennie and Urwin have taken this all in and have put two and two together.

URWIN

(*Crossing and sitting on the arm of Lennie's chair*) Here Barra, your old lady reckons that you and Mrs Jamieson have got a little thing going, does she?

BARROWCLOUGH

Certainly not.

URWIN

I bet she didn't believe all those late shifts you've been working.

LENNIE

Now, Reg, this thing between Mr Barrowclough and Mrs Jamieson is sheer speculation.

BARROWCLOUGH

(*Getting up*) There is no 'thing' Godber. Our relationship is purely professional.

Mrs Jamieson comes in and walks across to the desk.

MRS JAMIESON

Should I clear these cups up, Mr Barrowclough?

URWIN

(*Crossing over to her*) No need to be so formal, love. We know all about you and him.

Mrs Jamieson blanches and bristles towards Barrowclough.

MRS JAMIESON

Henry, how could you!

BARROWCLOUGH

Dorothy, I never said a word.

MRS JAMIESON

Well, it never came from my lips!

She storms out, taking the tray.
Fletcher wakes up, stretching
himself, unaware at first of his
whereabouts. He starts on seeing
the fish, then looks around him, and
notices Lennie.

FLETCHER

Where am I?

LENNIE

(*Getting up and going over to Fletcher*)
We're in the Governor's office,
remember?

Fletcher gets to his feet
and launches straight into
his defence.

FLETCHER

Oh yes, sir, about Mr Mackay's
allegations, Godber and me weren't
drunk, we never drink. Sometimes we
chew on the occasional sock, but . . .

Lennie is trying to stop him.

LENNIE

Fletch, Fletch . . . The Governor isn't
here! Don't you remember?

He points to Urwin.

FLETCHER

Hello, Reg, you the new Governor?
What are you doing here?

URWIN

I'm hijacking Barrowclough, don't you
remember?

FLETCHER

How could I nod off in the middle
of that?

BARROWCLOUGH

The coffee you drank was drugged.

FLETCHER

Drugged?

LENNIE

It was meant for Reg, but
Barrowclough messed it up.

FLETCHER

I do feel a bit queer.

He sits down.

LENNIE

Could be dangerous, Fletch. Those
drugs on top of all the booze
we had.

BARROWCLOUGH

Thank you, Godber, I'll
remember that.

FLETCHER

So will I, my son.

Suddenly Mrs Jamieson comes
back with a transistor radio.

MRS JAMIESON

Listen, we're on *The World at One*.

Urwin stands up and Lennie moves
to the radio. They all listen.

VOICE

(*Offscreen*) A government spokesman
said that the Home Secretary
could not be reached for comment
regarding the situation at Slade Prison.

Details are still confused, but it appears that the Governor's secretary, Mrs Dorothy Jamieson . . .

Despite the situation, she is pleased at hearing her name on the radio, and Lennie gives her a little 'that's you' look.

VOICE

(*Offscreen*) and a Prison Officer . . . are being held at gunpoint by three desperate prisoners.

FLETCHER

Three!

He stands up, holds his head and sits down again.

VOICE

(*Offscreen*) They are demanding transportation and a large sum of money. In the City today, shares suffered a further decline when . . .

Urwin turns the radio off.

Mrs Jamieson takes it back into the outer office.

FLETCHER

(*Walking to the desk*) Here, what's this about three desperate men?

BARROWCLOUGH

They said that details were confused.

He sits down.

FLETCHER

Oh, yes, but next thing, they'll be issuing names.

LENNIE

What's my family going to think?

FLETCHER

What's my wife going to think?

BARROWCLOUGH

I hope she shows a little more consideration than mine.

URWIN

(*Getting up*) Hey, hey, hey. Never mind your naffing families, what about me? It's on the wireless so everybody knows about it. So why am I still stuck here, where's my helicopter?

Fletcher takes charge, the pacifier.

FLETCHER

Reg, Reg . . . a word of caution. I don't want you to build your hopes too high, my son.

URWIN

What d'you mean?

FLETCHER

I think you should get used to the idea that they may not play ball. Put yourself in their shoes. They have to demonstrate to an anxious public that they ain't going to bow down to every nutter with a gun and fly him off to sunnier climes.

URWIN

Here, I'm no nutter.

FLETCHER

I'm taking the Establishment viewpoint, Reg. Nothing personal.

LENNIE

'Nother thing – ten thou's a lot of money.

BARROWCLOUGH

Doesn't seem an excessive amount for a Prison Officer with twenty-three years' unblemished service.

URWIN

(*Sitting at the desk*) Let me get this straight. What you're saying like, is they're calling my bluff. They haven't been taking me seriously?

BARROWCLOUGH

(*Triumphantly*) Right. And there's nothing you can do about it now.

URWIN

There is one thing I could do.

BARROWCLOUGH

What?

URWIN

I could always shoot you.

He points the gun at Barrowclough.

BARROWCLOUGH

Yes, yes, I suppose you could do that.

FLETCHER

Wouldn't advise it, Reg. Any wave of public sympathy you might attract would go right out of the window if you was to maim a screw.

LENNIE

Listen to Fletch, and just keep cool.

FLETCHER

That's the ticket, son. 'Cause I have been through this before, you see.

URWIN

Have you?

BARROWCLOUGH

(*Disbelievingly*) Really, Fletcher?

FLETCHER

Yeah. First nick I was in. There was this bloke called Popplewell. He was a trusty like you, Reg. That's how he

come to be on an outside work party. Repainting the Governor's house. Well, the next thing we knew he was barricaded in there with Mrs Bailey.

BARROWCLOUGH

Mrs Bailey?

FLETCHER

Yeah. Mrs Bailey, the Governor's wife, Mrs Bailey. That was her name. The Governor's name was Bailey, and she was married to him so she was Mrs Bailey. Follow all that, so far?

He looks round at Lennie and raises his eyes.

LENNIE

I suppose you called him Old Bailey?

FLETCHER

(*To Lennie*) Do you want to tell the story, Godber?

LENNIE

I'm sorry, I was just . . .

FLETCHER

(*Moving back to Urwin*) Yeah well.

LENNIE

Please go on, Fletch.

FLETCHER

Don't know if I can now. I've lost the thread.

URWIN

(*Pointing gun*) Get on with it.

FLETCHER

All right, all right. Well now, before you could say Jack Robinson the house was surrounded by the screws, and the law, and of course there was newspapers and television cameras. If I remember rightly, even Fyfe Robertson turned up but he soon cleared off. Anyhow, for three days all sorts of people made appeals to Popplewell, like the Chaplain, and the psychiatrist. But there was never a word from him or Mrs Bailey. Remember Mrs Bailey?

BARROWCLOUGH

What happened?

FLETCHER

On the fourth day Mrs Bailey let him go.

He sits down.

LENNIE

You mean she was holding him. Why?

FLETCHER

Why? Well, I think to use a catchphrase what was prevalent at the time, Len . . . she'd never had it so good.

15. OUTER OFFICE

The camera shows the clock on the wall which says half-past four. Mrs Jamieson is putting files in the filing cabinet. Fletcher and Lennie walk in from the Inner Office.

FLETCHER

You all right, Mrs Jamieson?

MRS JAMIESON

What is happening in there?

LENNIE

Oh, we've won a little victory. He's extended his deadline till five o'clock.

MRS JAMIESON

Oh good, then I'll probably have time

to finish this before he shoots us all. Or must I expect a fate worse than death?

FLETCHER

Is there a fate worse than death?

Mrs Jamieson thinks about it for a moment.

MRS JAMIESON

No, I don't suppose there is.

FLETCHER

That's the spirit. Here listen, are those prisoners' files?

MRS JAMIESON

Yes.

FLETCHER

Fish Urwin's out for me, would you?

MRS JAMIESON

Why?

FLETCHER

Might help, who knows? Have a quick shifty, Len.

He goes back into the inner office, while Lennie and Mrs Jamieson move to the filing cabinet.

16. INNER OFFICE

Urwin is sitting in the chair and Barrowclough is sitting at the desk.

URWIN

Listen, I'm getting bloody angry, now. When are we going to get some action around here?!

BARROWCLOUGH

I'm still waiting to hear from the Governor.

URWIN

Well, I can't wait much longer, remember that.

Fletcher feels the onus is on him to cool Urwin down.

FLETCHER

Here, Reg, you seem kind of tense.

URWIN

I got to get out, Fletch. Can't take any more.

BARROWCLOUGH

That's exactly how I feel.

URWIN

You feel like that after half a day. I've been in stir half me life.

BARROWCLOUGH

But you're up for parole soon, Urwin.

URWIN

Parole – they won't give it to me. Not a snowball's. They never have and they never will. And I just got to get out of here.

FLETCHER

But why this way, Reg?

URWIN

Because if I stay Inside much longer, I'm going to top myself.

FLETCHER

Suicide. You wouldn't do that, would you?

URWIN

Tried it once before.

FLETCHER

Oh yes? How d'you make out?

Urwin stares at Fletcher for a moment.

URWIN

I failed, didn't I? Typical. I was in a supermarket. Trying to steal a tin of pork luncheon meat. Suddenly I thought, 'Is this what my life has come to? Stealing luncheon meat?'

FLETCHER

You tried to kill yourself in a supermarket. How?

URWIN

I just put me head down and charged towards the glass doors.

FLETCHER

What went wrong?

URWIN

(*Motions doors opening*) Electric. I ran head first into an off-duty cop . . . he booked me for nicking a tin of pork luncheon meat.

FLETCHER

Always one about when you don't want one. What you should realise, Reg, is you're one of those people who doesn't get the breaks. Not even with glass doors. Today's typical. Obviously you've been planning to hijack the Governor for months. The day you choose he gets the runs.

LENNIE

(*Offscreen*) Er, Fletch . . .

Fletcher goes through to the outer office.

17. OUTER OFFICE

As Fletcher comes in, Lennie hands him Urwin's file.

LENNIE

Look at this.

FLETCHER

(*Reading the file*) Would you Christmas Eve it.

LENNIE

Three times in the past two years, Urwin's been recommended for psychiatric treatment.

FLETCHER

Only he never got it, did he? The system did this to Reg. I've got to talk to him. Mrs Jamieson, would you come through here a minute, please.

He opens the door for her.

18. INNER OFFICE

Fletcher walks in, holding the file, followed by Mrs Jamieson.

FLETCHER

Sit down, love. Reg, can you come through and have a word with me and Godber? Private, like.

Urwin looks a little doubtful.

URWIN

I dunno.

LENNIE

Come on, Reg. These two can't get up to nowt.

He casts a look in their direction.

LENNIE

Well, they can, but I don't think they'd want to with us in the next room.

URWIN

Okay then.

Lennie goes across to the desk with the file.

LENNIE

Read this, Mr Barrowclough. It should interest you.

Lennie returns to the Outer Office.

19. OUTER OFFICE

Fletcher escorts Urwin to the bench.

FLETCHER

Here, Reg, sit down. You trust me, don't you?

URWIN

Maybe.

He sits.

FLETCHER

Well, I got to tell you, son. You ain't going to make it.

Lennie moves in behind Fletcher.

URWIN

Got to make it, Fletch. I'm a three-time loser.

FLETCHER

I swear to you there ain't no way. They got all the arguments on their side. Worst thing that could happen is if they say okay.

He sits.

FLETCHER

'Cause you know you'd never make it to that helicopter. They've got blokes out there could shoot a fly's eyebrows off at four hundred yards. And if flies had anything else they could shoot them off an' all. Know what I mean? And say you got to Mexico. Where next? Look at you. You think you're going to check into the Acapulco Hilton looking like that?

LENNIE

They'd never let you in without a tie.

FLETCHER

Reg . . . me and lad could have jumped you over the last few hours. But we didn't. You know why?

URWIN

Why?

FLETCHER

Because that would have dropped you in even further than what you is now. They have to see that you chucked in the towel yourself. Voluntary, like. Look, I won't lie to you. They're going to throw the book at you. But I've been reading your file. You've got some kind of case . . . if you give yourself up.

Urwin considers, then shakes his head negatively.

URWIN

No, Fletch. I'm going through with it.

FLETCHER

Think, Reg.

URWIN

No . . .

He stands up.

URWIN

I'm going the distance.

Fletcher stands up.

FLETCHER

In that case, you leaves me no choice. I'm going to have to take that gun off of you.

URWIN

You're what?

He backs off, brandishing the gun. Lennie stares at Fletcher astonished. He holds out his hand.

FLETCHER

Give me the gun.

URWIN

Stay where you are, Fletch.

Fletcher starts to walk towards him – John Wayne never did it better.

FLETCHER

Reg, you're my mucker, you ain't going to shoot me.

URWIN

Don't bank on it!

LENNIE

Hey, Fletch, give over. He's serious.

FLETCHER

Not to worry. Reg and me is mates.

URWIN

Don't push it – mate!

Fletcher reaches out a hand. The gun is in Urwin's hand. Fletcher very deliberately pushes a finger into the barrel of the gun.

Fletcher gently takes the gun from Urwin and puts it in the desk drawer. Urwin crumples into the chair.

FLETCHER

(*Arm round Urwin*) Now, Reg, on your feet, son. Don't let go. Don't pack it in. Now's the time you have to be in control.

URWIN

What's the point?

FLETCHER

Every point. Mustn't let Barra think we overcame you. You go in there and tell him this was your decision. And Len and me will back you up.

LENNIE

He's right, Reg. It's your only chance.

URWIN

You'd back me up?

FLETCHER

'Course we will, like I said we're still on the side of us. There's still them and us.

URWIN

But you two could be heroes. For what you two have just done you could probably get a free pardon.

Fletcher stands up and looks at Lennie.

FLETCHER

Well – what d'you think, Len?

LENNIE

'Tis Christmas after all.

FLETCHER

Goodwill to all men and all that swaddling. (*To Urwin*) On your way, son.

URWIN

Maybe you're right.

He gets up and starts to go, then stops and turns.

URWIN

But I'm still calling the shots, aren't I?

FLETCHER

'Course you are. Main thing is, you didn't shoot the shots.

Urwin walks through to the inner office.

URWIN

(*Offscreen*) Mr Barrowclough . . .

Lennie walks over to the door and shuts it.

LENNIE

Fletch, you are a ruddy marvel. I've never seen anything like it.

FLETCHER

What – oh, the gun, yes well . . .

He gets the gun from the drawer.

LENNIE

No, no, don't denigrate what you just done. I never seen anything like it. Not even in *Kojak*.

FLETCHER

Yeah well, I had an advantage over Lollipop head, didn't I, I knew the gun weren't loaded.

LENNIE

Wasn't it?

FLETCHER

No . . . I been working in the machine shop with Reg. He's been making that gun for months, it's only a toy.

Lennie takes the gun.

LENNIE

You knew that all along?

FLETCHER

Yes, but as I just said, if I'd mentioned it I'd've dropped him deeper in the clarts.

He takes the gun.

LENNIE

Looks very authentic to me – are you sure it's a toy?

FLETCHER

'Course I am. Look.

He points the gun towards the ceiling and pulls the trigger. There is a bang followed by a shower of plaster falling on their heads.

20. CELL

Fletcher is putting up a pathetic paper chain when Barrowclough enters. He clears his throat.

BARROWCLOUGH

Evening, Fletcher.

He walks over to the bunk.

FLETCHER

Oh hello, Mr Barrowclough.

BARROWCLOUGH

This is very nice. Is Godber about?

FLETCHER

No, he wanted to prove that his Christmas pudding was not the cause of the Governor's indisposition. So he ate three helpings to vindicate his reputation.

BARROWCLOUGH

Three!!! Oh I see, where is he then?

FLETCHER

Still in the bog. Two more to go.

He moves to the table and picks up the paper chain.

BARROWCLOUGH

How are you feeling then, after our terrible ordeal?

FLETCHER

I'm all right, Mr Barrowclough. But me and the lads are still a bit concerned about Reg Urwin.

He stands on the chair to pin up the paper chain.

BARROWCLOUGH

I have been assured that Urwin will be undergoing psychiatric treatment. He will not be punished so much as helped.

FLETCHER

(*On chair*) Yeah well, not before time.

BARROWCLOUGH

And I had a word with the Governor and in appreciation of your conduct the charges against you and Godber will be dropped.

FLETCHER

(*Getting down from chair*) Charges! Oh you mean those unfounded allegations about us making booze. Well good, only right and proper.

BARROWCLOUGH

'Nough said.

FLETCHER

Yeah, we don't get our booze back though, do we? (*Picking up the paper chain*) Hold this.

He moves the chair.

BARROWCLOUGH

In . . . in . . . in return, of course, I would like to think that you could forget certain things that may have been revealed during those desperate hours.

He moves towards Fletcher.

FLETCHER

(*On chair*) Like what?

BARROWCLOUGH

The rather delicate matter of Mrs Jamieson and myself. I'd like it to go no further.

FLETCHER

(*Getting down*) I don't know what you're on about, Mr Barrowclough.

BARROWCLOUGH

That's the spirit, Fletcher.

FLETCHER

If you're trying to tell me there's something I'm supposed to forget, I think you're overlooking the fact I was asleep most of the time. I didn't hear anything.

BARROWCLOUGH

You mean . . . you didn't know about myself and Mrs Jamieson?

FLETCHER

No, sir. Just don't worry . . . I do now, Henry . . .